INTERNATIONAL ASSOCIATION OF
CRIME ANALYSTS

Exploring
Crime Analysis
Readings on Essential Skills

The International Association of Crime Analysts

Editors:

Christopher W. Bruce
Danvers (MA) Police Department

Steven R. Hick
University of Denver

Julie P. Cooper
Irvine (CA) Police Department

IACA
Overland Park, KS
http://www.iaca.net

International Association of Crime Analysts, Overland Park, KS 66212
© 2004 by the International Association of Crime Analysts
All rights reserved. Published 2004
Printed in the United States of America
13 12 11 10 09 08 07 06 05   2 3 4 5 6 7

ISBN: 1-59457-980-6

Library of Congress Control Number: 2004114901
Publisher: BookSurge, LLC
North Charleston, South Carolina

Cover photo by Bruce Stirling

http://www.iaca.net/exploringca.html

Contents

About the Editors

Christopher **W. Bruce** has served as a public safety analyst at the Danvers, Massachusetts Police Department since 2001. He was a crime analyst for the Cambridge, Massachusetts Police department between 1996 and 2001 and a crime analysis intern at that department from 1994 to 1996. Bruce has been the Vice President of Administration for the International Association of Crime Analysts since 2000, and was the President of the Massachusetts Association of Crime Analysts between 2000 and 2004. He has given over three dozen presentations on crime analysis at various crime analysis and policing conferences. He teaches crime mapping and analysis for for Suffolk University's Graduate Program in Criminal Justice.

Julie **P. Cooper** is currently the Supervising Crime Analyst for the Irvine Police Department in Irvine, California. She was a Crime Analyst and Operations Administrator for the Los Angeles County Sheriff Department between 1996 and 1999. She has been active in crime analysis for the past 10 years and has served as the Secretary for the Southern California Crime and Intelligence Analysts Association as well as numerous committees for the International Association of Crime Analysts. She has been a past presenter at various crime analysis and policing conferences. She teaches Crime Mapping and Analysis for the National Law Enforcement & Corrections Technology Center's Crime Mapping and Analysis Program in Denver, Colorado. Ms. Cooper has her B.S. in Criminal Justice and her Master's in Public Policy and Administration from California State University, Long Beach.

Steven **R. Hick** is the GIS Director and faculty member in the Department of Geography at the University of Denver. For the past ten years, Steven has been directing the Geographic Information System (GIS) education and research activities in the Department. Mr. Hick is currently the Director of the *GIS Certificate Program* and was instrumental in the creation of one of the nation's first Master of Science degrees in Geographic Information Science. During the past five years, Steven has been an instructor in the Crime Mapping and Analysis Program working with the National Law Enforcement and Corrections Technology Center, a National Institute of Justice program at the University of Denver. He also provides crime mapping and analysis technical assistance to law enforcement agencies across the country. Before joining the University of Denver, Mr. Hick was a technical consultant at UGC Consulting from 1989 until 1994. Before moving to Denver, Mr. Hick was a cartographer with the Defense Mapping Agency, based in Fort Sam Houston, Texas, between 1985 and 1988. While living in Texas, Mr. Hick taught in the University of Texas system on the San Antonio and Austin campuses.

About the Contributors

Jonathan Alston received a BSc in Sociology with an emphasis in Deviance from Brigham Young University. He earned an MA in Criminology from Simon Fraser University after studying the selection patterns of serial rapists. He has been involved in a number of research projects that have included academic research as well as projects with the Royal Canadian Mounted Police, Ministry of Attorney General (BC), Legal Services Society (BC), and the Canadian government. He went to the University of Alberta and began working on his PhD in Criminology but has since become employed with the Edmonton Police Service as a crime analyst in its Intelligence Analysis Unit. He has been employed with the EPS since early 2000. Since joining the EPS, Mr. Alston has worked as a spatial crime analyst, as a crime analyst on several major case files, and as a research analyst for a service-wide strategic analysis project, and is currently assigned to the Sexual Assault Section.

Sean Bair is the Program Manager for the Crime Mapping & Analysis Program at the National Law Enforcement and Corrections Technology Center. His duties include establishing curriculum, providing technical assistance, supervising CMAP personnel, and instructing on a variety of GIS and analytical applications. Mr. Bair has trained over 1000 law enforcement personnel in the use of GIS as a tool for the analysis and reduction of crime and calls for service. He is a former police officer with assignments as a field training officer and sexual assault investigator. Before becoming a police officer, Mr. Bair was a crime analyst for the Tempe, Arizona Police Department. In his five years as an analyst, he has performed all aspects of crime analysis including Tactical, Strategic, and Administrative Crime Analysis. Mr. Bair has over 20 years of computer programming experience and has written several software applications to improve police operations including a Tactical Crime Analysis application that is in use worldwide.

Rachel Boba is an assistant professor at Florida Atlantic University in the Criminology and Criminal Justice program. At FAU, she teaches methods of research, criminal justice systems, crime prevention, problem solving, and analysis in policing and conducts research in the areas of problem solving, problem analysis, crime analysis, regional data sharing, and technology in policing. From 2000 to 2003, Dr. Boba was Director of the Police Foundation's Crime Mapping Laboratory where she directed federally funded grants in the areas of crime analysis and crime mapping, problem analysis, and school safety. Before her position at the Police Foundation, she worked as a crime analyst at the Tempe, Arizona, Police Department for five years where she conducted a wide variety of crime analysis and crime mapping work as well as applied research and evaluation. She holds a PhD and an MA in sociology from Arizona State University and a BA in English and sociology from California Lutheran University.

Barbara Brookover has worked with the Chula Vista Police Department in California for over 15 years. Before her recent transfer to the position of Police Support Services Manager, Ms. Brookover held positions as a crime analyst, senior crime analyst and crime analysis manager. Ms. Brookover worked as a crime analyst for the Oceanside, California Police Department for two and a half years before beginning her career in Chula Vista. While managing tactical, strategic, and administrative crime analysis functions in Chula Vista, Ms. Brookover has managed the Crime

Prevention Unit, Senior Volunteer Patrol, Data Entry Section and False Alarm Program. After coordinating the development of effective crime analysis units in both Oceanside and Chula Vista, Ms. Brookover was invited to serve on the State of California Career Criminal Apprehension Program Advisory Committee. She also assisted with development of the Expanded Applications-Crime Analysis training course sponsored by the California Department of Justice Advanced Training Center. Ms. Brookover holds a Bachelor of Arts Degree in Geography from the University of New Mexico and a Master of Science Degree in Human Resources Management from Chapman University. She has extensive professional writing experience and tutors high school students enrolled in Advanced Placement courses, assisting with writing assignments and competitive essays.

Donald W. Chamberlayne has been with the Worcester Police Department as its crime analyst since January 1995. He is currently Vice President of Administration for the Massachusetts Association of Crime Analysts, having previously served as the editor of the Crime Analyst's Round Table. He is a member of the International Association of Crime Analysts and in 2001 was the recipient of its award for "outstanding contribution to the field of crime analysis." His educational background includes degrees from the University of Virginia and the University of Massachusetts. Before coming to the field of crime analysis, he taught in the areas of urban planning and social science, and later served in research and analysis positions pertaining to demographics, housing markets, and labor markets, as well as database systems design and development.

Donald R. Dixon received his Bachelor of Arts Degree as a double major in History and Government and Politics from the University of Texas at Dallas in 1985. He received his Master of Arts Degree in Political Economy from the same institution in 1986. Dr. Dixon taught government and economics at area community colleges and lectured in political science at UT Dallas for several years while beginning his studies toward a PhD at UT Dallas. In 1994, Dr. Dixon was hired as a crime and intelligence analyst by the Dallas Police Department. In December of 2001, he was awarded the degree, Doctor of Philosophy of Political Economy. His dissertation was titled, "The Social Ecology of Juvenile Violence." In 2002, he accepted a position with California State University at Sacramento as an Assistant Professor of Criminal Justice. Dr. Dixon's research interests include information systems for criminal justice, computer crime, juvenile violence, GIS applications to criminal justice research, and social ecological analysis. He remains active in the crime analysis community through the International Association of Crime Analysts and the Northern California Association of Crime Analysts.

Noah Fritz is the founder and director of the Crime Mapping and Analysis Program (CMAP), a training and technical assistance program sponsored by the U.S. Department of Justice. In his career, Mr. Fritz has been a youth advocate, a juvenile probation officer, a research analyst for Arizona State University and the Arizona Department of Public Safety, the first Crime Analyst and Information Management Bureau Commander for the Tempe (AZ) Police Department—where he supervised the Crime Analysis and Police Systems units—and a Criminal Justice Strategic Planner for Jefferson County, Colorado. Mr. Fritz is also the 2000–2006 president of the International Association of Crime Analysts. His accomplishments include undergraduate degrees in Sociology and Criminal Justice from Illinois State University, and a Master's degree and current PhD work in Justice Studies from ASU. He has authored articles in *Sociological Quarterly*, the *Encyclopedia of Criminology and Deviant Behavior*, publications for the National Institute of Justice, and appeared nationally on ABC's "Weekend News Edition" featuring crime mapping. He currently teaches at the University of Colorado and the University of Denver.

Dan **Helms** is the Director of Analysis for Bair Software, Research & Consulting. He is the developer of GeoGenie Enterprise, Trend Tracker, and TimeScan analytical software, which is in use across the United States and internationally in Africa, Asia, and Europe. Mr. Helm's analytical tools are in use with U.S. military security forces, and have been credited with helping to resolve crime series in the United States. He is also the Crime Analyst, and GIS Specialist for the National Law Enforcement & Corrections Technology Center (NLECTC). As primary instructor for the Crime Mapping & Analysis Program (CMAP), Mr. Helms has trained hundreds of police investigators, analysts, and agents in crime analysis and mapping methods. Mr. Helms is a former intelligence specialist with the U.S. Air Force, fluent in the Arabic language, and has worked closely with the national intelligence community since 1987. He was formerly a crime analyst with the Las Vegas Metropolitan Police Department, where his innovative methods and programs won several national and international awards. He is also a licensed Police Firearms Instructor.

Dennis **Kessinger** served for twenty-one years in full-time public safety positions, including eight years as a firefighter for the Long Beach (CA) Fire Department, four years as an analyst for the University of California at San Diego, and nine years as an analyst for the Redding (CA) Police Department. At the Redding Police Department, Mr. Kessinger designed and built the crime analysis unit from concept to statewide model. He has written and administered more than $3 million in successful grants for public safety agencies, and he continues to consult and speak on both grant administration and presentation techniques. He created a popular "Life After Law Enforcement" seminar to show how public safety skills can be transferred to a post-law enforcement life. Mr. Kessinger is an adjunct faculty member at National University in the Criminal Justice and Masters in Public Administration Program. He has written more than twenty-three articles in national and international publications. He is the author of *Lawyercide: a Crime Analysis Novel*, published through Crimson Druid Publishing, which Mr. Kessinger founded. Mr. Kessinger assists at a shelter for domestic violence and sexual assault victims, providing counseling and legal assistance. When not traveling, teaching, speaking, or writing, he lives with his wife and son in Redding, California.

Deborah **Osborne Loewen** is a crime analyst with the Buffalo (NY) Police Department and holds a BA in Psychology and an MA in Social Policy with a criminal justice emphasis. She has served as a consultant to the Analysis Center of the Police Service of Northern Ireland (PSNI) and has been successful in identifying placement opportunities for PSNI analysts in North America. Ms. Loewen was co-chair of the International Association of Crime Analysts certification committee and served on the IACA by-laws committee. She is a co-founder and the vice-president of the Western New York Regional Association of Crime and Intelligence Analysts, and is a member the Southwestern Ontario Chapter of IALEIA. Ms. Loewen has co-authored the book *Introduction to Crime Analysis: Basic Resources for Criminal Justice Practice*, published in 2004 by the Haworth Press. She has taught in the crime analysis program at Mercyhurst North East College, PA.

Christopher **G. Mowbray** is a Criminal Intelligence Analyst with the Royal Canadian Mounted Police (RCMP). He is a member of the Integrated Response to Organized Crime Team, a provincial initiative to investigate and disrupt all forms of organized crime groups. Before joining the RCMP in early 2004, Mr. Mowbray was employed as an Intelligence Analyst with the Edmonton Police Service where his duties involved criminal analysis on a joint forces operation dealing with high risk missing persons and unsolved homicides in Alberta Canada. He is particularly experienced in spatial analysis of sexual assaults and gang activity and homicides in the city of Edmonton. Mr. Mowbray has a Masters degree in Criminal Justice Studies from the University of Leicester in the United Kingdom where his area of study was spatial pattern analysis and target selection of serial sexual offenders in Edmonton Canada. Mr. Mowbray earned a Bachelor of Science with a major in Biological Sciences from the University of Alberta and earned a second Bachelors degree from the University of Alberta (Bachelor of Arts) in Anthropology and Sociology.

Jamie Price is an assistant professor in the department of behavioral sciences at Kentucky Wesleyan College. Mr. Price is a certified instructor of the National Law Enforcement and Corrections Technology Center's Crime Mapping and Analysis Program (CMAP). His teaching interests include criminology, research methodologies, statistics, policing, and criminal courts. His research interests include the spatial-temporal analysis of crime, hot spot methodologies, police effectiveness, and evaluation research. Before joining Kentucky Wesleyan College, Mr. Price was an assistant professor in the department of criminology and criminal justice at Florida Atlantic University. He has received a B.A. in criminal justice from Kentucky Wesleyan College, a M.S. in criminal justice from the University of South Carolina, and is completing his PhD in criminal justice at the University of Cincinnati.

Karin Schmerler is a public safety analyst with the Chula Vista (CA) Police Department. In this capacity, she researches city-wide and neighborhood-level crime and disorder problems; interprets original data on traffic and pedestrian stops; and makes presentations on research and problem-solving projects to a variety of local and national audiences. Ms. Schmerler is currently working on problem-solving projects to reduce auto theft, and crime and disorder in budget motels. Before working for the Chula Vista Police Department, she spent six years as a social science analyst at the Office of Community Oriented Policing Services, U.S. Department of Justice, and seven years as a researcher at the Police Executive Research Forum. Ms. Schmerler is an author of *Problem-Solving Tips: A Guide to Reducing Crime and Disorder through Problem-Solving Partnerships*, and a co-author of "Primary Data Collection: A Problem-Solving Necessity." She holds a bachelor's degree in public policy from Duke University.

Paul E. Tracy is Professor of Criminology and Political Economy in the School of Social Sciences at the University of Texas at Dallas. His research interests focus on the measurement and analysis of juvenile delinquency careers, legal and policy issues in juvenile justice, prediction models of criminal careers, and drug prohibition policy. He is a recognized expert in the application of longitudinal research designs to the study of delinquent and criminal careers. His study of a large Philadelphia birth cohort of 27,160 people is the largest study of delinquency and crime ever conducted and is now in its twenty-fifth year. Dr. Tracy has published six books and numerous articles in criminology journals. Through his appointments to crime and justice commissions by Governor Rick Perry and former Governor George Bush, he is extensively involved in working to improve the criminal justice system by applying his research and policy interests to "real life" applications. Dr. Tracy holds a PhD in sociology from the University of Pennsylvania.

Mary **Velasco** is an Intelligence Analyst for the Federal Bureau of Investigation in Washington, DC. She was previously employed as a Research Associate in the Police Foundation's Crime Mapping Laboratory. Much of the Crime Mapping Laboratory's work is focused on encouraging analysts to conduct in-depth examinations of crime and disorder problems that are both informed by, and contribute to, the growing body of crime analysis and policing literature. This work required Ms. Velasco to be aware of which publications are most relevant for crime analysis professionals as well as how to access and interpret the information within these resources. Through training and technical assistance contacts, Ms. Velasco has sought to acquaint practitioners with practical resources, including government reports, academic publications, and professional books and periodicals. Ms. Velasco has also worked as a Crime Analyst for the Tempe, Arizona, Police Department, where she conducted a comprehensive study of Tempe's auto theft problem, co-authored protocols on tactical crime analysis, and administered a citizen survey. Ms. Velasco received her BS in Justice Studies at Arizona State University and her MS in Justice, Law, and Society at The American University.

Julie **Wartell** is the Crime Analyst Coordinator for the San Diego District Attorney's Office. Before this position, Ms. Wartell was the Project Director of the East Valley COMPASS Initiative (a regional analysis effort), worked as a crime analyst for the San Diego Police Department, served as a researcher for the Institute for Law and Justice and the Police Executive Research Forum, and completed a Fellowship at the National Institute of Justice Crime Mapping Research Center. Ms. Wartell has performed a wide range of research on and analysis of various crime problems and police-related issues, worked on the San Diego Police Department's strategic planning effort, and coordinated the development of a series of crime mapping training modules. She has done extensive training and presentations to officers and analysts throughout the country on topics relating to crime analysis and problem-oriented policing and has edited or authored numerous publications. Ms. Wartell has a Masters in Public Administration with an emphasis in Criminal Justice Administration.

Deborah **Lamm Weisel** is an assistant research professor at North Carolina State University. She teaches graduate and undergraduate classes in Applied Research Methods in Criminal Justice and Crime Analysis. Weisel has conducted numerous studies on effectiveness of policing, including studies on drug enforcement tactics, safety and security in public housing, police responses to gangs, motor vehicle theft, burglary, street prostitution, and speeding. Dr. Weisel's publications focus on providing policy-relevant guidance to police practitioners and include "Form and Sequence of Analysis in Police Problem-Solving" in *Crime Prevention Studies* (2003), "Assessing the Impact of Specialized Gang Units" in *Policing and Program Evaluation* (2004), and monographs on burglary and graffiti in the "Problem-Oriented Guides for Police" series published by the Office of Community Oriented Policing Services. Dr. Weisel holds a doctorate in Political Science and Public Policy Analysis from the University of Illinois at Chicago.

Herbert **Williams** is a lieutenant with the Woodbridge Township Police Department in New Jersey, where he commands the Crime Analysis Unit. Lt. Williams trains officers throughout the state, teaches the Methods of Instruction course that certifies police instructors, and has taught overseas for the U.S. Department of Justice. A graduate student at John Jay College, he is the principal investigator for a study on racial profiling, and is co-editing a book on Intelligence Analysis. Lt. Williams and his wife, Liz, have two exceptionally bright and handsome sons, Dillon and Zachary.

About the IACA

The International Association of Crime Analysts is a non-profit professional association, established in 1990, dedicated to advancing the effective use of crime analysis by law enforcement agencies. Its activities and goals include:

- Providing training and networking opportunities at annual conferences
- Collaborating with other associations to offer analytical training
- Providing technical support to agencies developing crime analysis programs
- Researching, analyzing, and publishing information relevant to crime analysts
- Fostering multi-agency collaboration and information sharing
- Certifying analysts through its Certified Law Enforcement Analyst program

Membership is open to analysts, police officers, educators, students, and anyone interested in the field of crime analysis. See http://www.iaca.net for more information, or contact us at 9218 Metcalf Avenue #364, Overland Park, KS 66212, (913) 940-3883.

International Association of Crime Analysts

Noah J. Fritz
NLECTC
University of Denver
President

Christopher W. Bruce
Danvers (MA) Police
Vice President of Administration

Gerald Tallman
Overland Park (KS) Police
Vice President of Membership

Samantha L. Gwinn
San Diego (CA) Police
Treasurer

Carolyn Cassidy
Gainesville (FL) Police
Secretary

Sgt. Mark Stallo
Dallas (TX) Police
Past President

Acknowledgements

The editors of *Exploring Crime Analysis* are grateful to the Executive Board of the International Association of Crime Analysts for its guidance, support, and patience. We must also acknowledge the members of the larger committee who, with the editors, selected the authors for this book: Chief Thomas K. Casady of the Lincoln (NE) Police, Dr. Donald R. Dixon of California State University at Sacramento, Douglas Hicks of the Minneapolis (MN) Police, Dr. Jerry Ratcliffe of Temple University, and Susan Cné Wernicke of the Shawnee (KS) Police.

We thank Herbert Kuehne of the Sioux City (IA) Police for his research on publishing; Officer Thomas Callahan of the Woburn (MA) Police for providing an integral piece of the cover art; and Omalley Abel, the IACA's Administrative Assistant, for preparing the glossary. Finally, we are indebted to our fastidious proofreaders: Carol Fitzgerald of the New England HIDTA, Heather Gundersen of the Cambridge (MA) Police, Samantha Gwinn of the San Diego (CA) Police, Casey Hatchett of the Brookline (MA) Police, Jamie May of the Overland Park (KS) Police, and Debra Piehl of the Newton (MA) Police.

List of Common Abbreviations

AFIS	Automated Fingerprint Identification System
CAD	Computer-Aided Dispatch
CFS	Call(s) for Service
CMAP	Crime Mapping and Analysis Program (NIJ/NLECTC Program)
CPTED	Crime Prevention Through Environmental Design
DEA	Drug Enforcement Administration (U.S.)
FBI	Federal Bureau of Investigation (U.S.)
FI	Field Interview
GIS	Geographic Information Systems
GPS	Global Positioning System
IACA	International Association of Crime Analysts
IACP	International Association of Chiefs of Police
IALEIA	International Association of Law Enforcement Intelligence Analysts
IT	Information Technology
MAPS	Mapping and Analysis for Public Safety (NIJ Program)
M.O.	*Modus Operandi*
NIBRS	National Incident-Based Reporting System
NIJ	National Institute of Justice (U.S.)
NLECTC	National Law Enforcement and Corrections Technology Center (U.S.)
ODBC	Open Database Connectivity
POP	Problem-Oriented Policing
RMS	Records Management System
UCR	Uniform Crime Report(ing)
USDOJ	United States Department of Justice
VBA	Visual Basic for Applications

Exploring Crime Analysis

Reader Alert

In a profession as young and dynamic as crime analysis, there are few universal truths. With only a few exceptions, this book is composed of ideas, concepts, theories, and opinions—not of objective facts. Some readers, including many experienced analysts, will find statements within this book with which they do not agree, or which they feel should be discussed further within the profession. Such debates are a sign of strength and vitality; a profession that lacks debate is a stagnant profession.

The material within this book does not represent the "official position" of the International Association of Crime Analysts, because the "official position" of the IACA is to encourage open, constructive, and thoughtful discussion. It is, however, our position that the authors we have assembled have shown, through skill and experience, that they are the representatives of the field who are best equipped to lay the foundation on which such discussions will take place. As you read these chapters, we encourage you to think critically about the profession of crime analysis and the methods, techniques, and concepts applied in it. Then, join the debate on the IACA's e-mail Discussion List, on the IACA Web site's discussion boards, and in forums at our annual conferences. Only in this way will our profession grow.

Foreword

Joseph M. Polisar

T he CompStat phenomenon that was pioneered in the New York City Police Department was the beginning of a sea of change in how the law enforcement profession viewed and used crime analysis. No longer is crime analysis an obscure function within our departments; it has taken its rightful place alongside other important tools such as photography, fingerprint analysis, DNA analysis, and the like.

My agency, the Garden Grove (CA) Police Department, has aggressively pursued the new technology that is critical to our crime analysis efforts. We rely heavily on technology, using geographic information systems (GIS) software; special crime mapping applications to perform spatial and temporal analyses; a spatial statistics program for distance, hot spot, journey-to-crime, and space-time analysis of crime incidents; and an application for geographic profiling of serial property crimes.

The following are crime analysis "success stories" here in Garden Grove:

- Using both geographic profiling software and training, we were able to successfully investigate the "Ski Mask Bandit Series." Our crime analysis unit identified the anchor point (area of highest probability where offender[s] live, work, and play) in a 2004 multi-agency robbery series. Ski-masked suspects targeted thirty-two liquor and video stores, hotels, and motels within a 546-square-mile area of Orange County. The geographic profile identified, with a 70 percent probability, that the suspects' anchor point was within an eight-square-mile area. The suspects were eventually arrested at a motel in which they were living, which was within the top 0.7 percent of the geographic profile.

- Our crime analysis unit was also able to investigate a "Baskin Robbins Bandit Series." The unit identified two anchor points in a 2004 multi-agency robbery series in Orange County. A male and female pair targeted eighteen locations, primarily Baskin Robbins ice creams stores, within a 433-square-mile area. The geographic profile identified two anchor points, with a 70 percent probability that the suspects lived in an 8.7-square-mile area. After the apprehension of both suspects, it was determined that each suspect had a parent with who he had been living within the peak profile. The residence of each parent was within the top 0.5 percent of the geographic profile.

- Our crime analysis unit has also been successful in crime forecasting. One example is a school burglary series. Crime analysis techniques identified a multi-agency series where multiple suspects targeted elementary schools, prying classroom doors to gain entry and

1

take select computer and audio-visual equipment. Analysts forecasted probable days, times, and locations to assist investigators and patrol officers in their tactical plans to address the problem. The suspects hit one of the three targets.

- Finally, our crime analysis unit has also been successful in helping identify suspects. One example is an indecent exposure series. The crime analyst mapped all incidents within the series, overlaying the hunting area with those subjects who matched the suspect description. The search was narrowed to a small number of possible suspects. Additional research and surveillance led to the identification and apprehension of the offender.

Crime analysis is a tool that has revolutionized the way that police do their jobs, and I have no doubt that it will continue to do so for years to come.

Joseph M. Polisar

Chief of Police
Garden Grove, CA

President
International Association of Chiefs of Police

Introduction

E*xploring Crime Analysis: Readings on Essential Skills* is the first of (I hope) many manuscripts written by dedicated professionals of the International Association of Crime Analysts (IACA). It represents a new beginning for a young but growing profession.

I have been in this business now for over 15 years, beginning my career as the first crime analyst for the Tempe (AZ) Police Department. I was hired as a requirement of the Commission on Accreditation for Law Enforcement Agencies (CALEA), which no longer includes hiring a full-time crime analyst as a mandatory standard. The week I started my new job, I walked around the department and asked the command staff members what they wanted me to do. To my chagrin, they couldn't tell me. They told me to go and read CALEA standard 15 (which concerns crime analysis). Over 150 applicants had applied for the job—a job for which the hiring authority did not have a clear idea about what it expected or hoped to achieve or produce.

The literature of the time was of little help. My review of available books on crime analysis resulted in the recovery of only one text: *The Police Crime Analysis Unit Handbook*, a 138-page manual, published in 1973, developed to encourage local law enforcement agencies to create crime analysis units. This text, already 16 years old, laid the foundation on which I would create the first crime analysis unit within the state of Arizona.

The lack of literature, knowledge-sharing, and training in crime analysis led a group of us to form the International Association of Crime Analysts in 1990. Both the founding of Tempe's crime analysis unit and the IACA occurred during a time when federal funding for such initiatives was scarce, falling between the LEAA boom of the 1970s and the COPS funding explosion of the 1990s (see the "History of Crime Analysis" in Chapter 1). The initiation and development of crime analysis, or any program vital to police operations, should not depend on the availability of federal funding for such programs, but unfortunately it often does.

How well has the situation improved since then? There is more available literature: today, an Amazon.com search for books with the title "crime analysis" produces 23 books (a list that includes some search engine errata but omits some of the books most often cited by analysts.) Many of these books have been written in the past three years, and they cover a wide range of subjects, including problem analysis, GIS, computer applications, CompStat, and data mining. Certainly, there is more training: analysts can now choose from a variety of professional training conferences, non-profit training, and corporate training.

But police use of crime analysis has arguably remained static. The United States of America alone has more than 17,000 police agencies, but the IACA has representatives from only 540 of them. Even if only one-quarter of individuals assigned to crime analysis choose to join the IACA, and if only one-half of America's police agencies were large enough to justify an analysis capability (fairly liberal figures), that leaves 75 percent of America's police agencies without an assigned analytical position. Moreover, those agencies with analysts don't often make full use of them: I know of many analysts, starting in new agencies, who tell stories identical to my experiences 15 years ago. Around the world, analysts complain of bulletins that took hours to produce discarded in trash bins and littered across the roll-call room floor. Finally, departments have yet to widely embrace the principles of problem-oriented policing, which requires a strong analytical function to study crime *problems*—an in-depth, qualitative process that goes beyond the standard series identification, forecasting, and statistical trend charts that have characterized much of what crime analysts have done in during the past 30 years.

Thus, after one hundred years of professional policing, and more than forty years since "crime analysis" was first found in print,[1] crime analysis is still a struggling profession—struggling to find its way into a majority of agencies, struggling to be considered a core rather than peripheral function, struggling to find legitimacy even with in police departments ostensibly dedicated to community policing, and struggling to find a niche beyond basic tactical analysis.

Crime fighting is a complex endeavor. Given all the emerging technologies that can be employed to the task—such as computers, night goggles, DNA analysis, and geographic information systems, to mention only a few—you would think that our arrest rates would be better, our inner cities safer, and our cars and electronic gadgets more secure. Unfortunately, they are not. Even though crime rates have decreased in the most recent decade and we have incarcerated a record number of offenders in are prisons and jails—two million and counting—we continue to conduct police work in the vast majority of cities and towns across the globe in remarkably the same way we did at the beginning of the twentieth century. Thanks to a number of innovative chiefs and pragmatic academics with support from the federal government, "police science" or "applied criminology" is now taking hold. This book represents the *beginning* of a formulation of the knowledge, skills, and abilities necessary to get the job done. Much more work remains to be done.

Tactical crime analysis or crime series analysis represents the essence of our tradition, but a much more robust enterprise must be conceptualized, designed, and implemented before we can realize the power and effects of this approach. Herman Goldstein has offered a new vision for an effective, outcome-based policing style. He tells us:

> Crime analysis, which has been an important part of the professional model of policing, is a base on which police can build in meeting the much wider and deeper demands for inquiry associated with problem-oriented policing.... Initially, it consisted of a review of reports on similar crimes to identify those that may have been committed by the same individual or group, with the hope that the sum of information from a number of reports might better enable the police to identify and apprehend the offender(s). If an offender was apprehended, similar analysis might enable the police to solve other crimes for which the offender was responsible and to increase the strength of the case against him or her. As crime analysis developed, attention focused on discovering patterns of criminal activity, enabling analysts to alert patrolling police officers to individuals suspected of committing a particular type of crime and to the area in which they might commit

---

[1] O.W. Wilson, *Police Administration,* 2nd ed. (New York: McGraw-Hill, 1963), 103.

it….At its best, crime analysis has been used to identify offenders and interrupt crime patterns rather than to gain the kind of knowledge and in-sights that might be used to affect the conditions that accounted for the criminal conduct…[1]

Problem-oriented policing [POP] actually provides an *incentive* to make much more effective use of the data typically collected as part of crime analysis and to expand beyond the current *limited* objectives of the most advanced crime analysis models. This would first require focusing more broadly on all of the problems police handle rather than on just traditional categories of crime. It would require trying to understand the nature of these problems as a basis for *critical review* of the agency's response, rather than limiting inquiries to narrower operational goals. It would use more sources of information than just the reports filed by police officers. To understand all aspects of a problem, police would have to become adept at *conducting literature searches, using telephone and door-to-door surveys, interviewing those having the most direct knowledge about a problem (including citizens, officers, representatives of various government agencies and private services, and ex-offenders), and making use of data collected by other government agencies and in the private sector.* Finally, the type of systematic inquiry contemplated as part of problem-oriented policing would *place a much higher value on the accuracy and preciseness* of the data used and the conclusions reached than has been characteristic of studies conducted within police agencies. [2]

It is clear: the challenge has been made, and it is time to summon up our human and technological resources to prevent crime and improve our quality of life, the original mandate for which policing was intended to achieve. Nick Ross, the Chairman of the Jill Dando Institute of Crime Science, in the Foreword of Ronald Clarke and John Eck's step-by-step guide, *Become a Problem-Solving Crime Analyst,* calls us out:

In reality POP involves some pretty sophisticated stuff. It requires smart thinking. Crime science can create new tools to make POP possible, but who are the professionals who will do the analysis of data and identify patterns at the local level? Who will construct hypotheses on how to intervene and put those ideas to the test? Who will create strategies that the police and other crime reduction partners can then act on? Who can gently but firmly lead society away from being so reactive to the new smart way of detecting baddies quickly and heading off trouble before it starts? Need I say it? You.

Police analysts will become more important, indeed increasingly will be seen as crucial, if we are to tackle crime more intelligently. You are the brains, the expert, the specialist, the boffin. [3]

Exploring Crime Analysis was written to help you to become that kind of expert analyst. In conjunction with a Professional Certification Program and the development of a Professional Training Series, the IACA hopes to be a leading force in moving crime analysis and policing toward a more professional problem-solving model, based on a high standard of knowledge, skills, and abilities.

I have had the opportunity to speak to a number of crime and intelligence analysts about these endeavors, and I have heard complaints that the skill set was too narrowly focused, or that a

---

[1] Herman Goldstein, *Problem-Oriented Policing* (New York: McGraw Hill, 1990), 37.
[2] *Ibid*, 37–38, emphasis added.
[3] Ronald V. Clarke and John Eck, *Become a Problem-Solving Crime Analyst in 55 Small Steps* (London: Jill Dando Institute of Crime Science, 2003), foreword.

certified set of standards for knowledge, skills, and abilities either already exists, or that the standards are too rigid for most to obtain. For every standard we must find a level that serves as a benchmark, and until we draw a line in the sand—so to speak—we will not have a measuring stick on which to move forward. Others have told me that this skill set does not serve or adequately address the functions or processes that are required for quality crime analysis. To them I give an analogy or two:

The sport of baseball requires a variety of skills and knowledge to be mastered before one can expect to effectively play the game. While it is rather simple to turn on the television and grab a beer or travel to the stadium to experience the sound of screaming fans, the smell of hotdogs, and the taste of cotton candy; to be able to even remotely duplicate the performance of major league ball players or even slow-pitch softball players, a number of fundamental skills are required. Running, hitting, throwing, and catching appear to be rather simple or even mundane skills, but anyone who has attempted to hit a baseball squarely on the threads will attest, it's a whole lot harder than it appears. Hand and eye coordination needed to combine these skills into specific plays and outcomes calls for a concerted effort of all the players. Knowing what to do (and executing it) with one out and runners on first and third, with a two run lead in the bottom of the ninth inning, takes a great deal of practice and intuitive skills. Given the variety of scenarios that develop in the course of a game, each calling for a different strategy or tactic, not to mention the symbols and signals that one needs to watch for, players have to be well-trained and well-orchestrated. Overlay that with the fact that the opposition is planning and devising ways to trick you or outplay you, and you have a contest only a trained eye can depict. But it all boils down to one's ability to effectively hit, run, catch, and throw as the basis for excellence.

Others might envision cooking in the same fashion. There are certainly different ways in which one can prepare food—broil it, bake it, fry it, grill it, boil it—each having a certain effect on the outcome of taste and texture. Cooking too long or too short, or using too much spice or too little of an ingredient, can turn a delicacy into a doggie treat. Chefs soon learn that the over-reliance on any one piece of technology—such as a microwave—can spoil an otherwise well-prepared meal. Similarly, analysts should not learn to depend too heavily on any one tool or technology (e.g., GIS, database querying, statistics), however new or powerful. Like the seasoned baseball player or the epicure chef, the competent crime analyst is in the best position to succeed at his or her chosen profession, and those that excel must be able to demonstrate a clear grasp of the basic skills and fundamentals of their trade.

This book serves as the foundation for understanding the essential knowledge, skills, and abilities it takes to become a master crime analyst, albeit perhaps wanting for process and function. You will need to know the significance of criminal behavior, how the criminal justice system operates, and how criminological theory might inform a particular pattern or trend. As you become proficient at using computers, reading comprehension, and writing clearly and concisely, your products will improve. When you become adept at applying research methods, calculating statistics, and deciphering qualitative information from within reports and observations about your jurisdiction, you will able to convert raw data into information, and information into organizational knowledge. The outcome will be a police organization that understands the scope and nature of crime and disorder, and one that can offer efficiency, effectiveness, and improved quality of life to its constituency. When an analyst has become proficient at the knowledge, skills, and abilities proffered in these pages, the different scenarios and challenges facing police will become more manageable and, ultimately, preventable. It is at that point you can declare yourself a "local crime expert" as described by Clarke and Eck in *Becoming a Problem Solving Crime Analyst*, or what Nick Ross called a "boffin" above.[1]

As each of you achieves this core level of competency, a more comprehensive model of analysis is possible that will prepare us to almost effortlessly identify current crime series, and more robustly develop strategies to address re-occurring patterns and develop solutions to a variety of community problems. These skills will become as second-nature to us as fielding a ground ball is to a professional baseball player. Crime series analysis will become a daily routine, as simple as boiling water but one as critical as this simple skill is to gourmet cooking. Our capability to monitor short-term patterns and series will provide us with a long-term understanding of emerging problems, and will offer us a systematic model for problem solving that will allow time for assessments and the refinement of tried-and-true responses to which we can turn when new challenges confront us. It is time to move beyond performing only tactical crime analysis and take on these new challenges.

This book lays the foundation on which this future is possible. I strongly urge you to become an expert on crime and crime analysis techniques, both for the advancement of your career and the betterment of policing. Your efforts will have a distinct influence on the quality of life within our society. I wish you well in your endeavors.

> **Noah J. Fritz**
> *President*
> International Association of Crime Analysts

---

[1] According to Nick Tilley, a renowned British criminal justice scholar, a "boffin" is British slang for a technical expert who provides quantum discovery for the application of another profession or discipline—one who offers key contributions without being a practitioner himself or herself, such as a crime expert assisting the police.

PART I
Foundations of Crime Analysis

1
Fundamentals of Crime Analysis

Christopher W. Bruce

Information is the most valuable commodity in the world. It's more valuable than money, for with it one can make money. It's more valuable than power, for with it one can achieve power. It's more valuable than goods, for with it one can build, acquire, and improve goods. In any business, in any industry, in any part of the world, the right information is absolutely priceless.

Businesses invest a great deal of money, time, and resources in the quest to acquire information—information about their products, and how to improve them; information about their competitors, and what they're up to; information about customers and what they want; information about the business itself, and how its various divisions are doing. Governments rise and fall on information—information about the opinions and attitudes of their citizens; information about allies; information about enemies. Information wins wars, builds cities, heals the sick, enriches the poor, and—most relevant to the crime analysis community—solves and prevents crime.

Industries, organizations, and companies realize these principles on an operational level. Consequently, they devote individuals, units, and sometimes entire divisions to collecting, processing, and disseminating information. Businesses have product researchers and testers, budget analysts, management analysts, and market researchers. Every division of government has policy analysts, and the federal government hires and trains spies and intelligence specialists. Insurance companies employ actuaries and claims analysts. Every time you see the word "analyst" in a person's job title—research analyst, budget analyst, policy analyst, business analyst, market analyst, stock analyst, intelligence analyst, and so on—you're dealing with someone whose job revolves around information—information designed to help a company, agency, or organization do its job better.

Such is the case with crime analysts. Crime analysts provide information to police agencies about crime, disorder, calls for service, police activity, and other areas of police interest, all with the goal of helping the agencies do their jobs better. Specifically, crime analysts help police agencies:

- Solve crimes
- Develop effective strategies and tactics to prevent future crimes
- Find and apprehend offenders
- Prosecute and convict offenders
- Improve safety and quality of life
- Optimize internal operations
- Prioritize patrol and investigations
- Detect and solve chronic problems
- Allocate resources
- Plan for future resource needs
- Enact effective policies
- Educate the public

This list applies primarily to municipal police departments, but other law enforcement and criminal justice agencies can enjoy the benefits of crime analysis even if their charters do not include some of the goals listed above. Wherever a crime analyst is employed, his or her job is to provide information support for the agency's overall mission.

Data, Information, and Knowledge

Information shares some characteristics with other "commodities" like metals, grain, or automobiles. First, human effort has to go into the production of these commodities. Metals must be mined from the Earth, grain must be planted and harvested, and automobiles must be manufactured on an assembly line. Second, all commodities are created from raw materials—ore, seeds, and parts in our examples—and the raw materials might, in turn, be composed of even rawer materials. Third, the production of these commodities serves little purpose until they are delivered to a consumer.

An analyst's effort is what creates information, whether that information is "built" or "mined." A metaphor that works well is to see the analyst as a sculptor. Some sculptures are created by combining and molding pieces of clay, much as an analyst creates information by combining pieces of data. Other sculptures are created by chipping away extraneous pieces of stone to reveal a shape inside, much as an analyst filters out extraneous pieces of data to find the one that reveals a fact or truth.

Either way, the analyst's raw material is *data*, which might come from numerous sources. Out of this data, the analyst seeks to create *information*, which he then delivers to his "consumer"—the police agency. This information, once internalized, becomes *knowledge* that informs police action. Two processes are at work:

1. *Data* becomes *information* when it is effectively *analyzed*.

2. *Information* becomes *knowledge* when it is effectively *communicated*.

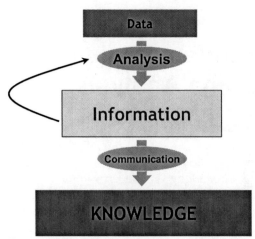

Figure 1-1: The transition from data to knowledge

Though the title *crime analyst* focuses on the analysis process, both analysis and communication fall within the crime analyst's area of responsibility. Section 2 of this book, "Processes of Analysis," is primarily concerned with the analysis function, while Section 3, "Tools of Crime Analysis," offers suggestions for communicating information.

In the chart, note the line from "Information" back to "Analysis." The transition of data into analysis is a self-feeding loop, as new data is juxtaposed against existing information to create further levels of analysis.

Table 1-1 shows some ways in which this process works in a typical municipal police agency, with examples of tactical, strategic, and operational applications.

A History of Crime Analysis

The practice of crime analysis probably predates the profession. Some of the most essential functions of crime analysis—such as identifying hot spots for extra patrol—were likely performed in ancient times. In the modern era, crime analysis techniques and products were used in the first modern police

Table 1-1: Examples of the transition from data to knowledge in a typical police agency

Data		Information		Knowledge		Result
Individual Incident Reports in a records management system	Analysis	Six of the reports are related in a series of robberies	Communication	Robbery series is prime topic of discussion in next detective's meeting	Strategy & Action	Robbery offender is apprehended
Statistics showing number of officers per capita throughout the state		Your police department has 20% fewer officers per capita than average		Chief has this information in mind when preparing his budget proposal		Agency is granted additional officers by city
Crime volume of current year compared to past years; individual records in RMS; jurisdictional information		Auto theft is up 20%, with most of the increase in Police Beat 5 on the midnight shift, probably influenced by new sports arena		Officers internalize this information and consider it when patrolling Beat 5		Auto theft is reduced

force, the London Metropolitan Police, in the 1800s. "Detectives," who identified patterns of crime, were first assigned in London in the 1840s, crime statistics are available for the city as early as 1847, and it was within this department that the concept of *modus operandi*, and of classifying offenders and crimes based on it, first appeared in the second half of the nineteenth century.

As other police around the world adapted or emulated the London model, they developed their own versions of these techniques. Methods of pattern identification and analysis are performed by every patrol officer in the regular course of his or her duties. As one early crime analysis manual observes:

> Informal crime analysis, in its simplest sense, is performed by all officers as they investigate crimes. Crime analysis is the quality of examining one crime occurrence and comparing it with similar past events. In essence, the officer is a walking crime analysis unit as he compares his investigations with his past experiences and with the experiences of others.[1]

American police reformers in the twentieth century began to formalize the use of crime analysis techniques. One early proponent of the use of analysis, August Vollmer (1876-1955), has been called "the father of American policing." Vollmer served as the Chief of Police of Berkeley, California, from 1905 to 1932. His innovations range from vehicle patrol to radio communication to fingerprinting, and include (relevant to our purposes) pin mapping, the regular review of police reports, and the formation of patrol districts based on crime volume.

> When Vollmer mobilized his beat officers on bicycles in 1909, he laid out beats in accordance with the number of calls anticipated from each part of the city.[2]

Though the term "crime analysis" had not yet appeared in law enforcement literature, one quote from Vollmer's "The Police Beat" shows he was familiar with its concepts:

> On the assumption of regularity of crime and similar occurrences, it is possible to tabulate these occurrences by areas within a city and thus determine the points which

---

[1] Robert Austin et. al., *Police Crime Analysis Unit Handbook* (Washington, DC: Law Enforcement Assistance Administration, 1973), 3. Note, though, that the text implies a limited definition of the term "crime analysis" that focuses only on pattern analysis.

[2] G. Hobart Reiner et. al., *Crime Analysis in Support of Patrol* (Washington, DC: Law Enforcement Assistance Administration, 1977), 8.

have the greatest danger of such crimes and what points have the least danger.[1]

Vollmer's protégé, Orlando Winfield Wilson (1900-1972), served as a police executive in a number of agencies, including the Chicago Police Department, where he was Superintendent from 1960 to 1971. Wilson wrote several influential books, including *Police Records* (1942), *Police Administration* (1950), and *Police Planning* (1957). It is in Wilson's second edition (1963) of *Police Administration* that we find the first written citation of "crime analysis":

> **Crime Analysis.** The crime-analysis section studies daily reports of serious crimes in order to determine the location, time, special characteristics, similarities to other criminal attacks, and various significant facts that might help to identify either a criminal or the existence of a pattern of criminal activity. Such information is helpful in planning the operations of a division or district.[2]

Though this is the earliest known source of the term, Wilson's use suggests that there were already crime analysis units in existence at the time of his writing. His third edition of the book offers several pages on crime analysis and contributed to the growth of the profession in the late 1970s.

During the late 1970s, many formal crime analysis programs developed across the country with funding from the Law Enforcement Assistance Administration (LEAA). To support these programs, the LEAA published a series of manuals on crime analysis between 1973 and 1977. Crime analysis became one of four facets of the LEAA's Integrated Criminal Apprehension Program (ICAP), and to this day, long after

the death of ICAP, some crime analysis units are known colloquially as the "ICAP Unit."

When the LEAA lost the last of its funding in 1982, the profession of crime analysis entered a dry spell. Few new units developed, except in certain states where local support was strong. Many crime analysts funded through the LEAA and ICAP lost their jobs.

The 1990s brought a "Golden Age of Crime Analysis," characterized by:

- The 1990 publication of *Problem-Oriented Policing* by Herman Goldstein, who worked with O.W. Wilson in Chicago.

- The formation of the International Association of Crime Analysts (IACA) in 1990, and the association's first conference in 1991.

- A certificate program in crime analysis offered by the California Department of Justice, starting in 1992.

- New and plentiful funding from the U.S. Department of Justice. Much of it focused on community policing and problem-oriented policing.

- Powerful, affordable technology, including crime mapping applications, desktop publishing, and relational databases.

- The development of the "CompStat" system of strategy development and management accountability within the New York City Police Department. (The first CompStat meetings were held in 1994.) The CompStat process relies heavily on mapping and analysis.

---

[1] Quoted in Reiner, *Support of Patrol*, 9.
[2] Orlando W. Wilson, *Police Administration*, 2nd ed. (New York: McGraw-Hill, 1963), 103.

- The establishment of the National Institute of Justice Crime Mapping Research Center (now called the Mapping & Analysis for Public Safety program) in 1997.

- The foundation of the National Law Enforcement and Corrections Technology Center's Crime Mapping and Analysis Program (CMAP) in 1998.

This combination of factors caused a proliferation of new crime analysts and crime analysis units throughout the 1990s. Moreover, these new analysts had access to new ideas, literature, professional standards, support, and training that were not available to their 1970s counterparts.

Unfortunately, a few years into the new millennium, we seem to have left the "golden age." Political changes and an economic downturn have greatly reduced the amount of money available to local police agencies, and the development of new crime analysis programs has slowed to a crawl. The threat of terrorism has shifted the focus of law enforcement away from traditional crime analysis toward criminal intelligence analysis (a separate analysis discipline that has evolved along a parallel track). At the same time, however, the professionals within the field have banded together to develop training, literature, and certification. It remains to be seen whether the forces of progress or regress will prevail.

Classifications of Law Enforcement Analysis

Crime analysis is one of several types of analysis that fall under a macro-heading variously called "law enforcement analysis," "public safety analysis," or "police analysis." "Law enforcement analysis" is probably the most common. We may define it as follows:

Law enforcement analysis: Processes, techniques, and products that provide information support to the mission of law enforcement agencies.

("Law enforcement agency" is a common term that comprises municipal police, state police, and investigative or special-purpose agencies with local, state, national, or international jurisdiction. It is generally understood, however, that these agencies—particularly local police—do much more than simply enforce the law. The different types of analysis under this heading support *all* the missions of these agencies, and not just those geared toward "law enforcement.")

Within this overall field, we find crime analysts, criminal intelligence analysts, and criminal investigative analysts.[1]

Crime analysis is focused on the study of criminal incidents; the identification of patterns, trends, and problems; and the dissemination of information that helps a police agency develop tactics and strategies to solve patterns, trends, and problems.

Criminal intelligence analysis concentrates on the collection and dissemination of information about criminals, particularly organizations and conspiracies. Intelligence analysts hunt for leads on the structure and hierarchy of criminal organizations, the flow of money and goods, relationships, current activities and plans, and personal information about the participants—usually with the goal of arrest, prosecution, and conviction of the offenders involved.

---

[1] Steven Gottlieb, Sheldon Arenberg, and Raj Singh, *Crime Analysis: from First Report to Final Arrest* (Montclair, CA: Alpha Publishing, 1994), 11-13. This is the earliest known text to divide the functions of analysis this way. The authors include "operations analysis" as a category of law enforcement analysis, but other crime analysts seem to recognize operations analysis as a function specific to crime analysis; it is presented that way here.

The Crime/Intelligence Controversy

In the United States, crime analysis and criminal intelligence analysis have for most of their histories been considered distinct professions. Criminal intelligence analysis traces its history to military intelligence techniques and their application to domestic "enemies" such as drug cartels, extremist groups, and organized crime. Crime analysis is more rooted in the concerns of local law enforcement, crime reporting, problem-oriented policing, and community policing. Though they have always shared some common ground, they developed on separate tracks. The literature of each discipline rarely mentions the other, and both have their own international professional association: the International Association of Crime Analysts (IACA) and the International Association of Law Enforcement Intelligence Analysts (IALEIA).

In recent years, however, some members of both professions—and both associations—have begun to question whether the functions, skills, and processes of crime analysis and criminal intelligence analysis are really different enough to justify two distinct professions. There are analysts at one extreme who believe strongly that the professions are separate and should remain so, and there are those at the other end who think there should be no distinction at all.

As we cover in the section on Defining Crime Analysis, most analysts working for medium or small police agencies will likely perform *all* types of analysis, no matter what their titles. For such analysts, the perception is naturally strong that crime analysis and criminal intelligence analysis are part of the same profession.

To our perception, the difference between a crime analyst and a criminal intelligence analyst (and, to some extent, the difference between the IACA and the IALEIA) lies primarily within the missions of the agencies that employ them. Most criminal intelligence analysts seem to work for state, national, international, or special-purpose agencies in which the mission is the investigation, apprehension, and prosecution of offenders. There are also a number of intelligence analysts working in investigative units of large police agencies, in which the unit's mission is also apprehension and prosecution. Criminal intelligence analysis is thus primarily an *investigative* process.

Most crime analysts, on the other hand, work for local police agencies, where the mission is not so much to capture and convict offenders as it is to reduce crime and disorder through multiple strategies (of which apprehension is one). Crime analysis is primarily a *problem-solving* process.

It makes sense, then, that in countries other than the United States, where most police agencies are fairly large and the distinctions between federal, state, and local levels are less severe, that analysis units perform all types of analytical work. This likely accounts for the position of non-U.S. analysts that there is little or no distinction between the two.

The IACA's position is that crime analysts and criminal intelligence analysts share common tools, techniques, and skills, but different audiences, products, and goals. Thus, the traditional model makes sense to us: crime analysis and criminal intelligence analysis are related—but not identical—disciplines, existing side-by-side under a common banner.

Criminal investigative analysis refers to the procedures and skills used to create a physical, behavioral, or psychological profile of an offender based on the characteristics of the crimes that he or she has committed. "Profiling" is a synonym. It is an intense, time-consuming process, requiring a great deal of skill and training, and generally only applied to cases of murder, rape, and arson—particularly serial murder, rape, and arson. Crime analysts might use some investigative analysis techniques to help the agency solve an individual crime, as when an analyst compares a suspect's actions in a particular incident to a database of offenders known to commit crimes the same way. Investigative analysis applied to a crime series also shares some territory with tactical crime analysis, as when an analyst uses his knowledge of criminal behavior to "profile" a serial burglar. Nevertheless, these are informal applications of criminal investigative analysis, and investigative analysis is usually regarded as a unique profession, distinct from crime analysis.

Defining Crime Analysis

The definition that we provided is one of numerous ways that crime analysis has been defined throughout its history. Sometimes these varying definitions complement each other. Other times, they contradict.

The earliest known definition is O.W. Wilson's, cited above, and focuses primarily on what we now call tactical crime analysis (see below) but does not anticipate the variety of demands that would be placed on crime analysis units in smaller police agencies.

By the 1970s, federal publications were defining crime analysis in a manner that included strategic analysis, administrative analysis, and operations analysis (see below):

[T]he crime analysis function is defined as a set of systematic, analytical processes directed at providing timely and pertinent information relative to crime patterns and trend correlations, to assist operational and administrative personnel in planning and deployment of resources for prevention and suppression of criminal activities, aiding the investigative process, and increasing apprehensions and clearance of cases. Within this context, crime analysis supports a number of department functions, including patrol deployment, special operations and tactical units, investigations, planning and research, crime prevention, and administrative services.[1]

In recent years, there have been attempts to simplify this definition. The Web site of the International Association of Crime Analysts says:

Crime analysis describes the techniques and processes used to study crime patterns and trends, the way they affect a particular jurisdiction, and how police agencies respond to them.[2]

But other recent definitions have sought to broaden the scope of crime analysis to include any activity that provides information support to a law enforcement agency, as in this definition from a local crime analysis association flyer, intended for law enforcement executives:

The individual or unit in a police department charged with processing data and providing information that the agency

---

[1] G. Hobart Reiner et. al., *Crime Analysis Operations Manual* (Washington, DC: Law Enforcement Assistance Administration, 1977), 1-3.
[2] International Association of Crime Analysts, "Frequently Asked Questions," http://www.iaca.net/resources/faq.html (accessed January 23, 2004).

can use to reduce, prevent, and solve crime, disorder, and quality of life issues.[1]

This definition, which could conceivably include intelligence analysis and investigative analysis, would seem to suit "law enforcement analysis" or "public safety analysis" better than crime analysis.

The difficulty in defining crime analysis is tied to how crime analysis positions are defined and structured within individual police agencies. Many analysts in small agencies provide *every* type of law enforcement analysis for their organizations, but it is rare to find these analysts titled "law enforcement analyst" or "public safety analyst." Instead, the agencies call them "crime analysts" or "intelligence analysts" or some combination of the two. Meanwhile, a large agency might employ several "crime analysts" whose job responsibilities are limited to the identification and analysis of crime series—called tactical crime analysis. Crime trends and other strategic problems are handled by a different unit, perhaps with a different title. The point is that depending on the size of the agency, you might find individuals with a "crime analyst" title whose actual job functions are either broader or narrower than the traditional definition of the term. This is not necessarily a problem, but it is something that we must take into consideration when studying the field.

Classifications of Crime Analysis

Crime analysis functions are usually assigned to one of four classifications:[2]

1. Tactical Crime Analysis
2. Strategic Crime Analysis
3. Administrative Crime Analysis
4. Police Operations Analysis

We describe each of these in turn:

Tactical Crime Analysis

This term describes the daily identification and analysis of emerging or existing crime patterns, including series and hot spots. The goal of tactical analysis is to:

1) Identify emerging crime patterns as soon as possible
2) Complete comprehensive analyses of any patterns
3) Notify the agency of the patterns' existence
4) Work with the agency to develop the best strategies to address patterns

Tactical analysis is, again, a daily process, and should probably be the first priority on an analyst's to do list. It is an *action-oriented* process—the goal is to help the department intercede patterns quickly and effectively.

Analysts use several methods to identify crime patterns, but the most frequent (and most successful) involves the daily review of crime reports, and the comparison of those reports to past incidents. In making this comparison, the analyst looks for enough commonalities between a past incident and a present incident to suggest a pattern of crime.

---

[1] Massachusetts Association of Crime Analysts, "What Is Crime Analysis?" http://www.macrimeanalysts.com /articles/whatiscrimeanalysis.pdf (accessed January 23, 2004).

[2] Crime analysis was divided into "tactical analysis" and "strategic analysis" in the Integrated Criminal Apprehension Program manuals of the 1970s. See, for example, Richard G. Grassie et. al., *Crime Analysis*

Executive Manual (Washington, DC: Law Enforcement Assistance Administration, 1977), 1-2 to 1-6. Gottlieb, *Crime Analysis*, 14–15, is the earliest known source for the term "administrative analysis" and is primarily responsible for making this categorization scheme known among crime analysts. Gottlieb includes "operations analysis" as a type of law enforcement analysis, distinct from crime analysis, but we believe that operations analysis is now generally understood as a crime analysis function.

To perform these comparisons, analysts of yore kept paper logs of crimes and their various factors, but most modern analysts use databases and database querying techniques. There are also crime mapping and statistical techniques that will aid in the identification of patterns.

Analysis of a crime pattern typically focuses on the who, what, when, where, or how factors that are common across a significant number of the incidents. Identifying these commonalities is often the key to the pattern's solution. For instance, in a street robbery pattern in which each incident features the same offender description (making it a series), the analyst might focus on the offender, searching a database of known offenders who match that description. In a burglary pattern in which Oriental rugs are stolen, the solution might lie in finding the outlets of sale for the stolen rugs. A purse snatching pattern localized in one section of a park might be suppressed through environmental re-design. If the incidents in a series show temporal or geographic commonalities, the analyst may try to predict where and when the offender will strike next.

Most analysts notify their agencies of a crime pattern through some sort of printed crime bulletin, though e-mail and intranets are becoming more common means of communication. In agencies with CompStat

or similar meetings, the analyst might have to give a presentation on the pattern. Depending on the nature of the pattern and the policies of the agency, the analyst might also have a role in notifying the public.

Let's examine a typical tactical analysis scenario: the analyst arrives for work on Wednesday morning and begins reviewing the crime reports taken during the previous 24 hours. Among them is a report of the "smash & grab" burglary of a jewelry store at 02:30 that morning (a witness observed the incident, fixing the time). The analyst, because she reads the agency's burglary reports every day, at once recalls a similar incident during the previous week. A database query reveals, in fact, *two* recent burglaries that show some similarities to the current incident. The analyst then examines the who, what, when, where, and how factors (Table 1-2).

With the similarities that these three incidents show, the analyst confidently announces the existence of a crime pattern. She immediately creates and distributes a bulletin to the police agency. The bulletin helps the Public Information Officer prepare a press release, and helps the communications director prepare a teletype for dissemination to surrounding agencies.

Table 1-2: A commercial burglary series

Time	Target	Point/Method of Entry	Property Stolen	Offender Info.
Tuesday June 9 03:45	Aiken Jewelers 123 Main St	Front window smashed with brick	5 watches, 3 rings, 2 necklaces	None seen
Thursday June 19 00:00 to 07:30	Bobbitt's Baubles 456 Elm St	Front door kicked in	8 necklaces, 3 rings, 4 earrings, 1 watch	None seen
Wednesday June 25 02:30	Candice's Cameos 789 Pine St	Front door window smashed with rock	3 watches, 1 ring, 4 necklaces	Two white males, both tall (over 6 feet), both with brown hair, driving an older-model green American sedan

The analyst reflects on the pattern. Since the burglars have struck once per week for the past three weeks, always on a weeknight during the middle of the week, she anticipates another incident the next week. The commonalities in the pattern give the agency several avenues for strategy development:

- The pattern is focused on jewelry stores. The analyst could compile a list of all jewelry stores in the area and disseminate it to the patrol division. Patrol officers could watch jewelry stores closely during the next week. Though this might prove impractical if the jurisdiction has too many stores.

- The agency could contact all the jewelry stores in the area and encourage them to take extra security measures during the coming weeks.

- The agency could focus on outlets of sale: where are the burglars selling the stolen jewelry? The analyst or one of the detectives in her agency might check pawn records in her town and in surrounding towns for some of the stolen items.

- The offender description is somewhat vague, but it might prove valuable. The analyst could conduct a database query of all known offenders who drive older-model green American sedans, focusing specifically on anyone over six feet tall with a history of burglary.

With these options, the pattern could have several successful outcomes. We'll pick one: the analyst compiles a list of potential suspects based on the vehicle and offender description. She crosschecks this list against a list of individuals who have been reported pawning items lately, and finds a match: a Robert Schlimm of Hillcrest Drive.

Detectives visit the pawnshop and identify several pieces of jewelry stolen in the burglaries—jewelry pawned by Schlimm. The next week, starting Tuesday night, a team of officers tails Schlimm and catches him and a companion in the act of committing their fourth burglary. The ultimate result: three burglaries have been solved and perhaps dozens have been prevented.

Strategic Crime Analysis

Strategic analysis focuses on trends, problems, and their causes.

Trends are long-term increases and decreases in crime, or changes in the characteristics of a particular crime over a long period of time. Crime trends can occur over months, years, decades, even centuries, but are rarely discussed in terms shorter than a month or longer than a decade. Sometimes they can be traced to a single cause (e.g., a new shopping mall, fluctuations in the price of heroin); more often, they have numerous obscure and indirect social, environmental, economic, political, and geographic causes. These causes, and the trends that follow from them, are generally what is meant by the term "crime problems."

Crime trends can be positive (increases in a type of crime), negative (decreases in a type of crime), or neutral (shift in the characteristics of crime with consistent volume). ("Positive" and "negative" in this sense refer to the direction of change in the volume of crime from one time period to the next, not to the desirability of the trend.) It is equally important to study negative trends as it is to study positive ones; knowing the factors behind a decrease in crime is as important as knowing the factors behind an increase. Decreases might be duplicated with other crimes and in other geographic areas.

Some examples of crime trends include:

- A new strip mall erected along a major street becomes a hot spot for auto theft and auto burglaries

- Aggressive police action against "chop shops" over a decade leads to a dramatic decrease in auto theft

- A statewide recession causes widespread unemployment, indirectly leading to increases in numerous crimes

Analysis of trends usually starts with some kind of statistical report or map that gives a broad overview of crime. From here, the analyst can drill-down into the specific characteristics of each crime, looking for substantial changes and attempting to determine their causes (see Chapter 6 for insight into this involved process).

The police agency's response to a crime trend is not to immediately mobilize officers into tactical action. Most responses that work well with patterns do not work well with trends. When faced with a trend, the agency looks toward problem-solving strategies and policies that will have a long-term effect.

Assume, for example, that the analyst's annual report reveals that robberies in 2004 are 20% higher than average for the city.

The analyst queries those robberies, and further discovers that while individual or "street" robberies held steady, commercial robberies increased significantly. A closer look at the commercial robbery data shows that the bulk of them occurred at convenience stores during the nighttime. However, suspect descriptions and *modus operandi* differ considerably, suggesting that multiple independent offenders are involved. There was a single arrest.

The analyst has now identified a specific trend, and he begins to question its cause. He maps the offenses, and notes that the targets are clustered on or near a local route that traverses half a dozen towns. A phone call to analysts in these other towns confirms that they have also seen a jump in convenience store robberies. Thumbing through a file of newspaper clippings, the analyst recalls that a Greyhound racetrack, which allows gambling, opened eight months ago in one of the towns along the afflicted route.

The analyst hypothesizes that the convenience store robbers are racing gamblers looking for some quick cash. He investigates the one robber arrested for a convenience store hold-up and he finds that the offender is known to the police in the town containing the racetrack. He has been arrested twice for disorderly conduct at the track. Physical descriptions of the other robbers, behavior, and direction of flight point to gamblers as suspects in the other convenience store robberies as well.

The analyst writes up his findings for his agency, which must now take action to intercede. Some possibilities include:

1) Staking out convenience stores at likely days and times in an attempt to apprehend offenders.

2) Re-designing patrol routes to give the afflicted area more attention.

3) Saturating the afflicted area with extra patrol cars, instructing the officers to frequently visit convenience stores and park in store lots.

4) Conducting aggressive traffic enforcement along the afflicted route. (If data shows that gambler-robbers are more likely than average people to have

revoked registrations, suspended licenses, and active warrants, this may indirectly result in apprehension and suppression of offenders.)

5) Conducting security surveys at convenience stores in this area, helping them decrease their chances of victimization through better lighting, increased visibility, visible security cameras, drop safes, and other prevention strategies.

In general, trends are best solved through strategies that *reduce the desirability of the targets* or that *reduce opportunity*, as opposed to strategies that apprehend offenders.

Administrative Crime Analysis

Administrative crime analysis is a broad category including an eclectic selection of administrative and statistical reports, research, and other projects not focused on the immediate or long-term reduction or elimination of a pattern or trend. Examples would include:

- A report on demographic changes in the jurisdiction
- A historical research project on crime during the Prohibition period
- Miscellaneous crime statistics to support grant applications
- Preparation of Uniform Crime Report (UCR) or Incident-Based Reporting System (IBRS) reports
- Creation of charts and graphs to support the chief's presentation to the City Council
- Creation of patrol deployment maps for a special event
- Provision of a list of individuals with warrants by police beat and seriousness of offense

Administrative analysis has gotten a bad rap over the years—it is traditionally regarded as a low-priority category—but this category is, in fact, what keeps many analysts employed. The presence of an individual who can answer any question, provide information on demand, and arrange data in any desired form is of great value to most police agencies. Furthermore, many tasks that are categorized as "administrative analysis" might substantially affect public safety—see the last two examples above, for instance.

Police Operations Analysis

Police operations analysis describes the study of a police department's own operations and policies—including its allocation of personnel, money, equipment, and other resources, geographically, organizationally, and temporally—and whether these operations and policies have the most effective influence on crime and disorder in the agency's jurisdiction. Because many operations analysis tasks require good evaluative research, analysts who engage in it should have a solid understanding of social science research methods. Some questions that operations analysis might seek to answer include:

- What is the best way for the police agency to divide the city into beats?
- What is the optimal allocation of officers per shift?
- What effect has the department's mandatory arrest policy for misdemeanor domestic assault had on domestic violence recidivism?
- Can the agency justify a request for more police officers?
- How much time and money would the department save if it enacted a policy that limited its response to unverified burglar alarms?

Operations analysis goes hand-in-hand with strategic crime analysis, as many operations decisions (including geographic and temporal allocation of officers) are based on long-term crime trends.

The Crime Analysis Process

The crime analysis process involves six steps:

1. Data collection and management
2. Data scanning and querying
3. Data analysis
4. Information dissemination
5. Strategy development
6. Evaluation and feedback

In this section, we cover the various aspects of this process.

Background Knowledge

Before the crime analysis process even begins, analysts come to the table with certain knowledge. The quality and extent of this knowledge will inform everything they do as analysts, for better or worse.

The specific areas of knowledge most valuable to crime analysts are:

- **Knowledge about crime and criminal behavior:** Analysts need to understand how criminals actually behave in the real world, and why they behave that way. They need to understand the nature of various crimes, including how and why they are committed. Chapter 3 provides a solid foundation for this knowledge.

- **Knowledge about policing and police strategy:** Analysts also need to understand how police behave in the real world—their mission, duties, schedules, tactics and strategies, and

limitations. Chapter 2 introduces readers to this knowledge.

- **Knowledge about the jurisdiction:** Good analysis is informed by a thorough knowledge of the police jurisdiction—where people live, work, and play; how they get from one place to another; the jurisdiction's commerce, economics, demographics, politics, geography and environment; and dozens of other factors that will make a difference in the analysis of any pattern or trend.

- **Knowledge about the police agency:** Every agency has its own character, traditions, and style. Analysts will need to work within this style to be effective.

Data Sources

A crime analyst must become a connoisseur of several different types of data:

1. Data about **incidents** that occur within the analyst's jurisdiction. This is an analyst's primary data. Such data might include crime reports, arrest reports, call for service records, and traffic accident reports. Chapter 10 helps with the distinctions between these data types.

2. Data from **other agencies** that might help an analyst identify cross-jurisdictional phenomena. These include National Law Enforcement Telecommunications Service (NLETS) teletypes, postings in police Internet discussion groups, other agencies' bulletins and reports, verbal information from meetings, news stories, or sophisticated cross-jurisdictional information sharing systems.

3. Data about the **jurisdiction** that might help explain or predict crime patterns or trends. These types of data include demographic statistics, business profiles, political information, economic indicators, and news reports.

4. Data about **persons and businesses,** to identify and learn about offenders, and to analyze their activities. These include traditional intelligence data—informants' reports, financial data, phone records, property deeds—as well as more mundane sources of data, such as telephone books, voter registries, criminal histories, parole release notices, sex offender registries, and pawn reports.

5. Data on **police activity**, including calls for service, activity logs, patrol rosters, citation records, directed patrol schedules, and other similar logs.

6. **Geographic information system (GIS) data**, which spans all these categories but exists in a specific format (see Chapter 15).

Analysts will review each of these data types regularly, but some more frequently than others:

Incident data—daily, to find crime patterns as they happen.
Other agency data—daily, or as often as the analyst can obtain it, to compare with the analyst's own jurisdiction's data.
Jurisdictional data—reviewed as analysts receive it, filed or stored in a database for later reference; consulted as needed to analyze patterns and trends.
Person & business data—generally, analysts will seek this data for a specific purpose (e.g., to identify possible suspects in a pattern).

Police activity data—sought specifically for operations analysis reports

There are four factors that can influence the quality of data and, therefore, the way analysts handle and use it:

1. **Accuracy.** How accurate is the data? Do the people entering the data spell things correctly? Are the reports coded correctly? Are the address ranges in the street files correct? There are opportunities to spoil data accuracy with every type of data. See Chapter 7 for a discussion of data integrity.

2. **Reliability.** How reliable is the source of the data? Is it logical that the source would know what it purports to know? What is the source's reputation for data quality? What sort of history does the source have with data quality?

3. **Completeness.** Does the data contain all the information the analyst needs? Are there fields missing? Has the source neglected to provide important facts?

4. **Timeliness.** Does the analyst get the data in time to analyze it while patterns and trends are still current?

CAD records entered by overwhelmed dispatchers may suffer from accuracy problems. One might question the reliability of newspaper articles from frankly partisan sources. Pawn reports from indifferent pawnshops may plague analysts with their incompleteness. Crime bulletins that analysts receive at monthly meetings can be of dubious value because of timeliness problems. Crime reports filled out by harried police officers and entered by bored, frustrated records clerks may suffer from all of these issues.

Data Sources Checklist

Listed below are many sources of data that a crime analyst might want to obtain.

INCIDENT DATA

❑ **Crime Reports** from a records management system (RMS) or from paper copies.

❑ **Arrest Reports**, which may be the same as crime reports.

❑ **Call for Service Records,** which include both criminal and non-criminal policing issues. Again, in some departments, these are kept in the same system as crime reports.

❑ **Accident reports.**

OTHER AGENCY DATA

❑ **Teletypes**, received from the antiquated but venerable NLETS system. Most departments have at least one terminal and printer in the dispatch center.

❑ **Bulletins and Reports**, issued by crime analysts in surrounding cities and towns.

❑ **Regional Newspapers** that cover the analyst's area. Many newspapers now offer their articles on the Internet.

❑ **Meetings** of analysts, detectives or other groups in which intelligence is shared.

❑ **Online Bulletin Boards & Discussion Groups**

❑ **E-Mail Discussion Lists**

OTHER AGENCY DATA (cont.)

❑ **Regional Crime Analysis Network** (available in select locations)

❑ **Police Magazines, Newsletters, and Journals** sometimes carry pattern and trend information.

❑ **Web Sites** maintained by other police departments.

JURISDICTIONAL DATA

❑ **Demographic Data**, published by the U.S. Census Bureau (see Chapter 12).

❑ **Local Newspaper Articles** on demographic, social, economic, and physical changes in your area

❑ **Business Listings** to identify the different types of commercial establishments

❑ **Tax Assessment Information** provides economic information and ownership for properties.

❑ **Government Web Sites** for news, political information, statistics, other information about the jurisdiction.

PERSONS & BUSINESSES

❑ **Field Interview Reports** (certain agencies only)

❑ **Intelligence Reports** from informants and other sources.

PERSONS & BUSINESSES (cont.)

❑ **Parole Release Notices** from your local corrections agency.

❑ **Criminal Histories**

❑ **Known Offender Files**

❑ **Motor Vehicle Registration and Licensing Data**

❑ **Deeds and Tax Assessment Data**

❑ **Telephone Directories** (including online "reverse" directories)

❑ **City and Town Registers** (in certain jurisdictions)

❑ **Pawn Data** (if required by local laws)

❑ **Sex Offender Registries**

POLICE ACTIVITY DATA

❑ **Call for Service Records**

❑ **Arrest Records**

❑ **Patrol Rosters** showing which units and areas were staffed on each shift.

❑ **Case Histories**

❑ **Citation Records**

❑ **Directed Patrol Logs**

❑ **Budgets**

Intelligence analysts are often trained to give each piece of intelligence a numerical ranking for each of these factors, but for most crime analysts, it's usually enough to simply know the answers to these questions—and to do their best to fix any problems.

Data Management

Data management constitutes its own discipline of police science, occupying far more depth and detail than we can hope to cover in the scope of this book, let alone this chapter. The means by which various police agencies approach this critical process are as varied as anything in police science. In many agencies, data management remains in its infancy, characterized by the collection of very little data in paper-based systems; in others, it is extremely advanced, characterized by elaborate computerized records management systems, with aggressive quality control and strong data querying capabilities. Whether an analyst finds his department's data management processes in fine order or in mind-breaking chaos, his goal is the same:

> To have **easy access** to a **quality set** of **timely, complete** data on which he can conduct **flexible queries** to find and analyze different crime phenomena.

The extent to which the department's data management systems allow or do not allow for each of these four crucial factors determines how much time the analyst must spend entering and managing his own data. In departments with utterly intolerable systems, the analyst may find that he needs to spend half his day simply entering and tracking reports in a database or matrix of his own design. In departments with superior systems, the analyst will be able to jump right into the process of data scanning and pattern identification first thing in the morning.

Depending on the quality of the department's records management systems, then, the analyst will take one of five approaches to data management:

Use the Records Management System. Police departments today find that there are hundreds of competing RMS vendors offering a variety of confusing packages, many of which lack the most basic functionality of modern mouse-and-menu-driven operating systems, omit important data fields, and fail to provide a flexible, robust querying capability. The sheer number of companies means that very few of them have a large market share, and thus very few of them make enough money to encourage innovation and aggressive product development. Agencies are likely to remain with the same system, however insufficient, for many years, both because of the high cost of a new system and the sharp learning curve (caused in part by the lack of standards from one vendor to the next) associated with the implementation of a new system.

Thus, almost a decade after the introduction of user-friendly operating systems, stable client/server networking, and powerful database technologies into the average police department, many agencies are running records management systems on VMS or VAX servers or 20-year-old mainframes. Analysts skilled with desktop database programs such as Microsoft Access could theoretically develop a far better RMS on their own. Some have.

Despite this disturbing situation, a handful of analysts will find themselves working for agencies with modern, intuitive, complete, robust records management systems that handle all their analysis needs. These analysts should consider themselves very fortunate. Analysts in this situation will find little need to pursue any of the other approaches to managing data, and will be able to focus the bulk of their efforts on information scanning and analysis.

Linking to RMS Data. Linking to RMS data through modern technologies such as ODBC is a good solution when the RMS captures enough information (and captures it accurately) but doesn't provide enough flexibility for querying. The analyst can circumvent the limits of the RMS's reporting capabilities by linking directly to the data with a modern database program, such as Microsoft Access or Filemaker, or with a reporting tool, such as Seagate Crystal Reports. Any of these programs should allow the analyst to design the queries and reports he or she needs.

Exporting/Importing RMS Data. In some cases, the necessary software is not available to establish a direct link to a particular RMS's data tables. Many of these RMS's still offer the capability to export data in a format that can be read by database programs. Once imported, analysts can perform the same queries as with linked data—the information just won't be "live."

Exporting and importing is also a good option if the analyst wants to make changes to the data, but does not have permission (or time) to change it in the RMS.

Linked/Imported Data Joined with Analyst's Data. This option is for analysts who can establish either a link or a successful export/import routine, but who want to track data that the RMS simply doesn't record. For instance, the RMS may have fields for the address, but not for the type of location. It may contain data on offenders and victims, but not on the relationships between them. The analyst can set up his own tables to track this additional information and (using a database system) link those tables to the RMS data.

Going it Alone. Some analysts will find that their agency either has no RMS or has one so

irredeemable (in terms of completeness, accuracy, or timeliness) that it can't be used. Such analysts will have to track their own data, using one of three methods, in order of sophistication:

1. *Paper matrixes and logs.* This was the only solution in the pre-desktop computer era. Each matrix or log is based on a single crime type and lists information specific to that crime. For instance, a robbery matrix might show the type of weapon used, the description of the suspect and victim, and the type of property stolen.

2. *Spreadsheets.* Tracking data in spreadsheet format, such as Microsoft Excel, provides great benefits over tracking it in paper-based format. Entry is simpler, you're not limited by the physical size of a page, and you can sort, search, and filter the data. The drawback is that a spreadsheet can only track one type of data (incidents, people, property) and can't effectively link two tables together.

Chapter 18 covers spreadsheets, and offers advice on when to use a spreadsheet and when to use a database.

3. *Relational Databases.* The most effective solution to tracking your own data is to take the time to learn a desktop database program like Microsoft Access or FoxPro. You can track multiple types of data, link data tables together, and design sophisticated queries to filter, sort, or aggregate data.

Methods of Analysis

Once an analyst has a handle on data sources and data management, he or she is ready to begin actually *analyzing* data. But what does it mean to analyze?

To begin, there are two approaches to analysis, just as there are two approaches to reasoning (see Chapter 5): inductive and deductive. Inductive analysis begins with individual pieces of data, which the analyst puts together to form patterns. Tactical crime analysis is very much an inductive process.

Deductive analysis begins with a large amount of data, which the analyst filters, queries, or *mines* to find patterns or trends within. Strategic crime analysis is primarily a deductive process.

Remember the metaphor of the sculptors? The inductive analyst is the sculptor who builds his sculpture out of individual pieces of clay; the deductive analysis creates his art by chipping away at extraneous rock to find the image within.

Another, perhaps better, way to approach the issue of what it means to *analyze* is to look at the different things that analysts actually *do* with data to create information. These methods of analysis fall into seven categories:

1. **Filtration.** Analysts remove extraneous data to focus on what's important. This applies to individual pieces of data (an analyst may have to filter out dozens of paragraphs from an officers' narrative to find the information important to the analyst) and to large data sets (an analyst searching for patterns of nighttime burglary filters out daytime incidents and non-burglaries).

2. **Categorization.** Analysts categorize, classify, or cluster pieces of data into logical groups—robbery or burglary, purse snatching or carjacking, Beat 4 or Beat 5, offender or victim—to help identify, analyze, and communicate information. Some categories are obvious, such as the year (2003 or 2004); others require more

intellectual effort, such as when an analyst creates situational types (domestic assault, gang assault, or road rage assault).

3. **Aggregation.** Analysts count, summarize, average, or otherwise aggregate data into categories. Examples of aggregation include taking 20,000 police calls for service and showing the number during each shift; arranging 365 auto thefts by counting the make and model of cars stolen; and showing the average dollar value stolen by crime type for 16,500 property crimes.

4. **Comparison.** Analysts may compare individual incidents to determine if they are related. They may also compare large data sets (e.g., 2004 crimes vs. 2005 crimes, crimes in New York vs. crimes in Los Angeles, Beat 4 calls vs. Beat 3 calls) to determine trends and deviations from the norm. Most crime statistics are meaningless unless compared to previous time periods or other geographic areas.

5. **Correlation.** Correlation is a statistical technique that determines if one set of data is related to another set of data (e.g., increased population is related to increased calls for service; decreased average income is related to increased crime rates). The term "correlation" is sometimes used informally to denote any observed relationship between two variables (e.g., robberies seem to cluster around subway stops, burglaries decline during school hours.)

6. **Causality & Explanation.** This process takes correlation a step further by determining whether one factor *causes* another. Did the new shopping mall "cause" auto burglaries to increase in the area? Have increases in the price of heroin "caused" an increase in burglary?

7. **Projection**. Analysts can use existing data to project or predict the future. If we've already had 19 robberies this month, how many are we likely to have by the end of the month? If the offender's activities continue as they have in the past, where and when is he likely to strike next?

Most analytical projects require a combination of several of these techniques. We'll look at two examples, one tactical and one strategic:

Tactical. The analyst reads a crime report concerning an offender who stuck a gun in a man's face and drove away in his car. The analyst *categorizes* this as a carjacking and begins a search for similar incidents by *filtering* the crimes in his database to exclude everything except robberies. The analyst *compares* the current robbery to past robberies and finds seven that seem similar. He *aggregates* the incidents by hour of day and determines that six occurred between 15:00 and 18:00. He finds a *correlation* between the incidents and the presence of a methadone clinic and infers *causality*. Based on the offender's past incidents, he *projects* that the offender is likely to strike again within the next four days between 15:30 and 17:45, within four blocks of the methadone clinic.

Strategic. By *comparing* year-to-date incidents in 2001, 2002, 2003 and 2004, the analyst finds that auto theft (a *category*) has increased 25% over the past three years, which *correlates* precisely with an increase of thefts of car parts at local used car dealerships during the same period. By *aggregating* by year, make, and model, the analyst discovers that most of the cars targeted have been mid-1990s model Toyotas and Hondas, and that few of these stolen cars have been recovered, suggesting that they have been sold whole or disassembled for parts. The analyst brings this information to a local meeting, where she receives intelligence that a new chop shop has opened in a nearby town, suggesting an *explanation* for the trend. Based on year-to-date figures, the analyst *projects* 345 auto thefts by the end of the year if nothing is done to intercede this trend.

Products of Analysis

The fourth step of the crime analysis process is *information dissemination*. Analysts disseminate information through a variety of procedures and products, from the formal to the informal. These include:

o In-person briefings to officers at roll calls and other events
o Regular (daily, weekly) crime bulletins and reports
o Special (as needed) alerts, bulletins, and reports
o Monthly, quarterly, and annual reports
o E-mail updates
o Intranets and internal electronic bulletin boards
o Informal interpersonal communication between analysts and officers

Paper bulletins have long been the flagship products of crime analysis units, but they suffer from quick obsolescence. In many agencies, patterns and trends emerge and change every day, and unless the analyst is willing to issue a bulletin at each change, published information will always lag behind available information. To solve this problem, many analysts are turning toward intranets and other means of live electronic communication, updated as needed.

Chapters 9 and 16–19 cover products of analysis in detail, including tips on effective visualization of information, effective writing, creating bulletins, and effective presentation.

Strategy Development

At the strategy development stage, the analyst loses direct control: it is for the police department as a whole to take the analyst's work and develop strategies based on it. Still, the analyst has a vested interest in making sure that his information is used, and used effectively. To this end, the analyst can work, overtly or subtly (depending on the atmosphere of the agency), to encourage his agency to make effective decisions.[1]

Left alone, some agencies lack creativity when it comes to strategy development. Whether a series or hot spot, pattern or trend, the solution is the same: more officers. Directed patrols (often involving paid overtime) become the primary or only strategy. Unfortunately, while extra patrols work to combat some problems, they are not an effective solution—or not the *most* effective solution—for others.

Figure 1-2, known colloquially as the "San Diego Wheel," suggests three avenues of strategy development for certain crime patterns: apprehension, suppression, and target hardening. Each avenue focuses on one part of Cohen and Felson's Routine Activities Theory, which fixes crimes at a convergence of a motivated offender, a suitable target, and absence of capable guardianship.[2] Remove any of these elements and the crime will not occur. Apprehension seeks to remove the offender; hardening makes targets less suitable; and suppression supplies capable guardianship.

---

[1] Recent literature has encouraged analysts to take a more active role in developing responses. See, for instance, Ronald V. Clarke and John Eck, *Become a Problem-Solving Crime Analyst in 55 Small Steps* (London: Jill Dando Institute of Crime Science, 2003), step 32.

[2] For the genesis of this theory, see Lawrence E. Cohen and Marcus Felson. "Social Change and Crime Rate Trends: a Routine Activity Approach," *American Sociological Review* 44 (1979): 588-607.

Problem-oriented policing literature suggests a more expansive approach to crime prevention. Ronald Clarke's Situational Crime Prevention, for instance, argues that crimes can be prevented by one of five strategies:[3]

1. **Increase the effort** that criminals must expend to commit crimes through methods such as target hardening, access control to facilities, control over tools and weapons, and other security measures.

2. **Increase the risk** that offenders incur while committing crimes through methods such as surveillance and security.

3. **Reduce the rewards** of crime through methods such as hiding property, etching expensive property with identification information, and disrupting markets for sale.

4. **Reduce provocations** for offenders to commit crimes, including frustration, stress, disputes, and peer pressure.

5. **Remove excuses** for crime, by setting clear rules, posting signs, and controlling drugs and alcohol.

Agencies should focus apprehension efforts on short-term series, whereas more creative crime prevention and problem-solving strategies should be employed for long-term trends and problems. Analysts would do well to familiarize themselves with the relevant literature on both apprehending offenders and solving problems.

---

[3] Ronald V. Clarke, "Situational Crime Prevention," in *Building a Safer Society: Strategic Approaches to Crime Prevention*, ed. Michael Tonry and David P. Farrington (Chicago: University of Chicago Press, 1995), 91–150.

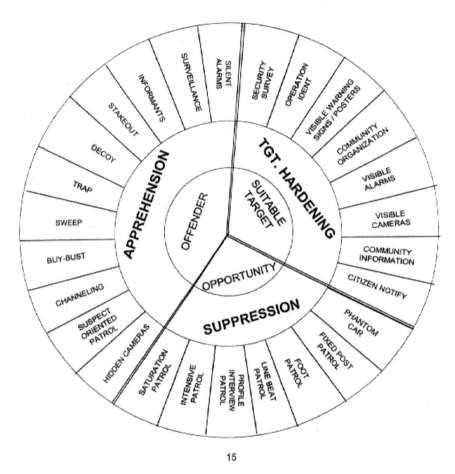

15

Figure 1-2: "The San Diego Wheel." This diagram was created by George J. Sullivan of the San Diego Police Department in 1979. It suggests a number of strategies to combat predatory crimes.

Evaluation and Feedback

Evaluation & Feedback is often called "the forgotten step of the crime analysis process."[1] One of the most frequent complaints heard among analysts is that they issue loads of information, but their agencies don't actually *do* anything with it. Sometimes, this happens because the agency has not adopted a pro-active policing model, but just

as often it happens because the style or substance of the analyst's information is not particularly valuable to the agency. If the officers don't read the analyst's bulletins, is the problem with the officers, or with the bulletins?

Agencies should periodically examine their crime analysis programs by asking the following questions:

o Are the analysts identifying patterns and trends as they occur? Are the analysts disseminating information about these

---

[1] Susan C. Wernicke, "Feedback: the Forgotten Step of the Crime Analysis Process" (lecture, annual conference of the Massachusetts Association of Crime Analysts, Falmouth, MA, May 2–5, 2000).

patterns and trends to the agency? Are the analysts considering all relevant factors? Is the format of this information adequate and timely? Is the information getting to everyone who needs it?

o Can the department, based on the analysts' information, develop effective problem-solving strategies?

o Are the analysts' reports well-written, concise, and complete? Are reports distributed too frequently or too infrequently? Are the reports really necessary, or do they serve a purpose that has expired in the department? Are there reports that would be beneficial that the analysts do not provide?

o Is the program supporting all divisions in the agency, or is it focused exclusively on the needs of a single division? Are the analysts accessible and approachable by all members of the agency?

o Is the crime analysis unit adequately staffed, trained, situated, and equipped? (See below.)

Spontaneous constructive criticism is, unfortunately, rare. To answer these questions, the analyst must regularly solicit feedback through surveys, focus groups, process research, and informal networking. Though it can be discouraging to discover that the analyst's favorite product isn't really needed by the agency, the effective analyst will welcome this criticism and tailor his information to the agency's needs.

Administration of Crime Analysis

The effectiveness of a crime analysis unit hinges on how the police agency administers it. There are a number of ways to make certain that crime analysis is *ineffective*:

o Understaff it
o Assign the wrong person to do it
o Assign it to the wrong organizational location
o Assign it to the wrong physical location
o Don't offer opportunities for training and professional development
o Ignore it

We'll tackle these issues one by one.[1]

Staffing

We begin with the most basic question of all: how much analysis does a police agency need? There are various formulas. Some consider the number of officers in the agency; others look at the jurisdiction's population; and still others are based on the volume of crime. Of the three, only the last one really makes sense, lest an agency with too few officers or a high commercial population understaff itself with analysts.

A police agency needs roughly one analyst for every 1,500 UCR Part 1 or every 1,800 NIBRS Group A reports it takes each year (see Chapter 10 for more on UCR and NIBRS reporting). Alternately, you may use calls for service: an agency needs roughly one analyst for every 30,000 "calls" (include police-initiated responses) per year.

If an agency records only 750 Part 1 crimes and has only 15,000 calls for service, it needs a part-time analyst—someone who can analyze crime 20 hours a week and perform other duties (e.g., patrol, investigations, dispatching, information systems management, records management, grant administration) for the other 20 hours.

---

[1] For a longer discussion of all of these issues, see Deborah A. Osborne and Susan C. Wernicke, *Introduction to Crime Analysis: Basic Resources for Criminal Justice Practice* (New York: Haworth Press, 2003), 88–101, though note that we disagree on staffing formulas.

Agencies that require more than one analyst have to choose how to allocate them. The three most popular methods are:

o **By Crime Analysis Categorization:** one analyst performs tactical analysis, another performs strategic analysis.

o **By Jurisdictional Division:** each analyst covers one precinct, division, or beat.

o **By Crime Type:** one analyst handles violent crimes, another covers property crimes. Very large agencies might assign one analyst to each crime category: a burglary analyst, a robbery analyst, an auto theft analyst, and so on.

The second option works best in large agencies with multiple physical facilities; the first works best in mid-sized agencies with only one building. The third option is most appropriate for large agencies that may have a number of facilities but have centralized their analysis unit at the headquarters.

Hiring and Appointment

The most common question about appointing or hiring analysts is: officer ("commissioned," "sworn") or civilian? There are advantages to both. Officer analysts usually take to the job detailed knowledge of the jurisdiction and its criminals. They understand how the police department works, and they may also have more immediate credibility with the other officers in the agency.

Officers, however, tend to be police officers first and crime analysts second. Civilian analysts may stay in the field longer, more aggressively pursue training, develop their skills, become certified, and provide their agencies with the benefits associated with having a full-time career professional. Civilian

analysts don't usually get re-assigned or promoted, forcing the agency to appoint and train a new person.

Agencies that can justify more than one analyst can give themselves the best of both worlds: a mixture of officers and professional civilian analysts in the same unit. For agencies with only one analyst, we recommend that they hire a civilian and keep their patrol and investigations levels at full strength.

When choosing either officers or civilians, agencies should favor the following characteristics:

o Exceptional intelligence
o Creative, inquisitive disposition
o Computer proficiency
o Experience with statistics and research methods
o Strong writing and communications skills
o Education or background in criminology or criminal justice
o Capability to get along with other members of the agency

Organizational Location

There are many schools of thought on the best organizational location for a crime analyst or crime analysis unit. O.W. Wilson recommended that it be placed within a planning unit (which many smaller agencies lack). Some writers have recommended that it fall within the patrol division; others would place it in the investigations division. Most agree that it should be kept clear of the administrative divisions (e.g., personnel, information technology, records), where it is often accorded less respect from the officers and where it will more likely be used for non-crime analysis purposes.[1]

---

[1] See, for instance, Gottlieb, *Crime Analysis*, 83.

The simple truth is that each department should put its crime analysis unit within the section that works best for that department. This location will vary depending on the agency's structure, its division of responsibilities, its history and politics, and the personalities and management styles of the various division commanders. These questions will serve as a guideline:

o In what division will the crime analysis unit have the easiest, timeliest access to police incident information?

o Which divisions have a history of embracing creative problem solving, pro-active strategy, and change?

o Which division commanders are the most supportive of the developing crime analysis program?

o Which division will be most often responsible for developing strategies based on crime analysis information?

Agencies should be aware that the crime analysis unit is likely to take on the priorities and characteristics of the division to which it is assigned. A crime analysis unit located within the investigations division is more likely to focus its efforts on crime series and the apprehension of offenders. Crime analysis units within community policing divisions are more likely to focus on long-term trends and problem-solving. Operations analysis and the analysis of non-crime incidents are best fostered by placing the unit within the patrol division.

When practical, we prefer an autonomous crime analysis unit—one not localized within any specific division. Such units are responsible to all divisions and sections within the police agency, but outside the politics of any one of them.

Physical Location

When possible, the crime analysis unit should be centrally accessible to all members of the department—particularly patrol officers and investigators. Effective crime analysis depends on the liberal flow of information between analyst and officer, and nothing stifles this flow faster than putting the analyst in a back hallway or up on the fifteenth floor.

Officers should be encouraged to visit the analyst, share intelligence, and ask for information. Police administrators sometimes shield analysts from "drop-ins," either by physically blocking the office or by making officers submit a formal request for analysis information. Such policies are misguided and damaging to the analysis effort; isolated units are invariably the least effective ones.

Training & Professional Development

Training and professional development are extremely important in the analysis profession. New technologies and techniques emerge every year, and analysts need to stay on top of them to give their agencies the most benefit for their dollar. To this end, agencies should encourage their analysts to join professional associations, network with other analysts, and attend regular training events.

Professional associations also provide analysts with outlets for growth and advancement that they may not find within their police departments. The vast majority of agencies will hire or appoint only one analyst, and only a small percentage will have "layers" of analysts that provide opportunities for promotion. Professional associations offer opportunities for committee work and service in elected or appointed positions, which are important benefits for a career analyst.

A Crime Analyst's Task List

It's possible that readers may make it this far in the book, achieve a solid understanding of what crime analysis is, but not have a clear practical picture of how to approach day-to-day crime analysis. This "to do" list outlines the various functions of the typical crime analysis unit. Analysts will, of course, have to modify this list to meet the needs of their unique jurisdiction or mission.

FREQUENT/DAILY TASKS

Review crime reports from the previous day, compare with past reports, looking for patterns and series (aspects covered in Chapter 8). Track information in databases as required.

For identified patterns and series, thoroughly analyze the who, what, when (Chapter 11), where (Chapter 15), how, and why factors; disseminate pertinent information to the department for follow-up.

For individual crimes and crime series with suspect descriptions, search databases of known offenders for possible matches; forward leads to investigative officers.

When an offender is arrested for an offense likely to be part of a pattern, search past incidents for possible matches with the offender's *modus operandi*; forward leads to investigators and prosecutors.

Prepare a regular newsletter or bulletin for your agency (see Chapters 16 and 17 for tips).

Scour local newspapers, teletypes, journals, other-agency bulletins, and other sources for information that may have an effect on, or be connected to, crime in your jurisdiction.

Network with other analysts in your area to share intelligence, strategies, and techniques.

Network with officers and detectives in your agency to gather intelligence that may not be found in written records.

Disseminate information on patterns, trends, and hot spots to residential and business communities (depending on policies of the department)

Meet with departmental decision makers in strategy development forums (New York City's COMPSTAT system is one such forum)

PERIODIC (WEEKLY/MONTHLY/ANNUALLY)

Scan for emerging or changing crime trends through statistical (Chapters 10 and 13), mapping, or data querying techniques.

Prepare periodic statistical reports.

Prepare the department's quarterly or annual crime report.

Research (Chapter 6) crime trends and crime problems, with a focus on identifying root causes.

Prepare a workload analysis for your agency (by shift/division/beat) to assist administrators with resource allocation.

AS NEEDED/ASSIGNED

Analyze traffic accidents for hot spots and causes, with an eye toward enforcement and re-engineering.

Analyze the effectiveness of police programs to determine if resource use is justified.

Conduct and analyze community surveys (see Chapter 14 for sampling issues).

Develop crime prevention tips and strategies based on the observed characteristics of crime in your jurisdiction.

Provide database queries, statistics, and other crime information on demand.

Prepare charts (Chapter 19), graphs, statistics, maps for reports, community presentations, grant applications, courtroom presentations. Present (Chapter 9) as required.

RMS/CAD/GIS database maintenance and quality control.

Proper Use

Effective crime analysis requires that agencies actually use the products of analysis. In too many agencies, the crime analysis process stops at "Information Dissemination," with no strategy development based on the analyst's work.

Crime analysis should not simply be a person or unit within the police agency—it should be an important part of the agency's mission and plan. Just about any pro-active policing model, from problem-oriented policing to CompStat to Weed & Seed, requires analysis as a basis for action. Police agencies that are not effectively using crime analysis are not effectively policing.

Conclusion

Crime analysis is an essential component of pro-active policing, and every law enforcement agency should have some kind of analysis capability. Good analysis requires a number of skills, which are covered by the rest of the chapters in this book.

As the variety and scope of these chapters suggest, crime analysis calls on an eclectic collection of abilities and knowledge, requiring a "renaissance" individual who can juxtapose techniques and processes often considered in opposition. Crime analysis is both left-brained and right-brained, both intuitive and conscious, both scientific and artistic. It requires a strong analyst (as the name of the profession would suggest), but also a strong communicator. There are loads of data to analyze, but the data concerns human activity and thus requires a human perception.

By asking and answering questions about crime patterns, trends, and problems, analysts help their agencies concentrate their limited resources in a way that helps them prevent or solve the most crime for the least effort. When a police department stops a robbery pattern after four incidents instead of letting it run a course of 15, the victimization of 11 citizens has been prevented. When an agency works with a shopping center to increase security in its parking lot, hundreds of shoppers may be prevented from having their property and vehicles stolen over the course of several years. When used properly by police agencies, crime analysis reduces crime, reduces victimization, reduces loss, reduces suffering. For the analytically-minded, there are few callings more noble or fulfilling.

Recommended Readings

Boba, Rachel. *Problem Analysis in Policing*. Washington, DC: Police Foundation, 2003.

Clarke, Ronald V. and John Eck. *Become a Problem-Solving Crime Analyst in 55 Small Steps*. London: Jill Dando Institute of Crime Science, 2003.

Goldstein, Herman. *Problem-Oriented Policing*. New York: McGraw-Hill, 1990.

Gottlieb, Steven, Sheldon Arenberg, and Raj Singh. *Crime Analysis: From First Report to Final Arrest*. Montclair, CA: Alpha Publishing, 1994.

Grassie, Richard G. *Crime Analysis Executive Manual*. Washington, DC: U.S. Department of Justice, Law Enforcement Assistance Administration, 1977.

Osborne, Deborah A. and Susan C. Wernicke. *Introduction to Crime Analysis: Basic Resources for Criminal Justice Practice*. New York: Haworth Press, 2003.

Reiner, G. Hobart et. al. *Crime Analysis Operations Manual*. Washington, DC: U.S. Department of Justice, Law Enforcement Assistance Administration, 1977.

2
Understanding the Criminal Justice System

Donald R. Dixon

This chapter provides an overview of the constitutional and legal framework in which the modern American criminal justice system operates. From this foundation, a discussion of the police, courts, and corrections systems at the local, federal, and state levels, their operations and interrelationships, is undertaken. Finally, the role and place of crime analysis at each level will be discussed. Given the constraints of this book, this chapter will necessarily provide no more than an overview of the topics. Readers interested in a more detailed examination of the criminal justice system and its component parts are directed to any good introductory college textbook on criminal justice, and to more specialized topical courses.

What is Criminal Justice?

In the early nineteenth century, Daniel Webster wrote, "Justice is the great interest of man on earth. It is the ligament which holds civilized beings and civilized nations together."[1] With this thought in mind, the reader is encouraged to remember that the modern criminal justice system is a very complex set of institutional relationships, guided, shaped, and constrained by the U.S. Constitution, acts of Congress, state legislatures and city councils, and decisions of the U.S. Supreme Court, and lower courts.

While the phrase, "criminal justice," is an oxymoron in the minds of some, the purpose of the system, at its most fundamental level, is to protect citizens' rights and properties.

> The justice system [is] divided into three main components: **law enforcement agencies**, charged with investigating crimes and apprehending suspects; **the court system**, in which a determination is made whether a criminal suspect is guilty as charged; and **the correctional system**, charged both with treating and rehabilitating offenders and with incapacitating them so that they cannot repeat their crimes.[2] (Emphasis added)

On occasion, at the societal level, we are forced to make choices between the rights of individuals and public order. This aspect of our political and social milieu is what makes the system confusing, frustrating, and very interesting to study and examine.

In theory, all three branches of the system (police, courts, and corrections) work together cooperatively to accomplish the goals of enforcing law, protecting citizens, and balancing competing rights and interests. In reality, the system is so complex, so large, and so confusing that it can hardly be called a system at all. Many of the decisions made and outcomes realized in the criminal justice system hardly seem fair or just. However, a more clear appreciation of the system helps us approach an understanding of its strengths and weaknesses.

Constitutional and Legal Foundations

The Preamble to the Constitution includes among its purposes establishing justice, promoting the general welfare and ensuring

---

[1] Cited in Frank Schmalleger, *Criminal Justice Today*, 7th ed. (Upper Saddle River, NJ: Prentice Hall, 2003), 3.

[2] Joseph J. Senna and Larry J. Siegel, *Introduction to Criminal Justice*, 9th ed. (Belmont, CA: Wadsworth, 2002), 5–6.

domestic tranquility. To this end, the Constitution creates the three branches of government: the legislative, the executive and the judiciary. Article I, Section 8 of the Constitution establishes the powers of Congress. Among these powers are, in order of appearance in the document's text, the "power to provide for the common Defence [*sic*] and general Welfare of the United States," the power to regulate commerce, to coin money and fix the standards for weights and measures, provide punishment for counterfeiting, establish patents and copyrights, establish lower courts (to the Supreme Court), call up the militia, and to "make all Laws which shall be necessary and proper for carrying into Execution the foregoing Powers and all other Powers vested by this Constitution in the Government of the United States...."[1] In this section, the Congress is given both "enumerated powers" and "implied powers." The Founding Fathers of this country were farsighted enough to mandate certain laws be created (weights and measures, coining of money, and punishment of counterfeiting, for example), and to realize that Congress would have to create new laws and rules to meet the changing demands of society.

Article I, Section 9 of the Constitution establishes certain specific limits on the powers of Congress. Among these limits are, importantly, the injunction that the right of *habeas corpus* may not be suspended except in times of war or rebellion, and then only if public safety demanded it, and that no *ex post facto* (after the fact) laws be passed. This latter injunction prevents Congress, and by extension state legislatures or city governments, from passing laws that would become effective retroactively.

Section 10 of this Article requires that states may not usurp any powers of the federal legislature. Thus, the federal government is established as the highest law making body in the country. State governments may not pass or enforce laws contrary to federal law.[2]

Article II of the Constitution creates the presidency, the executive branch of government. The president is in charge of all federal agencies, and is required to implement and enforce all laws passed by Congress and decisions made by the Supreme Court. Although the presidential Cabinet and other agencies of government are not specified in the Constitution, Congress has created the various agencies as the need has arisen. Different presidents have exercised their enforcement powers according to their political philosophies and the exigencies of the times.

Article III establishes the U.S. Supreme Court. This court was intended to be the highest tribunal in the land. This section of the Constitution provides that the Supreme Court has "original jurisdiction" over certain cases (i.e., those cases involving foreign ambassadors and countries where the United States in a party, cases between states, and other cases where original jurisdiction cannot be located equitably in one state), and final appellate jurisdiction over all other cases, whether such cases originate at the federal or the state level. Decisions of the Supreme Court stand as precedent for decisions in future cases that are similar.

The first ten amendments to the Constitution are known as the Bill of Rights. The purpose of the Bill of Rights is to establish certain protections for citizens against possible

---

[1] Theodore J. Lowi and Benjamin Ginsberg, *American Government*, 4th ed. (New York: W.W. Norton, 1996), A14.

[2] This was tested and settled by the American Civil War. Laws, Court decisions, and executive actions subsequent to the Civil War have had to reinforce this principle.

abuses or usurpations by the government. Some of these individual rights are especially important for the accused.[1] The Amendments that have had the most significant effect on the criminal justice system are the First, Fourth, Fifth, Sixth, Seventh, and Eighth (and the Fourteenth, which is not a part of the Bill of Rights). A significant number of Supreme Court decisions have given form and substance to these Amendments. It is these cases that have shaped, perhaps as much as any other force in our society, the ways in which our criminal justice system acts toward individuals.

The First Amendment reads:

> Congress shall make no law respecting an establishment of religion, or prohibiting the free exercise thereof; or abridging the freedom of speech, or of the press; or the right of the people to peaceably assemble, and to petition the government for a redress of grievances.

Are these rights absolute? Of course not. Few paragraphs are more familiar to Americans, and fewer are less well understood. The cumulative effect of numerous Court decisions concerning this Amendment on the criminal justice system is that agents of the government must protect citizens' lawful exercise of their rights, whether those agents agreed with the exercise or not.

The Fourth Amendment protects citizens from "unreasonable" searches and seizures, and requires a search warrant to be issued based on probable cause. *Mapp vs. Ohio* (1961) established the "exclusionary rule" barring the introduction of illegally seized evidence at trial. Similarly *Katz vs. U.S.* (1967) prohibits electronic surveillance conducted "outside the judicial process."[2] The purpose of this amendment and these and other related court decisions is to prevent the government from harassing or otherwise abusing its citizens' rights to "be left alone."

The Fifth Amendment requires examination of evidence before issuing an indictment, protects the accused from "double jeopardy," protects the accused from being compelled to be a witness against himself or herself, and outlines the right of due process. Among the more important cases related to this amendment are *Escobedo vs. Illinois* (1964) and *Miranda vs. Arizona* (1966). Both decisions spoke to the right of an accused or arrested person to remain silent and to have an attorney present during questioning.[3] *Argersinger vs. Hamlin* (1972) established the right to counsel for persons accused of misdemeanor offenses.

The Sixth Amendment addresses the right to a speedy and public trial and the right to an attorney. The Seventh Amendment also addresses the right to trial by jury (in civil cases), and establishes that trial appeals can only be based on procedural matters; the "facts of the case" are decided at the original trial. The case of *Gideon vs. Wainwright* (1963) helped establish the right to counsel. *Duncan vs. Louisiana* (1968) addressed the issue of the right to trial by jury in state cases where the accused faces serious charges and sanctions.[4]

The Eighth Amendment simply says, "Excessive Bail shall not be required, nor excessive fines imposed, nor cruel and

---

[1] I am in the habit of asking introductory-level students whether they can imagine confessing to a crime they did not commit. None of them can imagine doing such a thing until I begin describing some of the less pleasant "interrogation techniques" that have been used over time. The point, of course, is to get them thinking about the powerlessness of the individual against the power of the state.

[2] Lowi and Ginsberg, A55 and 344.
[3] Lowi and Ginsberg, A53 and A57, 521, and 329–330.
[4] Lowi and Ginsberg, A53 and 114.

unusual punishments inflicted." The most controversial cases arising from this Eighth Amendment involve the death penalty. In the late 1970s, the Supreme Court placed a moratorium on imposition of the death penalty (*Furman vs. Georgia*) until it could be determined whether the manner in which this sanction in imposed is consonant with the Constitution. Today, 38 of the 50 states have death penalty statutes.[1] The Fourteenth Amendment (1868) "incorporates" the Constitution to the states, saying, in part "[n]o state shall make or enforce any law which shall abridge the privileges or immunities of citizens of the United States...." It took over 100 years and very many Supreme Court decisions, and the active cooperation of several presidents, to fully enforce the intent of this amendment. The bottom line is that the U.S. Constitution is intended to guide and restrict the relationships between citizens and their government, and in a very real way, between each other as individuals.

The constitutional mandates, amendments, and cases discussed above shape the functions of the criminal justice system at every level. It is important to understand that the law and precedents apply to all citizens. Many people complain that the convicted "have too many rights." It may seem that way, but it is more accurate to think in terms of the convicted having the same rights as all Americans. They have the right to be protected from harassment or abuse by the government, and they have the right to fair and equal treatment under the law.

System Models: From Due Process to Crime Control

A number of perspectives toward the criminal justice system have been articulated.

To help develop a perception on how and why it functions, a brief discussion of these perspectives follows.

Herbert Packer (1975) describes the criminal justice process in terms of being:

> [A]n assembly line conveyor belt down which moves an endless stream of cases, never stopping, carrying them to workers who stand at fixed stations and who perform on each case....the same small but essential operation that brings it one step closer to being a finished product....a screening process in which each successive stage....involves a series of routinized operations, whose success is gauged primarily by their tendency to pass the case along to a successful conclusion.[2]

Packer, and later James Q. Wilson (1983)[3] helped to develop what is now known as the "crime control model." This perspective emphasizes control of offenders and protection of society through the use of harsh sanctions. This approach has been the dominant approach since the early 1990s and has been criticized for causing prison overcrowding.[4]

At the other end of the spectrum is the "due process model," so called because of its emphasis on ensuring the rights of individuals at all stages of the criminal justice process.[5] "Due process is a central and necessary part of American criminal justice. It requires a careful and informed consideration of the facts of each individual case....Due

---

[1] Schmalleger, 431.

[2] Herbert L. Packer, *The Limits of the Criminal Sanction* (Stanford, CA: Stanford University Press, 1975), 25, as cited in Senna and Seigel, 12.
[3] James Q. Wilson, *Thinking About Crime*, rev. ed. (New York: Vintage Books, 1983).
[4] This is mainly because society has come to view all offenders as dangerous, and thus in need of imprisonment.
[5] Packer, in Senna and Seigel, 22.

process is intended to ensure that innocent people are not convicted of crimes."[1]

Other perspectives worth mentioning briefly include the "justice perspective" which holds that all people should receive the same treatment under the law, and favors the use of determinate sentencing, an end to parole, and the cessation of any pretense of rehabilitation—it believes the purpose of prison is punishment.[2] The restorative justice perspective, on the other hand, draws inspiration from various religious traditions. This view believes the role of the criminal justice system is to resolve conflict between victim and offender.[3] The "rehabilitation perspective" believes the proper role of the criminal justice system is treatment for the offender in order to return them to full and proper participation in society.

Since the early 1990s, the crime control and justice perspectives have held sway among policymakers in the United States. "Truth in sentencing" laws and "three-strikes" laws have reflected a renewed "get tough" attitude on the part of society and its elected officials. The results have included serious crowding in prisons, a massive prison building campaign to accommodate the surge of new prisoners, reexamination of the rights of the accused and of the incarcerated, and renewed enthusiasm for the death penalty.

The various models discussed here illustrate the wide ranging attitudes and expectations placed on the criminal justice system. Senna and Seigel say criminal justice is both a system and a process. To better appreciate what they mean, discussion of each element of the system—police, courts, and corrections—follows.

The Police

Over 650,000 police officers, in more than 17,000 agencies, are the most visible and most frequently encountered agents of the criminal justice system.[4] Most people are most familiar with municipal (or city) police departments. Other police agencies include county sheriffs, state police and the variety of federal agents. Often called the "front line" in the "war against crime" police are charged with upholding the law, investigating crimes, pursuing and bringing to justice those who break the law, keeping the peace and protecting the community.

Local police have evolved from the watchmen, "thief takers," and Reeves of the Shire of centuries past into highly skilled, well trained, educated modern officers we know today. Local agencies today employ over 730,000 sworn and civilian employees.[5] New York City has the country's largest police force, with 44,000 full time employees (37,000 sworn). There are other large agencies, also. The majority of all police forces in the country, however, employ ten or fewer officers.[6] Police agencies' jurisdictions are limited to the boundaries of city or town. Typically, chiefs of these agencies are appointed by either mayors or the city councils. These agencies are the most common consumers of crime analysis services.

Sheriffs, on the other hand, are elected county officials. Their deputies typically patrol the unincorporated areas of the county, although their jurisdiction includes the entire county. Sheriffs, therefore, frequently work in cooperation with local police. Sheriff's Departments also run the

---

[1] Schmallager, 28.
[2] Senna and Seigel, 24.
[3] Senna and Seigel, 25.

[4] Senna and Seigel, chapter 5.
[5] Bureau of Labor Statistics (2000), cited in Schmalleger, 199.
[6] Schmalleger, 199.

county jails. Some departments have their own crime analysis units.

Crime analysis units at the city and county levels gather and store data on calls for service, crimes reported, arrests, traffic, and any other related issues deemed a priority by their agency. Large departments, such as the Dallas Police Department, employ over two dozen crime analysts and are well resourced in terms of computers and automatic data retrieval systems. More common are the departments who have one full time person, or one or two part time personnel, who perform the crime analysis function.[1] Many police departments and sheriffs departments have no formal crime analysis unit or staff.[2] Some have begun cooperative, cross-jurisdictional efforts to gather and make sense of the data they have.

According to Schaub (2003), most crime analysis at the local level is administrative (limited to report generating) or tactical, identifying "information to assist operations personnel…in the identification of *specific* and *immediate* crime problems and the arrest of offenders"[3] (emphasis in the original). She argues that strategic crime analysis techniques are not used frequently enough. (See Chapter 1 for more on the distinctions between these classifications.) Nevertheless, local police agencies increasingly use crime analysis, and the field is growing both in stature and professionalization.

State-level agencies began to emerge in the nineteenth century. Such agencies perform police functions at the statewide level. These functions include criminal investigations, patrol of the state's highways, maintaining a statewide criminal records database, operating identification departments, and helping local law enforcement agencies in investigations when asked.[4] Some states, such as North Carolina, have two state-level police agencies, the State Highway Patrol and the State Bureau of Investigation.

Crime analysis at the state level frequently involves data gathering and dissemination to local agencies, generating annual and ad hoc reports, and analysis to aid specific investigations. Many states have statewide crime analysis units today. Some, such as the Michigan State Police, seem to focus on making reports and information available to the public, although they do participate in Automated Fingerprint Identification System (AFIS) and LiveScan and undoubtedly aid the state police with investigations.[5] Other states' crime analysis units, such as in Connecticut, provide the reporting services common to most crime analysis units, but also provide specific services to the state police, the Department of Fire, Emergency and Building Services, Homeland Security and the Computer Crimes and Electronic Evidence Unit.[6] The emergence of crime analysis units at the state level is a very encouraging development and will certainly become a great help to both investigations and service to the citizens.

Before the creation of the Department of Homeland Security (DHS), there were 21 separate federal law enforcement agencies across eight federal government

---

[1] Christina M. Schaub, "Modern Crime Analysis: Proactive or Reactive," (master's thesis, California State University at Sacramento).

[2] No formal, nationwide study has been conducted to date; however, anecdotal evidence suggests this to be the case.

[3] Schaub, 15.

[4] Schmalleger, 198.

[5] Michigan State Police, "Criminal Justice Information Center," http://www.state.mi.us/msp/cjic.htm (accessed June 26, 2003).

[6] State of Connecticut, Department of Public Safety, "Crime Analysis Unit," http://www.state.ct.us/dps/Crime_%20Analysis_%20Unit/Index.thm (accessed June 26, 2003).

departments.[1] Several of these have now been brought under the umbrella of the DHS. Perhaps the most famous federal law enforcement agency is the Federal Bureau of Investigation (FBI). The FBI "mission [can be] divided into five functional areas: criminal law enforcement; law enforcement services; foreign counterintelligence; investigative and operational support; and direction, control, and administration."[2] The FBI maintains a number of offices useful to crime analysis functions. Among these are its Identification Division, the Crime Laboratory, the National Crime Information Center (NCIC), the Uniform Crime Reports (UCR), the Automatic Fingerprint Identification Service (AFIS), the Combined DNA Index System (CODIS), and many other such offices.

The Drug Enforcement Administration (DEA) has a more narrowly focused mission than the FBI. They are charged with drug interdiction and enforcement of drug laws. Other agencies have similar missions. The FBI, especially, but other agencies as well, perform analytic functions similar to crime analysis units at the state and local level. These federal agencies frequently make their offices and expertise available to state and local agencies for assistance in investigations. This is a more cooperative relationship structure than one might believe from news reports and politicians.

Of particular interest to the crime analysis community is the National Institute of Justice (NIJ), an agency of the Department of Justice. The NIJ provides a variety of training, publications, software, grants, and other resources to the criminal justice community that are enormously helpful in the fight against crime at the state and local levels. The Mapping and Analysis for Public

Safety (MAPS) Office (formerly the Crime Mapping Research Center) is only one example of a NIJ agency that has provided support and training for crime analysts through national conferences, free software, free publications, and other means.

Federal agencies also provide grants and funding for the technology necessary to start up a crime analysis unit (e.g., computer hardware and software, training). These agencies also cooperate with researchers to develop and test anti-crime strategies that are then made available to police agencies across the country.

Federal, state, and local police, "are primarily providers of services. Among the services they provide are law enforcement, order maintenance, and crime prevention."[3] The division of duties, responsibilities, and jurisdictions is a function of the constitutional system we know as federalism. While the federal government is "superior" to the states, which are in turn superior to local police agencies, in terms of governing structure, the various federal agencies also provide support and assistance to the state and local agencies. In practice, local police are the most numerous and the most visible to the citizens.

The Role and Function of the Courts

The U.S. Constitution established one Supreme Court, and gave the Congress the power to establish lower courts. Each state has the authority to establish courts, and most state court systems are modeled on the federal model, with one supreme court, appellate courts, and lower courts.[4] The

---

[1] Schmallager, 193.

[2] Schmallager, 195.

[3] Steven M. Cox and John E. Wade, *The Criminal Justice Network: An Introduction*, 4th ed. (Boston: McGraw-Hill, 2002), 116.

[4] Texas, however, has two supreme courts, the State Supreme Court hears civil cases, the State Court of

function of both federal and state courts is to decide issues of law. In the case of criminal law, the courts hear evidence, decide guilt or innocence and apply appropriate sanctions. Civil courts hear evidence related to disputes and make decisions as appropriate.

Some of the basic concepts of the court system include jurisdiction and the types of law that affect the court's decisions. Jurisdiction is the authority to hear a case. No American court has unlimited jurisdiction. Even the Supreme Court has certain limits. Federal courts, generally speaking, hear cases arising under federal law and state courts hear cases arising under state law. Some federal courts can hear cases arising from state law, but this happens only on appeal and only at the federal District Court of Appeals level, and the Supreme Court. Otherwise, there are two types of jurisdiction: original and appellate. Original jurisdiction refers to the court charged with hearing the original case. Appellate jurisdiction refers to higher courts that have the power to hear appeals arising from the original decision. It should also be noted that some courts have general jurisdiction and some have limited jurisdiction. Courts of general jurisdiction hear a variety of cases. Many district and county courts hear both civil and criminal cases. Courts of limited jurisdiction hear only specific types of cases. For example, juvenile courts hear only cases involving juveniles; probate courts hear only cases involving wills and estate settlements.[1]

Additionally, there is the issue of overlapping, sometimes even competing, jurisdictions. The case of the Washington Beltway snipers is a good example of this. The two men who, in 2002, terrorized the greater Washington D.C. area by shooting at randomly selected victims violated both federal law (civil rights) and the laws of both Virginia and Maryland (murder and aggravated assault). Attorney General John Ashcroft, determined that Lee Boyd Malvo should stand trial in Virginia first. Maryland will have the opportunity to try him later. Federal courts may also have the opportunity to try him.

Our courts operate with a variety of legal traditions. Statutory law arises from the acts of the congress and state legislatures, passing laws (or statutes). This is the law most people think of when they think of someone "breaking the law." Criminal law arising from statute typically involves efforts by the federal or state government to protect the health, safety, and property of individuals or businesses. In these cases the government will always be the plaintiff.

Civil law involves "disputes between citizens, or between government and citizens where no crime has been alleged."[2] Contracts and torts (obligations inherent in social life) are examples of common civil disputes. Common law, which is only found in state and local cases, is the application of previous decisions to current cases. Administrative law involves rules and regulations made by government agencies that have the effect of law. Occupational Safety and Health Administration regulations are an example of this type of law. "Constitutional law involves judicial review of…a government's action in relation to specific clauses of the Constitution."[3]

The concept of precedent is of critical importance to our understanding of the court system. A precedent is a decision issued by the high court by which future decisions must be guided, or with which future actions

---

Criminal Appeals is the highest court of criminal appeals in the state.
[1] Cox and Wade, 153.

[2] Lowi and Ginsberg, 313.
[3] Lowi and Ginsberg, 313.

must be governed. It is possible for a Supreme Court precedent to be applied retroactively, but this is rare. When the Supreme Court ruled that suspects must be advised of certain rights before questioning (Miranda vs. Arizona), the decision established a precedent that all police agencies are required to follow.

There are more than 375,000 people employed in the court system, including judges, clerks, bailiffs, and administrators. The budget of the court system involves many billions of dollars. These courts operate in what is known as a dual system—one system of courts for federal cases and one for state cases. There are 94 federal district courts including three special territorial courts (for U.S. possessions such as Puerto Rico and Guam). Appeals from these courts, and from the U.S. Tax Court, are heard by one of the 12 United States Courts of Appeals (each serving a region of the country). There are special federal courts, such as the Court of International Trade, Claims Court and the Court of Veteran's Appeals. These courts' appeals go to the Court of Appeals for the Federal Circuit. There are Courts of Military Review for each branch of the service, and Courts of Military Appeal.[1] All federal judges are appointed by the president subject to Senate confirmation (it is very rare for a presidential appointment to not be confirmed). Once confirmed, federal judges serve for life although they can be impeached and removed from the bench for "treason, bribery or other high crimes and misdemeanors." Lifetime tenure is a subject of some debate, but the original reason for such an appointment was to remove judicial decision making from partisan politics and political pressure.

State courts follow a similar structure to the federal courts. All have courts of limited jurisdiction and of general jurisdiction. Justice of the Peace courts, municipal courts, and traffic courts are examples of the former. Superior courts and circuit courts, which hear serious criminal and civil matters, are examples of the latter. These courts "make full use of juries, prosecutors, defense attorneys, witnesses, and all the other actors we usually associate with American courtrooms."[2] Thirty-nine states have intermediate courts of appeals, and all fifty states have at least one state supreme court.

States select their judges following one of four models, depending on state law. Some states use the appointment system, similar to the federal model but the judges serve specific limited terms. Some states elect judges in partisan political contests. Some elect judges in non-partisan political contests. A growing number use what is known as the Missouri system, in which the governor appoints a judge, subject to legislative confirmation, and when the judge's term of office has ended he or she stands uncontested in what is called a retention election. If they are retained by the voters, they serve another term and then stand for another retention election, and so on. None of these systems are perfect and all have supporters and critics.

The court system in the United States is known as an adversarial system. There are two sides in each case, both trying to be declared "the winner" by the judge or jury. All criminal defendants have the right to be represented by counsel. The indigent are most often represented by public defenders. In fact, some 75 percent of prison inmates were represented by public defenders.[3] Many

[1] Schmallager, 327.

[2] Schmallager, 330.
[3] Cox and Wade, 177.

public defenders are young and relatively inexperienced. Prosecuting attorneys, often called district attorneys, are elected public officials whose continuance in office depends on good performance as a prosecutor.

In courts of original jurisdiction juries may be selected to hear the evidence and make a determination of guilt or innocence.[1] Juries are selected from among citizens in a random selection, subject to some qualifying criteria. During the course of the trial the prosecuting and defending attorneys present evidence and call and cross-examine witnesses in an effort to prove their side of the case. The judge defines for the jury what the facts of the case are and what evidence is admissible and which is not. The judge instructs the jury as to what alternative verdicts exist. The judge also defines what alternative sanctions may be applied if the defendant is found guilty. However, a judge may alter or set aside a jury's decision if he or she finds that doing so would serve the interests of justice.[2] Appeals courts may change or overturn decisions of the trial court when procedural errors are found. Under the 7th Amendment to the Constitution, "no fact tried by a jury shall be otherwise re-examined in any Court of the United States...." Thus, the only basis for an appeal is in the case of some error in procedure during the course of the investigation, arrest, questioning, or trial.

During trial, evidence is presented by both prosecuting and defense attorneys. It is typically at this stage that data from crime analysis units are used. The defense attorney may try to use, for example, evidence of crime rates in an area, or specific types of crimes, or arrests of certain types of suspects by certain types of officers, to cast doubt in the minds of the jurors about the guilt or innocence of the defendant, of about the arrest was made, and so on. Prosecutors may ask crime analysis units for suspect descriptions, maps indicating what happened during a crime spree,[3] and other forms of supporting information.

Only a small percentage of crimes that occur result in an arrest.[4] Of those that do result in an arrest, some 90 percent are resolved by a plea bargain.[5] A plea bargain is the trading of a guilty plea for some consideration, such as dropped or reduced charges, or leniency at sentencing. The advantages to the criminal justice system are numerous: the expense of a trial is avoided, the crowded schedules of the nation's courts are significantly relieved, and the perpetrator is convicted and punished. Many people believe that plea bargains circumvent "true justice." However, without plea bargains the criminal justice system would be bogged down even more than it is now.

Following the trial, if the defendant is found guilty, the judge will impose sanctions as defined by law. Some states allow sentencing by the jury, but this is typically limited to death penalty cases.[6] When plea bargains have been entered into, the judge normally accepts the recommendation of the

---

[1] Juries are required by the Constitution in criminal cases, and in civil cases where the amount exceeds $20. Jury trial may be waived by the defendant.

[2] As was the case in the trial of Louise Woodard, a 19-year-old British nanny, who was sentenced to 15 years in prison by the jury, but the judge ordered the conviction reduced to involuntary manslaughter and changed the sentence to time already served (see Schmallager, 376).

[3] As happened in Dallas, TX in 2000, when the prosecutors obtained a map detailing the particularly gruesome happenings during a brutal kidnapping and murder in which the victim was kidnapped on one side of the city, driven to different locations where he was beaten and tortured, and finally his body dumped on the other side of the city. The map was introduced at trial and the suspects received the death penalty.

[4] Senna and Seigel, 14.

[5] Cox and Wade, 221.

[6] Cox and Wade, 234.

prosecutors. Judges typically have a good deal of discretion in imposing sentences and committing the newly convicted person to the corrections system.

Corrections: Home Confinement to Federal Prison

There are typically five goals considered in sentencing an offender to the corrections system: retribution, incapacitation, deterrence, rehabilitation, and restoration.[1] Retribution is the age-old demand for vengeance. Modern retribution follows the "just deserts" model of sentencing.[2] This perspective holds that criminals deserve to be punished because of their choices and actions. Imprisonment is the primary tool of retribution and has been especially favored since the early 1990s.[3]

Incapacitation is the removal of the convicted person from society so that he or she cannot commit further crimes. Modern innovations, such as electronic surveillance, offer ways to incapacitate the offender without imprisoning them.

There are two types of deterrence. Specific deterrence is aimed at the original offender and has the goal of convincing him or her that the punishment that is visited upon them is greater in "cost" than any perceived "benefits" of the crime committed. General deterrence seeks to persuade others from committing crimes by holding the original offender as an example. From either perspective, the goal of deterrence is behavior modification.

The goal of rehabilitation is another form of behavior modification. "Rehabilitation seeks

to bring about fundamental changes in offenders and their behavior."[4] Rehabilitation programs seek to improve prisoners' education and literacy levels and to provide them with job skills in hopes that they will lead full and productive lives upon release from prison. Recidivism studies in the 1970s and later found unacceptably high rates of prisoners returning to lives of crime after release. This fed the public's growing desire to punish as a primary goal of corrections.

The fifth goal of sentencing is restoration. The idea is to make the victim and the community whole again. Sentencing options through this goal typically involve payments the offender is required to make to either the victim or to a community fund.[5] Supporters of this approach to sentencing argue restitution payments and work programs serve the dual purpose of benefiting the victim and rehabilitating the offender.[6]

Traditionally, courts have used indeterminate sentencing when sentencing people to jail or prison. One goal of this form of sentence was to allow judges to tailor the punishment to fit both the crime and the offender by considering both aggravating and mitigating circumstances. Another goal of this sentence is to give wardens and parole boards latitude in rehabilitating offenders. By using the promise of early parole as a possibility, the behaviors of inmates can be changed. Indeterminate sentencing is still in use in at least 18 states.[7]

In recent years, with "truth in sentencing" laws and "three strikes laws," determinate sentencing has become more the norm. When a person is sentenced he or she will serve the majority of the sentence. California

---

[1] Schmallager, 405-406.
[2] Schmallager, 406.
[3] Schmallager, 406.
[4] Schmallager, 407.
[5] Schmallager, 408.
[6] Schmallager, 409.
[7] Schmallager, 409.

now requires prisoners to serve a minimum percentage of their sentences, typically 80%, before they become eligible for parole.

Criticisms of indeterminate sentencing include the possibility that sentencing inequalities can result from biases due to racism, sexism or social characteristics. Criticisms of determinate sentencing include charges that it hampers the discretionary powers of judges and prosecuting attorneys, that it ignores specific circumstances of crimes and criminals, and that it has led to overcrowding of prisons.

The Federal Bureau of Prisons was established in 1930, and is divided into five regions. The different prisons vary in size from over 2,000 inmates per facility to just a couple of hundred per facility. These institutions are for the purpose of incarcerating those who have violated federal laws. Some federal correctional facilities, such as the one at Ft. Leavenworth, KS, are designed to hold the more serious and dangerous offenders. Others, such as the one at Seagoville, TX (outside Dallas) are designed for the less serious offenders.[1]

The majority of corrections facilities exist at the state level. In the year 2000, more than 2,000,000 inmates were incarcerated in state prison facilities.[2] Most inmates are involved in some type of work each day. Some still work on prison farms. Others work in industrial-style laundries, kitchens, and so on. The well educated may work in prison offices or libraries. Most, however, perform menial tasks with no other purpose than to keep them occupied.

Prisons are divided into different levels of security depending on the nature of the population of the prison. So-called "super-max" prisons have emerged in the last decade or so to house the very violent and those that pose serious escape risk. "The emphasis is on security and control."[3] Security includes double fences and razor wire, surveillance cameras, and significant restriction of movement. Inmates may be locked down for up to 23 hours in a day.[4] Contact with the outside is severely restricted.

More conventional are the maximum, medium, and minimum security prisons. Maximum security prisons typically house long-term inmates and dangerous inmates. Such prisons normally have high concrete walls and guard towers, armed guards and dogs, and floodlights. Medium security prisons house younger and less dangerous prisoners. They allow greater freedom of movement and contact with the outside world. Rehabilitation and education programs are more common in these prisons than in their higher security counterparts as well. Minimum security facilities house non-violent offenders and typically do not have armed guards and high walls. The normally have dormitory-style housing and use work release and educational release programs, and home furloughs. These prisons are criticized as "country club" by some, but others consider them to offer the best opportunity for rehabilitation for low-level offenders.[5]

All prisons keep records on their inmates, including their criminal histories and their personal and demographic data. When a prisoner is paroled to a community, his or her data is normally sent to the local police department. In Dallas, TX the crime analysis unit receives a computer disk each month

---

[1] Indeed, many of the inmates at Seagoville Prison ride into town each day to work in offices and other businesses, and then return each night to the prison for dinner and sleeping.
[2] Cox and Wade, 286.

[3] Cox and Wade, 287.
[4] Cox and Wade, 287.
[5] Cox and Wade, 288.

containing the parolees' data. This data has been instrumental in developing suspects on numerous occasions. One such occasion happened in 1998. A series of rapes began to occur in an area of Dallas where a significant number of parolees lived. The lieutenant of the Sex Assaults Unit approached the supervisor of the Crime Analysis Unit for help in identifying possible suspects. The corrections data was loaded into a spreadsheet, and the data was sorted by area of the city. A recent parolee matched the description given by the victims, and he even lived in the same apartment complex where one of the assaults had occurred. This address was also very close to the location of several of the other offenses. This particular parolee had been sent to prison for sex offenses. The lieutenant had his investigators go interview this man. He turned out to be the perpetrator. Obviously, sharing data between the state prison system and local police departments is a very valuable crime analysis tool.

"Jails are usually the first, and sometimes the only, contact offenders have with corrections."[1] Jails are run by local authorities, frequently the sheriff's department. Jails are properly thought of as short-term holding facilities for people awaiting arraignment, trial, and sentencing. They serve many other functions today. They hold probation, parole, and bail bond violators, and they temporarily hold many different types of people who are waiting for transfer to appropriate facilities. They also house inmates for federal and state authorities due to overcrowding. They hold inmates sentenced to short sentences (under one year). Frequently they run community-based programs such as home detention and electronic monitoring.[2] Many jails are old,

staffed by poorly trained guards and administrators, and are low budget priorities for the cities and counties that run them.

An article by Zupan and Menke, published in 1991, argues that the problems found in many jails arise from "overuse and misuse of detention, overemphasis on custodial goals, and political and public apathy."[3] The problems associated with traditional jails, including physical and sexual assaults, transmission of communicable diseases, and dilapidated physical conditions of the jails themselves, have led to the development of new management strategies. "Direct supervision" jails emerged in the 1970s. This management philosophy creates an open atmosphere in which guards mix freely with the inmates, affording more direct contact between the two, leading to more effective supervision and thus putting the authorities back in control of the jails.[4]

Not all persons convicted of offenses need to be, or should be, incarcerated. "As an alternative to the expensive, generally ineffective, and sometimes inhumane practice, the concepts of intermediate sanctions and community corrections have evolved. Intermediate sanctions are less severe than incarceration, but are more restrictive than probation."[5] This level of sanctions includes "boot camps," electronic monitoring, intensive probation, home confinement, restitution, fines, and similar sanctions that stop short of prison or jail. This level of sanction is appropriate for low level and first-time offenders, non-violent offenders with limited contact with police authorities, certain drug offenders, and similar offenders that do not pose a danger to

[1] Cox and Wade, 288.
[2] Schmallager, 511.

[3] Linda L. Zupan and Ben A. Menke, "The New Generation Jail: An Overview," cited in Schmallager, 516-17.
[4] Schmallager, 517.
[5] Cox and Wade, 304.

society, and who may be susceptible to behavior modification.

"Community corrections programs include probation, parole, work release, halfway houses" and similar programs.[1] The assumption behind these programs is that the offenders directed into them, and the interests of justice, are best served in community settings where the offenders may continue to work and to have contact with their families and loved ones, and have access to supervision, and appropriate psychological and psychiatric care. Such programs are typically reserved for offenders who might have the best chances at rehabilitative success. The newest form of community based corrections is "restorative justice." This movement seeks to bring victims and offenders together to resolve differences and allow the victim to tell the offender the influence the offense has had, and for the offender to make restitution to the victim and confront the effects of their crime.

One of the most controversial aspects of corrections is the fact that prisoners have rights that the authorities must ensure. Before the 1960s, authorities took what is known as a "hands off" approach to the prisons. That is, judges relied on the professionalism of the prison administrators to do their jobs without undue interference from the bench. Prisoners, upon conviction, experienced a kind of "civil death" which prevented them from voting, holding office, holding certain jobs, and in some states, from marrying. Even today, nearly four million American citizens are prevented from voting because of previous felony convictions.[2]

In 1969, a federal court declared the entire Arkansas prison system to constitute an unconstitutional form of cruel and unusual punishment because of overcrowding (more than double what it was designed for) and inhumane living conditions. The judge laid out 44 standards that had to be met before additional inmates could be transferred to the prison system. These conditions included "living space, staff-to-inmate ratios, visiting privileges, makeup of staff, food service modifications," and medical care.[3]

It was the 1974 Supreme Court decision in *Pell vs. Procunier* that established a "balancing test" to guide the decision trail between inmate rights and prison requirements. This case involved only First Amendment rights of prisoners. The Court held that prisoners do not forfeit their rights simply because of their status as inmates, if their claim is not inconsistent with legitimate penological objectives. In short, prisoners retain rights under the Constitution, so long as their exercise of those rights does not jeopardize the needs of the prison in terms of security, safety, and custody.[4] This is an example of the balancing act between individual rights and public order mentioned earlier.

In 1980, Congress passed the Civil Rights of Institutionalized Persons Act (CRIPA). This bill applies to all persons in adult or juvenile jails, prisons, mental hospitals, and other facilities operated by public entity. The law requires Attorneys General to bring suit if they find conditions in an institution to constitute "egregious or flagrant conditions which deprive such persons of any rights, privileges, or immunities secured or protected by the Constitution or laws of the United States...."[5]

Any number of cases since *Pell* have given scope and breadth to the reality of prisoners'

---

[1] Cox and Wade, 305.
[2] Schmallager, 550.

[3] Schmallager, 551.
[4] Schmallager, 551.
[5] Schmallager, 552.

rights. In a nutshell, prisoners have what we now recognize as conditional rights. That is, rights that are protected so long as they do not compromise the legitimate interests of the state and society with regard to incarcerating convicted felons. These interests include order-maintenance, security, and treatment needs with regard to prisoners. Institutions may restrict the rights of prisoners, but mere convenience for the institution is not a legitimate reason to do so. Generally speaking, prisoners have rights to religious freedom, freedom of speech, access to legal assistance, medical treatment, protection from foreseeable attack, and against unreasonable institutional punishments and disciplines.

In 1991, the Supreme Court signaled a willingness to return, at least in part, to the "hands off" doctrine. In *Wilson vs. Seiter*, the Court ruled that unless conditions are the result of "deliberate indifference" which constituted "malicious intent" then the claims of the plaintiff under the Eighth Amendment may not have standing. The deliberate indifference standard is still being developed, but an increasingly conservative Supreme Court seems less likely to be sympathetic to the claims of prison inmates, beyond the rudimentary requirements of life sustenance.

Conclusion

The U.S. criminal justice system is a confusing hodge-podge of laws, policies, constitutional requirements, and attitudes toward what is appropriate. The founders of this nation built in numerous safeguards against the abusive exercise of power by the government against its citizens. These rights apply today.

This chapter has surveyed constitutional provisions and legal cases that have guided and shaped the formation of the criminal justice system. Our system seeks to balance the rights and privileges of citizens against the state, citizens against each other, and convicted felons against political and emotional reactions.

The police are the enforcers of the law, but our constitutional system prevents the police from breaking the law as they enforce it. The court system applies the law and determines guilt or innocence. The court system is far from perfect. However, it does fundamentally protect the innocent, and provide at least a modicum of justice for those found guilty of breaking the law, while balancing the interests of private citizens. The corrections system is charged with enforcing sanctions as imposed by the courts. All of these functions are guided and constrained by the Constitution, laws, and Supreme Court decisions.

The role of the crime analyst in all of this is to provide useful, "clean," appropriate data. Federal level crime analysts are critical in gathering relevant data and producing analysis and reports crucial to protecting national security, whether threatened by terrorists, drug smugglers, or organized crime. State and local crime analysts' roles are every bit as important in identifying and solving local-level crime problems. The relationships built by these different crime analysts help the entire system to run smoothly and effectively.

Crime analysts provide important information to the court system. This information aids the system in providing evidence relevant to cases, and data so that suspects can be identified, tracked, and ultimately brought to justice. Analysts at the corrections level help detail complete records of prisoners, parolees, and those released from the corrections system. This information can assist police and prosecutors build cases, and to avoid unnecessary prosecution of the innocent.

While imperfect, the American criminal justice system has served the citizens well, and will continue to do so even as it continues to evolve and change in response to laws, court decisions, and social attitudes. The criminal justice system is the subject of numerous college courses. Each element of the system easily takes up an entire semester, or more, of intense study. Many, many books and articles have been written to analyze the system, discover its weaknesses and strengths, and point us toward continuing improvement so that the rights and privileges of all Americans may be ensured and protected more effectively.

Recommended Readings

Champagne, Anthony and Edward J. Harpham, eds. *Texas at the Crossroads: People, Politics, and Policy*. College Station, TX: Texas A&M University Press, 1987.

Cox, Steven M. and John E. Wade. *The Criminal Justice Network: An Introduction*, 4th ed. Boston: McGraw-Hill, 2002.

Lowi, Theodore J. and Benjamin Ginsberg. *American Government*, 4th ed. New York: W. W. Norton and Company, 1996.

Mika, Harry and Lawrence J. Redlinger. "Crime and Correction." In *Texas at the Crossroads: People, Politics, and Policy*, edited by Anthony Champagne and Edward J. Harpham. College Station, TX: Texas A&M University Press, 1987.

Packer, Herbert L. *The Limits of the Criminal Sanction*. Stanford, CA: Stanford University Press, 1975.

Schmallager, Frank. *Criminal Justice Today*, 7th ed. Upper Saddle River, NJ: Prentice Hall, 2003.

Senna, Joseph J. and Larry J. Seigel. *Introduction to Criminal Justice*, 9th ed. Belmont, CA: Wadsworth/Thomson Learning, 2002.

Wilson, James Q. *Thinking About Crime*, rev. ed. New York: Vintage Books, 1983.

Zupan, Linda L. and Ben A. Menke. "The New Generation Jail: An Overview." In *American Jails: Public Policy Issues*, edited by Joel A. Thompson and G. Larry Mays Chicago: Nelson-Hall, 1991.

3
Understanding Criminal Behavior

Jonathan D. Alston

The following are all case synopses of crimes that occurred in Edmonton, Alberta in the past year. Some may read very much like the kind of crime that has occurred in your jurisdiction:

- A twenty-something male, appearing drug-addled and nervous, runs into a gas station at 02:15, points a knife at a clerk and makes off with $27.00 in cash and ten cartons of cigarettes. It is believed that this is the thirteenth armed robbery he has committed in the past two months. This is the third time he has robbed this particular gas station and the second time he has robbed this clerk.

- A recently paroled child molester, in breach of his conditions, goes to a public swimming pool. While there, he befriends a young family, paying particular attention to their ten-year-old son. He asks if it would be all right to take their son for a sleepover at his house. They are reluctant but their son really wants to go and they agree. During the sleepover, the molester sexually assaults the boy.

- A group of aboriginal (Native American) juvenile females are hanging out at a convenience store. They begin talking with a group of three young white males who come out of the store. They invite the boys back to one of the girls' home. The boys readily agree. Once they reach the home, they enter and are taken down to the basement. They find a large group of young aboriginal males waiting for them. The boys are beaten, robbed, and terrorized for hours and are locked together in a bathroom. They then all escape from a small window in the bathroom. This is the third such violent interracial incident in this neighborhood in the past three months.

- A bank manager approves a loan for a fictitious person. He wires half of the money from this loan into the accounts of twelve other fictitious persons—all of whom have significant loans. The money in these twelve accounts is then wired in the form of loan payments back to the bank. The bank manager then takes the remaining half of the money and creates a thirteenth account. Next he withdraws most of it in cash and parses it out among a group of mistresses and escorts he has been frequenting. The amount of money embezzled approaches $16 million.

Almost all crimes, including those above, have three things in common: an offender, a victim and a location.[1] Some have more than one of each. As a crime analyst, one of your primary jobs will be to look at these and provide an analytical product that is going to deal with such crimes and help put these offenders, and others like them, in police custody.[2] All the crimes described above had

---

[1] There are a few exceptions. So-called "victimless" crimes such as drug use and prostitution may not have an obvious victim. However, even in these crimes there is a requirement for elements or persons coming together in space. For example, a drug user will get drugs from a supplier and a "john" will need to encounter a prostitute in order to journey to a space in which to commit the crime.

[2] In this chapter *crime analyst*, rather than *intelligence analyst*, is used in most cases. The methodology and applications of theory suggested here are applicable for either type of analyst. See Chapter 1 for a discussion.

an analyst assigned to them and because of their good work (and others'), all of these offenders ended up in police custody and, eventually, in prison.

The purpose of this chapter is to demonstrate how analysts can apply their knowledge and understanding of criminal behavior to tactical and strategic crime analysis. This chapter provides an overview of criminological theory, focusing on the theory known as the *criminal event perspective.*

The methodology that is presented in this chapter is *ideal.* Not every analysis needs to follow the format that will be presented here, as time or circumstance may not allow for such detail. After learning the most complex or comprehensive method, an analyst can then easily adapt the format to his or her own work. Finally, the methodology is not just the author's invention. Several analysts who, in turn, have been influenced by the work of other analysts worldwide, have developed this methodology over the past several years in the Edmonton Police Service's (EPS) Intelligence Analysis Unit.

This type of work is not easy, and it typically will be reserved for experienced crime analysts with intermediate to advanced analytical skills. Novice analysts may find it advantageous to first review the suggested readings noted at the end of the chapter.

The Role of Theory in Crime Analysis

Criminological theories all try to explain aspects of crime or criminal behavior. Most offer insight into this behavior that can be applied in crime and intelligence analysis. These theories vary in their degree of acceptance among criminologists. The theories that have the greatest acceptance usually have more empirical support than other theories. Some theories seem more

philosophical than theoretical. For example, critical criminologists look at the way "crime" is defined and who defines it.

Most criminology theories attempt to explain offenders' motivations for committing crimes. A few examine victim behavior to see if there are common reasons for why certain types of persons are more likely to be victimized. Recently, criminology has seen a rise in the popularity of theories that look more at places of crime rather than people of crime. Place-based theories try to explain why some sites or areas are more crime prone than others.

Crime analysts do not have the luxury of the academic. They cannot just pick a theory that only explains a portion of criminal behavior and apply that time and again throughout their professional life. The proficient crime analyst will take an integrated theoretical approach and will examine offender behavior *and* victim behavior *and* the place of the crime. Some criminologists have put a name to this type of integrated thinking and have called their approach the *criminal event perspective.* Sacco and Kennedy provide this definition:

> Criminal Event comprises its precursors, including the locational and situational factors that bring people together in time and space; the event itself, including how the interactions among participants define the outcomes of their actions; and the aftermath of the event, including the reporting to the police, their response, the harm done, and the redress required, and the long-term consequences of the event in terms of public reactions and the changing of laws.[1]

---

[1] Vincent F. Sacco and Leslie W. Kennedy, *The Criminal Event: an Introduction to Criminology*, 3rd ed. (Toronto: Nelson Thomson Learning, 2002), 35.

Another way of saying this would be that a crime occurs when the path of an offender crosses with the path of a victim. Where they meet is the crime scene. All three are vital elements of the crime. A distinct advantage of the criminal event perspective and others like it is that they look at the whole of a crime and are thus readily transferable to crime analysis.[1]

Criminological theorists try to make sense out of criminal behavior. They see patterns, make hypotheses, and test their theories. Crime analysts essentially do the same thing. The purpose of theory and crime analysis is to organize the chaos or to make simple what is complex. This is not an easy thing to do. There are reasons why some unsolved crimes go unsolved for so long and why it might take months or years to investigate a tip concerning an individual a police department contacted in the first week after a serious crime was committed. Likewise, there are important reasons for why a particular high crime neighborhood has been a problem area for decades. The good news is that a proficient crime analyst can be part of the solution to these problems.

Effective analysis of crime always result in some sort of analysis product. This can be a map, chart, timeline, written report, or otherwise. Generally, analysts will provide these products with either a tactical or strategic focus. In the next section, we will see how an understanding of criminal behavior can be used in tactical analysis.

Applying a Knowledge of Criminal Behavior in Tactical Analysis

As noted in Chapter 1, tactical analysis provides information or intelligence that will assist in the identification of immediate crime problems and, hopefully, in the arrest of a specific criminal. This type of analysis is not new. In the 1970s, the Federal Bureau of Investigation (FBI) began structuring a tactical analytical process known as psychological profiling. This process has been one of the foremost and successful in its application of a knowledge of criminal behavior in capturing violent criminals. The profiling process was heavily influenced by psychiatry and psychology and, as such, was centered on offender behavior.

In 1978, the FBI began the Serial Murder Project. Their goal was to conduct interviews with serial murderers who (presumably) had insight into their offending behavior that could be used to develop ways to assist the FBI in capturing future serial murderers more effectively.[2] They then developed a mentorship-based curriculum for training other profilers. Today, profilers can be found working in the United States, Canada, South

---

[1] Research examples include: Erin G. Van Brunschot, "Assault Stories," in *Crime in Canadian Society*, 6th ed., ed. Robert A. Silverman, James J. Teevan, and Vincent F. Sacco (Toronto: Harcourt Brace, 2000); Robert F. Meier, Leslie W. Kennedy, and Vincent F. Sacco, *The Process and Structure of Crime* (Piscataway: Transaction, 2001), see esp. Patricia L. Brantingham and Paul J. Brantingham, "The Implications of the Criminal Event Model for Crime Prevention"; and Laura A. Thue, "Gender and the Social Processes of Violence: the Interaction Between Personal and Situational Factors" (PhD dissertation, University of Alberta). The criminal event perspective is also reminiscent of Routine Activities theory; see Lawrence E. Cohen and Marcus Felson, "Social Change and Crime Rate Trends: a Routine Activities Approach," *American Sociological Review* 44 (1979): 588–608. Routine activities theory sees crime as the interaction of a motivated offender, a suitable target, and a lack of capable guardianship.

[2] G. Maurice Godwin, "Reliability, Validity, and Utility of Extant Serial Murder Classifications," in *Criminal Psychology and Forensic Technology: a Collaborative Approach to Effective Profiling*, ed. G. Maurice Godwin, 61–78 (Boca Raton, FL: CRC Press, 2001).

Africa, the United Kingdom, Australia, across Western Europe, Japan, and elsewhere.[1]

Crime analysts will be called on to perform similar duties. This may be in a homicide or rape series but will often be something more mundane and common like a burglary or robbery series. They may also be called on to provide an analysis on a single crime such as a homicide or sexual assault.[2]

As discussed in the previous section, the best approach is to take an integrated look at the crime series. Rather than an offender profile, a crime analyst using an integrated approach will likewise produce an integrated product. The author proposes that a useful name for such a product would be a *Series Profile*. The name emphasizes that the entire series is being profiled and not just the offender or victim or place.

A Series Profile is the written product of a crime analyst versed in a knowledge and understanding of criminal behavior. Depending on the crime, the complexity of the investigation, and the time on hand this could be anywhere from a couple of pages to hundreds of pages long. It is a virtual dissection of a criminal event in which all known aspects of a crime are taken out, examined in part, and considered within their contribution to the whole. It will be a vital contributor to the "intelligence process"[3] and

is designed to guide an investigation. The Series Profile will discuss all three components of the criminal event. These components will take the form of sections. This will include offender characteristics, victim or target characteristics, and spatial characteristics. In each of these sections the Series Profile will indicate what is known and what is not known about a series and, if not known, what could be found out through further investigation. Analytical comments and recommendations for investigative follow-up will need to be made after each of the sections. The following pages describe the sections of a Series Profile.

Offender Characteristics

The first major section includes all that is known about the offender. When writing this section, assume that the readers of the report will know little to nothing about the case and are relying on the report to give them the background they need. Time permitting, this section can be supplemented with images, charts, graphs, tables, timelines, and so on. Maps should be reserved for the spatial characteristics section.

The offender characteristics section is made up of a number of sub-sections that include the following: classification of the series, physical description of the offender, vehicle or mode of transport description, crime or a sequence-of-events description, *modus operandi* description, and signature and motive description. Following these sub-sections, a discussion could be provided of any suspects in the series. Finally, a sub-section covering analytical comments will need to be offered.

Classification of the Series

A series is defined as two or more criminal offenses committed by an individual or group

[1] see: Robert K. Ressler, Ann W. Burgess, and John E. Douglas, *Sexual Homicide: Patterns and Motives* (Washington, DC: Lexington, 1988); John E. Douglas et. al., *Crime Classification Manual* (New York: Lexington, 1992); Vernon J. Geberth, *Practical Homicide Investigation*, 3rd ed. (New York: Elsevier, 1996); and Ronald M. Holmes, ed., "Psychological Profiling," in *Journal of Contemporary Criminal Justice* 15 (1999).
[2] Though this chapter focuses on series, the techniques discussed in this section can be easily adapted to single case analysis.
[3] Charles C. Frost, "Criminal Intelligence: the Vital Resource; an Overview," in Godwin, 61–78.

of individuals. Alston notes these separate and specific classifications of series:

- Class I: a single offender acting alone in all reported offenses.
- Class II: two or more offenders acting together, where all offenders are common to all cases.
- Class III: two or more offenders committing some offenses together, some alone, and some with others in which a binding or overarching element keeps the group together and the series continuing.[1]

An offender can belong to more than one series but one crime cannot exist in more than one series. In some cases it may be difficult to classify a series. Even after an arrest, the true nature of the series may not be known. Classifications are made on what the best intelligence indicates is the truth. As always, direct evidence such as DNA, a confession, or eyewitness testimony is the best support for a classification.

Murderers such as Norman Simons (South Africa), Andrei Chikatilo (Russia, Ukraine), Clifford Olson (Canada), Ted Bundy, Jeffrey Dahmer, Aileen Wuornos, John Gacy, Arthur Shawcross, and Robert Yates are examples of Class I serial criminals. From serial burglars to serial murderers, these appear to be the most common type of serial criminal.

Ian Brady and Myra Hindley (UK), Douglas Clark and Carol Brady, and John Allen Muhammad and John Lee Malvo (the DC area sniper killers), are examples of Class II serial murderers. Partner serial murderers are relatively common. Steven Egger calls them

"team killers."[2] Eric Hickey found that in his sample of serial murderers 37% had at least one partner (either Class II or Class III).[3] This type of serial criminal is also common for less serious crimes such as robbery and burglary.

Kenneth Bianchi and Angelo Buono, the infamous Hillside Stranglers, are an example of Class III serial murderers. These two cousins were bound together by both blood (i.e., they were relatives) and by their compulsion to commit such crimes. However, they also committed several offenses on their own, especially Bianchi. A youth gang who uses rape as a method of initiation and a way to ensure loyalty to the gang is another example of a Class III series.

A Class III rape series that occurred in the early 1990s in the Vancouver, British Columbia area is instructive. The series began with a group of three individuals, all of whom worked together at an auto-body shop (the binding reason that initially kept the group together; later it would be the thrill of the crimes and the fear of capture that kept them cohesive). Interestingly, they were all different races—one white, one East Indian, and one aboriginal (Native American). Separately, each of these men was merely a petty criminal, but when together, a group identity apparently formed that made them capable of much worse. They committed a number of brutal rapes in the Greater Vancouver area of British Columbia. The white offender emerged as the leader of this group and was involved in most of the offenses with at least one of the other offenders. However, some offenses were committed by the other two of the group,

---

[1] Jonathan D. Alston, "The Serial Rapist's Spatial Pattern of Target Selection," in Godwin, 2001.

[2] Steven A. Egger, *The Killers Among Us: an Examination of Serial Murder and Its Investigation* (Upper Saddle River, NJ: Prentiss Hall, 1998).

[3] Eric W. Hickey, *Serial Murderers and Their Victims* (Pacific Grove, CA: Brooks-Cole, 1991).

and in some, all three were present. Class III series also appear to be common.

For the sake of simplicity, if a series becomes too lengthy or complex it may be helpful to divide the series into different sub-series. Take for example, the offenses of Paul Bernardo in the metro-Toronto area (Ontario, Canada). During the late 1980s, Bernardo committed a large number of sadistically motivated rapes, and was given the moniker of "the Scarborough Rapist" (Scarborough is a suburb of Toronto). That series ended soon after a composite sketch was released to the public that looked very much like Bernardo. He soon moved from Scarborough to live with his fiancée Karla Homolka and her family in St. Catharines (near Niagara Falls) in 1990. Bernardo and Homolka then moved to another location near St. Catharines in early 1991. The criminal expression of his sexual deviance seemed to change as his relationship with Karla developed. From the time he moved in with her they began a series of crimes that they committed together (although there may have been a few other offenses where Bernardo acted alone). Bernado and Homolka "accidentally" killed Karla's sister in a botched drugging and sexual assault; abducted and sexually assaulted a woman in January 1991; allegedly drugged and sexually assaulted at least one teenager; and twice abducted, tortured, and killed two young women. Given the chronology and nature of the offenses, the Scarborough Rapist crimes would be its own Class I series and the Bernardo-Homolko crimes would be a Class II series.

Examining offense patterns in this way allows the crime analyst to organize the files in a consistent manner and ensures that no offense or item is missed. More important, offender behavior changes by type of class. Paul Bernardo did not commit any murders

until his wife was involved in his offense behavior. A group of three offenders will act differently than a single offender.[1] Methods of capture and interrogation for Class II serial criminals will be much different than those employed with a Class I serial offender.

Physical Description

In a series where the offender is unknown, the physical descriptions offered by victims and witnesses reported in different files can be a blessing or a curse. Research has repeatedly shown and established that eyewitness testimony, though compelling in court, is frequently erroneous.[2] Other forms of obtaining a physical description, such as security cameras, are more reliable. In recent years, forensic enhancement of these images has had great influence on obtaining good physical descriptions of offenders.

Information that should be examined should at least cover the basics: gender, race, height, weight, hair color, hair length, eye color, facial hair, body shape, clothing, and approximate age. Depending on a number of factors, the police reports available to the analyst may not have recorded all of this information. Obvious attempts to disguise any of these features should be noted. Any especially exclusionary or specific information should be prominently noted (e.g., tattoos, scars, birthmarks, an accent).

This information can be summarized in tables or charts. An analysis of this information *must* be offered. The analysis may be brief, but is necessary to draw

---

[1] Psychologists call this phenomena *gestalt*.
[2] See, for instance, David P. Farrington and Sandra Lambert, "Predicting Offender Profiles from Victim and Witness Descriptions," in *Offender Profiling: Theory, Research, and Practice*, ed. Janet L. Jackson and Debra A. Bekerian, 133–158 (Chichester, West Sussex: Wiley, 1997).

attention to the patterns that may be obvious to the author of the table or chart, yet which others may see differently or not at all.

For example, suppose a crime analyst working in Salt Lake City is examining a series of armed robberies. In the physical description table, she creates a column for "clothing." In the first robbery, the offender's clothing includes a Washington Wizards jersey with the number 23. In the second, third, and fourth robberies there is nothing distinguishable in the clothing. In the fifth robbery, the offender's clothing includes sweat pants with a Green Bay Packers logo. In the sixth and seventh robberies, there is again nothing distinguishable. In the eighth and latest robbery his clothing includes a Chicago Blackhawks baseball cap.

It may be obvious to this analyst that this sports clothing has something to do with the Chicago to Milwaukee areas, given that #23 of the Washington Wizards was Michael Jordan's number (an ex-Chicago Bull), that the Packers play in Green Bay (north of Milwaukee) and that the Blackhawks are Chicago's hockey team. However, not everyone will be aware of this information. If the analyst had access to a list of suspects, one of whom had moved from Racine, Wisconsin recently (located between Chicago and Milwaukee), she would want to draw attention to him.

Remember that one of the jobs of a crime analyst is to notice things that others have missed. Do not just ask what could have been missed but what *was* missed and what has been accepted in the case as absolute fact. If unwarranted, the analyst will have to question such "fact." Often points about physical description can become so entrenched that they form almost a dogma about the criminal. Cold case files are replete with examples of offenders who were

originally written off because they did not match the dogma. No doubt, pointing out this problem will cause consternation among some officers and will require significant diplomacy on the part of the analyst.

Vehicle Description

Like physical description, vehicle description can be either a blessing or curse. This is an area in which, in my experience, police officers can form blind spots. Generally speaking, police officers are very good at vehicle description. Years of observation on the street develop these skills to the point where most officers can tell the make, model, and even the approximate year of a car from some distance away. However, some officers forget that the average person is very poor at vehicle description. Thus descriptions given by witnesses or victims should be kept general—often truck, newer car, older car, motorcycle, mini-van is as far as one would want to go in this area.

In serious crimes with extensive media exposure, the crime analyst must be wary of vehicle descriptions that come in the form of tips. The general public has stereotypes about criminal behavior that are often erroneous. How many killers actually use customized vans to abduct their victims? A few examples spring to mind but these are few and far between and are often historical, such as in the 1970s and 1980s, when customized vans were popular. However, thanks to films such as *Silence of the Lambs*, *Red Dragon*, and others, vans are often believed to be the vehicle of choice among serial killers. Those in the U.S. will remember the white van descriptions of the DC-area sniper killings. In Canada, the infamous white van showed up years earlier in the killing of a little girl in Kelowna, British Columbia. In Edmonton, we had a full-sized van (though blue) as the suspect vehicle in a child homicide. Needless to say, vans were not used in any of these cases.

Crime Description / Sequence of Events

In this sub-section, the analyst should review the exact sequence of events that occurred in the offense. Often this information will already be available in the police reports and victim and witness statements that were completed when the crime was first discovered. A tactical crime analyst should review all of this material, as significant details may be left out of police reports that can be found in witness or victim statements. Particular attention should be paid to oral, physical, and sexual behaviors (if any). This process can be used regardless of the type of crime that is being analyzed.

Contrary to the more general description offered in the physical and vehicle description sub-sections, this information needs to be relayed in clinical detail—word for word and line by line. This can be disturbing, especially in violent crimes like murder or rape, but it is necessary. The information described in the sequence of events will be used or broken down in the next two sub-sections: *modus operandi*, and signature and motive.

Modus Operandi

Modus operandi refers to the method of operation. In criminal behavior, this refers to the method used by the offender to successfully commit the offense or offenses. In other words, it is *how* the offender committed the crime. These methods are not to be confused with motivation or *why* the offender committed the crime.

Cataloging these behaviors are important in linkage analysis, where decisions are made as to whether given crimes are likely part of a series. This is especially important for crimes that occur close together chronologically. Identifying the *modus operandi* helps to gain insight into the type of offender being dealt with. David Canter uses the metaphor of a shadow to describe *modus operandi* and signature behaviors. He argues that an offender may take measures to disguise himself, but they cannot prevent casting a shadow, just as an individual walking outside on a sunny day cannot prevent casting a shadow.[1]

Table 3-1 shows the *modus operandi*, and related factors, for an offender in a recent burglary series. In this case, note how the burglary of *Fein Canadian* stands out from the rest. Indeed, it was later found that the offender worked at this location.

Modus operandi will include activity carried out to gain access to and maintain control of the victim, activities that assist him or her in the commission of the offense, to prevent his or her identification, and those that help him or her in fleeing the final crime scene afterward. Studies have suggested that an *m.o.* will change or evolve. Hazelwood and Warren reported that an *m.o.* is valid in rape series for only three to four months.[2] With that in mind, crime analysts should draw attention to *m.o.* generalities rather than specifics of crimes. For example, if a glass cutter was used in one burglary, a lock pick in the second, and a crow bar in the third the analyst should note that though these are all different, they are all access tools that the offender would probably have had to take with him or her to the location. Brent Turvey offers a list of *m.o.* behaviors that have been adapted below:

---

[1] David Canter, *Criminal Shadows: Inside the Mind of a Serial Killer* (London: Harper Collins, 1994).

[2] Robert R. Hazelwood and Janet I. Warren, "The Relevance of Fantasy in Serial Sexual Crime Investigations," in Burgess and Hazelwood, 127–137.

Table 3-1: West-end Industrial Burglary Series (Master File #03-62877)
Factors Related to *Modus Operandi*

Target & Date	Disguise	Caution Taken	Damage	Items Taken	Transport	Direction of Flight	Notes (re: *m.o.*)
Ace Repair 12104 178 St. (W 03-Jan-01)	Balaclava, large coat	Gloves (surgical)	Incidental to crime	Computer Equipment	GMC Half-Ton (Red) (on tape)	East (toward Highway 16)	Subject seen on security tape
Acklands 11800 184 St. (F 03-Jan-10)	Balaclava, large coat	Gloves (winter mitts)	Incidental to crime	Tools (industrial)	unknown	North (toward Highway 16)	Subject seen on security tape
Nuts & Bolts 11304 178 St. (F 03-Jan-31)	Balaclava, large coat	Gloves (surgical)	Incidental to crime	Computer Equipment	"truck"	unknown	Subject seen on scty. tape & on Hwy. 16
Delta Porter 13704 170 St. (St/Su 03-Feb-08/09)	unknown	unknown	Incidental to crime	Tools (industrial)	unknown	unknown	No security tape
House of Tools 11987 170 St. (Tu 03-Feb-18)	Balaclava, large coat	Gloves (winter mitts)	Incidental to crime	Tools (industrial)	"red truck" (seen by witness)	North (toward Highway 16)	Subject seen on security tape; seen on Highway 16.
Delta Porter 13704 170 St. (St/Su 03-Mar-01/02)	unknown	unknown	Incidental to crime	Tools (industrial)	unknown	unknown	No security tape; same location as above
Calco 11818 178 St. (M 03-Mar-03)	Balaclava, large coat	Gloves (surgical)	Incidental to crime	Tools (industrial)	Red Truck (on tape)	North (toward Highway 16)	Subject seen on security tape
Bosch 12310 184 St. (F 03-Mar-07)	Balaclava; light coat	Gloves (surgical)	Incidental to crime	Tools (industrial)	Red Truck (on tape)	South (toward Highway 16)	Subject seen on security tape
Fein Canadian 11518 170 St. (M 03-Mar-10)	Balaclava, baseball cap; large coat	-none (apparently reckless)	Kicked in bathroom door; tip over fridge	Safe (in manager's office)	4 door car; late 80s; American; white	unknown	Subject seen on tape; was at location for 25 minutes
Jet Equipment 11302 170 St. (Su 03-Mar-23)	Balaclava; light coat	Gloves (surgical)	Incidental to crime	Petty cash box; tools	Red Truck (on tape)	North (toward Highway 16)	Subject seen on security tape

- Method of protecting offender's identity (e.g., wearing a mask, covering a victim's eyes, wearing gloves, killing a witness to offense)
- Amount of surveillance of the target
- Use of a weapon during a crime
- Method of restraining victim (in violent crimes)
- Nature and extent of injuries to victim (in violent crimes)
- Property damage
- Nature and extent of precautionary acts
- Position of the victim's clothing (in violent crimes)
- Position of the victim's body (in violent crimes)

- Items taken from the crime scene(s) to profit or prevent identification
- Method of transport; focusing on information not noted in the vehicle description sub-section (e.g., if the car was stolen)
- Direction of escape from final crime scene[1]

As a general rule a complex *modus operandi* indicates an intelligent offender. Criminally inexperienced yet intelligent offenders will often excessively plan their *m.o.* Typically,

---

[1] Turvey, Brent E. *Criminal Profiling: an Introduction to Behavioral Evidence Analysis*, 2nd ed. (San Diego: Academic Press, 2002).

such offenders simplify their *m.o.* early into the series.

In serious violent offenses such as rape and murder, the FBI developed a typology regarding the method of approach and attack that is best discussed under this *m.o.* sub-section. This typology can also be used in less serious violent offenses. It includes the blitz, con, and surprise approach.[1]

The "blitz" approach involves the offender getting as close to the victim as possible and then suddenly confronting and overpowering him. The "confidence" or "con" approach involves establishing some ostensibly friendly contact with the victim and then overpowering her once she is in the offender's control. The "surprise" approach involves the offender secreting himself at a location where it is believed a potential victim will pass by (e.g., the utility room in the hall of an apartment complex). The offender then lunges out once the victim is chosen.

One of the disadvantages to the FBI approach is that the categories are not mutually exclusive. The differences between blitz and surprise are, to some extent, subjective. D. Kim Rossmo develops a more geographic based method of approach typology. He suggests the term "raptors" for those offenders who attack their victims upon encounter, "stalkers" for those who first follow their victims then attack, and ambushers who attack their victims after enticing them to a location controlled by the offender, such as a residence or workplace.[2] Both the FBI and Rossmo typologies are useful.

---

[1] Ann W. Burgess and Robert R. Hazelwood, eds. *Practical Aspects of Rape Investigation: a Multi-Disciplinary Approach*, 2nd ed. (New York: CRC Press, 1995).

[2] D. Kim Rossmo, *Geographic Profiling* (Boca Raton, FL: CRC Press, 2000).

Signature and Motive

As noted above, *m.o.* refers to *how* the offender committed the crime. Signature (a term popularized by the FBI) has much more to do with *why* the offender committed the crime. It comprises the behaviors that reflect the emotional or psychological needs that the offender satisfies through his or her criminal behavior. In this way, signature is closely related to the motive for committing a crime and can be thought of as the behavioral expression of the motive.

In contrast to the *m.o.*, the signature and motive for a crime will change only slowly over time, if they change at all. Typically, offender motivation of this type is not couched in the terms of criminological theories such as strain, social control, or self-control theories, as discussions are specific to the series in question.

A signature and motive may be difficult to determine and will vary widely by crime type. It may also overlap or become confused with the *m.o.* A motive may be something as simple as money or drugs. If this is the case, this sub-section will be one of the shortest in the Series Profile. However, even in the everyday crimes of burglary and robbery, a crime analyst should not forget motive.

Remember the example given at the beginning of the chapter of the twenty-something male that robbed a clerk of $27.00 in cash and ten cartons of cigarettes? It was not until the analyst began this section and was ready to write this off as a money motive that she realized just how much money was involved. Canada has high taxes on cigarettes (a pack of 25 cigarettes costs around $10.00). With ten packs of cigarettes per carton this robber had made off with a $1000 worth of goods. In the previous two robberies he stole a combined 18 cartons (worth $1800). So, it became apparent that with such a valued commodity that he might be selling them rather than using them. Beat members were asked about anyone they knew of that had been selling cigarettes on the street recently and they quickly identified a few targets, one of whom turned out to be the culprit.

Signature is often defined as the fantasy-based impulses that satisfy emotional, psychosexual or psychological needs.[1] It has usually been reserved for serious violent crimes such as rape or murder, but this need not be the case. For example, in most burglaries the motive seems to be straightforward—easily liquidated items stolen to obtain money. But consider a burglary where the offender defecates on a bed, urinates in a child's room, and steals underwear; or another where family photo albums and precious heirlooms are destroyed. In such cases, there is a clear signature or psychological need that the crime is fulfilling that goes beyond the *m.o* or method used to successfully engage in the crime.

For many crime types, typologies exist that may help the crime analyst understand the type of offender they are dealing with. When dealing with a rape series the Groth typology of power, anger, and sadism is useful.[2] An FBI typology builds on Groth's and consists of descriptions of the power reassurance, power assertive, anger retaliatory, anger excitation, and opportunistic rapist.[3]

Other typologies are less helpful. Many feel that the FBI's classification system of organized vs. disorganized and asocial vs. nonsocial offenders is problematic and confusing. G. Maurice Godwin and Brent Turvey are two among several authors that have called this system into question.

Keppel and Birnes discuss the utility and problems of looking at the signature in criminal behavior. They suggest focusing on extraordinary violence similarities such as if victims are beaten beyond a point needed to control them, if the offender is preoccupied with the victim's behavior or characteristics, or with the crime scenes.[4] Similarly, Hazelwood and Warren report that by noting the signature the profiler (or crime analyst) can then take the next step of determining what type of material, if any, the person would have accumulated to complement his fantasies.[5] Miethe and Drass note significant differences between crimes that are instrumental (i.e., for some type of tangible gain) and those that are expressive (i.e., emotion based).[6]

Suspects

If suspects have been identified in the crime series, they could be discussed in this sub-section. However, depending on how the analysis is to be used, suspects could also be examined in an additional report. A separate report is best used when discussing suspects in a longer series, or one with more serious offenses.

If a series has numerous suspects, a brief paragraph or two may be all that is provided in this sub-section. If there is a prime

---

[1] For example, Robert R. Hazelwood and Janet I. Warren, "The Relevance of Fantasy in Serial Sexual Crime Investigations," in Burgess and Hazelwood, 127–137.

[2] A. Nicholas Groth, *Men Who Rape: the Psychology of the Offender* (New York: Plenum Press, 1979).

[3] Burgess and Hazelwood, 1995.

[4] Robert D. Keppel and William J. Birnes, *Signature Killers* (New York: Pocket Books, 1997).

[5] Hazelwood and Warren, 17.

[6] Terrance D. Miethe and Kriss A. Drass, "Exploring the Social Context of Instrumental and Expressive Homicides: an Application of Qualitative Comparative Analysis," in *Journal of Quantitative Criminology* 15, no. 1 (1999): 1–21.

suspect, or if the offender is known, this sub-section would need to be comprehensive. Depending on how much information is available, this sub-section could become very lengthy and, again, may need to be completed in a report in addition to the Series Profile.

Regardless of whether a paragraph or full report is completed, information on the suspect's physical description, vital statistics (including contact information), biographical details, criminal history and his or her awareness space (areas of familiarity—residence, past residences, hang-outs, and so on) should be included.

Analytical Comments and Recommendations

This final section can be used to summarize the analysis in each of the above sub-sections; make new inferences about the offender, based on the premises established above; and make suggestions or recommendations for investigative follow-up.

Initially crime analysts may feel apprehensive about doing this, believing such analyses should only be performed by trained profilers. However, consider a recent study where crime scenarios were given to a group of profilers, police investigators, psychologists, college students, and psychics. They report that profilers performed only slightly better than the other groups and there was no practical difference between any of the groups.[1] Given how much time and effort many analysts expend in their work, by the time they get to this section they may well be the *most* qualified to offer insight into offender characteristics.[2]

Depending on where one works and how the analysis is to be used, this sub-section can be used to offer information that could be considered more opinion than analysis. Analysts will want to be careful with opinions, but they should not hesitate to include them if they are based on sound consideration of the series and are believed to be of value to the investigation.

Victim or Target Characteristics

The second major section will include all that is known about each victim or target in the series. "Victim" is the term generally given to living targets, while "targets" is used for property related targets. These terms are used interchangeably in this next section.

As with the offender characteristics section, this section should be written with the assumption that the reader knows little to nothing about the case and is relying on this analysis to provide the background. As before, images, charts, graphs, and tables will often supplement this section.

One caveat should be considered continually as this section is put together: a crime analyst must not make judgments about victims or their lifestyles. Even judgments about targets such as the location of a home should be made with care. Remember, depending on how it is used, the analysis may be disclosed and the author called to testify in a court proceeding. If an analyst were to make significant judgments regarding a victim's character, he may find himself testifying for the defense.

This section will consist of a number of sub-sections that will include at least the

---

[1] Richard N. Kocsis et. al., "Criminal Psychological Profiling in Violent Crime Investigations: a Comparative Assessment of Accuracy," in Godwin, 79–94.
[2] A psychological profile the author came across recently while completing a series profile, concluded

that the offender "thought white" and had a mental age of twenty—a comment of uncertain definition and very dubious value to the investigation.

following: physical description; risk level, which may include their social networks and awareness space; offender-victim association; and analytical comments and recommendations.

Physical Characteristics

The victims of crimes are most often known. Thus, this sub-section will often be one of the most reliable and invaluable sources of information about the series. Steven Egger, among others, has noted that one of the strongest similarities among serial offenders is their consistent choice of victims.

In property crimes, the type of property that was targeted needs to be described. Avoid discussing the geographic layout of the location as that will be discussed in the next section (spatial characteristics) but focus on the target itself. Other than geography, address why you suppose the property was targeted. Was it in plain sight? Was it easily accessible? Was there a lack of guardianship? If dealing with a burglary series, knowing the type of establishments being targeted is critical. For example, whether the site is a town house, bungalow, mansion, an apartment, or a condo may indicate much about the offender.

In personal crimes, information that should be noted includes age, gender, hair color, eye color, body type, race, height, weight, clothing, facial hair (if any). Particular attention should be made to any differences between the *actual* physical characteristics and *apparent* physical characteristics. Further, a brief discussion of how the victim would have likely appeared at the time of the offense should be brought to the attention of the reader. For example, a three-year-old girl who is big for her age and playing alone would likely cue in as older than three to a potential abductor some distance away.

In crimes with property and personal elements such as commercial robberies, the crime analyst will have to look at both the physical characteristics of the property and the person. This will be more time consuming. It is certainly tempting to ignore the human victims in such cases; yet this would not be prudent as for years studies based on interviews with commercial robbers have reported that the physical characteristics of human victims are a major contributor to their decision to commit a robbery.[1]

Table 3-2 shows the physical characteristics of the victims of a serial rapist. As can be seen the offender has no *absolute* victim preference, other than females. However, it would seem that he is primarily targeting attractive white women.

Risk Level

In this section, as much detail as possible should be provided about any factors or behaviors that may have led to the victim or target being selected by the offender. These factors may not be immediately obvious until a number of victims or targets are found in a series. In violent crimes, preliminary analysis could be conducted on the following (if known): marital status, occupation, education, medical history, criminal record, and psychosexual proclivities (be careful here, but if it is in the report include it). Include the street address of the victim, even if the address had apparently nothing to do with the crime, as well as the general area of the victim's address (e.g., west side, downtown, the Meadows neighborhood). If disclosure

---

[1] See Floyd Feeney, "Robbers as Decision-Makers," in *The Reasoning Criminal: Rational Choices on Offending*, ed. Derek B. Cornish and Ronald V. Clarke (New York: Springer-Verlag, 1986), 53–71; and Frederick J. Desroches, *Behind the Bars: Experiences in Crime* (Toronto: Canadian Scholar's Press, 1996).

Table 3-2: Mill Creek Rapist (#02-118707)
Victim Physical Characteristics

Name	Age Range	Hair Color	Body Type	Height/ Weight	Race (Apparent)	Clothing	Notes (re: appearance)
Rita McCormack (68-Oct-16)	30s	Blonde	Thin	(not recorded)	White	Sports-wear	Attractive
Jessica Cardinal (79-Jan-10)	20s	Blonde (dyed)	Thin	5' 4" 90 lbs.	Aboriginal or White	Nothing unusual	Victim lives in valley (homeless)
Elaine Crossing Eagle (80-Feb-11)	20s	Brown? (not recorded)	Thin	5' 9" 118 lbs.	Aboriginal	Nothing unusual	Attractive
Donna Harris (86-Jun-28)	Youth (late teens)	Blonde	Medium	5' 2" 135 lbs.	White	Mini-skirt; T-shirt	Walking with toddler in stroller (*i.e.*, may have appeared older).
Gillian Forsythe (61-May-03)	40s	Brown/ Blonde (highlights)	Thin	(not recorded)	White	Mini-skirt; tank top	Working near area (prostitute)
Helen Marshall (69-Sep-06)	30s	Brown	Medium	5' 8" 140 lbs.	White	Sports-wear	Attractive
Jessie Burns (71-Dec-10)	30s	Blonde	Thin	5' 0" 95 lbs.	White	Sports-wear	Attractive

issues are a concern, just include the general area of the city or jurisdiction.

More thorough analyses that could be placed in this section would include a delineation of the victim's social network. In cases of child victims, an analysis of the children's family trees and the social network of their parents or guardians could be included. Depending on their complexity this may take some time to complete.

This information would then be followed by a discussion of any risk factors that were evident at the time of the offense (remember to save a discussion of the location of the crime scenes for the next section). For example, were the victims intoxicated? Were they alone? Were they just getting off a late shift? In property offenses such as auto-theft one might ask: was the car left unattended for some time? Were any of the doors or windows left open?

In summarizing this sub-section, draw attention to two things. First, in general, was the victim or target at high risk? That is, would one expect that similar individuals in the community are also at risk? Second, was the victim or target at risk at the time of the offense? Both of these assessments must be made.

Why? Take for example; a street prostitute (risky lifestyle) sleeping in her bed who is attacked by a stranger who breaks into her fifth story apartment (little risk at the time of the offense). Similarly, a college-educated, reserved married man walking to his car after a party through a rough area late at night may not be living a risky lifestyle but is, at the moment, at a relatively high risk for armed robbery or assault. This analysis will be necessary in informing a method for capturing the offender, such as patrol saturation, and may be used to make a determination on whether a public warning is warranted.

Offender-Victim Association

One of the simplest but most important sub-sections will be a discussion of how the offender and victim or target first came into contact. Obviously, this will be more difficult for property targets. If this information has been covered in the sequence of events, *m.o.*, or signature portions of the offender characteristics section, just revisit it briefly.

Analytical Comments and Recommendations

As with offender characteristics, this final sub-section should be used to summarize the analysis in each of the sub-sections; to make new inferences about the offender, based on the premises established above; and make suggestions or recommendations for investigative follow-up.

Historically, not many police investigations have focused on analyses of victim characteristics. Thus, this section could include suggestions and recommendations that would be of particular value to a current investigation.

Spatial Characteristics

The third major section includes all that is known about the different spatial locations involved in the criminal event. This section should be supplemented with maps. Time permitting, images, charts, graphs, and tables could also be included. In the other sections, supplementary material is usually interesting and often very valuable, but in this section, such material is critical.

An analyst may be called on to perform spatial analysis in serious crime series. This chapter is not meant to be a primer on complex spatial analysis such as geographic profiling. If inexperienced with examining spatial characteristics of crimes, the reader

may want to peruse Chapter 15 of this book and Rossmo's *Geographic Profiling* (2000). Rossmo discusses the theory and practice behind this developing form of profiling and crime analysis. If the crimes in the series are especially serious, a law enforcement agency may call in the services of a geographic profiler. However, this will not be feasible in every crime series, especially if it is a property related or robbery series. Regardless of who performs the spatial analysis, a thorough examination of each crime scene will help make determinations about whether a given offense belongs in a current series.

The spatial characteristics section is made up of a number of sub-sections that include one or more of the following: the initial contact scene, the abduction scene, the assault scene, and the dump site and recovery scene. A sub-section of analytical comments and recommendations will also need to be provided.

Initial Contact Scene

Each crime will have at least one crime scene. If there is only scene, the job of the analyst will not be as difficult. The initial contact scene is the location where the offender and victim (or target) first come into personal contact; in other words, where the offender first sees the target. If the offender and victim were previously known to one another then this scene will be the location where they came into contact immediately before the crime. Obviously, this may or may not be known depending on the crime. The purpose of this section is to find out why the space or path of the offender and the space of the victim intersected.

Essentially, in spatial analysis everything that is believed to be relevant should be discussed in this sub-section. For example, in writing about convenience store robberies D'Alessio and Stolzenberg found that parking lot size, number of hours open, whether gasoline service was provided, and the degree of social disorganization in the surrounding area were major contributors in target selection.[1]

Also, this may seem obvious, but crime mapping and reading police reports cannot substitute for actually going to the crime scenes, even if they occurred years ago, and making personal observations. Questions to answer are whether the initial contact scene is on public or private space and what the sight lines are to the initial contact scene (e.g., could the offender have seen the target from further away?). As noted above, the questions to be answered are what it is about the scene that led to the crime occurring, and if the area is a place where similar victims or targets are often found.

It is important to determine whether the space is a congregating location for victims similar to those in the series. Steven Egger discusses several groups and offers ideas for how and why they are commonly targeted.[2] For example, are vagrants, homeless people, prostitutes, homosexuals, runaways, youths, children, single women, the elderly or other groups that offenders have been known to target commonly found in the area?

With this in mind, some determination of the spatial selection patterns of the offender can be made. Research has shown that the initial contact scene is of prime importance when discussing criminal events. Brantingham and Brantingham have offered *environmental criminology*, a theory that suggests that most

offenders select targets close to their homes or in areas with which they are most familiar.[3] This has been found to be the case with serial murderers and arsonists,[4] serial rapists,[5] serial robbers,[6] and many others.

A number of spatial selection typologies have been created that may be vitally important in determining the identity of the offender. Most of these use the initial contact scene. One spatial selection typology developed by Alston and based loosely on a study by Canter and Larkin included marauders, commuters, and hybrid offenders. A "marauder" was defined as an offender who is predisposed in target selection to the primary activity nodes of his awareness space.

---

[3] See Patricia L. Brantingham and Paul J. Brantingham, "Nodes, Paths, and Edges: Considerations on the Complexity of Crime and the Physical Environment," in *Journal of Environmental Psychology* 13 (1993): 3–28; and Patricia L. Brantingham and Paul J. Brantingham, "The Implications of the Criminal Event Model for Crime Prevention" in Meier, Kennedy, and Sacco, 2001.

[4] See Rossmo, *Geographic Profiling*.

[5] See James L. LeBeau, "Pattern of Stranger and Serial Rape Offending: Factors Distinguishing Apprehended and At Large Offenders," in *Journal of Criminal Law and Criminology* 78 (1987): 309–326; James L. LeBeau, "Four Case Studies Illustrating the Spatial-Temporal Analysis of Serial Rapists," in *Police Studies* 15 (1992): 124–145; David Canter and Paul Larkin, "The Environmental Range of Serial Rapists," in *Journal of Environmental Psychology* 13 (1993): 63–69; Anne Davies and A. Dale, *Locating the Stranger Rapist* in *Special Interest Series: Paper 3* (London: Home Office Police Research Group, 1995); Janet I. Warren, Roland Reboussin, and Robert R. Hazelwood, *The Geographic and Temporal Sequencing of Serial Rape* (Washington, DC: U.S. Government Printing Office, 1995); Jonathan D. Alston in Godwin, 2001; and Christopher Mowbray, *Target Selection and Spatial Pattern Analysis of Serial Sexual Offenders in Edmonton Canada* (master's thesis, University of Leicester, 2001).

[6] See Thomas Gabor and Edward Gottheil, "Offender Characteristics and Spatial Mobility: an Empirical Study and Some Policy Implications," in *Canadian Journal of Criminology* 26 (1984): 267–281; and Jonathan D. Alston, "Applications of Spatial Profiling in Armed Robberies" (paper presented at the Western Canadian Robbery Conference, Edmonton, AB, 3 April 2001).

---

[1] Stewart J. D'Alessio and Lisa Stolzenberg, "A Crime of Convenience: the Environment and Convenience Store Robbery," in *Environment and Behavior* 22, no. 2 (1990): 255–271.

[2] Steven A. Egger, "Victims of Serial Killers: the 'Less Dead,'" in *Victimology: A Study of Crime Victims and Their Roles*, ed. Judith M. Sgarzi and Jack McDevitt (Upper Saddle River, NJ: Prentice-Hall, 2003), 9–32.

Most victims or targets are chosen near activity nodes that interact with the space of his or her preferred victim type. A "commuter" is an offender whose primary activity nodes and awareness space do not overlap with his or her criminal activity space. They are less common than marauders and Alston found that they tended to select targets near major thoroughfares. A "hybrid" exhibited both "marauder" and "commuter" patterns. He found that their target selection evolved with their *m.o.*—many started out as commuters and became marauders (and vice versa).[1]

Figure 3-1 shows an example of a marauder pattern in a recent arson series. Note how the offender's residence and workplace are both within his criminal activity space.

Rossmo developed a selection typology focused on serial murderers. He notes as "hunters" those who specifically set out to search for victims and who base their search from their residence. "Poachers" are those who specifically set out to search for victims but do so from an activity node other than their residence. They may even commute or travel from city to city looking for victims. "Trollers" are said to opportunistically encounter victims while involved in other non-predatory activities. "Trappers" assume positions or occupations or create situations that allow them to encounter victims within a location under their control.

Last but not least, a discussion of temporal characteristics would be included in this sub-section. Time of day, day of the week, date, season of the year, and weather are temporal characteristics that affect criminal behavior including victim and spatial selection patterns.[2] Chapter 11 of this book examines crime and temporal characteristics further.

These predictions are usually most accurate in longer series. Often, temporal characteristics are valuable in linkage analysis, especially in deciding to *include* a crime in a series. However, given the many reasons for temporal preferences in target selection they are less valuable in making the decision to *exclude* a crime from a series.

An analyst may prefer to include this type of information in the Offender Characteristics section. This could be advantageous if there is limited time data for a series, such as if there were information on only initial contact scenes. However, discussions about temporal factors will usually fit best in this section.

Abduction Scene

The abduction scene is the location where the offender interacts with the target and alters the path of the victim or target to the extent that only the offender's path is then taken. Obviously, not all crimes will have an abduction scene. This may seem unnecessarily complex but there are instances, such as in "con" approaches, where the abduction scene does not fit the "blitz" stereotype that first comes to mind. An "abduction" then, can be non-violent. The word "abduction" suggests a violent crime, but could also be adapted to a discussion of property (e.g., auto theft).

Most often, in violent abductions the initial contact scene and the abduction scene will be at, or nearly at, the same location. Again, anything believed to be relevant about the scene should be discussed in this sub-section.

---

[1] Alston, Jonathan D., *The Serial Rapist's Spatial Pattern of Target Selection* (master's thesis, Simon Fraser University, 1994), based on David Canter and Paul Larkin, "The Environmental Range of Serial Rapists," *Journal of Environmental Psychology* 13 (1993), 63–69.

[2] See, for instance, Keith Harries, *Crime and the Environment* (Springfield, IL: Charles C. Thomas, 1980).

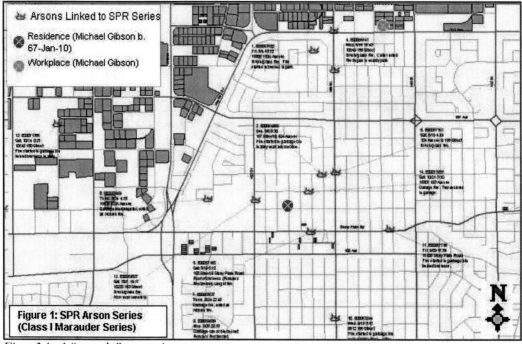

Figure 3-1: A "marauder" arson series

The first question to be answered is what it was about the scene that led to it being chosen as the abduction scene. For example, whether the abduction scene was on public or private space, or what sight lines to the abduction scenes existed.

A lot of information about the offender can be inferred from this information. An abduction that took place in public space with many sight lines around would suggest recklessness or disregard. An abduction that occurs in private space with few sight lines indicates more organization, thought, and perhaps a fear of identification (i.e., he or she is known to people in the area).

This is not meant to be a criminalistics or identification section, but perhaps a brief discussion of physical evidence such as blood drops, clothing, bullet casings, weapons, and the like that are found at the scene may be very important to flesh out the nature of the abduction scene. If any temporal

characteristics differ from that of the initial contact scene, discuss them here.

Assault Scene(s)

The assault scene is the location where the offender commits the most serious criminal offense against the victim. Depending on the crime, there may be one or even several assault scenes. For example, consider the following homicide: The event begins as an altercation inside a bar (the initial contact scene) when the male victim, looking for a fight, confronts two male individuals, who are friends, one of whom had stepped on the eventual victim's boot. They go outside to the parking lot for what the victim thinks is going to be a fistfight. Once there, one of the two friends brings out a secreted butterfly knife and fatally stabs the victim in the heart (the first assault scene). The victim flees and the two friends follow. They catch up with him at the gas bar of a service station a few blocks away. The knife-wielding offender stabs the victim in the back, puncturing one of his lungs, while the other kicks and punches the victim (the second assault scene). The victim gets away again, jumps over a short fence, and runs down a few more blocks. The two offenders continue to follow and eventually catch up with him again and the knife-wielding attacker stabs him until the victim no longer moves (third assault scene). Because all the criminal offenses (the stabbings) are of a similar nature, they are all, by definition, assault scenes.

As before, anything that is believed to be relevant should be discussed in this sub-section. In the example above, the public nature and sight lines of the three assault scenes indicates offenders who are reckless. This is related to the offender characteristics of *m.o.* where the number of wounds indicated a great deal of anger. That one of the offenders had brought a weapon indicates some premeditation and suggests someone with a violent past.

Remember to attempt to answer what factors of the assault scene(s) led to it being chosen. A lot of information about the offender can be inferred from this information. As before, an assault that takes place in public space with a number of sight lines indicates recklessness or disregard. An assault that occurs in private space, with few sight lines indicates more organization, thought, and perhaps a fear of identification.

Physical evidence will much more likely be found at the assault scene(s) than at the initial contact scene or abduction scene. The location of this physical evidence could be found on maps discussing such evidence (there were lots of blood drops at and between the assault scenes discussed above). These will help out in the analysis and will also be invaluable as future court documents (e.g., prosecutorial exhibits). If any temporal

characteristics are different than that of the initial contact or abduction scenes, discuss them here.

Dump Site / Recovery Scene

The dump site is the location where the offender's path and the victim's path or space diverges after the crime has taken place. In terms of property, it may be the parking lot where the car or bike is left or the garbage bin where the wallet is thrown away (minus its cash and credit cards). In violent crimes such as murder, it will be where the victim's body is left.

The recovery scene is usually the same location as the dump site. If they are different it will usually be because some other factor removed the victim or target from the dump site. For example, a body dumped into a river may float several miles. As a crime analyst the dump site is important as that location will usually be the last scene explicitly chosen by the offender.

A crime analyst should make some careful suggestions as to why the offender chose the site. Significant information about the offender and the series can be inferred from an examination of this scene. For example, suppose you were working on a long rape and robbery series in Los Angeles whose victims, mostly prostitutes and vagrant drug users, were being targeted, sexually assaulted, robbed, and then left along hillsides in Pasadena. The dump sites may tell you much more about the offender than the initial contact scenes, as street prostitutes and vagrant drug users are localized or concentrated in set areas of the city. As before, sight lines and the nature of the space (e.g., public, private, commercial, industrial, park, schoolyard, river valley) will indicate information about the series that will assist in linkage analysis and suspect identification.

This is the one scene where, by definition, there is physical evidence. A brief discussion of this evidence (specifically, its location) should be offered in this sub-section. If any temporal characteristics differ from the other crime scenes, discuss them here.

Analytical Comments and Recommendations

As with offender characteristics, this final sub-section should be used to summarize the analysis in each of the pervious sub-sections; to make new inferences about the offender, based on the premises established above; and to make suggestions or recommendations for investigative follow-up.

This final sub-section should be used to summarize the spatial analysis offered above. This is the place to make more speculative statements and even suggest investigative courses of action. For example, if an analyst was dealing with a sex crime series and he had access to a sex offender registry, he may want to include a map showing the crime scenes of interest and their proximity to any addresses of sex offenders who fit the offender characteristics and the preferred victim type set out earlier. This could be of particular value to a current investigation.

Applying a Knowledge of Criminal Behavior in Strategic Analysis

As noted in Chapter 1, strategic analysis provides information that will assist in the identification of long-range crime problems and crime trends. For strategic analysis to be useful it must inform or suggest strategies or actions that could be employed to deal with the crime problem.

Strategic analysis also includes the preparation of statistical reports that focus on exceptions or deviations from the norm, and the provision of resource acquisition and allocation information, with the intention of dealing with identified crime problems. In many jurisdictions, a single crime analyst may be responsible for both tactical and strategic analysis (along with other non-analytical duties). Since the 1990s, police agencies have begun to recognize the need to develop *problem analysis*.[1] In this chapter, as in others in this book, the concept of strategic analysis is closely related to the concepts of problem analysis and problem-oriented policing.

Strategic crime analysis is difficult. It requires skill sets markedly different than those used in tactical analysis. Good tactical analysts do not necessarily make good strategic analysts and vice versa. Good strategic analysis will require a background in criminology theory, research methods, and statistics, as well as the ability to apply such knowledge of criminal behavior to "real" crime problems rather than experimental situations or analyses of large data sets. Many crime analysts that perform effective strategic analysis come from an academic background and have significant post-graduate experience.

This type of analysis can have a huge influence on the focus and abilities of a police service. For instance, the Edmonton Police Service has a number of specialized units that were created with the assistance of strategic analyses. This includes, among others, a spousal violence breach team, a rapid response children-at-risk team, a high-risk parolee apprehension unit (recall the case of the child molester who assaulted the son of the naive parents?), a hate crime unit (remember the case of the aboriginal youths who lured the white boys back to a home?), a gang task force, a helicopter flight operations

---

[1] See, for instance, Herman Goldstein, *Problem-Oriented Policing* (New York: McGraw-Hill, 1990); and Rachel Boba, *Problem Analysis in Policing* (Washington, DC: Police Foundation, 2003).

unit, a horse and rider unit, two neighborhood empowerment teams, and four intelligence-led policing teams. The EPS also has a planning and evaluation section and an intelligence-led policing special project that conduct strategic analysis.

Like the Series Profile proposed for tactical analysis, the written product of a strategic analyst needs to take an integrated approach. The author proposes that a useful name for such a product would be Strategic Analysis Report. This emphasizes that the focus of the report will be strategic, a point that would be redundant in a Series Profile were it called a Tactical Series Profile. This could be followed up by a name given to the crime problem. For example, "Strategic Analysis Report: Football Hooliganism in Liverpool," or "Strategic Analysis Report: An Examination of Personal Robberies in St. Louis; 2001–2003." Depending on the complexity of the problem this report could be anywhere from a few pages to hundreds of pages long and may take anywhere from a few days to several months to complete.

The same criminal event process discussed for crime series can be used for larger crime problems—that is a focus on offenders *and* victims *and* geography. The first section of the report will provide a background or synopsis of the problem. The second section will include an examination of the problem from offender-based perspectives and sets of solutions. The third section will examine the problem from victim-based theories. The fourth section will examine the problem from spatial-based criminological theories. In the final section, recommendations for how the strategic analysis could be rolled out tactically are offered. Ideally, this final section will be written in cooperation with the tactical crime analyst(s) assigned to the area(s) in question.

Synopsis of the Problem

One of the most consistent factors of crime problems is their repetitiveness and consistency. In other words, identified problems from the abuse of drugs to traffic enforcement to youth gangs have probably occurred in the jurisdiction before and, if not, a similar problem has likely occurred in a nearby city. The distinct advantage of this is that it allows the strategic crime analyst to build off the work of others and offer strategies that have been tried and tested elsewhere. Some crime problems are so repetitive and consistent that criminological theories have been developed to explain their repetitiveness and consistency. In criminology, this theoretical development has mostly focused on offender-based explanations. However, as noted earlier, there is a good argument for providing analyses that take an integrated approach in that they examine offender behavior, victim behavior, and the places of crime.

Thus, in strategic analysis, the crime analyst does not so much as apply a knowledge of criminal behavior based on a dissection of a series as in the Series Profile, but rather, examines a crime problem and uses his knowledge of past research and theories to understand that problem. The strategic crime analyst must know what "tools" (i.e., theories) are needed to "fix" what is broken (i.e., the crime problem).

Remember, that in an integrated approach numerous approaches or theories can be applied. The Strategic Analysis Report will not just review one method for dealing with a crime problem but at least three avenues for dealing with it: an approach to deal with the offenders, another to deal with victims or targets and a third to deal with the places of the crime problem.

Identification of the Crime Problem

The first paragraphs of the report provide a brief introduction to the analytical process used for the report. Following this, a review of recent statistical reports is offered that shows how the crime problem was identified. Charts and graphs could be included to supplement this sub-section.

Justification for "Resourcing" the Crime Problem

Law enforcement and related government agencies usually have limited resources and time. The demands for these limited resources are great. Thus, once the crime problem is identified, a justification for dealing with the problem, with these limited resources in mind, should be established. This should follow easily from the previous subsection. Depending on the nature of the problem this subsection may be anywhere from a paragraph to several pages long.

Strategic Analysis of the Crime Problem: Offenders

As noted above, the purpose of this section is to look at the problem from an offender-based perspective. Unfortunately, it is beyond the scope of this chapter to show how each theory could be used in strategic analyses. It would be difficult to review all or even most of the theories in academia that have been used to deal with crime problems. Therefore, only quick explanations are provided about some of the more germane theories. Suggestions for what type of modern day crime problems the theory is best suited for are also given. Essentially, what is being proposed is that the strategic crime analyst would select the best theory or "tool" from those reviewed below (or others known to them) and then use that theory to explain the nature and scope of the crime problem and set a strategic direction for dealing with it.

Classical School / Rational Choice / Deterrence. These approaches are similar in background and philosophy, suggesting that people have free will and choose either criminal or lawful behaviors. People choose to commit crime because they feel that the benefits they will gain outweigh the risks that they will be caught and punished. Eighteenth- and nineteenth-century social philosophers such as Cesare Beccaria and Jeremy Bentham held that increasing the certainty, swiftness, and severity (in moderation) of punishments can deter criminal behavior. [1]

The theories are suited for many crime problems. Attempts to solve traffic related crime problems have traditionally been based in these strategies. Crime displacement can also be explained by the theory.[2] Methods to increase the certainty of detection such as neighborhood foot patrol programs and neighborhood watch programs are also based on this approach. Finally, changes in correctional philosophy, especially in the United States, in the 1970s and later shifted toward a more neo-classical approach.[3]

Differential Association / Differential Association-Reinforcement. Central to these theories is the position that criminal behavior is learned. Edwin Sutherland opines that criminal behaviors result when a person associates with more definitions favorable to law-breaking than law-abiding definitions.

---

[1] See Cesare Beccaria, *On Crimes and Punishments* (1764), trans. Henry Palolucci (New York: Bobbs-Merrill, 1963) and Jeremy Bentham, *An Introduction to the Principles of Morals and Legislation* (1823) (Amherst, NY: Prometheus Books, 1988).

[2] For instance, Derek Cornish and Ronald V. Clarke, "Understanding Crime Displacement: an Application of Rational Choice Theory," *Criminology* 25 (1987), 933–947.

[3] Robert Martinson, "What Works?: Questions and Answers About Prison Reform," *Public Interest* 35 (1974), 22–54 and Charles A. Murray and Lewis A. Cox, *Beyond Probation* (Beverly Hills, CA: Sage Publications, 1979).

These definitions are encountered in intimate groups. Sutherland goes on to argue that these differential associations vary by frequency, duration, priority, and intensity.[1]

Differential association-reinforcement theory also posits that criminal behavior is learned. Proponents of this theory, such as Ronald Akers, incorporate the principles of operant conditioning found in psychology. They suggest that criminal behavior occurs as the result of direct conditioning where the positive rewards gained from a crime outweigh the perceived punishments or negative reinforcement.[2]

Strategic directions based on this theory might focus on attempts to provide positive definitions for a community or persons at risk. The establishment of a neighborhood empowerment team or beat officers in a problem area are examples of such strategies. By design, this team or officers are supposed to integrate themselves into the community and provide law-abiding roles or definitions. The daily presence of a police officer in a high school may also help counteract the influence of "pro-crime" definitions.

Social Learning. Like differential association theory, social learning theory states that criminal behavior is learned. Social learning theorists, such as Albert Bandura, argue that delinquent and criminal behavior is essentially imitated. They suggest that individuals will emulate persons they have a strong positive identification toward, whether they are family members, friends, sports heroes, or characters in television or movies. If criminal behavior is approved of and rewarded, it becomes even more likely that a person will act out.[3] John Winterdyk notes how less than two weeks after the Columbine High School mass murder in Littleton, Colorado, a boy in a small town in Alberta, Canada, dressed similarly to the two killers in the Colorado tragedy, came into a high school and shot two boys who he felt had been tormenting him. Winterdyk's notes this as an example of the modeling that Bandura suggests.[4]

Strategies in this regard will most likely be long-term and not have an effect that can be easily measured. This would include presenting law-abiding stereotypes such as publicizing positive interactions of the police with the community and continually presenting officers as community role models. The community based policing philosophy, where officers are encouraged to foster leadership roles in a community, are examples of this type of theory in practice.

Culture Conflict / Cultural Deviance / Differential Opportunity. These theories suggest that many people commit crimes because of adherence to values and norms that are expected or approved of in their subculture, but that run contrary to the larger culture. Thorsten Sellin argues that law, especially criminal law, is an expression of the morality of the dominant culture. However, a society or nation is composed of many social groups based on ethnicity, race, religion, and

---

[1] Edwin H. Sutherland, *Principles of Criminology*, 3rd ed. (Philadelphia: J.B. Lippincott, 1939).

[2] Robert Burgess and Ronald Akers, "A Differential Association-Reinforcement Theory of Criminal Behavior," *Social Problems* 14 (1966), 128–147; Ronald Akers, *Deviant Behavior: a Social Learning Approach*, 2nd ed. (Belmont, CA: Wadsworth, 1977); and Ronald Akers, Lonn Lonza-Kaduce, and Marcia Radosevich, "Social Learning and Deviant Behavior: a Specific Test of General Theory," *American Sociological Review* 44 (1979), 636–655.

[3] Albert Bandura, "Vicarious Processes: a Case of No-Trial Learning," in *Advances in Experimental and Social Psychology*, vol. 2, ed. Leonard Berkowitz (New York: Academic Press, 1965); Albert Bandura, *Aggression: a Social Learning Analysis* (Englewood Cliffs, NJ: Prentice Hall, 1973); and Albert Bandura and Richard Walters, *Adolescent Aggression* (New York: Ronald Press, 1959).

[4] John A. Winterdyk, *Canadian Criminology* (Scarborough, ON: Prentice Hall, 2000), 193.

so on. Culture conflict or deviance results when the norms of these smaller groups, or subcultures, clash with the dominant culture.[1] Albert Cohen, for example, argues that the delinquency among lower-class youths is actually a protest against the dominant culture. Higher rates of delinquency among the lower class are a result of being evaluated against the "middle-class measuring rod."[2] Richard Cloward and Lloyd Ohlin suggest that deviance, especially with street gangs, result when these subcultures are blocked from achieving societal goals.[3]

As noted, some subcultures have a minority or ethnic base that further differentiates them from the larger society. Some subcultures are lifestyle and behavioral oriented (e.g., skateboarders, ethnic street gangs, speeders and ravers, taggers and other graffiti vandals, punks, hip-hop or rap fans, club hoppers).

Strategic directions that could be offered with this theory in mind might be to try to fuse subcultural values with the law-abiding values of the larger society. For example, setting aside a separate location for skateboarders to congregate may solve a vandalism problem in a city mall where skateboarders are felt to be contributing to the problem. Patrol officers could then encourage any boarders congregating at the malls to go to the location. Taggers or graffiti artists may be given set locations to paint. Community groups may organize supervised all-night rave parties with the assistance of the police.

Strain / Anomie. Strain theory, also known as anomie theory, states that social instability is caused by an erosion of standards and values.[4] It relates to differential opportunity theory (above). Robert Merton and Robert Agnew write that in every society there are common goals held by most persons. In western countries, the goal of success is especially pervasive. Yet the means to attain this goal, and others like it, are unequally distributed across groups within the society.[5]

Strain results when legitimate goals such as success cannot be achieved by legitimate means. Some people then decide to "adapt" and achieve their goals through illegal means (e.g., drug dealers, pimps, Mafioso). Others reject the goals and means altogether and dropout of society or seek to overthrow society and establish a new set of goals and means (e.g., terrorist cells, extremist groups).

Step-up programs, such as affirmative action, are examples of attempts that have been made to deal with some of the differences in access. Typically, strategic solutions dealing with strain problems are societal, and will be difficult for a single police agency to try to implement.

Social Control / Bond / Self-Control (General). These theories argue that people are naturally pleasure seeking. Simply put, people commit crime because, "it feels good." Often these theorists are as interested in explaining conformity as they are in deviance or criminality. Travis Hirschi contends that if a person is not properly bonded to society, he or she will likely choose criminality. He further argues that the strength of bonds are affected by a persons commitment to society, attachment to others,

---

[1] Thorsten Sullin. *Culture Conflict and Crime* (New York: Social Sciences Research Council, 1938).

[2] Albert K. Cohen, *Delinquent Boys* (New York: Free Press, 1955).

[3] Richard Cloward and Lloyd Ohlin, *Delinquency and Opportunity* (New York: Free Press, 1960).

[4] Emile Durkheim, *Rules of Sociological Method* (1895) (New York: Free Press, 1965).

[5] Robert K. Merton, "Social Structure and Anomie," *American Sociological Review* 3 (1938), 672–682; Robert K. Merton, *Social Theory and Social Structure* (London: Glecoe, 1949); and Robert Agnew, "A Revised Strain Theory of Delinquency," *Social Forces* 64 (1985), 151–166.

involvement in law abiding activities, and belief in the morality of the law.[1]

In a restructuring of social control theory, Michael Gottfredson and Travis Hirschi suggest that certain persons are characterized by an impulsive, risk-taking and physically aggressive personality that is consistent with a lack of bonding or social control. Criminality is only one result of this lack of self-control. Such people may become the chronic criminals that commit a disproportionate amount of crime in society. They call this theoretical reformulation, self-control theory or general theory.[2]

Strategies from this perspective would focus on going into problem areas or identifying problem groups and getting them involved in legitimate activities. Midnight basketball leagues and community sponsored sports programs are examples of strategies that are reflective of a social control or bond approach. Approaches based in self-control theory would include intelligence-led policing initiatives that emphasize policies that support the targeting of the most chronic and dangerous criminals in a jurisdiction.

Labeling. The labeling perspective argues that society plays a large part in the creation of criminals and deviants, because, once "labeled" as a criminal or deviant, a person will find it very difficult to remove the stigma. Eventually, the individual comes to believe in the accuracy of the label, internalizes it as part of his or her identity and acts out in other criminal behaviors.[3] Frank Tannenbaum referred to this label as a "tag."[4] Howard Becker notes that the difficulty in removing a societal label is directly related to the seriousness of the sanction that is applied.[5]

A labeling based strategy would attempt to prevent formal sanctioning or punishment of problem persons as criminal or deviants. An example might be a vice section sponsored "john school" where those arrested for prostitution offenses are given the option of attending a one-day seminar put on by community groups on the dangers of prostitution. In exchange for their attendance they are not formally charged with a crime. Alternative measures programs for first-time young offenders are other examples of labeling based strategies.

Psychodynamic. Psychodynamic theory is heavily influenced by the writings and analysis of Sigmund Freud. The theory suggests that an imbalance of deviant personality traits that occurs in early childhood will have long-term effects and produce individuals predisposed to juvenile delinquency and then adult criminality. The personality is made up of three elements: the id, the ego, and the superego. The id consists of the basic pleasure seeking impulses and, if not controlled by the two other elements of the personality, it will express itself, usually negatively, in an instinctive and amoral manner.[6] Marguerite Warren and Michael Hindelang argue that chronic criminal behavior is the product of an uncontrolled id.[7]

[1] Travis Hirschi, *Causes of Delinquency* (Berkeley, CA: University of California Press, 1969).
[2] Michael Gottfredson and Travis Hirschi, *A General Theory of Crime* (Stanford, CA: Stanford University Press, 1990).
[3] Edwin M. Lemert, *Social Pathology: a Systematic Approach to the Theory of Sociopathic Behavior* (New York: McGraw-Hill, 1951).
[4] Frank Tannenbaum, *Crime and the Community* (Boston: Ginn and Company, 1938).
[5] Howard S. Becker, *Outsiders: Studies in the Sociology of Deviance* (New York: Free Press, 1963).
[6] Sigmund Freud, *The Ego and the Id* (New York: W.W. Norton, 1961).
[7] Marguerite Q. Warren and Michael J. Hindelang, "Current Explanations in Offender Behavior" in *Psychology of Crime and Criminal Justice*, ed. Hans Toch (Prospect Heights, IL: Waveland Press, 1986), 166–182.

These theories have had a strong influence on the tactical analytical process of psychological profiling used by the FBI. For example, Hazelwood and Warren (1995) discuss aberrant and uncontrolled sexual fantasies and psychosexual impulses among select individuals. These impulses motivate some of these individuals to become serial rapists, serial killers, or both. Samuel Yochelson and Stanton Samenow also draw attention to a "criminal personality."[1]

Patrol officers and detectives will frequently be exposed to individuals who suffer from mental disorders. Crime and intelligence analysts may find themselves working on a series or strategic plans that involve such individuals or groups. The American Psychiatric Association's *Diagnostic and Statistical Manual of Mental Disorders* (1994) notes numerous dangerous disorders. For example, persons with personality disorders such as conduct disorder, anti-social personality disorder (a.k.a.: criminal psychopathy), borderline personality disorder, and narcissistic personality disorder will often find themselves in contact with law enforcement. Persons with mental disorders such as schizophrenia, paranoid disorders, and paraphilias (e.g., sexual sadism and pedophilia) may come to the attention of law enforcement.

Unfortunately, other than therapy and psychoanalysis, there are no applications that are known to effectively treat such people.[2] Police support of community services that try to deal with early developmental problems

may be influenced by such theory. However, police response and crime and intelligence analysis will be greatly improved if a background is fostered for understanding and recognizing mental disorders.

Personality / Biosocial. Personality is the relatively stable set of traits that influence thought, emotions, and behavior. Personality theories focus on qualities or traits that make some individuals more prone to criminality than others. Hans Eysenck argues that two traits are especially related to antisocial behavior: extraversion and neuroticism. Extraversion is the need for stimulation. Neuroticism is the tendency toward emotional instability, frustration, and anxiety.[3]

A related branch of research and theory is known as biosocial theory or sociobiology. Socio-biologists such as Edward Wilson contend that genetics and brain chemistry are major factors in predicting criminal and deviant behavior.[4] This work is not new and goes back at least as far as the nineteenth century with Cesare Lombroso, who theorized the existence of a born criminal who had "atavistic anomalies" (i.e., animal-like traits) that made them more crime-prone.[5] This theory has gone through various stages of acceptance over the past century. Current research has shown promising links to body chemistry and resultant behavior.[6]

[1] Samuel Yochelson and Stanton E. Samenow, *The Criminal Personality: a Profile for Change*, vol. 1 (New York: Jason Aronson, 1976); and Stanton E. Samenow, *Inside the Criminal Mind* (New York: Random House, 1984).

[2] However, with regards to *tactical* applications, many law enforcement agencies have paid for the training of their own officers in profiling techniques or have occasionally called upon the services of trained psychological profilers.

[3] Hans Eysenck, *Crime and Personality* (London: Routledge and Kegan Paul, 1964).

[4] Edward O. Wilson, *Sociobiology* (Cambridge: Harvard University Press, 1975).

[5] Cesare Lombroso, *Crime: Its Causes and Remedies* (1899), trans. Henry P. Horton (Montclair, NJ: Patterson Smith, 1968).

[6] Alan Booth and D. Wayne Osgood, "The Influence of Testosterone on Deviance in Adulthood: Assessing and Explaining the Relationship," *Criminology* 31:1 (1993), 93–117; and Roger Masters, Brian Hone, and Anil Doshi, "Environmental Pollution, Neurotoxicity, and Criminal Violence" in *Environmental Toxicology*, ed. J. Rose (London: Gordon and Breach, 1998), 13–48.

As with psychodynamic theory, there is no real strategic application of personality or biosocial theories that would deal with crime problems in quick order. Police support of community services that try to deal with early or adolescent developmental problems may be influenced by such theory. Some agencies, such as the Correctional Service of Canada, use a test designed to identify psychopaths in prison populations. Keeping in mind the ethical issues arising from such identification, this information could be made available to specialized areas, such as high-risk offender units, for use in prioritization.

Strategic Analysis of the Crime Problem: Victims

The purpose of this section is to look at crime problems from the perspective of victims and offer strategic direction based on that insight. Victimology began to develop significantly as a discipline during the victim rights movements of the 1960s.[1] At first, victim-based theories were strongly one-sided and tended to villainize offenders, but these have evolved in recent years. As before, it is beyond the scope of this chapter to review all or even most of the theories in academia that address crime victimization. Therefore, only quick explanations are provided on three of the more germane victimology theories.

It will also be useful for strategic crime analysts to keep crime victimization studies on hand and be aware of victimization trends.[2] This should help such analysts determine the extent of crime problems. Also, knowledge of victimization statistics could be modified for tactical purposes, such as in linkage analysis. For example, suppose three white elderly ladies were beaten up during armed robberies by a young, white male and all of these crimes occurred within a three-block radius. Is this a common occurrence? The answer is that, in most places, such victimization of the elderly is extremely rare. This allows the analyst to make stronger inferences about the likelihood that the offenses are related.

Situated Transaction. This theory is based on the research of victim-participation theories and is reminiscent of the criminal event perspective emphasized in this chapter. Instead of assuming the complete innocence of the victim and the complete culpability of the offender, transaction theorists see violent criminal activity as the result of a full round of interactions between the two principal parties (the offender and victim) and also any witnesses to the event. Thus, the crime is seen in its whole context.[3]

For example, research in spousal related violent crimes would suggest that the eventual victim, that is the person who was harmed the most, influenced the original violence. Or, in examining a schoolyard fight where two individuals are assaulting each other as a group of schoolmates circles and cheers them on, they would point out that the actions of the group in this setting have much to do with how the altercation is carrying on. Individuals that are rarely violent may, in some instances, become extremely violent and even homicidal (e.g., a crowd of intoxicated but jubilant individuals becomes a riotous rabble when the police are seen arresting some in the crowd).

---

[1] Harvey Wallace, *Victimology: Legal, Psychological, and Social Perspectives* (Boston: Allyn and Bacon, 1998).

[2] For instance, Leslie W. Kennedy and Vincent F. Sacco, *Crime Victims in Context* (Los Angeles: Roxbury, 1998).

[3] See, for example, Erving Goffman, *The Presentation of Self in Everyday Life* (Garden City, NY: Doubleday, 1959); Erving Goffman, *Stigma: Notes on the Management of Spoiled Identity* (Englewood Cliffs, NJ: Prentice Hall, 1963); and David F. Luckenbill, "Criminal Homicide as a Situated Transaction," *Social Problems* 25:2 (1977), 176–186.

Suggestions for strategic action based in this approach may involve a school resource officer encouraging a policy where persons who fight are suspended along with any who are seen encouraging the altercation. It may also provide such officers with an understanding of the dynamics of schoolyard fights. Similarly, patrol saturation and staggered bar closing times would discourage crowds of drunk revelers from forming.

Lifestyle-Exposure. Some theorists argue that many persons live lifestyles that expose them to greater risks of victimization. Essential lifestyle-related factors will increase a persons exposure to crime. They include the time spent in public spaces, the time spent with groups known for criminal behavior (e.g., young, urban, males), the time spent among non-family members, the ability to isolate oneself from those with offender characteristics, and a lifestyle or manner that indicates that an individual is a convenient and desirable target.[1]

This theory does not transfer easily to strategic action. However, it is reflected in criminal justice policies such as those that prohibit a sanctioned offender from associating with persons who share a lifestyle that contributed to their criminal behavior.

Routine Activities. The Routine Activities theory has become increasingly popular. The criminal event perspective discussed earlier in the chapter is influenced by this theory.[2] Cohen and Felson argue that the motivation to commit crime is a constant. There is, and always will be, a steady stream of motivated offenders willing to engage in crime. Crime occurs when motivated offenders are presented with suitable targets and a lack of capable guardianship.[3]

Victim-based strategic directions with Routine Activities theory in mind often attempt to decrease the suitability of targets or victims. An approach called "target hardening" is used for such measures.[4] For example, customers may be warned about areas of a mall or public space that is prone to criminality, thus making potential targets more aware. Employees of a large business who park at a lot that is being targeted by car thieves may be warned to purchase steering wheel lock mechanisms.

The design of modern gated communities in the U.S. is an example of this approach. These communities are purposefully designed to have very little public space or public walkways. Easy neighbor interaction in many of these communities is discouraged by physical design. This greatly discourages criminal opportunity. Crime prevention units often use such approaches when informing the general public about how to avoid victimization.

Strategic Analysis of the Crime Problem: Spatial

The purpose of this section is to look at the crime problem from a spatial point of view. There are a number of criminology theories that look at the effect of place on crime. For years criminologists have noted that certain areas of cities seem to be consistently crime prone. Moreover, they note that these areas tend to overlap with concentrations of other social ills such as disease outbreaks, mental illness, poverty, and others.

---

[1] Michael J. Hindelang, Michael R. Gottfredson, and James Garofalo, *Victims of Personal Crime: an Empirical Foundation for a Theory of Personal Victimization* (Cambridge, MA: Ballinger, 1978).

[2] Sacco and Kennedy, 2002.

[3] Lawrence E. Cohen and Marcus Felson, "Social Change and Crime Rate Trends: a Routine Activities Approach," *American Sociological Review* 44 (1979), 588–608.

[4] Clarke, Ronald V., *Situational Crime Prevention: Successful Case Studies* (New York: Harrow and Heston, 1992).

A few of these theories are reviewed briefly below. As before, suggestions for what type of modern day crime problems the theory is best suited for are also given. The strategic crime analyst can select the best theory or "tool" from those reviewed below (or others known to them) and use that theory to explain the nature and scope of the crime problem and set a strategic direction for dealing with the problem.

Social Ecology / Social Disorganization. This theory links crime and deviance to the ecology or physical make-up of a city. Robert Park, Ernest Burgess, and Roderick McKenzie argue that high crime rates tend to occur in concentrated areas and these high rates are correlated with concentrations of other forms of urban decay.[1] Clifford Shaw and Henry McKay write that these areas are incapable of producing the social capital necessary to resist criminal groups. They note that these areas become "socially disorganized."[2]

Historically, as in Shaw and McKay, social disorganization has been measured by looking at the presence of three social variables: social mobility (how permanent is the population—is there high turnover? Do they own their own homes? How many renters?); the average socioeconomic status of the area; and ethnic heterogeneity (how racially mixed is the area?). It has been found that areas that have high social mobility, a lower than average socioeconomic status, and a high degree of ethnic heterogeneity will often not form the social barriers necessary to resist the incursion of social problems such as crime and public disorder. It is the three variables interacting together that lead to social disorganization.

This theory can be used to deal with the spatial aspects of certain crime problems. For example, the development of prostitute strolls and centers of drug activity can usually be explained by social disorganization principles. Social ecology theories emerged in Chicago and several large strategic analyses, including the Chicago Area Project,[3] have been developed that trace their roots back to these theories.

Routine Activities. As discussed earlier, many crime rates and trends can be explained through this theory first posited by Cohen and Felson. For example, a downturn in robbery may be explained by the overall societal trend toward a card-based vs. cash-based economy. Further, a corresponding increase in commercial robberies may be explained by the same societal trend.

As noted, this theory makes no explicit statements about offender motivation and is thus particularly suited for explaining only a part of the criminal event. The closest in spirit or philosophy, of the offender-based explanations, is the Rational Choice perspective discussed earlier.[4]

Spatial-based strategic (and tactical) directions with routine activities in mind often attempt to increase the amount of capable guardianship. Oscar Newman coined the term "defensible space" to describe how physical space can be designed to prevent criminal opportunity.[5] For example, an area that is having problems with burglary may be encouraged to trim any trees or foliage that

---

[1] Robert E. Park, Ernest W. Burgess, and Roderick D. MacKenzie, *The City* (Chicago: University of Chicago Press, 1925).
[2] Clifford R. Shaw and Henry D. McKay, *Juvenile Delinquency and Urban Areas: a Study of Rates of Delinquents in Relation to Different Characteristics of Local Communities in American Cities* (Chicago: University of Chicago Press, 1942).

---

[3] See: http://www.chicagoareaproject.com
[4] Clarke and Felson, 1993.
[5] Oscar Newman, *Defensible Space: Crime Prevention Through Urban Design* (New York: Macmillan, 1973).

cover up any windows or doors. Crime Prevention Through Environmental Design (CPTED) programs are examples of Routine Activities strategies.

Analysts involved in crime mapping, especially those who conduct "hot spot" research find much in common with this perspective.[1] It has become popular among both academics and crime analysts and is readily transferable to both tactical and strategic crime analyses. Chapter 1 also covers the effect of the Routine Activities theory in modern law enforcement.

Environmental Criminology. Paul Brantingham and Patricia Brantingham are the most significant contributors to this theory. The Brantinghams argue that individuals develop an awareness space made up of the areas surrounding their personal activity nodes (e.g., home, workplace, favorite hangout) and the routine pathways taken between these activity nodes. This awareness space is tied to the environment, or structural backcloth, around them and includes social, cultural, legal, spatial, and temporal dimensions. Persons who are criminals tend to select victims or targets within their awareness space, or structural backcloth.[2] This theory was introduced earlier in the tactical analysis section and its application has typically been for tactical crime problems

such as a crime series. Strategic applications of environmental criminology are similar to those offered by Routine Activities theory.

Recommendations

This is the final section of the Strategic Analysis Report. At this point the crime problem has been identified and a justification for dealing with it has been developed. The crime problem has been examined using the integrated approach and at least three possible strategic directions have then been offered—including one approach based on dealing with offenders, another to deal with victims, and a third to deal with the spatial elements of the crime problem.

These recommendations need to mesh with tactical activities. An open and consistent communication process will be necessary in jurisdictions where strategic crime analysis and tactical analysis are conducted by different areas. Of course, if one analyst performs both functions this will be much easier. This is necessary because, on its own, strategic analysis may be unpalatable to front line decision-makers (e.g., a patrol sergeant). Essentially, in this final section a method is provided for dealing with the crime problem in a piecemeal manner that identifies tactical steps in dealing with a problem.

For example, strategic crime analysts that are part of a citywide gang task force may set out a strategic direction for disrupting and reducing gang activity in the city. However, the entire strategic plan would not be presented in daily patrol meetings. Instead, after a short briefing, a patrol squad may be given a small number of specific targets that have been selected by the tactical crime analyst to work on for the next month. The patrol squad would be given a sheet containing a photograph, an address, a list of

---

[1] See John E. Eck and David Weisburd, eds., *Crime and Place* (Monsey, NY: Police Executive Research Forum, Criminal Justice Press, 1995); Keith Harries, *Mapping Crime: Principle and Practice* (Washington, DC: U.S. Department of Justice, 1999); and John E. Eck, *Preventing Crime at Places* in *Evidence-Based Policing*, eds. Lawrence W. Sherman et. al. (New York: Routledge, 2002), 241–294.

[2] Patricia L. Brantingham and Paul J. Brantingham, "Nodes, Paths, and Edges: Concentrations on the Complexity of Crime and the Physical Environment," *Journal of Environmental Psychology* 13 (1993), 3–28; and Patricia L. Brantingham and Paul J. Brantingham, "The Implications of the Criminal Event Model for Crime Prevention" in Meier, Kennedy, and Sacco, 2001.

hangouts, any conditions they may have (if on parole on probation), and a synopsis of their criminal involvement. The work they do on the targets would then be forwarded back by the tactical crime analysts and from them back to one of the gang task force strategic crime analysts.

Conclusion

The purpose of this chapter has been to show how knowledge of criminal behavior can be applied in both tactical and strategic analyses. It has been demonstrated that an integrated approach that examines criminal behavior from the perspective of offenders, victims, and the places or spaces of crime should be the basis for both types of analysis.

The analytical processes discussed in the chapter have been developed over the past several years in the Edmonton Police Service's Intelligence Analysis Unit. They have been presented as ideal forms but that is not to say that they could not be improved. Another agency may have different functions or abilities and may need to adapt some of these techniques. It is hoped that this chapter will have provided some direction on how to make the job of the crime analyst a little easier, more structured, and ultimately more fruitful.

Recommended Readings

American Psychiatric Association. *Diagnostic and Statistical Manual of Mental Disorders,* 4th ed. Washington, DC: APA, 1994.

Bartol, Curt R. *Criminal Behavior: a Psychosocial Approach,* 6th ed. Englewood Cliffs, NJ: Prentice Hall, 2002.

Boba, Rachel. *Problem Analysis in Policing.* Washington, DC: Police Foundation, 2003.

Brantingham, Paul J. and Patricia L. Brantingham. *Patterns in Crime.* New York: Macmillan, 1984.

Burgess, Ann W. and Robert R. Hazelwood. *Practical Aspects of Rape Investigation: a Multi-Disciplinary Approach,* 2nd ed. (New York: CRC Press, 1995).

Canter, David. *Criminal Shadows: Inside the Mind of a Serial Killer.* London: Harper Collins, 1994.

Eck, John E. and David Weisburd, eds. *Crime and Place.* Monsey, NY: Police Executive Research Forum, Criminal Justice Press, 1995.

Geberth, Vernon J. *Practical Homicide Investigation,* 3rd ed. New York: Elsevier, 1996.

Gottlieb, Steven, Sheldon Arenberg, and Raj Singh. *Crime Analysis: from First Report to Final Arrest.* Montclair, CA: Alpha Publishing, 1994.

Harries, Keith. *Mapping Crime: Principle and Practice.* Washington, DC: U.S. Department of Justice, 1999.

Osborne, Deborah A. and Susan C. Wernicke. *Introduction to Crime Analysis: Basic Resources for Criminal Justice Practice.* New York: Haworth Press, 2003.

Rossmo, D. Kim. *Geographic Profiling.* Boca Raton, FL: CRC Press, 2000.

Sacco, Vincent F. and Leslie W. Kennedy. *The Criminal Event: an Introduction to Criminology,* 3rd ed. Toronto, ON: Nelson Thomson Learning, 2002.

Turvey, Brent E. *Criminal Profiling: an Introduction to Behavioral Evidence Analysis,* 2nd ed. San Diego: Academic Press, 2002.

4
Practical Literature: What to Read and How to Read It

Mary Velasco

Literature reviews are an important component of crime analysis efforts in that they allow us to learn from others' successes and failures and use that information to inform future research projects. Crime analysts should have the skills to obtain the relevant literature and the ability to synthesize information about a topic for various audiences, including police personnel, government officials, and the community. Analysis efforts can be greatly enhanced by reviewing academic literature in addition to relying on practical knowledge that has been accumulated through the efforts of other law enforcement professionals. Unfortunately, time constraints frequently prevent analysts from being able to conduct a comprehensive literature review. In addition, many analysts are unaware of the vast amount of literature that is available to them or they do not know how to access the information.

This chapter will acquaint readers with practical resources that are available to inform their analytical and problem-solving efforts. Examples of these resources are publications such as the Problem-Oriented Guides for Police Series, online resources such as the Crime Reduction Toolkits and the National Criminal Justice Reference Service (NCJRS), and practical research journals such as *Police Practice and Research*. In addition, through discussion and examples, this chapter will focus on how to interpret and organize this information through the

creation of an annotated bibliography and a practical literature review and how to apply this information to one's own analysis efforts. The ability to access, understand, and apply both academic and practical literature is a fundamental skill for today's crime analysis professionals.

Every day, crime analysts are called on to prepare products ranging from simple statistical reports to more in-depth, problem-specific research reports. Often it is not possible to conduct a thorough review of the literature pertaining to a topic; however, academic and professional literature can be excellent resources for understanding the current state of knowledge about a particular crime or disorder problem as well as learning what methods others have employed to better understand and respond to the problem. With this knowledge, analysts can more effectively assist in the analysis and response to problems in their own jurisdictions. For example, an analyst assigned to an auto theft task force is asked to analyze the problem and help police officials determine which response will be more effective—encouraging local businesses to hire security patrols and parking lot attendants or conducting a city-wide lock-your-car campaign. After reading this chapter or attending the corresponding training class, analysts will be aware of numerous resources to consult for assistance with this task. One example of a valuable resource is the Problem-Oriented Guides for Police Series publication titled *Thefts of and From Cars in Parking Facilities* by Ronald V. Clarke. This guidebook not only reviews what we know about auto theft and theft from vehicles, but it also provides questions to help guide one's analysis as well as reviews the effectiveness of common responses such as educational campaigns, parking lot attendants, and decoy vehicles. Consulting the literature reminds crime analysts that they are part of a community—a group of professionals who learn from their experiences, share their knowledge with others, and work toward achieving a common goal.

This chapter is divided into several sections that are meant to serve more as a quick-reference manual than as a standard book chapter. The first section lists and briefly summarizes the contents and availability of various practical literature resources (books, periodicals, reports), academic journals, abstracts databases, and online resources. The resources included in this chapter are those most relevant for crime analysis efforts based on the judgment of this author. These resources provide a good starting point for learning more about a particular topic and informing future research endeavors. The final sections of the chapter provide guidelines for understanding and synthesizing the information and writing a literature review. This information will also be organized as a reference manual that includes tips drawn from the author's experience. Currently, most crime analysts are not regularly called on to perform traditional literature reviews; however, knowledge of the literature as well as an understanding of how to apply it to one's work is an integral skill for today's crime analysis professionals.

Practical Literature: Resources by Topic

To facilitate queries for literature on a specific topic, the resources listed in this section are divided into several categories, including literature on crime analysis and problem analysis, crime mapping, practical theory, problem solving, and research methods and evaluation. It should be noted that the term "literature" is used fairly loosely throughout this chapter to refer to both academic and professional writing available through a variety of resources, including the

federal government, membership and non-profit organizations, and the Internet.

In recognition of the budget constraints that analysts often face, the chapter primarily includes resources that are available free of charge. Resources that can be freely obtained via the Internet or by contacting the publishing entity are denoted with an asterisk (*) in front of the citation. The resources are listed in alphabetical order. When relevant, more information about a particular resource (e.g., specific topics covered in past issues of the publication *Crime Mapping News*) are provided to the reader. Lastly, to ensure that this chapter is relevant and up-to-date in the coming years, specific information such as telephone numbers or Web links are rarely included. Generally, literature published by the federal government can be obtained by visiting the agency's Web site, contacting the agency via telephone, or downloading the report from the Web site of the National Criminal Justice Reference Service (described later in this chapter). Literature prepared by professional organizations can typically be obtained by contacting the organizations or by visiting their Web sites. Lastly, books can be obtained through the publisher or by visiting a bookstore or an online book retailer.

Crime Analysis & Problem Analysis Literature

*Boba, Rachel. *Guidelines to Implement and Evaluate Crime Analysis and Mapping in Law Enforcement*. Washington, DC: Office of Community Oriented Policing Services, 2001.

This document is meant to serve as a guide for the processes of implementing and evaluating crime analysis and mapping for police agencies that do not currently have the function in place as well as those that are looking to reevaluate and restructure their current functions.

*Boba, Rachel. *Introductory Guide to Crime Analysis and Mapping*. Washington, DC: Office of Community Oriented Policing Services, 2001.

This guide is a basic introduction to crime analysis and mapping, including definitions, concepts, and examples.

*Boba, Rachel. *Problem Analysis in Policing*. Washington, DC: Police Foundation, 2003.

This report introduces and defines problem analysis and provides guidance on how it can be integrated and institutionalized into modern policing practices.

*Clarke, Ronald V & John Eck. *Become a Problem-solving Crime Analyst in 55 Small Steps*. London: Jill Dando Institute of Crime Science, 2003.

This is a practical manual for the working crime analyst. The guidebook encourages analysts to incorporate the principles of problem-oriented policing and practical theory into their daily work.

Goldstein, Herman. *Problem-Oriented Policing*. New York: McGraw-Hill, 1990.

This book introduces the concept of problem-oriented policing and discusses how it can be implemented within a police agency.

Gottlieb, Steven, Shelton Arenberg, and Raj Singh. *Crime Analysis: From First Report to Final Arrest*. Montclair, CA: Alpha Publishing, 1994.

This text introduces and defines crime analysis, outlines the process of implementing a crime analysis program, and reviews a variety of data collection and analysis techniques.

International Association of Crime Analysts. *Forecaster* (multiple issues).

This periodical is the quarterly newsletter of the International Association of Crime Analysts (IACA). It contains articles authored by crime analysis professionals on a variety of topics.

Osborne, Deborah A and Susan C. Wernicke. *Introduction to Crime Analysis: Basic Resources for Criminal Justice Practice*. New York: Haworth Press, 2003.

This book provides practical resources for the working crime analyst, including an overview of the analyst's toolbox, GIS, crime analysis products, and training resources, among other topics.

Reuland, Melissa M. *Information Management and Crime Analysis: Practitioner's Recipes for Success*. Washington, DC: Police Executive Research Forum, 1997.

The chapters in this book cover crime information, database structures, administrative crime analysis, the use of information technology to assist investigations and tactical planning, and how crime analysts use computer mapping.

*Scott, Michael. *Problem-oriented Policing: Reflections on the First 20 Years*. Washington, DC: Office of Community Oriented Policing Services, 2001.

This publication reviews how the problem-oriented policing model has developed over the 20-year history of the concept and proposes future directions.

Crime Mapping Literature

*Bair, Sean** et. al., eds. *Advanced Crime Mapping Topics: Results of the First Invitational Advanced Crime Mapping Topics Symposium.* Denver: National Law Enforcement Corrections and Technology Center, 2002.

This publication includes articles describing advanced analytical and mapping efforts in four areas: crime series or investigative analysis, operations research or resource allocation studies, problem solving or applied research, and discrete site analysis.

*Crime Mapping Laboratory.** *Crime Mapping News.* Washington, DC: Police Foundation (multiple issues).

This quarterly newsletter includes articles authored by practitioners and researchers on issues pertaining to crime analysis and crime mapping. Past topics include:

Volume 2
- Implementing crime mapping
- Tactical crime analysis
- Regional data sharing
- Using non-traditional data

Volume 3
- International mapping efforts
- School safety
- Interactive mapping on the Web
- Analysis and mapping of drug activity

Volume 4
- Mapping terrorist events
- Problem analysis
- Partnerships between law enforcement and vendors
- COMPASS

Volume 5
- Problem analysis

- Miscellaneous topics
- Project Safe Neighborhoods
- Problem analysis training

*Harries, Keith.** *Mapping Crime: Principle and Practice.* Washington, DC: National Institute of Justice, 1999.

Through discussion and a number of practical examples, this text provides an introduction to crime mapping.

LaVigne, Nancy & Julie Wartell, eds. *Crime Mapping Case Studies: Successes in the Field,* vol. 1. Washington, DC: Police Executive Research Forum, 1998.

LaVigne, Nancy & Julie Wartell, eds. *Crime Mapping Case Studies: Successes in the Field,* vol. 2. Washington, DC: Police Executive Research Forum, 2000.

These two books highlight various criminal justice agencies' successes with applying mapping to their problem-solving, crime prevention, and enforcement efforts. Below are selected topics from each volume:

Volume 1
- Auto theft
- Burglary
- Mapping by community organizations
- Open garage door burglary
- Serial rape
- Traffic accidents

Volume 2
- Campus crime
- Construction site crime
- Environmental design
- Gangs
- Gun violence
- Indecent exposure
- Serial robbers

LaVigne, Nancy & Julie Wartell. *Mapping Across Boundaries:* Regional crime analysis. Washington, DC: Police Executive Research Forum, 2001.

Through examples, this guide outlines how regional mapping efforts began; how they were implemented; decisions regarding software, hardware, data sharing, and privacy agreements; and how cross-agency mapping has been used in practice.

*Mapping and Analysis for Public Safety Program (MAPS) Conference Papers (Multiple years).

Papers prepared for the annual International Mapping and Analysis for Public Safety Conference are available free of charge online. The papers are a valuable resource for learning about new spatial analysis techniques and research projects. Sample topics from previous years include:

- o Advanced statistics
- o Analytical techniques to support crime prevention
- o Crime and place
- o Cross-jurisdictional data sharing
- o Forecasting
- o Improving crime pattern detection with theory
- o Offender travel behavior
- o Problem solving
- o Victimization

*Rich, Thomas F. *Mapping the Path to Problem-solving.* Washington, DC: National Institute of Justice, 1999.

This eight-page report briefly reviews risk-focused policing, the Strategic Approaches to Community Safety Initiative (SACSI), mapping for corrections, and hot spot mapping.

*Wartell, Julie and J. Thomas McEwen. *Privacy in the Information Age: A Guide for Sharing Crime Maps and Spatial Data.* Washington, DC: National Institute of Justice, 2001

This report provides guidance to police personnel, researchers, and others who plan to create and share crime maps. It demonstrates a variety of techniques that promote privacy and data confidentiality.

Practical Theory Literature

Clarke, Ronald V., series ed. *Crime Prevention Studies* (multiple volumes). Monsey, NY: Criminal Justice Press.

This book series is dedicated to research on situational crime prevention and other initiatives that aim to reduce opportunities for crime. Some of the topics addressed in previous volumes include:

- o Crime and place (Vol. 4)
- o Crime mapping and crime prevention (Vol. 8)
- o Repeat victimization (Vol. 12)
- o Analysis for crime prevention (Vol. 13).

Clarke, Ronald V. *Situational Crime Prevention: Successful Case Studies,* 2nd ed. Guilderland, NY: Harrow and Heston, 1997.

This book explains the general principles of situational crime prevention and presents over 20 examples of effective prevention initiatives.

*Clarke, Ronald V. *Hot Products: Understanding, Anticipating, and Reducing Demand for Stolen Goods* (Police Research Series Paper 112). London: Home Office Policing and Reducing Crime Unit, 1999.

This report reviews the research on hot products, which are the consumer items most attractive to thieves. It is important to understand what types of property criminals prefer and why, since their distribution may help explain patterns of theft.

*Felson, Marcus and Ronald V. Clarke. *Opportunity Makes the Thief: Practical Theory for Crime Prevention* (Police Research Series Paper 98). London: Home Office Policing and Reducing Crime Unit, 1998.

This paper discusses criminological theories such as Routine Activities, Rational Choice, and crime pattern theory and their practical implications for crime prevention efforts.

Felson, Marcus. *Crime and Everyday Life*, 3rd ed. Thousand Oaks, CA: Sage, 2002.

This book includes a discussion of crime problems from the Routine Activities perspective and discusses how simple changes in the physical environment can substantially reduce crime rates.

*Pease, Ken. *Repeat Victimization: Taking Stock* (Crime Detection and Prevention Series Paper 90). London: Home Office Police Research Group, 1998.

This report reviews the state of repeat victimization research—what we currently know and how to make the most of this knowledge.

Problem-Solving Literature

*Bynum, Timothy S. *Using Analysis for Problem-Solving: a Guidebook for Law Enforcement*. Washington, DC: Office of Community Oriented Policing Services, 2001.

This guide provides an introduction to analyzing problems within the context of problem-oriented policing. It also includes a discussion of police data and explores the various methods of primary data collection.

*Multiple Authors. *Problem-oriented Guides for Police* Series. Washington, DC: Office of Community Oriented Policing Services.

The Problem-Oriented Guides for Police consist of 22 problem-oriented guidebooks that focus on assessing specific response strategies. Although most of the guides are dedicated to discussing responses, there are good tips for understanding your local problem that include a list of questions to ask about the crime or disorder problem and a discussion of evaluation measures. The guides also include a general discussion of the state of knowledge of each problem, a list of references, and recommended reading. The COPS Office plans to produce more guides in the future. Among the topics available as of September 2004 are:

- Acquaintance rape of college students
- Assaults in and around bars
- Bullying in schools
- Burglary of retail establishments
- Burglary of single-family houses
- Check and card fraud
- Clandestine drug labs
- Disorderly youth in public places
- False burglar alarms
- Financial crimes against the elderly
- Graffiti
- Loud car stereos
- Misuse and abuse of 911
- Rave parties
- Robbery at ATM machines
- Shoplifting
- Speeding in residential areas
- Street prostitution
- Theft of and from cars in parking facilities

*Office of Community Oriented Policing Services. *Problem-solving Tips: A Guide to Reducing Crime and Disorder Through Problem-solving Partnerships*. Washington, DC: Author, 1997.

This brief guide provides a brief introduction to the SARA model and the problem-solving process. It also provides detailed recommendations and three brief problem-solving examples.

*Police Executive Research Forum. *Excellence in Problem-oriented Policing: The Herman Goldstein Award Winners*. Washington, DC: Author, 1997–2004.

These reports include descriptions of award-winning examples of problem-oriented responses to community problems.

*Read, Tim and Nick Tilley. *Not Rocket Science? Problem-Solving and Crime Reduction* (Crime Reduction Research Series Paper 6). London: Home Office Policing and Reducing Crime Unit, 2000.

This report examines the role of problem solving in crime reduction through questionnaires and interviews with police forces in England and Wales. It includes a discussion of both successful and failed problem-solving efforts.

*Sampson, Rana and Michael Scott. *Tackling Crime and Other Public-Safety Problems: Case Studies in Problem-solving*. Washington, DC: Office of Community Oriented Policing Services, 2000.

The book presents case studies of successful problem-oriented policing efforts for a wide variety of crime and disorder problems. Notes from the editors, detailing the noteworthy aspects of each effort, are included after each section. Among the topics included in this book are:

- Alcohol-related crime
- Apartment complex crime
- Burglary
- College-related crime
- Cruising
- Domestic violence
- Drugs
- False alarms
- Gangs
- Graffiti
- Group homes
- Homeless-related crime
- Mental illness
- Neighborhood disorder
- Parks
- Prostitution
- Robbery
- Theft from vehicles

Research Methods/Evaluation Literature

*Bureau of Justice Assistance. *Police Guide to Surveying Citizens and Their Environment*. Washington, DC: Author, 1993.

This monograph describes the basics of surveying the public and the physical environment. It includes a number of examples, survey instruments, and tips for making surveys more cost-effective.

Eck, John E. and Nancy LaVigne. *Using Research: a Primer for Law Enforcement Managers*, 2nd ed. Washington, DC: Police Executive Research Forum, 1994.

This short book was developed for police officials who have no background in research or statistics. It addresses the fundamentals of research and serves as a bridge to introductory texts.

*Eck, John E. *Assessing Responses to Problems: an Introductory Guide for Police Problem Solvers.* Washington, DC: Office of Community Oriented Policing Services, 2001.

This publication, part of the Problem-Oriented Guides for Police Series, provides useful guidelines for measuring and evaluating problem-oriented policing efforts.

*Weisel, Deborah Lamm. *Conducting Community Surveys: a Practical Guide for Law Enforcement Agencies.* Washington, DC: Bureau of Justice Statistics and Office of Community Oriented Policing Services, 1999.

This report provides practical pointers for conducting community surveys; it is accompanied by computer software.

Relevant Academic Journals

By reviewing academic and professional journals, crime analysts can build knowledge about criminal justice research efforts. While not every article may be relevant for the daily responsibilities of a crime analyst, the analyst is the research specialist in the police agency; therefore, he or she should be aware of the current state of research concerning criminal justice issues. Subscriptions to many criminal justice journals are relatively inexpensive; as of December 2003, annual subscriptions to most of the journals listed in this chapter range from $60 to $200. Journals can also be searched through abstracts databases and viewed at many university libraries free of charge (discussed in the next section). The following journals, listed in alphabetical order, were selected by the author as those most relevant to crime analysis professionals.

Crime & Delinquency
This quarterly journal, available from Sage Publications, includes practical research findings, debates on current issues, reviews of current literature, and detailed research findings concerning a variety of criminal justice issues.

Criminology & Public Policy
This journal, published three times each year, is available through membership in the American Society of Criminology (ASC). The journal presents criminology research findings to assist in the formulation of criminal justice policy.

Journal of Interpersonal Violence
This monthly journal, available from Sage Publications, presents research relevant to the study and treatment of victims and perpetrators of crimes such as domestic violence, child sexual abuse, sexual assault, physical child abuse, and violent crime.

Journal of Research in Crime and Delinquency
This quarterly journal, available from Sage Publications, presents research examining the social, political, and economic contexts of criminal justice, victims, and offenders.

Justice Quarterly
This quarterly journal is available through membership in the Academy of Criminal Justice Sciences (ACJS). The journal provides articles on current qualitative and quantitative criminal justice research.

Justice Research and Policy
This journal, published two times per year, is available through membership in the Justice Research and Statistics Association (JRSA). The journal provides articles on applied criminal justice research efforts.

Police Practice and Research
This quarterly journal, available from Taylor & Francis, presents current police research as well as operational and administrative practices from around the world.

Policing: An International Journal of Police Strategies and Management

This quarterly journal, available from Emerald, provides discussion, analysis, and strategies pertaining to topics such as community policing, performance measurement and accountability, crime trends and analysis, victimology, and crime prevention.

Abstracts Databases

An abstract is a summary of the main points of a work of literature; therefore, an abstracts database provides summaries and bibliographic information for literature such as journal articles, books, government reports, conference proceedings, and periodicals. Access to an abstracts database allows crime analysts to quickly search thousands of books, journals, reports, and other sources for information pertaining to a particular criminal justice topic. Advanced search functions allow analysts to narrow their queries to those items most relevant to the task at hand. For example, upon noting that 94% of burglar alarms are false, a crime analyst decides to conduct a study of the false alarm problem and prepare a list of recommendations for reducing the problem. One of the first tasks in a study of this nature is to consult academic and practical literature to learn about the problem and how other agencies have analyzed or responded to it. An abstracts database such as the one provided through the National Criminal Justice Reference Service (NCJRS) (discussed below) is a good starting point for this study. A quick search of this database for the term "false alarm" yields a number of useful results, such as the Problem-Oriented Guides for Police Series report False Burglar Alarms, by Rana Sampson, and an article in the FBI's periodical, Law Enforcement Bulletin, titled "False Alarms: Cause for Alarm." Both of these resources provide general information

about the prevalence of the false alarm problem as well as useful case studies describing actions taken by police agencies to combat the problem.

There are two abstracts databases listed in this section; the first is a free online service and the other database is available by subscription. Since subscriptions can be expensive, analysts are encouraged to visit their local college or university library to determine whether criminal justice databases are available for public use on library computers (they generally are).

*National Criminal Justice Reference Service (NCJRS) Abstracts Database

This online database contains summaries of federal, state, and local government reports; books; research reports; journal articles; and unpublished research. The subject areas covered by the database include police, corrections, courts, crime statistics, domestic preparedness, victims of crime, drugs and crime, and juvenile justice. The NCJRS database is a valuable tool for analysts as it is comprehensive and easily accessible.

Criminal Justice Abstracts

This resource, available in both database and paper format, indexes and summarizes journal articles, books, reports, dissertations, and unpublished papers on criminology and related disciplines. Some of the relevant topics covered include crime trends, crime prevention and deterrence, juvenile delinquency, and policing.

Online Resources

This section outlines a number of resources that are freely available over the Internet. In this author's opinion, crime analysts should always conduct a thorough, yet discriminating, search of the Internet when conducting a literature review. Information available over the Web is not only quickly and easily accessible, but in many cases, it is also free. The following resources, listed in alphabetical order, were selected as those most relevant for both daily and long-term crime analysis tasks. Web addresses are provided and are current as of August 2004; however, if a Web link is no longer active, readers are encouraged to enter the name of the resource into an online search engine to obtain the updated Web link.

*Center for Problem-Oriented Policing
(www.popcenter.org)
This online information center, which debuted in June 2003, is dedicated to encouraging the practice of problem-oriented policing. The site provides general information about problem-oriented policing and problem solving in addition to full-text access to many of the publications discussed in the first part of this chapter. Some of the publications available through the site are:

- Assessing responses to problems: An introductory guide for police problem solvers
- Conducting community surveys
- Crime prevention studies series
- Herman Goldstein Award winners and finalists
- Opportunity makes the thief: Practical theory for crime prevention
- Problem-oriented guides for police series
- Situational crime prevention: Successful case studies, second edition
- Using research: A primer for law enforcement managers, second edition

*Crime Reduction Toolkits
(www.crimereduction.gov.uk/toolkits)
The toolkits are a free, interactive Web-based resource where practitioners and policymakers can access information on

effective police practice. Each toolkit is problem-specific and provides links to information such as:

- What we know about the problem
- How others have tackled the problem
- Assessing the local situation
- Developing a local strategy
- Resources (e.g., sample action plans, evaluation checklists)
- Contact information

Analysts are encouraged to consult this resource before beginning a problem analysis project. The comprehensive information contained within the toolkits will allow them to learn from and expand on similar crime reduction efforts. As of August 2004, some of the topics covered in the Crime Reduction Toolkits are:

- Alcohol-related crime
- Antisocial behavior
- Arson
- Business and retail crime
- Communities against drugs
- Domestic burglary
- Fear of crime
- Mentally disordered offenders
- Persistent young offenders
- Racial crime and harassment
- Repeat victimization
- Rural crime
- Street crime and robbery
- Trafficking in people
- Using intelligence and information sharing
- Vehicle crime

The following is an example of the subject areas explored in the Repeat Victimization (RV) Toolkit.

Introduction/What is RV?
What do we know about RV?
- Facts & figures
- Risk factors
- National context

Developing local solutions for local problems
- Assessing the local situation
- Drawing up a local strategy

Tackling RV
Making it happen
Resources
Innovation
Practical tools
Contact points
Useful publications

*Home Office Research Development and Statistics Directorate (RDS)
(www.homeoffice.gov.uk/rds/)

The Home Office is the agency responsible for internal affairs in England and Wales. The RDS Web site is similar to NCJRS in that it provides full-text access to criminal justice research publications. The site is a valuable source of information about crime-specific prevention strategies, repeat victimization, and problem-oriented policing strategies in the UK. The Police Research Series publications listed below are a sample of those that may have practical relevance for crime analysts. Sample titles include:

- Preventing car crime in car parks
- The prevention of street robbery
- Thinking about crime prevention performance indicators
- Local crime analysis
- Tackling local drug markets
- Arresting evidence: Domestic violence and repeat victimization
- Preventing residential burglary in Cambridge: From crime audits to targeted strategies
- Police use of decoy vehicles

*National Criminal Justice Reference Service (www.ncjrs.org)

NCJRS provides a number of services to criminal justice researchers. The abstracts database (discussed in the preceding section) provides summaries of more than 170,000 criminal justice publications. Also available through the Web site are the:

- Virtual library: Offers free online access to over 7,000 full-text publications. Many of the documents published since 1995 by NCJRS-sponsoring agencies such as the National Institute of Justice, the Office for Victims of Crime, the Bureau of Justice Statistics, and the Bureau of Justice Assistance are available in full-text online.

- Information network: By registering with NCJRS, you will receive regular updates about NCJRS services and resources through the 1) NCJRS Catalog, a bimonthly report detailing new publications available through NCJRS; 2) JUSTINFO, a biweekly electronic newsletter detailing new publications, conferences, and funding opportunities; and 3) periodic e-mail notifications about resources that match your specific interests.

- Reference and referral services: NCJRS staff can provide statistics and referrals, compile information packages, search for additional resources, and provide tailored technical assistance. Send criminal justice-related questions via e-mail to: askncjrs@ncjrs.org.

Government Resources

The preceding section is focused on specific online resources that are available to inform crime analysis research efforts. While many publications available through government agencies can be searched or accessed through clearinghouses such as the National Criminal Justice Reference Service, analysts should also be familiar with the information and services provided by individual agencies. The following alphabetical listing includes those federal agencies that are most relevant to crime analysis professionals. Web addresses are provided and are current as of August 2004; however, if a Web link is no longer active, readers are encouraged to enter the name of the resource into an online search engine to obtain the updated link.

Bureau of Justice Assistance (BJA)
(www.ojp.usdoj.gov/bja)
This site provides information on BJA funding programs and includes a searchable database of all federally funded and supported training opportunities for state and local law enforcement practitioners.

Bureau of Justice Statistics (BJS)
(www.ojp.usdoj.gov/bjs)
The site provides statistics, trend information, and datasets for a variety of criminal justice topics, including crime and victims, criminal offenders, homicide trends, and criminal record systems.

FedStats (www.fedstats.gov)
This site provides access to official statistics collected and published by over 100 federal agencies. Criminal justice statistics can be readily searched by topic (e.g., offenders, victims, violent crime), federal agency, or geographic region.

Mapping and Analysis for Public Safety Program (MAPS)
(www.ojp.usdoj.gov/nij/maps)
The MAPS site provides crime mapping-related publications, conference proceedings, software, mapping tutorials, and information on funding and training opportunities. The

site also provides information for subscribing to Crimemap, an electronic listserv devoted to discussions of crime mapping and analysis.

National Institute of Justice (NIJ)
(www.ojp.usdoj.gov/nij)
The site provides information on NIJ programs and funding opportunities and includes publications on a variety of topics, including law enforcement, drugs and crime, victims, and research and evaluation.

Office for Victims of Crime (OVC)
(www.ojp.usdoj.gov/ovc)
The OVC site provides information on funding opportunities and victim-related statistics and publications prepared by a variety of federal agencies.

Office of Community Oriented Policing Services (COPS) (www.cops.usdoj.gov)
The COPS Web site provides full-text access to a variety of publications relevant for crime analysis and problem solving. The site also provides details about COPS funding and training opportunities.

Office of Juvenile Justice and Delinquency Prevention (OJJDP)
(www.ojjdp.ncjrs.org)
The site provides juvenile justice and delinquency information and resources, including publications, conferences, funding opportunities, and discussions of strategies for combating youth crime.

In addition to the federal agencies outlined above, a number of non-profit and membership organizations provide information and publications that are relevant for crime analysts. Examples of these organizations include the Institute for Law and Justice (ILJ), the International Association of Chiefs of Police (IACP), the International Association of Crime Analysts (IACA), the International Association of Law

Enforcement Intelligence Analysts (IALEIA), the International Association of Law Enforcement Planners (IALEP), the Justice Research and Statistics Association (JRSA), the Police Executive Research Forum (PERF), the Police Foundation, the Urban Institute, and the Vera Institute of Justice. Readers are encouraged to visit the Web sites of these organizations to learn more about the information and services they provide.

Literature Review Checklist

The following checklist is meant to serve as a reminder of all the resources that are currently available to crime analysts. While this chapter has primarily focused on the type and availability of literature and online resources, analysts are also encouraged to employ other methods for developing a body of knowledge to inform their crime analysis and problem-solving efforts. Other methods for obtaining information for a literature review include contacting one's colleagues. This can be accomplished both through personal contact and through electronic discussion lists such as those maintained by the IACA and the MAPS Program. Electronic lists allow analysts to post queries and obtain feedback and ideas from a larger community of analysts and researchers. As analysts carry out their daily duties and undertake complicated research tasks, it is important to remember that there is a large body of literature available to inform their efforts, and a helpful community of professionals who have likely faced similar challenges and developed workable solutions.

By consulting the resources discussed in this chapter and reviewing the following checklist at the start of an analysis or research endeavor, you will save valuable time and generate ideas to assist you in analyzing and responding to crime and disorder problems.

Have you consulted:

❏ Government resources? Examples include the Problem-Oriented Guides for Police Series, published by the COPS Office and the abstracts database and virtual library offered through the Web site of the National Criminal Justice Reference Service.

❏ Professional periodicals and books? Examples of professional books and periodicals include the Crime Prevention Studies Series, edited by Ronald V. Clarke, and the Police Foundation's Crime Mapping News.

❏ Abstracts databases? Abstracts databases such as Criminal Justice Abstracts allow searches of academic literature such as books, journal articles, and dissertations.

❏ Online resources? Examples include the Center for Problem-Oriented Policing, the Crime Reduction Toolkits, and the Home Office Research Development and Statistics Directorate.

❏ Conference materials? Organizations that post conference proceedings on their Web sites include the IACA and the MAPS Program.

❏ Your colleagues? Obtain information from colleagues through telephone contacts, electronic listservs, and by attending regional and national crime analysis meetings.

When you have compiled all the relevant information about your topic, you have completed the first phase of the literature review process. The next step involves summarizing and synthesizing the literature.

Summary and Synthesis

A literature review typically generates a great deal of information, which must then be organized into manageable categories or themes. The most efficient technique for organizing one's resources is through the creation of an annotated bibliography. An annotated bibliography is simply a list of the resources (e.g., books, periodicals, Web sites) consulted during the literature review process that includes bibliographic information and comments concerning the content of the resource. The purpose is not only to help you organize and understand large amounts of information, but also to begin organizing your thoughts around what is known about a particular criminal justice issue. In addition to bibliographic information for each resource (consult a style manual such as those published by the American Psychological Association [APA] or the Modern Language Association [MLA] for guidelines), each entry is followed by a paragraph in which you:

• Briefly summarize the resource: Identify the major points, research findings, and conclusions.

• Identify common themes and concepts: This allows you to group similar resources together.

• Critically assess the material: Do more than summarize—determine the strengths and weaknesses of the information and evaluate the study's methods and findings.

• State how the material relates to your research question(s): Determine whether the resource is relevant to your problem or study. If the resource is not informative or relevant, it should be excluded from the literature review.

The preceding list describes the basic material to be included in an annotated bibliography. Only a few sentences are required for each resource; entries should be kept brief to ensure that the information does not become overwhelming. The comments can be written informally, though writing concise, complete sentences will allow you to easily copy the information into a literature review or a research report at a later date. Below is an example of an annotated bibliography entry. The citation style is APA (American Psychological Association); however, you are encouraged to use the citation style with which you are most comfortable.[1]

National Institute of Justice. (1999, January). *Inventory of state and local law enforcement technology needs to combat terrorism* (Research in Brief). Washington, DC: Author.

This report discusses the results of an NIJ-sponsored survey of state and local law enforcement officials concerning their technology needs to combat terrorism. The first phase of the project, reported in this research brief, involved surveys of all 50 states and the District of Columbia to determine their needs. The survey identified key issues including the need for a national intelligence database and for improved communications technologies. Although the report cites a number of relevant technologies (e.g., bomb robots, protective gear, electronic listening devices), it does not specifically mention mapping technology.

This entry is from an annotated bibliography that is provided in its entirety at the end of this chapter. The use of the complete citation ensures that this information can be easily copied into the reference list of another document. In addition, the comments

---

[1] *Exploring Crime Analysis* follows the *Chicago Manual of Style* guidelines.

following the citation include the main components of an annotated bibliography—a summary of the report, the research findings, and a critical assessment of the report's relevance to the research question.

Writing a Literature Review

Once the annotated bibliography is complete, you will have a good understanding of the information that you have compiled and how it relates and contributes to your project. If the annotated bibliography is thorough and well-constructed, then the last stage of the process—using the annotated bibliography as a foundation to write the literature review—is quite easy. A literature review is a summary and critical analysis of the knowledge and empirical research relevant to your topic. In other words, it is a more organized, more concise version of the annotated bibliography. The literature review is typically used to support a hypothesis, research findings, or a particular point of view. Some general guidelines to follow when constructing the literature review are:

- Critically analyze the literature; do not just summarize what is known about the topic.

- Consider the audience of your report—this will dictate the level of specificity of the information.

- Identify areas of controversy in the literature.

- Focus on how the literature pertains to your research question(s).

- Formulate ideas for further research.

Generally, the literature review should include an introduction, body, and conclusion, even if it is part of a larger report. Although there are no length requirements,

the review should adequately convey the state of knowledge concerning your topic and lead the audience to your research question. For example, a literature review prepared for a study of residential burglary in Anytown, USA would include general descriptive information about the problem of residential burglary, empirical findings from other studies of the problem, and a discussion of how these studies informed the Anytown study or left gaps in knowledge that the Anytown study attempts to fill.

Since every individual has his or her own writing style, it is difficult to provide more specific guidelines for preparing a literature review. Therefore, readers are encouraged to review the annotated bibliography and literature review examples at the end of this chapter. These documents were prepared by members of the Police Foundation's Crime Mapping Laboratory (CML) for a proposal in which the CML would identify and document strategies of state and local law enforcement agencies and policymakers who are using data and analysis for counterterrorism efforts.

Conclusion

As crime analysis moves toward more systematic, in-depth analysis of crime and disorder problems, crime analysts will rely on literature reviews with greater frequency than they do today. While not every crime analysis task will require a review of the literature, the crime analyst is the research specialist in the police agency; therefore, he or she should be aware of the current state of research on criminal justice issues. By conducting literature reviews, analysts become aware of the many (mostly free) resources that are available to inform their work. Furthermore, a literature review adds authority to an analyst's work product and assures the audience that the analysis is theoretically based and empirically sound. Reviewing the literature and basing one's work on what others have learned saves a great deal of valuable time and leads to more informed, and ultimately more effective, crime analysis.

Annotated Bibliography Example

The following annotated bibliography was prepared by members of the Police Foundation's Crime Mapping Laboratory (CML) for a proposal in which the CML would identify and document strategies of state and local law enforcement agencies and policymakers who are using data and analysis for counterterrorism efforts. Note that the annotated bibliography is organized by agency (theme) and that the full citation is used so that the information can later be copied to the reference list of the proposal. Throughout the document, you will also find that informal notes are included to help organize the writer's thoughts.

Office of Community Oriented Policing Services

Chapman, R. & Scheider, M.C. (2002, Fall). *Community policing: Now more than ever.* On the Beat, 19, 6-7. Retrieved 13 Jan 2003 from http://www.cops.usdoj.gov /pdf/otb/e08021676.pdf.

This article emphasizes the relevance of the community policing philosophy for terrorism prevention and response efforts. Through the promotion of problem-solving efforts and the development of external partnerships, community policing can help police agencies prepare for and prevent incidents of terrorism and also respond to the fear that such incidents create in the community. The authors note that, since 9/11, "America's law enforcement agencies have provided a visible security presence at potential terrorist targets, partnered with federal intelligence agencies, responded to an increasing number of hate crimes, and investigated a large number of terrorism related leads" (Chapman and Scheider, 2002, p. 7). The authors do not review these efforts or specifically discuss the importance of crime mapping; the primary purpose of the article is to reinforce the role of community policing in local law enforcement efforts to combat terrorism.

Chapman, R., Baker, S., Bezdikian, V., Cammarata, P., Cohen, D., Leach, N., Schapiro, A., Scheider, M., Varano, R., & Boba, R. (2002). *Local law enforcement responds to terrorism: Lessons in prevention and preparedness.* Washington, DC: Office of Community Oriented Policing Services.

The authors note that a high level of responsibility for responding to threats of terrorism rests at the local level. Therefore, this report outlines the types of resources that police agencies may want to consider when developing their own terrorism prevention and response plans. It also highlights the efforts of COPS grantees who have used COPS funding to improve their response to terrorism. These efforts include improving data and intelligence collection, capitalizing on technological advancements, communicating with other public safety agencies, responding to citizen fear, and preparing to assist victims. The report is designed to assist police with conducting their own security needs assessments and implementing effective response procedures.

Mapping for homeland security is addressed throughout the report. One example describes how the Seattle Police Department used COPS funding to implement crime mapping software that can be used to create emergency mobilization maps to assist response efforts in the event of a terror attack. In another example, developed by the Crime Mapping Laboratory, a map is used to depict burglaries of ammonium nitrate suppliers. This publication provides a brief introduction to the use of crime mapping for homeland security through examples, but it is limited in that it only refers to a small number of agencies that have received COPS funding.

Office of Community Oriented Policing Services. (2002). *Providing homeland security.* Retrieved January 13, 2003, from http://www.cops.usdoj.gov/default.asp?Item=109.

This Web site is a resource for reports, training, and technical assistance opportunities, and links related to homeland security. The site includes a great deal of information, ranging from reports on how to identify suspicious packages and physical security planning to domestic preparedness training and technical assistance. The site is a helpful resource for local law enforcement agencies seeking information related to the preparation, response, and prevention of terrorism incidents.

Wichita State RCPI. (2002). *Training: A police response to terrorism in the heartland: Integrating law enforcement intelligence and community policing.* Retrieved January 14, 2003, from http://www.wsurcpi.org/docs/A_Police_Response_to_Terrorism _Registration_Kansas.pdf.

This training course, held at the Regional Community Policing Institute at Wichita State University, focuses primarily on police ethics and homeland security. Topics presented during the day-long training course include: appropriate use of law enforcement intelligence, protection of citizens' rights from unsupported accusations of involvement in terror groups, avoidance of unwarranted investigations, issues in profiling potential terrorists, confrontation and investigation of people perceived to be non-U.S. citizens, and how community policing can address expressed concerns regarding the erosion of citizens' rights.

National Institute of Justice

Much of the information available through the National Institute of Justice relates to equipment for first responders; examples are the reports "An Introduction to Biological Agent Detection Equipment for Emergency First Responders," "Guide for the Selection of Personal Protection Equipment for Emergency First Responders," and "Guide for the Selection of Communication Equipment for Emergency First Responders."

Riley, K.J. & Hoffman, B. (1995). *Domestic terrorism: A national assessment of state and local law enforcement preparedness.* Santa Monica, CA: Rand.

The purpose of this project, initiated through funding from the National Institute of Justice, was to analyze states' and municipalities' terrorism preparedness to provide law enforcement agencies with information about the prevention and control of terrorist activities. The research involved a three-phased approach—a national survey of state and local law enforcement agencies designed to assess the terrorist threat perceived by these jurisdictions and to identify promising programs; the selection of ten locations as case studies to examine in detail how different jurisdictions have adapted to the threat of terrorism; and the identification of programs to counter potential threats along with the development of a research agenda. Generally, the study found that a variety of successful terrorism preparedness formulas existed in both large and small communities.

This study is similar to the research we wish to conduct in its use of the case study approach. However, it can be argued that the results are not completely relevant since the research was conducted almost ten years ago.

National Institute of Justice. (1999, January). *Inventory of state and local law enforcement technology needs to combat terrorism* (Research in Brief). Washington, DC: Author.

This report discusses the results of an NIJ-sponsored survey of state and local law enforcement officials concerning their technology needs to combat terrorism. The first phase of the project, reported in this research brief, involved surveys of all 50 states and the District of Columbia to determine their needs. Overall, a total of 195 individuals representing 138 agencies took part in the survey. The survey identified key issues including the need for a national intelligence database and for improved communications technologies. Although the report cites a number of relevant technologies (e.g., bomb robots, protective gear, electronic listening devices), it does not specifically mention mapping technology.

National Institute of Justice. (2002). *A method to assess the vulnerability of U.S. chemical facilities.* Washington, DC: Author.

This report discusses the development of risk assessments for chemical facilities, focusing on terrorist or criminal actions that could have a national influence or cause the airborne release of hazardous chemicals. The report does not explicitly discuss the use of mapping technology but does recommend the use of site plans and environmental assessments of the facilities. A simple drawing of possible entry points to a chemical facility is included (p. 26 of the PDF); however, GIS is a much better tool for compiling and representing the information obtained in the site analysis.

International Association of Chiefs of Police
Conference: Local response to terrorism: lessons learned from the 9-11 attack on the Pentagon. March 19-21, 2003, Arlington, Virginia.

The purpose of this conference is to convene high-level policymakers from local jurisdictions to learn from Arlington County's experiences in responding to the terrorist attack on the Pentagon and to work in teams to analyze the response capacity within their own jurisdiction. The conference will address: activities that must be under way before a response begins; how incident and unified command really work in a major response; security considerations during the operation; evidence collection and its influence on operations; and details from more than 235 lessons learned.

International Association of Chiefs of Police. (2001). *Leading from the front: Law enforcement's role in combating and preparing for domestic terrorism.* Alexandria, VA: Author.

I copied the following description from the COPS Web site: "The International Association of Chiefs of Police (IACP) published this document, which identifies areas that law enforcement practitioners should consider as they tailor and strengthen their own security strategies."

Police Executive Research Forum. *Community policing in a counter-terrorism context.* Retrieved January 17, 2003, from http://www.policeforum.org/active.html

The following information is from the "Active Projects" sections on the Police Executive Research Forum Web site. It sounds similar to what we hope to accomplish, although there does not seem to be the emphasis on data sources, analysis, and mapping that we envision for our project: "PERF has received funding from the COPS Office to examine the role of local law enforcement in homeland security and "counter-terrorism" policing. The overarching goals of this initiative are to: 1) evaluate how September 11 has so far affected local law enforcement; 2) assist community policing agencies as they work to improve their terrorism response capabilities; and 3) examine contentious issues and potential initiatives that could impede the continued evolution of community policing. PERF will accomplish these goals through a national survey of law enforcement leaders, a series of executive sessions, follow-up fieldwork to identify model programs, and a comprehensive written manual for police agencies."

Police Executive Research Forum. (2002). *Terrorism resources: Anti-terrorism and disaster response programs exist for law enforcement.* Retrieved January 17, 2003, from http://www.policeforum.org /justtrrsm.pdf.

This brief, five-page report is a partial listing of funding opportunities, training, and technical assistance resources, reports, and Web sites related to anti-terrorism and disaster response. The guide provides a description and contact information for each resource, and it is meant to serve as a starting point for state and local law enforcement agencies that are developing anti-terrorism and critical incident response plans. The report does not include any resources specific to analysis or mapping; most of the information is very general (e.g., state and local anti-terrorism training).

Federal Emergency Management Agency

Federal Emergency Management Agency. (2000, January). *Partnerships in preparedness: A compendium of exemplary practices in emergency management,* vol. 4. Retrieved 13 Jan 2003 from http://www.fema.gov /pdf/rrr/partners_v4.pdf.

Since 1995, FEMA has been producing compilations of exemplary practices in emergency management. The objective is to share information regarding innovative emergency management programs so that

these programs can be adopted elsewhere to respond to natural or man-caused disasters. Volume 4 describes public and private-sector emergency management practices that include coordination among organizations, volunteer projects, and resource sharing. The information provided about each program is brief (one page) and includes information such as contact, target population, description, and budget. It should be noted that the practices cited in the report do not specifically focus on terrorism.

Federal Emergency Management Agency. (2002, July). *Managing the emergency consequences of terrorist incidents: Interim planning guide for state and local governments.* Retrieved January 23, 2003 from http://www.fema.gov/pdf/onp/managi ngemerconseq.pdf.

This document provides state and local emergency management planners with a framework for developing supplemental emergency operations plans for addressing the consequences of a terrorist act involving weapons of mass destruction; a consistent planning approach that will foster efficient integration of state, local, and federal terrorism consequence management activities; and the most current information regarding the planning and operational challenges faced by communities that have dealt with terrorist events. There is a discussion of maps as an important element of an emergency operations plan (p. 18); however, there are no examples of how various agencies have used mapping in the development of their emergency plans.

National Emergency Management Association

National Emergency Management Association. (2001, December). *Trends in state terrorism preparedness.* Retrieved January 17, 2003, from http://www.nemaweb.org/Trends_in_T errorism_Preparedness/index.htm.

In October 2001, NEMA conducted a survey of states to identify trends in state terrorism preparedness. This report provides a snapshot of some common and unique approaches to addressing domestic preparedness. The report is broken down by region and provides general information in the areas of emergency operations, National Guard activities, incident command, public health, legislative initiatives, and key issues such as funding and coordination with the federal government. The report does not provide specific examples of counter-terrorism efforts nor does it specifically mention mapping and analysis. It is generally a good introduction to what is being done to combat terrorism at the state level.

Oklahoma City National Memorial Institute for the Prevention of Terrorism Office of Homeland Security. (2002, July). *State and local actions for homeland security*. Retrieved January 28, 2003 from http://www.mipt.org/pdf/statelocalhom elandsecrpt.pdf.

This report, compiled by the Office of Homeland Security, provides an overview of measures that state and local governments have taken to improve homeland security. These measures include efforts to provide security, maintain public safety, protect public infrastructure, and respond to terrorist attacks through disaster relief and public health agencies. For example, the government of Washington, DC has created a Domestic Preparedness Task Force, transformed its emergency operations plan, made a commitment to secure proper equipment for emergency responders, and developed interoperability among key federal, state, and district agencies. This report is a useful resource for state and local governments in their efforts to improve homeland security and develop emergency response plans; however, the

report does not specifically address the issues facing local law enforcement.

Other Resources
Camp, D.D. (2000). *Domestic terrorism*. In L.S. Turnbull, E.H. Hendrix, & B.D. Dent (Eds.), Atlas of Crime: Mapping the Criminal Landscape (pp. 162-170). Phoenix, AZ: Oryx Press.

This chapter addresses the various types of domestic terrorism groups in the U.S. and notes that the geographic display of information on terrorist groups may assist in efforts to identify heavy concentrations of activity and locations of home bases.

I also looked at the Web sites for the Centers for Disease Control, Federal Geographic Data Committee, and Office of Domestic Preparedness but did not find any information specific to law enforcement analysis and mapping efforts. There are bits of information on various sites about efforts in specific jurisdictions; however, there is nothing that refers specifically to mapping.

Literature Review Example

The following literature review is based on the annotated bibliography above. The review was prepared by members of the Police Foundation's Crime Mapping Laboratory (CML) for a proposal in which the CML would identify and document strategies of state and local law enforcement agencies and policymakers who are using data and analysis for counterterrorism efforts. Note that the information from the annotated bibliography (about six pages) has been reduced to a concise two pages that summarize and evaluate what is known about efforts to document the counterterrorism efforts of state and local law enforcement agencies.

Documenting Counterterrorism Practices

There have been a number of efforts in the last several years to catalog innovative counter-terror measures implemented by state and local governments for the purpose of developing a body of literature describing model programs (Federal Emergency Management Agency, 2000; National Emergency Management Association, 2001; Federal Emergency Management Agency, 2002; National League of Cities, 2002; Office of Homeland Security, 2002). These reports provide snapshots of measures that state and local governments have implemented to improve homeland security, including information such as program descriptions, budget requirements, and contact information. The reports serve a valuable function in that they can provide guidelines to state and local governments as they begin to develop their own counterterrorism and critical incident response plans.

A recent report compiled by the Office of Homeland Security details state and local efforts to maintain public safety, protect public infrastructure, and respond to terrorist attacks through public safety and health agencies. For example, the government of Washington, DC has created a domestic preparedness task force, transformed its emergency operations plan, made a commitment to secure proper equipment for emergency responders, and developed interoperability among key federal, state, and district agencies (Office of Homeland Security, 2002). While these reports are valuable resources for state and local governments in their efforts to improve homeland security and develop emergency response plans, many of the studies do not specifically address the issues facing state and local law enforcement decision making.

Fortunately, a number of studies have also been undertaken that focus specifically on the challenges law enforcement agencies face in planning, preventing, and responding to terrorism and how the agencies have met these challenges. Over the last several years, researchers have identified model counterterrorism measures developed by law enforcement agencies (Riley and Hoffman, 1995; National Institute of Justice, 1999; Chapman, Baker, Bezdikian, Cammarata, Cohen, Leach, Schapiro, Scheider, Varano, and Boba, 2002; International Association of Chiefs of Police, 2001; Office of Community Oriented Policing Services, 2002; Police Executive Research Forum, 2002).

One study of innovative approaches, initiated through funding from the National Institute of Justice, involved a national survey of state and local law enforcement agencies designed to identify promising programs and the selection of ten locations to serve as case studies of how different jurisdictions have adapted to the threat of terrorism (Riley and Hoffman, 1995). An ongoing study of the role of law enforcement in homeland security, initiated through funding from the Office of Community Oriented Policing Services (COPS Office), seeks to provide law enforcement executives and policymakers with practical recommendations for implementing counterterrorism policing (Police Executive Research Forum, 2002). Generally, previous studies have demonstrated that a variety of innovative and effective counter-terror programs have been developed for use by law enforcement.

A review of the research documenting law enforcement strategies reveals that much of the current work is dedicated to discussions of immediate public safety concerns such as critical incident command. For example, an upcoming conference for public safety officials is focused entirely on responding to a terrorist attack, covering topics such as incident management, security considerations, and evidence collection. While these topics are relevant law enforcement concerns, there is a limited amount of work focused on the importance of systematic data collection, acquisition, and analysis to police agencies' counter-terrorist strategies. When data analysis is discussed, it is usually in the context of how it can support response strategies, such as in a recent report that addresses the use of spatial analysis for determining possible entry points to a chemical facility (National Institute of Justice, 2002). The report includes a simple illustration, but it does not provide practical examples from law enforcement agencies that are already using environmental assessments and spatial analysis to conduct risk assessments of vulnerable facilities nor does it provide sufficient detail to enable duplication of this process.

Law enforcement agencies have come to rely on analysis to inform and assist their policing efforts, and many agencies have applied data, analytical tools, and techniques to their counter-terror efforts. A recent publication prepared by the COPS Office is the first to highlight the importance of improving data acquisition and analysis for homeland security through discussion and practical examples. In fact, the use of analysis and mapping is addressed throughout the report. One example describes how the Seattle, WA, Police Department implemented GIS software to create emergency mobilization maps to assist response efforts in the event of a terror attack. Also included in the report is an analytical map, prepared by the Police Foundation Crime Mapping Laboratory (CML), that depicts burglaries of ammonium nitrate suppliers (Chapman et al., 2002). This publication provides a brief introduction to the importance and use of analysis for homeland security, but

it is limited by the fact that the practical examples are only briefly described and highlight a small number of agencies that are recipients of COPS Office funding.

Another resource that addresses counterterrorism efforts from an analytical perspective is a recent issue of the Police Foundation Crime Mapping Laboratory's publication, Crime Mapping News. The articles in the newsletter include a discussion of the ways in which analytical tools and techniques can be used to assist investigation, prevention, and emergency operations (Helms, 2002), as well as an example of how GIS technology was used to assist rescue and recovery efforts after the collapse of the World Trade Center buildings (Howard, 2002). Both of these articles are useful for law enforcement analysts; however, similar to the COPS Office report, the utility of this resource is limited in that it provides a snapshot of only two analytical methods, rather than a comprehensive review of analysis strategies employed by a large number of law enforcement agencies.

To date, there has been no systematic effort to document the variety of innovative data collection, acquisition, and analysis strategies that have been employed by state and local law enforcement agencies to improve their counterterrorism efforts. As previously mentioned, reports by federal agencies such as NIJ and the COPS Office and organizations such as the International Association of Chiefs of Police mention the importance of intelligence gathering and data analysis; however, they do not attempt a comprehensive review of law enforcement agencies' efforts in this area. These reports do provide examples, but they are illustrative rather than instructive (i.e., not providing enough detail for replication).

Literature Review References

Chapman, R., Baker, S., Bezdikian, V., Cammarata, P., Cohen, D., Leach, N., Schapiro, A., Scheider, M., Varano, R., & Boba, R. (2002). Local law enforcement responds to terrorism: Lessons in prevention and preparedness. Washington, DC: Office of Community Oriented Policing Services.

Federal Emergency Management Agency. (2000, January). Partnerships in preparedness: A compendium of exemplary practices in emergency management, vol. 4. Retrieved January 23, 2003, from http://www.fema.gov/pdf/rrr/partne rs_v4.pdf.

Federal Emergency Management Agency. (2002, July). Managing the emergency consequences of terrorist incidents: Interim planning guide for state and local governments. Retrieved January 23, 2003, from http://www.fema.gov/pdf/onp/man agingemerconseq.pdf.

Helms, D. (2002, Winter). Closing the barn door: Police counterterrorism after 9-11 from the analyst's perspective. Crime Mapping News, 4(1), 1-5.

Howard, J. (2002, Winter). Incident-level GIS. Crime Mapping News, 4(1), 6-8.

International Association of Chiefs of Police. (2001). Leading from the front: Law enforcement's role in combating and preparing for domestic terrorism. Alexandria, VA: Author.

National Emergency Management Association. (2001, December). Trends in state terrorism preparedness. Retrieved January 17, 2003, from http://www.nemaweb.org/Trends_in _Terrorism_Preparedness/index.htm.

National Institute of Justice. (1999, January). Inventory of state and local law enforcement technology needs to combat terrorism (Research in Brief). Washington, DC: Author.

National Institute of Justice. (2002). A method to assess the vulnerability of U.S. chemical facilities. Washington, DC: Author.

National League of Cities. (2002, November). Homeland security: Practical tools for local governments. Retrieved January 13, 2003, from http://www.nlc.org/nlc_org/site/file s/reports/terrorism.pdf.

Office of Community Oriented Policing Services. (2002). Providing homeland security. Retrieved January 13, 2003, from http://www.cops.usdoj.gov/default.as p?Item=109.

Office of Homeland Security. (2002, July). State and local actions for homeland security. Retrieved January 28, 2003, from http://www.mipt.org/pdf/statelocalh omelandsecrpt.pdf.

Police Executive Research Forum. (2002). Community policing in a counter-terrorism context. Retrieved January 17, 2003, from http://www.policeforum.org/active.h tml.

Police Executive Research Forum. (2002). Terrorism resources: Anti-terrorism and disaster response programs exist for law enforcement. Retrieved January 17, 2003, from http://www.policeforum.org/justtrrs m.pdf.

Riley, K.J. & Hoffman, B. (1995). Domestic terrorism: A national assessment of state and local law enforcement preparedness. Santa Monica, CA: Rand.

5
Foundations of Critical Thinking

Deborah Osborne Loewen

The analyst's most important working "tool" is his or her mind. In this chapter, the analyst will learn something about how the mind works in the process we call *thinking*. This is a basic introduction to the very complex concept of thinking. There is much more an analyst may read and study about this subject. However, many experts agree that reading about thinking skills cannot improve them—only by applying the knowledge gained by reading to real thinking situations can one improve one's thinking.

What is Critical Thinking in Crime Analysis?

The concept of "critical thinking" is like the concept of "crime analysis" in that it does not have a standard definition. For the purposes of this chapter, the definition of critical thinking is adapted from the Army Management Staff College as follows:

> Critical thinking in crime analysis is disciplined, self-directed thinking. It includes recognition of one's strengths and weaknesses with the objective of improving one's thinking processes to conduct better analytical work. [1]

"Critical" thinking can be defined as "indispensable" thinking. This chapter describes indispensable thinking skills—applied skills that are essential to becoming a more effective analyst.

Thinking can be improved by asking good questions. In fact, asking *and answering* relevant questions are the foundations for critical thinking. Critical thinking skills also depend on having an adequate knowledge base: good critical thinkers possess comprehensive knowledge in relevant and multiple subject areas

Thinking
The Brain and Thinking

Thinking is centered in the brain. The brain has two hemispheres, which function differently, yet work in an interconnected fashion.[2] The left brain's functioning is logical, linear, numerical, verbal, and specific. The left brain perceives the parts, the order, the numbers, and the words. It tends to focus on questions of dichotomy (either/or choices) and analyzing the whole into parts.

Left brain thinking is linear, focused on cause and effect. Linear thinking is the foundation of reasoning skills and is the basis of centuries of scientific thought. Another term for linear thinking is reductionism. Reductionism involves breaking down wholes in to parts to study them.[3]

The right brain's functioning is global, non-verbal, emotional, intuitive, and integrative. The right brain perceives the whole, the

---

[1] See R. Eichhorn, "Developing Thinking Skills: Critical Thinking at the Army Management Staff College," Army Management Staff College, http://www.amsc.belvoir.army.mil/roy.html (accessed June 23, 2003).

[2] Studies of injuries to the brain have uncovered the differing functioning of the brain's hemispheres

[3] Fore more information on linear and non-linear thinking, see Tom Czerwinski, *Coping with the Bounds: Speculations on Nonlinearity in Military Affairs* (U.S. Department of Defense, Command and Control Research Program, 1998).

relationships, and the interconnections. It tends toward inclusiveness (this *and* that) and the perception of the whole of a problem or situation and the interactions within the whole. Face recognition is a right brain activity.

Right-brain thinking is non-linear. Non-linear thinking is the foundation of intuition and creative thinking skills. Non-linear thinking is also the basis of systems thinking, a type of thinking that views whole systems (for example, ecosystems, communities, criminal organizations, economies) and the agents within the systems as dynamic, self-organizing entities.[1]

To dissect, name, and explain, we use linear thinking. To see the whole and the possible relationships within, we use non-linear thinking. A holistic approach to crime analysis involves using linear cause and effect analysis models along with non-linear, integrated, global approaches to analysis.

Elements of Thinking

Perception is the beginning of thought. We use our five senses to perceive the world and create knowledge. We process sensory input (sight, hearing, taste, smell, and touch) through use of mental patterns, which are based on prior learning. We classify the sensory input into categories through use of symbols comprised by language. Memory relies on established mental patterns, patterns that are based on subjective perceptions and patterns that are shared collectively by groups of people. Pattern recognition tasks are a central feature of the work of crime analysis.

---

[1] For a layman's guide to systems thinking, see Joseph O'Connor and Ian McDermott, *The Art of Systems Thinking: Essential Skills for Creativity and Problem Solving* (London: Thorsons Publishers, 1997).

Mental models are established thinking patterns that help us categorize sensory input, including new information, into familiar patterns. Mental models are assets that help us categorize and classify information quickly. Since we often use them automatically without conscious awareness, mental models may also interfere in accurately perceiving new situations.

Our **concepts** are dependent on shared definitions of the meaning of words. Errors in thinking are sometimes the result of problems in language interpretation or lack of a common language to express a concept. Clearly defining terms is necessary for quality thinking and communication of thoughts.

Perspective refers to the fact that thinking occurs relative to the thinker. The thinker's perspective is limited by his or her own view. Considering other perspectives is important for developing good thinking skills.

Problems are the precursor to thinking. We have a challenge, something to do or know, thus we think. Simple tasks, such as driving to work, can become automated and relegated to habit, requiring no conscious thought. Yet, if there is a roadblock, the driver has a "problem." He or she must think of an alternate route. Problems are why we think—we think to solve them. Common types of problems are further defined later in this chapter.

Abstraction involves the symbolizing of real persons, places, and things through use of words, labels, visual representations, and numbers. It is important to remember that "the map is not the territory"—the real world can be expressed in words and pictures, and ideas consisting of our symbols, but these are only representations of the real world (more discussion on real-world abstractions are discussed in Chapter 15 on crime mapping).

Reasoning
Types of Reasoning

Logic is based on premises that are known or thought to be true. *Reasoning* is the ability to draw accurate conclusions based on observations and knowledge of causes and effects.

Deductive reasoning involves taking a generally known fact and applying it to a specific fact or specific set of facts in a given situation. It is reasoning from the general to the specific. An example of deductive reasoning is to take a general category of crime, such as burglary, and apply it to a specific incident and then decide that it meets the definition of burglary.

Inductive reasoning involves taking a fact or set of facts about a particular incident and using the fact or set of facts to find a general explanation. It is reasoning from the specific to the general. An example of inductive reasoning is finding a number of individual burglary incidents with similarities and categorizing them as a series—the definition of a crime series being the general fact, the particular incidents of burglary each fitting into that general category.

Abductive reasoning is also known as **inference to the best explanation**, or IBE. Abduction involves inferring causes from effects. An example of abductive reasoning is the analysis of gang graffiti reports and photos combined with analysis of intelligence information and arriving at the conclusion that a specific gang is using graffiti as a method to claim territory in a specific neighborhood.

We use deductive, inductive, and abductive reasoning to come to conclusions. The thought process is complex—generally, we do not use one type of reasoning in isolation

from other types of reasoning.[1] We deal with both general facts (deduction) and specific incidents (induction) in our work, and we seek to explain what causes the findings we discover through analysis (abduction).

In **dialogical reasoning**, we reason by comparing multiple perspectives. For example, we may employ dialogical reasoning through reading different research reports and coming to a conclusion through considering different perspectives. Using dialogical reasoning helps us consider other points of view and expands our awareness of issues. Discussing issues with others is another way to reason dialogically.

In **dialectical reasoning**, we reason by considering opposing views. For example, when we determine that there is a serial rapist in our community, we consider the possible arguments against our conclusion in order to be ready to answer any questions about our judgment. Considering the arguments against a finding helps determine if our conclusions are based on missing or inadequate information, follow incorrect assumptions, or are illogical. Lawyers use dialectical reasoning when arguing cases.

Analogous reasoning involves comparing a situation to a past situation that is similar in some way. One way we reason by use of analogy is to remember situations similar to the current situation and then compare them. Looking at relevant case studies or looking for best practices related to a current problem involve analogous reasoning. Analogous reasoning is one of the reasoning skills used when linking crimes in a crime pattern or series.

---

[1] John Dewey, *How We Think* (Toronto: Dover Publications, 1997), 79.

Using dialogical, dialectical, and analogous reasoning together in our work will improve its accuracy and the depth. If we measure our thinking process and our conclusions with consideration of alternative perspectives and opposing views, as well as by comparing new situations to similar situations, we are apt to improve the quality of our thinking.

Elements of Reasoning in Crime Analysis

Basic elements of reasoning can affect the quality of analytical thought.[1]

An **assumption** is an unstated premise or belief. False assumptions will lead to incorrect conclusions. Valid assumptions simplify our work—we do not have to think about everything we know before beginning our work. For example, we assume that certain crimes are in fact crimes and that criminals behave in certain ways. Examining our assumptions to determine validity and eliminating false assumptions will improve reasoning.

Observation is the act of noticing. Good analytical work involves noticing relationships, noticing contradictions in information, noticing gaps in information, noticing what is significant, and noticing what works.

We engage in input by gathering raw data, information, and knowledge, and create output in the format of information and knowledge. **Raw data** comprises individual, unorganized facts not yet interpreted for

meaning. **Information** is composed of processed data, loosely grouped with relative meaning. Examples of information include statements from officers and victims, news reports, government statistics, and charts, diagrams, or maps. **Knowledge** is interpreted, organized information.[2] An example of knowledge is the in-depth, well written analytical report on a particular crime problem revealing new, actionable information to officers.[3] The crime analyst may be considered a "knowledge worker," as the main purpose of the position is to interpret and organize information for law enforcement agencies.[4]

A **theory** consists of abstract principles, the collection of ideas about observed phenomena. We may come up with our own theories to explain the phenomena we observe. For example, theories about why we have more violent crime in our city, theories about a particular serial arsonist, or theories about why a particular park has become a crime hot spot.

Evidence is the data or information that may prove a conclusion to be true. Since we work in a field where we are not evidence collectors, in many cases we do not have control over the types of evidence gathered. Therefore, most of our reasoning involves inference to the best explanation and is not supported by physical evidence. Yet, processed data provides our evidence: evidence that crime is rising, evidence that specific crimes are occurring in a specific area, evidence that the same victims are being

---

[1] Definitions adapted from Foundation for Critical Thinking, "Critical Thinking Glossary," http://www.criticalthinking.org/k12/k12library/gloss/intro.nclk (accessed March 20, 2004). Richard Paul and Linda Elder gave their permission to use information from their book and Web site in this chapter. See their book *Critical Thinking: Tools for Taking Charge of Your Learning and Your Life* (Upper Saddle River, NJ: Prentice Hall, 2001) for a good critical thinking text.

[2] Wayne W. Reeves, *Cognition and Complexity: the Cognitive Science of Managing Complexity* (Lanham, MD: Scarecrow Press, 1996), 18; also Paul and Elder, 323.
[3] A full discussion of data, information, and knowledge in the crime analysis process can be found in Chapter 1.
[4] See Thomas H. Davenport and Laurence Prusek, *Working Knowledge: How Organizations Manage What They Know* (Boston: Harvard Business School Press, 2000).

targeted, evidence that more narcotics are being seized, and so on.

Relevance is the determination of what is pertinent, or what is connected to the matter at hand. A crime analyst must be able to determine what is relevant when collecting data and information, what types of analyses and products are most relevant in a specific situation or for a specific task, and the relevancy to the audience—who needs what product in what format.

Ambiguity refers to information that has more than one meaning. A tolerance for ambiguity is necessary to avoid misrepresenting the truth. Not everything can be neatly categorized and explained in definite terms. People do not always agree about how the same information should be interpreted. Open-mindedness and acknowledgment of ambiguity (when it exists) are important qualities for crime analysis work.

Analysis is the element of reasoning that involves breaking down a problem into parts and studying the parts. It is the basis of the scientific process.

Interpretation involves placing information in the context of a point of view to give it meaning. For example, what does the rise in robberies mean? To the robber? To the police? To the community? What is the meaning of the association link chart of a drug cartel? Who is in charge of the group? What does the map showing the flow of narcotics up from South America mean? To law enforcement agencies at various levels? To the drug user? To the courts? These examples illustrate the varying context of points of view. An effective analyst will be able to interpret information in various contexts and points of view.

Synthesis is the combining of separate elements to form a coherent whole. The ability to synthesize large quantities of information from a variety of sources and summarize it in a report, map, or bulletin is a hallmark of law enforcement analysis work.

Judgment is to determine authoritatively after deliberation, or to decide after achieving some understanding. When situations are complex and multi-faceted, rushing to judgment is apt to result in erroneous analytical work.

An **opinion** is like a judgment but is open to dispute. There is often less evidence to support an opinion, or the subject area is complicated and open to interpretation from a number of perspectives.

A **premise** is a statement that serves as the basis for an argument. A **syllogism** is a classic form of reasoning in which two premises are made and a logical conclusion drawn from them. For example, the premise *all robbers steal* and the premise *John is a robber* equals the conclusion that John steals.

A **conclusion** is a judgment or decision. Being willing to modify one's conclusions based on new information is a critical thinking strength.

Implications refer to what will be involved or affected. Analysts can reflect on the implications of their work to determine whether the work is meaningful or unintentionally harming innocent persons. If the implications are unduly negative, the work should be re-evaluated.

Evaluation involves deciding if something is valuable. Evaluation is most effective if it occurs throughout the thinking processes, from first question to final answer.

Reasoning Fallacies

There are a number of common reasoning fallacies that can pose problems in the reasoning of a crime analyst. [1]

The ***ad hominem* argument** involves attacking the person (or persons) rather than the idea. An analyst may refuse to believe something because he or she does not like the person presenting the idea. Such a fallacy is also work when, for example, an analyst's work is dismissed by a police officer because the analyst is a civilian.

In the **false dilemma** (presenting either/or choices when there are more choices than two) the audience is given a choice of something being true or not true, when reality often presents us with multiple options. Agencies that fail to implement crime prevention strategies because they don't have enough overtime funds are falling victim to a false dilemma: many strategies do not require officers to work overtime.

Oversimplification is a common reasoning fallacy in crime analysis, as when analysts describe a problem in broad categorical terms ("robbery") instead of specific situational terms ("convenience store holdups").

One might **divert attention from the issue** in crime analysis by blaming one's agency's shortcomings for one's inefficiency in crime analysis.

Appeals to questionable authority involve forming arguments based on theories or ideas from authorities who lack credibility, such as a relative or street officer as opposed to an authority who is recognized and respected as reliable by many.

Confusing "what should be" with "what is" is a reasoning fallacy that involves lack of acceptance of reality and over-idealization. Complaining that high-tech equipment is needed for crime analysis in an agency that cannot afford it would be a reasoning fallacy, because crime analysis can be done without high-tech tools, albeit not as well.

Confusing naming with explaining is a common reasoning fallacy in crime analysis. Listing crimes is merely naming. Explaining the "who, what, where, when, why, and how" of crime is explaining.

Arguments and Positions

One of the biggest challenges in crime analysis is to risk making predictions or identifying problems that may require arguments of persuasion or defense of one's position. To present a compelling argument or take a strong position, one must use good reasoning to support one's conclusion. Visualizing the supporting reasons for a conclusion as the structure of a building holding up a roof may be helpful to use when trying to construct a good argument.[2]

An example of the necessity of knowing how to take a strong position and argue for one's views is when an analyst identifies a crime series and police personnel doubt the analyst's judgment.[3] It is important for the analyst to articulate his or her reasoning

[1] See reasoning fallacy resources at "Stephen's Guide to the Logical Fallacies," http://datanation.com/fallacies/index.htm (accessed March 15, 2004).

[2] For more information on arguments, see Connie A. Missimer, *Good Arguments: an Introduction to Critical Thinking* (Englewood Cliffs, NJ: Prentice Hall, 1990).
[3] A real-life example of this type of situation is provided by Mel Rhamey, "Crime Analysis Success—Fighting the Credibility Battle," in *Introduction to Crime Analysis: Basic Resources for Criminal Justice Practice* by Deborah A. Osborne and Susan C. Wernicke (Binghamton, NY: Haworth Press, 2003), 103–104. Ms. Rhamey identified a serial rapist and had a difficult time persuading her agency that her information was credible.

clearly and explicitly in order to convince others of the severity of the situation.

Creativity

Creativity in thought involves synthesizing ideas from a variety of places to come up with new ideas to answer questions and solve problems. Although logic and reason are the foundations of crime analysis, the tool of creativity is as important.[1]

Effective crime analysts employ reasoning skills while incorporating the creative process when needed. When we imagine how crimes might be related, we use creative thinking. When we design a new database, we use creative thinking. The ability to imagine is the foundation of creative thinking.

Sociological imagination is one tool for creative thinking. It involves understanding history in terms of individuals, and individuals understanding themselves in the context of history and society.[2] To apply sociological imagination, a crime analyst can seek to look at a criminal group or crime problem in terms of historical, social, and biographical contexts. This technique might generate better theories about crime as it occurs in particular places and times, and as it involves particular individuals.

Cross-fertilization is another method of bringing creativity into crime analysis. Cross-fertilization involves learning and applying knowledge and practices from other disciplines. The more we know about other fields, the more we can bring to the creative process. Medicine is a field we may look to; tools such as differential diagnosis might be

adapted to "diagnose" crime problems. Business market analysis techniques might be useful in helping us learn more about markets for drugs and stolen commodities. New computer software helps us be more creative in analyzing and displaying information.

Examples of creative thinking in crime analysis include the development of geographic profiling, based on routine human activity patterns, the application of animal movement algorithms to study criminal movement,[3] the development of problem-oriented policing and problem solving concepts, the creation of interactive crime maps on the Internet, and the development of agency-specific analytical products.

Problem Solving Skills
Problem Identification

It is important to define the problem or problems before engaging in problem solving. Often, the first issue presenting itself as a problem is not the best problem to address. Asking the right questions will help clarify a problem. Larger problems may also have sub-problems. We should analyze problems to be certain that they are relevant to our purposes, and to be more likely to apply the most appropriate problem solving techniques. New problems may surface during a problem solving process—this is not unusual in problems as complex as crime.

When an analyst is using the scientific process, a problem is expressed in the form of a *hypothesis*. A hypothesis is an unproved theory tentatively accepted to explain certain facts. For example, an analyst may

---

[1] A good resource for creative thinking ideas is Roger Von Oeach, *A Whack on the Side of the Head: How You Can Be More Creative* (New York: Warner Books, 1990).
[2] C. Wright Mills, *The Sociological Imagination* (New York: Oxford University Press, 1959).

[3] See Sean Bair, "Geographic Information Analysis: from GIS to GIA; the Science of the System; Applying 'Animal Movement' Analysis Techniques to the Study of Crime." International Association of Crime Analysts, http://www.iaca.net/resources/articles/gis%20to%20gia.pdf (accessed April 22, 2004).

hypothesize that a group of juveniles are responsible for a number of vehicle break-ins at a shopping mall near a high school. This is the "problem." The analyst would likely use scientific methodology—to test this theory, gathering evidence through data analysis, spatial analysis, demographic analysis, and statistical analysis.

Types of Problems

The simplest types of crime analysis "problems" are *requests for information* that can be fulfilled by providing facts without analysis. Lists of crimes, answering questions that involve researching open source information (such as newspapers or online journals), looking up facts—these are the simplest "problems" and are more questions than problems, questions that need obtainable, ready-made answers available through basic reading research.[1]

Another type of problem in crime analysis is *the problem with one answer or multiple but limited correct answers*. It can be addressed by analysis and may require computations and data querying. Examples: What is the crime rate in the city? What is the average distance between the crimes? To what addresses are 911 calls for narcotics activity dispatched in a particular city? Who is committing a particular crime? These types of problems are types that analysts frequently address.

There are the more challenging types of *problems wherein one answer of many must be chosen*. These problems require the use of judgment to select best answers. Example: What area of a particular city should receive extra resources to combat gun-related violence? What tools and techniques should be employed in analyzing the burglaries in a particular jurisdiction?

Another challenging type of problem is *the problem in a multi-answer situation wherein the answer must be designed*. The solutions require synthesis and creative thinking. Examples: Why are these crimes occurring in this neighborhood? How can a particular individual be a more effective crime analyst? These problems are apt to have more than one "right" answer.

Problem Solving Techniques

Using appropriate problem solving techniques will improve the quality of thinking and work. The following problem solving techniques are linear (left brain) techniques.[2]

Analysis, the identification of the components of a situation and consideration of the relationships among the parts, is a linear problem solving technique. An example of analysis is reading the individual police reports in a geographic "hot spot" of burglaries to see if the specific crimes within that hot spot seem related.

Categorizing/classifying is the process of identifying and selecting rules to group objects, events, ideas, and people. An example of this common crime analysis technique would be to create a database of sex offenses by category and classifying the data by elements such as approach method, suspect demeanor, and use of ligatures.

---

[1] See more about problems and problem solving in Morgan Jones, The Thinker's Toolkit: 14 Powerful Techniques for Problem Solving (New York: Random House, 1995).

[2] William G. Huitt, "Problem Solving and Decision Making: Consideration of Individual Differences Using the Myers-Briggs Type Indicator," *Journal of Psychological Type* 24 (1992), 33–34. This article is re-printed at http://chiron.valdosta.edu/whuitt/files/prbsmbti.html. Dr. Huitt gave permission to use his problem solving type definitions for this chapter.

Challenging assumptions is the direct confrontation of ideas, opinions, or attitudes that have previously been taken for granted. An example would be to challenge the notion that a neighborhood in your jurisdiction is a crime cold spot by collecting citizen surveys that indicate the contrary.

Evaluating/judging is comparison to a standard and making a qualitative or quantitative judgment of value or worth. An example would be to compare an agency's crime maps to those of experts in crime mapping to determine if they are equal to or better than the experts' maps and suitable for the intended purposes.

Inductive/deductive reasoning is the systematic and logical development of rules or concepts from specific instances or the identification of cases based on a general principle or proposition using the generalization and inference. An example: reading crime reports and noting a similarity in times and locations of purse snatchings and then inferring that the crimes are related.

Thinking aloud is the process of verbalizing about a problem and its solution while a partner listens in detail for errors in thinking or understanding. To use this technique, an analyst might talk to a trustworthy detective about a recent rash of pocket picking to determine if ideas for deterrence are feasible.

Network analysis is an approach to project planning and management where relationships among activities, events, resources, and timelines are developed and charted. An example of this technique is the creation of an event flow chart depicting the criminal activity and non-criminal activity of a suspected serial arsonist in relation to the arson incidents to determine relationships between crimes and the suspect.

Task analysis is the consideration of skills and knowledge required to learn or perform a specific task. An example of task analysis is the creation of an activity flow chart that explains the general steps of money laundering to better understand and explain the process.

This next group is composed of non-linear (right brain) problem solving techniques:

Brainstorming involves attempting to spontaneously generate as many ideas on a subject as possible. Ideas are not critiqued during the brainstorming process; participants are encouraged to form new ideas from ideas already stated. An example: members of an analytical unit brainstorm to generate ideas about how to best distribute analytical products to the targeted end-users.

Imaging/visualization is producing mental pictures of the total problem or specific parts of the problem. An example is use of a "mind map" to explore the visual relationships of crime problems within your jurisdiction.[1] Figure 5-1 uses a mind map outline to analyze cigarette smuggling. This technique can be used with any problem.

Incubation involves putting aside the problem and doing something else to allow the mind to unconsciously consider it.

Outrageous provocation is making a statement that is known to be absolutely incorrect (e.g., the brain is made of charcoal) and then considering it; hoping to bridge to a new idea. For example, considering "the computer can do all the crime analysis work by itself" might lead to finding ways to automate some crime analysis work.

---

[1] See more about mind mapping in Tony Buzan's *The Mind Map Book* (New York: Plume, 1996). Information on mind mapping and other problem solving techniques can be found at www.mindtools.com.

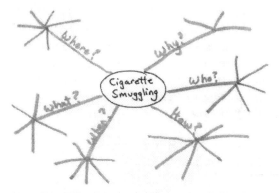

Figure 5-1: A mind map of cigarette smuggling

Overload is considering a large number of facts and details until the logic part of the brain becomes overwhelmed and begins looking for patterns. Example: Reading hundreds of crime reports in a week will lead an analyst to find some patterns.

Random word technique involves selecting a word randomly from the dictionary and juxtaposing it with problem statement, then brainstorming about possible relationships. For example, a random word such as "sky" may be combined with a problem such as gang graffiti—a relationship such as water falling like rain to wash away graffiti might be generated through brainstorming.

Synthesizing is combining parts or elements into a new and original pattern. An example of synthesis is to combine and map data on recovered guns, gun related calls for service, gun possession arrests along with data on shooting victims to uncover new relationships and patterns.

Taking another's perspective involves deliberately taking another person's point of view; referred to as "be someone else." For example, use the word "rape" and think about what it means to a rape victim, a rapist, the husband of a victim, the parent of a victim, the parent of a perpetrator, a defense lawyer, a prosecuting lawyer, and a judge.

Metacognition

The term **metacognition** refers to the self-awareness, self-examination, and self-correction of one's thinking. The ability and inclination to reflect on one's thinking are essential to improving critical thinking skills. [1]

Self-awareness is needed to understand and avoid bias. **Bias** is defined in two ways: a mental inclination or a prejudice. Mental inclinations (also called a mindset) result from personal conditioning. Personal history, personalities and temperaments, education, and social groups influence an individual. Personality, temperament, and emotions affect work habits and work style. Education influences analytical abilities and preferences. Self-examination involves learning how the influence of these variables might affect one's work.

Prejudice involves judging prematurely or unfairly. Its opposite is fair-mindedness. Fair-mindedness is an important trait for a crime analyst. It denotes the tendency to treat perspectives objectively rather than subjectively.

Egocentricity, a tendency to view everything in relation to the self, is natural in childhood but an obstacle to mature critical thinking in adulthood. *Sociocentricity*, the belief that one's own society or social group is superior, is a form of bias. The influence of political groups, religions, and social status influences individual thinking.

Ethnocentricity, a tendency to view one's race or culture as superior, is another form of bias. All persons have bias to some degree. Understanding one's biases is the first step to

---

[1]For a detailed description of metacognition, see Richards J. Heuer, *The Psychology of Intelligence Analysis.* Central Intelligence Agency, http://www.cia.gov/csi/books/19104/ (accessed May 5, 2004).

avoiding or correcting them. One cannot eliminate every bias, because some biases' influences are unconscious.

Groupthink is the tendency of individual group members to be more interested in getting the approval of others than thinking original thoughts that fall outside the group norm. The group may be the agency in which one works or the community of other analysts. In examining one's thinking, it is important to be aware that pressures to conform may limit one's thinking.

Metacognition requires ongoing self-regulation. Self-regulation of thinking involves self-direction, adjusting oneself to a standard, and adjusting oneself to improve accuracy. The ability to correct one's work in light of new knowledge, to admit error, to understand the implications of past and current influences on one's thinking, to welcome evaluation and collaboration—these are important qualities for good critical thinking.

Conclusion

We conclude with a set of questions designed to stimulate thinking and to guide analytical work, as well as to help the crime analyst assess his or her strengths and weaknesses in the critical thinking process.[1] It is up to the individual analyst to decide how much effort to put into improving thinking—improving thinking is possible by having a willingness to grow and by cultivating the ability to reflect on one's thinking. Although engaging in thinking for the pleasure of thinking has value, keep in mind that the fruits of our work must be practical and applicable to the real world. The results of our thinking in the workplace, in the form of analytical products, should be tailored to meet the objective of helping real people to protect real people, real places, and real things.

Critical thinking is an ongoing process—unlike this chapter, it does not end. Continually asking oneself questions about the methods, procedures, tools, and techniques one employs in crime analysis, assessing one's strengths and weaknesses and adjusting oneself accordingly, are central to the critical thinking process in crime analysis.

- What is your motivation for doing the work you are doing?
- What is the purpose of the work?
- Are the task-related problems or issues clearly articulated?
- Are there sub-problems?
- Is there a better problem to work on than the one currently considered?
- What assumptions are you making?
- Has the problem been examined from other frames of reference or points of view?
- Are there issues of personal bias involved?
- Who are the stakeholders? Who will be affected by your work?
- Is there pressure to conform to group thinking?
- What information do you have? What is its quality? Reliability? Validity?
- What information do you need?
- What information is missing? What are the limitations of your information?
- What relevant information is available to fill in your information gaps?
- How may you get the information you need?
- What does the information and evidence indicate?

---

[1] Adapted from Paul and Elder, 139

- Are there alternative interpretations of the data?

- Have you used different approaches to analyze and evaluate the information?

- Is there a better way to do this work?

- Do you need help in areas where you lack expertise?

- What concepts are central to your work?

- Are the theories in use applicable to the situation?

- What are the implications of your findings?

- Do your findings uncover new problems that should be addressed?

- What are the criteria for evaluating your work?

Critical Thinking Resources
Online Tools

A free interactive *Army Critical Thinking Training Module* and links to other critical thinking concepts:
http://www.cog-tech.com/projects/TrainingEvaluation.htm

Mission Critical: A Critical Thinking Tutorial
http://www.sjsu.edu/depts/itl/

Logic Tutor by Michael Green
http://www.wwnorton.com/logictutor/

Argumentation and Critical Thinking Tutorial
http://www.humboldt.edu/~act/

Mindtools: links to a number of critical and creative thinking tools
http://www.mindtools.com

Tools for Improving Your Critical Thinking
http://www.coping.org/write/percept/intro.htm

Stephen's Guide to thinking fallacies
http://datanation.com/fallacies/index.htm

HIDTA Resource

A Distance Learning CD-ROM, titled *So What's Next? Analysis and Critical Thinking*, is available through the National HIDTA Assistance Center at www.nhac.org.

Online Reading Resources

The Foundation for Critical Thinking
http://www.criticalthinking.org

Critical Thinking: What it is and Why it Counts
http://www.insightassessment.com/pdf_files/what&why98.pdf

Promoting Critical Thinking in Professional Military Education: U.S. Air Force Research Paper
http://www.au.af.mil/au/awc/awcgate/acsc/00-058.pdf

Improving Leadership Through Better Decision Making: Fostering Critical Thinking. U.S. Air Force Research Paper
http://www.au.af.mil/au/awc/awcgate/acsc/97-0506.pdf

Command and Control Theory: U.S. Marines
http://www.au.af.mil/au/awc/awcgate/mcdp6/ch2.htm#decisionmaking

Strategic Decision-making in the Information Age: by Lieutenant Colonel Stephen A. Shambach, U.S. Army
http://www.au.af.mil/au/awc/awcgate/stratdm.htm#RATIONALDECISIONMODEL

Training Critical Thinking for the Battlefield: U.S. Army
http://www.au.af.mil/au/awc/awcgate/army/critical/vol_1_research.pdf

PART II
Processes of Crime Analysis

6
Solving Crime and Disorder Problems through Applied Research

Karin Schmerler
Julie Wartell
Deborah Lamm Weisel

Despite technology advances and widespread adoption of advanced crime analysis techniques in the last decade, most people who cause public safety problems still don't get caught by the police. Despite some notable successes, crime analysis has been unable to make a significant contribution to improving overall public safety levels because crime analysts are generally relegated to tracking the ebb and flow of varied crime problems or are used to predict when the next relatively rare, high-profile crime will occur. Yet the potential for crime analysts to reduce crime and disorder problems is quite high, if they are in a position to spend time learning more about why these problems occur and ways of effectively preventing them.

Like police officers, crime analysts have generally focused on detecting individual or serial offenders. This strategy, however, has substantial limitations. Many crimes are never reported, only a small portion are cleared through the apprehension of an offender,[1] many offenders are never prosecuted, and only a few are actually punished. A wealth of

---

[1] Even if clearance rates for crimes such as residential burglary and auto theft—which average in the mid-teens—were doubled, offenders wouldn't be caught 70 percent of the time they commit these crimes.

research suggests that focusing on groups of offenders, victims, places, and on the context of public safety problems can be more effective than traditional policing methods in achieving crime reductions.

To improve the value of crime analysis, attention should be given to addressing three structural limitations of the current crime analysis paradigm:

- Crime analysis relies almost exclusively on police reports of crime while the majority of public safety problems do not involve criminal activity. Typically, fewer than 15 percent of calls for service are associated with Part I criminal offenses (and a large chunk of these offenses are high-volume, lower-level crimes on which analysts rarely focus, such as petty theft).

- Data available for crime analysis are consistently of poor integrity because of missing variables, underreporting, delayed reporting, data errors and reliance on broad crime classifications.

- Analysis of poor quality data produces little insight for police responses. The best that traditional crime analysis can offer is to summarize where and when reported offenses occur, generally pointing police to resource-intensive increased patrols or surveillance rather than more effective responses.

Despite these limitations, experience in applied research suggests that crime analysis has much to offer, in terms of increasing public safety, because analysts can help police understand that crime and disorder occurs in certain predictable patterns, and shed light on ways these patterns can be interrupted.

To better understand and prevent crime and disorder problems, analysts should transcend current data systems and employ applied research methods. These methods include:

- Use existing police data as an exploratory resource to initially identify or categorize specific sub-categories of problems, establishing prevalence and temporal and spatial patterns.

- Through research and local experience, identify key variables that may distinguish problem locations from similar locations without problems.

- Develop tools such as interview instruments and environmental surveys; use them to collect specific information about key contributing variables.

- Develop responses based on findings and monitor results.

Improving Responses to Public Safety Problems

Many police strategies focus on arrest, but most police work is not related to crime. For instance, only four of the top 10 calls for service received by the Chula Vista Police Department[1] in 2002 were criminal offenses and thus cannot be addressed through strategies focused on arrest (see Table 6-1).

As a routine strategy, enforcement is usually not an effective strategy because most crime is opportunistic. For example, nearly 70% of vehicles stolen are recovered, suggesting that most vehicles are stolen for joyriding or transportation rather than for profit. This evidence suggests that the majority of thieves are not high-level professionals and research shows that amateur car thieves—and even some professionals—are easily deterred by anti-theft devices and better security at large parking lots, among other things.

Table 6-1: Top 10 Citizen-Initiated Calls for Service in Chula Vista, CA, 2003

Call Type	Total	% of Total
False Burglar Alarms	8882	12%
Disturbance by Person	3977	5%
Domestic Violence	3692	5%
Traffic Collision	3580	5%
Noise Disturbance	2759	4%
911 Hang-up	2397	3%
Vehicle Theft	2327	3%
Petty Theft	2091	3%
Vandalism	1983	3%
Suspicious Person	1806	2%
Top 10 Total	**33594**	**44%**

Police responses guided by detailed analysis of problems have a track record of reducing crime (often preceded by heavy investments in enforcement with little result). Australia, for example, reduced car theft by 20% in a single year, through the increased use of passive immobilizers in new and used cars. Not all crime reductions related to problem analysis are large scale. Guided by crime analysis, two large shopping malls in San Diego County (CA) have been able to keep auto theft rates significantly below comparable malls in the county through the use of electronic gates at entrances and exits. Other examples of the crime prevention results related to crime analysis can be found at the Center for Problem-Oriented Policing.[2]

What Is Applied Research and Why Is It Important to Crime Analysis?

In crime analysis, applied research refers to the collection and analysis of information beyond the data already captured in existing police databases. Applied research methods include interviews, surveys, observations, and other techniques of collecting data about people and places. Applied research focuses

---

[1] Chula Vista is a Southern California city of 208,000, with a 2002 index crime rate of 4,324.

[2] Center for Problem-Oriented Policing. "The Herman Goldstein Award Projects." U.S. Department of Justice, http://www.popcenter.org/library-goldstein.htm, (accessed February 23, 2004).

strategically on collecting information on variables that can help you understand a specific crime or disorder problem.

In contrast to basic research, applied research focuses on key factors that contribute to specific problems and emphasizes those that can be modified in practical ways, whether through police efforts or other approaches. In contrast to basic crime statistics, applied research is not generic; it can be customized to examine unique features of problems. Applied research can be constructed to compare problem locations to similar locations without problems, for example.

Do You Need an Advanced Degree to Conduct Applied Research?

Applied research does not typically use complex statistical procedures, and does not require an advanced degree. One reason is that sampling is not usually used in applied research; we are often able to collect information from the entire population of concern for many problems. For example, we can identify all the budget motels in a jurisdiction—or at least those within a police division in a very large jurisdiction. This means we do not need to develop a sample or a sampling strategy, as do many statisticians, who use small groups to draw conclusions about much larger groups.

Descriptive statistics are usually sufficient for applied research. The most used statistics are univariate statistics that summarize variables by average or mean, range, percentage or rate, such as the number of thefts per parking spot. Simple multivariate statistics can be used to examine the relationship among multiple variables. Typically, this will consist of a simple table (a cross tabulation) that can be used to examine the interaction among variables we think are related to a particular problem. For example, if we were focusing

on a budget motel problem, we would want to do a cross tabulation on variables such as room price and calls for service.

How Does Applied Research Relate to Other Types of Social Science Research?

Applied research is a type of scientific research that is widely used in the social sciences. In contrast to more well known research methods, such as experimental designs, applied research does not generally reach the level of pure scientific standards because we cannot use techniques such as random assignment of subjects. The major limitation of applied research is that we can't say with certainty that our research would produce the same results in other settings.

Applied research designs are typically either quasi-experimental, in which we collect information to compare one area to another, or descriptive, in which we examine data about one problem or area, often over time.

Quasi-experimental designs are particularly useful for evaluation, as a police response can be enacted and data collected to measure effects in an experimental area compared to a designated control area. The designated control or comparison area is selected to be as similar as possible to the experimental area; in practice, it may be a challenge to find a comparison area but the effort will improve our certainty about the findings. A comparison area can be created by using a before-and-after design, to examine the effects after a response is implemented.

Descriptive designs are most commonly used in crime analysis because they involve passively examining existing data or collecting information about a problem. Descriptive designs are often used to identify and describe observed relationships between variables, such as time of day and burglaries.

The major limitation of descriptive designs is they point only to correlations between variables and cannot explain, with certainty, why those relationships exist. This limitation is not fatal for crime analysis because we can make a reasonable guess that burglaries occur in the daytime because no one is home.

In crime analysis, descriptive designs typically use existing data; applied research, however, involves collecting additional data about variables that are presumed to be related to the problem of interest. Data are usually quantitative or numeric, but they may be qualitative, reflecting information collected through interviews or observations. If the qualitative data are sufficiently numerous, they can often be converted into quantitative data to make analysis more straightforward. If there are only a handful of cases—interviews with five or six offenders—it is not necessary to quantify the data.

The selection of the type of research design to be used is not typically a major stumbling block in crime analysis. In practice, a crime analysis project may use several research designs—a descriptive design may begin with trend analysis of larcenies of gasoline from service stations and lead to a survey of store employees or observation of environmental features. The preliminary findings may lead to a quasi-experimental design in which stations with pre-pay policies are compared to those without pre-pay policies, and this design can even be created after the fact if historical incident data are available.

All research designs should be focused on answering research questions—hunches or hypotheses about why a problem occurs in a particular space or time. When creating research designs for applied research:

- Focus data collection on variables with potential for explanation

- Use data over time whenever possible
- Create or use comparison groups or areas when possible and practical
- Ensure that data are sufficiently numerous to suggest correlations

Why Does Crime Theory Matter?

Crime theory guides the use of applied research. Crime theory explains why crimes tend to occur in certain predictable patterns, and helps you understand what facilitates and inhibits crime. It can also provide you with a number of good ideas regarding the best solutions to specific crime problems. This information, in turn, helps you focus your crime analysis efforts on the lines of inquiry that are likely to be the most fruitful. In addition to helping develop a problem analysis plan grounded in research, crime theories can help you construct surveys, offender interviews, and observation tools.

Opportunity Theory: a Key Crime Reduction Concept

One of the most important crime theories is opportunity theory. A deceptively simple concept, opportunity theory is the idea that the amount of crime that occurs is closely linked to the amount of opportunity for its commission. While the idea is fairly straightforward, most criminologists have traditionally focused their attention on the "root" causes of crime such as poverty.

Understanding these root causes is not particularly helpful to an analyst who is trying to reduce the number of convenience store robberies. In contrast, understanding how the level of opportunity to commit convenience store robberies varies from one store to the next can be extremely helpful in figuring out how to reduce them. In other words, it is more important for police and crime analysts to understand why some persons or places are victimized than to understand why an offender initially became a criminal.

Opportunity theory is a relatively new concept in policing. Historically, policing has focused on deterrence—the idea that offenders will be caught by police and punished. The reality of the justice system is that deterrence is only effective in small settings such as hot spots when the real or perceived risk of detection is *actually* increased and can be sustained for at least short periods of time.

Opportunity theory has practical implications for crime analysts. If we can determine which factors make it difficult to commit specific crimes, we can reduce crime opportunities, and hence, crime itself.[1]

Situational Offending: a Framework for Reducing Offending in Specific Settings

Drawing on opportunity theory, Ronald Clarke developed the concept of situational crime prevention,[2] which is essentially a framework for reducing specific crime problems by blocking specific opportunities during risky times and at vulnerable places. There are four main ways of reducing or blocking crime (and disorder) opportunities:

- **Increasing the perceived effort involved in offending** (e.g., putting locks on brake pedals in cars to make them hard to steal)
- **Increasing the risk of offending** (e.g., installing surveillance cameras at ATMs)

- **Reducing the anticipated reward to the offender** (e.g., putting ink tags on commonly shoplifted items)
- **Removing excuses to offend** (e.g., putting up "No Loitering" signs in areas with drug and prostitution problems)

Understanding how situational crime prevention works can help analysts make crime targets less attractive to offenders.

Displacement and Diffusion of Benefits

Displacement, or the threat of it, has caused many crime analysts to question whether they can really reduce crime and not just move it around to other locations. Intuitively, displacement of crime problems seems likely: wouldn't offenders just find new locations to commit crimes if the old locations were harder, riskier or not as rewarding?

The answer is often "no." A review of more than 30 studies on displacement supports this contention.[3] Locations have problems for specific reasons; offenders don't randomly select them. They are selected because the locations offer ripe environments for crime; these choice settings facilitate or allow crime to occur more easily than do other locations. When displacement does occur, it is generally at a level that is lower than at the original site. The result is a net reduction in crime.

What researchers often find is the opposite of displacement: diffusion of benefits. In study after study, problem-solving efforts aimed at reducing one crime problem have actually resulted in reductions in related crime problems (for example, target neighborhoods have experienced a reduction in commercial burglary and residential burglary, even though the problem-solving efforts were aimed only

---

[1] Marcus Felson and Ronald V. Clarke, "Opportunity Makes the Thief: Practical Theory for Crime Prevention," Home Office, Research, Development & Statistics Publications, http://www.homeoffice.gov.uk/rds/prgpdfs/fprs98.pdf (accessed September 27, 2003).
[2] Ronald V. Clarke, *Situational Crime Prevention: Successful Case Studies* (New York: Harrow and Heston, 1992).

---

[3] John E. Eck, "The Threat of Crime Displacement," *Criminal Justice Abstracts* 25:3 (1993).

at residential burglary). On some occasions, the target problems were reduced in nearby neighborhoods that were not the focus of the problem-solving project.

The Problem-Solving Model

Problem solving, like situational crime prevention, provides a framework for systematically examining crime and disorder problems and developing effective responses. The acronym SARA is often used to describe the four stages of a model used by many crime analysts. They are:

- Scanning—identifying and selecting a problem
- Analysis—figuring out why a problem occurs
- Response—selecting and implementing responses tailored to analysis findings
- Assessment—determining whether the responses worked

The problem solving process is not completely linear; usually, problem solvers move from one stage of the model to the next and back again, as more information about a problem comes to light. Applied research focuses primarily on scanning and analysis, though the data collection methods described below can be often be used for assessment or evaluation purposes as well.

Long-Term Trend Analysis

Analysts perform long-term trend analysis to discover three things:

1. Is there a problem?
2. What is the problem?
3. How much of a problem is there?

Trend analysis should be your first step in analyzing problems; if you have not shown that there is a problem, there is no need to collect additional data, spend time researching other efforts, or survey stakeholders. Keep in mind, though, that what constitutes a problem in one city might be different than in the next. In a small city, three ATM robberies in one month can be a problem (if there are usually zero or one), while in a large city, three ATM robberies would not cause anyone to blink an eye (although 20 in a month might).

What is a Problem?

Although it may seem self evident, the definition of a specific problem is not always obvious. Crime categories are typically far too broad to adequately describe or shed light on problems. When dissimilar events are included in analysis, patterns are masked by the amount of variation within the data. For example, we often track robberies over time but we know there is usually a vast difference between a bank robbery and a carjacking. We often track burglaries, but the distinctions between commercial and residential burglaries—from typical time of day to types of property taken—are also vastly different. In selecting a problem on which to focus, it should generally be a specific behavior (or set of closely related behaviors) that occurs in a very specific location (or group of closely related locations). For example beer theft from convenience stores is a good, narrowly defined problem that can be more easily analyzed and addressed than the general problem of shoplifting.

In this chapter, "disorder at budget motels" is presented as a discrete problem that can be better understood and addressed using applied research methods. This particular problem is referenced throughout the chapter to provide examples of the results of applied research. The problem of disorder in budget motels includes a range of reported offenses and calls for service that do not result in offense reports. In this definition, the problem excludes other types of lodging and is not limited to reported incidents. While this definition is appropriate for many cities, a much larger or smaller jurisdiction might redefine the problem as experienced locally.

Types of Trends

Trends can come in a variety of forms—but what police should be most concerned with are upward, above-average numbers of crimes (or disorder) or aspects of a crime. In terms of long-term trend analysis, an upward trend for at least a month could signal the need for deeper analysis of a problem over a period of not less than six months. If there is a spike in a crime problem during a week or two, this is likely a series of related crimes that can be investigated and dealt with tactically. Although the trend may be an increase in the total numbers of a particular type of crime (the most obvious), analysis could show that the total number of incidents is staying constant but one type of victim or modus operandi may have become significantly more common. For instance, the number of residential burglaries may not have changed over the past year, but newly built single-family home victims may have become a much larger majority.

In general, a trend analysis should answer a number of questions, such as those bulleted below. Depending on the particular problem being analyzed, some questions will be more relevant and valuable than others.

- What is the nature and extent of the problem?
- How many offenses have occurred?
- How many locations or people have been victimized? How many have not been victimized?

- What is the rate of victimization (e.g., the number of auto thefts per 1,000 registered vehicles or the number of auto thefts per 100 parking spots)?
- How do the locations with problems and those without problems compare?
- What proportion of offenses is associated with repeat locations?
- What harms are associated with the problem in terms of costs, injuries, or community perceptions?
- How long has the problem existed?
- When does the problem occur?
- Who are offenders? What percentage are repeats?

It should be noted that the above list is not all-inclusive. Each specific problem will require additional analysis questions to determine trends (see the Problem-Oriented Guides for Police Series,[1] the Herman Goldstein Award projects and other published case studies for ideas).

To Answer These Questions, You Need Data!

Long-term trend analysis typically starts with existing police data. If possible, at least two years of data should be analyzed. The most common data sources used are crime reports, calls for service, and arrests. Others include citations, complaints, field interviews, and databases created for specific purposes. Each is described in more detail below:

Crime/incident reports are generally captured in a records management system (RMS). Traditionally, these systems were designed to collect crime data for the purpose of reporting this information to the FBI's Uniform Crime Reporting Program.

---

[1] Center for Problem-Oriented Policing, "Problem-Oriented Guides for Police Series," U.S. Department of Justice, http://www.popcenter.org/problems.htm (accessed February 23, 2004).

Therefore, many of the older systems do not capture the type of data that is useful for analysis. Useful fields that are typically present in most records systems are *date, time, address where the incident occurred, type of location* (e.g., residence, business), *modus operandi,* victim information, and in some cases a description of the offender.

Calls for service are stored in a computer-aided dispatch system (CAD). CAD data is often overlooked in problem solving and analysis, but can be very valuable. Some high-volume calls (such as noise complaints or alarms) may not be captured in the RMS. In addition, CAD has an advantage over the RMS in that it can help you determine how much time is being spent on a problem.

Arrests, kept in an RMS or a separate system, can illustrate trends in activities that may not be captured by calls or crime reports (drugs, prostitution). Remember, however, that arrests are an indication of police proactivity, and do not necessarily provide a complete picture of the problem. (For a longer discussion about crime reports, calls for service, and arrests, see Chapter 10.)

Traffic citations may be stored in a RMS or separate database. **Complaints** come in two varieties: citizen complaints about officer behavior and complaints about issues in the neighborhood (that may or may not lead to a crime case or arrest). **Field interviews** are extremely valuable but often a lower priority for departments in terms of maintaining the data electronically (and therefore are sometimes of little use for analysis).

Police agencies often create databases for specific needs such as graffiti, gang members, and narcotics complaints. Crime analysts need to find out about these databases (and hope they are created in a format conducive to exporting the data for analysis). Trend analysis of this information might reveal an increase in graffiti incidents in a particular area or by rival gangs.

Other specialized datasets exist in criminal justice and government agencies that can also assist the crime analyst in discovering and analyzing trends. These include databases that contain information on parolees, sex offenders, tax assessments, code compliance, and public housing. Think about the problem on which you are focusing and consider who else might be collecting data related to that problem. If your problem is disorder at motels, is there a motel association or local business group that might be aware of complaints against a particular property?

I Have Lots of Data; Now What Do I Do?

There are many software programs and tools for performing trend analysis. Which ones you use will depend on which question you are trying to answer. Spreadsheets and databases can be used to analyze trends such as time, *modus operandi,* or suspect or victim profiles. Much of this analysis can be done using relatively basic math and statistics. Statistical software packages can be used for some higher-level analyses, such as distribution. Spatial and temporal patterns and trends can be analyzed using a geographic information system (GIS). See Chapter 15 for more information about GIS.

Initially, you want to look at total numbers, rates (be sure to use the most relevant denominator as discussed in Chapter 10), and averages over time. These basic analyses can be done for the problem as a whole as well as aspects of the problem (e.g., time of occurrence, victim profile).

Let's go through an example, using the problem of disorder at budget motels.

How many calls for service, crimes, and arrests occurred over the last three years at all budget motels, by month? How much time are police spending at the motels? What is the rate of police activity per number of motel rooms? (Is an eight-room motel that generates 10 calls per month worse than a 50-room motel that generates 12 calls per month?). What types of crime and disorder calls are occurring? Which motels had the majority of the police activity? What time are most of the problems occurring? Who are the offenders? Besides age, sex, race, how about residents of the city or out-of-towners? Are the problems occurring inside the rooms or in the parking lot? How long has the motel problem been occurring?

Although this list is not complete, it gives you a basis for identifying trends on which you might want to focus further analysis and potential strategies.

How do I Present All This Information?

There are three types of products that can be used to present the information that you have generated with your analysis. They are tables, figures, and maps. (An explanation and tips on how to best present these products can be found in Chapters 16–19). Returning to our motel disorder problem, one output might be the chart in Figure 6-1.

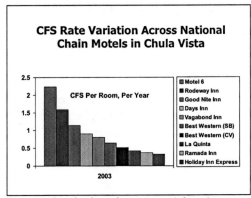

Figure 6-1: Sample column chart to present information

This chart shows the variation in the number of calls for service per room for 10 national budget motel chain properties in Chula Vista.

In reporting on your trend analysis, there are a number of things to consider: 1) Focus the problem as specifically as possible; 2) Know your audience; 3) Ensure you have used accurate and timely data; and 4) Don't stop with existing data and trend analysis tools—this is only the first step.

Background Development

What Experience Have Others Had with the Problem?

Once you have used readily available police data to establish that a problem exists, to identify how much of it there is, and to discover the overall trends in the problem, you can begin to craft a research plan that will help you delve more deeply into the problem. Rather than reinvent the wheel, you will want to know what experience others have had with the same or a similar problem. Often called a literature review or a background search (see Chapter 4), this initial investment of time and effort can save you much time in your research. The results of this inquiry will allow you to focus the rest of your problem research and crime analysis efforts.

What Type of Information Should I Look For?

As you begin to look for information, take note of what you already know or think about your problem. Then you will be able to collect pieces of information about the problem that either conflict with what you already know or think, or support or validate what you know or think. These concepts will frame questions about your problem that must be answered to find the best response.

During your investigation, use the following six goals to organize information:

1. Identify important sources of existing non-police data that could shed light on your problem. For instance, chambers of commerce have data about motels and hotels, rooms, occupancy, and rates

2. Identify key variables that illuminated someone else's problem—or justified a particular response, such as

   a. A large local clientele

   b. Many long-term guests

   c. A high number of visitors, especially those on foot

   d. The level of access control

   e. Use of the property by prostitutes

   f. The price of lodging

   g. Number of code violations or complaints

3. Identify variables that can be used to specify and test hypotheses, such as:

   a. Local guests are most apt to engage in problem behavior at motels; this suggests you need the home addresses of motel guests, possibly from a register, as well as calls for service information

   b. Motels with unimpeded vehicle and pedestrian access to rooms attract problem guests; this suggests you need to observe property and record data on physical features

   c. Cheap hotels attract problem customers, suggesting you need rate and calls for service information (see Figure 6-2)

   d. Motels with long-term guests cause more problems; this suggests you need data about length of stay and numbers of guests from all motels

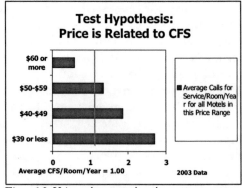

Figure 6-2: *Using a chart to test hypotheses*

4. Identify key interest groups or stakeholders, such as hotel/motel organizations, code enforcement, licensing boards, or chambers of commerce. In particular, take note of:

   a. What data or information may these groups have about the problem?

   b. Business licenses indicate number of customers and occupancy limits

   c. Tax records indicate motel income

   d. Motel registration logs show length of stay and residence of customers

   e. What role might these groups take in resolving the problem?

   f. What is their legal responsibility for the problem?

   g. What is their ability to influence the problem?

5. Note key differences between your own problem, or between problems examined by others

   a. Different types of problem motels— budget, tourist, business, and others

   b. Different population characteristics such as size, density, transportation routes, or crime rates

   c. Unusual factors, such as proximity to international borders or military bases, large tourist areas, high youth population, or sporting events

6. Ideas for potential responses. While you should be cautious about getting prematurely attached to someone else's response, you can get terrific ideas from others. Later, you will look for data that will support the need for a response or suggest that a particular response would not be effective.

So Where Do I Look for Information?

Searching for information can be a daunting experience because there is so much available. You'll want to streamline your search to save time. In general, consider that there are six primary sources of information:

Academic Journals. Journals contain scholarly writing about research on topics related to criminal justice or criminology. Journals contain published information about research projects that have been evaluated or met reliable standards of scientific accuracy. For many readers, journal articles may be dense and difficult to read. Nonetheless, there is much valuable information in them and a few tips may improve their usefulness. To be most efficient:

- Search for articles published within the last two or three years.

- Most articles contain an abstract or summary of the research. Read this to see if the article relates to your problem.

- Review the references included in every journal article. Academic references are usually very thorough and you may use this technique of "snowballing" to find even more useful articles.

- Most journal articles summarize prior research on the topic.

- Avoid spending too much time on the "Methods" and "Analysis" sections of the journal article. The conclusion or discussion sections will be more useful.

One of the best sources of information about journals is *Criminal Justice Abstracts*, a quarterly publication that provides summaries about recently published articles. Unless you have a subscription to this publication or on-line access to it—which we advise—you will need to visit a library to search this source. You can also try to obtain journals directly: a listing of academic journals is available through the American Society of Criminology. Many of these journals will be available in the library of your local college or university; many are available on-line through such libraries and you may be able to use dial up access to download the full-text.

Specialized journals are often available that contain articles about your specific problem. For example, *Security Management* or the *Journal of Travel Research* may provide more information about budget motel problems than *Criminology* or *Police Quarterly*.

Research Monographs or Reports. One of the best places to find recent research on public safety problems is through the National Criminal Justice Reference Service (NCJRS) Web site. This Web site includes both abstracts of recent research (and many academic publications) and the full text of many government-funded research reports. It is usually helpful to search the abstracts first by using key words in the subject line and reviewing the abstract. Then you may search the full-text database by the reference number, or look elsewhere for the document.

In addition to ncjrs.org (mentioned above), the Center for Problem-Oriented Policing, supported with funds from the Office of Community Oriented Policing Services

(COPS) of the U.S. Department of Justice, has a useful Web site. This site contains valuable information on specific problems, descriptions of problem-solving efforts by police, and links to other criminal justice information. For example, this site provides a detailed description of a police department's efforts to reduce motel-related problems. This site also contains the Problem-Oriented Guides for Police, which provide information on responses to specific problems that have been effective in other communities.

POP Guides: The Best Place to Start

The *Problem-Oriented Guides for Police* series offers analysts one-stop shopping for the most useful background research on a wide variety of common crime and disorder problems. Each guide synthesizes the best available research on the causes of the focus problem, and also provides a blueprint for effectively analyzing and responding to the problem. To date, 20 guides have been published on such topics as drug dealing in privately owned apartment complexes, auto theft in parking facilities, and burglary of single-family homes. Ultimately, 50 guides will be produced and available through the Center for Problem-Oriented Policing at www.popcenter.org. A full listing of guides can be found at the end of this chapter.

The Home Office in the United Kingdom is roughly the equivalent of the Department of Justice in the U.S. The Home Office produces a great deal of information about problems faced by police. Although the Web site's search engine can be unwieldy and take a bit of time, this is often a valuable Web site.

Using an internet search engine, such as Google, may lead you to valuable information. Be specific to avoid paging through too many "hits" that just waste your time. For instance, a Google search with the terms "motel," "crime," and "police"

produced nearly 60,000 hits. But if you add "prostitution" and "visitors," the search yields fewer than 700 hits with several highly relevant and informative publications and news articles in the first seven listings.

Newspaper, newsletter, or magazine articles. Many popular periodicals and publications for practitioners provide descriptions of public safety problems. These publications include *FBI Law Enforcement Bulletin* and *Police Chief* as well as general magazines and newspapers. Typically, these articles are fairly general and will not provide the detail necessary for background research.

Books. A few books have current and useful information about crime prevention. For example, the Crime Prevention Studies series, published by Criminal Justice Press in Monsey, NY, has a wide range of information on situational crime prevention. While chapters may not address every problem with respect to our example of budget motels, there is much information about the effect of lighting, target hardening, and other information related to protecting properties. Textbooks rarely have useful information about public safety problems.

Other police departments. Occasionally, other police departments can be a valuable source of information for gathering very general information. Typically, you will want to minimize the amount of information you collect from other police departments, as it is time consuming and often lacks the rigor associated with other data sources.

How Should I Look for Information?

Primary sources of information include:

Libraries. Libraries, especially university libraries, contain indices (such as Criminal Justice Abstracts), books not elsewhere available, access to many electronic databases and journals, and physical copies of many journals. In particular, librarian assistance is usually readily available and invaluable.

Electronic searches. Internet searches for Web sites and public information are quick ways to search for information. However, such searches may link you to unreliable or useless sources. Unless you have a subscription to indices or publications, many sources will not be available electronically, although some can be purchased.

Calling around or posting messages on electronic mail lists. Contacting other police departments may be useful if you want to learn more about a particular response. However, this may be time consuming, and it does not guarantee reliable information.

Since electronic searches can be time consuming, you may want to decide at the outset how much time you will allot to this task. An exhaustive search may take more time than you have available. As you search, keep detailed records of where you gathered useful information—note important publication information, such as title, author, publication, date, and page numbers.

How Do I Organize Data Collection?

Following your trend analysis and background research, you are ready to plan the collection of data that doesn't currently exist or is not readily available. In this endeavor, you should focus on efficiently collecting data that will answer questions about your problem. Data collection is generally a linear process and these tasks should be organized so that each task can inform and more tightly focus the next task.

Each data collection task should answer one or more important questions about the

problem. Asking and answering these questions comprise the "analysis" plan and allow you to schedule data collection based on the research method you employ. In general, you should collect the most easily available data first and save time-consuming data collection tasks for later so that more difficult tasks can be as specific as possible. Thus, you will first use existing police data and then collect secondary data from other organizations (such as code violations). The next step would be to conduct an environmental assessment or observations, and lastly, interview offenders and victims, or conduct surveys.

Your data collection or research plan can be organized into a chart form, as shown below. Table 6-2 provides an example that you should modify to fit your own problem. It is a handy tool for reminding yourself and others of what needs to be done and why. The table organizes the information that confirms what you know or think about the problem, and shows what empirical evidence—weak or strong—supports the assumption. By pointing to weak data, the table suggests alternative or additional data that could be collected. However, one must consider what value the data would have if you collected them. For example, from additional data collection, we may learn that budget motel guests are low income, perhaps welfare recipients. Could this information help us frame a response? If we don't plan to prohibit poor people from securing overnight lodging, learning about their income level may not be so important. On the other hand, if we were to learn that budget motel guests are often criminals—have outstanding warrants, or are probationers or parolees—we may be able to develop an effective response that invokes the "handlers" of these types of problem guests based on this information.

Table 6-2: Sample Analysis Table

What we think or know to be true	How we know it	Specific questions that when answered will confirm or disprove what we think
Poor management practices contribute to problems	Police knowledge Research	What practices are used by motel operators with few problems and many problems?
Historical problems with certain budget motels	Police officer experience Citizen complaints Convention and Visitors' Bureau	How long and how much of a problem is there across the range of overnight lodging in the community?
Budget motels attract troublemakers	Police experience Low room rates Arrest data	If not price, what attracts offenders to the property?
Budget motels with crime problems are deteriorated properties	Police experience Code enforcement experience	What is the nature and scope of code issues at problem properties?
Troublemakers are local residents and long-term guests	Police experience Demographic data on clientele Arrest data	Are troublemakers local residents? How many guests have been staying at problem and non-problem motels for more than 30 days?
Law-abiding guests often victimized by troublemakers	Police experience Call data weak because of underreporting	How much and what type victimization occurs?
Nearby residents often victimized by troublemakers; fearful	Police experience Call data weak because of underreporting	How much and what type victimization occurs?
Problem motels have little control of ingress to property; visitors to motel customers cause problems; poor lighting	Police experience	What is the physical layout of problem and non-problem properties? What are the visitor policies at problem motels?
Police have responded with "john" stings, traffic stops, extra patrols and surveillance; limited effectiveness, problems recur	Arrest data Call data	Is there a relationship between police-initiated CFS and citizen-initiated CFS?

"What we know and what we need to know"

Information needed to answer these questions	Data Source or Method of Collection	Implications for response
Management practices CFS at each property	Manager interviews CAD	Set expectations regarding motel management practices and CFS levels; Provide training, ensure compliance
CFS at each property for at least three years Number of rooms at each property to calculate CFS per room ratios	CAD, mgr. interviews, or telephone requests for number of rooms, or Internet listings of number of rooms	Compare calls at different motels; suggests motels should more responsibility for reducing problems
Pricing information Perspective of motel users on motel reputation/ benefits of use	Manager interviews, or telephone requests for room price, or Internet listings of room price Offender interviews	Suggests some motels are known by "troublemakers" – could publicize new policies to target groups such as parolees, navy personnel, students, or truck drivers
Prior code violations Current code violations	Code enforcement records Code inspections	Use code compliance to improve quality
Home address of motel offenders Guest length of stay	Arrest records Offender interviews Guest registers	Management practices should vary for short-term stays and local residents
Victim experiences	Surveys of guests using guest register	More victimization could justify abatement/civil action against motel
Resident experiences and opinions	Neighborhood/business surveys	Citizens could encourage changes in management practices, and support threat of civil action
Environmental features of motel properties Visitor policies and the level of adherence to these policies	Environmental survey Manager interviews Surveillance	Situational crime prevention techniques suggested
Citizen-initiated CFS split out from officer-initiated CFS	CAD	Traditional tactics/ enforcement alone are not effective; may combine with other responses

Methods of Data Collection

Applied research involves collection of primary data about the problem; information that is often easily available but that has generally not been collected.

Primary data collection tools and techniques include the following:

- Surveys
- Interviews
- Focus groups
- Environmental surveys
- Observations

These methods can be classified as collecting information from places and collecting information from people. The following two sections describe these approaches.

Collecting Primary Data From Places

Environmental Surveys

Both criminological theory and evaluated research projects have shown that the environment plays a large part in either facilitating or controlling crime. For this reason, environmental surveys are an important tool in analyzing a crime or disorder problem. There's no substitute to a first-hand observation to get a true feel for why a certain location has problems. (Plus they, and other primary data collection efforts, can be a lot of fun, especially if you don't have a lot of other opportunities to get away from your computer!)

There are three main types of environmental surveys:

Assessments of physical and social features. Recording the physical features and other aspects of both problem and non-

problem locations, such as the amount of visible litter, enables you to see if there is an association between specific property variables and the level of crime or calls for service generated by the property. Conducting environmental surveys such as these can produce statistically significant correlations between variables that help explain why a problem occurs at some properties and not others.

With respect to budget motel problems, the results of this type of environmental survey have been very useful. A survey conducted in Chula Vista, California, found strong positive correlations between calls for service rates and pedestrian accessibility to the property. The more freely pedestrians can come and go from various directions, the more calls for service. This finding fits closely with the situational crime prevention technique that recommends making it harder to access problem locations. Another finding of the survey was that having a pool on motel property is a risk factor for high calls for service. Again, crime theory can provide likely explanations and support for this finding. If a pool is inoperable, it is a clear sign to potential offenders that there is a lack of capable guardians at the location; if it is operable, the motel is probably more apt to be a social destination that attracts boisterous people than motels without pools.

CPTED surveys. These instruments typically comprise a checklist of physical features that are generally known to affect crime and disorder. Examples of such features include sufficient lighting and natural surveillance, the presence of low-growth landscaping or fencing that can prevent or inhibit illegitimate users of the space from easily trespassing; and basic security measures, such as door chains and locks. In essence, CPTED surveys are used to identify obvious problems in the layout, design, appearance, or physical security.

Safety audits. Sometimes used as an adjunct to CPTED surveys, safety audits involve users of the property in identifying locations that feel unsafe or are cause for concern. Like CPTED surveys, the audits should be done both during the day and at night, as perceptions of safety often vary by time of day, as do lighting needs. Safety audits are conducting by walking around a property with a group of people, led by a trained observer, who asks pertinent questions about the property. In the case of a motel project, the trained observed might ask the group what sections of the parking lot they would avoid and why, where they would prefer to be assigned a room and why, and what path they would take to walk from point A to point B, among other things.

Observations

Watching a problem location for a while can give you a great sense of who uses the space and in what ways; this, in turn, provides important clues regarding the nature of the problem and responses that may be effective. Recording your observations, either in writing or through the use of videotapes or photos, can also provide compelling evidence about the nature and volume of problem behavior at a property to those not able to personally visit the location.

To illustrate, let's return once again to the budget motel problem. An analysis of calls for service to motels would probably not be particularly enlightening regarding the nature of the problem. As mentioned earlier, the most frequent call to motels generally relates to a disturbance of some sort. To get a better handle on the character of the problems at motels in Chula Vista, officers observed four properties. Two had high calls for service

rates, one had a moderate call rate, and the last generated very few calls. Officers conducted their observations in undercover vehicles posted at strategic locations on the properties. They worked from a series of bulleted items that would provide richer detail on the property users that were thought to be markers of specific problems. Officers logged the license plate numbers of all people entering the premises in vehicles; recorded subject descriptions; counted the number of people who came onto the property on foot; noted suspicious behaviors, such as loitering; and watched to see which areas of the parking lot or sections of the motels seemed to attract problem people.

These observations confirmed that one of the worst motels had a significant drug problem, based on the fact that more than 90 percent of the traffic at the property was on foot. They also demonstrated that the best motel provided lodging to people engaged in a variety of suspicious behaviors, but because the people were relatively discreet or a predominantly legitimate clientele diluted their behaviors, problems at that property did not translate into high calls for service rates. Finally, the observations confirmed that the other high call for service property was a veritable free-for-all, with a substantial portion of the users approaching the motel from all directions, heading to party rooms, and cruising the parking lot.

Tips on conducting observations:

- Watch places in 20-minute increments over a series of representative time periods (weekdays vs. weekends; night versus day).

- Try to be relatively unobtrusive.

- Use a simple protocol (for a motel problem, this might include bullets that remind observers to look for people loitering, record license plate numbers, and so on) and a site map to record information.

Collecting Primary Data from People

Interviews

Talking with people provides some of the best insight into why a problem is a problem; this understanding, in turn, increases your chances of developing effective, long-term responses to problems. In some cases, interviews or focus groups are the only way you can determine the dynamics of a particular crime problem or confirm your suspicions regarding how things work (or don't work) with respect to a focus problem.

To illustrate, let's continue with the example of a budget motel problem. Your background research on the problem indicates that good motel management practices are among the most effective ways of maintaining safe, orderly properties. However, it is sometimes difficult to convince motel managers and policymakers that motel personnel—not police—have the greatest ability to reduce crime problems. Your best bet in this situation would be to interview motel managers about their business practices and then see if there is an association between certain business practices and motels with high calls for service. (In Chula Vista, high call levels were positively correlated with the average length of stay by guests, a practice that can be curbed.) How is the best budget motel run and how does that contrast with the worst? If you can confirm locally what is known or suspected to be true generally, your case on behalf of improved management changes is stronger.

In the case of a budget motel problem, interviews with managers will yield other benefits. You will learn:

- How widespread problems are at the motels—since most motel problems don't rise to the level of a crime, much problem activity is never reported to police

- How much variation there is with respect to management practices across motels

- More about the concerns of motel managers and the specific practices they have found to be most effective at reducing problems

- How interested managers of problem motels are in working with you to address issues of concern

Interviews, as opposed to written surveys, would be the best method for obtaining information from motel managers because they allow for in-depth, structured discussions of sensitive issues with a relatively small group of people. Interviews also allow you to clarify questions that could be misinterpreted, which could be particularly helpful if you expect communication difficulties due to language barriers.

Interviews can be very time-consuming, however, so it's important to reserve them for the most important players—those stakeholders with the most critical information on the causes of the problem, typically place managers and offenders. In the case of a motel problem, managers have the broadest view of motel operations. They can provide the perspective of motel owners, who have the ability to make significant changes, but are also in touch with the day-to-day operations of the motel, including guest screening and security policies.

It's important to keep the interview instrument as short as possible. Interviewees usually can only spare so much time and often become restless after about 20 to 30 minutes of questioning, if not sooner. In Chula Vista, researchers used a seven-page form to interview motel managers that was on the long side, in part, because little background research was available to inform the instrument's development. Future versions of the survey could be considerably reduced, based on the most relevant findings from the first administration. (Note: if interviews are known to be crucial elements of your analysis plan, it may be more cost-effective to combine the administration of environmental surveys with interviews of place managers.)

An example of a much shorter interview instrument administered by officers in the field to gain a different, but critical, perspective on problem motels is a motel user interview (see Figure 6-3). The purpose of the motel user interview was to determine how risky a motel's clientele is, and why high-risk guests and visitors patronize that particular motel—questions that could help us convince property managers to make changes and also help us figure how to make the problem motels less attractive to undesirable guests. To this end, the field interview included questions about the motel users' criminal justice status (whether they were on probation or parole, registered sex offenders, or narcotics registrants). It also asked motel users to describe the reputation of the motel and state their second and third choices of motels if their first choices were

Motel Name: MOTEL 6 **MOTEL SURVEY** 0455

1. Are you a Guest ☒ Visitor ☐ Neither ☐ ________ explain
2. Have you rented here before? Yes ☒ No ☐ How many times? 5-6
3. Have you visited here before? Yes ☒ No ☐ How many times? 1-2
4. What's the main reason you rented or visited here?
   Price ☒ Accommodation ☐ Reputation ☐ ________ explain
   Location ☒ TROLLEY explain Other ☐ ________ explain
5. How much did you pay? $ 50.00
6. Are you on Probation ☒ Parole ☐ Offense NARCOTICS
7. How did you hear of this place? Friend ☐ Advertisement ☐ On your own ☒
8. Gender: Male ☒ Female ☐ Age 20 Race: B ☒ W ☐ H ☐ As ☐ O ☐
9. City of residence: SAN DIEGO If you're just visiting, is the guest local? Yes ☒ No ☐
10. If you/guest is local (SD County), why staying at a motel? TRANSIENT
11. How did you get here?
    Trolley ☒ Car ☐ Cab ☐ Bicycle ☐ Walked ☐
12. Officer's reason for contact? Radio Call ☐ Observation ☒ Citizen Flag ☐

Figure 6-3: Chula Vista's Motel User Survey

booked. The purpose of this question is to predict and avoid displacement of problem motel activity if the "best" motels from the offenders' perspectives are cleaned up.

Focus Groups

Like interviews, focus groups are excellent ways of collecting in-depth information from key stakeholders in a problem, but they differ from interviews in several important ways:

- Key stakeholders are questioned as a group
- The discussion often stems from questions that may be more loosely constructed than formal interview questions
- The discussion is more free-flowing than structured interviews; tangents are not totally forbidden, if they identify new areas that should be explored
- The information collected is qualitative instead of quantitative

Focus groups can be used as follow-ups to large surveys, to delve more deeply into topics that do not lend themselves to multiple-choice answers. They can also be used to identify issues about which you may want to survey a larger group. For example, in the case of a motel problem, focus groups might be used to identify concerns of residents and businesses adjacent to problem motels, their perceptions of the motels, or their personal experiences with motel users. Police officers are also great sources of information about crime and disorder problems, and may prefer to share their knowledge in more casual settings, such as focus groups.

Tips on conducting focus groups for analysis purposes:

Select people who are at least somewhat knowledgeable about the crime or disorder problem in question and have somewhat similar backgrounds or perspectives (e.g., keep neighbor focus group separate from business focus group)

- Work with groups of seven to nine people
- Develop between five and seven bullet points for discussion
- Keep the discussion moving
- Try not to let one person dominate; formally seek input from all participants if necessary
- Aim to complete a focus group in a little over an hour

Written Surveys of Stakeholders

Surveys are particularly useful when you:

- Would like to know what large group of people (for example, between 50 and 500) think or know about a specific crime or disorder problem
- Want to be able to generalize findings from a large group of people to an even larger group of more than 500 to tens of thousands of individuals (however, this is rarely necessary when using applied research used to address crime problems)
- Need straightforward answers to simple questions, particularly relating to personal experiences with the focus problem (e.g., "during the past month, how often have you heard loud disturbances in the motel parking lot")

In the case of a motel problem, several groups of people might be surveyed: neighboring residents and businesses, community members-at-large, and members of citywide business and hospitality groups.

The different groups of people surveyed could provide various perspectives on the level of concern about the problem, identify which aspect of the problem is most bothersome to them (e.g., lack of safe, clean lodging in the city; the effect of run-down motels on real estate values of nearby properties; the effect notorious motels have on a city's image and ability to attract major events; thefts perpetrated by motel guests and visitors; or loud disturbances).

Because conducting written surveys can be both time-consuming and expensive, you should only employ this data collection method if you think it will provide critical information on the nature and scope of the problem. If you are far enough along in your analysis of the problem and familiar with responses that have worked in other, similar settings, the survey can be constructed to identify potential responses that might be acceptable to a large percentage of respondents. For example, respondents could be asked whether they would support a stronger business licensing program for motels, and abatement of the very worst properties.

Tips on conducting surveys:

- Field test the instrument to make sure people understand the questions
- Use close-ended questions
- Encourage the people being surveyed to respond via the Internet, if possible; Web-based surveys require no postage or data entry

Volumes have been written on such issues as question construction and instrument design, survey sampling, and other topics relevant to large surveys. For those interested in the finer points of conducting surveys, two of the best resources available on problem-solving surveys are *A Police Guide to Surveying Citizens* and *Their Environment*, and *Conducting Community Surveys: A Practical Guide for Law Enforcement Agencies* (see Recommended Readings).

Other general interview, focus group, and survey tips:

- Interview subjects or survey respondents should be informed whether the information they provide will be kept confidential, and if not, who will have access to it.
- Explain how participating in the interview or survey process will help them or their neighborhood
- Offer incentives for participating in the process
- Start with easy, non-threatening questions
- Generally, it's a good idea to place the more sensitive questions near the end of the instrument, at which point, the interviewees may be more comfortable with answering questions. Or, if they refuse to answer or continue, most of the data has already been collected.

Conclusion

Applied research bridges the gap between academic research and practice, providing information that police agencies can actually use to prevent crime and disorder. Its mechanisms are learnable by most crime analysts with little formal training. Applied research exercises the analyst's creative mind and often gets him or her out of the office and into the field.

Many of the chapters in this book offer techniques and tactics that focus on "tactical crime analysis" (see Chapter 1)—on apprehending the serial or pattern offender. While these techniques are an important part of the crime analyst's tool set, it is the analysis and response to long term problems, using applied research methods, that offers crime analysts the greatest opportunity to prevent the most crime and disorder.

Recommended Readings

Clarke, Ronald V. and John Eck. *Become a Problem-Solving Crime Analyst in 55 Small Steps*. London: Jill Dando Institute of Crime Science, University College London, 2003. http://www.jdi.ucl.ac.uk/publications/manual/crime_manual_content.php.

Eck, John *Assessing Responses to Problems: An Introductory Guide for Police Problem Solvers*. Washington, D.C.: Office of Community Oriented Policing Services, 2001. http://www.popcenter.org/Library/RecommendedReadings/Assessing%20Responses.pdf.

Eck, John and Nancy LaVigne. *Using Research: A Primer for Law Enforcement Managers* (2nd ed.). Washington, D.C.: Police Executive Research Forum, 1994.

Eck, John, and Nancy LaVigne. *A Police Guide to Surveying Citizens and Their Environment*. Washington, D.C.: Bureau of Justice Assistance, 1993. http://www.popcenter. org /Library/RecommendedReadings/Surveying%20Citizens.pdf

Felson, Marcus., and Ronald V. Clarke. *Opportunity Makes the Thief: Practical Theory for Crime Prevention*, Paper 98. London: Home Office, 1998. http://www. popcenter.org/Library/RecommendedReadings/Thief.pdf

Problem-Oriented Guides for Police Series. Washington, D.C.: Office of Community Oriented Policing Services, 2001–Present. [See box for full listing.] http://www.popcenter.org/default.htm

Schmerler, Karin and Mary Velasco. "Primary Data Collection: A Problem-Solving Necessity." In S. Bair et al (ed.), *Advanced*

Crime Mapping Topics: Results of the First Invitational Crime Mapping Symposium. Denver: National Law Enforcement & Corrections Technology Center, Crime Mapping and Analysis Program, 2002. http://www.nlectc.org/cmap/cmap_adv_topics_symposium.pdf

Weisel, Deborah Lamm. *Conducting Community Surveys*. Washington, D.C.: Office of Community Oriented Policing Services, 1999. http://www.popcenter.org/Library/RecommendedReadings/Conducting%20Surveys.pdf

Problem-Oriented Guides for Police Series
http://www.popcenter.org/default.htm

Problem-Specific Guides

Acquaintance Rape of College Students
Assaults in and Around Bars
Bank Robbery*
Bomb Threats*
Bullying in Schools
Burglary of Retail Establishments
Burglary of Single-Family Houses
Check and Card Fraud
Clandestine Drug Labs
Crimes Against Tourists
Cruising*
Disorder at Budget Motels*
Disorderly Youth in Public Places
Domestic Violence*
Drug Dealing in Privately Owned
    Apartment Complexes
Drunk Driving*
False Burglar Alarms
Financial Crimes Against the Elderly
Graffiti
Gun Violence Among Serious Young
    Offenders
Identity Theft
Loud Car Stereos
Mentally Ill Persons
Misuse and Abuse of 911
Open-Air Drug Markets*
Panhandling
Prescription Fraud*
Problem Drinking Among Young
    People*

Rave Parties
Robbery at Automated Teller Machines
Robbery of Taxi Drivers
Sexual Activity in Public Places*
School Break-ins (vandalism, burglary,
    arson)*
Shoplifting
Speeding in Residential Areas
Stalking
Street Prostitution
Street Racing*
Student Party Disturbance on College
    Campuses
Thefts of and from Cars in Parking
    Facilities

Problem-Solving Tools

Forming and Sustaining Partnerships
 with Businesses*
Using Offender Interviews to Inform
    Police Problem-Solving*
Repeat Victimization*
Researching Problems*

Response Guides

Crime Prevention Publicity Campaigns*
The Benefits and Consequences of
    Police Crackdowns
Closing Streets and Alleys to Reduce
    Crime*
Video Surveillance of Public Places*

*In production/future guides

7
Data Integrity

Dan Helms
Sean Bair
Noah J. Fritz
Steven R. Hick

Data is the basis for all analysis.

Data integrity is universally critical, because *every part of the analytical process that follows depends on the data on which it is based.* Crime and police data have always contained huge flaws, ranging from missing data to misleading data, typographical errors (typos) to redactions, even substandard English writing problems. Since the proliferation of desktop geographic information systems (GIS) in the latter 1990s, analysts have increasingly begun to *notice* the flaws in their data.

The overwhelming majority of crime analysts begin every day with the same vital chore: they download data from records management systems (RMS), computer-aided dispatch (CAD), and several other sources to get the day's job done. Most then take that data into a GIS application to make points appear on a map, using a process called "geocoding." Those records that do not geocode automatically must then be processed interactively to make certain they find a place on the map. If the majority of the records are represented on our maps—say 80-90%—we claim, "good enough for government work," and begin the analytical process. Everything that results from our work from this point forward will be limited by the quality and accuracy of this process.

Invariably, this process isn't perfect—and, therefore, all our analysis will also be imperfect. This is because the data we begin with will inevitably contain flaws. Data containing flaws that make it unreliable or unusable are called, "Dirty Data."

It is vital that we thoroughly and completely know and understand our data—with particular emphasis on flaws and weaknesses that might contaminate later analyses. We should also know how to clean our data to help reduce or eradicate these weaknesses. Although the chore of managing and cleaning data is thankless, mind-numbing, and only attractive to the most masochistic of crime analysts, it is absolutely unavoidable. This chapter will discuss how to identify and eradicate the most prevalent of data integrity issues before they disrupt or taint your analyses. We will also present suggestions to help you perform this vital task in the most efficient and least painful way.

Why is Data Integrity Vital?

Nowhere is the quality and accuracy of data more important than in law enforcement. Some of the ways in which dirty data can affect police work include:

- **Misrepresenting Problem Addresses**: Analysts may calculate the frequency of repeat addresses to determine the most problematic locations in their cities. Patrol assets may then be deployed to focus on this problem.
- **Spatial Analysis**: Points may be drawn at the wrong place. This means that the calculations of distance, direction, movement, and density will all be wrong. Many analysts study hot spots—this is impossible with dirty data.
- **Spatial Statistics**: An erroneously geocoded point could be associated to a polygon in which it doesn't belong, so choropleth maps (area symbol or multi-colored area maps) will be incorrect.

- **Missing Points**: Data that fail to geocode will result in failed analysis.
- **Search Errors**: The misspelled name of an interviewed suspect may not return when queried in a database.

Most of the examples provided in this chapter will center on crime mapping and spatial analysis data problems; however, it is important to remember that all types of data and all data usages are subject to data integrity errors. Examples include incorrect assignment of crime type based on call for service information, assigning new information to the wrong person in a database due to a one-digit mistake in Social Security Number, or a misspelled name.

The phrase "good enough for government work" should have no place in the analyst's lexicon. When dealing with life-or-death decisions, affecting millions of dollars of assets and the safety of thousands of citizens and officers, anything less than perfectionism is absurdly unprofessional. The attitude that "eyeballing" or getting "close enough" is acceptable for the police analyst is a dangerous conceit that may lead to serious problems for the analyst and the agency that promotes it. We're all familiar with the phrase "garbage in, garbage out." But how much attention do we really pay to this phrase? Is it our analytical creed? If not, why not?

What Is Dirty Data?

Although crime mapping (the use of a GIS to perform spatial analysis of crime and police activity) is only one part of the analyst's inventory, we will focus at first largely on the effects of dirty data on crime mapping. In particular, we will discuss how dirty data can influence the process of geocoding.

Most analysts first notice their dirty data, and gauge how bad it is, through geocoding. They rely on GIS applications to take dirty data and find where it exists on a map. One's geocoding score, called the "hit rate," often gauges the level of success. A score of 80-90% is often thought of as desirable for law enforcement. That is, 80-90% of the data are represented on the map, and only these data will be analyzed. Many agencies consider much lower scores "acceptable."

Even if an agency somehow attains a 100% hit rate, it does not follow that the data is clean. How can an agency that achieves 100% geocoding accuracy—a perfect score—still have unclean data? After all, aren't the points all on the map? Sure, we can see all the "dots"—but how do we know they are where they are supposed to be?

Also, even if data is clean enough to geocode, it may still be too dirty for other analytical purposes. Let's take a look at an example of "perfect" data that still has serious problems. Below are seven CAD records of police calls. The calls all occurred at the same location—123 E MAIN ST.

Address
123 E. MAIN ST.
123 E MAIN
123 E MAIN ST
123 E MAIN ST
123 E. MAIN ST
123 E. MAIN ST.
123 E. MAIN ST. #1

Let's begin by visually examining these addresses. Can you see the differences? Are there any duplications? In fact, although each record describes the same location, they are all actually unique. Some distinctions are obvious, such as the "#1" at the end of the seventh record. Others may be difficult to detect. Can you see the difference between the third and fourth records? To the eye, they appear identical, but the fourth record has an extra blank space at the end. The reader can't see this, but to a computer trying to analyze the address, it's an important difference.

All these cases found their mark on our map—that is, we achieved a 100% geocoding hit rate. Since 100% is perfect, this is clearly good enough for us, isn't it? Now we can begin our analysis. Our first order of business is to create a proportional symbol map—a map whose symbol size increases with the frequency of data. In this case, we should expect to see 123 E MAIN ST have a point representative of seven occurrences. Unfortunately, it doesn't—in fact, we will have seven points on top of each other at that location, each representing one unique address. Our data, although 100% geocoded and spatially accurate is fundamentally flawed—it is dirty. Each of these records contains small differences that make it unique and distinguish it from the others. It may be as simple as a punctuation mark, an extra space (which might be overlooked by the reader), or the addition of an apartment number. But they are different. When our analysis is performed, the results are only as good and reliable as the underlying data. If the data contains flaws, so does the analysis. We *must* first clean our data.

Certainly every agency has dirty data, and these problems absolutely must be resolved. The process of correcting data integrity errors is called "data cleaning" or sometimes "data scrubbing." Data cleaning (as we will refer to it throughout the article) is the process of taking tabular data and correcting mistakes before being used for analysis. Errors typically originate from keyboard entry, Optical Character Recognition (OCR) scanning, voice recognition software, ScanTron Forms, and field entry devices such as hand computers and Global Positioning System (GPS) units.

There are three sources of dirty data, depending on how the data was corrupted or weakened in the first place:

1. **Origination Errors,** which occur when the data is collected or transcribed
2. **Management Errors**, which occur when the data is stored
3. **Retrieval Errors**, which occur when we query or download data to analyze it

Each of these generates problems due to different problems in the process of handling data, and must be corrected differently. Let's examine each class in turn:

What Are Origination Errors?

By far the most universal problems that result in dirty data occur during origination, when the data is first collected, or whenever the data is transcribed from one system (such as a paper report) into another (such as an RMS database).

So, what do origination errors in data look like? Typical data errors include:

- Empties
- Typographical Errors
- Punctuation
- Abbreviations
- Omissions
- Aliases
- Malapropisms
- Generalizations
- Invalid Entries
- Extraneous Errors

Let's briefly discuss each of these:

Empties occur when an entire data field is null, or empty. This error usually cannot be "cleaned" away—there's simply nothing there to work with. However, empties can sometimes be overcome by either finding the data in a different field (the "Address" field in a police report might be blank, but the "Narrative" text might contain the necessary information), or by researching (calling up the officer or reporting individual and obtaining the necessary data).

Typographical Errors (or **Typos**) occur when keystrokes aren't what the operator intends. A common typographical error is transposition of characters; another is skipping characters. For example, instead of "1000 E UNIVERSITY DR," typographical errors might change the text into "UNIVERSTIY," "UNVERSITY," or "UNIVESITY." This could be a particular problem if the resulting typo might look like a correct entry—what if the "DR" in the above address was transposed? It would read "1000 E UNIVERSITY RD" which looks correct—worse, it might be a valid (but wrong) address itself. This sort of error is extremely tough to catch. This category includes honest mistakes—when the entry clerk actually thinks that "City Hall" is at "100 S Main St" when it's really at "102 W First St."

Punctuation errors occur when punctuation marks are used when they should not be, or excluded when they are expected. These include ".", ",", "#", "\", "/", quotation marks, apostrophes, "@", "-", "&", and so forth within the address field. These characters are often used to mark direction (E.), the indication of a suite or apartment number (1 E. MAIN ST. #A101), the use of place names ("123 E Main St @ Mall of America"), and are often the delineation between intersecting streets (E UNIVERSITY DR/S RURAL RD or UNIV&RURAL).

Abbreviations are used to shorten words, thereby decreasing the time and effort

necessary to enter them into a data table. This is particularly true in law enforcement RMS and CAD systems, where dispatchers need to type an address as quickly as possible in order to dispatch an officer to a location. Most often these abbreviations appear in the form of acronyms or other truncations of the proper full word. For instance, "1234 E. Vista Del Cerro Dr." was almost never seen typed into the Tempe Police Department's RMS system properly. Instead, it was entered "1234 E. VDC," "1234 E. Vista D.," or "1234 E. Vista Del C.," or worst yet, simply "VDC." The latter was because most often the officers knew that "VDC" represented the only apartment complex on that small strip of road.

Omissions (or **Blanks**) result when necessary data elements are erased or, more likely, not entered in the first place. This often occurs when the person entering the data intentionally or carelessly "skips over" a piece of data he or she considers useless or extraneous. One common example is street direction. The difference between "1005 W University Dr" and "1005 E University Dr" is more than two miles. However, the clerk entering an address from a crime report may skip over the directional element, because it seems extraneous—resulting in "1005 University Dr." This error can be compounded when street types are excluded as well: "1005 University." All of these addresses will probably geocode—that is, we can usually make a "dot" appear on our computer map. But will the dot be in the right place? Most GIS software will *guess* at that direction and street type, and it often guesses wrong. The result is flawed analysis.

Alias Errors result from the use of names and phrases that make perfect sense to a human being, but are useless to a computer. For example, the "Mall of America" may have an address of "123 E MAIN ST." If we type in the correct address, "123 E Main St," our GIS will geocode it correctly. But crime reports are seldom written for computers; they are written for people. The address will probably use the common place name instead of the correct physical address: "Mall," or, even worse, "MOA."

Malapropisms, more simply **Malaprops** or **Mals**, occur when the data is not the expected format or information. For example, instead of "123 E MAIN ST," the writer might enter "Behind the fence," or "100 yrds S/B from vacant lot." This type of error can be as difficult to clean as an **empty**.

Generalizations are data errors that are similar to common place names; they occur when, instead of recording a specific location, the reporter or data entry clerk enters a broad location. In law enforcement, by far the most common example of this is the use of "hundred blocks" in address fields: "1200 BLK W UNIVERSITY DR." A person reading this will know that the event took place somewhere between 1201–1299 W University Dr., and this may be good enough for most practical purposes. However, once again, our computers can't make any sense of this. Even if our computer does somehow convert this into a valid physical location, it will almost certainly be wrong, particularly if during the interactive phase of geocoding the user always selects the first, and lowest, closest address—a common practice. Now you have assigned all those hundred block addresses to the lowest address on those street segments. That's not accurate, is it?

Invalid entries look like correct data, but are not valid. For geocoding purposes involving address data, the most common type of invalid entry is the non-address. Non-addresses are addresses that look and sound like real physical locations, but which are actually invalid. An example of this error

might be "1000 W UNIVERSITY AV." Although this address is correctly formatted, contains no place names, nulls, abbreviations, or typos, it is still wrong—because there simply is no such place. The 1000 block of west University Avenue begins at 1001. The physical address listed as "1000" just doesn't exist. Once again, our computer will interpret this as a valid address and draw a dot on our street centerline map layer where it thinks this address should be. But in fact, since there really is no such place, the dot is of course in the wrong place.

Extraneous errors occur when extra data is entered into a field that should contain only limited data. This often happens in address fields in police records, especially dispatch records. Many RMS providers, as a matter of practice, allow a dispatcher to search for an address both by physical address and common place name. A dispatcher may type "123 E. Main St" which is at the "Mall of America" or he or she may type, "Mall of America." Either way, the RMS system will verify this location via a CAD geo-reference file and update the address field with the proper address. Often this "proper" address field will contain the common place name as a "feature" (e.g., "MALL OF AMERICA@123 E. MAIN ST." or "123 E. MAIN ST@MALL OF AMERICA").

Another type of extraneous data error occurs most often when dispatchers type in an address and unthinkingly use the remaining address field space for additional information. Common redundant data include suite or apartment information or related data about the call (e.g., 1005 W UNIVERSITY DR 2 X HMA RED P/U TRUCK AZ PHX-138 or 1005 W UNIVERSITY DR #1234). All these data much be cleaned from our address for valid and reliable analysis.

What Are Management Errors?

Management errors arise from how we store our data—usually in the form of computer data files, but not necessarily. Hopefully, our recordkeeping processes have been well thought out, and we won't be too troubled by data management errors; but all too often, police agencies are plagued by these easily-solved problems. Don't let these common data management errors happen to you:

- Record Truncations
- Field Truncations
- Field Conversions
- Physical Corruption

Record Truncations occur when a database or file system can't hold all the data that's been put into it, resulting in some records being deleted or not accepted. Although it may sound idiotic, this error is amazingly widespread in crime analysis. The biggest offender, by far, is the Microsoft Excel spreadsheet program; it's such a big problem that it deserves some separate discussion.

Many crime analysts choose for a variety of reasons to create Excel spreadsheets to keep records of crimes. Often these are typed (increasing the chance for data entry errors) by the analyst (arguably a waste of an expensive resource to perform a lower-level task); others prefer to download or import data from an RMS database into a spreadsheet. Spreadsheets in general, and Excel in particular, are widely used by analysts because they are seen as being extremely powerful and also very, very easy to use. Unfortunately, these programs do not duplicate the full power of a real database (See Chapter 18); Excel has a low record limit of only 65,535 lines. If the analyst loads more than 65,535 (65,536 if you don't have a header row) records into an Excel

spreadsheet, only the first 65,535 records are kept—the remainder is excluded and the analyst is never told this by the application. It's astonishing how many agencies think they've had 65,535 calls for service each year; and also 65,535 crime reports, and 65,535 known offenders. Quite a coincidence.

Make certain that your data repository has enough room for all the data you intend to store in it. Legacy databases (older systems from the early days of police computers) are notorious for falling short in storage capacity.

Field Truncations occur when specific fields aren't long or detailed enough to hold the information that's placed in them. The most common offenders are usually simple text fields. For example, the field "Address" might be 30 characters long, meaning it will hold up to 30 characters of text. This might be enough for most addresses, but when the writer enters "S TROPICANA AV & W MARTIN LUTHER KING JR BLVD" all that gets stored is the first 30 characters: "S TROPICANA AV & W MARTIN LUTH" and nothing more. This can also happen in numeric fields and date fields.

Field Conversion errors happen when data is changed from one type into another type. This usually occurs when we transfer data from one system into another electronically using some kind of automation. For example, a date field might inadvertently be converted to a numeric field, causing unpredictable changes in the resulting values. A numeric field might get converted into a string (text) field—it would look the same to the user, but now mathematical functions might not work as expected against that data. Some numeric data types have limits on how big their values can be, or how precise (in decimal places) they can be; unless the converting user is intimately familiar with the nuances and subtleties of data types and how to properly convert values, this kind of error may arise, unknown to the user, any time data is downloaded or imported from one application to another. Given the fact that most analysts still perform this kind of operation every day, this is clearly a potentially serious problem.

Physical data corruption is often forgotten in the modern, computerized workplace; however, it is still a source of many basic problems. Physical corruption occurs when the physical record containing the data is damaged or misplaced. This happens when a handwritten report falls into the crack behind the desk. It happens when a stack of Field Interview Cards is held up by interagency mail delays. It happens when a typist spills coffee on the report he's about to enter into the RMS. It can also affect computer storage products. We might like to pretend that in our new "virtual world" of information technology, we are independent of physical limitations, but that's clearly not true yet. Computer hard drives crash—regularly. Backup tapes can be misplaced, mislabeled, or stepped on. Floppy disks can be easily damaged. CDs and DVDs are susceptible to light, heat, scratching, and moisture damage.

It is essential that physical security of our virtual data be maintained by backing up databases, and ensuring the safety and operational lifetimes of the backups, which should be made redundant whenever practical.

What Are Retrieval Errors?

Some data errors may arise when the analyst retrieves information; even though the source data is accurate and reliable, the resulting search, query, or reporting functions can often lead to problems. In general, retrieval errors are identical to management errors— they include truncations and conversion errors. If the process of retrieval requires any data entry (such as "augmenting" fields downloaded from an RMS by adding an analytical synopsis), then the new entries are also subject to origination errors.

How Can Data Errors Be Overcome?

There are three ways in which data errors can be overcome. They can be avoided, repaired, or compensated for.

Avoiding data errors means not allowing them to occur in the first place. This is typically accomplished through policy and training, usually together.

Regular and quality training ensures that data entry personnel understand what it is they are entering and develop the necessary professional competence to perform at a satisfactory level. Although often denigrated as low-level and low-pay work, data entry is the basis of all that we do as analysts—it is therefore essential that our data entry be performed in as professional and thorough a manner as possible. It is important to distinguish exactly who is responsible for each step in the "chain of custody" for your vital police data. A typical data chain of custody looks something like this:

1. Victim
2. Officer
3. Records Clerk
4. Database Administrator
5. Crime Analyst

Errors introduced at each link of this chain will usually persist through all subsequent links. In other words, if the victim gets something wrong (e.g., lies about his name, forgets his phone number), the officer will usually get that wrong too, and so will everybody else after her. If the officer misunderstands what the victim is reporting and writes down the wrong information, the records clerk who later types that report into the RMS will seldom catch and correct the mistake. This cascade effect means that it is usually best to clear up errors as early in the data collection process as possible. We could introduce measures to help avoid errors at each step of the process:

1. **Victim**—Train officers on interview skills to make sure they get the correct information.
2. **Officer**—Practice good recordkeeping skills to ensure thoroughness, good spelling, good grammar, and so on.
3. **Records Clerk**—Make use of verification tools, learn to self-check quality, and so forth.
4. **Database Administrator**—Make certain the database is large enough and detailed enough, and thoroughly backed up and maintained.

Policy is the other factor that must be taken into account to avoid data errors. Many police agencies have tools such as address verification software, but don't mandate its use because it's unpopular. This attitude is understandable, but also unacceptable. If officers are never held accountable for their incomplete, inaccurate, and illegible reports, data errors are inevitable. Sergeants should regularly perform quality control on the work of their officers. Supervisors should regularly audit data entry specialists.

To make policy change effective, it's essential that the crime analyst—who is probably the only person at the police agency who understands and cares about the drawbacks of dirty data—gets everyone in the data chain of custody involved in the process. He or she should demonstrate to those responsible for producing and maintaining source data how vital it really is.

A good example occurred at the Las Vegas Metropolitan Police Department. At that agency, officers produced large volumes of Field Interview Cards every day. These cards, however, were often unusable due to the high percentage of blank fields, incomplete values, or illegible printing regularly used by the officers. Why did the officers do such a bad job of filling out FI Cards? Why bother to fill them out at all, if they would only do it so poorly? The answer was that patrol sergeants required their officers to fill out a certain volume of cards (hence the high number being produced); however, once a card was filled out, it was dropped in an inter-departmental mail envelope and never seen again. There was no system in place for officers to ever look up their own, or anyone else's, FI Cards. In other words, these cards were useless to the officers, who consequently didn't waste their time or effort making them good. Once a system was introduced to allow officers to query FI Cards, however, and the value of well-written FI Cards to actually solve crimes and find criminals was demonstrated by a few successes, the officers realized that the data was useful. Quality improved immediately, and has remained consistently high, because the persons primarily responsible for collecting and producing the data also use it.

Avoiding data errors is the most efficient way of overcoming them; however, a certain number of data errors are basically inevitable. Repairing the errors enables the analyst to overcome errors after they occur, but before they become a problem.

Repairing errors in source data is called data cleaning. This process is fairly straightforward, but like many simple concepts gives rise to much complexity, and will be treated in a later section.

The final way to overcome data integrity problems is to compensate for them. This method is by far the weakest and least desirable way to cope with data errors; it is commonly used by crime analysts.

Let's face it: cleaning data is boring, time-consuming, and difficult. Avoiding data errors in the first place requires training and policy—two things that few crime analysts can control. Therefore, the path of least resistance for the typical analyst is simply to compensate for errors he or she can identify.

Probably the most common example of compensating for dirty data without either attempting to avoid or repair it is the use of "alias tables" in GIS software.

An alias table converts a known erroneous address into a valid, matchable address: "City Hall = 400 E Stewart Av," or "3250 S Trop = 3250 S Tropicana Blvd." The technique of using alias tables is attractive to most crime mappers, who usually measure their success by their geocoding "hit rate"—a misguided if understandable standard. Implementing an alias table often radically improves hit rates and puts more dots on the map, which most would agree is a good thing. Unfortunately, there are still serious problems—the data is still dirty, we haven't repaired the damage; we've merely put a Band-Aid over it this one time. Tomorrow, the same record will cause the same problem. Furthermore, by bringing alias tables into our data preparation routine, we've added another level of complexity to our data—not only must our source data be precise, we now have to take the time and effort to manage an alias table, too.

Compensatory techniques like alias tables only work when the analyst is aware of the mistakes—in other words, she or he needs to know exactly what problems cause the data to be dirty, and what steps need to be taken

to fix it. Given this fact, it seems obvious that the analyst should take the tiny amount of extra effort required to actually clean the data, rather than just "cope with it."

There is a fourth way to deal with faulty data, in addition to avoiding, repairing, and compensating: the analyst can opt to ignore the faults. This is never acceptable, but it is also very prevalent.

Who Should Clean Data?

The simplest answer is, "everybody." The most common answer is, "anybody but me!"

Responsibility for data cleaning is an organizational issue that the agency must plan and enforce. It makes the most sense for those responsible for maintaining the data to ensure that it is clean and reliable. In most police agencies, this is the Information Technologies staff or the Records Unit.

In the absence of any organizational plan and enforcement, however, it is the crime analyst who must take responsibility for data cleaning. Though not part of an ideal crime analysis job description, it is, in the end, the analyst who most cares about the quality of the data that he or she uses.

How Can We Clean Our Data?

Data cleaning consists of a series of discrete operations. Each operation eradicates one problem. We just have to make sure we have enough operations in our list of cleaning operations to take care of all our problems—and, very important, that our cleaning operations don't result in creating more, different problems.

The overwhelming majority of data cleaning operations are basically "search and replace" functions. Most of us are already familiar with this type of function from software applications such as word processors, spreadsheets, and the like. Essentially, we look for instances of an error, and replace the erroneous text with correct text. The two elements of any data cleaning operation are the fault (the error we're searching for) and the fix (what we replace it with). Some simple examples include:

Fault:	Fix:
TRPCANA	TROPICANA
LVBS	S LAS VEGAS BLVD
CCDC	CLARK COUNTY DETENTION CENTER
CITY HALL	400 E STEWART AV
AVE	AV
ROAD	RD
BVD	BLVD

The idea is simple. Now, how do we go about doing it? There are three approaches to actually performing data cleaning operations: *Manual*, *Semi-Automatic*, and *Fully Automatic*.

Manual data cleaning consists of a human operator searching through records, spotting instances of errors, and replacing the faults with valid fixes. The advantage to this method is that the human operator will seldom make any additional mistakes by making this change; there will seldom by any unintended consequences that could cause trouble later on. The disadvantages, however, are many. This method is painfully time-consuming, and therefore very expensive in terms of work time; it is very slipshod, because human beings simply can't visually scan through thousands of records and spot every little flaw. Indeed, as we have seen, some flaws are literally invisible to the human eye (such as extra spaces at the end of a word). This approach is highly discouraged, except for rare occasions involving very exceptional errors or very low numbers of records (a couple of dozen, no more).

Semi-Automatic data cleaning is more widely used. This consists of the human operator using an automated function, such as the "Search and Replace" feature in Microsoft Excel, to quickly perform an individual operation. Unfortunately, this method is actually the weakest of the three. Although less time-consuming than the fully manual method, it still requires the analyst to manually type in fault/fix options and perform each operation, which takes time. Moreover, the operator can easily forget a step, or perform an operation out of sequence, causing potentially severe problems. Even though it still requires the operator to spend time, it doesn't even have the relatively feeble advantage enjoyed by the manual approach that the human operator's own judgment in applying fixes avoids unintended consequences.

Fully Automatic data cleaning is more rare, but increasingly popular, and is the strongest approach for most users. This method consists of preparing a list of fault/fix operations ahead of time, which are then followed in order by a completely automated set of search and replace actions. This method, like the semi-automatic approach, can result in unintended consequences (which we'll describe later). The cleaner must take great care when preparing the list of tasks and establishing their proper order to avoid unintended consequences; however, when properly created, this method is by far the fastest and most efficient.

The Many-Headed Hydra of Data Cleaning

The basic premise of data cleaning—take a known "fault" and replace it with a valid "fix"—is very simple; unfortunately, it's *deceptively* simple. If the analyst isn't extremely careful, cleaning one error can result in many more. This is because cleaning operations can often have unintended consequences that can be disastrous later on. These consequences occur when a given cleaning operation affect data other than that intended by the user (over-inclusion), or fail to clean all the targets intended by the user (under-inclusion).

Here's a simple example of over-inclusion: dispatchers in Las Vegas regularly abbreviate the names of streets. "Desert Inn Rd," for example, is often abbreviated "DI" rather than spelled out. Since "DI" is not a valid street name, all calls and crimes located on this street do not geocode—addresses such as "3101 S DI," "4505 DI," and "DI/TROP" will not match up. The obvious solution, of course, is to replace "DI" (the fault) with "Desert Inn Rd" (the fix).

Unfortunately, this pleasingly simple operation gives rise to numerous errors. Every time the search and replace function finds the letters "DI" together, it replaces them with "Desert Inn Rd." This means that valid addresses that contain these characters get changed. So, "1450 S Indian Springs Rd" is turned into "1450 S InDesert Inn Rdian Springs Rd"—we've taken a perfectly good address and screwed it up. That's an unintended consequence of over-inclusion.

How can we correct that problem? In the example above, we could use the technique of Padding, which means adding one blank space onto the beginning and end of a text block. We could pad the fault string to look for " DI " (see the difference? There are blank spaces before and after the word). This way, we would only find instances where the letters "DI" occurred by themselves. Problem solved.

Whoops! This technique, however, gives rise to the other kind of unintended consequence: Under-inclusion. When we restrict our search to " DI " (the padded text), this will only

identify addresses where "DI" occurs by itself with a space at the beginning and the end. So what about addresses like "3250 S DI"? This address is seriously flawed, but it won't get fixed because there is no terminal space after the "DI" fault, so it doesn't match exactly. If we're going to pad our faults, we also need to pad our fixes and also our target strings—that is, we need to add a blank space to the beginning and to the end of every string before searching it. Then we need to remember to strip them off when we're done.

And what about the flawed text, "DI/TROP"? That's the intersection of Desert Inn Rd and Tropicana Blvd. Our technique of padding the faults, fixes, and targets still doesn't work: " DI " does not occur in " DI/TROP " even when we've padded them, because the slash separating the two parts of the intersection doesn't have a space beside it. This is the sort of problem that crops up all the time? How can we fix it?

The answer is to perform several cleaning operations in a sequence. In the example above, we would first perform another cleaning operation to space out the elements of the intersection. We would replace "/" with " / " (that is, pad the fix but not the fault). This would separate the street names with a space from the delimiting character, the slash mark. This is getting complicated!

So, to clean the address "DI/TROP" without corrupting other addresses, we need to perform three cleaning operations, and in a specific sequence:

Fault:	"/"	
Fix:	" / "	
Result:	DI / TROP	

Fault:	" DI "	
Fix:	" DESERT INN RD "	
Result:	DESERT INN RD / TROP	

Fault:	" TROP "
Fix:	" TROPICANA BLVD "
Result:	DESERT INN RD / TROPICANA BLVD

Even these simple steps aren't perfect: intersections containing a "/" mark that already has spaces around it will now have two spaces around it. We have to clean up after that, too.

There is simply no way that every type of problem and factor influencing qualitative data cleaning can be addressed in this small chapter. Make no mistake, these are deep waters, and the crime analyst will need to develop and practice data cleaning skills just like any other professional requirement, such as learning to use a GIS or perform time series analysis. Data cleaning might not be as interesting as forecasting a crime series, but forecasting a crime series is impossible without clean and complete data.

Rules of the Road

Although there is no way we can offer all the information required to master data cleaning in this tiny space, we can certainly give a few pointers. The following rules will help ensure that data cleaning doesn't end up costing you more than it benefits:

1. Never clean source data—always use a copy.
2. Never replace numbers with other numbers.
3. Don't fix a problem with another problem.

Automation

As we've seen, fully automatic data cleaning is probably the most efficient approach for most agencies to take. But how can it actually be implemented?

There are three possible solutions: off-the-shelf, homegrown, or ad hoc.

An **Off-the-Shelf** data cleaning product offers professionalism and customer support; however, it may require an initial outlay of money. Be certain to carefully examine and evaluate a product before purchasing it to ensure it meets your requirements.

Homegrown data cleaning applications are programs written by someone at the local level, usually your agency's IT staff. This is a widely-used solution; many agencies develop in-house applications to clean their data. The advantages are that support is local and the product will be tailor-made to your specific needs. The drawbacks, however, are that the support is often weak (what happens when the "computer dude" who wrote the program for you gets transferred or fired?), and it is often highly time-consuming to build and to maintain. The cost in terms of salary to develop an in-house application is usually higher than buying something off-the-shelf.

Ad Hoc data cleaning applications are macro-type automations written at the local level, often by the crime analyst. Ad-hoc solutions usually employ macro automation technology, Visual Basic for Applications (VBA), or another macro builder such as Arc Macro Language (AML). This method is widely used because almost every crime analyst has macro-enabled software already available (such as Excel, a highly popular choice, as is Access, or even ESRI's ArcView). The analyst then develops the application herself by writing the necessary macro elements. Depending on the skill of the analyst, this can be a very effective solution. The advantages are that the analyst herself is in control of the elements of the program. One disadvantage is that the analyst is probably not going to be a very good program developer. Many crime analysts know enough to write a macro in Excel—but not enough to do it very well. In addition, the only future support for such an ad-hoc product is the analyst, so if the analyst is sick, or transferred, the product won't be supported any longer, making it a dubious choice for a police agency as a whole.

A well-written cleaning application, whether created internally or purchased from a vendor, should not have its cleaning parameters "hard-coded" in the application. It should be adaptable, able to remember its functions, procedures, and cleaning parameters. Macros are inflexible and contain hard-coded operations. Applications are typically (and hopefully) far more flexible. There should be no need for the user to know or modify the actual code that performs the cleaning.

Conclusion

Crime analysts often make two basic mistakes with regard to data integrity. The first is to ignore dirty data or treat it as somebody else's problem. The second is to take aggressive measures to clean data without thinking them through thoroughly ahead of time.

Data integrity is absolutely vital to all aspects of crime analysis and intelligence—without reliable data, there can be no reliable analytical products. Although it may be best for these problems to be addressed elsewhere in the police organization, such as in the Records or Information Systems area, since the analyst is the one who will eventually use the data, it is at the analyst's level that ultimate responsibility must lie.

Correctly addressing data integrity problems requires a methodical and conscientious strategy formulated well in advance. The process is straightforward:

1) The analyst must study each type of data (e.g., crime report, known offenders, calls for service) and analyze the chain of custody for each record, learning how data is changed and what data errors are introduced at each stage.

2) The analyst must craft a response for each type of error discovered using one or more of the possible strategies (compensation, repair, or avoidance).

3) The results of the data-cleaning, avoidance, or compensation efforts must be assessed, with particular attention paid to uncovering new errors introduced as unintended consequences of the data control process.

4) Data must be regularly audited for accuracy, to keep watch for new individual errors as well as new classes of errors introduced by such things as redistricting, new RMS software, database changes, policy and reporting changes, urban growth, and legislation.

This process, along with a comprehensive initial audit of available data, should be accomplished before analysis is performed. There is simply no point in mastering crime mapping, profiling, data mining, querying, or link-charting until the data necessary to make these powerful analytical techniques work properly is clean, timely, and accurate.

8
Qualitative Analysis

Noah J. Fritz
Sean Bair
Dan Helms
Steven R. Hick

A body of literature exists within the social sciences on the differences between quantitative and qualitative methods. Both have a place in the study of crime and criminals. Quantitative methods rely on statistics to ascertain the frequency and significance of criminal activity, the volume and density of crime, the correlations between crime and other factors, and future trends in crime and demand for police service. Various quantitative methods are covered in Chapters 10, 13, and 14.

Qualitative methods, according to some scholars, are the basis of all research and knowledge.[1] John Johnson points out that qualitative research "owes its good fortune of late to the insight that knowledge is a social enterprise…The major point is that the observation of naturally occurring everyday events yields the fundamental data for building a more abstract (or theoretical) understanding of the basic properties of human existence."[2] Qualitative analysis, unlike quantitative analysis, is based on direct observations or direct quotes from subjects, and on the assessment of field notes or source data. It attempts to focus on the meaning of behavior, and in many cases leads us to understand the very essence of human

interaction, whether legal or illegal. It calls for analysts to go directly to the source of information, to enter the field, to see themselves what is happening, and to study the context in which phenomena occur.

Qualitative analysis relies on field research, document or content analysis, open-ended interviews, and ethnographies. These methods can and should be used to better understand the scope and nature of patterns and problems, and to conduct in-depth assessments of public safety issues.

This chapter begins with an overview of how qualitative information applies to and is used by crime analysts. We discuss how qualitative information is critical to tactical, strategic, and administrative crime analysis.

The second section focuses on sources of qualitative information as it pertains to police work. We leave traditional sources of police data—records management systems and computer-aided dispatch—behind and explore more robust sources of data that lend themselves to a deeper understanding of crime and criminal behavior. The third section offers specific research methods for assessing and evaluating these data sources.

The fourth section shows how ethnography can be used to understand crime and criminals in their historical and geographic context. We look at some examples of urban ethnography as it relates to drugs and violence in an underground economy.

Sections five, six, and seven take readers through three qualitative examples: (1) an inductive document analysis of sexual assault reports; (2) a deductive problem-solving project using neighborhood ethnography; and (3) a content analysis of local newspaper articles related to crime and disorder. The chapter concludes by enticing readers to

---

[1] See, for example, John M. Johnson, *Doing Field Research* (New York: Free Press, 1978); David L. Altheide, *Qualitative Media Analysis* (Thousand Oaks, CA: Sage, 1996); and Jack D. Douglas, *Understanding Everyday Life* (Chicago: Aldine, 1970).
[2] Johnson, 19.

return to their jobs and begin using a variety of qualitative sources and techniques in their everyday applied research endeavors.

Qualitative Analysis and the Types of Crime Analysis

Crime analysis has been categorized in a variety of ways over the years. Traditionally, it has been classified into three distinct types, as discussed in Chapter 1: tactical, strategic, and administrative.

Tactical Crime Analysis

For the purposes of this chapter, tactical crime analysis refers to an inductive approach used to identify, describe, and forecast crime series. An analyst often begins this inquiry by reading a stack of police reports (particularly the narrative portion) one at a time, paying close attention to the elements and timeline of the criminal event. As each report is read, the analyst compares it to previous reports, with an eye toward identifying whether the elements are the same or similar to the extent that the reader strongly believes that the same person or persons have committed these crimes. This is the critical element that distinguishes a series from a pattern.

Reading police reports for the purpose of correlating crimes, offender characteristics, and specific *modus operandi* is a form of qualitative research. One may add to this preliminary form of document analysis the review of witness statements, offender interviews, audio and video recordings, and perhaps the physical observations of the crime location, the target, and the surrounding area. An understanding of the connection between time and space—of why crimes take place when and where they do—is paramount to crime prevention, target hardening, suppression, and apprehension. In this way, it is imperative that an analyst

follow an inductive model—that is, to go from the specific incidents to a more general profile of the overall series. For qualitative purposes, then, there are at least four major goals of this form of crime analysis:

1. Identify crime series by reading police reports each day and comparing them to past reports. Produce crime bulletins or other publications that alert readers to the existence of the series and inform them of its characteristics. Distribute the analysis to field officers, detectives, and possibly citizens or businesses in the affected area and time.

2. Use the series analysis to search known offender databases, read witness statements, review dispatcher comments, interview officers and detectives regarding any distinctive qualities of this series to shed additional light on the series and the unique signature of its offender. The second goal results in the development of investigative leads, not necessarily having probable cause, but which entice the investigating detective to look more closely at certain suspects.

3. Using temporal and spatial analysis (see Chapters 11 and 15), and other qualitative information, forecast a likely time and location of the next incident. The unique elements of the environment or the qualities of the victim or target should be assessed and any peculiar details should be articulated to officers and investigators so they can "be on the look out" when patrolling or continuing their investigation. This more in-depth forecast and criminal profile is the distinction between cursory forms of tactical crime analysis that simply regurgitate information and a more robust and informative examination that predict when and where the offender is likely to strike next.

4. Following an arrest, to take the offender's profile and compare it to past crimes

(perhaps without the previous unique detail) that feature similar geographic, temporal, or behavioral characteristics. This process may not only clear more cases, but may also build a stronger case against this offender. This work should subsequently convince the courts that he or she deserves a tougher sentence—commensurate to the volume and extent of the crimes. Few criminals only commit one crime and then stop. A suspect arrested for one crime may have committed many more crimes that can be identified by this retroactive qualitative process.

Detectives may take this additional information and challenge the offender by driving him past the target addresses and accusing him or suggesting that they know he committed crimes at these other locations. It is amazing the number of incidents for which offenders have "copped to" when directly confronted. Collecting this more in-depth information helps build better known offender databases, and provides more quality investigative leads in the future. A released offender who recidivates has a greater chance of being caught if police have detailed records of his past activities.

A progressive police department may take the time to conduct post-arrest interviews (a qualitative research method) to collect additional information about how and why offenders target certain victims or locations. Such information is invaluable for crime prevention and problem-solving. In some agencies, crime analysts conduct or participate in these post-arrest interviews.

Strategic Crime Analysis

Strategic crime analysis focuses on developing effective strategies to intercede in long-term trends and to solve crime problems. Those strategies may be related to problem solving, resource allocation, or general operational approaches in addressing crime related issues and service delivery. Qualitative methods, such as focus groups or interviews, citizen surveys, officer surveys and interviews, ride-alongs, and neighborhood ethnographies are appropriate for gathering additional information regarding crime and disorder, as well as police practices.

Community policing and problem-oriented policing embrace research models that rely on qualitative information and methods. Probably the most popular model, SARA, calls for officers or analysts to scan for problems, analyze them in depth, respond with effective solutions, and assess the effectiveness of the response. An abundance of articles and books have been written about community and problem-oriented policing, the essence of which is captured by Herman Goldstein himself in the box below.

This spectrum of information sources to which Goldstein refers has been more specifically articulated by John Eck and William Spelman.[1] They point to qualitative information sources involving actors, incidents, and potential responses—community versus institutional. Goldstein writes that this is a different form of crime analysis, one beyond traditional goals of identifying crime patterns and series. This form of strategic crime analysis or problem analysis calls for the extraction of many qualitative elements of information beyond what can be found in a police report or identified through crime statistics.[2]

---

[1] John E. Eck and William Spelman, *Problem Solving: Problem-Oriented Policing in Newport News* (Washington, DC: Police Executive Research Forum, 1987).

[2] For additional information on problem analysis, see Rachel Boba, *Problem Analysis in Policing* (Washington, DC: Police Foundation, 2003); and Ronald V. Clarke and John Eck, *Become a Problem-Solving Crime Analyst in 55 Small Steps* (London: Jill Dando Institute of Crime Science, 2003).

Goldstein on Problem-Oriented Policing

Excerpts from Herman Goldstein, *Problem-Oriented Policing* (New York: McGraw-Hill, 1990).

"Problem-oriented policing grows out of [a] critique of the current state of policing... In a narrow sense, it focuses directly on the substance of policing—on the problems that constitute the business of the police and on how they handle them. This focus establishes a better balance between the reactive and proactive aspects of policing. It also creates a vehicle for making more effective use of the community and rank-and-file officers in getting the police job done. In its broadest context, problem-oriented policing is a comprehensive plan for improving policing in which the high priority attached to addressing substantive problems shapes the police agency, influencing all changes in personnel, organization, and procedures..." (32)

"The first step in problem-oriented policing is to move beyond just handling incidents. It calls for recognizing that incidents are often merely overt symptoms of problems. This pushes the police in two directions: (1) It requires that they recognize the relationships between incidents (similarities of behavior, location, persons involved, etc.); and (2) it requires that they take a more in-depth interest in incidents by acquainting themselves with some of the conditions and factors that give rise to them." (33)

"Thus, focusing on the substantive, community problems that the police must handle is a much more radical step than it initially appears to be, for it requires the police to go beyond taking satisfaction in the smooth operation of their organization; it requires that they extend their concern to dealing effectively with the problems that justify creating a police agency in the first instance..." (35, emphasis removed)

"Problem-oriented policing actually provides an incentive to make much more effective use of the data typically collected as part of crime analysis and to expand beyond the current limited objectives of the most advanced crime analysis models. This would first require focusing more broadly on all of the problems police handle rather than on just traditional categories of crime. It would require trying to understand the nature of these problems as a basis for critical review of the agency's response, rather than limiting inquiries to narrower operational goals. *It would use more sources of information than just the reports filed by police officers. To understand all aspects of a problem, police would have to become adept at conducting literature searches, using telephone and door-to-door surveys, interviewing those having the most direct knowledge about a problem (including citizens, officers, representatives of various government agencies and private services, and ex-offenders), and making use of data collected by other government agencies and in the private sector.* Finally, the type of systematic inquiry contemplated as part of problem-oriented policing would place a much higher value on the accuracy and preciseness of the data used and the conclusions reached than has been characteristic of studies conducted within police agencies." (37–38, emphasis added)

In developing effective strategies to address problems, analysts should be prepared to perform ride-alongs, interview officers and citizens, and (when appropriate) conduct participant observation or field work. Once a neighborhood or area has been determined to be a hot spot or prone to a specific problem, the analyst should enter the field to directly observe behavior in and around the area of concern. If safety is an issue, the analyst should take precautions, like carrying a radio or cell phone or conducting observations with police escorts (although keep in mind that behavior will be altered with the presence of police). Interviewing citizens or witnesses is an additional way to gather qualitative information about the scope and nature of the phenomenon. Tapping into the intuition and experience of patrol officers who have worked the beat or precinct will shed additional light on the matter. All of these techniques, qualitative in nature, are effective tools for problem analysis. While police departments have effectively used participant observation in the form of surveillance, its primary purpose is investigatory, not research or knowledge building. First-hand observations of behavior remain the best source of data, particularly regarding criminal or deviant acts.

The point here is that by employing qualitative research methods—interviews and participant observations—an analyst can gather richer, more direct data than what can be extracted from police reports alone. Conducting an environmental scan, identifying the type of premise, studying its structure and location, and observing direct human interactions that occur at these locations may help develop better solutions to chronic crime or disorder problems. Developing effective solutions to underlying causes of community problems is the primary aim forwarded by problem-oriented policing. To appropriately analyze and assess community concerns, qualitative information and methods can play a critical role, as the example in subsequent sections will illustrate.

Administrative Crime Analysis

The analysis of crime and police related information for administrative purposes— political and budgetary in nature—can be better informed by qualitative data sources and document analysis. Administrative crime analysis calls for analysts to address political and monetary elements of the business at hand; that is, providing public safety.

Local newspapers, Web sites, public e-mail forums (chat-sessions) and the like lend themselves to content or document analysis. Newspapers and electronic media print more information on crime than on any other topic. If one wants to understand the broader picture about how crime and police work is viewed and discussed within a local context, there is no better source than the local newspaper or newscast. (The relationship between the police and the press is often adversarial—something that analysts can work to change—but this does not impugn the quality of the reporting.) Reporters, both print and electronic, interview politicians, citizens, attorneys, victims, witnesses, and offenders, and report their findings.

Conducting content analysis over a single year or a decade can produce volumes of knowledge about what is important to a given community. Comparing what is written or said in the local press or nightly news to your agency's message or stance can offer critical insight into public relations, community policing efforts, and department image and morale. Administrative crime analysis must focus on the politics of crime, the financial accountability of service delivery, and the fiscal considerations of delivering public safety. Contemporary issues, like gangs, drugs, prostitution, terrorism, domestic violence, and school safety, must be addressed as an administrative concern.

Administrative crime analysis can employ content or document analysis to identify pressing issues and concerns, measure police satisfaction, and help focus limited departmental resources. The example in Section 7 will demonstrate how to use commercial software to search for police related topics within a local newspaper. If you cannot afford the software or do not have access to a college or university library, you can simply commit yourself to regularly reading your local paper and clipping police related articles for future reference.

Sources of Qualitative Information

Sources for qualitative data abound within policing. Most of this qualitative data goes unnoticed, or at least undocumented. Patrol officers' intuition and experience leave with each retirement. Localized knowledge about troubled youths, hangouts, gang turf, hot spots, informants, snoopy neighbors, and the like is collected day in and day out by patrol officers without formal documentation. The way people describe things (e.g., color, size, odor, noises, flavor, and texture) are based on our five senses: seeing, smelling, touching, hearing, and tasting, not to mention our sixth sense of intuition. Most of what we rely on in crime analysis has been based on sight, focusing on when and where crime occurs. What people say, smells relating to drugs or meth-labs, or noises they hear in the night are examples of qualitative information that can be used in crime analysis. What follows is a list of data source for qualitative information within police work. The list is certainly not exhaustive but is illustrative of the abundance of data sources we have at our fingertips:

- Police incident reports, more specifically police narratives or synopses
- Arrest or booking forms
- Audio and video recordings
- Photos
- Witness and victim statements
- Interviews with:
  - Officers regarding their observations and intuition
  - Citizens / Neighbors
  - Victims / Witnesses
  - Offenders (post arrest)
- Field Interview Cards
- Traffic tickets or citations
- Internet Web sites
- Newspapers and other periodicals (preferably local in nature)
- Direct observations and field notes
- Ride-alongs and field work/environmental scans
- CPTED surveys (Crime Prevention Thru Environmental Design)
- Drawings, sketches, floor plans
- Open-ended survey results
- Newscast, reporter interviews, commentary.

A good source for a comprehensive list of factors to consider when analyzing a problem is found in John Eck and William Spelman's *Problem-Solving: Problem-Oriented Policing in Newport News[1]* and is titled "A Guide for the Analysis of Problem Information." It suggests dozens of factors to investigate about victims, offenders, third parties, environment, and police response.

Qualitative Research Methods and Crime Analysis

Document or Content Analysis

Arizona State University Professor David Altheide suggests that almost anything can be considered a "document." He divides "documents" into three categories:

1. **Primary documents**, which include newspapers, magazines, television newscasts, radio transcripts, e-mails, and diaries;
2. **Secondary documents**, such as field notes, published reports, or other accounts one step removed from primary documents; and
3. **Auxiliary documents**, a catch-all category that might include such odd subjects as a collection of garbage to study consumer behavior ("garbology").

"Document analysis," says Altheide, "refers to an integrated and conceptually informed method, procedure, and technique for locating, identifying, retrieving, and analyzing documents for their relevance, significance, and meaning."[2] Document or content analysis, therefore, is the primary qualitative method for identifying and analyzing police reports or narratives for patterns and series.

---

[1] Washington, DC: Police Executive Research Forum, 1987.
[2] David L. Altheide, *Qualitative Media Analysis* (Thousand Oaks: Sage Publications, 1996), 2.

Analyzing secondary police documents like witness or victim statements is an example of qualitative research pertinent to tactical crime analysis. Investigating newscasts or newspaper articles to identify themes and socio-political issues is an example of how a crime analyst can perform administrative crime analysis. Or simply searching for a subject (or topic) or a specific premises within news reports (written or electronic) can develop valuable knowledge about a given problem, problem location, or specific names of individuals related to a given issue.

The simplest way to conduct a periodical literature review is to employ commercially available software that allows a keyword or phrase search. The most popular application, available at most colleges and universities, is LexisNexis. LexisNexis allows the user to search both national and local magazines, newspapers, and newscast transcripts. If you do not have access to something like LexisNexis, you can search most local newspapers via the Internet from the desired city (e.g., www.denverpost.com) or use search engines like Google (www.google.com) to find sites or specific information on a given topic. There is a fee associated with using the software or the direct newspaper service, but it is worth inquiring at your local library (public or educational) to see if you could "piggy-back" on an existing software agreement. Enrolling in an independent study or a readings-and-conference at a local college would be well worth the access to LexisNexis. Most direct Web-based sites charge per inquiry and download, but if you are researching a given topic, the time and effort saved will be well worth the cost.

The least expensive form of document analysis is to read your local paper regularly, clip or scan those documents you find relevant for police work, and store them in a file (computer or physical) for future reference. Often you can search local electronic newspaper articles for the past few days without a fee. Simply saving relevant paragraphs in a Microsoft Word document will allow you to search on the contents at a later time. You can store documents by topic, dates or even geography for easier access in the future. Content or document analysis can be a valuable qualitative research method to crime analysts, if you give it try.

Observer Participation

Observer participation, as opposed to participant observation (see below), refers to the process of watching what is going on, usually from a distance, and removed from any direct interaction with the subjects. Ride-alongs are the best example of conducting observer participation. Watching what officers do, what victims do, what arrestees say and do, or simply keeping your eyes and ears open while you drive around a beat or precinct is what this qualitative research approach is all about. It is rather simple, but the trick is to be methodical about seeking and gathering information relevant to your study or focus. Police officers achieve this valuable instinctive method almost intuitively. Have you ever done a ride-along in which the officer pulled a u-turn and asks you if you saw that kid in the dark alley? Officers really do have eyes in the back of their heads, just like second-grade school teachers. This is what we are referring to when we speak of observer participation: the knack for seeing, hearing, smelling, feeling, tasting, and even intuitively knowing what is going on around you. The analytical difference is that the applied researcher (i.e., the crime analyst) must document these observations methodically and purposefully. Other ways to conduct observations are by hanging out in a coffee shop, café, bar, bus stop, or the bus itself. Of course, it must be "with a purpose"—that is what makes it scientific.

Participant Observation

Participant observation, another form of field research, calls for the analyst to take a more active role in the environment. In some cases, the analyst will assume a role in the community, sometimes gaining access through an informant or insider. Participant observation is risky, as any undercover narcotics officer will testify; safety ought to be the primary consideration when employing this research strategy. Going "covert" may best be left to sworn investigators, but by simply getting involved in a community or a neighborhood non-profit program, the analyst will have the opportunity to speak with neighbors and patrons about community issues. These interactions can provide invaluable insights into the social and cultural dimensions of a specific group or neighborhood.

Open-Ended Interviews

A less risky or vulnerable research approach is to merely conduct open-ended interviews with officers, victims, witness, citizens, and offenders. This direct approach is surprisingly successful, even with known offenders. Criminals have a knack for bragging, and simply asking them what they do and how they do it has led many researchers to insightful findings. Remember, myths and urban legends abound. Conducting open-ended interviews, as opposed to a survey, has a greater tendency to allow for meaningful dialog, and the pursuit of newly-tapped topics resulting from that dialog. It provides the analysts with the immediate opportunity to seek clarification and supporting documentation. Surveys have their place, and the authors are not suggesting that one research method is better than the other, but qualitative methods lend themselves to a richer, more in-depth picture of the phenomenon under study. Understand, though, that these qualitative research techniques take more time and energy, so if you are considering them, do it right—systematically and methodically. Take good field notes, write them up (document your findings), and store them in a manner that is amenable to querying and retrieving the information at a later time.

For a comprehensive reading about qualitative data sources and methods, see Denzin and Lincoln's *Collecting and Interpreting Qualitative Material* and Emerson, Fretz, and Shaw's *Writing Ethnographic Field Notes* (full information in the "Recommended Readings" below).

Criminal Behavior, Crime, and Culture: Ethnographies

Comprehensive ethnographies are probably both too time consuming and too academic for the working crime analyst to pursue, but conducting a neighborhood scan or hot spot assessment in an ethnographic way can be quite enlightening. Whether the analyst does an observer participation or a participant observation (see above), valuable information can be obtained from getting out into the field and seeing directly what the area looks like, or what type of premise it is that continues to be targeted, or is the source of victim contact. For an analyst to get a fuller understanding of criminal behavior, crime, and the culture in which it occurs, doing field research is the answer. If safety concerns, time constraints, or departmental policy preclude you from conducting mini-ethnographies of hot spots, repeat victimization locations, geographic patterns, or "red-light" districts, taking the time to read well-documented urban ethnographic accounts is the next best thing. In this section, a few accounts will be reviewed and commented on in regard to their relevance to crime analysis and community policing. The three selections discussed hereafter are Elijah Anderson's dual publications: *Streetwise* (1990) and *Code of the Street* (1999); and Adler's study of drug culture, *Wheeling and Dealing: An Ethnography of an Upper-Level Drug Dealing and Smuggling Community*.

Streetwise

In *Streetwise*, Elijah Anderson offers an insider's view of life on the streets of an eastern city. This ethnographic work consists of Anderson's ongoing qualitative research, in which he spent the better part of ten years roaming the streets of the worst crime area in Philadelphia. Comedian Richard Pryor alludes to it in a number of his routines (a possible source for qualitative documents about being a minority and living in the inner city). Do not take offense at profanity or immorality while you are a researcher; remain open minded to slang, rap music, and the like. It speaks tenfold about the sub-cultures and counter-cultures within our society. As a person, choose your own morality, but as a researcher, you must remain open to social realities, ways of life, diverse cultures, and the coarse veracity within the criminal world. You do not have to like it, but as a crime analyst you should be aware of it. Anderson shares with us the common-sense or "streetwise" elements of our more impoverished areas. *Streetwise* is the epitome of this level of awareness that occupies our inner cities and ghettos. The essence of Anderson's message within *Streetwise* follows.

Around the nation, urban residents feel intimidated by their streets, parks, and other public places, particularly after dark or when too many strangers are present. The national problem of safe streets has become especially acute in the city. Particularly in underclass ghetto communities and adjacent areas undergoing transitions in race, class, and culture. The margins of the ghetto can be scenes of tension as they become gentrified and are slowly absorbed by a wider community made up primarily of middle- and upper-income people who for the most part are white...

Through public experience, a person becomes deeply familiar with elements of the neighborhood-drug dealers, policemen, the local grocer, poor people, homeless people, and middle class families and individuals making up the community's social fabric. But perhaps most important, one gains some working conception of how these elements fit together.

In these circumstances the person neither takes the streets for granted nor recoils from them but becomes alive to dangerous situations, drawing on a developing repertoire of ruses and schemes for traveling the streets safely. In a word, the person learns street sense, how to behave in a sensible manner. In becoming something more than a passive reactant to public situations, the individual becomes proactive and to some degree the author of public actions.[1]

Code of the Street

Anderson offers his most recent insights into the violence and drugs that are associated with the underground economy in *Code of the Street* (1999).[2] He meticulously describes life for "decent" versus "street" kids or families and the struggle they encounter on a daily basis trying to survive the streets. "Saving face," or defending one's honor—through violence—becomes a primary need, and the desire to achieve the American Dream—wealth and fortune—versus the honorable acceptance of taking a minimum-wage job

---

[1] Elijah Anderson, *Streetwise: Race, Class, and Change in an Urban Community* (Chicago: University of Chicago Press, 1990), 1–6.

[2] The first book of the series is Elijah Anderson, *A Place on the Corner* (Chicago: University of Chicago Press, 1978).

flipping hamburgers or mopping floors is the harsh reality of most minority youth today, at least according to someone who has dedicated his entire life and career studying it. Anderson grasps the inward and hidden nature of things, and has a knack for penetrating the truth about growing up in poverty, growing up around crime and drugs, growing up on the streets, and the toll it takes on decent kids desiring an alternative. Every analyst should understand the "code of the street." Anderson shares with us the primary elements in his book, something to which a few words cannot give justice. While the following section attempts to paraphrase the highlights, the authors strongly urge you to obtain a copy of this astonishing account of the inner-city and read it for yourself.

> The primary aim in this work is to render ethnographically the social and cultural dynamics of the interpersonal violence that is currently undermining the quality of life of too many urban neighborhoods. In this effort I address such questions as the following: How do the people of the setting perceive their situation? What assumptions do they bring to their decision making? What behavioral patterns result from these actions? What are the social implications and consequences of these behaviors? This book therefore offers an ethnographic representation of the code of the street, and its relationship to violence in a trying socioeconomic context in which family-sustaining jobs have become more scarce, public assistance has increasingly disappeared, racial discrimination is a fact of daily life, wider institutions have less legitimacy, legal codes are ignored or not trusted, and frustration has been powerfully building for many residents.[1]

Anderson employs field research that describes the accounts of blacks and Hispanics as a struggle between being "decent" and "street," and the strong hold on "decent" kids that at times forces them to "code switch" to survive the everyday life of the ghetto. Anderson's research provides evidence of an underground economy and a propensity for violence that rule the code of conduct in the inner city, something white people and upper middle class minority people can push out of their everyday life experiences. In the 1980s and early 1990s, white people physically moved out of the inner city to "nicer" suburban neighborhoods. Now, many are moving back, neighborhoods are becoming gentrified, and the clash between "decent" and "street" has emerged once again.

Wheeling and Dealing

In the final illustration of field research on crime and criminals, Patricia Adler's *Wheeling and Dealing* takes us inside the upper-level drug dealing and smuggling community. Adler takes advantage of her tenure in a coastal California community where she lived and conducted participant observation, fieldwork, and extensive interviews for six years. She did this by "befriend[ing] a group of people engaged in a rather risky, and illegal, occupation." In her own words:

> ...I became friends with our next-door neighbor, gaining access through him to a whole community of upper-level marijuana and cocaine dealers and smugglers. This book describes what I found in this hidden drug subculture, from the easy money, to the casual sex, the vast drug consumption, the big deals, the hopes, the dreams, and the nightmares. People have found this book of interest, partly, because of its descriptions and analyses of this rarely seen world, bringing with it answers to questions about recruitment, community, lifestyle, motivation, relations to law enforcement, and retirement. These

---

[1] Elijah Anderson, *Code of the Street: Decency, Violence, and the Moral Life of the Inner City* (New York: W.W. Norton, 1999), 11.

traffickers embodied an ironic paradox, as they were caught in the contradiction of trying to work rationally in order to live hedonistically and irrationally.[1]

Wheeling and Dealing exposes the life of drug dealing and smuggling. Adler's second edition updates the reader on her subjects' activities since the original publication and concludes with a comprehensive review of more recent literature on drug trafficking in America and the socio-political response to what is considered deviant or illegal behavior. Adler gives her honest and non-judgmental account of this type of human behavior, from the eyes and feelings of the subjects, and within the context in which they find themselves. Crime analysts interested in drug trafficking and its social ramifications should put this book on their "must-read" list.

While the list of ethnographic accounts is limited due to the time and personal energy it takes researchers to conduct their studies, the information garnered from their reading is well worth the time it takes to examine these works. A short bibliography of crime-related ethnographies is offered at the end of this chapter. The authors strongly urge the reader to obtain them and extract the valuable message about the sociology of everyday life.

Reading and Assessing Police Reports: a Qualitative Inductive Approach to Crime Series Analysis (A Tactical Example)

Using three actual police reports of sexual assault, the reader should be able to find the discerning elements of a serial rapist. A subset of these reports may in fact be perpetrated by the same individual, but the criminal elements contained within the report

do not offer enough confidence to include them in the series. You be the judge. Your task: read the reports in chronological order, and determine which reports are categorically part of the series, and why. You should think about your reasoning or rationale, and point to the specific criteria you used to make the determination. Below are copies of these three reports, as officially documented by the police and reported by the victims. Names and identifiers have been removed to ensure privacy and compliance with victim rights legislation.[2]

A brief description of the pattern will be added following the reports, identifying the reports that make up the series and those that are not, and a depiction of the contributing data elements that make up the defining profile.

Warning

The attached police reports are of a graphic nature representing a number of sexual assault incidents. You will be asked to read these reports as an exercise in content analysis as it applies to tactical crime analysis. If you find this kind of material offensive, you may want to skip this exercise, but it is certainly possible that as a crime analyst you may be required to review this kind of material for your job. This series was not chosen to shock you, but offered as an excellent example of how the detailed content within the police report narrative and within the description of a criminal event, a crime analyst will find the elements of the crime that allows him or her to link cases together into a crime series, the fundamental job duty of a tactical crime analyst.

---

[1] Patricia A. Adler, *Wheeling and Dealing: An Ethnography of an Upper-Level Drug Dealing and Smuggling Community* (New York: Columbia University Press, 1993), 5.

[2] The following police reports are used with permission from the originating agency.

...CE DEPARTMENT
...ENSE REPORT
...ND MULTI-PURPOSE
REPORT FORM

	18. REP AREA	19. DIST	20. WATCH			
UNIT			12x8			

1. VICTIM'S NAME (LAST, FIRST, MIDDLE) — ~~[redacted]~~
2. CASE NO. 01-03399
3. VICTIM'S ADDRESS — ~~[redacted]~~   PHONE ~~[redacted]~~

SEX. Fem	RACE. Blk	D.O.B. 6-20-77	SOC. SEC. NO ~~[redacted]~~

5. VICTIM'S PLACE OF EMPLOYMENT OR SCHOOL ~~[redacted]~~   6. BUS. PHONE ~~[redacted]~~

22. DISPATCHED AS:
23. DISP ACKN A.M. / P.M.
9. REPORTING PERSON'S NAME ~~[redacted]~~

24. ADDRESS DISPATCHED TO
25. RET'D. SERV. A.M. / P.M.
11. REPORTING PERSON'S ADDRESS.   CITY ~~[redacted]~~   10. RES. PHONE ~~[redacted]~~

26. DESCRIBE LOCATION--TYPE PREMISES
8. LOCATION OF OFFENSE (ADDRESS) ~~[redacted]~~   12. BUS. PHONE

27. VICT OCCUPAT. Cocktail Waitress	28. HOURS OF EMPLOY. 1900-0500	29. SOBRIETY

13. DATE AND TIME OCCURRED 2-25-01 0415
14. DATE AND TIME REPORTED 2-25-01 0625
16. CLASSIFICATION

15. CRIME OR INCIDENT
Home invasion / Confinement / Sexual Battery
Sex Offense / Burglary / Threats + Intimi / Crim...

30. REQUESTED
- CORONER ☐
- NCIC CK ☐
- OTHER ☐
- CRIM INV ☐
- AMB ☐
- APB RADIO ☐
- TOW ☐
- T TYPE ☐

WITNESS PARENT GUARDIAN

31. NAME
[1]
[2]

AGE	BEST CONTACT ADDRESS	BEST PHONE	OTHER PHONE

SUSPECTS

32. NAME AND ADDRESS, SEX, RACE, AGE-DESCRIP--ARR. NO
[1] Mike
[3]

NAME AND ADDRESS, SEX, RACE, AGE-DESCRIP--ARR. NO
[2]

VEH. COLOR(S)   YEAR MAKE MODEL LIC. YEAR-STATE-NO.

STOLEN PROPERTY

33. QTY	DESCRIPTION-(SIZE-COLOR-MODEL-STYLE-MATERIAL-CONDITION)	SERIAL NO.	WHERE LOCATED	VALUE, NEW	AGE	VALUE NOW
1	Printer (Computer)					
1	Cell Phone					
1	Gold Herringbone Neckless					

INJ/PER

34. VICTIM TAKEN TO
35. TRANSPORTED BY
36. DESCRIBE INJURIES
37. CONDITION

MISSING PERSON

38. HT. WT. HAIR EYES COMP. HAT COAT JACKET SWEATER BLOUSE/SHIRT SKIRT/TROUSERS SHOES JEWELRY

39. POSSIBLE CAUSE OF ABSENCE
DESTINATION
40. COMPETENCY: PHYSICAL / MENTAL
41. PAST RECORD, OTHER DATA-IQ, MONEY CARRIED ~~[redacted]~~

BURGLARY

BURGLARY OF
- BUSINESS ☐
- RESIDENCE ☐
- GARAGE ☐
- OTHERS ☐

TYPE OF OFFENSE
- FORCED ENTRY ☐
- NON FORCED ENTRY ☐
- ATTEMPT ☐

HOW ENTERED
- DOOR FRONT-SIDE-BACK ☐
- WINDOW FRONT-SIDE-BACK ☐
- ROOF ☐
- GARAGE DOOR ☐
- OTHER ☐

MEANS OF ENTRY
- PRIED OPEN ☐
- BROKEN OUT ☐
- UNLOCKED ☐

- DAYLIGHT ☐
- DUSK ☐
- DARK ☐
- UNKNOWN ☐

NARRATIVE

On 2-25-01 at aprox. 0410 Victim received a phone call advising
her that she had left the lights on in her 01 Pont. Sunfire. When
victim went out to turn her lights off she left the door to her
apt. unlocked but secured the exterior door to the building.
After turning the lights off in her veh. Victim went back to her

OFFICE USE ONLY

REPORTING OFFICER ~~[redacted]~~ 1110   NO
OFFICER   NO
SUPERVISOR APPROVING   NO

44. CASE STATUS (STATUS MUST BE INDICATED FOR ALL CASES, INCLUDING NON-CRIMINAL INCIDENTS)
☐ OPEN (PENDING) ☐ CLOSED ☐ SUSPENDED

CASE DISPOSITION (DISPOSITION OF CRIMINAL CASES MAY BE INDICATED AS APPROPRIATE)
☐ UNFOUNDED
☐ CLEARED BY ARREST ☐ CLEARED EXCEP

46. DATE/TIME TYPED NO   47. REPRODUCED BY NO.
48. UNIT REFERRED TO: 49. UCR DISPOSITION
50. REVIEWER   NO   PAGE NO OF

51 COMPLAINT NO

CONT. SHEET

1. TIME AND DATE		01-03399
0625	2-25-01	

apt. and went to bed aprox five minutes later she heard some-one in her apt. when victim turned to see she noticed a thin built body standing over her bed with a stick in hand, then suspect put a pillow over victim's face and told her (victim) if she screamed he would kill her.

Victim is unable to tell if the voice in the apt. was the same as the one on the phone.

Suspect blind folded victim and walked victim to living rm. turned on the light. suspect told victim to get on the floor. At this time suspect asked victim for vaseline or grease, then suspect took victim back into bed room. Before suspect took victim back into bedroom while still in living room suspect tore victim's gown off of her.

Once victim was back in bedroom suspect made victim lay on her bed face down and put his hand in her vigina. suspect then told victim to "Play with yourself" Victim also states that suspect also put what she thought was the stick she saw in her vigina.

After this went on for aprox. fifteen minutes suspect told victim that he was taking her printer and neckless. and if she called the police he (suspect) would kill her (victim). Victim further states that suspect told her (victim) that he (suspect) has been watching her victim for a long time and the he (suspect) was very close and would continue to watch er.

Suspect then left taking victim computer printer and a gold Herringbone necklace.

Note x suspect left only after victim's cell phone rang and was ad-vised by victim that it might be her boyfriend suspect also took cell phone

16. REPORTING OFFICER	NO	2ND OFFICER	NO	17. SUPERVISOR APPROVING	NO

...olice Department

CASE NUMBER:01-03399

DATE:2/25/01

TIME: 3:05 PM

THIS IS A STATEMENT BY: ▓▓▓▓▓▓▓▓▓▓▓

Q. DO YOU KNOW WHO DID THIS OFFENSE?

A. I WAS IN BED AND I GOT A CALL, PRIVACY MANAGEMENT. SO I DIDN'T THINK TO WAIT, TO HEAR THE NAME. SO I JUST HIT 1 1 TWICE. HE SAID, ▓▓▓▓▓▓▓, YOU KNOW THAT YOUR PARKING LIGHTS ARE ON. HE SAID THAT I KNEW THAT MY BATTERY COULD BURN OUT IF YOU DON'T TURN THEM OFF. I ASKED WHO IS THIS AND HE SAID MIKE. AND I WAS GETTING READY TO SAY MIKE WHO BUT HE JUST HUNG UP. I JUST THOUGHT IT WAS ONE OF MY SISTER'S FRIENDS, SO I GOT UP AND I PUT MY PANTS, MY SHIRT AND MY SHOES ON. I WENT DOWN STAIRS. I DIDN'T LOCK MY DOOR BUT I DID MAKE SURE THAT THE MAIN DOOR DOWNSTAIRS DID CLOSED. I WENT TO MY CAR AND I UNLOCKED IT AND CUT MY PARKING LIGHTS OFF. I LOCKED MY DRIVERS SIDE DOOR BACK AND WENT IN. BUT WHEN I GOT TO THE MAIN DOOR, I NOTICED THAT THE DOOR WAS OPENED A LITTLE BIT. SO I WENT BACK UPSTAIRS AND I NOTICED THAT MY DOOR WAS CRACKED A LITTLE BIT. I DIDN'T THINK ANYTHING ABOUT IT. I WENT IN AND HUNG MY JACKET BACK UP. I TOOK MY CLOTHES OFF ALL EXCEPT FOR MY GOWN. I CUT THE BEDROOM LIGHT OFF AND GOT RIGHT BACK INTO BED. LIKE THREE MINUTES LATER, I HEARD SOMEONE IN THE ROOM. I TURNED AROUND AND IT WAS A GUY STANDING OVER ME WITH A STICK. HE PUT A PILLOW OVER MY FACE AND ASKED ME WHERE WAS A SCARF OR BLINDFOLD OR SOMETHING. I TOLD HIM ON THE FLOOR, I DIDN'T KNOW. THEN HE FOUND A SHIRT AND A SCARF AND TIED THEM AROUND MY HEAD. AND HE ASKED ME WHERE WAS THE MONEY AT BITCH. I SAID THAT I DIDN'T HAVE ANYTHING EXCEPT 26 DOLLARS. HE ASKED ME WHERE WAS THE JEWERY OR THE DVD PLAYER. AND I TOLD HIM THAT I DIDN'T HAVE ANY JEWERY OR A DVD PLAYER. HE SAID THAT I DIDN'T HAVE ANYTHING VALUBLE AROUND HERE AND I SAID THAT THE ONLY THING I HAVE IS WHAT HE SEES. HE WAS MUBBLING THAT HE WANTED THE COMPUTER. I WAS STILL BLINDFOLDED. HE SAID BITCH, GET UP AND WE ARE GOING TO THE LIVINGROOM. AND HE WAS ASKING ME WHERE WAS THE LIGHT SWITCH. I TOLD HIM IT WAS OVER ON THE WALL AND I WAS REACHING FOR THE SWITCH. ONCE I TURNED ON THE LIGHT, HE TOLD ME TO TAKE OFF MY GOWN. HE TOLD ME TO GET ON THE FLOOR. HE TORE MY PANTIES OFF. HE WAS ASKING ME WHERE WAS THE PHONE CORD AND I TOLD HIM THAT IT WAS OVER ON THE TABLE. HE TIED ME UP AND HE CONTINED TO LOOK FOR ITEMS. HE WENT INTO THE BEDROOM AND THEN HE CAME BACK INTO THE LIVINGROOM. HE UNTIED ME AND TOLD ME TO PLAY WITH MY SELF. HE THEN TOLD ME THAT I DIDN'T HAVE MY LEG OPEN ENOUGH AND THAT HE WAS GOING TO KILL ME. SO THEN HE ASKED WHERE WAS THE VASELINE. I SAID IT WAS IN THE CALINET IN THE BEDROOM. HE

Page 2 of 5 Signature of person giving statement _____

Date _____

Signature of witness _____

olice Department

CASE NUMBER: 01-03399
DATE: 2/25/01
TIME: 3:05 PM

THIS IS A STATEMENT BY: _____

WAS SAYING WHERE AND I SAID IN THE BEDROOM. HE WAS LOOKING IN THE BEDROOM AND THEN HE YELLED HE COULDN'T FIND IT. THEN HE CAME BACK INTO THE LIVINGROOM WITH HAIRGREASE. HE TOOK THE BLINDFOLD OFF ALITTLE BIT AND ASKED WAS THIS THE VASELINE. I TOLD HIM NO, THAT IT WAS HAIR GREASE. HE ASKED WHERE WAS THE VASELINE. HE TOLD ME TO GET UP AND HE MADE SURE THE BLINDFOLD WAS TIED BACK REAL GOOD. HE WALKED ME BACK INTO THE BEDROOM AND THEN PUT HANDCUFFS ON ME. HE TOLD ME TO GET ON THE BED FACE DOWN. THEN HE TOOK THE VASELINE AND PUT SOME ON HIS GLOVES AND INSERTED HIS HAND INTO MY VAGINA. AS HE HAD HIS HAND UP INTO MY VAGINA, HE WAS SAYING TELL ME THAT IT FEELS GOOD BITCH. I TOLD HIM NO, THAT IT HURTS. THEN I MOVED MY HANDS DOWN A LITTLE BIT AND I FELT A POLE OR STICK AND HE INSERTED IT INTO MY VAGINA. ALL WAS HE SAYING WAS AHN. THEN HE CONTINUED TO LOOK FOR ITEMS AFTHER THAT. HE WAS ASKING ME WHERE DID I PUT THE PHONE AND WHERE DID I PUT THE HERRINGBONE. I WAS STILL TIED UP. HE WAS FUMBLING AROUND IN MY PURSE AND TAKING CHANGE. THEN HE ASKED ME IF I HAD ANY FOOD STAMPS. I TOLD HIM THAT I DIDN'T GET FOOD STAMPS. HE WAS IN MY PURSE AND FOUND A FOOD STAMP CARD. I HAD TO EXPLAIN THAT I DIDN'T GET FOOD STAMPS ANYMORE. HE SAID TO ME THAT HE WAS GOING TO TAKE MY ID, HE ASKED WAS THIS THE ONLY ID I HAD AND I TOLD HIM YES. HE THEN SAID THAT HE WOULDN'T TAKE IT THEN. HE ALSO SAID THAT HE WATCHES ME ALL THE TIME AND THAT I WAS SO PRETTY. HE SAID THAT IF I CALLED THE POLICE, HE WOULD BE BACK AND HE WOULD KILL ME. HE SAID THAT IF I DIDN'T HAVE ANY MONEY, HE WOULD KILL ME. THEN THE CELL PHONE RANG. IT WAS PRIVACY MANAGEMENT AND HE ASKED WHO WAS THAT. I SAID IT WAS MY BOYFRIEND. THEN HE ASKED IF HE WAS COMING OVER THERE, WAS HE DOWN THERE OR IS HE OUT THERE AND I TOLD HIM THAT I DIDN'T KNOW. THEN HE SAID THAT HE WAS GOING TO TAKE MY PRINTER AND MY HERRINGBONE. HE CAME OVER TO THE BED AND UN CLICKED OFF ONE OF THE CUFFS. THEN HE ASKED ME WAS I OKAY. I TOLD HIM YES. HE TOLD ME TO COUNT TO ONE THOUSAND AND I SO I STARTED TO COUNT. I LAYED THERE FOR ABOUT TWO MINUTES. I GRABBED MY NIGHT GOWN AND WENT ACROSS THE HALL. I KNOCKED ON THE DOOR AND _____ ANSWERED THE DOOR. I TOLD HER WHAT HAD HAPPENED AND I USED THE PHONE AND CALLED QUITE AFEW OF MY FAMILY MEMBERS. I PPUT SOME CLOTHES ON AND CAME DOWN HERE. THAT IS WHEN I NOTICED THAT HE HAD BROKEN INTO THE CAR TO PUT ON THE PARKING LIGHTS. THAT'S IT.

Q. DESCRIBE THE MAN THAT WAS IN YOUR APARTMENT?
Page 3 of 5   Signature of person giving statement _____

Date _____
Signature of witness _____

OFFENSE REPORT
AND MULTI-PURPOSE
REPORT FORM

1 VICTIM'S NAME (LAST, FIRST, MIDDLE)			2 CASE NO.
	AT 1.11		0106583
3 VICTIM'S ADDRESS			

SEX F	RACE B	D.O.B. 1-19-72	SOC. SEC. NO.

17 UNIT 83	18 REP. TEA	19 DIST A.DAM	20 WATCH 12X8	5 VICTIM'S PLACE OF EMPLOYMENT OR SCHOOL	6 BUS. PHONE/WK

22 DISPATCHED AS: ROBBERY	23 DISP ACKN. 2:45 P.M.	9 REPORTING PERSON'S NAME

24 ADDRESS DISPATCHED TO APT	25 RET'D SCENE 4:10 A.M.	11 REPORTING PERSON'S ADDRESS	CITY	10 RES. PHONE

26 DESCRIBE LOCATION--TYPE PREMISES RESIDENTIAL APARTMENT	7 LOCATION OF OFFENSE (ADDRESS)	12 BUS. PHONE

27 VICT OCCUPAT NURSE	28 HOURS OF EMPLOY EVENINGS	29 SOBRIETY SOBER	13 DATE AND TIME OCCURRED 4-15-01	14 DATE AND TIME REPORTED 4-15-01 3:04 AM.	16 CLASSIFICATION

30 REQUESTED	CRIM INV ☒	15 CRIME OR INCIDENT
CORONER ☐ AMB ☐ TOW ☐		SEX OFFENSE / ROBBERY
NCIC CK ☐ APB RADIO ☐ T TYPE ☐		
OTHER ☐		

WITNESS PARENT GUARDIAN

31 NAME	AGE	BEST CONTACT ADDRESS	BEST PHONE	OTHER PHONE
①				
②				

SUSPECTS

32 NAME AND ADDRESS, SEX, RACE, AGE-DESCRIP--ARR. NO.	NAME AND ADDRESS, SEX, RACE, AGE-DESCRIP--ARR. NO.
① BLACK/MALE BLUE BANDANA	② BLACK SCULL CAP DEEP VOICE
③ BLUE NIKEY JACKET/BLUE JEANS	BLACK JERREY SHOES SILVER GUN

STOLEN PROPERTY

33 QTY 4	DESCRIPTION--(SIZE-COLOR-MODEL-STYLE-MATERIAL-CONDITION) GOLD BRACELETS	SERIAL NO.	WHERE LOCATED ON PERSON	VALUE, NEW AGE UNK	VALUE NOW UNK

INJ PER

34 VICTIM TAKEN TO	35 TRANSPORTED BY	36 DESCRIBE INJURIES	37 CONDITION

MISSING PERSON

38 HT	WT	HAIR	EYES	COMP	HAT	COAT	JACKET	SWEATER	BLOUSE/SHIRT	SKIRT/TROUSERS	SHOES	JEWELRY

39 POSSIBLE CAUSE OF ABSENCE	40 COMPETENCY: PHYSICAL	PAST RECORD, OTHER DATA-IQ, MONEY CARRIED
DESTINATION	MENTAL	

BURGLARY

BURGLARY OF	TYPE OF OFFENSE	HOW ENTERED	MEANS OF ENTRY	
BUSINESS ☐	FORCED ENTRY ☐	DOOR FRONT-SIDE-BACK ☐	PRIED OPEN ☐	DAYLIGHT ☐
RESIDENCE ☐	NON FORCED ENTRY ☐	WINDOW FRONT-SIDE-BACK ☐		DUSK ☐
GARAGE ☐		ROOF ☐	BROKEN OUT ☐	DARK ☐
OTHERS ☐	ATTEMPT ☐	GARAGE DOOR ☐	UNLOCKED ☐	UNKNOWN ☐
		OTHER ☐		

NARRATIVE

STATES THAT ON 4-15-01 AT APPROX SHE WAS LETTING HER FRIEND OUT OF HER APARTMENT DOOR, WHEN SHE OPENED THE DOOR, A BLACK MALE SUBJECT WEARING BLUE JEAN, BLUE SHIRT AND A BANDANA OVER HIS FACE AND A SCULL CAP, ARMED WITH A SILVER HAND

OFFICE USE ONLY

43 REPORTING OFFICER NO. 1386	44 CASE STATUS (STATUS MUST BE INDICATED FOR ALL CASES, INCLUDING NON-CRIMINAL INCIDENTS)	46 DATE/TIME TYPED NO	47 REPRODUCED BY NO.
2ND OFFICER NO	☐ OPEN/PENDING ☐ CLOSED ☐ SUSPENDED	48 UNIT REFERRED TO:	49 UCR DISPOSITION
45 SUPERVISOR APPROVING NO	CASE DISPOSITION (DISPOSITION OF CRIMINAL CASES MAY BE INDICATED AS	50 REVIEWER NO	PAGE NO 1 OF 2
	☐ UNFOUNDED ☐ CLEARED BY ARREST		

41 COMPLAINT NO

172

PAGE ...

CONT. SHEET 1. TIME AND DATE 3:30 AM 4-15-01   CASE NO 0106583

GUN ENTERED AND DEMANDED THAT EVERYONE IN THE
RESIDENCE GET DOWN ON THE GROUND OR HE WOULD KILL
THEM, AND DO NOT LOOK AT HIM. SUBJECT THEN BEGAN
ASKING WHERE IS THE MONEY. EVERYONE WAS IN THE
LIVING ROOM ON THE GROUND. THE SUBJECT THE BEGAN
DEMANDING THAT THE FEMALES BEGIN TO STRIP, AND
PERFORM ORAL SEX TO EACH OTHER. THE SUBJECT THEN
MADE THE FEMALES TAKE OFF ALL OF THEIR JEWELRY, THE
VICTIMS THEN DID SO, AND HAND OVER THEIR MONEY.
THE SUBJECT THEN BEGAN TO GO THROUGH THE VICTIMS
HOUSE. THE SUBJECT THE BEGAN UNPLUGGING THE PHONES
WHILE STILL MAKING VERBAL THREATS TO THE FEMALES.
HE THEN TOLD THE FEMALES TO COUNT TO (100) ONE HUNDRED
A NOT TO LOOK UP. FEMALES THEN BEGAN COUNTING.
THE SUBJECT THEN WENT TO THE PATIO DOORS AND OPENED
THE BLINDS (VICTIM UNKNOWN TO WHAT SUBJECT DID) THEN
LEFT OUT. VICTIM STATES BEFORE THE SUBJECT LEFT
SHE COULD HEAR A PLASTIC BAG NOISE. AT THE SCENE,
THE ITEMS OF ONE OF THE FEMALES WAS FOUND AT
THE DOOR IN A PLASTIC BAG. (FIVE DOLLARS IN SINGLES AND
PINK PAIR OF PANTIES). SUBJECT ALSO TOOK THE PHONE OUT
OF THE KITCHEN AND TOOK THE BATTERIES OUT OF IT.
VICTIM STATES THAT HER PATIO BLINDS WERE OPEN AND
THAT SOMEONE COULD HAVE BEEN ABLE TO SEE IN. THE
FEMALE VICTIMS IN THE RESIDENCE OTHER THAN THE
VICTIM ARE AS FOLLOW:

6. REPORTING OFFICER   NO   2ND OFFICER   NO   17. SUPERVISOR APPROVING   NO

CASE NUMBER:01-06583

DATE:4-28-01

TIME:3:12 PM

THIS IS A STATEMENT BY: ████████████

WENT AROUND TO GET CLOSER TO THE DOOR AND TO GET MY SHOES TO PUT ON. WHEN I GOT TO THE DOOR, THIS MAN CAME INTO THE DOOR AND HE STUCK A GUN INTO MY FACE. I PUT MY HANDS UP IN THE AIR AND I COULD HARDLY GET IT OUT THAT THE MAN HAD A GUN. I DID SAY IT AND THE MAN SAID FOR EVERYONE TO GET DOWN ON THE FLOOR. HE KEPT SAYING FOR EVERYONE TO GET DOWN. HE CLOSED THE DOOR AND LOCKED THE DEADBOLT. HE WALKED PASSED ME AND I GOT DOWN OVER BY THE DOOR. HE WAS CUSSING AND STUFF. THE BLINDS WAS SHUT BECAUSE I COULD HEAR HIM CLOSING THEM. HE WAS SAYING FOR ALL OF US TO TAKE OFF OUR JEWERLY AND FOR US TO GIVE HIM OUR MONEY. THEN HE SAW A PURSE ON THE TABLE. AND HE ASKED WHO'S PURSE WAS THIS. ████████ SAID THAT IT WAS HER PURSE AND SHE TOLD HIM THAT ALL SHE HAD WAS FIVE DOLLARS. HE WAS TELLING US TO STOP LOOKING AT HIM. HE THEN SAID QUIT LOOIKING UP. HE THEN SAID SOMETHING TO SOMEONE ABOUT, WHAT WAS THAT, IS THAT A KNIFE. HE WAS ASKING US WHERE WERE WE WORK AT. SOMEONE SAID ████████████. HE ASKED WHEN DO WE GET PAID. THEN HE ASKED ████ HOW MUCH MONEY DID SHE HAVE. SHE SAID SOME LIKE TWENTY OR THIRTY DOLLARS. HE SAID FOR HER TO NOT LIE TO HIM OR HE WOULD KILL HER. HE WALKED HER TO THE BACK FOR HER TO GET HER PURSE. I COULD HEAR HIM TALKING AND HIM WALKING AROUND. WE WERE ALL IN THE LIVINGROOM SCARED. I KEPT MY FACE DOWN ON THE FLOOR. WHEN HE CAME BACK INTO THE LIVINGROOM, HE SAID FOR US ALL TO GET UNDRESSED. I WAS FIGURING THAT WE COULDN'T CHASE HIM WENT HE LEAVES IF WE WERE NAKED. HE TOLD ████ TO HAVE ORAL SEX WITH ME. HE SAID THAT HE WANTED TO SEE TWO WOMEN 69 EACH OTHER. I WAS CRYING AND HE HAD TOLD ME TO GET UP AND FOR ME TO MOVE OVER INTO THE LIVINGROOM. I WAS CRYING AND HE CAME OVER TO WHERE I WAS AT AND HE PUT THE GUN ON MY LIPS AND IN MY MOUTH. HE TOLD ME TO SHUT UP. THEN HE SAID, DOES ANYONE OF US HAVE CONDOMS. HE SAID THAT HE WAS GOING TO SHOOT ONE OF US. THEN HE WENT OVER TO ████ AND THEN HE ASKED HER HOW OLD WAS SHE. SHE SAID THAT SHE WAS TWENTY. THEN I HEARD A PLASTIC BAG MOVING AROUND. HE WAS TALKING TO ████ AND HE TOLD HER TO TURN OVER OR BEND OVER OR SOMETHING LIKE THAT. THEN HE SAID, WHO IN HERE SUCK DICK. HE SAID THAT HE WOULD SHOOT ONE OF US. HE ASKED ████ AND THEN HE ASKED ████. SHE SAID YEA. IT SOUND LIKE WHEN SHE SAID YEA, HE WENT OVER TO SOMEONE ELSE. THEN HE SAID HE WANTED YOU TO DO IT. HE WAS TALKING TO ████ HE TOLD ████ TO WATCH. HE KEPT WALKING AROUND IN THE

Page 3 of 7   Signature of person giving statement ████████████

Date _____████████████

Signature of witness _____████████████_____

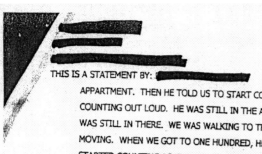

CASE NUMBER:01-06583

DATE:4-28-01

TIME:3:12 PM

THIS IS A STATEMENT BY: █████████

APPARTMENT. THEN HE TOLD US TO START COUNTING TO ONE HUNDRED. WE STARTED COUNTING OUT LOUD. HE WAS STILL IN THE APPARTMENT. WHEN WE GOT TO NINETY, HE WAS STILL IN THERE. WE WAS WALKING TO THE PATIO DOORS AND I HEARD THE BLINDS MOVING. WHEN WE GOT TO ONE HUNDRED, HE WAS STILL THERE. THEN ██████ STARTED COUNTING AGAIN. WE ALL JOINED IN WITH HER. THEN I HEARD THIS PLASTIC BAG AGAIN BEING MOVED AGAIN. HE WAS STILL MOVING AROUND IN THE APPARTMENT AND HE WAS OVER TO THE APPARTMENT DOOR. HE HAD ASKED ABOUT IF ANYONE HAD A DVD PLAYERS AND OTHER STUFF. WE WERE STILL COUNTING THE SECOND GROUP OF HUNDRED. THEN HE HEARD THE DOOR SHUT. THEN ██████ SAID THAT SHE THINKS HE GONE.' I LOOKED UP AND LOOKED OVER TO THE BLINDS. THE BLINDS WERE LEFT CRACKED OPENED SO THAT ANYONE COULD LOOK IN. I THOUGHT THAT I COULD SEE SOMEONE OUT THERE AND WE WERE ALL STILL CRYING AND SCREAMING AND NO CLOTHES ON. I SAID FOR SOMEONE TO CLOSE THE BLINDS BECAUSE I DIDN'T WANT HIM SHOOTING US. WE WERE PUTTING OUR CLOTHES ON AND WE WERE ALL WORRIED THAT HE COULD SHOOT US THREW THE WINDOWS OF THE PATIO. SOMEONE PUT A CHAIR AGAINST THE DOOR TO SECURED THE DOOR AND THEN WE ALL STARTED TO MOVE DOWN THE HALL TO FEEL SAFE. THEN WE ALL WANTED TO CALL THE POLICE BUT THAT IS WHEN WE ALL DESCOVEREED THAT THE PHONES WERE ALL UNPLUGGED. AND THE PHONE IN THE BEDROOM WAS GONE. THE BATTERIES IN THE CORDLESS PHONE WAS GONE AND CELL PHONE WAS GONE. HE MUST HAVE TOOK IT BECUSED IT WAS ON THE TABLE. ██████ REMEMBER THAT SHE HAD A CELL PHONE IN HER PURSE. I I WENT BACK INTO MY BEDROOM AND I FOUND MY EARPIECE TO MY BEDROOM PHONE IN THE CLOSET. I TOOK THAT AND PUT IT INTO THE WALL IN THE KITCHEN. WE BOTH HAD PHONES NOW. WE WERE BOTH CALLING THE POLICE AT THE SAME TIME. AFTER I TALKED TO THE POLICE, I CALLED THE GIRL THAT LIVED UPSTAIRS. SHE CALLED HER MOTHER BECAUSE I COULDN'T REMEMBER HE SECURITY NUMBER FOR WOODLAKE VILLIAGE. WHEN SHE GOT THE NUMBER, SHE CALLED THEM AND SHE TOLD ME THAT THEY WERE ON THEIR WAY. SHE THEN TOLD ME THAT SHE WAS ON HER WAY DOWN THERE. I TOLD HER TO BE CAREFUL BECAUSE THAT WAS THE WAY THAT HE HAD CAME DOWN THE HALL. I HEARD A BANGING ON THE DOOR. I ASKED WHO WAS IT AND IT WAS HER. I OPENED THE DOOR AND ██████ WAS HAVING A AXNEITY ATTACK. ████ WAS CALLING FOR ME TO GET A PAPER BAG. I KNEW THAT I DIDN'T HAVE ANY BAGS, AND THAT IS WHY I KNEW THAT HE HAD BROUGHT IN HIS OWN BAG THAT HE WAS RATTLING. I TOLD RAT THAT I DIDN'T HAVE ANY BAGS AND

Page ⁊ ⌐ of 7   Signature of person giving statement ████████████████

Date _____ ████████████████

Signature of witness ____ ████████████████

OLICE DEPARTMENT

OFFENSE REPORT

AND MULTI-PURPOSE
REPORT FORM

1 VICTIM'S NAME (LAST, FIRST MIDDLE)		2. CASE NO. 01- 41910
2. VICTIM'S ADDRESS		PHONE
SEX. FEMALE	RACE. BLACK	D.O.B. 11181974	SOC. SEC. NO.
3. VICTIM'S PLACE OF EMPLOYMENT OR SCHOOL		6. BUS. PHONE

17 UNIT 17	18. REP AREA B	19. DIST BAKER 6	20. WATCH 0000-0900
22 DISPATCHED AS: 31-ROBBERY-RAPE		23 DISP ACKN 0600 A.M. P.M.	9 REPORTING PERSON'S NAME
24 ADDRESS DISPATCHED TO		25 RET'D.SERV. A.M. P.M.	11) REPORTING PERSON'S ADDRESS CITY	10. RES. PHONE
26 DESCRIBE LOCATION--TYPE PREMISES APARTMENT COMPLEX			8. LOCATION OF OFFENSE (ADDRESS)	12. BUS. PHONE
27 VICT. OCCUPAT DIRECT-CARE COUNSELOR	28 HOURS OF EMPLOY 0000 - 0800	29 SOBRIETY SOBER	13. DATE AND TIME OCCURRED 101001 0600	14. DATE AND TIME REPORTED 101001 0636	16. CLASSIFICATION
30. REQUESTED CRIM INV ☑			15. CRIME OR INCIDENT
CORONER ☐ AMB ☐ TOW ☐ NCIC CK ☐ APB RADIO ☐ T TYPE ☐ OTHER ☐			RAPE / ROBBERY

	31 NAME (FIRST RAPE VICTIm)	AGE 19	BEST CONTACT ADDRESS	BEST PHONE	OTHER PHONE
WITNESS PARENT GUARDIAN	①				
	②				

SUSPECTS	32 NAME AND ADDRESS, SEX, RACE, AGE-DESCRIP -ARR. NO. ①		NAME AND ADDRESS, SEX, RACE, AGE-DESCRIP -ARR. NO. ②
	③		VEH COLOR(S) YEAR MAKE MODEL LIC-YEAR-STATE-NO

STOLEN PROPERTY	33 QTY 1	DESCRIPTION--(SIZE-COLOR-MODEL-STYLE-MATERIAL-CONDITION) LADIES WEDDING RING	SERIAL NO	WHERE LOCATED	VALUE, NEW	AGE	VALUE NOW

INJ PER	34 VICTIM TAKEN TO	35 TRANSPORTED BY	36 DESCRIBE INJURIES	37 CONDITION

MISSING PERSON	38. HT.	WT	HAIR	EYES	COMP.	HAT	COAT	JACKET	SWEATER	BLOUSE/SHIRT	SKIRT/TROUSERS	SHOES	JEWELRY
	39. POSSIBLE CAUSE OF ABSENCE			40 COMPET-ENCY: PHYSICAL			41. PAST RECORD, OTHER DATA-ID. MONEY CARRIED						
	DESTINATION			MENTAL									

BURGLARY	SURGLARY OF BUSINESS ☐ RESIDENCE ☑ GARAGE ☐ OTHERS ☐	TYPE OF OFFENSE FORCED ENTRY ☐ NON FORCED ENTRY ☑ ATTEMPT ☐	HOW ENTERED (DOOR FRONT) SIDE-BACK WINDOW FRONT SIDE BACK ☑ ROOF ☐ GARAGE DOOR ☐ OTHER ☐	MEANS OF ENTRY PRIED OPEN ☐ BROKEN OUT ☐ UNLOCKED ☑	DAYLIGHT ☐ DUSK ☐ DARK ☑ UNKNOWN ☐

NARRATIVE

MS ██████████ REPORTED ON THE ABOVE DATE AND TIME, SHE

WAS AWAKEN INSIDE OF HER APARTMENT BY AN UNKNOWN BLACK

MALE WEARING ALL BLACK CLOTHING WITH HIS FACE COVERED WITH

WHAT APPEARED TO BE A BLACK SCARF AND BLACK HOODED

SWEATSHIRT ARMED WITH WHAT ALSO APPEARED TO BE A 9MM

OFFICE USE ONLY

43 REPORTING OFFICER	NO	44 CASE STATUS (STATUS MUST BE INDICATED FOR ALL CASES, INCLUDING NON-CRIMINAL INCIDENTS)	46 DATE/TIME TYPED NO	47 REPRODUCED BY NO
2ND OFFICER	NO	☐ OPEN (PENDING) ☐ CLOSED ☐ SUSPENDED	48 UNIT REFERRED TO:	49 UCR DISPOSITION
45 SUPERVISOR APPROVING	NO	CASE DISPOSITION (DISPOSITION OF CRIMINAL CASES MAY BE INDICATED AS APPROPRIATE) ☐ UNFOUNDED	50 REVIEWER NO	PAGE NO OF

51 COMPLAINT NO

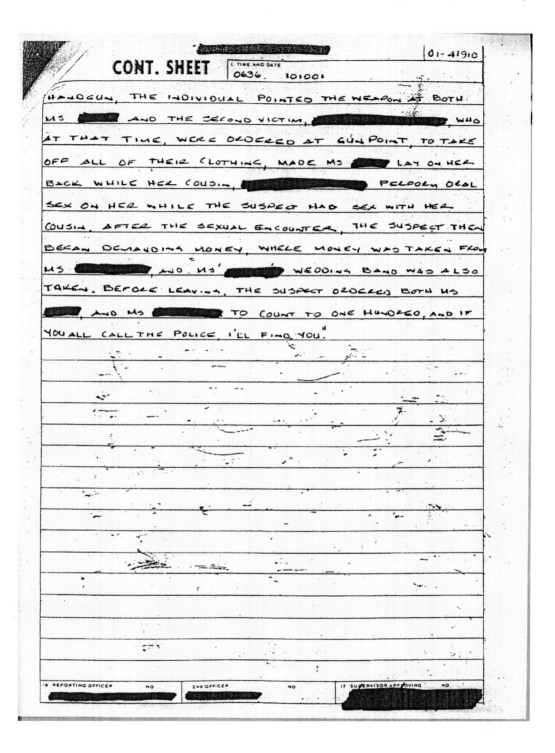

CONT. SHEET

01-41910

I. TIME AND DATE
0636   101001

HANDGUN, THE INDIVIDUAL POINTED THE WEAPON AT BOTH MS ████ AND THE SECOND VICTIM, ██████████, WHO AT THAT TIME, WERE ORDERED AT GUNPOINT, TO TAKE OFF ALL OF THEIR CLOTHING, MADE MS ████ LAY ON HER BACK WHILE HER COUSIN, ██████████ PERFORM ORAL SEX ON HER WHILE THE SUSPECT HAD SEX WITH HER COUSIN. AFTER THE SEXUAL ENCOUNTER, THE SUSPECT THEN BEGAN DEMANDING MONEY, WHILE MONEY WAS TAKEN FROM MS ██████, AND MS' ██████ WEDDING BAND WAS ALSO TAKEN. BEFORE LEAVING, THE SUSPECT ORDERED BOTH MS ████, AND MS ██████ TO COUNT TO ONE HUNDRED, AND IF YOU ALL CALL THE POLICE, I'LL FIND YOU."

16 REPORTING OFFICER	NO	2ND OFFICER	NO	17 SUPERVISOR APPROVING	NO
██████████		██████		██████████	

Case # 01-41910

Date: 10/14/01

Time: 9:51 AM

Voluntary Statement of: ▓▓▓▓▓▓▓▓

Q. IN YOUR OWN WORDS, TELL ME WHAT HAPPENED AS YOU KNOW IT?

A. MY COUSIN ▓▓▓▓ CAME IN LIKE A QUARTER TILL SIX AND I WAS SLEEPING. I DIDN'T KNOW THAT SHE WAS THERE UNTIL THE GUY RANG MY BUZZER. ▓▓▓▓ GOT UP OUT OF THE BED AND ANSWERED THE BUZZER AND ASKED WHO WAS IT. AND THE GUY SAID THAT ▓▓▓▓ SAID THAT I HAD LEFT MY LIGHTS ON. ▓▓▓▓ WALKS BACK INTO MY ROOM AND I THINK SHE WAS LIKE, I DON'T THINK I LEFT MY LIGHTS' ON. THEN I SAID, ▓▓▓▓ WAS ASLEEP AND THEN I SAID THAT SHE LEFT LAST NIGHT. BUT SHE DID COME BACK I JUST DON'T KNOW WHEN SHE CAME BACK. ▓▓▓▓ WENT OUT TO SEE IF SHE LEFT HER LIGHTS ON. AS SHE SLIPPED OUT, HE SLIPPED IN. ▓▓▓▓ RAN BACK INTO THE HOUSE. SHE LOCKED THE DOOR. SHE WALKED BACK INTO THE BEDROOM, SHE LAYED BY MY NIGHTSTAND ON THE FLOOR. AND SHE SAID, SOMEBODY IS PLAYING GAMES WITH US. AS WE WERE TALKING, ▓▓▓▓ SEEN A SHADOW AND THAT WAS WHEN HE MADE HIS PRESENT'S KNOWN. THAT IS WHEN HE SAID TO PUT YOUR FACE INTO THE FLOOR. HE PRECEED TO WALK TOWARDS ▓▓▓▓ AND HER BACK WAS TO HIM. BY THAT TIME THAT IS WHEN I OPENED MY EYES AND HE POINTED A GUN AT ME. HE THEN SAID FOR ME TO TURN OVER AND PUT MY FACE INTO THE PILLOW. I WAS STILL PEEKING AFTER THAT, HE POINTED THE TO ▓▓▓▓'S BACK. HE WAS BEING VERY AGGRESSIVE ABOUT WHERE WAS THE MONEY. HE WAS SAYING, IF WE DIDN'T GIVE HIM THE MONEY, HE WAS GOING TO KILL THIS BITCH. SO I SAID, I DIDN'T HAVE ANY MONEY, THAT I MY PAYDAY HADN"T COME YET. HE ASKED ▓▓▓▓ THE SAME THING AND SHE SAID THAT SHE HAD THIRTY DOLLARS IN HER PURSE. HE SAID WHERE IN YOUR PURSE AND SHE SAID IN THE SIDE IN A LITTLE POUCH. AFTER THAT, HE SAID TAKE OFF ALL OF YOUR CLOTHES SO THAT WE COULDN'T CHASE AFTER HIM WHEN HE LEAVES. AFTER THAT HE TURNED ON THE BEDROOM LIGHT. MY SONS WERE LYING IN THE BED WITH ME AND ▓▓▓▓ STARTED TO CRY. AND HE PUT THE GUN IN HIS FACE AND HE SAID IF I DIDN'T SHUT HIM UP, HE WAS GOING TO KILL HIM. HE MADE ME GET OUT OF THE BED WITH MY BACK TURNED TO HIM AND HE MADE ME PUT AN ORANGE SHIRT ON MY FACE. HE MADE ME GET MY KIDS OUT OF THE BED. HE MADE ME WALK MY KIDS TO THEIR ROOM BACKWARDS. ▓▓▓▓ THEN ASKED HIM IF HE WAS GOING TO KILL MY MOMMY AND HE SAID NO. HE MADE ME WALK BACK TO THE ROOM WHILE HE HAD THE GUN TO MY BACK. BY THAT TIME, WE BOTH DIDN'T HAVE ON ANY CLOTHES. THEN HAD ASKED US IF WE WERE LEISBIANS AND HE TOLD HIM NO, THAT WE WERE COUSINS. THEN HE MADE US

Page 2 of 7 Signature of subject giving statement _____

Date _____

Signature of witness _____

Police Department

Case # 01-41910

Date: 10/14/01

Time: 9:51 AM

Voluntary Statement of:

PREFORM ORAL SEX ON EACH OTHER. HE WAS HAVING A GEENERAL CONVERSATION WITH US. HE WAS ASKING US WHO WAS MARRIED AND I TOLD HIM IT WAS ME. HE WAS LOOKING AROUND WHILE HE WAS HAVING US DO THAT TO OURSELVES. HE WAS IN THE NIGHTSTANDS, THE DRAWERS, THE CLOSETS AND OUR PURSES. HE WENT INTO THE KITCHEN BECAUSE HE HAD ASKED WHERE WAS THE GARBAGES BAGS AT. HE KEPT WALKING IN AND OUT CHECKING ON THE KIDS. HE HAD ASKED US IF WE SUCK DICK AND WE TOLD HIM NO. HE ASKED HWERE WAS OUR MAN'S AT AND I SAID HE WAS NOT HERE RIGHT NOW. BY THAT TIME HE MADE ME GET OFF OF HER AND TO GET ON MY BACK. HE SAID TO KEEP THE PILLOW ON MY FACE AND HE SAID SCOOT DOWN TO THE END OF THE BED. I WASN'T MOVING FAST ENOUGH AND SO HE GRABBED ME BY MY LEFT LEG. THAT IS WHEN HE MADE ▓▓▓▓▓ PREFORM ORAL SEX ON ME. THAT IS WHEN HE WAS SAYING DID WE HAVE ANY CONDOMS OR BABY OIL. HE PRECEED TO LOOK FOR THOSE THINGS AND HE WAS SAYING IF HE FOUND ANY OF THOSE THINGS. HE WAS GOING TO KILL US. SO ▓▓▓▓▓ SAID THERE WAS SOME VASELINE IN THERE AND HE ASKED WHERE AND SHE SAID IN THE BATHROOM. HE LEFT AND WENT INTO THE BATHROOM TO GET THE VASELINE. HE CAME BACK INTO THE ROOM AND THAT IS WHEN HE ASKED IF SHE HAD HAD ANAL SEX BEFORE. SHE TOLD HIM NO, THAT IT HURT TOO MUCH. SO HE PRECEED TO HAVE SEXUAL INTERCOURSE WITH HER ANYWAY. AFTER HE CAME, HE GOT UP. HE PICKED UP THE BAG AND AS HE WAS LEAVING, I WAS PEEKING. HE THEN TOLD US TO COUNT TO ONE HUNDRED. WE WERE COUNTING TOO FAST SO HE TOLD US TO COUNT MORE SLOWLY. THEN HE LEFT. WHEN I HEARD THE LOCK CLICK, I GOT UP AND LOCKED THE DOOR. THEN I GRABBED THE PHONE AND CALL 911 AND MY HUSBAND. THAT'S IT.

Q. DID YOU KNOW THE GUY THAT GOT INTO YOUR APARTMENT?
A. NO, BUT I KNOW HIS VOICE.

Q. COULD YOU IDENTIFY THE VOICE?
A. IF I HEAR IT AGAIN, YES I WILL KNOW IT.

Q. CAN YOU DESCRIBED THE MAN?
A. HE WAS A LITTLE BIT TALLER THAN ME, I AM 5'8 AND HE WAS THIN BUILT. MY SON TOLD ME THAT HE WAS LIGHT COMPLEXED. HE ALSO TOLD ME THAT THE MAN HAD ON BLACK AND

Page 3 of 7 Signature of subject giving statement _____

Date _____

Signature of witness _____

The Inclusion/Exclusion Dichotomy

How did you go about including or excluding a given report from the series?

As you read the reports, did you systematically classify the offender's characteristics, his actions, what he said to the victim, and in what order he completed his criminal act? Extracting data from the narrative is document analysis. Identifying key phrases or words and actions are the crux of crime series analysis, and represent the essence of this chapter: analyzing qualitative information and applying qualitative research methods. Did you take notes or simply "register to memory" information from one report to the next? Did something trigger in a subsequent report that caused you to return to a previous one, identifying a common theme across the series? This is the process of using the inclusion-exclusion dichotomy: always asking yourself whether the information provided in this report is linked to the series (include it) or not (exclude it).

What were the critical elements of the crime that lent support for their inclusion? In this collection of reports, offender characteristics, at least race and gender, do not assist the analyst in determining what to include or exclude from the series. The suspect in all of these reports remains the same. In a community or neighborhood where the demographics of the victims and offenders are homogenous, other qualitative factors must be pursued: hair styles, quality of teeth (e.g., split, gold, decaying), clothing (e.g., favorite baseball cap or jacket), cologne smells, alcohol on the breath, and certainly the perpetrator's actions and utterances.

The three reports are only a sample of a sexual assaults series that includes more than 25 cases. Within them, the offender consistently threatened to kill the victims,

used a handgun, and called them "bitch." He forced his victims to perform oral sex or "play with themselves." He targeted money, jewelry, and, in multiple cases, asked the whereabouts of any DVDs or DVD players as part of the home invasion-burglary-rape. He tied his victims up with materials found inside the home (telephone cord, rope) and used Vaseline or baby oil. In several cases, he asked if the victims had condoms or used a plastic bag instead. In many cases he told his victims "to remove your clothes so that you can't chase me," and had the victims count to 100 or 1000 when he was ready to leave. The encounters that definitively make-up this series also share the fact that the offender knew something about the daily routines of each victim, and that she did not have a boyfriend or husband, even to the extent that he was defiant when the victim said her significant other would be home soon.

It is to this type of detail that effective crime analysts must look when assessing qualitative information, whether the crime is as serious as a rape or not. Qualitative information can be extracted from reports of commercial or residential burglaries, robberies, peeping toms, thefts from cars, and just about any other police report. The challenge for crime analysis is to pay particular attention to detail, look closely at the specifics of the behavior, and focus on the peculiar nature of every crime report the analyst assesses. Offender signatures can include the chronology or sequence of events leading up to and in the commission of their crimes. They can also include the targets of their aggression, victim traits, characteristics of certain homes or businesses, property stolen, and property seized as mementos of the event (e.g., panties, bras). In some cases it may be a bizarre gesture or act, like writing a note on a bathroom mirror in lipstick, leaving a half empty beer can on the kitchen table, or defecating in the living room. These qualitative pieces of information are the difference between identifying and solving a series and simply reporting crime statistics.

As you reviewed the crime reports, did you recognize the inductive method or process you used to develop a series? Did you recognize how you intuitively responded to a document? Could you replicate this process every day?

If so, then you are capable of being a qualitative researcher. The methodical and systematic manner in which you reviewed and extracted pertinent information from these reports illustrates the use of qualitative data sources and the qualitative method of document and content analysis.

Neighborhood Field Research: A Case for Problem Solving (A Strategic Example)

Today, many crime analysts use crime mapping to identify crime hot spots. These techniques have become rather simple to use—some are automated—but identifying these hot spots are not the end product, and in many cases they only verify the intuitive police knowledge we already hold. As a crime analyst, you must find ways to bring value to your department beyond regurgitating information from police reports or common knowledge. Agencies embracing community policing and problem solving must be prepared to conduct in-depth analysis of troubled areas. Systematically identifying hot spots is the beginning, but supplementing this finding with documented officer knowledge of the area, creating mental maps, entering into the field to conduct ride-alongs, and making and recording observations gets to the crux of what Herman Goldstein intended. Interviewing officers, victims, witnesses, offenders, neighbors, and businesses will shed a great deal of light on the scope and nature of the problems within the targeted area.

Hot Spot Analysis

See Chapter 15 to learn about choropleth mapping, which aggregates crime by geographic area. Use these techniques to rank order the seriousness of crime, violence, or fear based on frequency or rate (see Chapter 10). Use these priorities to narrow your research focus and limit your energies to issues most important to your citizens or department. In assessing crime data, we urge you to use at least six months' worth—a larger set (a year or more) is preferable. In this way, you eliminate the changing priorities of crisis management or responding to vocal minorities or political nuances. Knowing the extent of community problems, and placing them in historical and geographic context, puts your agency in control of your limited resources and will improve your ability to carry solutions to their successful ends.

Having set some priorities for problem solving, it is now time for the crime analyst to conduct a more in-depth analysis of the top-ranking hot spots or neighborhoods. This is where qualitative information and qualitative research methods come in to play. Now that you have a sense of place, you need to gather more information about the environmental, socio-economic, and cultural factors affecting the problem. Conduct open-ended interviews with officers working the area, neighbors, and business owners, and schedule ride-alongs during different shifts to obtain first-hand observations about what is happening, to whom it is happening, and to what extent it is happening within the area of inquiry. Conduct both observer-participation and participant-observations—that is, ride-alongs as well as "covert" field research discussed previously.

Finally, while remaining objective throughout the study, take copious, detailed field notes. While this chapter does not lend itself to a full discussion of taking effective field notes, leave it to say that meticulously and regularly documenting your observations makes all the difference in your ability to make use of the qualitative information you collect while conducting field research.[1]

We now turn to a deductive scenario—beginning with aggregate data about a community and narrowing the focus and "zooming" in on specific issues or hot spots. Two different jurisdictional studies are offered as examples to better understand the scope of the projects and the tasks at hand. In both cases, crime mapping techniques established priorities, which guided these more ethnographic studies of time and place.

Tempe Beat 11 Study

The Tempe (AZ) Police Department conducted an in-depth analysis of the most northern beat within the city. The unit looked at one year's worth of crime and call-for-service data to determine the top ten most frequent crime and CFS locations. Among the top ten locations were a water park, a discount motel, an apartment complex, and a series of troubled businesses. The problem-solving team followed up with open-ended interviews of patrol officers working the beat, and identified an additional location (hot spot) of concern—a city park frequented and nationally publicized as a location known for obtaining sexual favors, sexually transmitted disease (STD), and public displays of sexual

misconduct. It was only through these open-ended interviews that details of the deviant behavior were collected and understood.

Participant observations were conducted at these hot spot locations at various times to observe both the legitimate and illegitimate behavior occurring at and around the areas. Crime analysts watched and recorded what people did, witnessing legal and illegal activities. The team saw prostitution, drug sales, and assaults—as well as people assisting others in times of need, people waiting for public transportation, and the like. The primary concern or issue at the water park turned out to be criminal damage and theft from automobiles; the discount motel problems were related to drugs and prostitution; and domestic violence and commercial thefts were among the concerns in the remaining locations. Additional daytime security, controlled access, and other crime prevention solutions proved successful in reducing crime and calls for service at our target locales.

The analysis of sexual misconduct at the city park illustrates the importance of qualitative information and the use of ethnographic research. Two analysts conducted covert observations (parked in a car within the park's parking lot) and documented the rather bizarre behavior, which turned out to involve homosexual activity among men.

Since "decent" citizens did not frequent the park, there were few documented calls for service, which made it difficult to establish peak times. Traffic counters were placed at the entrances and exits of the park to record the times and days with the most activity. This information was not used for enforcement purposes, but instead was used to determine a schedule for which outreach counselors from the county's health department entered the park, interviewed

---

[1] For more in-depth information on writing effective field notes, see Robert M. Emerson, Rachel I. Fretz, and Linda L. Shaw, *Writing Ethnographic Fieldnotes* (Chicago: University of Chicago Press, 1995); or John Lofland and Lyn H. Lofland, *Analyzing Social Settings: A Guide to Qualitative Observation and Analysis* (Belmont, CA: Wadsworth, 1984).

park-goers, and offered them information on programs and STD prevention. The nature of the problem was not addressed as a criminal matter but one of health and disease control, particularly AIDS transmission. This more in-depth assessment and creative response led the community to better understand that the problem was not a matter of homosexual misconduct, but one of estranged, sex-addicted heterosexual males potentially infecting their spouses with AIDS. The project leaders have determined that group therapy does not appear to reduce this behavior, but that treating these individuals as if they were suicidal—thus putting them on suicide watches and getting them into one-on-one counseling—is the only limited solution working to date.

Five Points Ethnography

As part of a PhD dissertation research effort, one of the authors has conducted both hot spot and ethnographic research of high-crime neighborhoods in Denver, Colorado. Using neighborhood-based crime data offered via the Internet, neighborhoods were ranked by crime volume and prioritized for further research. The Five Points neighborhood has had a long reputation for being the most crime ridden area in town. In an attempt to better understand the scope and nature of crime and community concerns within this area, observer-participation and newspaper content analysis were conducted. While this research effort is continuing and will include police ride-alongs and open-ended interviews with police officers and citizens alike, the following discussion is offered to illustrate the utility of collecting qualitative information and using qualitative research methods during problem solving efforts.

As in the previous example, GIS and demographic analysis of census data and officially reported crime data spanning multiple years were used to understand the extent and longevity of crime in the area of concern. Historical accounts of Five Points were collected, including manuscripts about the historic Curtis Park neighborhood, the predominately prosperous African-American community around the apex of Five Points, and the more current transformation of the gentrified Ballpark neighborhood laced with luxury condos and expensive lofts near the home of the Colorado Rockies baseball team.

In addition to this historical and geographic contextual analysis, a content or document analysis was conducted to ascertain pertinent issues and social concerns within Five Points. LexisNexis was used to search for newspaper articles in *The Denver Post*, querying for keywords like "Five Points," "crime," "police," and the like. The search returned over 150 articles, published over a decade. Discussions of crime, violence (particularly the "Summer of Violence" in 1993), poverty, public housing, gangs, drugs, police brutality, the underground economy, and other socio-economic topics prevailed. All of these discussions allowed the research to be put in a better social and historical context, something to which general statistics or anecdotal police data do not lend themselves.

Participant observations shed additional light on the types of activities, human interactions, and financial enterprises (legal and illegal in nature) that were witnessed first-hand. Time was spent riding the light-rail to and from the area, restaurants and taverns were frequented, and walking and driving the various streets in Five Points shed a great deal of insight into the community, its neighbors, and its culture. Crime analysts cannot afford to be ethnocentric if they hope to remain objective about research projects and problem solving efforts within community policing agencies. Collecting qualitative information about troubled neighborhoods, parks, business districts, drinking establishments, and community hang-outs is paramount to designing and implementing effective solutions. Qualitative research is vital to achieving sound findings.

The production of crime, like the research endeavor, is a social enterprise, and gathering more robust and contextual information will better inform decision and policy makers. Not every community is ready to commit to Goldstein's POP paradigm, but those that are will find greater success using qualitative information and research methods than in any other contemporary policing model. Knowing how crime, poverty, racism, gentrification, gangs, drugs, violence, and the underground economy interplay lends itself to more creative solutions and more long-lasting effects.

Newspaper Document Analysis: Public Opinion and Citizen Perception of the Police (an Administrative Example)

Administrative crime analysis calls for an understanding of the political and social aspects of police work. Whether the analyst is trying to figure out if the community has a positive image of the police, or is attempting to ascertain the socio-political issues surrounding a particular neighborhood, document analysis of the local newspaper is a good way to collect and assess this kind of information. Newspaper document analysis has become easier since the introduction of computers, the Internet, and periodical databases. This section takes a brief look at three techniques that can assist the analyst in researching administrative issues.

LexisNexis

LexisNexis began in 1973 as an online (private telecommunications network)

research tool for legal research. Since then, the company has expanded its offerings to include search tools for numerous public and private sector professions. The product used most often by social science researchers is LexisNexis Academic.

LexisNexis Academic allows users to search full-text articles from more than 5,600 national and regional newspapers, wire services, broadcast transcripts, business and news journals, state and federal laws, and court case citations. Articles for some of these sources go back 20 years or more.[1]

Analysts can use LexisNexis to search local newspaper or national news for topics of interest or to find out about how other cities may be dealing with crime or community problems can be a time saving endeavor, but it does have a price associated with it. If you can get a local college or university library to allow you to use the system as a community service, you might be able to save some money while gaining access to a wonderful resource for qualitative information.

Figure 8-1. A LexisNexis search for crime in the Five Points neighborhood.

---

[1] LexisNexis, "LexisNexis Academic," http://www.lexisnexis.com/academic/universe/academic (accessed June 3, 2004).

Newspaper Web Sites

Most newspapers are now online, and some maintain archives of past articles that you can search. This simple and affordable method for monitoring crime and police related issues is a form of qualitative document or content analysis. You can "cut-and-paste" any articles of interest into a word processing document or database for future reference or queries. You can search the archives for past articles, though there is typically a fee to read the full text. If you are working a major case or researching an important topic, this fee is well worth the time and energy you will save by searching these automated systems rather than going to the library and scanning months or years of microfiche or paper copies, assuming you would do it in the first place. Newspaper document analysis can be a great way to look into current social or political issues, find names and dates, and get quotes from local politicians, business leaders, or residents. Document analysis can be used effectively for administrative, strategic (problem solving), or tactical crime analysis. Finding names of relatives, associates, hang-outs, advocates, social programs, and the like can assist you in bringing an added value to your applied research efforts.

Figure 8-2. The Cape Cod Times *is one of many newspapers to offer its articles online.*

Paper Newspapers

Simply monitoring your local newspaper can provide valuable knowledge and information about your community. Either clip relevant articles and develop a filing system that will allow you to search and locate related articles at a later time, or scan the articles into a document or database and index the material so you can search for it later. The key to using qualitative information is being systematic and methodical. By indexing these kinds of articles, you begin to build a knowledge base about your community: what's happening, what is planned, what people are doing (both legal and illegal), and with whom they are doing it. You can provide valuable information to your chief, problem solving team, or investigators, who may not have the time or opportunity to research this level of detail. You become a valuable resource to your agency by taking the time to gather and record this kind of information.

Conclusion

Crime analysts rely on many forms of applied research methods, both quantitative and qualitative. This chapter focused on the use of observer participation, open-ended interviews, participant observation, document analysis, and the reading of ethnographies to better understand crime and criminals—and the social and political context in which they operate. A number of qualitative sources of information were identified, and a series of examples showed how these sources could be applied at the tactical, strategic, and administrative levels.

While crime analysts tend to focus on statistics and crime mapping as the basis for sound research, this chapter suggests that a well-rounded analyst looks to multiple methods and data sources to verify his or her findings or to add additional insights to the analysis. Qualitative research methods and qualitative information sources allow crime analysts to better understand the context in which crime occurs, and to gain a better understanding of the historical and geographic environment in which police officers must operate. Qualitative analysis should be seen as a tool for (1) better identifying crime series and building known offender databases, (2) gathering and assessing social and political issues surrounding a particular neighborhood problem or hot spot, and (3) keeping informed about police-community relations that inform police policy, training, and pubic relations efforts. It is the authors' hope that after reading this chapter, you are more equipped to conduct all three types of crime analysis, and that you are more prepared to gather additional information. You will become a major resource for your agency, from the chief to the patrol officer, and to your community, from the mayor or county commissioner to the local resident.

Recommended Readings

Adler, Patricia A. *Wheeling and Dealing: An Ethnography of an Upper-Level Drug Dealing and Smuggling Community.* New York: Columbia University Press, 1993.

Altheide, David L. *Qualitative Media Analysis.* Thousand Oaks, CA: Sage Publications, 1996.

Anderson, Elijah. *A Place on the Corner.* Chicago: University of Chicago Press, 1978.
———. *Streetwise: Race, Class, and Change in an Urban Community.* Chicago: University of Chicago Press, 1990.
———. *Code of the Street: Decency, Violence, and the Moral Life of the Inner City.* New York: W.W. Norton, 1999.

Boba, Rachel. *Problem Analysis in Policing.* Washington, DC: Police Foundation, 2003.

Consortium for Community Policing. *Understanding Community Policing: A Framework for Action.* Washington, DC: U.S. Department of Justice, 1994.

Denzin, Norman K. and Yvonna S. Lincoln, eds. *Collecting and Interpreting Qualitative Material.* Thousand Oaks, CA: Sage Publications, 1997.

Douglas, Jack D. *Understanding Everyday Life.* Chicago: Aldine, 1970.

Eck, John E. and William Spelman. *Problem Solving: Problem-Oriented Policing in Newport News.* Washington, DC: U.S. Department of Justice, 1987.

Emerson, Robert M. *Contemporary Field Research: Perspectives and Formulations.* Prospect Heights, IL: Waveland Press, 2001.
———, Rachel I. Fretz, and Linda L. Shaw. *Writing Ethnographic Fieldnotes.* Chicago: University of Chicago Press, 1995.

Goldstein, Herman. *Problem-Oriented Policing.* New York: McGraw-Hill, 1990.

Johnson, John M. *Doing Field Research.* New York: Free Press, 1978.

Lofland, John and Lyn H. Lofland. *Analyzing Social Settings: A Guide to Qualitative Observation and Analysis.* Belmont, CA: Wadsworth, 1984.

Sanders, William B. *Gangbangs and Drive-bys: Grounded Culture and Juvenile Gang Violence.* New York: Aldine de Gruyter, 1994.

9
Effective Presentations

Dennis Kessinger

Reading about how to give a Microsoft PowerPoint presentation to elected officials or how to effectively handle a high-stress press conference is a lot like reading about how to ride a bicycle or enjoy a romantic evening—the reality is in the doing. There was a time—admit it—when you didn't know the difference between GIS and GPS or how least squares analysis could help police work. Was a "rape kit" something a predator took to his crime or was it what hospital triage workers used, or both? You mastered all of those issues by understanding the concepts, seeing their relevance to your duties, experimenting with them, and then applying them. Giving an effective presentation to your commander or to a conference of 4,000 attendees is no different: learn the technology, master the techniques, apply the tools, and then go do it.

When Walter Cronkite was asked how he got rid of the butterflies in his stomach he said, "I always have butterflies; the trick is to get them to fly in formation." This chapter will provide the written flight plan so that your butterflies will assist you in your take off to a higher level of professional presentation. In addition to presenting your analyses to patrol or detectives, you will soon be equally comfortable being interviewed on television, responding to hostile media questions, or stating your case to your state's legislature.

How Mastering This Skill Will Enhance Your Professionalism and Value to Your Agency

One morning, you are sitting at your desk, safely surrounded by your computers and pin-maps. The keyboard responds easily to your deft touch and the database reveals patterns and trends that can be cleverly crafted into deployment bulletins, investigative leads, and command staff advisories.

> Wait a minute! I'm a crime analyst, not a public speaker!

Unexpectedly, the chief (sheriff, commander, or your pass-the-buck-supervisor-who-shouldn't-have-been-promoted) comes to you and says, "Hey, crime dog! I need you to give a twenty-minute talk at my service club luncheon today. There will be about 250 business and civic leaders and I want you to talk about how burglaries are down since I've been in charge. I also want a PowerPoint presentation with those cute moving graphics, and then be prepared for a ten-minute question-and-answer session on how crime analysis uses cutting edge technology to fight crime."

You suddenly remember the statistic—quite relevant right now—about how people fear public speaking more than death. You realize there will be 500 eyes watching you and 500 ears listening to what you say. However, you relax as you know you are a professional who has already mastered the technique of presenting complex crime and operational information in simple-to-understand formats—in the form of bulletins and flyers—that both persuade and inform. You now have the opportunity to present this same information in a different format—a presentation—that can have a broader community influence.

The skill of public speaking and presenting has a direct benefit to you and your career as well as advancing the professionalism of your agency. Within the organization, there are specialized fields: field evidence technicians, forensic specialists, homicide detectives, parolee tracking teams, SWAT members, hostage negotiators, and the hierarchy of patrol and investigations. Each of these experts may give a media interview or appropriate public talk regarding specific issues in their field: a particular case, a unique tool, or an unusual occurrence.

On the other hand, as a crime analyst, your skill area involves the agency-wide application of information that the public, media, and decision-makers will rely on to understand how the agency works and the changing environment in the community: Are the number of rapes up or down? How will the new shopping mall affect traffic in the area? How many registered sex offenders live near schools? How will the addition of two new patrol cars affect response times in Beat 2? What type of technology is available to reduce consumer fraud?

Your existing skills in being an "information disseminator" make you the logical professional to develop responses to these questions and to respond to the inevitable follow-up questions. As you expand your abilities to clearly present agency information, you will create a niche for yourself as an exceptional support person who can aid the chief executive in providing the necessary information to those who request it and allow police executives to set policy responses based on accurate data analyses.

The idea of creating an "aura of indispensability" because of your exceptional presentation skills is exciting. But how do you go from stomach churning, knee-knocking, deer-in-the-headlights reality to a comfortable and professional presenter who creates the best possible image of the organization? By simply realizing that the process you used to become a skilled crime analyst—learning the technology, mastering the techniques, applying the tools, and then doing it—is the same. Making an effective presentation is a just another skill set you can easily master.

Let's Get Started

There are three components to effective presentations: technology (equipment and verbal), technique (style and materials), and tactics (appropriate application of knowledge). Like an orchestra conductor, you will soften one component and increase the volume on another depending on the circumstance. However, the strategic blending of the presentation tools is what will produce the final product.

The technology aspect deals with applying external tools to support and define the presentation. These can be overhead transparencies, easels with colored marking pens, PowerPoint slides, show-and-tell items, pin-maps, pointers, laptops, props, or other items to display to your intended audience. This also includes the use of language to sustain a professional presentation. Technology is what supports the presentation.

> **Your Presentation Tools:**
> 1. Technology
> 2. Technique
> 3. Tactics

The technique (style and material) is how you present yourself to the audience. What do you wear? How to stand? What information is appropriate to relay? How do you move on stage, in front of the camera, in front of a panel of experts? How do you use your voice to create the impression you need? How to react to those 500 eyes staring at you? Technique is how you give the presentation.

> There are always three speeches for every one presentation:
> 1. The speech you *planned* to give.
> 2. The one you *actually* gave.
> 3. The one you *should have* given.

The tactics (appropriate application of knowledge) are where you present the concepts you wish to get across. You know where you want to go and you craft your presentation to cover the key issues and then have the audience draw the logical conclusion. You begin by determining the result you want (e.g., generating a call to action, providing scary or reassuring information, stating critical facts to support a change of attitude) and by giving honest and accurate supporting data you create the premise for the presentation. Tactics are the themes you want the audience to know.

You've been asked (ordered) to give a presentation. What do you do first?

What Is the Goal?

The first question in preparing for any presentation is what is the intent, the purpose of the talk? Is it to persuade, inform, frighten, inflame, or motivate? That is, what do you want the audience to get out your presentation? Do you want them to agree to a particular perspective? To provide information so they can draw their own conclusions? To frighten or inflame them into taking a desired course of action? Or to motivate them to become involved in an issue? Once you determine the goal, you can create the themes.

Who Is the Audience?

How you structure your presentation will depend on the audience. Clearly, an interview on the local news channel will require a different style than talking to the Garden Club. Similarly, speaking to your peers at a conference is formatted in a different manner than how you would address your state legislature. Nevertheless, the techniques you employ—eye contact, gestures, voice modulation—are consistently applied.

What Is the Subject Matter?

Are you to talk about blood splatter analysis? Elder abuse? Sexual predators? How geographic information systems (GIS) improve response times? What is crime analysis? To refine your presentation you need to know how general or how specific is your talk. Also, how much information can be discussed? Ongoing cases require extreme caution as to confidentiality and case preservation. Descriptive analyses of burglary trends are generally safe. Determining the subject matter borders will help structure the talk and create a thematic approach.

How Long and How Many?

How much time will you have? A TV or radio interview may literally be thirty seconds. A keynote speech may be twenty minutes and a presentation to a legislative body could take hours. Also, how many will be listening? An informal "Neighborhood Watch" question-and-answer presentation is presented differently than a keynote speech in a hotel ballroom—not so much text, but in logistics: visibility to materials, voice amplification, responding to questions, how you will be introduced, and so on.

Planning the Presentation:
- What is the goal?
- What are the themes?
- What is the structure?
- How much time is available?
- How many people are you addressing?

Let's use the topic of burglary in the community as our example.

The Chief walked in to your office and told you he heard from a service club friend that there is an "epidemic rise in burglaries." The Chief wanted you to show how burglaries are actually down and how his adopting crime analysis as a proactive tool benefits the community and the agency. "Get started," he said, "the luncheon is in three hours."

Goal? You want to counter the perception of an "epidemic," show that burglaries are down, and that crime analysis is a positive addition to police services. You know you have twenty minutes to fill and you must be prepared for ten minutes of Q&A. Your goal is to show burglaries are in fact down, crime analysis is proactive, and the Chief is a very progressive leader (while not stated bluntly, it is implied with supporting evidence).

Themes? As a rule of thumb, focus on three themes. The "rule of threes" in public speaking is a proven technique to provide information, explain concepts, and give the audience (and you) an outline to follow and remember. The "themes" can be one group of three for a very short presentation (30-second spot) for one topic, or multiple groups of threes for as long a speech as is necessary. For the luncheon presentation, the burglary and crime analysis themes could be an expanded set of threes, such as:

1. Past burglary data compared to current burglary data,
2. The positive effect of crime analysis on department personnel when providing proactive burglary information, and
3. The correlation between the Chief's actions and the decline in burglaries.

The crime analysis component could be:

1. An overview of what crime analysis is,
2. How it is applied at the agency, and
3. How cops (deployment, crime/suspect correlation) and citizens (faster response times) benefit.

For a 30-second TV interview spot, themes and the rule-of-threes could be that since he became Chief:

1. Burglaries have declined 8% every year. This is due, in part, because
2. He instituted a crime analysis unit that proactively uses data to effectively deploy personnel, and
3. That links known suspects to crimes, which increases arrests and improves public safety.

The benefit to you of this "theme" and "rule of threes" approach is in the ease of following prepared notes or speaking from memory. Even if you are asked to give a two-hour presentation at a conference, expanding each component in groups of three can make a speech flow logically and without skipping crucial points or having to backtrack.

Structure? Here is where you adjust the presentation to "fit" the audience. Speaking to a group of elderly burglary victims requires a distinctly different approach than speaking to a legislative body. Here is where voice modulation, enunciation, eye contact, and gestures can all assist the audience in following your presentation and letting the audience "connect" with you.

Time? It has been said that the average speaker can talk at 400 to 600 words a minute while the average reader reads around 200 words a minute. People generally absorb new concepts and discussions at a slower pace than a speaker can talk. Once you know—or have an approximate—time allotment for your talk, adjust the themes so that you can address them appropriately without rushing; you're a professional explaining important concepts of interest to your audience, not asking them to buy household products.

On the other hand, a fast-talking, energetic speaker can truly "pump-up" an audience. If you are giving a motivational talk—such as to recruit Neighborhood Watch volunteers—then speak rapidly with enthusiasm. Just be aware that the older the audience is or with an audience that may be less familiar with the topic (how methamphetamine labs damage the environment), you should plan on speaking at a slower pace to inform and persuade them.

People? If your audience is briefing room or living room sized, the talk can be more informal and you may wish to allow for questions during the talk. In smaller venues, informality is appropriate. Here the themes and rule of threes have great value because you can answer questions and then return to the theme at hand. On TV and radio interviews, you will be interrupted and directed by the interviewer. Keep the themes in mind and try to cover each one if possible, even if just for a sound bite. In large hotel ballrooms, presentations can actually be the easiest, as you can stay within the themes and your planned presentation, generally without audience input or mid-speech questions.

Format? An old public speaking axiom holds that all you have to do during a speech is 1) tell them what you are going to talk about, 2) talk about it, and then 3) tell them what you said. (Rule of threes again.) In planning of the format of your speech, determine the audience needs (voice amplification, view-ability of the screen if using visual aids) and how best connect with them. In large room presentations, an easel with markers is worthless and in small rooms, a PowerPoint presentation may be overkill. Determine the best method of making your presentation easy to follow and absorb; be less concerned with making a good impression and more concerned with providing valuable information.

Getting Ready for the Presentation
Gathering the Materials

This is the easy part. You already have advanced skills in accessing and manipulating data. The presentation attribute you want to refine here is in editing and refining of material for maximum effect. In our burglary scenario, you would retrieve your burglary data—both descriptive and inferential—to create the necessary data elements. What are the key points to discuss? The method of entry? Point of entry? Day of week? Time of day? Type of structure? Any or all of these could provide a good starting point to format a presentation.

The Chief wanted you to talk about the decrease in burglaries. What if the data shows an increase? First, never manipulate the data to create a false impression. This can be misusing hard data such as time ranges, categories, or definitions, or misusing charts and graphics to mislead. If possible, you could try to show the decrease in burglaries in certain sectors or beats, or by showing that when adjusted for population, there was a decrease despite the increase in raw numbers.

The point here is that never create a false or inaccurate presentation because—as experience has often demonstrated—someone in the audience or who later acquires your presentation will invariably "test the data" and it is far worse to be shown either misleading or incompetent. If, after your best ethical attempts, you are unable to give the Chief the data he wants, explain the dilemma and ask for guidance. If you are giving the presentation it is your reputation on the line; keep it honest and ethical.

Multiple Use of the Same Material

One of the advantages of being a crime analyst is your ability to target the analyses for various clients. You can create a burglary analysis that provides deployment options for patrol, known offender correlation for detectives, administrative updates for command, and public release data for the media. When creating your presentation, think ahead about other presentations you could make with the same material: Rotary Club today, City Council next week, public access TV the week after, and then the citizen's patrol monthly meeting. When gathering material for presentations, always think of multiple uses.

When to Use—and Not to Use—Technology

Have you ever been to a workshop or conference where the PowerPoint presentation didn't work properly because the hardware locked up? Have you ever watched a group of techies try to fix a laptop and adjust cables and do multiple reboots while the speaker looked on in panic? Have you observed the bulb in the overhead blink out or the microphone constantly squelch with feedback? Most of us have. Technology can be a powerful addition to a presentation…it can also make you look very

unprofessional when it doesn't work right and you're caught flat-footed.

The best use of technology is where it is limited to supporting your talk, not the focus of the talk. An easel, an overhead, of a multimedia display should only be used to make clear a concept that could be explained orally. Think of the supporting tool as a way of emphasizing certain points. In our burglary example:

- In a small venue presentation, you could write on the easel the first theme "Burglaries are down" and circle it with a different color. Then write the statistic and draw an arrow to it. Reconnect to the audience—visually by eye contact and physically by facing them—and continue with the explanation. Only return to the easel as needed for other themes or highlights.

- In a mid-sized conference room where an overhead projector or PowerPoint style presentation can be used, you show a slide and then emphasize the points. Do not read the side as if it were part of the speech! You should concentrate on expanding the information with anecdotes or stories that support the slide. If you are using a text slide—"Burglaries are down 8 percent"—you let the display give the data and you provide the reasons: "Due to analyzing crime statistics, we found patterns in the burglaries that let us focus on certain known criminals."

- In ballroom size venues, even projections are sometimes too small to be effective. If appropriate, handouts with charts and data can be used for reference. Here, though, do not give them an outline of your speech itself, just the data supports and they can supplement that, if they choose, with the language from your talk.

- In radio spots, your technology is literally your voice; more on that later.
- For TV interviews, supply the studio with "bullet-points," phone numbers, diagrams, pictures or whatever you're using as support to them before the interview. Ask in advance what format they need (such as digital files). Then, during your interview, the control room will overlay your visuals when appropriate or display statistics on the screen. If it is merely an interview, your "technology" will be voice and body language. More on that later.

Any formal technology used in a speech should be expendable. You should be able to be just as effective and just as persuasive without the technology. If you use easels or overheads as the focus of the talk—or as a crutch—you will fail if they do.

Even if all your technology (and the building's technology) fails—lights, power, air conditioning, heating, projectors—you want to be able to take the presentation outside and be just as persuasive and dynamic in the presentation. Technology is a marvelous enhancement, but it is like the wrapping on a gift box, the real value is what is inside the box. The great orators of Athens and Rome could project their voice and persuade their audiences with their words and presentation style alone—so can you.

A single word about using all the "bells-and-whistles" on PowerPoint and other slide-show software that makes technology so appealing: don't. Although it is very tempting to have the cute animated graphics and the fade-in, shutter, snowflake, slide, and a dozen other transition tools, they are only distracting and lose their audience appeal very quickly. Perhaps one animated graphic at the beginning and then leave the animation out.

As to the slides themselves, keep the background the same color throughout the presentation and limit the typestyle and font size to no more than three; otherwise the effect is confusing. On pie charts or graphs, keep the number of data elements (pieces of the pie or bars on the chart) to as few as possible, and don't mix types (pies and bars) on the same page. The point is to have the slide highlight the point you want to make.

Always proofread your overheads and slides. With the marvelous power of spell-check and the crush for time, we can often speed through creating a file and then—since we've read it so often—we overlook an obvious error. At a large conference a presenter had an overhead describing how his department addressed issues of sexual assault in the community. The audience began chuckling and giggling and then laughing uproariously. The presenter turned around and read the slide to discover the error. It said his department was very concerned "with protecting pubic safety." He meant to say, of course, "public" safety but the spell-check approved word, in the context of the subject matter, created a different effect. Of course, it was quite a memorable presentation!

Season your presentation with appropriate and limited technology. But, like any good spice, technology should only enhance an otherwise outstanding presentation.

How to Adjust Emphasis, Vocabulary, and Body Language Depending on the Target Audience

You may have heard the old adage, "It's not what you say, it's how you say it." Studies have shown that the majority of information received and retained by the listener from a speech is based on the presentation accompanying the words rather than the mere words themselves.

Emphasis

Consider the following statements:

- "*I* didn't say you were stupid." (Someone else said it)
- "I *didn't* say you were stupid." (Denial)
- "I didn't *say* you were stupid." (I implied it, though)
- "I didn't say *you* were stupid." (I meant someone else)
- "I didn't say you *were* stupid." (You are now)
- "I didn't say you were *stupid*." (I meant something else)

Although the same words are used, the emphasis presents different impressions. When giving a presentation, you must be conscious of how words are emphasized. It may be subconscious, but if the emphasis—the tonal quality of the word—reflects a personal bias, it shows to the audience.

Emphasis includes sarcasm and enthusiasm in tone, as well. The words "he is a great president" can be complimentary if "great" is said with an enthusiastic tone. It can be just the opposite if said sarcastically. When making a presentation, you will want to emphasize certain points and that can be done best with an enthusiastic inflection: "Burglaries are *down* over 8 percent due to the Chief's *commitment* to public safety." Of course, don't overdue it, but emphasis and inflection on certain words can paint a powerful picture.

> Don't use **sarcasm, anger, or disdain** when giving an interview…it will seem exaggerated and obvious and you'll be far less effective.

As a caveat, do not use sarcasm, anger, or disdain, especially during a TV interview. Although certain issues can raise strong emotions, a presentation is most effective when the presenter is professional and sticks to issues and does not engage in displays of personal opinion. In the televised 2000 presidential debates, one candidate huffed and sighed, rolled his eyes, and spoke with sarcasm. The words were also calculated to indicate disdain and the delivery was so obvious it appeared tactless and unprofessional. Further, when on TV or giving a radio talk the use of sarcasm, anger, or disdain seems amplified and will only damage the presentation.

Use vocal variety on words where you want to convey more meaning. Vocal variety can also be in how loud or soft and how fast or slow you speak. You will find that a quiet voice can heighten the sense of compassion toward a burglary victim when describing the loss and sense of violation. A more forceful and faster deliver can indicate a committed response and sense of authority. A staccato delivery—"We. Will. Never. Tolerate. Crime. In. This. Town."—can propel the words far beyond their normal usage.

Consider the classic Winston Churchill quote: "We shall go on to the end. We shall fight in France; we shall fight on the seas and oceans; we shall fight with growing confidence and growing strength in the air; we shall defend our island, whatever the cost may be; we shall fight on the beaches; we shall fight on the landing grounds; we shall fight in the fields and in the streets; we shall fight in the hills. We shall never surrender."

A rather long single sentence with an almost annoying repetition of the word "fight," but such a speech! If you listen to sound recordings of Churchill's speeches, you will find they are masterpieces of vocal emphasis.

Vocabulary

"I ain't gonna give you no bad examples of more poorly words." Ouch. Okay, the use of proper vocabulary can be over- (and under-) rated. Your goal is to connect with your audience so they can absorb what you have to say and respond as appropriate. You should never "dumb down" a speech, but you should also never attempt to show off your erudition either. As an example, you may get blank stares if you say, "Burglaries have been causally repressed due to crime analysis being an efficacious use of technology." The average newspaper is written at the eighth-grade level and your speech should be equally straightforward.

Even if you are speaking to a group of your peers, avoid jargon. Not everyone knows the secret-handshake argot of the chosen. They may not know the meaning of: "He's 10-8, 10-19, on the 11-10." Drop the "paradigm" and "penumbras." Avoid "concatenations" and "interstices." Also avoid catchy slang such as "that's a no-brainer" or "he's a real Adam-Henry." If you continue in such word abuse, you'll likely get a "bi-labial fricative" (aka "raspberry").

Don't play word games unless your speech calls for it. Speak appropriately with common words and if you must use a technical term for a subject, go ahead and say it, but give an understandable definition as well. Again, your goal is to connect with the audience and keep their attention.

Body Language

This area of presentation technique deals with all the non-speechifying parts of the delivery. How you stand and move can help you relax and help keep the audience tuned in to your talk.

```
Showing off your body...
  1.  Don't do the "fig-leaf"
  2.  Don't jingle all the way
  3.  Dress appropriately
  4.  Over-acting is okay
```

In small venues, if you are seated your movements may be limited. You can still lean forward and—with restrained movements—use your arms and hands for emphasis. Leaning back and opening your arms can be seen as expansive and inclusive of the group. Leaning forward and lowering your voice gives an appearance of sharing confidences. Like technology, how you move your body will enhance your presentation.

In larger rooms or if you have a stage-like area, movement is critical. Do not do the "fig leaf." This is where speakers stand rock-still with their hands in front them, imitating an Adam or Eve statue. In addition to getting odd looks from the audience, you run the real risk of passing out if your knees are locked. Movement does several beneficial things during a speech. It gives you a chance to remain loose, it keeps the audience engaged, and you can gesture as needed.

Do not spend your nervous moments jingling the change in your pocket (men) or adjust undergarments (women—and men too; you think no one sees?). Jingling change or adjusting clothing is a nervous habit that you may not be aware of, but now that you are you won't want to do it again.

Also, always dress appropriately for the audience. As a general rule, dress "one-level-up" on the fashion ladder. At a casual beach conference, dress with an upscale print shirt and deck shoes (not t-shirt and flops). In a business environment, dress slightly above the corporate norm. It won't hurt and it will show your professionalism.

Finally, in conference ballrooms or very large venues it is okay to overact on stage.; that is, to make your movements larger and more flamboyant. If you ever see a stage actor up close, you'll see the makeup is greatly exaggerated because at a great distance normal makeup can't be seen. The same holds for presentation. Make arm movements more expansive. Move more forcefully and if necessary—even step down into the audience and then back up to the stage. Use a portable microphone or handheld microphone and move about. Here is one place where you can, and should, overact. It will help the audience keep their focus on you.

How to Feel Comfortable Speaking to Large Groups (or how to make the butterflies fly in formation)

Public speaking can be intimidating. All those people looking at you and expecting you to dazzle them with your innate brilliance. A huge crowd all focused on you. So how do you handle it? Try the following:

- Don't "picture them naked." Someone once thought this would help a speaker. Perhaps the intent was to think of them as all the same, but I've never heard of anyone who tried this and could concentrate on what they had to say!
- You don't need to get eye contact with everyone. In a large group you'll want to look at every portion of the room and you'll find that looking at their foreheads is sufficient and gives the impression that you are looking at them. (You may need to make eye contact with the first few rows, but if this is difficult, try the forehead look here as well.)
- Never try to read your speech unless you have it on a TelePrompTer. The first word you miss or sentence you skip will cause you to hesitate and soon you'll be fumbling around and will become hopelessly befuddled.

- To avoid befuddlement, keep to the themes and the rule of threes. If you know your themes you can address the subject matter in the proper order. The rule of threes will help you to remember each segment and your speech—seemingly all from memory—will be far more impressive than constantly referring to notes.
- Ignore those who talk to their neighbors, get up to go outside, talk on the cell phone, or who are snoozing.
- Never apologize or say you're nervous. It doesn't gain sympathy and it makes you nervous and look unprofessional.
- Remember that the audience wants to hear what you have to say.
- Don't "throw away the notes" or roll-up-your-sleeves. These gimmicks always look false and pretentious; politicians use them a lot. This is where, with false sincerity, the speaker puts down the notes and says how he is going just to talk to you from the heart. Similarly, the speaker will take off his coat and roll up his sleeves to be "one of the working class." This too smacks of patronizing the audience and is seldom believed.

You are a professional and the audience expects you to inform them, perhaps entertain them, and certainly to treat them with respect. Keep on track with your themes and rules of threes and don't fall into gimmicks or over-reliance on technology.

The Different Presentation Styles for Radio, TV, and Print Media

When giving a presentation to these outlets you'll still want to keep "on message" ("burglaries are down thanks to crime analysis and the Chief's commitment to public safety") but how you approach the delivery will be different.

On **radio**, you'll likely be interviewed with a question and answer format. Voice alone is your tool: no handouts, not overheads, no gestures. Keep your voice well modulated. Speak normally and do not sound like a robot. Emphasizing words is fine but consciously avoid sarcasm, anger, and disdain. Although you may feel it is appropriate, given the question, such inflection in your voice will seem amplified and you'll sound petty. Keep the responses brief and accurate. Don't ramble and don't editorialize. Finally, don't be drawn into an argument by the interviewer. Keep to the themes and the facts. If you don't know an answer, say you don't know and drop it. Don't speculate.

On **TV**, you may be able to forward in advance digital images, digital slides, or data that can be displayed on the screen during the talk, such as phone numbers to call. If it is a studio interview, wear basic and subdued colors (just watch a couple of professional newscasters to get an idea). Wild ties and casual clothes detract from the discussion. Keep your gestures to a minimum and avoid excessive head movement. Don't always nod in agreement with the interviewer and watch the facial expressions. Again, during the 2000 presidential debates, one of the candidates pursed his lips, frowned, looked angry, and was clearly annoyed. It was obvious and detracted from the substance of the message. Look at the interviewer with interest and don't shift your eyes to the camera. Consider the camera as just a piece of equipment; your task is to present the issues to the interviewer.

The **print** media will often use a question and answer format or a more informal dialogue. They may ask pointed questions or attempt to get you to disclose information by acting like an old friend. Remember, they are professional reporters who want to get an angle others are missing and they hope you disclose more than you should. As stated many times, remain focused on the themes and respond professionally.

How to Professionally Respond to Unexpected Questions and Nothing is Off-the-Record

You're giving a TV interview at the police station about the decline in burglaries and the talk is going well. While on-camera with the tape rolling, the interviewer asks, "What do you think of the sexual harassment suit against your Chief?"

> The pause that refreshes...that saves the interview—and your job.

Pause. Don't do the deer-in-the-headlights look, just pause. It is very unlikely the interviewer would ask that question or any controversial comment live and since it is probably being taped any lengthy pause will be edited out. This pause allows you time to regroup and get back to the themes. Never engage in a shocked or angry response; don't argue. Pause and then respond—pause again—and redirect the interview: "I don't have any information about that"—(pause to allow that comment to be edited out later and then continue)—"The Chief's commitment to crime analysis has laid the groundwork for increasing public safety."

The "unexpected questions" will also arise on radio as well as the print media. They are merely attempts to get an utterance from you that is newsworthy. You'll find the pause is marvelous tool to allow you to stay focused.

Nothing is off-the-record. Do not be misled by the earnest request of an unknown, or new-to-you interviewer, who tells you that anything you say on a particular topic is "off-the-record." Always assume everything you say is on the record. Also watch out for the cameraman or interviewer who lowers the shoulder camera to ask some more questions. You assume the "formal" interview is over. However, this can be a ploy where he or she will leave the tape running to catch you saying something inappropriate.

After you develop a working relationship with a reporter who has proved to be responsible and reliable you may be able to be "off-the-record" and provide some case background information that is non-confidential. Caution is appropriate, but many times a good working relationship with the media can benefit law enforcement operations as well.

Remember that hostile questions only work if you take the bait and respond. When asked a hostile or inappropriate question, pause, and remain focused on the themes at hand.

Ready for the Big Time?

Giving an effective presentation to your cubicle-partner, command staff, the state legislature, or 4,000 conference attendees is really just a matter of scale and style. The key techniques are adaptable to the venue and you get to choose the format: how to package the crime data to present the case for the agency; what technology to use to enhance and support the presentation; how to emphasize words; how to adjust body language for the venue; simple techniques to apply have the butterflies fly in formation; and how to pause to respond to hostile questions and cagey interviewers.

However, just like riding a bicycle or having a rapturous evening, public speaking requires doing it and not just reading about it. This truly is a topic that requires the "practical" application. Many community colleges offer public speaking courses. One of the best places to practice public speaking—in supportive safety—is at a local Toastmasters International club. This is an excellent place to master public presentation skills. Before you know it, you will be able to comfortably give an effective presentation.

10
Interpreting Crime Data and Statistics

Rachel Boba

The goal of this chapter is to provide knowledge of how to appropriately apply and interpret statistics relevant to crime analysis. This chapter includes a discussion of data, statistics, and application of statistics in crime analysis. The chapter does not cover all types of statistics but focuses on those that are most useful in crime analysis. Additionally, this is not a "how to" chapter in which formulas are included, but a discussion of data and statistics and their practical application. Throughout the chapter, there are additional resources recommended. One should view this as a first step to learning about applying and interpreting statistics for the purposes of crime analysis.

To understand crime and law enforcement statistics, one must first understand the data systems. A brief overview of systems in which police data are collected and housed is included. In addition, knowledge of what the data describe and what they may not describe is important in applying and interpreting statistics accurately and effectively. Even though there are many types of data used in crime analysis, for the sake of brevity, only three are discussed in this chapter, as they are the primary data sources for crime analysis. They are crime, arrests, and calls for service.

After a discussion of the data types and their effect on the interpretation of the statistics, the next section includes a specific discussion of selected statistics relevant to crime analysis work. Basic statistics, such as frequency and

percent, are not discussed, as they will be covered in Chapter 13. Discussion of rates, measures of central tendency, inference, statistical significance, t-tests, and correlation are included.

Police Data Systems

Police departments typically have two data systems in which crime, arrests, and calls for service, among other data, are housed. Even though these systems are slightly different from agency to agency, the basic purposes and functions are the same and thus these systems are discussed generally here. The two types of systems are referred to as a computer aided dispatch system (CAD) and a records management system (RMS). Although many small agencies may not have these systems and others may have additional specialized databases housed in specific units, the CAD and RMS are key systems for data in policing and crime analysis.

A CAD or a computer-aided dispatch system is a highly specialized telecommunications and geographic display technology created to support police and public safety response operations. CADs are typically used for all emergency operations, which in addition to police include fire and ambulance services. In a police department, calls for service that are dispatched to or initiated by officers are collected and warehoused in a CAD system. All activity concerning these calls is recorded in the CAD, which includes the information about the call recorded by the call taker and dispatcher (e.g., officers dispatched to the scene, when they arrived, the disposition of the call) and correspondence between officers and dispatchers over the system (e.g., vehicle lookups, officers taking lunch). This information is typically called "unit history" as it records the activity of each police unit during a call. It is important to note that a CAD system does not record all phone calls coming into the police agency, but those dispatched to or initiated by officers. Because of the vast information contained in a CAD system, information is often purged after a certain amount of time. However, it is standard to retain a summary or snapshot of a call for service for a longer period of time for analysis purposes. This information is often downloaded into an RMS.

An RMS or records management system is a technology in which police records are stored as databases. The main purpose of an RMS is to store crime incidents and related data such as property data, evidence, vehicle data, and persons data (e.g., suspects, arrests, witnesses). Many departments also include other types of data in their RMSes, such as personnel data, investigation information (cases), traffic stop data, and calls for service information (summary data). An RMS is used in a police agency for quality control evaluation, to look up individual incidents, to track cases, and to run reports.

Historically and still today, it is a struggle for crime analysts to retrieve data from their agencies' CAD and RMS systems. In many cases, software vendors create functions for producing paper reports and retrieving one case at a time without creating functions for downloading large amounts of data needed for analysis purposes. When they do have access to the systems, crime analysts typically have access to the RMS system but not to the CAD system directly since the summary information is exported to the RMS. Less often, a police agency will not have an RMS at all, and the analyst only has access to the CAD system and, consequently, may access data directly through the CAD. However, in either case the data used is a summary of the calls for service instead of the complete CAD records. The primary exception is when data are used for staffing allocation, when all unit history and back up unit data is needed.

Key Crime Analysis Data Sources

To understand crime and law enforcement statistics, one must first understand the data on which the statistics are based. Knowledge of what the data do and do not describe is important in applying and interpreting statistics accurately and effectively. This section covers the primary types of data crime analysts use—crime, calls for service, and arrests. There are many considerations that must be taken into account with these data types as these issues can affect the selection and interpretation of subsequent statistical analyses.

Crime

Crime data is the primary type of data used in crime analysis. There are many issues about crime data that can lead to misinterpretation or misuse of statistics. The section covers some of the general issues with crime data and then discusses the various ways in which crime can be counted.

Crime represented by police crime data does not represent all crime occurring in society. Thus, we typically see reports that name this type of data, "reported crime" or "crimes known to the police." This is an important distinction for anyone interpreting or trying to understand crime problems based on police data: that is, that we may not be aware of the entire problem and the police data may portray a biased picture. For example, we know that a very low number of rapes are reported to the police. Thus, if we report rape statistics rising or falling we must be very cautious and mention the fact that even though the police are seeing an increase or decrease, the actual number may be changing in a different way since we do not know the actual number of rapes being committed. This is particularly relevant for certain types of crimes (domestic violence, drug crimes, white collar crimes) and not as much for others (motor vehicle theft, arson, murder).

Crime data captured by police agencies is dynamic, not static. In other words, information about crime incidents is constantly being updated. For example, a person may report a crime that occurred two days before to an officer who then takes a day or two to complete the report. The case is assigned to a detective who begins to investigate the crime by identifying suspects a few days, weeks, or years later. The victim may call the police department with new information about the crime or correct erroneous information from the original report. The officer may arrest a suspect and clear the case. As you can see, the data for this incident are constantly being changed and updated, and a report including this case could change based on when the crime analyst downloaded the data for statistics.

That the data surrounding crime incidents are constantly changing creates an issue for analysis. One of the issues is "real-time" data. Many agencies emphasize performing statistics on the most recent data—as recent as an hour ago. Yet the likelihood of that data changing soon after the initial report is recorded is fairly high because of additional information from investigation, identification of suspects, errors in the original report, and so on. Theoretically, however, after a certain amount of time, the likelihood of the data being changed substantially is significantly lower. Unfortunately, there is no research in this area and analysts must take an educated guess about when the likelihood for further changes to the data is low. In many cases, crime data will be downloaded around the fifteenth of the month following when it is reported and then updated in six month or one year intervals to capture arrests and clearances. In any case, the use of "real-time" data should be done with extreme caution.

All crime data recorded by the police have two sets of dates. The first is the date the report of the crime was written. (In some cases, the time the report was written is also recorded, but this information is not essential, except for certain operations studies.) The second is the date(s) and time(s) the crime actually occurred. This is included in crime data because the date a crime was reported is not always the same as when it occurred.

In many cases, the exact date and time that the crime occurred are known (e.g., robbery, assault); however, in other types of crime, the exact date and time of the crime are not known because they were not witnessed by anyone (e.g., burglary, auto theft, larceny). In these crimes, victims report their best estimate of when the crime "could" have occurred. These are called "first possible" and "last possible" date and time or "from" and "to." The difference between these two sets of dates (when the crime was reported vs. when the crime occurred) is very important as they serve different purposes depending on the nature of the analysis.

All crime reported to the police is counted based on the date it is reported, because it would be impossible to count it by when it occurred, since this is not always known. As noted above, crime data is dynamic and crimes can be reported days, weeks, months, even years after they occur. Counts would need to be constantly updated based on date of occurrence and the ranges would cause further issues in counting. Date of report is constant, it does not change, and thus counts of crime are based on this variable. However, it can affect the interpretation of crime statistics. For example, if a large number of burglaries occur over the Christmas/New Year's holiday, victims may not report them until after the new year when they return home. Thus, a large number of crimes would be counted in the following month and even the following year when they may have occurred the previous month and year. Although there is nothing an analyst or police can do to correct this problem, it should be considered during the analysis process. Finally, the date of occurrence, though not adequate for counting crime, is important for analysis and is used for identifying patterns and series—when the crime occurred is much more important that when it was reported.

The various ways in which crime is measured affect statistics created from them. Below are the four major ways in which crime is measured and considerations for each.

Crime Reports

"Crime reports" refer to individual crime incidents that are reported to the police and are contained within the agency's RMS. It is important to note that even though all crime data collected by police agencies is generally the same, how and when incidents are recorded can vary by region, state, and even by police agency. For example, one agency may call tools taken from the back of a truck a theft, whereas another may call it a burglary from vehicle, two very different crime classifications even though it is the same crime. Thus, how an agency records its data will affect its statistics. Because each agency has its own policies, procedures, and RMS (there are no national standards for recording crime incidents), it is problematic comparing statistics based on crime report data across agencies. This is why crime statistics of different agencies are compared using federal standards (e.g., UCR or NIBRS).

Uniform Crime Report (UCR)

The UCR is a national standard of classifying crime uniformly that disregards state laws (see www.fbi.gov/ucr for further details). It

was created to provide a way to consistently count crime across the United States. The UCR does not collect information from agencies about all crime, only selected types (e.g., homicide, rape, robbery, aggravated assault, burglary, larceny, motor vehicle theft, and arson) and has a hierarchical coding system (i.e., if a rape and a murder are committed to the same person, only the murder is counted). However, it does collect information on all arrests no matter the type of crime. Compliance is voluntary, so not all police agencies report their statistics (though over 95 percent of the U.S. population is represented in the UCR statistics). The numbers are typically reported on a monthly basis to a state agency that then reports it to the FBI. These numbers are not updated (static). The most important differences between crime reports and UCR for a crime analyst are that UCR are only aggregate numbers that can not be broken down once reported, they only include certain types of crimes counted hierarchically, and the numbers are static. These are key reasons why UCR crime statistics and crime analysis statistics for the same jurisdiction will rarely match.

National Incident Based Reporting System (NIBRS)

The NIBRS system is an attempt to improve the UCR but is similar in nature.[1] For example, it also requires a standard of classifying crime uniformly that disregards state categories. It is an improvement over UCR in that additional primary crime types are tracked; that individual cases (not aggregate counts) are submitted voluntarily to the FBI; and that the system allows agencies to update incident submissions as new data becomes available. Often, analysts use UCR or NIBRS categories for analysis of incident

---

[1] See www.fbi.gov/ucr for further details.

data. Many records management systems recode the incidents accordingly. There are no national NIBRS statistics because a minority of agencies report their data in this way.

National Crime Victimization Survey (NCVS)

The national survey of crime victimization is another way in which criminal activity is measured, but it focuses on the experiences of victims. The purpose of the survey is to avoid counting only crimes reported to the police and to have statistics independent of police activity. It began in 1973 and samples 100,000 residents age 12 or older, from nearly 50,000 households.[1] Respondents are interviewed every six months over a 3-year period. The survey gathers information such as location of the crime, month, time of day, physical setting, characteristics of the victims (e.g., sex, race, income, extent of injury, self-protective actions and results of those actions, and relationship with the offender) and provides additional information on crimes that rarely are reported to the police (e.g., rape and domestic violence). It does not collect information on homicides, arson, societal crimes, or commercial crimes; and victims determine whether the incident was a crime, not the law. The NCVS is most helpful to social scientists and provides national trends of victimization, but local level police agencies are less apt to use this information in their jurisdictions. The primary reason is because a sample is taken from the nation, and there are not enough surveys conducted at smaller levels to generalize to a local population. If we ask: for a city of 150,000, how many would be surveyed in the NCVS? The following estimate can be generated:

---

[1] See www.icpsr.umich.edu/NACJD/NCVS/ for further details.

NCVS	City
100,000 surveyed=	X surveyed
200,000,000	150,000
Estimate of U.S.	City
population over 12	Population

$$X = 100,000 * 150,000 / 200,000,000$$
$$X = 75 \text{ would be surveyed in the city}$$

Even though 75 surveys may be enough to conduct statistics, it would not inform about the prevalence of crime victimization in that jurisdiction. In addition, the survey does not provide information about crime incidents but experiences of victims. While the national survey may not provide sufficient cases for local findings, many police agencies conduct their own citizen victimization surveys to help inform their crime prevention and control activities as well as the satisfaction with their activities.

Crime Data Summary

All of these types of data serve a purpose in providing a picture of crime. However, depending on which data are used the picture may be very different. A major issue crime analysts confront is why their statistics do not match the "official" statistics reported to the FBI. From the discussion above, we can see how this happens; any of the following could be true:

- The crime analyst downloaded the data at a different time than the UCR or NIBRS data were downloaded
- The crime analyst uses state crime codes, not UCR or NIBRS codes
- The crime analyst uses only those crimes determined by the police (not the victim) to be a crime.
- The crime analyst counts by number of reports, not number of victims or by a hierarchy of crimes.

Arrests

Arrests occur when there is sufficient evidence (probable cause) that a person has committed a crime. In crime analysis, the arrest is usually the final outcome of a crime incident, and we are not concerned with whether the person was actually found (or even is) guilty or sentenced for the crime. Police agencies are often measured by how many arrests occurred for a certain number of crimes (clearance rate). This will be discussed in the next section. This section discusses the nature of arrest data and how it affects crime statistics.

On aggregate, there are more crimes than arrests. However, theoretically there can be more arrests than crimes, if numerous people commit a single crime. Because many crimes have very low levels of arrests (e.g., the 2001 national clearance rate for property crime was 16.2 percent vs. 46.2 percent for violent crime, from Crime in the United States, 2001), rarely will one see more arrests than crimes in aggregate.

For some types of crimes, arrests are the only way to measure the number of incidents. These tend to be crimes detected by the police, not reported by victims, such as driving under the influence, drug offenses, and prostitution. Thus, analysis of particular types of crimes based on arrest data tends to reflect police activity more so than actual crime occurrences.

With this said, arrest data should be used sparingly for analysis. The following are additional considerations:

- When an individual is arrested, it does not mean he or she is guilty.
- Arrestees may not represent the offenders of the crimes because of overall low arrest rates.

- There may be a bias in those who are arrested (e.g., less experienced, less intelligent), so analysis of arrests may not generalize to all individuals committing these types of crimes.
- A small number of individuals may account for a large number of arrests.
- Police sting operations or special enforcement will greatly influence arrest counts.

However, arrests are often the only way to examine certain types of crimes. In these cases, the analyst should provide a detailed discussion of the limitations and be aware of police activities that may have influenced the number of arrests.

Calls for Service

A "call for service" is a request for police service in which an officer is dispatched or it is an incident found by a police officer. A phone call to the police station is not necessarily a call for service, and not every call for service results in a crime report. There are two types of calls for service, typically called "citizen-generated" and "officer-generated" calls. As the names denote, a citizen-generated call for service is one in which a citizen calls the police department and an officer or other police employee responds to the call. The response can be either in person or by phone. The type of activity can range from a homicide to a dog barking to a neighbor dispute. An officer generated call for service is one in which an officer identifies activity, responds, and calls it in to the dispatcher. These types of calls primarily include vehicle stops, subject stops, but can also be a range of activity.

Call-for-service data used by crime analysts are typically summary data downloaded from a CAD into an RMS. As noted earlier, the CAD data contains all the activity and

204

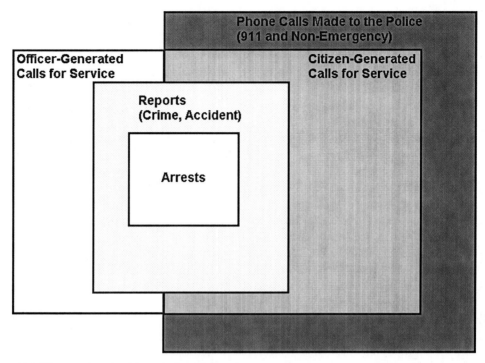

Figure 10-1: The approximate breakdown of police calls for service

communication of officers and dispatchers; thus, the officer is the unit of analysis. However, in the summary data, the call is the unit of analysis. Subsequently, when counting calls for service, each line represents one call (in CAD data, each line can represent one activity of one officer on one call; thus, there would be multiple lines of data for each call). Individuals sometimes refer to call-for-service data as "CAD data." This is incorrect most of the time, as they are referring to the summary "call for service" data, not the actual unit history data contained in CAD (unless they are conducting staffing analysis). There are a few exceptions to this based on an agency's individual system. By and large, this type of data should be called "calls for service" data and can be further identified as "citizen-generated" or "officer-generated."

"Calls for service" statistics reported by crime analysts are typically only citizen-generated calls for service unless otherwise noted. This is because, like arrests, officer-generated calls for service indicate the officer activity and not the demand for service. Counts of officer-generated calls are highly influenced by citizen-generated calls for service and thus should be used cautiously (i.e., the more citizen-generated calls, the less time officers have to generate their own activity).

Figure 10-1 shows the approximate breakdown of police calls for service:

- Citizens call the police with various emergency and non-emergency issues.
- A sub-group of the phone calls are dispatched to officers for response.
- Officers generate calls for service on their own.
- From a sub-group of calls for service, reports are generated, primarily crime and accident reports.
- Finally, arrests are made from a sub-group of officer and citizen-generated reports.

When using call-for-service data, there are various issues to consider. There may be data entry errors because dispatchers are often under extreme pressure, or the wrong button is pushed, or the correct information is just not known (e.g., addresses, apartment numbers). There also may be inaccurate reporting by victims. For example, a victim may report being "robbed," but the officer finds out he was burglarized. In many CAD systems, the dispatchers cannot or do not go back and change the original call type; however, in some they do. It is important to know whether a system is in place to account for these changes. The codes that are used for calls for service are very specific: many times there are five or six codes for the same type of incident. These are not practical for analysis and may need to be combined. Finally, types codes and policies for using them depend on the agency, so comparison is very difficult between departments.

Using Call-for-Service data as a Proxy for Measuring Crime

One of the main issues in the use of call-for-service data is that analysts use them to conduct analysis of crime incidents. They select those calls for service in which a crime report was taken for analysis to represent crime incidents. In some cases, analysts do not have a choice because crime data is not available electronically, but others do this for convenience. Analysts should be aware of the following problems with this practice.

As noted above, depending on the capabilities of a particular CAD system, a call for service is coded one type at dispatch and once the officer arrives it may be determined to be something else. Thus, a call that comes in as a robbery may actually be a burglary or a totally unrelated type of activity. In fact, this author did a test with a subset of data from a police agency and found that most of the robbery calls for service resulting in a report were actually burglary reports. This was done by matching the call data to the crime data.

In some cases, agencies use call-for-service data for a report, label it as an analysis of crime, but include non-criminal calls for service in the analysis (e.g., including calls such as "check welfare" and "suspicious behavior"). This causes confusion for the customer of the analysis as to what is a crime and what is not (this is more common with data provided to the public on the Internet).

The date and time variables of a call reflect when the call was received and dispatched by the police agency, and not when the crime occurred. Even though these times and dates would represent when the crime was reported, it provides no information about when the crime occurred. This is relevant for all crimes not reported immediately after they have occurred but is particularly relevant for property crimes or those crimes in which the exact time is not known (i.e., the crime occurred within a time span).

Similarly, the location listed on the call may not be the location of the incident, but a nearby location or the location from which the call was made. Recording apartment numbers in call-for-service data is often haphazard and depends on the amount of information available (e.g., "a loud fight coming from the next building") and the diligence of the call taker (e.g., determining the apartment number at which the incident is occurring, not where the call is originating).

If the data used to represent crime are only citizen-generated calls for service, crimes identified by officers will not be included.

A call for service may have several dispositions (e.g., "arrest" and "police report"). In some cases, the summary data downloaded from CAD into the RMS may only include one disposition; therefore, information is missing. In a similar vein, if only calls resulting in reports are examined, those resulting arrests may not be included. In addition, the type of disposition, "report" may not necessarily mean it was a crime (e.g., lost or found property also generate reports).

Calls for service summary information is static. That is, once it is exported it typically is not updated with new information from an investigation. For example, the data from a call for service resulting in a report would not reflect an arrest that was made two days later.

In conclusion, it is very problematic to use calls for service as a proxy for crime data for the stated reasons. One should use call-for-service data when:

- Examining police officer activity (e.g., officer generated traffic stops).
- Examining disorder activity that does not result in a crime report but may indicate problematic activity. Types of disorder calls might include suspicious behavior, drug activity (not crime necessarily), disorderly behavior, public drunkenness, noise complaints, and code violations.
- When there is no other choice, be sure to clearly define the data being used and the analysis resulting from the data. For example, analysis of time of day of calls for service only indicates when the calls were received by the police department, not when the corresponding crime occurred. Remember that analysis of crime based on call-for-service data will yield faulty results and is very limited in interpretation.

And use crime report data when:

- Studying crime problems in any way.

Understanding and Interpreting Statistics

The second section of this chapter covers the application and interpretation of various statistics that are appropriate for crime analysis. This chapter does not include formulas or descriptions of how to conduct the statistics, but is an overview of when and how to use these particular methods. For information on the calculations and methods, consult Chapters 13 and 14 in this book.

Rates

A rate is a ratio or proportion of one variable to another. It is also called "normalizing." For example, crime rate is typically the number of crimes in an area divided by the population of an area or the "number of crimes per person." However, there are three types of rates that are used regularly that a crime analyst should understand. Those are crime rate, arrest rate, and clearance rate.

Crime Rate

As stated above, a crime rate is typically the number of crimes in an area divided by the number of people living in the area. However, it is not as simple as this. The "crime rate" that is typically reported by police agencies and the FBI through the UCR program is in fact called the rate of "index crime." Index crime refers only to those crimes that the UCR tracks: homicide, rape, robbery, aggravated assault, burglary, larceny, motor vehicle theft, and arson. The index crime rate does not take into account other types of crimes. This is important for analysts to understand because if an analyst computes a jurisdiction's crime rate by using all reported crimes, the number will be quite different, and higher, than the index rate.

Another important point is that the index crime rate is reported as the number of index crimes per 100,000 persons. Reporting crime rate by 100,000 persons may not be realistic for jurisdictions in the U.S. that have fewer than 100,000 persons because it gives the perception that there are more crimes occurring than there actually are. For example, a town of 50,000 residents has 3,000 index crimes. This computes to an index crime rate of 6,000 crimes per 100,000 persons. Although it is important to use 100,000 when comparing rates to national or state levels, smaller jurisdictions can use 10,000 or 1,000 persons depending on the purpose. This is particularly relevant when comparing crime rates of smaller areas within a particular jurisdiction (e.g., census tracts, beats, precincts).

Another consideration in using index crime rates at the local level is distinguishing between property and persons crimes. When thinking about crime, most people, even police officers, think violent crime. So, when reporting crime rates, most think the information is referring primarily to violent crime, when in reality most index crime is property crime. Analysts should report an overall rate along with a property crime rate and persons crime rate separately.

Lastly, at the local level it is not always recommended to use population to determine a crime rate. Depending on the purpose of the statistic, population may not be relevant or can contradict what the analyst is trying to show. For example, an analyst may want to compare the commercial burglary rate of ten beats in a city. Because people do not live at commercial businesses, the burglary rate will show very high rates in commercially zoned areas. Even though this is not inaccurate, it may not be helpful for analysis. The analyst might instead examine the number of commercial burglaries by

number of commercial businesses or by area zoned commercial. This would show how many burglaries by beat according to the number of relevant targets, not population.

Although crime rates based on population are those that are publicized most often in policing, there are many other types of rates that can be used for crime analysis. The following are some additional examples:

- Per dwelling (e.g., to compare the number of residential burglaries since the target is the house and not the number of people living in it)
- Per apartment unit (e.g., to compare apartment communities since number of residents is constantly changing in these types of properties)
- Per person (occupancy) (e.g., to compare bars or night clubs since actual number of patrons is hard to measure)
- Per parking space (e.g., to compare parking lots since spaces are how many cars it can hold)
- Per acre (e.g., to compare parks)
- Per square foot (e.g., to compare businesses)

Arrest Rate

An arrest rate is similar to crime rate and is the number of arrests per person. Arrest rates are typically broken down by age, race, sex, and other census variables—for example, arrest rates are highest for men between the ages of 18 and 24. Arrest rates are typically used at the national level to indicate patterns of crime. National statistics come from UCR figures of arrests for almost all crimes, not only index crimes. Although individual jurisdictions compute their arrest rates, local level crime analysts do not regularly use them because census data can be quickly outdated, and the information is not easily broken down to compare within a jurisdiction.

Clearance Rate

A clearance rate is the percent of reported crimes resulting in an arrest or an exceptional clearance according to the FBI's standards. A crime is cleared by arrest if at least one person is arrested or charged with the commission of the crime, or if the case is turned over to the court for prosecution. The number of crimes cleared is counted, not the number of individuals arrested, and the arrest of one individual may clear several crimes or the arrest of many individuals may clear only one. A crime is cleared by exceptional means if circumstances beyond police control prevent a clearance by arrest. However, the police must gather specific information about the crime to satisfy this type clearance (e.g., the police must identify the offender, gather enough evidence to support an arrest, make a charge, turn over the offender to the court for prosecution, and identify the offender's location so that law enforcement could make an arrest).[1] National clearance rates are based on index crimes only. Typically, clearance rates are reported by type of crime. Historically, homicide has the highest clearance rates. There are several issues that must be considered when understanding and interpreting clearance rates.

As noted above, crime incident data is dynamic, which is particularly relevant for the computing of clearance rates. For example, this author would download the crimes reported in the previous month on the fifteenth of the following month. Thus, crimes that are not cleared by arrest in the same month they are reported are not recorded as cleared. Because arrests do not always occur close in time to when the crime report was made, clearance rates underestimate the number of clearances.

Typically, official crime and clearance counts are done monthly, in aggregate, and never updated.[2] The only exception is homicide rates: local agencies are required by the UCR program to update homicide clearances, no matter when they happen. Even though the UCR program requires monthly reporting of counts, a local crime analyst can update the counts yearly; that is, after several months into the next year, go back and download the number of crimes cleared. Theoretically, an analyst could do this every year for every previous year (since clearances can occur at any time), but with most crimes one year should be sufficient.

Updating clearance rates separate from the UCR process is important for crime analysts to do because clearance rates can be used for many different purposes in crime analysis. When looking at the nature of arrests for a particular crime, it is important to know the clearance rate for that crime. For example, if an analyst finds that most burglars arrested are juveniles, this may or may not be an important finding. We know that clearance rates for property crimes are typically very low. So, if we find that 75% of our burglars (the ones arrested) are juvenile, but we only arrest someone in 7% of the burglaries, we know that juveniles have committed 5.25% of the burglaries (0.75 * 0.07). Conversely, we know nothing about the offenders in 94.75% of the cases.

Measures of Central Tendency

Measures of central tendency are important statistics for crime analysts for describing a distribution of data and comparing variables. However, their use is limited as most of them depend on having interval or ratio variables (numeric), whereas most variables in crime

[1] Federal Bureau of Investigation, "Uniform Crime Reports—Frequently Asked Questions," http://www.fbi.gov/ucr/ucrquest.htm (accessed June 15, 2004).

[2] The UCR program requires monthly reporting.

analysis are ordinal or nominal. The measures of central tendency discussed here are mean, mode, median, range, and standard deviation. Below is a brief description of each statistic, its importance, and an example of its use:

Range

The range is the span of the data distribution for a particular variable. It is the maximum value of the variable subtracted by the minimum value. These values may not be reported formally, but are an important part of the analysis process. It is important to know the range of values for a particular variable before conducting analysis, particularly if there are outliers. For example, in examining the emergency response time for calls for service, this author found the data had a range of 20 hours, but that most of the cases clustered around 5 to 7 minutes. This was an indication there was something very wrong with the data and after some investigation, it was found that there was a technical problem with the CAD system.

Mode

Mode is the value that occurs most frequently in a distribution of a variable. It can be used with all types of variables (e.g., numeric or nominal) and is used regularly in crime analysis in a slightly modified form. Crime analysts use mode often in their analysis to answer the questions: where are the most calls for service occurring? How do the beats compare in crimes? Typically, mode is used

by providing a frequency list of values sorted by descending frequency. Table 10-1 shows the five most frequent accident locations. Instead of listing the intersection alphabetically, the analyst uses the descending frequency, which shows the mode at the top of the table, but follows with the next most frequent values, which is helpful for analysis.

Rank	Intersection	Accidents
1	E Main St & S University Blvd	26
2	E California Blvd & S University Blvd	25
3	W Grand St & S Downtown Av	21
4	W Maple Av & S Uptown St	20
5	E Main St & S Uptown St	19

Table 10-1: A frequency list of accident locations

This type of analysis can also be used in a cross-tabulation format (i.e., two variables together). Table 10-2 provides a breakdown of the three addresses with the most calls for service and then the three most frequent types of calls for service occurring at those addresses. This table allows the analyst to see the different types of calls that occur at the addresses. In addition, one can see that even though 454 S University Blvd has 49 calls for service, the most frequent type of call, "loud noise" had only 6 calls. This indicates that this address has a number of different types of calls occurring, unlike 976 W Maple, which has less variation in call types since the top three types of calls make up 27 of the 36 total calls for service.

Rank	Address	Total Calls	Type of Call for Service (Frequency)		
			#1	#2	#3
1	123 E Main St	54	Alarm calls (9)	Check welfare calls (7)	Shoplifting calls (5)
2	454 S University	49	Loud noise (6)	Suspicious persons (4)	Check welfare (3)
3	976 W Maple St	36	Shoplifting calls (10)	Alarm calls (9)	Illegal parking calls (8)

Table 10-2: The most frequent calls at selected addresses

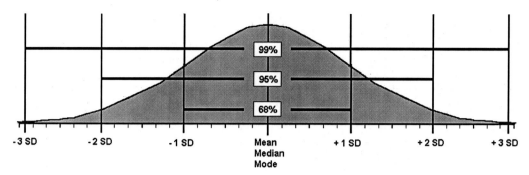

Figure 10-2: A normal distribution

Median

The median is the score or potential score (in that it does not necessarily occur in the distribution) above which and below which one half of all the scores lie. It is known as the fiftieth percentile. Median can be used instead of an average in crime analysis when a distribution is very skewed. For example, the average amount of time for a call for service may be 45 minutes, but the median may be only 15 minutes. The mean, in this case, is influenced by a small number of calls that were exceptionally long. Using the median communicates the information that "half of the calls for service were 15 minutes or shorter in length." In addition, other percentiles can be used to indicate the nature of a variable, such as "95 percent of calls for service were 30 minutes or shorter."

Mean

This mean is the average of a set of numbers. Means can be statistically tested against one another for examination of difference (see below). However, their use in crime analysis is somewhat limited as they require ratio or interval variables (e.g., response time, number of crimes per beat), while many variables in crime analysis are ordinal or nominal. In addition, they can be very sensitive to outliers, especially when used with small amounts of data (fewer than 35 cases).

Standard Deviation (SD)

The standard deviation is a measure of dispersion around the mean. In a normal distribution, 68 percent of cases fall within one SD of the mean and 95 percent of cases fall within two SD. For example, if the mean age were 45, with a standard deviation of 10, 95 percent of the cases would be between 25 and 65 in a normal distribution. Figure 10-2 is an example of a normal curve:

However, even if a distribution is not normal (i.e., skewed) the statistics (e.g., mean, mode, median, and standard deviation) still are accurate. Standard deviation is important in determining the nature and skew of a distribution. For example, if a distribution of a number of crimes has a mean of 5 with a standard deviation of 10, we know that the distribution is skewed because one standard deviation below the mean is –5, which is not possible.

Measures of Central Tendency Example

Table 10-3 and Figure 10-3 are examples of a statistical output and a bar chart for an analysis of emergency response time.

Emergency Response Times

Number of Cases:	2678
Missing:	0
Mean:	0:06:02
Median	0:02:54
Mode	0:02:16
Standard Deviation:	0:17:21
Range:	7:45:30
Minimum	0:00:01
Maximum	7:45:31
Percentiles:	
25	0:01:46
50	0:02:54
75	0:04:57

Table 10-3: Statistical output of emergency response times

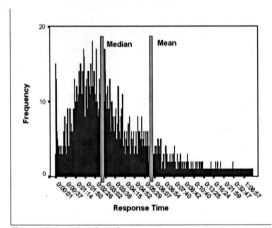

Figure 10-3: A bar chart showing emergency response time.

By looking at the chart without the statistics, we can see that the distribution is not normal, but skewed. That is, there are more values that are clustered in the lower time values. The fact that the mean and median are different numbers also tells us that the distribution is skewed (see the statistics and the chart). By looking at the range, we can see that the largest value for an emergency response time is over 7 hours. Note that this value is not on the chart as it is such a high number (outlier) that the statistical program did not include it (i.e., if it was on the chart there would be a very long tail to the right).

The standard deviation is very high (just over 17 minutes), and since the average response time is just over 6 minutes, we know there are extreme values influencing the mean. Lastly, from the median and percentiles we can see that 50% of our emergency calls for service are answered within 2:54 minutes, 75% in 4:57 minutes. By looking at all of these together, we may ask why a few calls have such a high response time, prompting further investigation. A standard statistical way of removing outliers is to conduct a 5% trimmed mean in which 2.5% of the data are taken out from the lowest and highest values. The result for this distribution is 3:41, a significant decrease in response time and much closer to the median.

Measures of Central Tendency Summary

It is important for analysts to understand data and statistics and their limitations. Even though these statistics work well to describe data, they can be affected greatly by outliers, especially when few cases are examined at once. Often, an analyst may calculate these statistics as part of the analysis process, but never publish them in a report. By applying these statistics to a data distribution, analysts can understand the data to choose an effective method for analysis. These statistics are also a good way to assess the quality of data. Measures of central tendency are used in crime analysis in the following situations:

- Mode is used often, as lists of descending frequency.
- Median and percentiles are used instead of mean when distributions are skewed.
- Mean is used only with ratio and interval variables, which are rare in crime analysis.
- Standard deviation is used to indicate the nature of a distribution, but is not often included in regular reports.

Statistics in Action: Standard Deviation

The following table and map detail are an identified bank robbery series comprising 5 incidents:

#	Weekday	Time
1	Monday	12:15
2	Tuesday	14:40
3	Monday	13:30
4	Monday	16:10

Challenge:
What prediction about the future events would you make based on these results?

Answer
If the offender behaves as he or she has in the past, you can predict that he or she may rob a bank on a weekday, more likely on a Monday, and more likely in the afternoon.

Challenge:

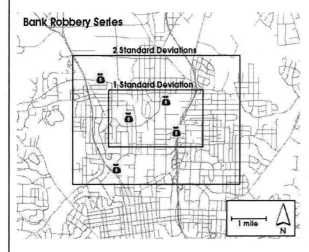

A sergeant wants to deploy surveillance resources on Mondays, from 1100 to 1500 in the area encompassed by the first standard deviation rectangle. Based on these past incidents, what is your estimate of the probability the officers catch the offender during the next robbery through this strategy?

Answer
At the most, there is a 21% to 24% chance that the officers will catch the offender during the next robbery through this strategy. Stated simply, the probability of an outcome is the likelihood that the outcome will occur within a given number of observations. For example, the probability of obtaining heads on a single coin flip is ½, or 0.50.

In this example, the sergeant is assuming that all of these events will occur together; that is, the bank robber will strike on Monday, *and* between 1100 and 1500, *and* in the area encompassed by the first standard deviation rectangle. This assumption invokes the multiplication rule, which states that, for independent events, the probabilities of two or more events must be multiplied together in order to determine the probability that the events will occur simultaneously.

Assuming that time of day, day of week, and location are independent of one another, the 0.21 probability is derived from the formula: 0.60 x 0.60 x 0.60 = 0.216, where 0.60 is the probability that the offender will strike on Monday (3 of the 5 incidents have occurred on a Monday), 0.60 is the probability that the offender will strike between 1100 and 1500 (3 of the 5 incidents have occurred during this time span), and 0.60 is the probability the offender will strike within the first standard deviation rectangle (3 of 5 incidents). Even though the question uses the percentage based on the real number of cases in the rectangle, there is an issue in using the standard deviation rectangle: the standard deviation rectangle does not seem to appear in the quantitative geography or spatial analysis literature. It is used in crime analysis, but the only definition we could locate with an equation was in Gottlieb's *Crime Analysis: From*

First Report to Final Arrest, which states: "This rectangle now represents the geographic area in which 68% of the crimes (one standard deviation) have occurred."[1] But according to the suggested method of calculation, X and Y values are treated independently, resulting in such a rectangle encompassing only 46% of the incidents (0.68 x 0.68). But in the map shown in this question, we used a true standard deviational rectangle (or approximation thereof) that encompassed 3 of the 5 crimes (.60).

The 0.24 probability is derived from the formula: 0.40 x 0.60 = 0.24, where 0.40 is the probability that the offender will strike on a Monday between the hours of 1100 and 1500 (2 of the 5 incidents have occurred on Monday during this time span), and 0.60 refers to the probability that the offender will strike within the first standard deviation rectangle.

We do not recommend using statistics to predict future incidents in a crime series, especially when the statistics are based on a low number of cases, as they are much less reliable. All predictions of future behavior are based on the assumption that the criminal will continue to behave in a similar fashion. Thus, we can state that, "based on the offender's past behavior, he or she may rob a bank on a weekday, more likely on a Monday, and more likely in the afternoon." (Note the lack of use of specific statistics.) However, many other variables, such as suspect description, property value, and the availability of targets should be considered in addition to time, day, and location.

[1]Steven Gottlieb, Sheldon Arenberg, and Raj Singh, *Crime Analysis: From First Report to Final Arrest* (Montclair, CA: Alpha Publishing, 1994), 452.

Inference

Inference is the process of taking a random sample of data to estimate the characteristics of a population. Most of the time this is done because studying the entire population is not realistic or possible. Measures of central tendency can be used inferentially to describe the characteristics of a population based on a sample. In policing, this is most often used in citizen surveys. That is, a random sample of citizens in a city is asked to complete a survey in order to generalize to the population of the entire city about police-related topics (e.g., victimization, fear of crime, satisfaction with police).

However, inference is typically not used in crime analysis as most of the data examined is a population. For example, call-for-service data represent "all" calls received by the police agency by definition; therefore, it is a population. Also, crime data represent "all" crime reported to the police agency. Even though reported crime is a subset of all crime, it is a biased sample, not random, thus inference cannot be used to generalize to all crime. See Chapter 14 in the book for more information about inference.

Statistical Significance

Statistical significance is a term used to denote that a statistical test has been conducted and the findings are significant at some predetermined level. However, in everyday speech people often use the term "significant" to mean "important." For example, "there were 100 burglaries in Beat 2 and 200 in Beat 3. This is a significant difference." Actually, we do not know if there is a statistically significant difference because a test of significance was not conducted. It does appear that there is a difference in the levels of burglary for these beats. Yet, it could be because Beat 3 is twice as large in area or has twice the number of houses. Consequently, one should be cautious about using the word "significant" in any case.

Statistics in Action: Statistical Significance

Challenge
Analysis of individuals arrested for auto theft during the past year reveals that of the 68 individuals arrested, 60 were known drug offenders. The Chief asks if this is statistically significant. How would you answer?

Answer
Based on the information given, you cannot determine statistical significance. A test of significance provides an estimate of how likely a sample is representative of the population from which it is drawn, and it requires a specific statistical test. There is insufficient information in this question to conduct such a test. However, what the Chief really seems to be interested in is whether there is a relationship between drug use and the commission of auto theft. With the information provided, it can only be stated that approximately 88% of the individuals arrested for auto theft in the past year were known drug offenders, and no conclusion about the entire population of auto thieves can be made. Because the 68 arrestees were not selected randomly from the population of auto thieves, one could say that there is bias since these were only the thieves that were caught. In addition, it may be the case that drug users are likely to be more careless in the commission of the crime, thus making them more likely to be arrested than professional auto thieves or joyriders.

The key question that is asked when a statistical test of significance is conducted is: what is the probability that what we think is a relationship between two variables is really just a chance occurrence? We can never be 100 percent certain that a relationship exists between two variables, since there are too many sources of error to be controlled (e.g., sampling error, researcher bias, problems with reliability and validity, simple mistakes). Thus, social science researchers have chosen a specific probability that is acceptable: 95 percent. In other words, if we are 95 percent certain that the relationship is not a coincidence, we say the relationship is statistically significant. In a statistics program, this number is usually displayed as a p-value with significance at the .05 (or 5 percent) level. Any p-value at or lower than .05 means the findings were statistically significant.

On the other hand, even when conducting a statistical test for significance, there can be a statistically significant finding, but the implications of that finding may have no practical application. For example, we may find that there is a statistically significant relationship between a citizen's age and fear of crime. It may be that older citizens are three percent more fearful than younger citizens. But is three percent a large enough difference to be concerned about? When differences are small but statistically significant, it is often due to a very large sample size; in a sample of a smaller size, the differences would not be enough to be statistically significant.

The following are a number of statistics most relevant for testing relationships for crime analysis purposes. All the following statistics produce a p-value that indicates the significance of the test. The exact formulas for computing these statistics are not included, but how and when to use them are discussed. (For further reading see an undergraduate statistics text.) It is important to note that when using these types of statistics, having more cases is preferable. A minimum of 35 cases is desirable because the fewer cases, the less reliable the statistics because they can be greatly influenced by non-normal distributions. This is a consideration in crime analysis, as many of the distributions in question do not have sufficient number of cases (e.g., tactical crime analysis). One final note, it is important that in crime analysis the term "significance" is only used when a statistical test has been conducted.

One-Sample T-test

A one-sample t-test tests whether the mean of a single variable differs from a specified constant. A statistically significant result indicates that the mean is different than the specified constant. However, this statistic does not indicate why or how the mean is different from the constant, only that the difference is statistically significant.

Examples:

- A police department may want to test whether an average number of reports taken by police officers differs from a constant (e.g., a number decided to be an acceptable number of reports).
- A researcher might want to test whether the average IQ score for a group of students differs from 100.
- A cereal manufacturer can take a sample of boxes from the production line and check whether the mean weight of the samples differs from 1.3 pounds at the 95 percent confidence level.

Paired-Samples T-test

A paired-samples t-test statistic compares the means of two variables for a single group. It computes the differences between values of the two variables for each case within the group and tests whether the average differs from 0. This is particularly useful in a pre- and post- measurement test for one group as each case is measured against itself.

Example:

- Twenty apartment communities are participating in a crime prevention campaign. The amounts of crime six months before the campaign and six months after the campaign (with three months in between for implementation) are measured for each apartment community. The difference between the measurements for each community before and after is tested. Significant results would indicate that this difference between Time 1 and Time 2 for all the communities is different than 0; thus, there is a change from Time 1 to Time 2 overall.

Independent T-test

An independent t-test compares means for two groups of cases to determine if they are different (e.g., experimental and control group). Ideally, for this test, the subjects should be randomly assigned (i.e., independent) to two groups, so that any difference is due to the treatment (or lack of treatment) and not to other factors. This is not the case if you compare average income for males and females. A person is not randomly assigned to be a male or female. In such situations, you should ensure that differences in other factors are not masking or enhancing a significant difference in means. Differences in average income may be influenced by factors such as education and not by sex alone. Note that in most policing examples, subjects or cases are not assigned randomly. This statistic is still used but the interpretation should be done very cautiously.

Examples:

- To test the difference between the average response time by different types of calls for service (e.g., domestic calls or robbery calls).

- To test the difference between the average age of victims by sex (e.g., male or female).
- To test whether different groups of dispatchers (e.g., day and night shift) take, on average, a different amount of time to dispatch calls.

In the context of problem solving, paired and independent t-tests can be very helpful to test differences between and within groups. Figure 10-4 illustrates that independent t-tests would be used to determine whether the experimental and comparison groups are different before the response and after. For a successful project, one would expect no significant difference between the groups in the pre-test and a significant difference in the post-test. Paired t-tests would be used to determine if the same group had changed over time. For a successful project, one would expect no significant difference from the pre-test to the post-test for the control group and a significant result for the comparison group.

Correlation

Correlation tests the level of association of the variables or the extent and direction in which two variables are related in a linear fashion. Note that correlation only tests linear relationships. There are two types of correlation statistics: Pearson's *r* (continuous variables) and Spearman (ordinal variables). See a statistics textbook for specific differences. In either case, the resulting coefficient is an *r* value ranging from −1 to +1, with values closer to −1 and +1 being stronger correlations and closer to 0 weak. Most statistical programs provide a p-value to indicate statistical significance of the correlation coefficient. Correlation can provide important information about the relationship between two variables because unlike t-tests, the coefficient has a sign that indicates the direction of the relationship. A positive sign means that as one variable increases or decreases, the other does as well. A negative sign means as one variable increases the other decreases or vice versa. Figures 10-5 to 10-9 are examples of scatter plots with two variables and their correlation coefficients.

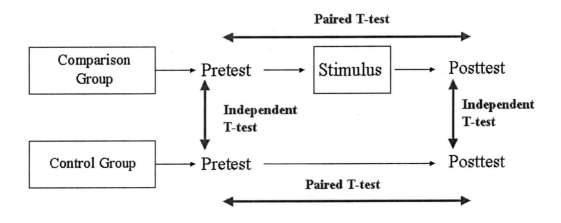

Figure 10-4: The function of independent t-tests

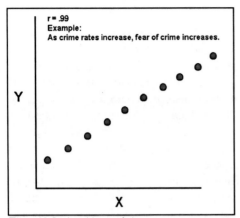

Figure 10-5: A positive correlation

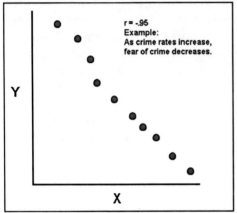

Figure 10-6: A negative correlation

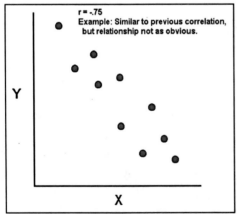

Figure 10-7: A weaker negative correlation

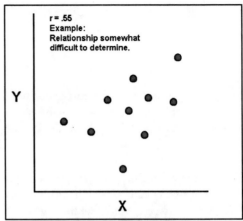

Figure 10-8: Correlation difficult to determine

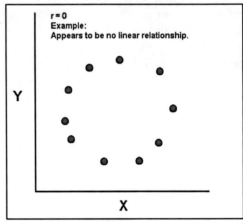

Figure 10-9: No correlation

When using correlation, one should be cautious. Correlation does not indicate causality; that is, one variable caused another. It only shows that there is a relationship. In addition, two variables can be perfectly related, but if the relationship is not linear (see Figure 10-9), the correlation coefficient is not an appropriate statistic for measuring their association. Finally, two variables may be correlated, but it may be because of a third variable (e.g., as photo radar tickets increase, accidents go down, but actually the speed of drivers is related to both).

Example:

- An analyst wants to determine whether beats in his or her jurisdiction with higher rates of crime also have higher rates of poverty. A correlation would determine if these variables were related by beat for the entire city.

Summary

The intent of this chapter is to provide issues to consider when using and interpreting statistics with crime analysis data. Although this chapter is lengthy and covers many of the data consideration and statistics, it by no means covers all that needs to be considered when applying and interpreting statistics. In many cases, data are unique to a particular department and only the informed crime analyst will be able to provide accurate interpretation. Never take police data at face value; question its validity and reliability at all times. Doing this and using statistics appropriately will improve the data quality as well as the quality of crime analysis.

11
Temporal Analysis

Dan Helms

Temporal analysis is the study of time. As crime analysts, we should all realize that clearly understanding the timing of events, whether they are crimes, calls for service, arrests, movements, or any other police-related acts, is fundamental to our ability to perform our jobs. We analyze time for two reasons: first, to understand what has already happened; second, to predict what will happen in the future.

As we shall see in this chapter, comprehensive temporal analysis is not as mysterious as it might be made out. The reliable and proven methods for analyzing time that have been used for decades (in some cases, centuries) by other professions can be quickly and easily put to use by the crime analyst. Here we will discuss method and theory—the techniques presented can be applied in any modern software environment using a variety of tools. They do, however, require the firepower of desktop computing—the days of the pocket calculator, slide rule, abacus, and counting on fingers are definitely behind us. Fortunately, a variety of tools and tactics exist to enable every crime analyst to perform powerful, comprehensive, and above all reliable temporal analysis of any police problem.

At the same time, although temporal analysis doesn't need to be difficult or time-consuming, neither is it very easy. Analysis of human behavior with respect to time is complex and requires serious thought. Weak and simplistic methods are likely to result in erroneous results and mistaken forecasts, some of which can be difficult to detect. By taking a comprehensive approach to temporal analysis—thinking out every part of the problem and crafting ways to tackle those problems well in advance—we can be ready to quickly and smoothly take advantage of our techniques when we need them.

Measuring Time

Information on the timing of crimes, calls for service, arrests, and other police and criminal activities is usually analyzed using computer software. This temporal information is stored in database tables, spreadsheets, and electronic reports. Before we can meaningfully subject this data to analysis, it is important that we understand a few elemental facts about how that temporal data is stored and retrieved.

Although most of us are intimately familiar with measuring time using calendars and clocks in our everyday lives as a matter of practical experience, a review of some fundamentals is called for.

Editors' note: Because of the large number of graphs and figures in this chapter, and the importance that they appear in exact positions relative to the text, we have presented this chapter in single-column format.

There are two elements that typically combine to identify a discrete temporal location—that is, an exact time. These elements are the date and the time.

Dates in the western world are measured on a calendar. The calendar used in the English-speaking world (with the partial exception of India) is the Gregorian calendar. The Gregorian calendar is a Renaissance improvement implemented in 1582 by Pope Gregory XIII, based on the ancient Julian calendar used in ancient Rome. It is interesting that the United States does not recognize an official calendar; the use of the Gregorian standard calendar stems from an English Act of Parliament in 1751, and has held over to modern times. Other nations use different calendars; among the most important are the Muslim Hijra Lunar Calendar, the Hebrew Calendar, and the Chinese Calendar. Dates measured using these divergent calendars will be highly distinctive. Consider the following examples, each of which shows exactly the same day:

Gregorian Calendar:	October 1, 2003
Julian Calendar:	September 18, 2003
Muslim Calendar:	4th Sha'ban, 1424
Indian Civil Calendar:	9th Asvina, 1925
Hebrew Calendar:	5th Tishri, 5764
Persian Calendar:	9th Mehr, 1382
Chinese Calendar:	6th Jiu Yue, 4700

In addition to these traditional and historical calendars, modern computer software and operating systems also assign date values in different ways:

Gregorian Calendar:	October 1, 2003
UNIX System Date:	1064966400
ISO-8601:	Day-3, Week-40, Year-2003
Windows Excel Date:	37895
Macintosh Excel Date:	36433

Times in the western world divide each day into periods of seconds, minutes, and hours. As we all know:

60 seconds = 1 minute
60 minutes = 1 hour
24 hours = 1 day

The hours of the day in civilian society are organized into two periods of 12 hours each. These periods are the *ante meridian* (A.M.) in the morning and the *post meridian* (P.M.) in the afternoon and evening. These periods derive their names from the position of the sun—below the meridian, or half-way mark in the sky, or beyond it, indicating a setting sun. Confusingly, the first hour of each period is numbered 12, rather than zero. So 12:00 A.M. indicates the middle of the night, while 12:00 P.M. (noon) is the middle of the calendar day. The 60 minutes of each hour are expressed as a number following the hour, separated by a colon. Thus, 12:15 A.M. is a quarter of the way through the first hour of a new day. Additional precision is obtained by expressing the

60 seconds of each minute as a number following the minute, separated by a second colon: 6:35:41 P.M. indicates forty-one seconds after six thirty-five at night.

Military time is measured on a 24-hour clock. The differences between military and civilian timekeeping are that military times are not separated by colons, always contain leading zeroes, hours are measured from 0–23 rather than 1–12, and there is no mention of meridian periods. In this system, post meridian hours are measured from 12–23 (adding 12 to the civilian equivalents). Therefore, 6:35 P.M. in civilian timekeeping equates to 1835 in military format.

Dates and times have traditionally been measured separately. After all, calendars and clocks are different instruments. More recently, however, these two halves of temporal measurement have been merged into a single "date/time" or "datetime" measurement that combines the calendar date with the clock time to define each unique point in time. These measures are carried over into the world of computer data storage. There has been a consistent evolution in the way in which dates and times are stored as computer data.

The most primitive computer storage of date or time information is in the form of text fields— that is, data columns designed to accept any alphanumeric characters—which contain dates, times, or both in written form. Although the human eye, reading these textual values, understands that they contain temporal information, a computer is merely aware that some characters have been entered into the field. There is no comprehension as to what that information might mean. Therefore, text fields must be adapted for use in date-based computations.

An alternative is numeric date or time fields, which will accept only numerals. This type of field can contain date or time information without delimiting characters. Because numeric fields are decimal-based, and temporal measurements usually are not, once again this often calls for some type of conversion routine.

A third possible format is the combined and specialize date/time field type. This field actually contains a single, highly precise number, which can be translated into a legible date and time. There are several variants of this field type, including the Microsoft date, Excel date, UNIX system, and Macintosh date systems.

Microsoft date fields consist of a long integer number. This number represents the number of milliseconds since midnight, January 1, 1900. Negative numbers describe datetimes before this origin date. This field type is capable, therefore, of handling values precise to the millisecond, which is accurate enough for most crime analysis functions.

Macintosh date fields are similar to Microsoft date, but use 1904 as the year of origin.

The popular Microsoft Excel spreadsheet program uses its own date/time format, "Excel Dates." An Excel Date field consists of a single-precision decimal number. This number represents the number of days since January 1, 1900, followed by a decimal fraction reflecting the fraction of that day expressed by the time portion of the value. Therefore, a value of "1.5" would indicate noon of January 2, 1900.

UNIX system dates are measured in the number of seconds since January 1, 1970.

Each of these formats—simple text fields, numeric fields, and specialized date/time fields—can be interpreted by software programs to display the results in nearly any way the user desires. It is easy, therefore, to change the way that dates and times are displayed in a software application—but remember, changing the format you view the data in does not change the data itself.

It's important for crime analysts to be aware of how these different systems store and manipulate dates and times. We need to be very aware of how our data is organized in order to query it efficiently and accurately. It's even more critical to understand these things when we transform data from one format to another through exporting.

Consider the following common scenario: A police department stores crime reports in a Microsoft SQL Server relational database. Every day, the database administrator automatically downloads recent data into a flat file using an automated export query. The crime analyst then imports this flat file into an Excel spreadsheet to sort and manipulate. Later, she saves her spreadsheet out at a dBASE-IV file to load it into ArcView, where it is geocoded and converted to a shapefile.

In this scenario, date and time values are translated between four different formats. Each time a conversion is performed, the chance for some sort of error occurs. Even if this error rate is very small—say, one in a million—over the course of years, this will result in some noticeable data discrepancies. When the error rate is higher, such as one in a thousand, the consequences are correspondingly more severe.

Schedules

Like any other person, the serial or professional criminal has only so many hours in the day. Crime takes time and effort, and the criminal must allocate his finite resources of both to carry out his attacks. Obviously this is true of any behavior: it takes a certain amount of time to go to school, to eat, to sleep, to earn a living, to commit a sexual assault. Like any other person, the offender must allocate his 24 hours among the many tasks he is driven to pursue. When we study the temporal allocation of time by any person, how we view the rational process of this allocation varies greatly with our unit of analysis.

For example, if we choose to examine temporal behavior on the basis of a 24-hour day, we are likely to uncover certain regular patterns that will allow us to make general predictions about a subject's temporal behavior. For example, activities such as eating and sleeping are typically performed every day. We could analyze these behaviors in the context of a 24-hour day and discover cycles: Perhaps something like a 8/12 (= 2/3) hour ratio between sleeping and waking, for example, and regular patterns of eating three times per day, with additional cyclic variances for snacks and naps. On the other hand, if we attempted to analyze certain other types of behavior, such as working, in this 24-hour context we would meet with both success and failure. Success, because we would probably notice that the subject exhibited something like a 8/12 hour ratio between working/not working for example. Failure, because our findings would likely be skewed by the fact that our subject doesn't work every day. Some days he will work for eight hours, and those hours will be predictable; on other days, however, he will not work.

Therefore, it is necessary for us to analyze this type of behavior using a different measurement schema: in this case, the seven-day week. By analyzing the subject's temporal allocation of time to work against the backdrop of a seven-day schedule, we will quickly be rewarded (in the case of an average worker) with the discovery that he exhibits a clear and reliable pattern, a ratio of 5/2 of working/non working days. We could then apply the principle of recursion—going back over previous analysis—with this new data, and by only including those days in which the subject went to work (Monday–Friday, for example), our discovery of a regular pattern to the hours spent at work would make much more sense. To illustrate this point, let's briefly consider an example of temporal activity.

The Figure 11-1 illustrates one way to keep track of a very simplistic temporal activity allocation schedule. In this example, we've used John Doe, a very dull individual, who engages in a very limited number of activities: "sleep," "work," "drive," "eat," "read," "watch TV," and "movie." Perhaps he is a crime analyst. These activities describe his actions, and by using this matrix we can see how John Doe allocates every hour of this week. Our <u>unit of analysis = 1 hour</u>, and our timeframe = <u>24 hours x 7 days</u>. Though only one of many means to display and relate temporal activities, this matrix should be self-explanatory:

Activity Matrix		Monday	Tuesday	Wednesday	Thursday	Friday	Saturday	Sunday	
Subject	Hour (0-23)	Activity	Activity	Activity	Activity	Activity	Activity	Activity	Modal
John Doe	0	Sleep	Sleep	Sleep	Sleep	Read	Watch TV	Read	Sleep
John Doe	1	Sleep	Sleep	Sleep	Sleep	Sleep	Read	Sleep	Sleep
John Doe	2	Sleep	Sleep	Sleep	Sleep	Sleep	Sleep	Sleep	Sleep
John Doe	3	Sleep	Sleep	Sleep	Sleep	Sleep	Sleep	Sleep	Sleep
John Doe	4	Sleep	Sleep	Sleep	Sleep	Sleep	Sleep	Sleep	Sleep
John Doe	5	Sleep	Sleep	Sleep	Sleep	Sleep	Sleep	Sleep	Sleep
John Doe	6	Sleep	Sleep	Sleep	Sleep	Sleep	Sleep	Sleep	Sleep
John Doe	7	Eat	Sleep	Eat	Eat	Sleep	Sleep	Sleep	Sleep
John Doe	8	Drive	Drive	Drive	Drive	Drive	Sleep	Sleep	Drive
John Doe	9	Work	Work	Work	Work	Work	Sleep	Eat	Work
John Doe	10	Work	Work	Work	Work	Work	Eat	Drive	Work
John Doe	11	Work	Work	Work	Work	Work	Read	Drive	Work
John Doe	12	Work	Work	Work	Work	Work	Watch TV	Read	Work
John Doe	13	Eat	Eat	Eat	Eat	Eat	Watch TV	Eat	Eat
John Doe	14	Work	Work	Work	Work	Work	Eat	Drive	Work
John Doe	15	Work	Work	Work	Work	Work	Watch TV	Drive	Work
John Doe	16	Work	Work	Work	Work	Work	Watch TV	Watch TV	Work
John Doe	17	Work	Work	Work	Work	Work	Watch TV	Eat	Work
John Doe	18	Drive	Drive	Work	Work	Drive	Watch TV	Watch TV	Drive
John Doe	19	Eat	Eat	Drive	Eat	Movie	Eat	Watch TV	Eat
John Doe	20	Watch TV	Watch TV	Eat	Watch TV	Movie	Watch TV	Watch TV	Watch TV
John Doe	21	Eat	Watch TV	Watch TV	Eat	Drive	Watch TV	Read	Watch TV
John Doe	22	Read	Read	Watch TV	Read	Eat	Watch TV	Sleep	Read
John Doe	23	Read	Sleep	Sleep	Read	Drive	Read	Sleep	Sleep
	Modal	Work	Sleep	Work	Work	Work	Watch TV	Sleep	Work

Figure 11-1: An activity matrix

The modal values assigned to each hour and to each day describe the modal activity type predominant for that hour or day. Thus, given this matrix, if someone were to ask us, "What will John Doe be doing at Midnight?" we might consult the modal value for midnights (Hour=0) and answer, "Sleeping," with some degree of confidence. Of course, if we were asked more specifically, "What will John Doe be doing during midnights over the weekend?" we would instead answer, "probably reading," with somewhat less confidence but still supported by our statistical expectations based on past observation.

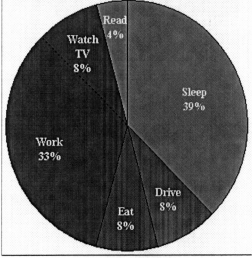

Activity	Hours	Percent
Sleep	9	37.50%
Drive	2	8.33%
Eat	2	8.33%
Work	8	33.33%
Watch TV	2	8.33%
Read	1	4.17%
Total	24	100.00%

Mr. Doe in our example leads a pretty dull week by most standards: He rises, grabs a bite of breakfast (unless he oversleeps), and drives downtown to the basement of City Hall to work the day away in his cubicle. He'll take a break for lunch at 1:00 P.M. (1300), and then work through the afternoon. Next it's the rush-hour drive back home, where he'll usually grab a bite of dinner about 7:00 P.M. (1900) (unless he works overtime, or is held up in traffic). Some television, perhaps another

Figure 11-2: modal values for John Doe's week

chapter of the latest Ann Rule or David Canter thriller, and then to bed. Friday night, poor Mr. Doe steps out to take in a movie and a late dinner, but then he goes home, stays up a short while longer, and sleeps in the next day. What's to do on the weekend? Mostly watch more television, perhaps go for a Sunday drive and a picnic in the country before an early night; after all, he has to work the next morning.

When we examine John Doe's extremely limited and simplified schedule, we easily see how regular are his habits, and how susceptible his schedule to analysis. We have little difficulty cataloging his temporal allocation of hours, and can make some easy generalizations about his life based on our observations. These, in turn, might lead us to make predictions of greater or lesser accuracy, depending on the regularity of Mr. Doe's lifestyle, the reliability of our data, and the level of detail of our analyses.

How useful is this to a practicing crime analyst? Consider the matrix in Figure 11-3. Here we are making a few substitutions, and now John Doe, in addition to the rest of his dull, predictable life, is a rapist. His schedule, therefore, includes two new activities: "stalk" and "attack." In this case, the offender is still doing what everyone else does: allocating a finite amount of time and energy toward his various pursuits. It just happens that one of these is criminal. We've already seen that modeling a subject's schedule using various methods can allow us to make some predictions, of varying accuracy, as to his future actions. This is no less true of criminals than crime analysts.

Activity Matrix		Monday	Tuesday	Wednesday	Thursday	Friday	Saturday	Sunday	
Subject	Hour (0-23)	Activity	Activity	Activity	Activity	Activity	Activity	Activity	Modal
John Doe	0	Sleep	Sleep	Sleep	Sleep	Stalk	Stalk	Drive	Sleep
John Doe	1	Sleep	Sleep	Drive	Sleep	Stalk	Stalk	Attack	Sleep
John Doe	2	Sleep	Sleep	Stalk	Sleep	Drive	Stalk	Drive	Sleep
John Doe	3	Sleep	Sleep	Drive	Sleep	Sleep	Sleep	Sleep	Sleep
John Doe	4	Sleep	Sleep	Sleep	Sleep	Sleep	Sleep	Sleep	Sleep
John Doe	5	Sleep	Sleep	Sleep	Sleep	Sleep	Sleep	Sleep	Sleep
John Doe	6	Sleep	Sleep	Sleep	Sleep	Sleep	Sleep	Sleep	Sleep
John Doe	7	Eat	Sleep	Sleep	Eat	Sleep	Sleep	Sleep	Sleep
John Doe	8	Drive	Drive	Drive	Drive	Drive	Sleep	Sleep	Drive
John Doe	9	Work	Work	Work	Work	Work	Sleep	Sleep	Work
John Doe	10	Work	Work	Work	Work	Work	Eat	Drive	Work
John Doe	11	Work	Work	Work	Work	Work	Read	Drive	Work
John Doe	12	Work	Work	Work	Work	Work	Watch TV	Read	Work
John Doe	13	Eat	Eat	Eat	Eat	Eat	Watch TV	Eat	Eat
John Doe	14	Work	Work	Work	Work	Work	Eat	Drive	Work
John Doe	15	Work	Work	Work	Work	Work	Watch TV	Drive	Work
John Doe	16	Work	Work	Work	Work	Work	Watch TV	Watch TV	Work
John Doe	17	Work	Work	Work	Work	Work	Watch TV	Eat	Work
John Doe	18	Drive	Drive	Work	Work	Drive	Watch TV	Watch TV	Drive
John Doe	19	Eat	Eat	Drive	Eat	Movie	Eat	Watch TV	Eat
John Doe	20	Watch TV	Watch TV	Eat	Watch TV	Movie	Watch TV	Watch TV	Watch TV
John Doe	21	Eat	Watch TV	Watch TV	Eat	Drive	Watch TV	Read	Watch TV
John Doe	22	Read	Read	Watch TV	Watch TV	Eat	Watch TV	Sleep	Watch TV
John Doe	23	Read	Sleep	Sleep	Drive	Drive	Read	Sleep	Sleep
	Modal	Work	Sleep	Work	Work	Work	Watch TV	Sleep	Work

Figure 11-3: John Doe's activity matrix with criminal activity added

Unfortunately, the typical law enforcement crime analyst does not have access to a reliable matrix of the offender's schedule. Usually, the only information he or she has available is data on criminal events. Therefore, instead of the detailed matrix as seen previously, the analyst only sees something like Figure 11-4.

Clearly, the analyst has his work cut out for him. But perhaps by applying sociology and psychology to the problem, we might infer more pieces of the puzzle than are readily apparent.

226

Activity Matrix		Monday	Tuesday	Wednesday	Thursday	Friday	Saturday	Sunday	
Subject	Hour (0-23)	Activity	Activity	Activity	Activity	Activity	Activity	Activity	Modal
John Doe	0	Unknown	Unknown	Unknown	Unknown	Unknown	Unknown	Unknown	Unknown
John Doe	1	Unknown	Unknown	Unknown	Unknown	Unknown	Unknown	Attack	Unknown
John Doe	2	Unknown	Unknown	Unknown	Unknown	Unknown	Unknown	Unknown	Unknown
John Doe	3	Unknown	Unknown	Unknown	Unknown	Unknown	Unknown	Unknown	Unknown
John Doe	4	Unknown	Unknown	Unknown	Unknown	Unknown	Unknown	Unknown	Unknown
John Doe	5	Unknown	Unknown	Unknown	Unknown	Unknown	Unknown	Unknown	Unknown
John Doe	6	Unknown	Unknown	Unknown	Unknown	Unknown	Unknown	Unknown	Unknown
John Doe	7	Unknown	Unknown	Unknown	Unknown	Unknown	Unknown	Unknown	Unknown
John Doe	8	Unknown	Unknown	Unknown	Unknown	Unknown	Unknown	Unknown	Unknown
John Doe	9	Unknown	Unknown	Unknown	Unknown	Unknown	Unknown	Unknown	Unknown
John Doe	10	Unknown	Unknown	Unknown	Unknown	Unknown	Unknown	Unknown	Unknown
John Doe	11	Unknown	Unknown	Unknown	Unknown	Unknown	Unknown	Unknown	Unknown
John Doe	12	Unknown	Unknown	Unknown	Unknown	Unknown	Unknown	Unknown	Unknown
John Doe	13	Unknown	Unknown	Unknown	Unknown	Unknown	Unknown	Unknown	Unknown
John Doe	14	Unknown	Unknown	Unknown	Unknown	Unknown	Unknown	Unknown	Unknown
John Doe	15	Unknown	Unknown	Unknown	Unknown	Unknown	Unknown	Unknown	Unknown
John Doe	16	Unknown	Unknown	Unknown	Unknown	Unknown	Unknown	Unknown	Unknown
John Doe	17	Unknown	Unknown	Unknown	Unknown	Unknown	Unknown	Unknown	Unknown
John Doe	18	Unknown	Unknown	Unknown	Unknown	Unknown	Unknown	Unknown	Unknown
John Doe	19	Unknown	Unknown	Unknown	Unknown	Unknown	Unknown	Unknown	Unknown
John Doe	20	Unknown	Unknown	Unknown	Unknown	Unknown	Unknown	Unknown	Unknown
John Doe	21	Unknown	Unknown	Unknown	Unknown	Unknown	Unknown	Unknown	Unknown
John Doe	22	Unknown	Unknown	Unknown	Unknown	Unknown	Unknown	Unknown	Unknown
John Doe	23	Unknown	Unknown	Unknown	Unknown	Unknown	Unknown	Unknown	Unknown
	Modal	Unknown	Unknown	Unknown	Unknown	Unknown	Unknown	Unknown	Unknown

Figure 11-4: A realistic crime analysis activity matrix

Temporal Distribution

Persons already familiar with spatial analysis will be comfortable with the idea of distribution. Distribution describes how events are situated throughout the study area in relation to one another. There are three classes of distributions: clustered, random, and uniform.

- **Clustered** events tend to occur in close proximity to one another.
- **Uniform** events tend to occur far apart from one another.
- **Random** events are neither clustered nor uniform.

On a map, these distributions are relatively easy to perceive. Less commonly considered is the fact that the timing of events can also be measured in term of distribution along a timeline, and can be classified in the same way. This is an absolutely critical consideration for the crime analyst.

In spatial analysis, we could use tests like the Nearest Neighbor Test, Ripley's K, Moran's I, or others to measure distribution. All of these techniques also work on a timeline to determine temporal distribution; instead of comparing distances in feet or miles, we simply compare intervals in hours or days.

A clustered distribution occurs when events tend to happen close together:

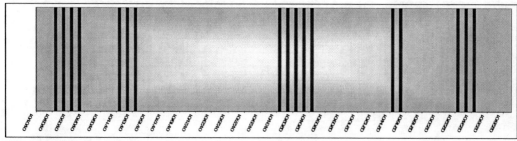

Figure 11-5: A clustered distribution

A uniform distribution occurs when events happen far apart from one another—this may result in a regular, even spacing between events, however, it might not always have that appearance:

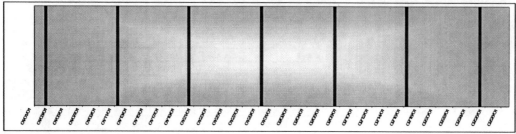

Figure 11-6: A uniform distribution

Finally, a random distribution fits neither of these categories well; it might be the result of a combination of clusters and uniformity, or truly chaotic phenomena:

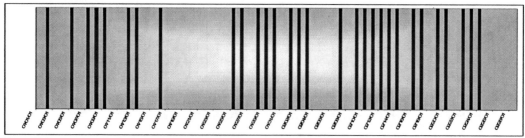

Figure 11-7: A random distribution

Remember that these distributions can be combined together—for instance, events might be clustered, but the clusters could be uniform:

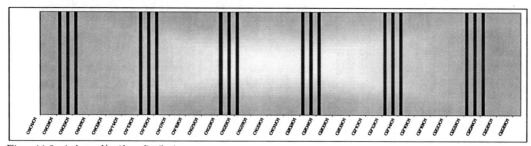

Figure 11-8: A clustered/uniform distribution

Tempo

In addition to the three types of distribution, because time only moves in one direction, we can also meaningfully measure its tendency—its tempo. There are three types of tempo: accelerating, decelerating, and stable.

- **Acceleration** occurs when the interval between events decreases as the number of events increases.
- **Deceleration** occurs when the interval between events increases as the number of events increases.
- **Stabilization** occurs when the interval between events neither increases nor decreases as the number of events increases.

Like distribution, tempo can be measured easily as a function of the change in interval over the change in number of events—in other words, the change in X over the change in Y, the same simple calculation for the slope of any line.

It is easiest to visualize the tempo of events using a tempogram. A tempogram is a bivariate chart that shows change in time along the X (horizontal) axis, and change in interval on the Y (vertical) axis:

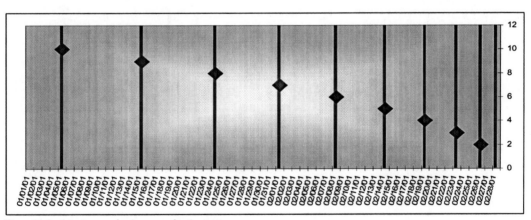

Figure 11-9: A tempogram showing an accelerating tempo

Notice that we can't plot the interval (Y mark) for the last known event—because of course we don't know how long it will be until the next (future) event.

The graphic power of tempograms can be uses to visualize any dynamic variation, and is an extremely powerful tool at the analyst's disposal for a variety of problems. The above tempogram demonstrates an accelerating tempo (the interval between events gets smaller as the series progresses), while the below tempogram demonstrates a decelerating tempo (the interval increases as the series goes on):

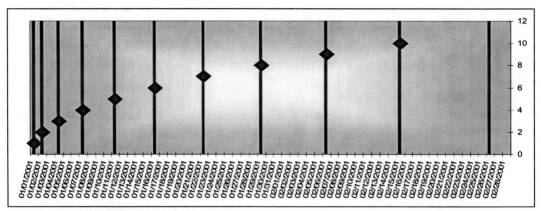

Figure 11-10: A tempogram showing a decelerating tempo

Some inconsiderate series don't seem to either accelerate or decelerate clearly—we consider these to be stable, until we find out otherwise:

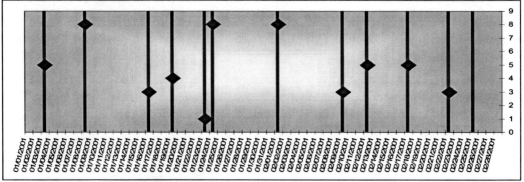

Figure 11-11: A tempogram showing a "stable" tempo

One of the best features of the tempogram technique is that it allows us to calculate a trend line using a method such as the Least Squares Linear Best Fit method or one of its many variants. By extrapolating this line through the last case, we can then make some meaningful predictions about when the next case will occur:

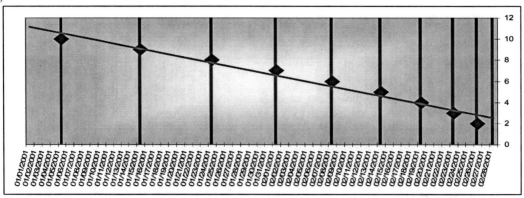

Figure 11-12: A tempogram with a trendline

Velocity

There are some limits to tempos—especially to accelerating tempos. Just look at the illustration showing the trend in an accelerating series of cases. This linear trend is accelerating fast—maybe too fast. Pretty soon, in fact, the predicted interval between cases should be zero (meaning an infinite number of cases will occur at the same time); even worse, they will start to have negative intervals. What does that mean? It means that the series is accelerating so fast it will soon be going backward in time. Outside of "Star Trek," this is a pretty ridiculous concept, so there must be something wrong with our logic, right?

What we've forgotten is that in the real world events have to have some minimum interval between them. In other words, there is a sort of "speed limit," which we call the terminal velocity, which is the fastest rate at which events can occur. Instead of a linear acceleration, it is often better to use a logarithmic trend line, which approaches, but never exceeds, this terminal velocity.

The terminal velocity will differ for different offenders and offenses—finding out what it is remains part of the challenge of serious temporal crime analysis, which can be at least partly resolved using statistical calibration.

Correlation

Sometimes the tempo or distribution of a series may seem chaotic:

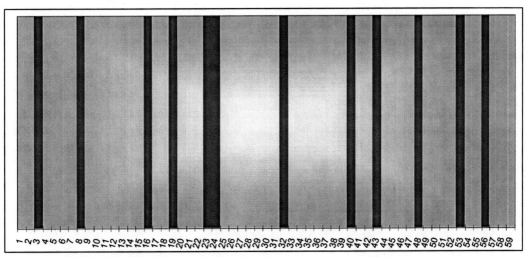

Figure 11-13: A so-called "chaotic" tempo

In the above example the overall trend (a very minute acceleration) is not a good predictor for future intervals. In other words, there is no temporal pattern—or is there? Perhaps a pattern exists, but involves data that we haven't looked at yet. Maybe the timing of cases depends on something else. There could be a correlation between one variable (interval) and another. But what could it be?

There are many possibilities. To make a sensible guess, we must first re-evaluate how and why the offender commits crimes at all. After all, there is a risk associated with committing crime, so why do it in the first place?

Some offenders are motivated by a compulsive obsession—pedophiles, for example, are often describes as being "driven" to their crimes. Other sexual offenders are often similarly categorized. Most offenders, however, are typically motivated by financial drives—they commit crimes to obtain money.

If the crimes we are examining are property-oriented, it might be reasonable to imagine some relationship between the amount of money obtained by the offender and the interval between cases. There could very well be some sort of correlation between these two factors. For example, if a drug addict uses $500 worth of drugs every week, he or she must steal at least $500 per week to support that habit (and, since this individual is unlikely to be holding down much of a job, any other expenses such as rent, groceries, and car payments, must also be paid for by crime). One of the few things police analysts usually know about the crimes we study is how much money (or property value) was taken by the offender—so it should be possible for us to measure any correlation between these factors (property value and interval between crimes).

We can do this by calculating the mean score obtained by dividing the property value by the matching interval. If the standard deviation for this mean is low, it means that this correlation coefficient seems to be valid and that one value predicts the other. So, if we know how much money was taken, we can project how long it will be (give or take) until the next crime.

This kind of prediction is called bivariate analysis—we can even use a tempogram to visualize it. Once we do, it's easy to see that there is a clear relationship between the two variables. In some cases, this relationship can be so clear that it's even possible for an expert to determine the type and amount of drugs to which a perpetrator is addicted by the curve of his property value/interval tempogram.

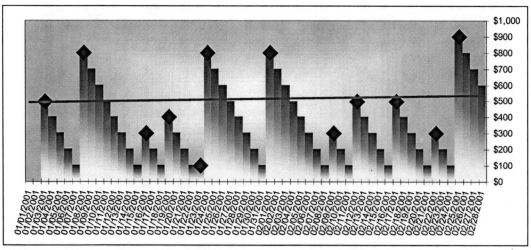

Figure 11-14: A bivariate tempogram showing the time between incidents in relation to the dollar value of stolen property

Temporal Influences

One of the keys to predicting temporal behavior is to identify the factors, environmental, psychological, physiological, geographic, and social, which influence it. There are many elements worth pondering.

When we consider an offender's temporal behavior, in addition to the demands on his time from non-criminal activity, we must also inquire into the nature of the offender's motivation to commit his crimes. As we have seen, if the offender is a robber or burglar motivated by a drug habit, the temporal characteristics of his crimes may exhibit a certain signature influenced by his situation. They are likely to be regular, because his addiction will drive him to crime until he has obtained enough cash to satisfy his habit. In fact, based on the regularity of the cases, and the relationship of the interval to the amounts taken, we might even be able to infer the nature and severity of his addiction, which in turn would help prioritize any list of suspects.

Thrill-seekers, on the other hand, might be much more opportunistic in their criminal endeavors, and might exhibit little obvious temporal regularity. However, there's no such thing as "random violence." There are underlying causes and patterns to every type of human activity, and we can discover them if we try hard enough. Even when the offender is simply walking along and happens to spot a potential victim, then makes a snap decision to risk committing a crime, this is not random, nor truly unpredictable. Something took the offender and victim to the same place, at the same time, and these actions can be observed or inferred.

Sexual offenders of certain types might be driven to crime in much the same manner as a drug addict: by an irresistible compulsion. This type of offender might commit his first crime after a long period of fantasizing and "practicing" through lesser offenses, building up his courage. Once he succeeds, future offenses may increase in frequency. Indeed if, as is likely, his real exploits fail to live up to his fantasies, he may be driven to increase the pace of his crimes by a regular and predictable acceleration to support his sexual drives.

Organized crime offenders are likely to exhibit some sort of fairly obvious temporal pattern; however, because the behavior of the series might be orchestrated by some sort of command authority rather than by the criminal agents themselves, it may be difficult to relate the tempo of events to any intuitive pattern. For example, the pace of auto thefts orchestrated by an organized criminal enterprise might be related to the demand cycle for stolen vehicles in Mexico— something that might not be apparent at all to a U.S. crime analyst.

By visualizing the temporal distribution of cases, it might be possible to infer a great deal about the nature of the offender. However, we must be wary to avoid some of the fallacies that pervade any type of modeling process.

Misleading Correlations and Patterns

The tactical analyst must beware of several pitfalls when attempting to perform temporal analysis. There are a variety of potential fallacies that might seem to indicate a pattern or a statistically significant relationship where in fact none exists.

A terrific example of a temporal fallacy that might sneak past an unsuspecting analyst has to do with storks and babies. In Norway, years ago, several researchers performed a temporal analysis of the birthrates of Norwegian citizens against the migration pattern of storks (probably as a joke). In fact, the data showed a definite correlation. Statistical testing proved that, in fact, as more and more storks returned from the south, more and more babies were born; conversely, when the storks dwindled, the birthrate declined. Moreover, the general trend in annual stork populations did, indeed, exhibit conformity with the overall annual birthrate—when the stork population as a whole declined over the years, so too did the birthrate. The conclusion, of course, for a researcher unprepared to identify a spurious relationship, is that storks bring babies. Obviously, this isn't true. How, then, can we explain the correlation between births and storks?

Well, it's simple enough. The cyclic pattern had more to do with temperature than anything else. Winters get cold in Norway, and when Norwegian couples spend more time indoors, apparently, they find ways to keep warm. One thing leads to another, and nine months later babies begin to appear. The storks don't like the cold either; they head to milder climes during the winter months. As the seasons turn and conditions become gentler in spring and summer, the storks return. They stick around until autumn, before feeling the bite and migrating again. There is a clear relationship between the two factors, but it's spurious, having nothing to do with one another. Instead, they are both dependent on a third, unstudied variable: climate.

It is easy to identify examples of spurious temporal anomalies to be found in the course of law enforcement analysis. Consider the problem of identifying when burglaries occur. A statistical analysis of crime report times and dates might indicate a prominent spike at 6:00 P.M. on Sundays. Does this indicate that more police should be out patrolling during these times? Hardly. The analyst has failed to ask the right question. Instead of identifying when burglaries are occurring, he or she is identifying when they are being reported. The explanation for the anomaly is that people who go away from home over the weekends are returning on Sunday afternoon to find they've been burglarized. In fact, there is likely to be another anomalous spike at 8:00 A.M. Monday mornings, because many might be instructed to fill out a report during business hours. The crimes are actually occurring much earlier, probably on Saturday, and possibly at night. We don't know for sure, but we can be sure that our initial findings are misleading.

Another example might be an apparent correlation between crime events and phases of the moon. The analyst might notice that a long-period terrorist attack series seems to relate statistically to the lunar cycle. This might be the case; however, there might be other explanations as well. For example, if the analyst was studying the activities of a Middle Eastern terrorist organization, the correlation might have more to do with the fact that the Islamic calendar is lunar in nature. Perhaps the terrorists commemorate anniversaries on the Islamic calendar, or receive funding on a schedule set by lunar months. Is there a correlation between the phases of the moon and the attacks? Certainly. Is it significant? No. The moon itself is merely setting the parameters for a terrestrial calendar, and this is the salient factor, not the moon.

Analysts must therefore ask the following questions when confronted by an apparent temporal correlation:

- Is the correlation logical? (Is there some obvious, reasonable explanation for why such a relationship should exist?)

- Is the correlation causal? (If you change one variable, will it result in a change in the other?)

- What have you forgotten? (Is there some shared attribute between the factors, some common relationship to another variable that might in fact be the crucial link?)

Activity Matrices

To understand a concept, it is important for the analyst to be able to thoroughly and completely grasp it. One of the best ways to ensure this is to visualize the phenomenon in question. We have already seen how we can form an individual's temporal activity into a matrix. This is often the starting point for development of an Activity Time analysis.

Timelines

The original matrix displays our data categorized by both hour of day and day of week, each of which is a useful timeframe against which to measure activity. Obviously, however, these are only two of many cycles against which temporal activity must be measured and described. Mr. Doe's timetable might alter substantially if viewed against a different temporal context, such as day of the month, month of the year, season of the year, or day of the year (Julian date). Analysis of Doe's activity allocation against these different matrices may result in discovery of patterns completely undetectable using other methods. For example, if Doe gets paid monthly, his activities are likely to reflect this. His expenses, such as rent, insurance, gas, and groceries are likely to be regular, and therefore predictable. If we are privy to Doe's accounts, we might create a timeline of calendar days, plotting the amount of money he withdraws each day:

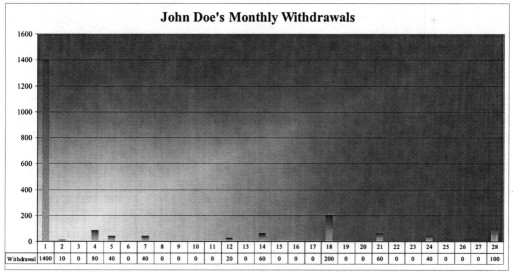

Figure 11-15: A timeline showing John Doe's daily withdrawals over the course of a month

In the above example, we are for simplicity's sake using a 28-day lunar month. Naturally, in the real world, it is necessary to use a combination of calendars to reflect the real temporal backdrop in which we operate. At first glance, some features immediately attract our attention. The month begins with an enormous withdrawal, against which all others pale in significance. Why is this? Because John Doe promptly pays his rent, utility bills, and auto insurance on the first week of each new month. These, therefore, constitute the sum of his $1,400 needs.

This large monthly withdrawal is followed by several much smaller withdrawals. Why is this? Naturally, John Doe needs money throughout the month. After covering his rent, utilities, and so forth he finds he still needs gas and groceries, lunch money, money to pay for dinners, and cover a variety of incidental expenses that come up unexpectedly. Therefore, as his ready cash is depleted, he writes more checks and visits the ATM to get more.

Looking at the actual amounts that John Doe spends each month, we can graph his actual expenditures into a timeline showing amount per day. When we iterate this 28-day false-month cycle, we arrive at something like this:

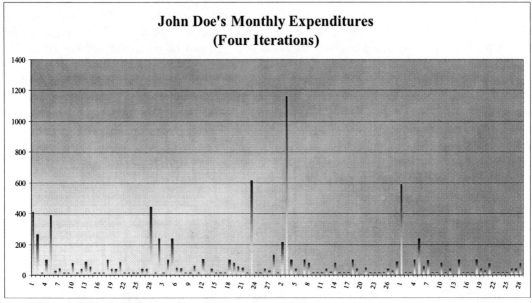

Figure 11-16: A timeline of John Doe's monthly expenses over four months

This frequency graph presents a seemingly complex picture. Many analysts would be tempted to call it "random." Indeed, a routine distribution test will confirm its "random" character; however, this is inaccurate. In fact, this seemingly chaotic mishmash of expenditures is the result of several repeating patterns, each superimposed on each other. If we simply look at the whole set of expenditures, it may be very difficult for us to try to pick out individual patterns; but look how easy it is when we examine them one at a time:

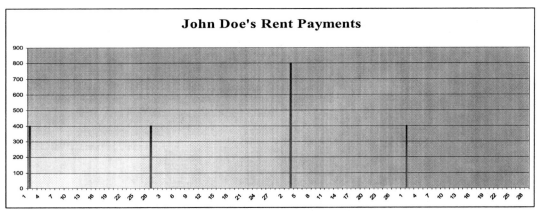

Figure 11-17: John Doe's rent payments over four months

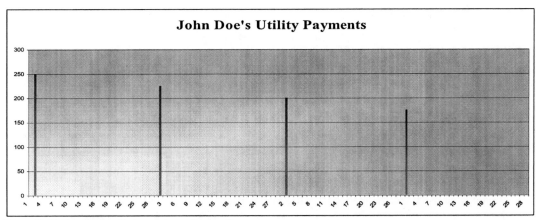

Figure 11-18: John Doe's utility payments over four months

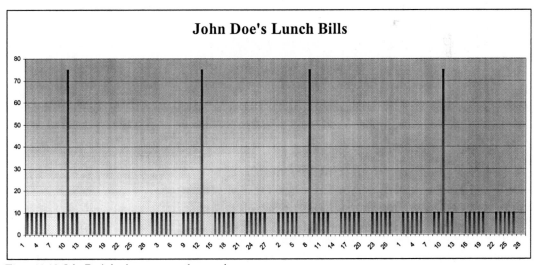

Figure 11-19: John Doe's lunch expenses over four months

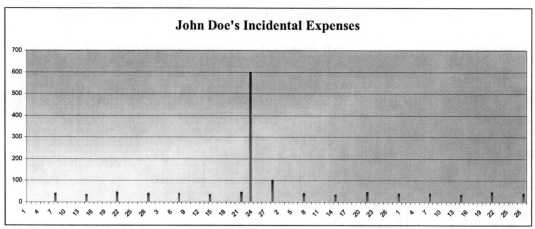

Figure 11-20: John Doe's incidental expenses over four months

By examining each individual contributing element of the overall pattern, multiple, somewhat different, patterns emerge. Minute variations and anomalies in each one can then be detected and explained.

For example, Doe pays about $400 in rent each month, except the third month, when he pays more than double. Why is that? Because Doe had a roommate who shared the cost, but who moved out for a month. Doe had to pay the whole rent by himself, doubling his expense. Notice that he was also a little bit late that month—he had to scare up more cash than usual, and perhaps things were a bit tight.

Doe's utility payments have been very regular, but they've been regularly decreasing. Why is that? Because summer is coming to an end, and Doe is using less electricity and water to run his air conditioner and keep his lawn green.

Doe pays ten dollars for lunch every workday; he doesn't go out for lunch on weekends. But once each month his bill goes to about $75 for lunch. Why is that? Because once a month, Doe treats his coworkers to a meal.

Doe has routine minor incidental expenses every week of less than $100—except for one very large expense of $600. Why is that? Because Doe's car broke down, and he needed to pay to have a new clutch installed. A week later, the bill from the towing company came in, and he had to pay $100 for that, too.

Altogether, the myriad individual elements of Doe's expenditures come together as a set of clear, repeating patterns that can each be individually explained and predicted; but when taken all together, present a confusing picture, as in Figure 11-21.

This technique is useful for examining the temporal characteristics of those phenomena having measurable values that change over time (such as John Doe's regular spending, or the numbers of crime reports taken every day by a police agency). We can imagine this sort of timeline as a continuous tone from a musical instrument, like a trumpet: over time, the tone grows louder or

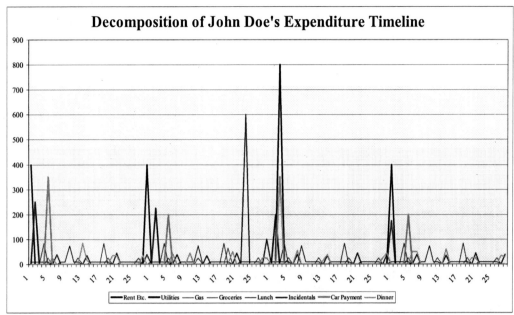

Figure 11-21: all of John Doe's expenses in a combined four-month timeline

softer, and changes in frequency according to the nature of the music being played. This type of timeline is much less intuitive, however, if we wish to examine "point" events—that is, phenomena that are not continuous (such as the discrete events in a sexual assault series). These events are more like the beats of a drum; they are all basically the same loudness and timbre, and their staccato pattern isn't as susceptible to continuous signal analysis techniques.

Why should a crime analyst need to use techniques like this? The answer is that he or she is often presented with a highly complex and confusing timeline. When attempting to analyze this timeline as a whole, the results can be unpredictable and chaotic, seemingly unintelligible. However, by breaking the overall pattern down into component elements, the analyst can succeed in finding numerous smaller patterns, which can be individually analyzed and predicted.

Examples from strategic analysis are obvious—trends in burglaries, crime in general, officer activity, and so forth. But tactical crime analysts can also clearly benefit from this technique: often what appears to be one crime series may in fact consist of more than one series that are basically similar. If the analyst attempts to study every similar case, the resulting timeline looks unpredictable; however, by breaking it down into component elements, each individual behavior pattern can be detected and forecast.

An example of this type of series occurred in Las Vegas in 2000. A series of armed robberies of coin-transport trucks emerged and quickly grew to more than forty cases. Analysis of the timeline of the series resulted in random, unpredictable findings. However, small discrepancies in the *modus operandi* indicated to the analysts and detectives that more than one team of offenders was involved. Eventually, eight teams, made up of eleven individuals who worked together in different combinations, were isolated. All but two teams operated with visible (and predictable) temporal patterns, which could be individually identified. Armed with this knowledge, detectives and patrol officers managed to abate the series with key arrests and interceptions.

This sort of visualization scheme is important when the temporal characteristics of a crime series change and evolve. This is a very common situation, and older, simpler temporal calculation models, such as forecasts based on the mean interval, typically fail in these instances

Sequential Analysis

A common objective for the tactical crime analysts is the extrapolation of a time series into the future. The obvious use is the prediction of when the next crime in a series might occur. Traditionally, this has only been accomplished by crime analysts using the technique of Mean Interval Forecasting. While this technique is simple and sometimes useful, it is operationally limited due to some hidden assumptions that must be true for the technique to work.

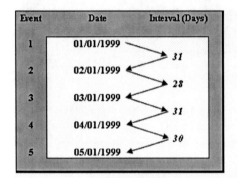

Mean Interval: 30 ((31+30+28+31+30)/4)
Standard Deviation: 1 ((1+2+1+0)/4)

Forecast: 5/30/99 - 6/1/99 (68%)
5/29/99 - 6/2/99 (95%)

Figure 11-22: intervals between hits, with mean, standard deviation, and a Mean Interval Forecast

Let's take a moment to explain the method. The analyst calculates the interval between each case and the one following (the unit of measurement varies with the specifics of the series; "hours" and "days" are typical units). The analyst then calculates the standard deviation of the intervals. The forecast consists of adding the mean interval to the date/time of the most recent case, then adding and subtracting a period based on the standard deviation, depending on the desired confidence level, to arrive at a time range in which the next event should occur, and an expected confidence value of the forecast.

Consider the series data in Figure 11-22. This example illustrates the "mean interval" forecast at its best: a regular series with a tempo like a heartbeat. This is a useful way to examine the temporal character of crime series and certainly a very easy way to arrive at a forecast.

Regrettably, this tempting method involves some serious flaws. Applying this statistical technique can lead to in misleading results. The foremost error is that the percentile confidence typically associated with these forecasts (68%, 95%, or 98%) is a misuse of statistics in this case. In fact, those percentages only apply when describing normal distributions—bell-curves—and cannot be used as "probabilities." [1] Unfortunately, the so-called "normal" distribution itself is atypical when examining the intervals between cases in a crime series.

---

[1] See Y.A. Rozanov, *Probability Theory: a Concise Course* (New York: Dover, 1969); and Donald R. Plane and Edward B. Opperman, *Business and Economic Statistics* (Plano, TX: Business Publications, 1981).

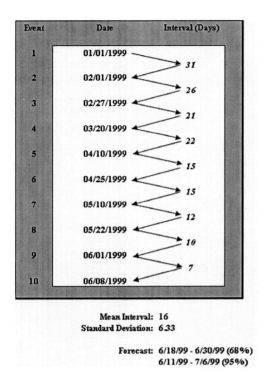

Event	Date	Interval (Days)
1	01/01/1999	31
2	02/01/1999	26
3	02/27/1999	21
4	03/20/1999	22
5	04/10/1999	15
6	04/25/1999	15
7	05/10/1999	12
8	05/22/1999	10
9	06/01/1999	7
10	06/08/1999	

Mean Interval: 16
Standard Deviation: 6.33

Forecast: 6/18/99 - 6/30/99 (68%)
6/11/99 - 7/6/99 (95%)

Figure 11-23: Intervals in a series with an increasing tempo

It is very common for a series to exhibit either an accelerating or decelerating tempo. And, of course, what happens if the crime series is increasing or decreasing in tempo? Or if you are missing some cases? Or if the offender had to skip a crime because he had the flu? The Mean Interval forecast fails. Consider the series timeline in Figure 11-23, in which the offense is sexual, and the offender is an "increaser," whose level of violence and frequency of activity both increase over time.

As you can see, the traditional Mean Interval method for a linear forecast result is unsatisfactory and misleading.

Even when the forecast does in fact contain the date of the next event, which analysts call a "hit," it is often impractical or even useless to law enforcement because it is too broad. The forecast period may be weeks or months in duration, making it unlikely that any effective law enforcement surveillance or response plan will remain in place. A more precise forecast is necessary.

However, when we use a simple tempogram to visualize the events, it's easy to make a sensible forecast, especially if we add a linear trend line to show the trend in intervals:

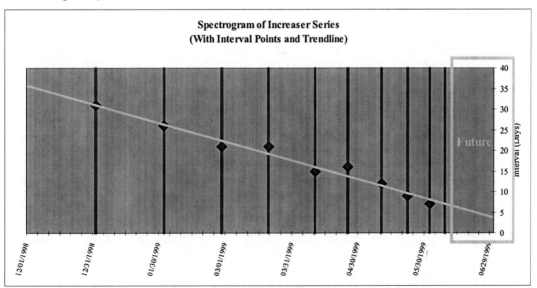

Figure 11-24: The same series as in 11-23, but on a tempogram with a trend line

Viewed this way, we see that, based on past behavior, the expected interval between the last known case (6/8/1999) and the next event in the series should be approximately five days. By analyzing the variation of our interval points to our trend line, we are able to be even more specific. Based on these results, we expect the next event to occur on 6/13/99 (68%); more broadly, we have a 95% expectation that the next event will occur between 6/12/99 and 6/14/99. This is a useful, practical, and reasonable forecast. In this example, a linear trend estimate works out very well; in reality, however, other types of trend estimates might be more advantageous, depending on the temporal characteristics of the series. Polynomial, logarithmic, and exponential trend lines might each be useful, depending on the series.

Example Lag Variogram (Interval/Ratio Technique)

Dan Helms, BSRC

Case	Interval in Minutes	Lag-1	Lag-2	Lag-3	Lag-4	Lag-5	Lag-6	Case
1	575	-450	375	4445	1940	-10	-440	1
2	125	825	4895	2390	440	10	820	2
3	950	4070	1565	-385	-815	-5	4150	3
4	5020	-2505	-4455	-4885	-4075	80	-2510	4
5	2515	-1950	-2380	-1570	2585	-5	-1935	5
6	565	-430	380	4535	1945	15	-425	6
7	135	810	4965	2375	445	5	820	7
8	945	4155	1565	-365	-805	10	4100	8
9	5100	-2590	-4520	-4960	-4145	-55	-2595	9
10	2510	-1930	-2370	-1555	2535	-5	-1940	10
11	580	-440	375	4465	1925	-10	-445	11
12	140	815	4905	2365	430	-5	860	12
13	955	4090	1550	-385	-820	45	4050	13
14	5045	-2540	-4475	-4910	-4045	-40	-2525	14
15	2505	-1935	-2370	-1505	2500	15	-1925	15
16	570	-435	430	4435	1950	10	-440	16
17	135	865	4870	2385	445	-5	790	17
18	1000	4005	1520	-420	-870	-75	4000	18
19	5005	-2485	-4425	-4875	-4080	-5	-2480	19
20	2520	-1940	-2390	-1595	2480	5	-1935	20
21	580	-450	345	4420	1945	5	-460	21
22	130	795	4870	2395	455	-10	830	22
23	925	4075	1600	-340	-805	35	4100	23
24	5000	-2475	-4415	-4880	-4040	25	-2480	24
25	2525	-1940	-2405	-1565	2500	-5		25
26	585	-465	375	4440	1935			26
27	120	840	4905	2400				27
28	960	4065	1560					28
29	5025	-2505						29
30	2520							30
Prediction (Case=31):		2587.00	5269.46	1213.89	195.19	610.00	2607.71	
Mean Variation:		67.07	244.46	253.89	75.19	25.00	82.71	
Standard Deviation:		1972.76	2617.96	2815.07	1942.50	30.80	1974.29	
Percentage:		-7%	-42%	-53%	-5%	98%	-7%	

Figure 11-25 a lag variogram

This is the advantage of studying the sequence of events, and examining their temporal relationships. We have already shown how to produce a simple variogram. A variogram is a matrix showing change between measurements. This visualization tool reveals how one event relates to the events immediately following and preceding it. But might not there be other, more complex temporal relationships between events?

The tool to study this question is the lag variogram. While a straightforward variogram displays only the sequential interval between cases 1-2, 2-3, 3-4, and so on, the lag variogram expands this to show a table of intervals between all cases. Each stage of the lag variogram is known as a lag. This number corresponds to the separation between cases being examined.

The lag variogram is a very simple idea, but very difficult to explain. In Figure 11-25, we display a table of time intervals between cases, but this technique works just as well with any numeric variable, such as distance between cases, measured in feet or miles, amount of money taken in dollars, or direction on a compass.

The technique of calculating the mean distance results in a very weak prediction. Instead of looking at the numbers themselves, we will instead examine the change in the independent variable (in this example "distance"). By doing so, we are no longer confined to static analytical processes. Although the results of lags 1–4 are disappointing, lag 5 presents some magnificent results. The series repeats itself every five cases. We can now reliably and accurately predict future behavior of this pattern.

Frequency Analysis

"Frequency" describes the speed with which events occur, or how many occur in a given period. Frequency analysis is one potentially useful, yet pleasantly simplistic, analytical tool at our disposal. Temporal measurements tend to be cyclical rather than linear. This means that we locate events based on a variety of overlapping, interacting, repeating patterns. These include day of the week, day of the month, hour of the day, and month of the year.

One easy way to examine the temporal characteristics of our data is to perform frequency analysis against the units of these various cycles. All we have to do is count up how many times events occur in each cyclical unit:

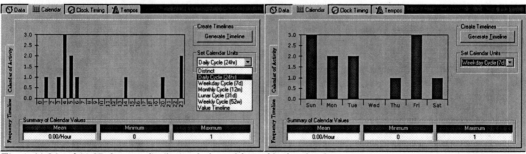

Figures 11-26 and 11-27: frequency distributions by hour of day and by day of week.

It's then easy to see exactly "when" our selected crimes are occurring. This technique is often used as a predictive method. After all, many criminals routinely strike on certain days of the week, and only at certain hours of the day. It seems only common sense to expect future crimes to follow similar behavior.

However, this method can also be misleading. In Figures 11-26 and 11-27, the hour with the highest frequency is 0400, or four in the morning. Two days of the week share the top honors, Sunday and Friday. Many detectives will ask the analyst, "What is the day of the week and hour of the day when the criminal strikes most often?" Can we answer that given this information? The answer is no. We can tell which hours are most active and, separately and independently, which days are most active, but that doesn't mean the two will work together. In the example above, for example, would you not expect crimes to be frequent on Sundays at 4:00 A.M.?

Virtual Temporal Topologies

Another, more elaborate way in which we can analyze the patterns of our subject's activity more closely and accurately by constructing a "Virtual Temporal Topology." A virtual topography is a surface, like a map, of an imaginary landscape. The landscape on a real map describes geography, which consists of an infinite range of points. Two coordinates describe each point (on a two-dimensional map, of course); the X and the Y values of a Cartesian plane. On a map, these coordinates might describe longitude and latitude; however, we can substitute other values.

The virtual topology substitutes values that have nothing at all to do with spatial coordinates. In the case of a virtual temporal topography, we will use temporal variables; and, in this example, we will use hour (0–23) and day (Monday–Sunday).

This technique not only allows the analyst to better visualize his data, but can be instrumental in performing a variety of sophisticated analytical and forecasting techniques. When we graph the occurrence of various types of activities on this virtual surface, we begin to see clear results.

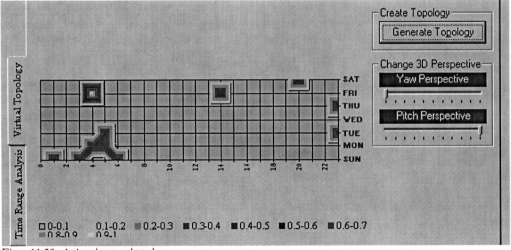

Figure 11-28: A virtual temporal topology

As you can see from the resulting virtual topology (Figure 11-28), created from the same sample data as our previous simple frequency measures, there is more variation in our overall temporal distribution than we might have thought. Although 4:00 A.M. is definitely our most active hour of the day, and Sunday is tied as our most active day, we don't have a single incident occurring at 4:00 A.M. on a Sunday.

We can detect this important discrepancy by performing cross-tabulation of days by hours to create a virtual surface. Other important bivariate temporal combinations include day of week and day of month, and hour of day and month of year.

It may be easier to see the actual temporal frequency distribution by rotating our surface in three dimensions to provide a perspective view:

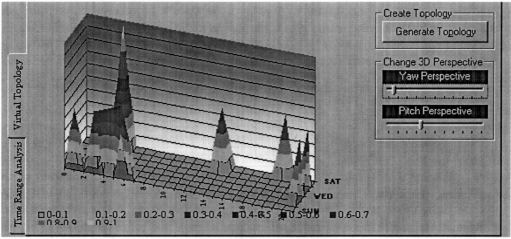

Figure 11-29: A virtual temporal topology seen from a three-dimensional perspective

Aoristic Analysis

Now we come to one of the biggest, most obvious flaws with our whole approach to temporal analysis so far: it is our assumption that we actually know when an event occurred.

So far, we have discussed a variety of methods, both weak and strong, to analyze the temporal behavior of crime; however, to do so, we need to know when the crimes we are studying have actually occurred. Regrettably, we don't always have this information.

In the case of crimes that are witnessed, such as robberies and sexual assaults, the chance that we will have accurate temporal information about each event is fairly strong. We might be off by a little bit, but usually the victim knows when he or she was attacked. Sometimes, however, even this is not true. Consider the case of a sexual assault committed using a "date-rape" drug, such as Rohypnol. The victim may have no idea whatever of the timing of the attack, except perhaps for the time of initial contact in a bar or on a date. If a crime such as a robbery occurs in a remote area, the victims may need to travel for a long period before they can report their crime, and may not be able to accurately time their victimization.

But the most troubling crimes from a temporal standpoint are also the most commonplace in law enforcement—unwitnessed crimes, targeting property: larceny, burglary, auto theft, and vandalism. In the cases of these crimes, we have almost no temporal information at all.

Well, if we don't know when crimes have occurred, what use are all these techniques we've discussed? The answer is that, although we don't actually know when unwitnessed or poorly-recorded crimes precisely occurred, we might be able to infer when they happened with a little bit of science and a little bit of luck.

Most police records systems allow for unwitnessed crimes to be timed by supplying an "earliest possible" and "latest possible" date/time stamp. So, the timing of a crime such as a burglary could be defined as falling between these two times: "0800 Monday—1730 Monday," for example. Police personnel are accustomed to thinking about the timing of crimes in terms of this boundary-based format, which we can use as a starting point to perform what some innovative analysts have termed "aoristic analysis."[1] Although methods for solving aoristic problems are as old as police work itself, the term "aoristic"—derived from the Greek "not fixed in time"—has only recently been applied to the police world.

There are two very common ways in which a working time can be interpolated for cases having no known exact time of occurrence: the midpoint method and the weighted method.

The **midpoint method**, also known as the split time method, involves identifying the midpoint between the bounding earliest and latest possible date/times. To calculate the midpoint of an aoristic time, divide the difference between the two bounding date/times (in hours) by two, then add this to the earliest date/time. The strengths of this method are that it is fast and easy to use; also, by definition its mean observed error will be smaller than any other method—so, if this method does guess wrong, on average it will guess *less* wrong than other methods. Drawbacks are that it is somewhat arbitrary. The accuracy of this technique is measurable in inverse proportion to the time span between the two bounding date/times—when there is a long range, this method is weak; when the range is narrow, it is stronger.

The **weighted method** is a much more creative approach. Here we evenly divide the "risk" of each crime among each temporal unit across its bounding span. That sounds complicated, but it's not—we just assign an increasing probability to each temporal unit (usually the hour of the day) based on the percentage chance that a crime occurred there. Then we sum up all the probabilities, and the result is a smoothed jeopardy curve that shows where the highest probabilities of crimes have landed. To calculate the weighted risk, for each case in your collection, divide the number one by the number of hours spanned, then add this fractional value to each hour as a "risk score." Repeat the process for every case, adding the fractional scores when they overlap. The strengths of this method are that it is far less arbitrary than the Midpoint process, and is particularly well-tuned for strategic applications. Weaknesses include the fact that

---

[1] Jerry H. Ratcliffe and Michael J. McCullagh, "Aoristic Crime Analysis" in *International Journal of Geographic Information Science* 12 (1998): 751–764.

the timing of cases influence one another; therefore, outliers that don't fit the rest of the temporal series are heavily de-emphasized and may lead to chaotic results.

Note how differently times are calculated by Midpoint and Weighted Methods in Figures 11-30 through 11-33:

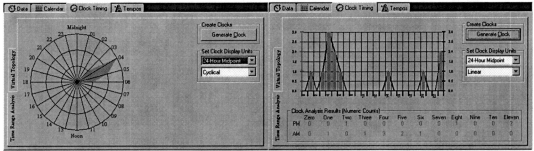

Figures 11-30 and 11-31: Hour of day distributions using the midpoint method

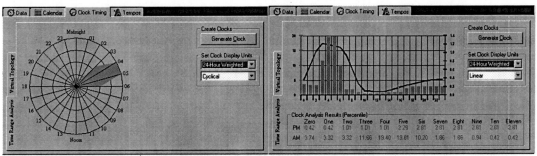

Figures 11-32 and 11-33: Hour of day distributions using the weighted method

Correlation Analysis

We know that the pace at which a crime series progresses might be in some way related to some of the other features of the case: the distance between crimes, the amount of money taken, the degree of violence shown toward the victim, close calls with the police, among others. If we can establish a relationship between these variables and the temporal sequence of the series, then we might be able to extrapolate when the next case is likeliest to occur. But how can we identify which variables might influence the offender's tempo?

The answer is to test each potentially critical variable for statistical significance. This process is broadly referred to in statistics as bivariate analysis. Bivariate analysis compares the value of one variable to the value of another, and tests to see if the one is related to the other. There are many techniques for accomplishing bivariate analysis, some very simple, others quite elaborate. To be truly valuable, some sort of function, a correlation coefficient, should be measured—this is a number that will allow us to predict one variable based on another (see Chapter 10).

One simple and effective method for deriving a correlation coefficient is merely to divide one variable value by the other, then calculate the mean. This results in a simple graph:

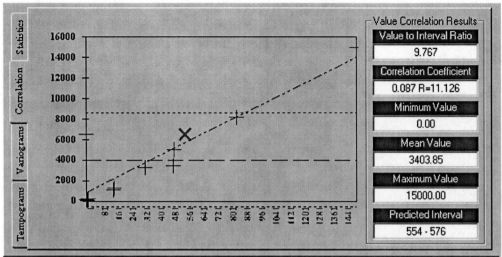

Figure 11-34: A line graph showing the relationship between two variables

In the example above, taken from a real Las Vegas crime series, we can see the extremely linear relationship between the amount of money taken (y-axis) and interval between cases in hours (x-axis). What does this mean? Probably that the offender needs a certain amount of money per week or per month. When he scores a large haul, he lays low for a long time afterward; but when he comes away with little or nothing, he strikes again quickly to get more. Since we know how much money he got in his last burglary (about $6500) we can calculate that he will strike again about 565 hours in the future—about 23 or 24 days.

Quite often, it is not a single dominant factor, but a combination of factors that is found to be significant. For example, both the hour of the day and the day of the week might be significant when examined together, but when examined separately they do not seem to influence the time series in any meaningful or predictable fashion. The amount of money taken and the day of the month might prove significant (perhaps the offender has monthly financial obligations). These individual variables may only reveal a noteworthy trend when studied together.

To examine how many variables interact with one another, we must expand from bivariate to multivariate analysis. The multivariate analytical method with which most analysts are familiar is the chi-squared test for statistical significance. The chi-squared test has the advantage not only of telling you what variables, or combination of variables, are relevant to a series' progression, but also of telling you how well they serve as a predictor. This can be very useful later when the analyst attempts to make a forecast and must know how confident he should be.

Spectral Analysis

Many timelines and tempograms exhibit a cyclic tendency. Some series may seem to accelerate every couple of months, or seasonally, or weekly. If we view our timeline or tempogram as a signal, we might be able to deconstruct it to identify what these cyclic rates really are. This, in turn, might prove valuable when we attempt to make a forecast.

One of the best methods readily available for deconstructing a timeline signal is the Discrete Fourier Transform, or DFT. The DFT is a mathematical algorithm that breaks down a signal into "real" and "imaginary" elements. These can then be recombined to reveal cyclical activity on hidden frequencies within our data.

Named for the inventor, eighteenth-century French mathematician Jean Baptiste Fourier, the DFT is a way to analyze the frequencies contained in a signal. Some readers unfamiliar with the concept might not clearly understand how "frequencies" can be nested and overlapped in a signal. We'll take a moment to explain the concept.

We've all seen old-fashioned vinyl record albums—some of us still prefer them. These work on a simple principle: A needle is dragged through a tiny groove cut into the vinyl, which causes the needle to vibrate. These vibrations are amplified into sound. There's only one groove, so why is it that you can plainly hear the distinct sounds of several instruments or voices simultaneously?

The answer is that the signal produced by the groove is composed of many subsignals. When these are superimposed on each other, the result is the combined sound of a song, a conversation, or what have you. Each musical note is a vibration wave in air, and each note vibrates at a specific and constant frequency. The higher the frequency (more vibrations per second) the higher the pitch of the note heard by the listener. When a musician plays a series of notes, she causes her instrument to emit vibrations in a series of specific frequencies. Every instant, our ears receive these vibrations and interpret their frequencies as sound. When many musicians play, our ears hear the total signal created by all the instruments playing at different frequencies and amplitudes. Our brains instantly decompose the signal into its component frequencies, and we can therefore identify both the brassy tones of a trumpet and the sinuous strings of a viola as being discrete, even though their combined signal is received whole.

Not only sound works this way; any phenomenon that occurs as a wave, or as a regular, repeating pattern, is susceptible to analysis of this sort. Light, radio, microwaves, sound, earthquakes, and various sociological phenomena can all be studied as waves and signals. Crime analysis is one of the beneficiaries of this type of study, because many types of crime and police activity exhibit regular patterns. Unfortunately, although our brains do an astonishing job of decomposing sound signals (and light waves), when we study other types of signal phenomena, we can seldom intuitively perceive the subsignals that go into the whole.

But if we split the signal by deconstructing it, we see that it is actually produced by several subsignals, which are superimposed and added to each other to produce the overall signal in our timeline. This example is simplistic; each subsignal is very regular, and the overall effect is also regular and predictable. In crime analysis applications, however, this is seldom if ever the case.

This is where the DFT comes in. By breaking down a "signal" and subjecting it to analysis through DFT, we can try to identify regular cycles in our timeline. Then, we can examine each of these apparent cycles to determine its specific frequency, amplitude, and regularity. If we can identify a hidden cyclic pattern, we can use this knowledge to identify possible cases to be added to the series; subtract cases from our series that might not belong; and, best of all, make a forecast as to the next occurrence in the series.

Figure 11-35 illustrates a complex tempogram line, derived from the number of sexual assaults reported for a period of one year:

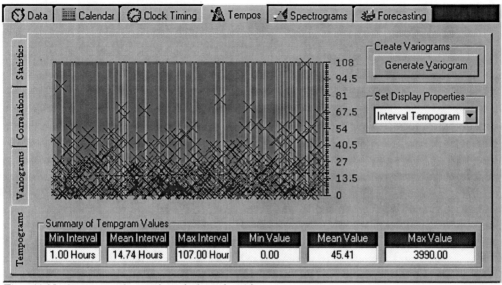

Figure 11-35: A tempogram of one year's worth of sexual assaults

As you can see, Figure 11-35 is highly confusing to the eye. The analyst might tempted to infer some possible pattern to the level of activity, or to call it all "random," but it's difficult to be precise, and to explain one's reasons.

Figure 11-36, on the other hand, is a Spectral Density graph of the above data after passing through the DFT:

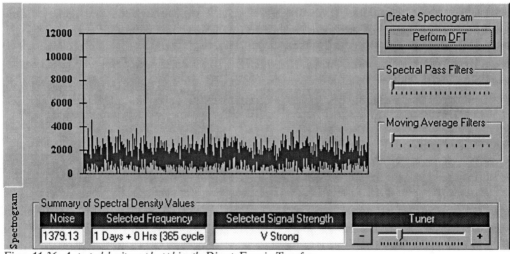

Figure 11-36: A spectral density graph applying the Discrete Fournier Transform

That does look complicated; but, if we apply a Moving Average filter to the Spectral Density graph above, we arrive at this:

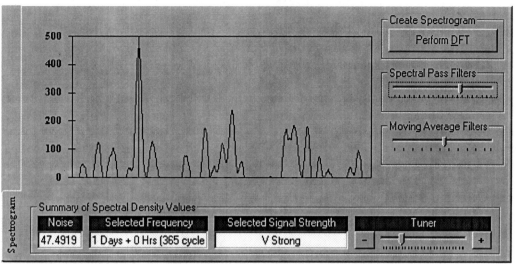

Figure 11-37: A spectral density graph applying the Discrete Fournier Transform and a moving average

Here we can see clearly where our highest frequencies lie. We can tune to each visible spike and then read out the appropriate signal strength. This tells us exactly how strong a repeating pattern occurs at each cyclic interval to which we've tuned.

The Science of Forecasting

Forecasting is what most crime analysts want from temporal analysis. Many are also intimidated by it—after all, as analysts we stake our credibility on each forecast. Many agencies or bureaus within agencies even have policies restricting forecasting. Should this be the case? Forecasting is definitely risky—nobody can read the future, and as professionals we shouldn't pretend that we can. But what's the point of analyzing crime if we never actually do anything about it?

The basic assumption that underlies all forecasting is that what will happen in the future will resemble what has happened in the past.

The term "forecasting" when used in reference to tactical crime analysis specifically describes the process of generating a prediction as to where, when, and how future events in a crime trend, pattern, or series will occur. Forecasts are generated by studying known events in the series to identify patterns that might prove susceptible to prediction. Most crime analysts who have performed any tactical analysis in their careers have made some attempt to forecast a crime trend, pattern, or series.

Strategic analysts also make forecasts. Their efforts, however, are almost entirely statistical in nature, and relate to the "big picture" view of crime and policing within the scope of their observations and analyses. It is perfectly in keeping with the nature of strategic forecasting to predict, for example, "There will be an 11 percent increase in sexual assaults over the next three months." This prediction can provide law enforcement agencies with broad intelligence on what their future efforts will entail, enabling them to prepare in advance by altering their patrol plans, investigative priorities and schedules, public awareness campaigns, and so on.

A tactical forecast, however, has as its goal the prediction of a specific crime, usually by a specific perpetrator. This is a vastly more complicated affair. Why so? The difficulty has to do with the nature of linear versus chaotic systems.

For thousands of years, scientists have attempted to describe the world in terms of "linear system" models. Linear systems follow clear-cut rules and are perfectly predictable. For example, the movement of stars and planets was early discovered to be precisely predictable, and is an example of a linear system. The movement of a pendulum is also an example of what is considered a linear system: with the right equations, one can precisely predict the movement of any pendulum. The trajectory of a ballistic projectile is a third illustrative example. If one knows the angle, inclination, mass, and force behind, say, an artillery shell, it is possible to predict precisely where it will fall.

Recently, however, scientists have begun to describe the world in terms of "chaotic system" models. Chaotic systems, unlike the clear and simple linear models, are very complex, and must take into account the interaction of an enormous number of variables. One of the most often-cited examples of a chaotic system is weather. It is impossible to predict the weather accurately, because so many variables intertwine in unpredictable ways that there is no mechanism for embracing them all. In fact, one accepted tenet dealing with the nature of subatomic particles (the "Heisenberg Uncertainty Principle") states that the specific characteristics of such particles cannot be measured without changing them, and therefore they cannot be known; this means that many phenomena are utterly impervious to prediction using linear models.

In fact, every one of the linear systems cited as an example above is now usually considered to be chaotic; in many ways this is much more realistic approach. For instance, consider the movement of a pendulum. A physics instructor will tell you that the movements of a pendulum are completely predictable, based on the formula $T = 2(L/g)^{\frac{1}{2}}$. While this is true of a "perfect" pendulum, which exists only in our minds as a mathematical illustration, it is demonstrably not true of a real pendulum. This is because a real pendulum will contain minute imperfections, resulting in slight distortions in its balance; it will be subject to microscopic influences from humidity and air pressure, and from the immeasurably tiny seismic disruptions from people walking nearby, trucks moving on the roads a mile away, and so forth. Even the effects of mere photons, shining in through its glass case (and themselves unpredictably polarized and distorted by the glass and the atmosphere) will impart their miniscule force, disturbing the perfection of our mathematical model. But the physicist need not despair totally: After all, the influence of these tiny forces is often too small to be measured at all. So, even if the prediction is wrong, perhaps it's only inaccurate by so tiny an amount that we don't notice it at all.

This is exactly the sort of abstract, arcane, math-oriented ground that makes most professional analysts wince. How is this relevant? Let's put our feet back on the ground for a moment, and take another look at forecasting tactical crime events. Is crime a linear or chaotic system? The answer, which we hope is obvious, is that it is most definitely chaotic. In fact, although at first it might sound absurd, the relationship between the movements of subatomic particles and the actions of an individual makes a reliable metaphor. Just as the movements of a pendulum are not perfectly predictable due to the large number of individually tiny (but cumulatively significant) influences of subatomic particles, yet remain almost predictable, at least as far as our imperfect instruments can measure, so too the actions of many people reacting to the stimuli of our complex social environment are unpredictable—but we can come close. The more broadly we measure, the more reliable our predictions.

Why can't we make a perfect tactical forecast? Too many imponderable factors, running down from the cosmic to the microscopic, can influence the behavior of the offender and his targets. We might formulate a reasonable forecast, yet miss our mark due to the offender coming down with the flu, or getting a flat tire. Perhaps the business he planned to rob closed early for the holidays, or burned down in an unrelated accident. Perhaps the offender's mother is staying with him over the weekend, and he can't very well sneak away to rape someone unnoticed. There are infinite reasons why no prediction, however artful, can ever be absolutely reliable and accurate.

Given these seemingly insurmountable difficulties, then, one might be tempted to wonder why we should try at all? The answer is that we might still come close. Remember how we noted earlier that it is impossible to predict the weather? That's true; however, we can come pretty close, if we're careful. Meteorologists can make informed guesses as to when and where it will rain or snow, and, with the current state of technology and methodology, they're right far more often than they're wrong, in the short-term, at least. Whether it will rain two months from now is anybody's guess; but whether it will rain three days from now is a matter where a trained meteorologist with access to reliable data can make an informed prediction. Forecasting the future of a crime series involves predicting the behavior of an offender, relative to his victim, in space and in time. If this behavior were purely a matter of random chance, we would have poor prospects for success indeed! Offender behavior, however, is not random. Offenders make decisions to commit their acts based on their needs and desires, based on their own prejudices, knowledge of their environment, and assessment of the risk to themselves. They base their actions on their own sense of morality (or more properly lack thereof). Although we might seldom call these actions "reasonable" (Who reasonably commits murder? Or rape?), we can still consider them "rational." That is, the crimes are committed for a purpose, and according to a plan. The purpose may be utterly mysterious, even to the offender; and the plan may be purely subconscious, and appear arbitrary and slipshod—but nevertheless the offender is surely influenced by them. By carefully studying what we know of his behavior from past crimes, by analyzing how he seems to move in and perceive time and space, and by identifying his pool of potential victims, we stand a small but very real chance of extrapolating what his future actions are likely to be, even when he himself does not know, consciously.

This tells us what we can safely expect from tactical forecasts. Although we can never hope to be perfect, no matter how powerful our computers or elaborate our methods, we can definitely hope to come close enough to actually intercept a crime—the Holy Grail of tactical crime analysis. Many practitioners have enjoyed success in predictions; some have even refined their process into a repeatable method.

There are three main families of temporal forecasting: Linear, Cyclical, and Leading Indicator.

Linear forecasts extrapolate what will happen based on an overall trend—a line—that is drawn from the past, through the present, and then carried on into the future. This is most easy to imagine in the context of linear visualizations of time: Timelines and tempograms. In linear temporal visualizations, the past and the future are in opposite directions, the farther you go in either direction, the more distant everything on the other end becomes.

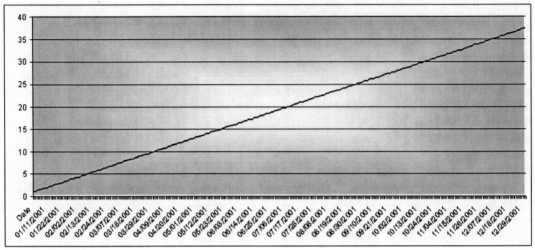

Figure 11-38: A linear timeline

Cyclical forecasts wrap around themselves—they make use of the circular, repeating patterns that we use to measure time. Things like seasons, months, days of the week, hours of the day— these things are extremely important to human behavior and, so, to criminal behavior too. But unlike a linear timeline or a tempogram of events, cyclical visualizations wrap around themselves. So, if we begin our week on Sunday, then proceed through the days of the week, we find, seven days later, we're right back where we started.

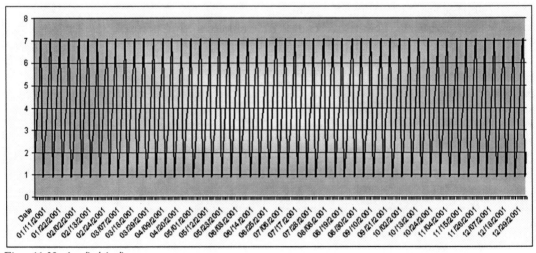

Figure 11-39: A cyclical timeline

These two main families give rise to a hybrid, more challenging family of temporal forecasting: complex forecasting. This type of forecasting incorporates both, by taking a linear trend and then either adding or multiplying cyclical values:

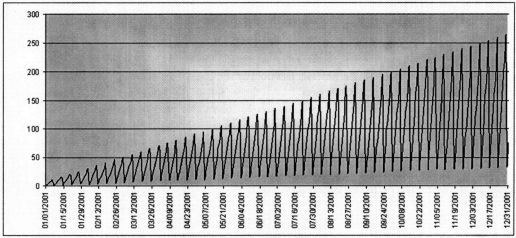

Figure 11-40: A hybrid timeline, with both linear and cyclical characteristics

The most commonly used model for performing complex temporal forecasting is known as ARIMA. This is an acronym for Auto-Regressive Integrated Moving Average, a process developed by the U.S. Census Bureau for population forecasting in the twentieth century. Several variations of the ARIMA algorithm have been employed for decades by a wide range of scientists and scholars. The X-12 variant is the current favorite; free utilities to implement this algorithm can be obtained from the U.S. Census Bureau.

Leading Indicator forecasting is bi- or multivariate in nature. Remember how we observed earlier that certain temporal behavior—like the timing of crimes—could be influenced by other variables—like the amount of money taken? Well, in that example, the amount of money taken would be a leading indicator—a variable that independently predicts the outcome of a dependent variable—timing. Financiers, demographers, and climatologists have long mastered the science of forecasting based on leading indicators. It can be surprisingly easy. As we've seen, bi- or multivariate analysis of our timeline might identify for us what variables may lead the timing of our series.

In temporal analysis, there are three things we can forecast: timing, frequency, and duration:

Timing forecasts attempt to determine when an event will take place. Tactical analysts use these forecasts to try to predict when the next event in a crime series will occur.

Frequency forecasts attempt to determine how many events will occur within a certain period of time. Strategic analysts use these forecasts to try to predict how many events will happen during some point in the future, such as how many robberies we will have next year.

Duration forecasts attempt to determine how long an event will last—we don't see these much, as crime analysts; however, administrative and operational analysts might attempt to determine how long officers are likely to spend on certain types of calls, how long it might take victims to report certain crimes, or how long it might take to peaceably disperse a crowd.

Timing forecasts are the particular challenge of the tactical crime analyst. A great many things have to go right for this type of forecast to succeed—but succeed it can, with thought.

How can we forecast when a crime will occur? At first approximation, that might seem as difficult as guessing the winning lottery numbers—but it's not that difficult, because the criminal's timing isn't random, and we can therefore study, model, and predict it. On the other hand, some analysts have forwarded simplistic forecasting methods, suggesting that something as simple as the mean interval method or hourly frequency forecasting can predict when a crime will occur—and indeed they can, sometimes. But, then, so can just guessing. The truth is that forecasting is neither impossible nor easy; it requires some careful consideration. When it comes to making temporal next-event forecasts, we have several options:

Linear Timing Forecasts

Based on the interval between cases, we can guess what the probable interval from the last known case to the next (future) case will be. The mean interval method satisfies this requirement, but only under very restricted circumstances. A tempogram approach will solve all problems that would work with the mean interval method, and most other types of series, too, including both accelerating and decelerating crime tempos. This is the preferred method for performing linear timing forecasts. We can accomplish tempogram forecasting using an extrapolated trend line based on previous intervals. The trend line can be either an ordinary least squares (OLS) trend line, or a variation, such as the logarithmic least squares, which curves to approach, but never exceed, terminal velocity.

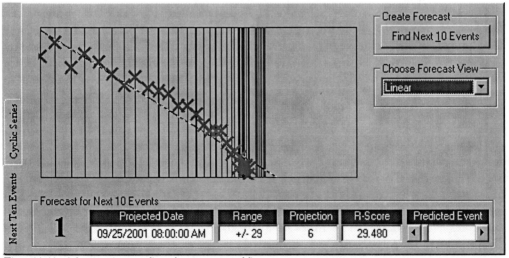

Figure 11-41: A forecast using an ordinary least squares trend line

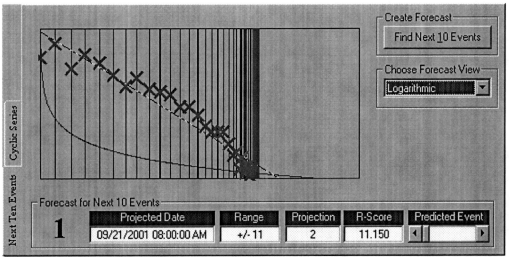

Figure 11-42: A forecast using a logarithmic least squares trend line

This process works easily with cases exhibiting a uniform temporal distribution, but what about clustered cases? The answer is for the analyst to calculate the temporal centroid for each cluster, then calculate the tempogram for these centroids. This method will enable the analyst to predict when the next cluster of crimes will occur. In addition, the use of a temporal lag variogram can reveal clustered trends in grouped cases that can then be coupled with a tempogram to formulate a linear timing forecast.

Cyclical Timing Forecasts

Cyclical timing forecasts are based on the percentage of previous cases occurring on units of a rotating cycle, such as day of the week, hour of the day, and so on. The best methods involve using cross-tabulations of two or more cyclical measures. The two temporal cycles with the strongest influence on almost every type of human activity are the 24-hour daily cycle, and the seven-day weekly cycle. The visualization of the cross-tabulation of these two frequency counts on a surface graph is called a virtual temporal topology. This three-dimensional matrix identifies an X-Coordinate (hour of the day), Y-Coordinate (day of the week,) and Z-Coordinate (number of events observed). This matrix has many uses, and can even be incorporated into a geographic information system (GIS) environment for spatial analytical processing, which can have great predictive potential. Even simply visualizing the virtual temporal topology can lead to insightful predictions based on previous activity levels.

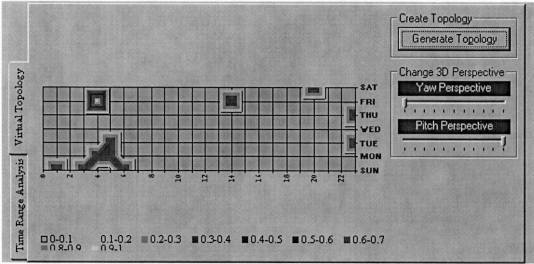

Figure 11-43: A cyclical timing forecast using a virtual temporal topology

Leading Indicator Timing Forecasts

Leading indicator timing forecasts are based on correlation with another, known variable. We can identify a relationship between one variable and the timing of events by determining the existence of a statistically significant correlation coefficient between the two. We might determine, for example, that an offender needs to obtain $1,000 per week—if his last attack netted $1,000, therefore, he will attack approximately one week later. There could also be a variety of other leading indicators, such as holidays, check mailings, bus schedules, flight schedules, swap-meets or gun shows, and so forth—each of which may influence the timing of crimes perpetrated by a particular offender.

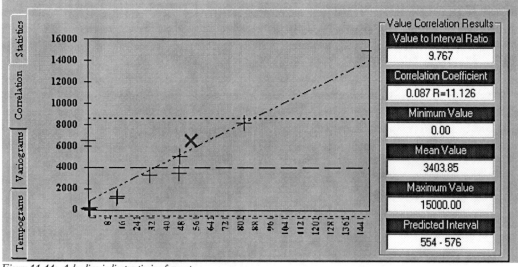

Figure 11-44: A leading indicator timing forecast

There are simply too many variations and combinations of analytical approaches to address them sensibly in this brief approach. Practical training in a laboratory setting or real-world experience with actual crime problems are really the way to learn and master temporal forecasting methods.

We should note, however, that there is no "best" way to analyze any given problem. Some methods are definitely weaker than others, but no one method or combination of methods has yet emerged as dominant at forecasting particular problems.

Also, we strongly advocate a "shotgun" approach to all forecasting problems: *Use every available method on every part of every problem.*

The approach should also be recursive. The analyst should use a variety of forecasting models and methods on each problem, then compare and contrast the results. These results should either confirm or refute one another—in other words, they will either predict the same thing, or different things. Rather than merely hedge our bets by making broad or self-contradicting forecasts ("The offender will strike on Tuesday; or Wednesday. Or possibly Thursday, Friday, or Saturday…."), we should instead put our trust in forecasts that confirm one another. If we're unable to confirm a prediction using multiple methods, we must rely on our analytical judgment to determine whether any forecast can be performed at all.

A Bigger Picture: Spacetime

In our previous introduction to activity models, we had occasion to allude to the marriage of space and time into "spacetime," an intrinsically important concept to crime analysts.

Historically, space and time have been considered separate concepts, unrelated to one another in any sensible way. This perception was forever altered with the publication of "The Special Theory of Relativity" (as it became known later) in 1905 by Albert Einstein. Among Einstein's many groundbreaking insights were the fundamental equality of all points of reference, the fact the matter and energy are actually the same thing, and, most salient to our discussion, that space and time were both just two different ways of looking at the same thing.

When we talk about "space," what we really mean is a system for measuring where something is located. For example, to describe the location of a vehicle in space, we might describe it using longitude and latitude, a relationship to a landmark ("500 feet south of the landfill"), or, more commonly seen in law enforcement, as a street reference ("the intersection of Hollywood and Vine"). When we talk about "time," what we really mean is a system for measuring when something is located. For example, to describe when a traffic accident occurred in time, we might describe it using a calendar (January 11, 2000), a clock (12:51 P.M.), a relationship to a temporal landmark ("two hours after sunrise"), or, more commonly, a combination of the above.

In science fiction in literature and popular entertainment, the public often hears talk of "dimensions," as if the subject was some other universe: "the Fourth Dimension," "the Fifth Dimension," "higher dimensions," and "inter-dimensional travel." However, as any architect, engineer, carpenter, or plumber can tell you, a "dimension" is nothing more than a direction of measurement. The dimensions of a footlocker might be expressed as 18" x 24" x 36". These three measurements express the size of a rectangular, regular solid in three dimensions: height, width, and length. In mathematics, these coordinates are typically signified obliquely by the variables X, Y and Z. In geography, they might be expressed as longitude, latitude, and elevation.

Most people think of themselves as living in a three-dimensional universe. All the material objects they encounter can be described and measured using three dimensions. In fact, this is a misconception. As illustrated by our traffic accident example, we can no longer limit ourselves to thinking about "objects" and "places," but must expand to thinking about "events" and "spacetime." Not only must we locate an event using a geographic or spatial reference in three dimensions, but we must add a fourth: time.

The two factors, place and time, are treated separately in almost every aspect of society, including law enforcement. Location and time are never put into the same data field; it seems contrary to reason. But space and time are inextricably linked, and we cannot as analysts consider one without considering the other.

To use the examples we've already discussed, imagine you wish to describe a particular event, like a traffic accident. To do so, you must describe both the time and the place in which it occurred. When we said earlier that we wished to describe the location of a vehicle in space, we implicitly assumed we were describing the vehicle's spatial position *now*. A few minutes ago, its spatial position might have been several blocks away. A few years ago, the car might not have had any spatial position; it might not have been built yet. A few minutes from now, in the future, it might have moved farther down the road.

Any movement involves a transition in both space and time. For a person or object to moved from Point A to Point B, let's say, he, she, or it must also move from Time A (the Start) to Time B (the Finish). The interrelationship between space and time has clear consequences for tactical analysts as it does for any other scientist.

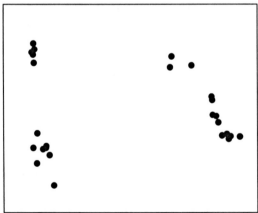

Figure 11-45: a crime series exhibiting several clusters

For an offender to commit a crime, for example, he must travel from where he is to where his victim or target is; the process of movement will involve a transition in time. The crime itself will have both a temporal and a spatial location, and it will have a duration. Each of these is an essential element in understanding how the offender behaves, and in attempting to forecast how he might behave in the future. Moreover, the relationship in spacetime between events in a crime series can give us a valuable insight into the mind, motivations, means, and methods of the offender. Having committed a crime in Neighborhood A, an offender might then commit his next crime in Neighborhood B, and then the next in Neighborhood C a few days later. After a few weeks, however, he might return to strike again in Neighborhood A.

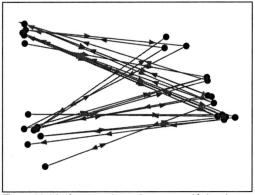

Figure 11-46: the same crime series, now considering time as well as space.

If we looked only at the spatial distribution of crimes—the pin map in Figure 11-45—we would see that two events, the first and the fourth, were close together in space, while the other two events were located farther away. Taken by itself, this datum would have little value. But if we expanded our visualization from space alone to spacetime, we would see that the offender has maintained a safe interval between strikes in the same area (Figure 11-46). This tells us something about his behavior. We have taken a seemingly random, nonsensical observation and turned it into a valuable insight, which might possibly lead to disrupting or intercepting the series in the future.

For these reasons it is critical that the crime analyst always perform both spatial and temporal analysis together, as two sides of the same coin, fully realizing that the results of one will invariably influence the other. This is a vital concern that cannot be neglected.

Visualizing temporal sequences over spatial positions is a powerful technique that is extremely simple to implement.

The addition of temporal analytical methods to spatial methods to create dynamic spatio-temporal analysis is a technique the modern crime analyst simple can't afford to overlook, and one that can often uncover meaning where either method alone finds only chaos.

Conclusion

Time is only one dimension of the problem of crime. In addition, spatial, behavioral, and evidentiary dimensions must be analyzed and explored thoroughly. Without doubt, these different factors should be taken together and studied simultaneously. As we have seen, changes in timing reflect changes in location, or behavior, or other factors, and vice versa.

Time may not be the most important dimension of a crime problem, either. Location or behavior could lead to much better insight into how a crime series is evolving, or how police are responding to problems. Still, the importance of time can never be ignored.

In this chapter we have reviewed how time is measured and how temporal data is stored and retrieved. We have discussed basic concepts such as distribution and tempo, and how these factors can be measured. We have discussed how offenders—and everyone else for that matter—schedules activities in time, and how we might reconstruct an unknown offenders activity schedule by interpolation. We have reviewed a variety of popular forecasting techniques and discussed their relative merits, including exposing some seldom-mentioned problems and defects, which could result in poor or inaccurate results.

Although it would require a tome many times larger than this entire book to thoroughly explore the topic of temporal analysis, we hope that this overview has provided you with some useful material.

Recommended Readings

Al-Taha, Khaled K., Richard T. Snodgrass, and Michael D. Soo. "Bibliography on Spatiotemporal Databases." *International Journal of Geographical Information Systems* 8 (1994): 95–103.

Golledge, Reginald G. & Robert J. Stimson. *Spatial Behavior.* New York: Guilford Press, 1997.

Plane, Donald R. and Edward B. Oppermann. *Business and Economic Statistics.* Plano, TX: Business Publications, 1981.

Ratcliffe, Jerry H. "Aoristic Signatures and the Temporal Analysis of High Volume Crime Patterns," *Journal of Quantitative Criminology* 18, no. 1 (2003): 23–43.
———— and Michael J. McCullagh. "Aoristic Crime Analysis." *International Journal of Geographic Information Science* 12 (1998): 751–764.

Rozanov, Yu A. *Probability Theory: A Concise Course.* New York: Dover Publishing, 1969.

Smith, Steven W. *The Scientist and Engineer's Guide to Digital Signal Processing.* San Francisco: California Technical Publishing, 1997.

Tufte, Edward R. *The Visual Display of Quantitative Information.* Hartford, CT: Graphics Press, 1983.

12
Demographic Analysis

Paul Tracy
Donald R. Dixon

This chapter will expose crime analysts to the principle that the most fundamental aspect of conducting research on crime volume and its distribution over place and time is that all crime measures are driven by demographic aspects of society. These demographic data concern first the fact that, as the age structure of a community changes the population-at-risk also changes, which in turn affects crime volume. The second consideration is that as particular demographic aspects of community structure change, so does the volume of crime. Thus, factors such as unemployment, poverty, housing density, residential instability, and other measures have a profound effect on the crime-proneness of an area. This chapter will expose crime analysts to the various demographic measures that must be considered when studying the volume, distribution, and patterns of crime.

Correlates of Crime

Historically, criminologists have recognized that macro-level features of society can have a profound influence on the nature and extent of crime. Criminologists have developed theories to explain the effect of these possible causal factors and have conducted numerous empirical studies that have attempted to document the strength and direction of these correlates of crime. This literature is too broad and too complex for in depth coverage in a short chapter such as this. Instead, we have decided to concern

ourselves with two basic correlates that may have the largest and most sustained effects on crime. These correlates are (1) age; and (2) socio-economic conditions.

Age and Crime

We know that crime varies by age. Crime generally begins in the early teenage years, rises sharply through adolescence, and then declines as people mature. Therefore, it is usually hypothesized that to the extent that the age structure of a community changes over time, there should be a corresponding change in crime. Further, one can posit the same basic hypothesis when studying crime across cities or even across areas within a city. Thus, to the extent that geographic areas reflect a different demographic profile, they should reflect a crime profile consistent with the underlying demographic situation.

There have been two basic types of research studying the age and crime connection. First, researchers have examined the age distribution in society and age-specific rates of offending.[1] Generally, these researchers have found that changes in age structure do indeed affect crime rates. Second, other researchers have studied the relative size of age cohorts over time and the effect on crime

---

[1] See, for example, Chester L. Britt, "Constancy and Change in the U.S. Age Distribution of Crime: A Test of the Invariance Hypothesis," *Journal of Quantitative Criminology* 8 (1992): 175–187; Thomas B. Marvel and Carlisle Moody, "Age Structure and Crime Rates: The Conflicting Evidence," *Journal of Quantitative Criminology* 7 (1991): 237–273; Darrell Steffensmeier, Emile Allan, and Miles D. Harer, "Age and Distribution of Crime," *American Journal of Sociology* 94 (1989): 803–831; Darrell Steffensmeier and Miles D. Harer, "Is the Crime Rate Really Falling? An Aging U.S. Population and Its Impact on the Nation's Crime Rate, 1980–1984," *Journal of Research in Crime and Delinquency* 24 (1987): 23–48; and Lawrence E. Cohen and Kenneth Land, "Age Structure and Crime: Symmetry Versus Asymmetry and the Projection of Crime Rates Through the 1980s," *American Sociological Review* 52 (1987): 170–183.

rates.[1] Generally, these studies have found an age effect on crime, but only partial support for the hypothesis that the effects are due to particularly large cohorts entering the crime prone years.

Other observers, however, have taken the link between the age structure of society and crime to extremes and have made astounding predictions for future crime rates. James Q. Wilson was probably the first to bring what we will call "Chicken Little Syndrome" to criminology when he suggested that:

> Meanwhile, just beyond the horizon, there lurks a cloud that the winds will soon bring over us. The population will start getting younger again. By the end of this decade there will be a million more people between the ages of fourteen and seventeen than there are now; this increase will follow the decade of the 1980s when people in that age group declines, not only as a proportion of the total but in absolute numbers. The extra million will be half male. Six percent of them will become high rate, repeat offenders—thirty thousand more young muggers, killers, and thieves than we have now. Get ready.[2]

John J. Dilulio echoed Wilson's concerns and noted that "Americans are sitting on a demographic crime bomb" because current projections indicate that by the year 2000, we will have an additional 500,000 persons in the crime prone age-group of 14–17. The consequence of this according to Dilulio is that, "in five years we will have 30,000 more young murderers, rapists, and muggers on the streets than we do now."[3] Dilulio offered a prognosis that was truly alarming:

> This crime bomb probably cannot be defused. The larger population of seven to 10-year-old boys, now growing up fatherless, Godless, and jobless— surrounded by deviant, delinquent, and criminal adults—will give rise to a new and more vicious group of predatory street criminals than the nation has ever known. We must therefore be prepared to contain the explosion's force and limit its damage.[4]

Alfred Blumstein continued the focus on the demographic stimulus to the expected rates of future violence. He argued that the current teenage cohort responsible for the majority of the (then) recent increases in juvenile violence is a small cohort in contrast to the much larger cohort of youth aged 5–15 who would shortly be moving into the crime prone years.[5] Specifically, he noted that between 1995 and 2010, population of 15–19-year-old males who commit the most crime will grow by 30 percent, including many in poverty with single mothers. Absent strategic public policy changes, it was his contention that the crime wave of the early 1990s that broke national homicide rate records will pale in comparison.[6]

Howard Snyder and Melissa Sickmund reviewed both F.B.I. arrest data and NCVS data, and showed that between 1988 and 1992, juvenile violence increased sharply after

---

[1] See, for example, Robert M. O'Brien, "Relative Cohort Size and Age-Specific Crime Rates: An Age-Period-Relative-Cohort-Size Model," *Criminology* 27 (1989): 57–78; Steffensmeier et. al. (1987); Daniel H. Klepinger and Joseph G. Weis, "Projecting Crime Rates: an Age, Period, and Cohort Model Using ANIMA Techniques," *Journal of Quantitative Criminology* 1 (1985): 387–416; and David F. Greenberg and Nancy J. Larkin, "Age-Cohort Analysis of Arrest Rates," *Journal of Quantitative Criminology* 1 (1985): 227–240.

[2] James Q. Wilson, "Crime and Public Policy" in *Crime*, ed. James Q. Wilson and Joan Petersilia (San Francisco: Institute for Contemporary Studies, 1995), 507.

[3] John J. DiLulio, "Arresting Ideas," *Policy Review* 74 (1995): 15.

[4] *Ibid.*

[5] Alfred S. Blumstein, "Violence by Young People," in *National Institute of Justice Journal* (Washington, DC: U.S. Department of Justice, 1995), 3.

[6] Alfred S. Blumstein, "An Interview with Professor Alfred Blumstein," *Law Enforcement News* 422 (1995): 10–13.

more than a decade of relative stability. But, they also made projections using a "constant rate" assumption in which violent crimes by juveniles between the years 1992 and 2010 would increase by 22 percent and an "increasing rate" model in which the rates of juvenile violence would increase as they have before 1992. Under this increasing rate assumption, the number of juvenile arrests for violent crime would double by 2010, with an increase of 145 percent for murder.[1]

Thus, whether based on the extrapolated projections of Wilson and Dilulio, or the empirical estimates generated by Blumstein or Snyder and Sickmund, the predictions were bleak. The future of juvenile crime was projected to be a "growth industry." Fortunately, the reality is that all these predictions were totally inaccurate, as the "crime bomb" has not detonated yet, and perhaps it never will. Fundamental to these false predictions for an increase in juvenile crime attributed to a large "echo-boom" birth cohort is that the exact relationship between changing age structure and crime has yet to be specified correctly. Researchers still agree that there is an age effect but we cannot seem to agree on what the effect is precisely.

In addition to age, researchers have studied changes in the demographic composition of society and whether increases or decreases in specific population subgroups may be related to crime. Previous investigations have identified that a very small number of habitual or chronic offenders are responsible for a disproportionately large number of offenses.[2] These researchers have found that

the prevalence and incidence of juvenile crime seems to differ by subgroups such as race, ethnicity, and gender divisions.[3] Particularly when measured by official records, minority groups are overrepresented and females are underrepresented among serious offenses, and females are over represented among status offenses and child welfare cases. Thus far neither the argument that these distributions reflect true behavioral differences nor the argument that police and other officials are selectively target subgroups has been found to be solely correct.

Some theories explain subgroup differences in crime as a function of conflicting cultural values,[4] or adaptations to other socially constructed barriers.[5] One recent explanation for youth violence attributes the subcultural adaptation to the inner cities' "ecology of danger," the value accorded to individual reputation, and behavioral norms that are regulated by "the code of the street."[6]

1978); Lyle W. Shannon, "A Longitudinal Study of Delinquency and Crime," in *Quantitative Studies in Criminology*, ed. Charles F. Wellford (Beverly Hills, CA: Sage, 1978); Paul E. Tracy, Marvin E. Wolfgang, and Robert M. Figlio, *Delinquency Careers in Two Birth Cohorts* (New York: Plenum Press, 1990); and Paul E. Tracy and Kimberly Kempf-Leonard, *Continuity and Discontinuity in Criminal Careers: The Transition from Delinquency to Crime* (New York: Plenum Press, 1996).

[3] Tracy and Kempf-Leonard, 1996.

[4] See Thorsten Sellin, *Culture Conflict and Crime* (New York: Social Science Research Council, 1938); and Marvin E. Wolfgang and Franco Ferracuti, *The Subculture of Violence* (London: Tavistock, 1967).

[5] See Elijah Anderson, "The Social Ecology of Youth Violence," in *Youth Violence*, ed. Mark H. Moore and Michael Tonry (Chicago: University of Chicago Press, 1998), 65–104; Albert K. Cohen, *Delinquent Boys* (New York: Free Press, 1995); Jeffrey Fagan and Deanna L. Wilkinson, "Guns, Youth Violence, and Social Identity," in Moore and Tonry; and Kimberly Kempf-Leonard, Meda Chesney-Lind, and Darnell F. Hawkins, "Ethnicity and Gender Issues," in *Very Young Offenders: Development, Interventions, and Service Needs*, ed. Rolf Loeber and David P. Farrington (Thousand Oaks, CA: Sage, 2000), 247–269.

[6] Anderson, 1998; and Fagan and Wilkinson, 1998.

---

[1] Howard N. Snyder and Melissa Sickmund, *Juvenile Offenders and Victims: A Focus on Violence* (Washington, DC: U.S. Department of Justice, 1995).

[2] See Marvin E. Wolfgang, Robert M. Figlio, and Thorsten Sellin, *Delinquency in a Birth Cohort* (Chicago: University of Chicago Press, 1972); Donna M. Hamparian et. al., *The Violent Few: A Study of Dangerous Juvenile Offenders* (Lexington, MA: Lexington Books,

Subcultural and structural correlates with youth crime for girls, particularly those who live in marginalized communities, link fear and victimization at home and norms about gender that may be especially problematic.[1]

Socio-economic Factors

Many theories suggest that economic prosperity will lead to a decline in crime. The general explanation for the recent downward trend may in fact be more widely accessible social capital now enabling more citizens, including those who have been very poor, to make strides toward achieving the "American Dream."[2] We agree with the position offered by Robert Sampson and William Wilson that criminology must develop a macro-social or community-level focus in order to investigate and disentangle the structural and cultural correlates of crime.[3] Two recent publications endorse and extend the these suggestions, offering valuable insights as to what a community-level research agenda might look like and how it might elucidate previously elusive aspects of crime.[4] Specifically, they suggest that:

Multilevel research designs and theories that reflect a variety of analytic methods

can further the study of serious and violent juvenile crime, especially when attempting to identify and account for ethnic and racial differences. The insights gained from such research have policy-related implication. Public policy aimed at reducing serious and violent juvenile offending should adopt the goal of transforming urban communities, especially in light of past trends in the concentration of urban poverty.[5]

The suggestions of these researchers are important. We maintain that a useful research agenda is one that acknowledges cultural differences, and then proposes a worthwhile strategy to understand and explain the many and complex effects of community structure and culture on crime. Moreover, the need to examine multi-level effects of economic well-being is underscored by a recent study that found crime was not attributable to social disorder, but rather the source of each was economic disadvantage, including concentrated poverty, and combinations of residential and commercial land use.[6] A multi-level orientation is critical if we are to identify, understand, and make progress in remedying the conditions that give rise to differential crime in the first place.

Data available from the census measures the prevalence of economic prosperity, including median income, families living below the poverty line, welfare recipients, owner-occupied houses, and female-headed households. The cleavages may actually have increased between the "haves" and "have nots" in the recent past so it is important to assess the extent to which the spatially concentrated areas of poverty observed previously now have diminished or become more diffused. Such improvement would

[1] Sibylle Artz, *Sex, Power, and the Violent School Girl* (Toronto: Trifolium Books, 1998); and Deborah R. Baskin and Ira B. Sommers, *Casualties of Community Disorder: Women's Careers in Violent Crime* (Boulder, CO: Westview, 1998).

[2] Steven F. Messner and Richard Rosenfeld, *Crime and the American Dream* (Belmont, CA: Wadsworth, 1994).

[3] Robert J. Sampson and William J. Wilson, "Race, Crime, and Urban Inequality," in *Crime and Inequality*, ed. John Hagan and Ruth Peterson (Stanford, CA: Stanford University Press, 1995).

[4] Darnell F. Hawkins, John H. Laub, and Janet L. Lauritsen, "Race, Ethnicity, and Sexual Offending," in *Serious and Violent Juvenile Offenders: Risk Factors and Successful Interventions*, ed. Rolf Loeber and David P. Farrington (Thousand Oaks, CA: Sage, 1998); and Darnell F. Hawkins et. al., *Race, Ethnicity, and Serious Violent Juvenile Offending* (Washington, DC: U.S. Department of Justice, 2000).

[5] Hawkins et. al., *Race, Ethnicity*, 4.

[6] Robert J. Sampson and Stephen Raudenbush, *Project on Human Development in Chicago Neighborhoods 1999 Annual Report* (Cambridge: Harvard University, 1999).

have significant effect on the crime attributed to relative deprivation, particularly the abject poverty of the underclass that Elliott Currie called "endemic."[1] New suggestions for understanding the spatial distributions of race and social disadvantage make clear the need also to examine concentration, exposure, city-level centralization, clustering, evenness, and a combination "hyper-segregation: index of these five dimensions.[2]

To encourage progress, it is important to understand the context in which economic changes occur. Economic, physical, and social isolation of the very poor has been blamed on the de-industrialization of cities, the attendant rise of the service economy primarily in suburban locations, and the inadequacy of public transit systems and public education. If job opportunities and wages have improved, we should know whether new conditions also suggest social and physical integration. We also must establish the legitimacy of financial sources; that waning violence, for example, is not due to increased property crime and other illicit activities from which there is financial gain.

Illustrations

The following illustrations apply the socio-demographic concepts we have been reviewing. We will use a data set of violent juvenile crimes in the city of Dallas between 1997 and 2001.[3] The unit of analysis is census

tracts, of which Dallas has 234. We have available the following offense-related dependent variables: frequency of violent juvenile crimes, frequency of juvenile robberies, and frequency of juvenile assaults. In addition we calculated offense rates for violence, robbery, and assault. The rates were calculated as follows:

$$\text{Offense Rate} = \frac{\text{Number of violent acts}}{\text{Juvenile Population}} * 1000$$

We used the unit of 1,000 as the constant because our juvenile population is in units of thousands rather than tens of thousands. We calculated offense rates because the frequency measure can be misleading. The volume of crime is partly a function of the population at risk (at risk to be an offender or a victim). Thus, a census tract could have a moderate volume of violent juvenile offenses and yet have a high rate because the particular tract has only a minimal number of juveniles. Of course the reverse can also be true: a tract can have a high frequency but yet a low rate because of the high number of juveniles at risk. We have used various census indicators pertaining to age and socio-economic conditions as predictor variables.

Age

Table 12-1 shows the results of a regression analysis of the violent juvenile crime rate and three predictor variables pertaining to the frequency of persons age 6–17 in the census tract. A multiple regression analysis seeks to explain variation in a dependent variable based on a group of independent variables. It usually involves the following statistics: (1) standardized beta is a measure of the strength of an independent variable in predicting the score on the dependent variable; (2) t-score is the value that is calculated in a t-test to determine if the independent variable is a

---

[1] Elliott Curie, *Reckoning: Drugs, the Cities, and the American Future* (New York: Hill & Wang, 1993).
[2] Douglas S. Massey and Nancy A. Denton, "The Dimensions of Residential Segregation," *Social Forces* 67, no. 2 (1988): 281–315; and Douglas S. Massey and Nancy A. Denton, "Hyper Segregation in U.S. Metropolitan Areas: Black and Hispanic Segregation Along Five Dimensions," *Demography* 26, no. 3 (1989): 373–391.
[3] Donald Dixon, *An Analysis of the Social Ecology of Violent Juvenile Crime* (PhD diss., University of Texas at Dallas, 2001).

significant predictor of the dependent variable; (3) probability value measures the chances that a particular t-score could have occurred by chance; (4) R-square is the amount of variation in the dependent variable that was explained by the independent variables (while it is reported in decimal form, it is usually expressed as a percentage); (5) F-test is like the t-test and measures whether the amount of variation explained by the regression analysis was significant; and (6) probability value measures the chances that a particular F-test score could have occurred by chance. Many of these statistics are discussed in Chapter 14.

The regression results reported in Table 12-1 indicate that it is the number of juvenile males residing in a census tract that represents a significant predictor of violent juvenile crime rather than the number of females or even the total number of juveniles. This simple three-factor model is significant and explains 25% of the variation in total violent juvenile crime across census tracts.

Table 12-1
Regression Analysis: Age and Violent Juvenile Crime

Variable	Standard-ized Beta	t-score	prob. value
Constant		2.936	.004
Females 6-17	.130	1.474	.142
Males 6-17	.377	4.390	.000
Total 6-17	.058	.567	.572
R-square = .252; F = 20.662; p= .000			

Table 12-2 reports the results of a multiple regression analysis of the juvenile robbery rate and the three predictor variables pertaining to the age structure of a census tract (i.e., frequency of persons age 6–17 in the census tract). None of the age-related measures is significantly associated with the dependent variable and the model overall is

barely significant at about .02, but there is only small amount of variation (5 percent) explained by the model. It appears from this analysis that the size of the juvenile population in a census tract is not related to the frequency of robbery.

Table 12-2
Regression Analysis: Age and Juvenile Robbery

Variable	Standard-ized Beta	t-score	prob. value
Constant		3.253	.001
Females 6-17	.134	1.343	.181
Males 6-17	.156	1.612	.109
Total 6-17	-.030	-.259	.786
R-square = .053; F = 3.409; p= .019			

Table 12-3 reports the results of a regression analysis of the juvenile assault rate and the three predictor variables pertaining to the frequency of persons age 6–17 in the census tract. Unlike the case of robbery, there is a substantial relationship between the number of juvenile males and the volume of assaults. The standardized coefficient (.479) for males age 6–17 is substantial and is significant at the .001 level. Further, the overall model is significant and explains an impressive 34 percent of the variation in assaults. This basic three-factor age model clearly indicates that the availability of juvenile males in an area is highly related to the assault component of juvenile violence.

Table 12-3
Regression Analysis: Age and Assault

Variable	Standard-ized Beta	t-score	prob. Value
Constant		2.498	.013
Females 6-17	.132	1.582	.115
Males 6-17	.479	5.931	.000
Total 6-17	.030	.312	.755
R-square = .337; F = 31.2; p= .000			

Age, School, and Employment

Table 12-4 displays the regression concerning the rate of juvenile violence and several predictor variables: (1) frequency of persons aged 16–19 in the census tract; (2) number of persons in the census tract that were or were not high school graduates; and (3) were either unemployed or not in the labor force. The regression model is significant and explains about 24 percent of the variance in juvenile violence. Three predictor variables were significantly associated with the juvenile violence rate. The number of juveniles aged 16–19 was the strongest predictor, followed closely by whether juveniles in this age group were not high school graduates. Last, a subject in this age group who was not a graduate and was unemployed was also significant. The results suggest that as a tract has increasing numbers of older juveniles who did not finish high school and are unemployed, there will be a corresponding increase in the rate of juvenile violence.

Table 12-4
Regression Analysis: Age, School, Employment, and Violence

Variable	Stand. Beta	t-score	prob. value
Constant		3.015	.003
Total 16-19	.482	4.331	.000
H.S. Grad. 16-19, unemployed	-.100	-1.447	.150
H.S. Grad. 16-19, not labor force	.084	1.099	.273
Not H.S. Grad 16-19	.396	2.145	.017
Not H.S. Grad, unemployed	.245	3.141	.002
Not H.S. Grad. 16-19, not labor force	.198	1.336	.183
R-square = .239; F = 9.495; p= .000			

Table 12-5 repeats this analysis and displays the results of a regression analysis of the juvenile robbery rate and several predictor variables: (1) frequency of persons age 16-19 in the census tract; (2) number of persons in the census tract that were/were not high school graduates; and (3) were either unemployed or not in the labor force. The regression model is not significant and explains only seven percent of the variance in juvenile robbery. There were no predictor variables that were significantly associated with the rate of juvenile violence.

Table 12-5
Regression Analysis: Age, School, Employment, and Robbery

Variable	Stand. Beta	t-score	prob. value
Constant		3.334	.001
Total 16-19	.088	.714	.476
H.S. Grad. 16-19, unemployed	-.018	-.232	.816
H.S. Grad. 16-19, not labor force	.079	.939	.349
Not H.S. Grad 16-19	.019	.103	.918
Not H.S. Grad, unemployed	.130	1.508	.133
Not H.S. Grad. 16-19, not labor force	.152	.315	.753
R-square = .071; F = 2.289; p= .037			

Table 12-6 displays the results of a regression analysis of the rate of juvenile assault and several predictor variables: (1) frequency of persons age 16–19 in the census tract; (2) number of persons in the census tract that were/were not high school graduates; and (3) were either unemployed or not in the labor force. The results for assault are similar to those for overall violence. The regression model is significant and explains about 30 percent of the variance in juvenile assaults. There were again three predictor variables that were significantly associated with the rate of juvenile assaults and the association was identical to that for overall juvenile violence. The number of juveniles ages 16–19 was the strongest predictor, and this was followed closely by a measure of whether juveniles in this age group were not high school graduates. Last, whether persons in this age group were not graduates and were unemployed was significantly related to the juvenile violence rate. Overall, the regression results show that as a census tract has increasing numbers of older juveniles who did not finish high school and are unemployed, there will be an increase in the rate of juvenile assaults.

Table 12-6
Regression Analysis: Age, School, Employment, and Assaults

Variable	Stand. Beta	t-score	prob. value
Constant		2.553	.012
Total 16-19	.539	5.026	.000
H.S. Grad. 16-19, unemployed	-.083	-1.241	.216
H.S. Grad. 16-19, not labor force	.079	1.082	.281
Not H.S. Grad 16-19	-.505	-3.202	.002
Not H.S. Grad, unemployed	.285	3.798	.000
Not H.S. Grad. 16-19, not labor force	.269	1.884	.061
R-square = .296; F = 12.696; p= .000			

Poverty

In the next set of analyses, we examine the connection between poverty and juvenile violence. We are now moving beyond the age factor and looking at whether the life situation of census tract residents influences the rate of juvenile violence activity.

Table 12-7 shows a simple two-factor regression model using the number of families living below the poverty line and the number of female-headed families as predictors. The latter measure was used because research has indicated that female-headed households experience greater likelihood of being poor, and the lack of economic status hits such families the hardest. The model is significant and explains 21 percent of the variance in the juvenile violence rate. The families in poverty measure was a significant predictor, while female headed families was almost significant as reflected in the probability value of 0.67 which is just beyond the required .05 value. Clearly, as one would expect, overall the regression analysis indicates that the poverty status of the residents in a census tract influences the rate of juvenile violence.

Table 12-7
Regression Analysis: Poverty and Juvenile Violence

Variable	Stand. Beta	t-score	prob. value
Constant		5.857	.000
Families in Poverty	.281	2.538	.012
Females Head	.204	1.846	.067
R-square = .213; F = 25.040; p= .000			

Table 12-8 repeats the two-factor regression model that uses the number of families living below the poverty line and the number of female-headed families as predictors, with the robbery rate the dependent variable. Overall, the model is significant, but the variance is only six percent. The families-in-poverty coefficient is almost significant, indicating that there is some importance to the effect of this measure on robbery.

Table 12-8
Regression Analysis: Poverty and Juvenile Robbery

Variable	Stand. Beta	t-score	prob. value
Constant		4.341	.000
Families in Poverty	.233	1.931	.055
Females Head	.019	.155	.877
R-square = .062; F = 4.341; p= .003			

As we have seen before, while the robbery rate has not been readily explainable with our statistical analyses, the rate of juvenile assaults has shown important findings. Table

12-9 reports the two-factor regression model for the rate of juvenile assaults across the census tracts. The model is significant at a very high level and could have occurred by chance in but one out of 1,000 trials. The model is also substantively important as it explains a substantial 31 percent of the variance in the juvenile assault rate. Unlike the situation for overall violence, both of the predictor variables had significant coefficients, thus indicating that families in poverty and children living in female headed families have substantial effects on the propensity for assault crimes by juveniles.

Table 12-9
Regression Analysis: Poverty and Juvenile Assault

Variable	Stand. Beta	t-score	prob. value
Constant		5.819	.000
Families in Poverty	.239	2.240	.026
Females Head	.307	2.884	.004
R-square = .270; F =34.117; p= .000			

Housing

In the last set of analyses we turn to the issue of the quality of the environment in which residents live as measured by two variables: housing vacancy and the value of the housing units. The first, number of vacant housing units for sale, is an indicator of whether the area has a stable residential population. When there are high numbers of housing units that are vacant and for sale, this can be construed as affecting the residential stability and cohesion. Similarly, the second measure, market value of the units for sale, reflects the approximate socioeconomic status level of an area. One might hypothesize that each of these measures would be related to crime.

Table 12-10 reports the two-factor model using these predictor variables. Overall, the model is significant. But, as we have seen above, the model only explains a minimal amount, seven percent, of the variance in overall juvenile violence. Yet, the median price measure of vacant units performs as we had expected. This variable is a significant predictor of juvenile violence and indicates that as median price declines there is a corresponding increase in the rate of juvenile violence in the census tract.

Table 12-10
Regression Analysis: Housing and Juvenile Violence

Variable	Stand. Beta	t-score	prob. value
Constant		12.126	.000
Vacant units for sale	.135	1.845	.067
Vacant units; median $	-.264	-3.621	.000
R-square = .071; F =7.052; p= .001			

Table 12-11 reports the results for the juvenile robbery rate. As we have seen before, the model is not significant and the variance explained, three percent, is minimal. Yet, the median housing price of vacant units still emerges as a significant predictor. This variable is significantly and inversely related to the rate of juvenile robbery and indicates that as median price declines there is a corresponding increase in the robbery rate. This result surely warrants further study. What is it about vacant units and declining property value that breeds higher rates of robbery activity on the part of juveniles?

Table 12-11
Regression Analysis: Housing and Juvenile Robbery

Variable	Stand. Beta	t-score	prob. value
Constant		8.213	.000
Vacant units for sale	.107	1.434	.067
Vacant units median $	-.181	-2.430	.000
R-square = .035; F =3.333; p= .038			

Table 12-12 gives the regression results for assault behavior. Although we have consistently obtained significant and important results for this measure before, this time the findings are less substantial. Overall, the model is highly significant, but for the first time, the regression model did not explain a substantial amount of the variance in the assault rate, only about 8 percent of the variance. Yet the two predictor variables have significant effects. The number of vacant units is directly related to the assault rate and is significant (below the .05 level). The median price of vacant units had a significant (.001 level) negative effect on the assault rate.

Table 12-12
Regression Analysis: Housing and Juvenile Assault

Variable	Stand. Beta	t-score	prob. value
Constant		12.300	.000
Vacant units for sale	.156	2.145	.033
Vacant units median $	-.385	-3.926	.000
R-square = .084; F =8.464; p= .000			

Obtaining Demographic Data

The analyses reported in this chapter illustrate that the demographic character of the census tracts across a community can be strongly related to crime measures. This suggests that the crime analyst should take demographic measures into account when analyzing the patterns, volume, distribution, and rate of crime. The most straightforward way to acquire demographic data for a jurisdiction is to use the United States Bureau of Census. The Census Bureau conducts a comprehensive counting of the population every ten years and makes these data available. Generally, a community will have an economic development office or a chamber of commerce and these offices will usually have the latest census data available.

Alternatively, the crime analyst can access the Census Bureau's Web page (http://www.census.gov) to get acquainted with the population data that are available.

There are also a number of private companies that specialize in providing access to jurisdiction-specific census data. For example, GeoLytics (http://www.geolytics.com) is a company based in East Brunswick, New Jersey, that has published detailed demographic and geographic data on CD-ROM for business, academic, non-profit, and government markets since 1996. GeoLytics specializes in compressing large amounts of government data, and packaging it with easy-to-use software. In addition to firms that supply data, there are also companies that will not only supply census and other demographic data, but will also provide training, either onsite or on the Internet. One such company is SmartGirlTechnologies (http://www.smartgirltechnologies.com/) in Portland, Oregon. This company provides what it calls a Local Demographic Analysis Workshop that was designed for human service providers, neighborhood activists, grant writers, planners or anyone who would like to easily look up and analyze basic demographic characteristics.

Conclusion

This chapter has discussed the issue of the effect of demographic conditions on crime. We have shown that a crime analyst must take into consideration the demographic and socio-economic character of a city's census tracts or neighborhoods when attempting to study comparative rates of crime.
Recognition of these causal factors is crucial because not all areas reflect the same rate or even trends in violent juvenile crimes. The question arises concerning what may be operating across census tracts to cause such differences in crime?

There are a multitude of possible explanations for the differences in juvenile crime or even adult crime for that matter. We have illustrated that even a few simple demographic models can produce significant analyses of crime rates. These illustrations serve to remind a crime analyst that the following issues should be addressed when preparing to conduct research:

1. Consider multi-factor explanatory models in the exploration of juvenile crime and violence rates and trends;

2. Conceptualize the competing explanations so as to develop a range of reliable and valid indicators of the demographic and socioeconomic aspects of the areas being studied;

3. Use sufficiently rigorous statistical modeling routines to provide for a definitive study. We would recommend that the best potential to achieve these goals is to develop and implement a research design that is responsive to the challenge. To develop such a design the crime analyst must employ a multi-disciplinary approach that:
    1. Blends disciplinary concepts and theories;
    2. Develops appropriate measurement strategies;
    3. Specifies a multi-faceted causal model or set of models.

Ultimately, we believe that the above features of research design and analysis strategies may have great utility for developing public policy and programs. The research will have investigated the various causal processes that may be operating and may have produced the crime rates or trends under scrutiny. There may be empirical verification for some theories and associated factors but perhaps not for others. More importantly, the research may be able to show where these processes were operative (i.e., individuals, neighborhoods, census tracts, schools, or even counties as a whole). By so doing, this research will have provided policy-makers with sophisticated statistical evidence that some community factors are related to crime and we will also have provided evidence about where these causal processes may be the most important.

Thus, it is crucial for crime analysts to appreciate that comprehensive research is needed that is capable of producing an empirically-based understanding of the reasons for crime rate differences. In turn, research that is guided by the principles discussed above can perhaps provide policymakers and planners with empirically validated tools that can be used to explain past tends, anticipate and explain future trends, and optimally, to plan effective prevention and intervention strategies.

PART III
Tools of Crime Analysis

13
Descriptive and Multivariate Statistics

Jamie Price
*Donald W. Chamberlayne**

Statistics is the science of collecting and organizing data and then drawing conclusions based on data. There are essentially three types of statistics: descriptive, multivariate, and inferential. Descriptive statistics summarize large amounts of information in an efficient and easily understood manner. Multivariate statistics allow comparisons among factors by isolating the effect of one factor or variable from others that may distort conclusions. Inferential statistics (covered in Chapter 14) suggest statements about a population based on a sample drawn from that population.

This chapter will familiarize readers with the principles of descriptive and multivariate statistics. Students and practitioners need to know the basic foundations of research and statistics so that they are better producers as well as consumers of research and police data. A fundamental understanding of descriptive and multivariate statistics is essential to job performance and evaluation.

Analysts should be able to perform a number of simple, though powerful, analyses to describe data and reach conclusions based on these data. Many people are intimidated by

mathematics and statistics. However, the role of statistics is very important with regard to reports, publications, policy, and the general understanding of information that we process every day.

Descriptive Statistics

In the following sections, readers will learn the following major goals: (a) summarizing large and small data sets, (b) examining the integrity of large and small data sets, (c) determining which statistics best portray the data, (d) comparing more than one variable to others, and ultimately, (e) applying descriptive statistics to problem solving and data driven decision-making.

Levels of Measurement

One concept that applies to both research and statistics is "levels of measurement." Indeed, measurement is the process of assigning numbers or labels to units of analysis or items under study. In other words, numbers are assigned to the "who" or "what" that are being studied. Numbers are assigned to make the data amenable to statistical analysis. There are four levels of measurement: nominal, ordinal, interval, and ratio. These distinctions are important because how data are analyzed depends on how data were collected. Each level conveys a different amount of information.

Nominal

The **nominal** level of measurement is the process of classifying data into categories. It is the lowest level of measurement and all categories must be *exhaustive*, thus covering all observations that may exist. In addition, the categories must be *mutually exclusive*: each observation can only be classified in one way. Nominal measures merely provide names or labels for distinguishing observations. For

* Editor's Note: Jamie Price and Donald Chamberlayne worked independently on their respective sections of this chapter. Mr. Price wrote the material on descriptive statistics; Dr. Chamberlayne's contribution begins with the heading "Multivariate Statistics."

example, we could classify respondents to a survey by race or gender. Each respondent's race could be coded as "African American," "Asian," "Caucasian," or "Other." For gender, each respondent is coded as "Male" or "Female." Each respondent falls into only one classification and there is an appropriate category for each respondent according to their race and gender. Though we could assign a numeric code to each category (e.g., "1" for male and "2" for female), the code is still nominal data—there is no logical way to rank-order or perform calculations with it.

Ordinal

The **ordinal** level of measurement consists of the characteristics of the nominal level—exhaustive and mutually exclusive—but also exhibits a degree of difference between the categories on a scale. This degree of difference indicates order or ranking between categories. The categories are ordered in some way, but the actual distance between these orderings would not have any meaning. Examples are opinion of police, crime seriousness, levels of fear. Response scales such as "good, better, best," "agree, neutral, disagree," or "very unlikely, unlikely, undecided, likely, very likely" are common ordinal scale measures.

Interval

The **interval** level of measurement consists of all the characteristics of nominal and ordinal levels of measurements. In addition, the interval level assumes that all the items on a scale have equal units or intervals of measurement between them. In contrast to ordinal scales, the distance between categories would have meaning. There are logical distances between categories expressed in meaningful standard intervals. Examples of interval measurement would be temperature readings and IQ.

Ratio

In addition to all the characteristics of the previous three levels of measurement, the **ratio** level of measurement contains a true zero point. A true zero point allows for measuring the total absence of the concept under measure. Income, weight, time, and age are examples of ratio level measurements.

Table 13-1 summarizes the different information conveyed by the four levels of measurement.

There are three implications regarding the level of measurement. First, ratio is the highest level of measurement because it contains all the characteristics of the other three. Second, researchers and practitioners should seek the highest level of measurement possible, within reasonable time, effort, and cost constraints of the study. Lower levels of measurement cannot be converted to higher levels of measurement, but higher-level measurement can be converted to a lower level. Third, and most important, the statistical technique to be applied will determine the level of measurement needed. Specific analytic techniques require minimum levels of measurement.

Characteristic	Levels Of Measurement			
	Nom.	Ord.	Int.	Rat.
Exclusive & Exhaustive	X	X	X	X
Rank Order		X	X	X
Equal Intervals			X	X
Absolute Zero Point				X

Table 13-1: A comparison of levels of measurement

Ideally, many concepts can be measured on different levels of measurement depending on how data are collected. For example, the concept "age" could be measured using the following response sets for each level of measurement:

Nominal: "Young" or "Old"
Ordinal: "0–6," "7–13," "14–20," "30+"
Interval: "1–20," "21–40," "41–60," "61+"
Ratio: 0,1,2,3,4,5,6,7,8,9,10,11,12,13,etc.

Based on the implications stated earlier, several points can be demonstrated regarding the different levels of measurement pertaining to the "age" example above.

1) Regardless of a person's age, there is a response set that applies to each individual (exhaustive).

2) Including the subjective nominal level, a person's age falls into only one classification (exclusive).

3) Although the ordinal level contains a zero, the intervals between each category are not equal; thus they cannot be interval or ratio.

4) The interval method does not begin with zero; thus it cannot be ratio.

5) The ratio level is based on the assumption that individuals under study could be less than one year of age (infant less than 365 days for example).

6) Working highest to lowest, a person's age collected on the ratio level could be converted into lower levels of measurement. Although, the interval level could not be converted using the ordinal level above, a new ordinal level could be created from the interval level such as 0 to 20, 21 to 40, 41 to 60, 61 and over. All three levels of measurement, ordinal, interval, and ratio could be converted to nominal.

7) Working lowest to highest, the data could not be converted into higher levels. For example, if a person's age is classified as only young or old, no determination could be made as to whether that individual was 0 to 6, 7 to 13, and so on. The last category of the ordinal level, 30+, could not be

converted into the more precise intervals such as 21 to 40, 41 to 60 and so on. Moreover the interval does not begin at zero. (For this reason, it is common for the interval and ratio levels to be treated as one level).

8) The age should be collected on the level necessary to the techniques the analyst is going to apply.

Data collection is very important. Likewise, two areas of great interest in descriptive statistics are describing the "average case" and describing how the "average case" compares to all the cases as a whole. These two areas complement each other. Indeed, measures of central tendency describe the characteristics of the average case and measures of dispersion indicate just how typical or average this case is.

Distributions

Before discussing measures of central tendency and dispersion, analysts should understand the distribution of data sets. Some data sets can be very large and cumbersome. Data should be described in a manner that is easily understood. One of the first steps in analyzing data is to construct a **frequency distribution**, which lists the number or frequency of scores or labels for each individual case. The frequency distribution allows for a basic description of the data set and for graphical representation.

Assume that we have collected data on the number of prior arrests for a group of 39 offenders and that we are interested in how many of them have more than three prior arrests. The **raw numbers** of prior arrests are hypothetically as follows:

1, 3, 7, 2, 5, 2, 4, 2, 1, 5, 6, 2, 3, 1,
4, 2, 3, 4, 3, 3, 5, 6, 1, 2, 3, 4, 6, 1,
3, 2, 2, 1, 3, 2, 4, 3, 12, 3, 1

If the data set is small, a visual inspection of the raw data set may reveal the answer relating to three or more arrests. However, if the data set is large it will probably be too difficult or impractical. For simplicity, we will use a small data set but assume it requires summation. Table 13-2 tabulates the number of prior arrests for 39 individuals.

Prior Arrests of Current Offenders

x (number of prior arrests)	f (frequency)	f x
12	1	12
7	1	7
6	3	18
5	3	15
4	5	20
3	10	30
2	9	18
1	7	7
	N = 39	Σ fx = 127

Table 13-2: A frequency distribution

From the frequency distribution above, the x column indicates that the data set of 39 offenders have between one and 12 prior arrests. Using the frequency column, it is easily determined that 13 offenders had more than three prior arrests. And among them, the group of offenders had 127 prior arrests.

In constructing a frequency distribution, the first step is to create an array or set of numerical values arranged in order from highest to lowest. This array is the first column or *x*. The second column is the frequency column (*f*). This column indicates how many times that particular score occurred in the data set. The third column, *fx*, indicates the total number of values by multiplying the first and second columns.

Once a frequency distribution has been created, analysts may want to further condense it to allow for easier, more meaningful graphing.

The **range** is a summary statistic that provides limited information but allows for condensing a frequency distribution. The range is the highest score minus the lowest score (H − L). From the example above, the range is: $12 - 1 = 11$.

To condense the distribution, the range is used to create groupings of information into class intervals.

$$\text{Class Interval} \atop i \quad = \quad \frac{\text{Range}}{N \text{ of desired intervals}}$$

Assume we want to group the number of prior arrests into four intervals:

$$i = \frac{12 - 1}{4} = \frac{11}{4} = 2.75$$

* 2.75 is rounded to 3

Thus, each interval will have three cases. Grouping the prior arrest data, the new **grouped distribution** would be:

Interval	f (frequency)
10–12	1
7–9	1
4–6	11
1–3	26
	n = 39

Table 13-3: A grouped frequency distribution

Although the data have been condensed and the distribution has changed, the nature of the data remains the same. Progressing from raw numbers to frequency distributions to grouped distributions allows for large data sets to be more easily managed and analyzed.

Data in frequency distributions or grouped distributions lend themselves to easy graphing. The purpose of **charts** and **graphs** is to portray the distribution of data for a quick and meaningful understanding. The following charts and graphs were created using Microsoft Excel; however, other graphing software is available.

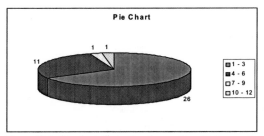

Figure 13-1: Pie chart illustrating the number of prior arrests, based on grouped frequency distribution in Table 13-3.

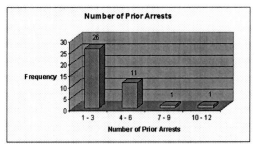

Figure 13-2: Column chart illustrating the number of prior arrests, based on grouped frequency distribution in Table 13-3.

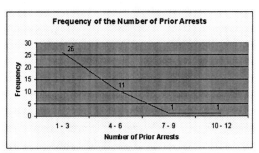

Figure 13-3: Line chart illustrating the number of prior arrests, based on grouped frequency distribution in Table 13-3.

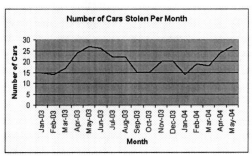

Figure 13-4: Line chart illustrating the number of stolen cars per month.

Graphing provides not only greater visibility of the distribution but also quick and simple interpretations. Pie charts (Figure 13-1) can present percentages or counts while comparing the relative size of various segments. Column graphs (Figure 13-2) also present percentages or counts while comparing the relative size of various segments. Histograms are special column graphs with continuous data. Line graphs (Figure 13-3) reveal plotted values and may reveal **skewness** or **trends** (Figure 13-4) over time.

In addition to frequency distributions and grouped frequency distributions, **percentages** and **cumulative percentages** can be calculated. Using the grouped frequency distribution for prior arrests, two additional columns have been added to indicated the percent of cases pertaining to each interval or segment as well as the cumulative percentage of each segment in combination with others.

Interval	F (freq.)	Percent %	Cumulative %
10–12	1	2.6	2.6
7–9	1	2.6	5.2
4–6	11	28.2	33.4
1–3	26	66.7	100.0
	N = 39	100.0*	

Table 13-4: A frequency distribution with percentages and cumulative percentages

The percent column is calculated by dividing the frequency of each interval by the total number of cases. For example, for the interval of ten to twelve prior arrests, one divided by thirty-nine equals 2.6% or approximately three percent of all cases. The cumulative percentage is determined by adding the percent column for each class interval. By adding the first two intervals, the cumulative percentage would be 5.2 percent (2.6 + 2.6). Adding the second and third intervals, the cumulative percentage would be 33.4 percent (28.2 + 5.2). And so on.

One question that often comes up is: what should you do with **missing data**? It is important because depending on how you treat missing data, the percentages and cumulative percentages as well as raw counts could be misleading. Percentages are determined by dividing the class intervals by the total number of cases. If cases contain missing data, you cannot determine whether the missing cases would have fallen into a particular segment or class interval. One solution is to create a segment labeled "missing cases" and include them in the total. This solution will deflate or reduce the other segments with regard to their relative percentages. Another option is to omit the missing cases altogether (i.e., do not have a "missing cases" interval and do not include them in the total number of cases as well). This may actually inflate the relative percentages for each class interval. Regardless of which method selected, always indicate whether missing cases have been included or excluded. This allows readers to determine for themselves whether the class intervals are inflated or deflated. Whether the missing cases are meaningful to your analysis pertains to validity and reliability issues and is beyond the scope of this chapter.

Measures of Central Tendency

Measures of central tendency are the most common forms of descriptive statistics. They describe the average or typical value from a distribution of values or scores. The primary measures of central tendency are: mean, median, and mode.

Mean

The **mean** ($\bar{x}$) is the arithmetic average. The mean is calculated by dividing the sum of scores by the number of cases. A distribution of data can have only one mean.

$$\bar{x} = \frac{\sum fx}{n}$$

f = frequencies
x = individual data points or class midpoints
n = total number of data items (sum of the frequency)

For example, for data set:
7, 6, 4, 3, 3, 1, 10, 12

x	f	fx
12	1	12
10	1	10
7	1	7
6	1	6
4	1	4
3	2	6
1	1	1
	n=8	$\sum fx$=46

$$\bar{x} = \frac{46}{8} = 5.75$$

The above example illustrates that the mean is 5.75 or approximately 6. Interestingly, notice that only one score has the exact value of 6. Four of the eight scores have a value less than 6 and three scores have a value of more than 6. It may be obvious, but the mean has one weakness. *It is affected by extreme score(s) in a distribution.* Extreme scores or **outliers** are single or small numbers of exceptional cases that deviate from the general pattern of scores. In the example above, if the last value in the distribution were 42 rather than 12, the mean would have changed from approximately 6 to approximately 10. Indeed, the mean involves *all* scores in a distribution and one score could inflate or deflate the mean.

The mean is useful with interval or ratio level data. Calculating a mean on a nominal variable is meaningless. For example, assume that a data set contained a nominal variable such as gender and is coded "1" for male and "2" for female. If the data set contained ten males and three females a mean could be theoretically calculated using the above formula, resulting in the mean score of 1.23. However, 1.23 is meaningless because the numbers "1" and "2" are used as labels rather than arithmetic numbers.

Median

The **median** (mdn) is the midpoint or middle score of a distribution. It is the point at which 50% of the scores lie above and 50% of the scores lie below. One of the strengths of the median is stability. Unlike the mean, the median is not significantly affected by extreme scores. Extreme scores or outliers can occur at either end of a distribution but have little effect on the median.

When there are few cases, it is simple to rank order the cases into an array of sequential numbers. Otherwise, when the number of cases is large, create a frequency distribution including a column of cumulative frequencies. Because the median measures position or location, the first step is to determine its location and the second step is to determine its value.

If the data set consists of an odd number of total cases, the location and value of the median is determined by rank ordering the individual scores and taking the middle one.

The formula to determine the position of the median is:

$$(n + 1)/2$$
n = the number of total cases.

For an array such as 1, 3, 3, 5, 6, 6, 9:

The position of the median is the fourth case [(7 + 1)/2], which has a value of 5 in the array above.

If the data set contains an even number of total cases, there is no middle case to represent the median. Instead, the median is located between two cases. The median can be determined by rank ordering the individual cases and taking the average of the middle two cases.

The formula to determine the position of the first case is:

$$N / 2$$

The formula to determine the position of the second case is:

$$(N / 2) + 1$$

For an array such as 1, 3, 3, 5, 6, 6, 8, 9:

The position of the first case is (8 / 2) = 4 or the fourth case, which has a value of 5.

The position of the second case is (8 / 2) + 1 = 5 or the fifth case, which has a value of 6.

The value of the median is determined by taking the average value of the above two cases. The formula to determine the value of the median in an array containing an even number of cases is:

$$Mdn = [X_{[N/2]} + X_{[(N/2)+1]}] / 2$$

$$or [5 + 6] / 2 = 11 / 2 = 5.5$$

The procedure for finding the median of a frequency table is similar to that for an array. Determine the position of the median as discussed above while using the column of cumulative frequency. Then determine the value or interval of its associated class or interval grouping.

Mode

The **mode** is the most frequent score or label. The mode is determined by directly observing the frequency distribution. If the distribution has one score or interval that occurs more frequently than the others, it is a unimodal distribution. If the distribution has two scores or intervals that tie for occurring the most, the distribution is said to be bimodal. Likewise, if there are more than two scores that are the same, the distribution is multimodal. For example, a multimodal distribution with three modes is trimodal.

Using Table 13-2, it can be observed that the distribution contains only one mode and the mode is 3 prior arrests (i.e., $f = 10$).

The mode indicates the most frequently occurring score(s) in a frequency distribution or interval(s) in a grouped frequency distribution. It provides limited information and is not subject to further statistical analysis. Although the mode applies to all four levels of measurement, because it uses very little information, it is most appropriate for nominal scale data.

Measure of Dispersion

The mean, median, and mode are important because they paint a picture of the "typical" case of a large data set. If all the values of a distribution or data set were the same, descriptive statistics would be of little value. Every item would portray the "typical" case. Indeed, variation is the foundation of statistics. Whenever means are used, we must be aware of extreme values.

It is important to examine measures of dispersion about the mean. There are three measures of variability: range, variance, and standard deviation.

Range

Although **range** was discussed earlier as a method used to create groupings of data into class intervals, it is also a simple measure of variation. The range indicates the distance between the highest and lowest values in a distribution. Because it uses the extreme values, it tells little about the other values in a distribution. This statistic can be unstable, as it relies on only two extreme values. There could be a great distance between the scores at the extreme ends of the distribution but little variation within the extremes. For example, consider these two data sets:

Data set #1: 1, 7, 7, 7, 8, 8, 8, 10
Data set #2: 1, 3, 4, 6, 9, 9, 9, 10

In the data sets above, both have a range of 9 but it is clear that data set #2 has much more variation among the values than data set #1.

Variance

The variance (s^2) is the sum of the squared deviations of each score from the mean, divided by the total number of cases. Stated another way, it is the mean of the sum of all squared deviations from the mean of any distribution. Essentially, it summarizes the dispersion of the scores around the mean.

The formula for variance is:

$$s^2 = \frac{\sum fx^2}{n-1}$$

The steps to calculate variance are:

(1) Calculate the mean of a distribution.
(2) Calculate the deviation from the mean for each score ($x = X - \overline{X}$).
(3) Calculate x^2 by squaring each x.
(4) Find the mean of the squared deviations.

Standard Deviation

Standard Deviation measures the average distance that each data item is away from the mean of all data items in a distribution. Thus, it suggests the average amount of variation about the mean. Standard deviation is meaningful because it provides insight to how scores in a distribution compare with each another. It also allows for comparison between two distributions.

With the potential of being influenced by outliers, means may be misleading. Thus, evaluating means along with standard deviations provides a better understanding of all scores collectively. In other words, if the mean is the average value of all observations in a group, then the standard deviation represents the average amount each individual observation varies from the mean. All scores in a distribution are used. As they are based on the mean, the variance and standard deviation require interval or ratio level data.

The formula for the standard deviation for array (ungrouped) data is:

$$s = \sqrt{\frac{\sum(x - \bar{x})^2}{n - 1}}$$

x : individual data scores
$\bar{x}$: mean
n: total number of data scores

As an example, we will calculate the standard deviation for a small data set of six values:

1, 6, 12, 17, 18, 24

We begin by calculating the mean:

$$\bar{x} = \frac{1 + 6 + 12 + 17 + 18 + 24}{6}$$

$$\bar{x} = \frac{78}{6} = 13$$

We then subtract each of the values from the mean. This gives us each value's *deviation*. We square each deviation and sum the squares. This is best illustrated in a table:

Value x	Deviation $x - \bar{x}$	Dev. Squared $(x - \bar{x})^2$
1	-12	144
6	-7	49
12	-1	1
17	4	16
18	5	25
24	11	121
Sum (Σ)		356

We then divide the sum of the square deviations by the number of scores minus one (in our case, 6 − 1 = 5), and take the square root of the result:

$$s = \sqrt{\frac{356}{5}} = \sqrt{71.2} = 8.438009$$

Note that 71.2 is in fact the variance for this data set—variance is a stop on the way to calculating the standard deviation. Finally, please note that modern computer programs, such as Excel or SPSS, quite rapidly calculate both variance and standard deviation, and largely remove the need to go through all of these steps.

There are three considerations regarding the interpretation of standard deviation.

(1) Any particular value for the standard deviation has no real intuitive meaning;
(2) It is most useful in a comparative sense;
(3) Comparing the relative values for the standard deviation and the mean indicates how much variation there is in a group of cases, relative to the average.

Skewness

Skewness illustrates the spread of scores weighted to one side of the mean. There are essentially three different patterns that may emerge from unimodal distributions: normal, positive, and negative.

A **normal distribution** (Figure 13-5) consists of scores evenly distributed throughout a distribution. In other words, there is no skewness and the spread of scores occurring before the mean is equal to those occurring after the mean. The mean, median, and mode are approximately equivalent.

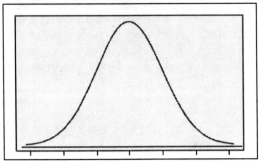

Figure 13-5: A normal distribution.

The properties of a normal distribution are:

- The normal distribution curve is bell-shaped
- The mean, median, and mode are equal and located at the center
- The curve is symmetrical about the mean
- The curve never touches the x-axis

Because the scores are evenly distributed around the mean, the area under the normal curve that lies within one standard deviation of the mean contains approximately 68% of all cases in the distribution. Approximately 95% of the cases reside within two standard deviations and approximately 99.7% of the cases lie within three standard deviations.

A **positively skewed** unimodal distribution consists of scores weighted to the left (i.e., the hump is located toward the left and the tail of the distribution moves toward the right). Its right tail is longer because a few scores have values much higher than the bulk of the distribution. The mode would be the largest value followed by the median and then the mean.

A **negatively skewed** unimodal distribution consists of scores weighted to the right (i.e., the hump is located toward the right side and the tail of the distribution moves toward the left). Its left tail is longer because a few scores have values much higher than the bulk of the distribution. Generally, the mean has a value that is larger than the median and the median value is larger than the mode value.

It is important to compare the mean, median, and mode while looking at a histogram in an attempt to determine whether the cases are normally distributed. If normal, statistical assumptions regarding the data can be made, and there is less concern over outliers distorting the mean.

In general, a normal distribution will produce essentially equal measures of central tendency while positively skewed distributions will have a larger mean and negatively skewed distributions will have a larger median. The farther apart the measures are, the more skewed the unimodal distribution is.

Whether the mean or median should be used to represent a skewed distribution depends on the nature of the data and the purpose of the research or project. If extreme scores or outliers are considered random deviations, the median should be used. When extreme scores or outliers are viewed as "normal," they should be taken into account and the mean will represent the distribution better.

Rates

Rates are used to standardize some measure for comparative purposes. Unlike raw numbers, rates allow comparison between items of different sizes. Rates are calculated by dividing raw numbers by a comparable denominator. This standardization equates raw numbers by creating rates in accordance to some baseline measure. The formula is:

$$\frac{a}{b}c = rate$$

a = raw number of occurrence
b = point of comparison (population, households, cars, individuals, etc)
c = unit of measure (10, 100, 1000, 100,00)

For example, to determine which city, Las Vegas or Miami, had a bigger problem with car theft, one method would be to compare the number of cars stolen from each city during a particular time period. According to The National Insurance Crime Bureau, Las Vegas had 15,503 cars stolen and Miami had 20,964 cars stolen in 2002. Upon inspection, one could argue that Miami has the bigger problem. Yet, this comparison may be unfair because one city may have more residents; thus, it may be assumed likewise that more cars are available to be stolen from that city.

Another method of comparison could be to standardize (increase or decrease) the number of cars stolen by creating rates based on the number of cars stolen relative to the population of each city. Using the population from the 2000 U.S. Census, the rate of stolen cars per 100,000 population would be:

Miami:

$$\frac{20,964}{2,253,370}x100,000 = 930.33$$

Las Vegas:

$$\frac{15,503}{1,563,275}x100,000 = 991.70$$

According to rates based on population, Las Vegas has approximately 61 more cars stolen per 100,000 people than Miami. Still, the denominator is important because of the complexity of comparison. For sake of argument, assume that Las Vegas and Miami are similar cities. Both are extremely popular tourist locations covering a relatively small area. Yet, more tourists rely on rental cars in Miami while tourists in Las Vegas use public transportation or walk. Moreover, perhaps more residents in Las Vegas use public transportation and residents of Miami drive their personal vehicle. Car-pooling may be another factor to consider. Another method could be to calculate the number of vehicles stolen divided by the number of vehicle registrations (while controlling for type of vehicle and type of registration).

Although rates provide for comparisons among units of unequal measure, consideration for the both the numerator and denominator is important when constructing rates and making appropriate comparisons.

Proportions, Percent, and Percent Change

A variable with only two categories is a **dichotomous** variable. With dichotomous data, the best description of central tendency is proportions. **Proportions** are the relation between two or more categories or values. In another words, a proportion is the relative frequency of a category or value. Proportions can be considered the mean of a dichotomous variable with a value range between 0 and 1.

Proportions are calculated by dividing the value of the part by the value of the whole. For example, what is the proportion of sergeants to line officers in a police agency with 15 sergeants and 60 line officers? The total number of people is 75; thus:

The proportion of sergeants would be: (15/75) = 0.20

The proportion of line officers would be: (60/75) = 0.80

If calculations were made regarding the police department as a whole given that the department consisted of 130 employees the proportions for each category would be:

The proportion of sergeants:
(15 / 130) = 0.12

The proportion of line officers:
(60 / 130) = 0.46

The proportion of other employees:
(55 / 130) = 0.42

Percentages are similar to proportions. A percentage is the mean of a dichotomous variable with values between 0 and 100. Indeed, percentages are the relation between two or more numbers for which the whole is accorded a value of 100, and the other(s) is given a numerical value corresponding to its share of the whole. Sometimes it is relevant to look at percentages to determine which part of the whole occurs the most frequent (see mode discussed earlier).

Percents are calculated by dividing the value of the part by the value of the whole and multiplying by 100. For example, what is the percent of males in a group consisting of 47 males and 28 females? The total number in the group is 75.

(47 / 75) * 100 = (0.6266666) * 100 = 62.66666 or 62.7% male

Thus, the number of males constitutes approximately 63% of the total group of people. The complement of such is that females would constitute approximately 37% membership in the group or:

(28 / 75) * 100 = (0.3733333) * 100 = 37.33333 or 37.3% female

In addition to percentages, the percent change between two time periods may provide needed information (i.e., trends). Or perhaps a policy intervention has been implemented and evaluators are interested in comparing the "before" characteristics to "after" characteristics.

Percent changes are calculated by subtracting "before" values from "after" values and then dividing the results by the original "before" values and multiplying by 100. A plus or minus sign (+/-) indicates an increase or decrease.

For example, we want to determine the percent change regarding money spent on ammunition during the first quarter of 2002 and the first quarter of 2003. Using the expense table below, the percent change would be calculated accordingly:

Quarter	Ammunition Expense
One (Jan–Mar 2002)	$ 2,650.00
Two (Apr–Jun 2002)	$ 4,740.00
Three (Jul–Sep 2002)	$ 5,100.00
Four (Oct–Dec 2002)	$ 4,330.00
One (Oct–Dec 2003)	$ 3,100.00

(3100 - 2650) / 2,650 * 100 = (450) / 2,650 * 100 = 0.1698113 * 100 = 16.98%

Percents and percent changes are popular and very useful regarding managerial reports and policy evaluations. Yet, there are two important points to consider. First, be careful comparing two time periods exclusively, especially with a long period of time elapsing in between. What may appear to be an increase or decrease over time may be derived from exceptions existing because of either one or both data points. It is suggested that trends or line charts should contain many data points in an effort to recognize fluctuations among the data.

Second, always report percents and percent changes along with their corresponding raw numbers. Otherwise, percentages may be misleading because of the instability of small numbers. For example, Police Department "A" experienced an increase in calls for service for domestic violence. The number of calls increased from one to four calls and reflects a percent increase of 300%. In comparison, Police Department "B" also experienced an increase in calls for service relating to domestic violence. Their calls increased from 1000 to 1100 calls reflecting a percent increase of 10%.

Multivariate Statistics

In the previous section we looked at ways to apply descriptive statistics to a set of data values, that is, to a *dataset*. These measures included a frequency distribution, the mode, the median, the mean, and the variance, as reflected in the standard deviation. In this section we consider the analysis of two or more variables simultaneously, looking for and assessing the strength and the potential implications of patterns of association between or among those variables.

Implicit in the datasets subjected to either *uni-* or *multi*-variate analysis is that the values, or numbers, of any variable represent consistently defined measures of some concept or entity, and that they are logically and definitionally related to each other in a

meaningful way. Otherwise, statistical measurements will be meaningless. While this point may seem obvious, it is a worthwhile practice to subject any dataset on which you are considering any kind of analysis to a series of questions to make sure everything is in order before proceeding.

It is helpful to consider a series of questions pertaining to any dataset before launching one's analytical arsenal. The first is whether the values representing the variable entity or concept are logically related to each other. Second is the data type, keeping in mind that there are statistical operations appropriate to data of each type and that use of inappropriate procedures leads to invalid results. A third question is whether the values can properly be compared directly with each other, a matter of their being based on the same standard of measurement, analogous to playing on a level playing field. The latter should come clear with an example or two. A few sample variables, each of which could be imagined to consist of some number of data values (readings, counts, measurements) are provided below to help think through the issues that have been outlined.

Dataset 1. Telephone numbers of local residents for whom arrest warrants are outstanding. We start with an easy one. Even though they look like numbers, telephone numbers are actually *nominal data*—code names using digits—and therefore are wholly unsuitable for any kind of mathematical computations or statistics. (To put them in order to facilitate searching might be useful but it would not be statistics.)

Dataset 2. Numbers of years of formal schooling completed by a number of adults arrested for any or selected types of offenses. Such measurements may be said to "operationalize" the concept of educational attainment; that is, to convert the abstraction of education into a more tangible, and measurable, format. Despite certain limitations, such as difficulties in accounting for various kinds of training programs outside the realm of K-12 school systems or colleges, such a measure can be said to be representative of educational attainment, and the data would be of the ratio type. There could be a problem, however, regarding the third criterion—that pertaining to the "level playing field." If some of the arrestees were too young they would not yet have had time to have completed as many years of formal schooling as older arrestees. (This is why the U.S. Census provides this data only for persons age 25 and over.) Amended to account only for arrestees of a minimum age the variable stands as an appropriately defined single variable for use in multivariate analysis for a variety of purposes.

Dataset 3. Numbers of motor vehicle thefts during a given year in cities with populations over 100,000. Counts of any recurring phenomenon, such as a crime type or category, can be considered valid data of the ratio type, provided the crime is defined and recorded in a reasonably similar manner in each city. However, the obvious problem here is that the sizes of cities vary over a wide range, such that the number of vehicle thefts in one city can not be fairly be compared with those in another of vastly different size. To put the cases (cities) on a level playing field it is necessary to *standardize* the dataset by converting crime *counts* to crime *rates*. It is customary to convert crime counts to rates per 100,000 persons. Use of such rates makes it possible to compare cities of varying population sizes (side-stepping issues regarding differences in data collection and coding procedures from city to city).

Dataset 4. Counts of disorderly conduct complaints (calls for service, or incidents, depending on local terminology and procedures), per month in a jurisdiction over a defined period of time. Since the geographic area remains constant, counts of disorder complaints (ratio data) constitute appropriate values of a single defined concept (however rough its definitional edges might be in practice). This variable contains a characteristic not seen in any of the preceding cases. It consists of two variables in one: counts of disorder, and intervals of time. As such, it offers a segue into the principal topic of concern here, multivariate analysis.

Statistical analysis is said to be "multivariate" in nature when two or more variables (usually, but not necessarily, of the ratio or interval type) are examined together with the focus on observable relationships, or patterns of association, between or among the variables. One of the most common venues for multivariate analysis is what we saw in Dataset 4 above: measurements of a variable over a number of intervals of time, the procedure commonly referred to as *time-series analysis* (see Chapter 11).

Given, say, 52 weekly counts of disorder calls (or any other recurring phenomenon of interest), we could determine the mean, the variance, and the standard deviation, as well as the high and low counts for the year. Thus we could report, or use in further analyses, that we have been "seeing" about 25 residential burglaries per week, "on average," plus or minus a few (based on the variance). Such descriptors may give us a better feel for the rate of occurrence of the problem, or at least make it easier to explain it to others. But would such a mean constitute a "best guess" as to the most likely approximate number of disorder complaints to be expected during the next, or 53rd, week?

Presented with such a dataset, a recommended practice is to put the data values into a spreadsheet and make a visual examination, using the "scatter diagram" graphic to plot each of the data-pairs. It is customary and useful for the sake of consistency to place time on the x-axis and the measurements of the principal variable on the y-axis. Because our data here represent accumulated counts over intervals of a week, a bar chart can be used to make the chart easier to read. (Later we will see reason to return to the scatter of points as the preferred technique for analytical work.)

Figure 13-6 shows, in the form of a vertical bar chart, a portrayal of 52 weeks of complaint calls pertaining to disorderly conduct. What is immediately obvious is that the data are not forming anything like a straight line. Instead, the shape of the line appears to suggest a seasonal effect, presumably reflecting underlying factors associated with the longer and warmer days of summer, such as a greater tendency for people to be outside, engaging in activities that sometimes lead some to go too far, resulting in calls to police regarding disorderly conduct (or loud parties, disturbances, and the like). This kind of seasonal pattern might be more prevalent in cities of more northerly climate where harsher winters may suppress some of the "street action" of the warmer months.

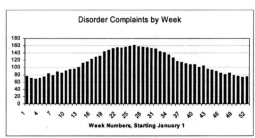

Figure 13-6: A bar chart of disorderly conduct over 52 weeks

Recalling the question posed earlier as to the usefulness of the mean (and the variance) of the 52 values, it is evident now that if we were to use the mean as the central tendency of a projection forward by one or a few weeks, we would be projecting as if it were early April! The procedural error causing

such a mishap would have resulted from the false assumption of linearity—that is, that the data values laid out over time would form a more or less straight line. They didn't, and they often do not. In the world of "societal phenomena" such as crime and disorder, various kinds of non-linear patterns of association are probably more numerous and of greater value than are linear patterns (see Chapter 11 for a further discussion of these concepts as they related to time).

Regression Analysis

In time-series analysis, the essential question is whether, and to what degree, there is a basic underlying trend at work. That is, do the known data values suggest the presence of some mythical trendline running *through* the scatter of data points, even if seldom actually touching, or passing directly through, any of the individual points on the graph. If such a trendline can be discovered and plotted, and if that line is found to be of sufficient quality as a representation of the pattern of the points, then it can be said to have a degree of predictive capability.

In essence, regression analysis is a procedure for pattern recognition—one of the principal goals of crime analysis. Even if the crime analyst seldom encounters an opportunity to conduct full-scale regression analysis, an elementary understanding of its concepts and place in the world of scientific analysis should prove valuable if for no other reason that to help hone one's thinking skills.

Regression and *correlation analysis* are two sides of the same coin. Regression locates the best line through the points and shows you what it looks like; correlation tells you how strong the association is and to what extent you can draw inferences from it. Given a strong enough pattern of association, a regression line suggests, as will be seen, possibilities for predicting future values.

The trendline seen in the disorder complaints data of Figure 13-6 would be called *non-linear*, and the statistical and algebraic methods used to determine the best approximation of that trendline would be referred to as *non-linear functions*. The most likely non-linear function underlying the seasonal effect in Figure 13-6 is what is known as the *sine* (or "sine wave") function. The sine function is represented in the rhythmic patterns of the seasons in response to the movement of the earth around the sun and the tilt of its axis.

A linear function is one in which the data points—that is, the junctions of the x and y coordinates—approximate more or less a straight line. A non-linear function is one in which the data points approximate some curved shape *that can be expressed by a known algebraic formula.* Not surprisingly, the algebra involved in some non-linear functions can get somewhat complex, quickly exceeding the limits of this introductory inquiry, but linear functions are comparatively simple. So we will focus here primarily on linear analysis, with an occasional glimpse into the non-linear arena. One crawls before walking, and walks before running.

Linear Regression: Procedures and Formulas

The objective of regression analysis is to find the "best line through the points." Therefore, the objective of linear regression is to find the best *straight* line through the points. This line is the one that, compared with all other possible locations, has the smallest *variance*, reflecting the gaps between the actual placement of the data points on the graph and the corresponding locations (per value of x) on the best straight line. More precisely, the location of the regression line is that which minimizes the sum of the squared

deviations—that is to say, the variance. (Note the similarity to the variance around the mean of a single variable, the square root of which was called the standard deviation.)

Consider each of the two "scattergrams" shown in Figures 13-7 and 13-8, each of which represents a series of data values, which are not shown and which are unimportant for present purposes.

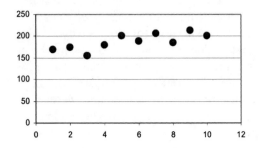

Figure 13-7: A scattergram with limited variance

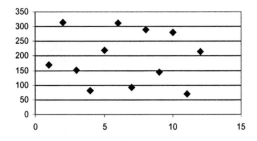

Figure 13-8: A scattergram with large variance

In both cases, a best straight line can be plotted through the points. In the case of Figure 13-7, it shouldn't be hard to imagine about where it would lie, and it might be fairly "realistic" and useful, but Figure 13-8 is a different matter. Although a "best" straight line can be found for 13-8, it is not likely to be of much value, given the large deviations of so many of the points from any such line. Figure 13-9 shows the result:

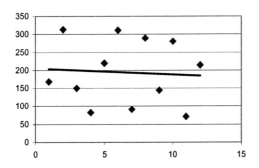

Figure 13-9: Figure 13-8 with a dubious trend line

The algebraic formula for a straight line is:

$$y = mX + b$$

Where:

m is a constant, known as the *coefficient of slope*, used as a multiplier of the value of *X*.

b is a constant representing the *y intercept*, that is the location on the y-axis where the line intercepts, which is to say the value of *y* when *X* = 0.

If *m* is found to be 1.35, then an increase in X of 1.0 will result in a corresponding increase in Y of 1.35. Thus, with reference to the

scales used on the x- and y-axes, the slope of the regression line is represented by *m*. Where the line of this slope sits on the graph is determined by the y-intercept. So the problem now is to solve for *m* and *b*. Brace yourself; here comes the math. But it's really not so bad:

$$m = \frac{n\sum xy - \sum x \sum y}{n\sum x^2 - (\sum x)^2}$$

where *n* is the number of data points (or value-pairs)

$$b = \frac{\sum y - m\sum x}{n}$$

Now let's solve one, using the data that underlay Figure 13-7, pertaining to residential burglaries. In Figure 13-10, we have used a Microsoft Excel spreadsheet to calculate the appropriate figures—see Chapter 18 for more information about spreadsheets.

(We could have used actual years, such as 1994–2003, in place of 1–10, but this way we have smaller numbers to work with. The actual numbers do not matter as long as they "scale" properly.)

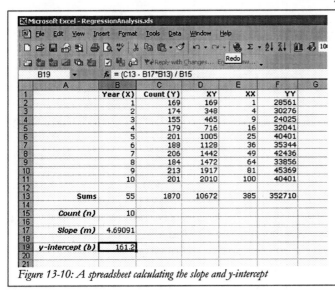

The formulas used in the spreadsheet are as follows:

D2	=B2*C2
E2	=B2*B2
F2	=C2*C2
B13	=sum(B2:B11)
B15	=count(B2:B11)
B17	=(B15*D13-b13*c13) / (B15*E13-b13*b13)
B19	=(C13-B17*B13)/B15

Figure 13-10: A spreadsheet calculating the slope and y-intercept

The slope of our data set is 4.6909 and the y-intercept is 161.2. The location of the trend line for any given year (i.e., the value of X) is:

$$4.6909 * X + 161.2$$

The predicted value for years 11 and 12 are thus:

$$4.6909 * 11 + 161.2 = 212.7999$$
$$4.6909 * 12 + 161.2 = 217.4908$$

Performing this calculation for each of the values of X allows us to create the regression line:

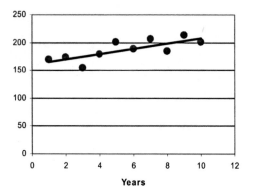

Figure 13-11: The regression line resulting from the calculations in Figure 13-10.

It was noted earlier that the regression formula operates to find the set of points (in this case linearly aligned) which minimizes the squared deviations of the actual from the predicted values of Y. Also recall from the previous section on descriptive statistics the concept of the variance around the mean: the mean sum of the squared deviations. In the case of a regression line, the variance is essentially the same thing, except that the deviations that are squared are those from the actual points to the predicted points along the y-axis for each value of X. Thus, the regression line takes the place of the mean in univariate analysis. Noting that the standard deviation was the square root of the

variance in the case of a single variable, the *standard error*, or *standard error of estimate*, is the square root of the variance in the case of regression. Clearly, the larger the standard error of the estimate, the less the accuracy, or quality, of the regression line, and the less the reliability of projections of future values.

In Microsoft Excel, adding a trendline to a scatter diagram (as in Figure 13-11) is a simple matter of right-clicking on one of the data points and choosing "Add Trendline." The program allows numerous types of trendlines, including the linear trendline we have demonstrated here. There are also options to see the equation and its results (as well as the R-squared value, which is covered below). Although a spreadsheet program can thus create a trendline without requiring analysts to know how to calculate the values themselves, it is important for to understand how the underlying process works.

Notice also our regression line extends beyond the highest value of x to Year 11 (another option that Excel gives; it's called "forecast forward"). This suggests the capacity of a regression line to project into the future, and it reflects the fact that the essence of mathematical projection is regression analysis. But, as previously noted, the matter of the quality, or reliability, of the projection remains to be considered.

Beyond Time Series Data

Regression analysis is by no means limited to time-series data. In fact, it is very common for two (or more) ratio-interval variables to be examined together to determine not only their trendline (linear or otherwise) but also the *degree of association* between or among them—that is, their *correlation*. To maintain a degree of simplicity in this introductory treatment of multivariate analysis, we will mention that one can conduct these procedures on three or more variables at once, suggest that the reader proceed to other sources as interested, and then restrain ourselves here to the analysis of simple pairs of variables. When three or more variables are involved, the procedures get a bit more complex, although software can handle the problem with ease, and all the user has to do is to understand the underlying nature of the process.

Usually, in the kinds of analyses that employ regression and correlation, one variable is conceived of as *dependent* on values of the other, the *independent* variable, as if following from it, with the possible, and often misleading, appearance of causality. There is a bit of an anomaly to be considered here: in regression analysis, we structure the research in such a way as to suggest, or look for the possibility of, causality—as if to say at least that "y appears to follow from x" to one degree or another. Yet it is not possible to determine causality merely from an observed pattern of association. The main reason for this is that there may be other factors "beneath the surface," that is, outside the realm of the immediate analysis, which are contributing to the values of the dependent variable, aside from the one established as the independent variable. Furthermore, it is possible that some "third force" is actually contributing to (or causing) the values of both of the variables under examination.

A final important observation: The ordinary course of events in the scientific process is to collect the necessary data (and enough of it to support valid findings) and to proceed with a testable *hypothesis* stating the relationship expected to be found, why it is expected, and its significance. Thus is established the purpose and meaning of the analysis. A brief example should help clarify the notions of independent and dependent variables in the context of a hypothesized finding.

Consider the relationship between the heights of a group of fathers and the heights of their sons. For reasons pertaining to heredity, we hypothesize that there will be a strong, positive relationship between the two, but one that leaves ample room for other contributing factors (such as Mom's genes, diet, and other health-related factors). The heights of the fathers will serve as the independent variable (x-axis), and the heights of the sons as the dependent (y-axis), for obvious reasons of *possible* cause-and-effect. The cases will be limited to one son to a father, and the sons must be age 18 or older in order to assure that they have had a chance to grow to full height.

Figure 13-12 shows the dataset for 12 father-son pairs (which, it should be noted, is wholly fabricated), along with the scatter diagram.

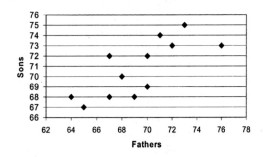

Figure 13-12: A scatter diagram comparing heights of fathers to heights of sons.

Can you imagine the location of the linear regression line through this scatter of points? Do you think the "fit," or degree of association of the points, will be as strong as it was in the previous example concerning residential burglaries?

Figure 13-13 shows the same graphic with the fitted linear regression line. The equation for the line was found to be:

$$Y = 0.6062*X + 28.719$$

Heights of Fathers and Sons

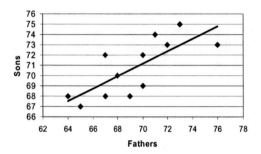

Figure 13-13: Figure 13-12 with a linear trendline

Recalling that these data are not real, we note that the parameters *m* and *b* suggest that for every inch in height of the fathers, the sons add just over 0.6 inches, but they begin with a "jumpstart" of nearly 29 inches. This being the case, what would you expect (as a best guess, plus or minus some range of values) would be the height of the son if a father who was 78 inches tall were added to the set? (Answer: Y = 0.6061*78 + 28.7 = 80 inches, or 6 feet 8 inches tall)

The matter of the reliability of the estimate remains to be examined; that is, the concept of correlation. Before turning to correlation analysis, however, let's take one more look at the father-and-sons data to open our analytical framework to encompass just a glimpse of non-linear analysis.

Looking back at the points in Figure 13-12, it seems feasible that there might be a better line through the points, one that is not linear (although such a line hardly seems likely to vary much from straight, given the appearance of the scatter of points). In Microsoft Excel, if you right-click on any of the data points and select "Add Trendline," you will see a number of options for non-

linear functions.[1] Figure 13-14 shows the result obtained when we select the polynomial function. Note that the line is gently curved such that as the fathers' heights increase so too do the sons', but at a decreasing rate.

Heights of Fathers and Sons

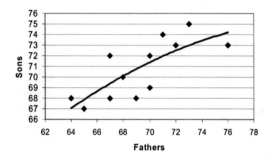

Figure 13-14: Figure 13-12 with a polynomial trendline

The formula for the polynomial equation is:

$$y = ax^2 + bx + c$$

The calculations derived by Excel for this example are:

$$y = -0.0216x^2 + 3.6211x - 76.2$$

This time the projected height of the son of a 78-inch-tall father is only 74.8 inches.

So which is the better way to go? Which regression function better expresses the relationship between the fathers and the sons? The answer lies in the "r-squared" values of each alternative, and r-squared is determined by correlation analysis.

---

[1] A little experimentation here won't hurt anything and you might begin to make sense of what is going on, especially if you examine the formulas which are displayed on the graphic when you check the designated boxes under the Options tab. Consult a statistics or algebra text, or do a little searching and reading online to explore some of these functions.

Correlation Analysis

Correlation measures the relative "fit," or degree of association, between two variables, or among three or more variables. This technique provides a measure of the quality of the regression line, and therefore of the reliability of any predictions based on it.

The method usually employed to measure the correlation of ratio or interval variables is known, after its author, as *Pearson's product-moment coefficient of correlation*, and is symbolized by the letter *r*. The formula for Pearson's *r* appears somewhat daunting at first, but like those for the *m* and *b* parameters of the regression line, it is not so bad when translated into spreadsheet format:

$$r = \frac{n\sum xy - \sum x \sum y}{\sqrt{(n\sum x^2 - (\sum x)^2)(n\sum y^2 - (\sum y)^2)}}$$

Looking back at the example dealing with residential burglaries, and at the simulate spreadsheet in Figure 13-10, we need now to add two cell formulas to enable us to solve for Pearson's *r*, as in Figure 13-15.

That's still a pretty awesome formula. But it's important.

Pearson's *r* operates within a range of 1.0, for a perfect (one-for-one) relationship in the positive direction (the higher the X the higher the Y), and -1.0, which is a perfect negative correlation (higher X, lower Y). A zero means no correlation at all, which is very unlikely because almost every conceivable pair of variables would show at least a slight, chance correlation. In general, a correlation approaching 1.0 (or -1.0) indicates a strong pattern of association, but how high is high? We need a way to link the *r scores* of the technique to something more tangible. The answer lies in the square of Pearson's *r*, the *r-square* indicator mentioned earlier.

Known as the *coefficient of determination*, *r-squared* represents the proportion of the variation in Y that is "explained" by the variations in X. Thus if r = 0.8, r-squared is 0.64, which translates as "64 percent of the variation in Y is explained by X." The other 36 percent is left to the influence of other factors.

Microsoft Excel - Correlation.xls

B19 =C13*C13

	A	B	C	D	E	F
1		Year (X)	Count (Y)	XY	XX	YY
2		1	169	169	1	28561
3		2	174	348	4	30276
4		3	155	465	9	24025
5		4	179	716	16	32041
6		5	201	1005	25	40401
7		6	188	1128	36	35344
8		7	206	1442	49	42436
9		8	184	1472	64	33856
10		9	213	1917	81	45369
11		10	201	2010	100	40401
12						
13	Sums	55	1870	10672	385	352710
14						
15	Count	10				
16						
17	$(\Sigma x)^2$	3025				
18						
19	$(\Sigma y)^2$	3496900				
20						
21	*r*	0.77532				

The formulas used in the spreadsheet are as follows:

B17	=B13*B13
B19	=C13*C13
B21	=(B15*D13-B13*C13)/ SQRT((B15*E13-B17)* (B15*F13-B19))

However, these were only used to illustrate how the equation above translates to Excel. Excel actually has a function called CORREL that calculates Pearson's *r* based on the cell ranges of the two variables. In this case, we would have used:

=CORREL(b2:b11,c2:c11)

Figure 13-15: A spreadsheet calculating Pearson's r

In the case of our earlier example concerning residential burglaries, the correlation coefficient, Pearson's *r*, was 0.775, yielding a coefficient of determination (r-squared) of 0.601, which can be interpreted as about 60 percent of the variance being "explained" by the independent variable. But obviously the passage of time, the x-axis variable here, can not be said to have "caused" the change in the number of burglaries; whatever causes more or fewer burglaries to occur, it certainly is not time itself. During the ten-year period many things might have changed in our community, including its total population. (Bear in mind that the use of burglary *rates* theoretically would have precluded a rise attributable to increased population, but between the takings of the decennial census it is difficult to gauge population change from one year to the next.)

In the case of the heights of the fathers and the sons, we looked at both a linear and a non-linear regression line. The r-squared values were 0.5749 for the linear and 0.5861 for the polynomial function, the curvilinear function "winning by a nose," although the difference would have to be called insignificant, especially in a computation based on so few cases. Thus, some 57-59 percent of the variance of the heights of the sons was attributable to the heights of their fathers, leaving the rest to the genes of their mothers, diet, and other environmental factors.

Regression analysis seeks the general pattern evident in observations on phenomena, including crime or disorder trends, relationships between socio-economic circumstances and behaviors, and other varied and complex aspects of the domain of the crime analyst. Regression involves pattern recognition and clear, if not quite perfect, placement of the pattern on a trendline, whether straight or curved in accordance

with some other mathematical function. Its partner, correlation analysis, tells us how strong the association is and to what extent we can assume it to be meaningful, useful, and reliable.

We have focused here primarily on linear functions because they are easier to comprehend and serve better to get one "up and running" in the intriguing theoretical landscape of regression analysis. But non-linear relationships are more common and are almost surely more essential to our understanding of the phenomena around us. As a way of encouraging the reader to use available texts, online sources, or even college courses to follow this introduction to the study of regression analysis (a.k.a. pattern recognition), we close with three examples of non-linear functions thought to be of particular interest.

First, the time-growth of money invested at a constant rate of interest, a common example of the exponential growth function. Figure 13-16 shows the growth over twenty years of $1000 invested at 10 percent. The inverse of such a curve would be the declining principle on a mortgage over the life of the payments.

$1000 at 10 percent, Annual Compounding

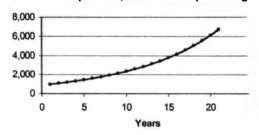

Figure 13-16: An exponential growth curve

Another very important, although lesser known, non-linear function is the "logistic" curve. In Figure 13-17, one can see the pattern of gradual takeoff, followed by a period of exponential increase, then a

298

slowing, or deceleration, of the rate of growth, until eventually a new and higher level is approached. Among the candidates for this pattern of curvilinear change are children growing to full height, the populations of metropolitan areas over the decades of their coming to maturity, and the diffusion of new technologies. In crime analysis, as well as other aspects of sociology, the logistic growth curve is often the better presumption to make regarding long-term change than is any kind of straight-line or, especially, exponential function. Thus, if something is increasing rapidly (a population, a crime rate), its growth rate is more likely to peak, slow down, and level off than it is to expand interminably. (Otherwise we'd have lots of cities with populations in the billions.)

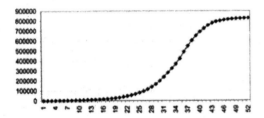

Figure 13-17: A logistic curve

Finally, Figure 13-18 shows the sine wave function mentioned earlier in the context of an apparent seasonal effect in a set of disorder counts.

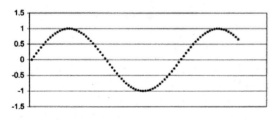

Figure 13-18: A sine wave function

Remember that each type of function consists essentially of a mathematical equation. So if the math doesn't scare you away, online sources that can get you going in these directions may be no more than a click away in your favorite search engine.

Conclusion

Whether making simple descriptions of the central tendency of various factors in a series ("the average time for the incidents is 15:33; 70% have occurred between 15:00 and 16:00") or using regression analysis to help forecast next year's call-for-service level, descriptive and multivariate statistics play an enormous role in crime analysis. Analysts' crime bulletins and annual reports overflow with averages, medians, modes, rates, percent changes, and correlations. Most often, these tools are used correctly, but sometimes they are used questionably, thus breeding questionable conclusions and questionable recommendations. A solid understanding of both descriptive and inferential statistics is crucial to good analysis and good decision-making.

Also crucial, however, is the need to reflect on, analyze, and interpret statistics. Always remember that crime analysis is a sociological field, and in sociology, all data, to some extent, is qualitative. A statistic is a foundation, not a product, of analysis. We encourage analysts to use this chapter hand-in-hand with Chapter 10 and Chapter 8 to properly understand how the ability to calculate and apply statistics fits into the wider spectrum of the modern analyst's work.

14
Inferential Statistics

Paul Tracy
Donald R. Dixon

This chapter covers the use of inferential statistics in crime analysis. It discusses the process of statistical inference and how the use of sampling allows analysts to conduct research that produces statistically valid inferences about crime that may be generalized to the city or county level. Since inferential statistics involve sampling, the chapter also addresses the various techniques for drawing random samples and the comparative strengths of these sampling designs. The chapter also illustrates the use of sampling to draw inferences about crime rates across census tracts.

Inference Measures

Generally, researchers use two types of statistical measures: descriptive and inferential. As you learned in Chapter 13, descriptive statistics are just what the name implies: measures that describe data in terms of the frequency with which a variable occurs, percentage distributions, measures of central tendency like the mean, and measures of dispersion around the mean like the variance or standard deviation. Descriptive statistics are thus used to describe the basic features of the data in a study. They provide simple summaries about the sample and the measures. Together with simple graphical analysis, they form the foundation of virtually every quantitative analysis of data.

Inferential statistics, on the other hand, have a different purpose: they are concerned with making decisions about a population (e.g., a city, or a unit of time like a calendar month or a quarter) by collecting and analyzing data based on a sample from the population. Inferential statistics thus lead to a concern about the statistical significance of sample results. Specifically, the pressing question confronting the crime analyst is: could the sample results have occurred by chance, or do they indicate differences that would be obtained if the entire population had been investigated and not just a particular sample?

Thus, with inferential statistics, a researcher tries to reach conclusions that extend beyond the immediate sample data—that is, to draw inferences from sample data concerning what the scores in the entire population might be. Or, a researcher can use inferential statistics to make judgments about the probability that an observed difference between sample groups is a reliable one, or alternatively a difference that might have happened just by chance. Therefore, a researcher uses inferential statistics to draw inferences from sample data to more general conditions, while a her or she uses descriptive statistics simply to describe what's going on in the data.

Crime analysts might wonder at this point why they would need to use inferential statistics, since much of the time they have available their entire populations of crime measures. For example, an analyst might have all the burglaries or robberies for the prior year, or offenders arrested for driving under the influence or some other offense type. Since crime analysts seemingly have all the data, they could legitimately question the need for a sample, which in turn raises a further question about why the need for inferential statistics at all. Clearly, this is a legitimate and important concern that must be addressed so as to avoid possible confusion between description and inference.

Inferential measures are primarily designed to help crime analysts when performing research studies that are sample-based and involve offender interviews or community surveys. Here, because a sample was used, inference measures are clearly necessary. For example, a crime analyst would use inferential statistics to infer the habits of *all* of a city's residential burglars, based on interviews with just a sample of them. Other prime occasions for the use of inference measures would be studying: (1) crime patterns across an entire city based on data from a sample of police reporting districts; or (2) the crime rate for an entire year based on a sample of months.

Thus, inference measures are only needed when a crime analyst has only partial data available, as is the case whenever a sample is involved. When an analyst has a complete enumeration of the relevant crime measures being studied, inference measures are not necessary. For the remainder of this chapter, therefore, it will be assumed that the analyst decides to draw a sample on purpose, or has only partial data available for analysis.

Sampling
Population

A "population" is the theoretical universe or aggregation of units from which a sample of units or elements could be drawn, or it represents the level of aggregation to which the researcher wants to generalize the results. The definition of a research population must stem from a careful specification of how membership is determined in explicit terms.

Study Population (or Survey Population)

Because a "population" is a theoretical or hypothetical universe of elements, a researcher seldom has the ability to ensure that each and every member of the population actually has a chance of being selected for inclusion in a sample. Thus, the study or research population is more

realistically that aggregation of elements from the population from which the sample is actually selected. For the crime analyst, this is a very straightforward issue. The study population usually involves an entire city or county, or in the case of a survey, the study population could be the resident population in the jurisdiction of relevance.

Sampling Unit

A "sampling unit" is that element or set of elements that forms the basis of selection. In a simple, single-stage sample, the sampling units are the same as the elements. But, in more complex samples, different levels of sampling units may be present. The researcher might begin with census tracts, then list the blocks contained therein, then enumerate the households within a block, and finally, draw a sample of adult respondents in the households.

Sampling Frame

The "sampling frame" is the actual list of sampling units from which the actual sample (or some stage of the sample) will be selected.

Observation Unit / Unit of Analysis

The observation unit, or unit of analysis, is that element or aggregation of elements from which data will be collected and analyzed. Thus, these two units may be the same, but not always. For example, the observation unit may be a particular adult in a household from whom data are collected about the entire family, which is the real unit of analysis.

Sampling Designs
Simple Random Sample

Simple random sampling is the most basic method of selecting a sample from a sampling frame. A simple random sample is one that is selected in such a manner that every member of the population from which the sample is being drawn has an equal chance of being chosen. Each selection is independent of any other selection, and at any given point in the selection process, all the remaining units have an equal probability of being picked. A simple random sample is selected by: (1) listing all the members of the larger target population; (2) setting the size of the sample; and (3) assigning a consecutive number to each member of the target population. Using a table of random numbers select the sample by taking numbers in succession from the table until the pre-set sample size has been obtained. For example, to choose a sample of 30 out of 100 patrol beats or police districts, consult a table of random numbers and select the first 30 different numbers between 001 and 100.

Systematic Random Sample

A simple random sample is seldom used in practice as it is not the most efficient method. It can be rather laborious if done by hand because it requires a complete enumeration of the sampling frame. Because of this, a systematic sample is often preferred.

Systematic random sampling (sometimes called interval random sampling) is very similar to simple random sampling. To draw a systematic sample, the researcher begins by using an existing master list of the members of the population (e.g., census tracts, blocks, or households) or developing such a list. The researcher then sets the basic interval by dividing the total number of units in the population by the pre-set size of the sample. To illustrate, if the researcher wants to select a sample of 100 persons from a population of 1,000, the basic interval would be 10. Once the interval is set, he or she selects at random (from a book of random numbers or by other appropriate techniques) a number (n) falling

within the designated interval. The sample is drawn by selecting every nth unit. Suppose that in the above example (a sample of 100 from a population of 1,000) the seventh person was selected. Then the sample would consist of numbers 7, 17, 27, 37, and so on.

Systematic sampling offers an alternative to simple random sampling. It is especially appropriate whenever a list is extremely long (e.g., a city directory or telephone book) or whenever a large sample is to be chosen. As with other types of sampling, the researcher should examine the master list carefully, determine how it was formed, and know the possible biases in the listing. This is important because systematic sampling may have problems. It assumes that there is no particular order to the elements as depicted in the sampling frame. This ordering is often referred to as "periodicity." In the event that periodicity is present in the sampling frame, a systematic sample may be biased because certain units are under-represented while others are over-represented.

Stratified Random Sampling

Stratified random sampling is an alternative method of drawing either a simple random sample or a systematic sample. Through a process of stratifying or classifying the elements in the sampling frame, a more representative sample may be achieved because the researcher divides the target population into categories of relatively homogeneous sub-populations. The researcher then draws independent random samples from within each of these strata or categories. In effect, the population is subdivided in accordance with theoretically or substantively meaningful categories. Each of the categories, or sample strata, itself represents a sampling frame and the selection of elements proceeds as in simple random sampling or systematic random sampling.

One important reason that a researcher should consider using a stratified sampling design is that there may be strong theoretical rationale that specific characteristics of the population may have an effect on the dependent variables being studied. A stratified sample insures representation of these important characteristics. Another reason for stratifying rather than taking a simple random sample is that a smaller number of cases can be drawn to achieve the same degree of accuracy (error rate). This is an important consideration because the smaller sample size required by stratified random sampling can reduce costs, sometimes substantially. Random sampling, by whatever method, is guided by concerns about sampling error. Sampling error can be reduced through: (1) drawing a larger sample or (2) using homogenous groupings or "strata" of a heterogeneous population.

Cluster Sampling

Cluster sampling is like stratified sampling because the study population is divided into unique and non-overlapping groups before sampling. But, in cluster sampling, the groups are naturally occurring units like census tracts or blocks as compared to stratified sampling where clusters are assumed to be homogeneous. The clusters form the sampling units and clusters are chosen randomly. If each member within the cluster is part of data collection, then the sampling method is known as single stage. If, however, another sample of units is taken from each selected cluster, then the sampling process is referred to as two-stage, which raises the principle of "multistage" sampling.

Multistage

Multistage sampling involves the repetition of two basic sampling concepts: listing and sampling. The example given previously (i.e.,

census tracts then blocks then households then a sample of adult respondents) is a multistage cluster sample. In multistage sampling the researcher must be concerned with the issue of selection probability. That is, the researcher must recognize that sampling can be either proportionate to size or disproportionate. One should not give all clusters an equal chance of selection if they are of unequal sizes. Similarly, in a two-stage or three-stage design, subsequent sampling must take the size of the sampling units into account. As a general rule, it is best to sample "proportionate to size." If, however, there are research-based needs to use a non-equal chance of selection (e.g., to ensure that underrepresented elements are included in the sample), then disproportionate sampling with weighting can be used.

Statistical Inference

After examining data using the descriptive methods described in Chapter 13, the researcher should, when appropriate and meaningful, perform tests of statistical inference. These statistical tests (including t-tests, f-tests, chi-square tests), based on mathematical probability theory, are called tests of statistical significance. Tests of statistical significance are predicated on the fact that the data have been obtained from a sample and that inferences are to be made from sample data to a larger population to which the researcher wants to generalize. Any time you examine sample data and want to reach conclusions about the population from which the sample was drawn, significance testing is necessary. A sample is only a partial reflection of the population, and whenever there is random variability in the sample there is always the possibility that the observed results represent nothing other than chance coincidence. Unless and until that possibility is rigorously evaluated, no conclusions can reasonably be drawn from a sample, one way or the other. Statistical significance is the mathematical means by which this evaluation is accomplished. This is far and away the most commonly encountered question of inferential statistics within the various fields of scientific research. If a researcher has sample data drawn from the real world, with all its complexities and interrelated causes and effects, how confident can he or she be that the sample results signify anything more than mere chance, mere random coincidence, or the luck of the scientific draw?

Thus, the purposes of tests of significance are twofold. First, they permit a determination of whether the statistical results of the particular project (that is, the differences between mean values, proportions or rates, correlations, and so on) under consideration are important and whether the findings can be generalized to the population. Second, statistical tests provide a basis for inference beyond the specific study—how likely are the results to be similar, within certain prescribed boundaries, if the study was conducted again in the same way, with the same factors operating, and with the same sampling parameters. A few of the common uses of significance testing are as follows:

- Test differences between measures of central tendency (usually the mean) for the project and comparison groups (tests can also be made among means of several groups to determine overall differences and between pairs of means);

- Test differences between or among percentages, proportions, and rates for project and comparisons;

- Test measures of association as well as differences between measures of association; and

- Test the direction and rate of change (slope) of trends (or differences between project and comparisons in direction or slope).

Some common statistical methods and tests, like the t-test or z-test, are used to test differences between two descriptive statistics such as means, rates, or proportions. The f-test is used along with analysis of variance to test differences among several sample means as well as the statistical significance of multiple regression and the slope and direction of trends. For discrete variables expressing group membership, the chi-square test measures the "goodness of fit" between a distribution of scores and a hypothetical distribution (e.g., whether the given distribution approximates a "normal" curve). Formulas, derivations, and the proper use of these and other tests of statistical significance can be found in most statistics textbooks.

The results of statistical significance tests are given as probabilities. Level of significance is the probability that the findings being tested are not true findings; that is, that differences between means or percentages are "really" zero, that the correlation is "really" zero. The significance level is expressed as a probability figure, such as .01, .05, and .10. These numbers refer to the chances of 1 in 100, 5 in 100, or 10 in 100 that the results (differences, measures of association, or slope of a trend line) are not true; that they are zero because they could have occurred by chance. The lower the probability value, the higher the level of statistical significance. Another way of expressing this is "level of confidence," which is the reverse of the significance level. It is usually stated as a percentage, which represents the probability that the findings are "true." For example, if the significance level were .001, the confidence level would be 99.9 percent. If the significance were .05, the level of confidence would be 95 percent.

When we talk about "true" and "not true" findings, we are concerned with what is called in statistical analysis the "null hypothesis." Most null hypotheses state that the differences between groups are really zero. In essence the researcher is saying that there are no differences or in other words that the sample results are not indicative of a larger population. If the tests show a high level of significance (the level used is arbitrary and depends on many factors), we reject the null hypothesis. Statistical tests thus provide evidence for or against the null hypothesis. The level of statistical significance thus becomes the probability that this null hypothesis is true (e.g., that the difference is at least 5 percent). In social science most researchers use .05 as the typical significance value. The significance value is related to the chances of making a Type I vs. a Type II error when testing hypotheses. The layout below shows the characteristics of Type I vs. Type II error situations.

Type I and Type II Error

Real Situation

H$_0$ (null hypothesis) true	H$_0$ is false
H1 (alternative hypothesis) false	H$_1$ is true
There is no difference	There is a difference

Decision	Our Theory is Wrong	Our Theory is Correct
Situation 1		
Accept null hypothesis (H$_0$)	No Error	Type II Error
We think there is no relationship, or our theory is wrong		
Situation 2		
Reject the null hypothesis (H$_0$)	Type I Error	No Error
We think there is a relationship, or our theory is correct		

Finally, an important but often neglected aspect of statistical testing, and one that may be very relevant to decision making, concerns confidence intervals. Confidence intervals are ranges of values around the sample statistic within which the "true" or population value lies. Testing the statistical significance of a sample value such as a measure of association or a difference between means or proportions provides a probability estimate concerning whether the sample value represents a population value of zero. This is testing the null hypothesis about that finding. By looking at confidence intervals, another dimension is added to statistical estimation. This dimension gives one an estimate of the range of values that can be expected given replications of the study drawing from the same population represented by the sample. Thus, a range of differences between means or proportions, a range of values of a measure of association or a range of slopes of trend lines can be determined.

For example, a project designed to reduce crime by implementing a new patrol regimen results in a 17 percent difference in favor of the project areas as compared to a comparison group. A confidence interval provides a range of values around the finding of 17 percent within which one could expect replications of the same project using samples from the same population (assuming most threats to internal and external validity have been controlled in the sample). A decision maker would be able to base decisions on more than whether the finding was a "true" finding (not zero), but on a possible range of findings that may be expected from future projects. The information from confidence intervals can be used along with cost data, *a priori* standards, the magnitude of the findings and other factors to make more enlightened decisions.

The size of the confidence interval around a sample finding varies. The narrower the range, the lower the probability that the population value lies within that range and vice versa. The confidence interval has a confidence level, that is, any range around the sample finding has a probability that the population value lies within that interval. Thus, the wider the interval, the higher the confidence level, since the population value is more likely to lie within a wide range than a narrow range around the sample value. However, for purposes of knowledge and decisions, the more narrow the interval the more information about the sample and the better the prediction of future results with samples from the same population. To illustrate, if the hypothetical project on crime reduction, mentioned above, with a 17 percent difference between project areas and comparison groups, shows a confidence interval of 13 percent to 21 percent, you have a better basis for making a decision than if the interval was 4 percent to 30 percent. The latter interval would provide more uncertainty about results of future projects than the former, if both intervals had the same confidence level. At times, given the findings from a project, decision makers may be faced with alternative ways of looking at the same data in terms of a narrower confidence interval with a lower confidence level or a wider confidence interval with a higher confidence level. The size of the confidence interval, given any particular confidence level for that interval, is based on: (1) the variability in the sample that is used to estimate the variability in the population; and (2) the size of the sample (which is also related to the estimate of variability).

As a researcher, it would be useful to present findings for which inferential statistics are calculated in terms of confidence intervals for various confidence levels as an aid to decision making. The significance level or confidence level used to decide whether a finding is meaningful is arbitrary and depends on many factors including educated guesses. In social science, the .05 significance level (95 percent confidence level) is usually used to reject the null hypothesis. Lower confidence levels are generally taken as not indicative of "true" findings (null hypothesis is accepted). However, these levels are arbitrary. They have no absolute mathematical truth. In criminal justice evaluation, you cannot arbitrarily determine the correct or right level of significance to use in order to make positive decisions about a project or program. Each project and decision context is different. It would be a mistake to automatically use any one significance level, such as .05 or better, to determine that a project's objectives have or have not been achieved for all projects. The level of significance should not be the only evaluative data input into the decision making process. It is also important to determine: (1) the extent to which results can be attributed to project activities (i.e., resolve threats to validity); (2) the size or magnitude of differences favoring success; (3) program costs; and (4) other support for the quantitative results such as qualitative findings. All these factors should be part of decisions and subsequent recommendations.

For use in decision making about projects, statistical data should supply more information than whether the results were statistically significant at some particular level of confidence. But statistical significance is not always the same as practical significance. There are instances in which a high level of statistical significance would not necessarily imply continuation or expansion of a project, and instances in which a low level of significance may nevertheless have such implications. In using statistical significance as a basis for decision about a project, observe two important cautions must be observed. First, the generalization of findings from the sample (the project being evaluated) to the larger population is dependent on the similarity (or representativeness) of the sample to that population and to the circumstances within which the project took place. Second, statistical significance does not offer incontrovertible proof in a logical, mathematical or empirical sense that what was assumed or hypothesized to lead to the findings was the actual cause.

Any project is only a sample. Results thus occur at a specific time, in a specific place, in a particular context, and with a specific set of factors that influenced results. Any inferences made by the use of statistical tests are limited by the similarity (in terms of the population being served, the project activities, and other influencing factors) of the sample to the situation to which one wishes to generalize. Statistical significance does not automatically allow the inference that if the project is continued or conducted in some other place, the results would be the same (within the confidence interval) as the sample.

For example, a study shows faster response time for calls for service in an experimental police patrol area over that of a comparison group of patrol areas that did not receive the enhanced activity. The level of statistical significance is .08 (92 percent confidence level). Assuming major threats to internal validity have been controlled, we still cannot say that the results would be the same (within a specific confidence interval) if the project is replicated in other patrol areas unless the project on which the results were obtained was representative, in all aspects relevant to outcomes, to that of the other patrol areas. Was the sample representative of the population? The similarity between sample (project) and population (that to which generalizations are to be made) will often be determined by expert judgment and best

guesses. The more similar the project is to the situation being considered for replication or continuation in terms of time, location, people being served, geographical location, people operating the project, specific project operations, organizational context, and extraneous factors, the more likely statistical tests will be useful for decision making.

The other caution concerns the use of statistical inference to provide evidence of the theoretical processes that were hypothesized to produce certain results. For example, if a program increased the arrest of career criminals over a comparison group at a high level of statistical significance, and all the major threats to internal validity have been accounted for, this does not offer proof that the processes that were theoretically hypothesized to produce the higher arrest rate in the experimental group were operating. Statistical tests may provide some evidence that the underlying processes have or have not been operating as hypothesized, but more and different types of evidence are needed to make a firm causal connection.

Though statistical inference has limitations, its use can be an important part of crime analysis research. Statistical tests provide objectivity in the analysis of quantitative data and provide an initial basis for judging whether objectives were achieved. Statistical tests can take descriptive statistics and put them into decision-relevant terms. Statistical tests are also familiar to most evaluators trained in the social and policy sciences, but often they should be used quite differently than in academic circles, where they are used to determine whether findings can be considered as contributing to knowledge or confirming hypotheses. If a crime analyst wants to use statistical tests as an input to decisions to continue, replicate, modify or discontinue a project, judgments should consider the following factors:

- The risk one is willing to take based on statistical inference—risks that results would or would not (in the case of a decision to discontinue or not replicate the project) be the same; that the null hypothesis is correct when rejected or not correct when accepted on the basis of an agreed-on significance level;

- Similarity of the population to which one wishes to generalize to that of the sample data used in the project;

- The applicability of statistical tests to the type of data and sample obtained from the project (technical considerations); and

- The specific decisions that have been made concerning the project—not all decisions need the type of inference that is obtained from statistical tests.

In summary, statistical testing is an important part of most quantitative analyses and can provide evidence, but not absolute proof of: (a) the relationships between activities and outcomes; and (b) the generalizability of project results to similar times, places, and situations. Additionally, statistical inference is only one in input into decision making and only one aspect of evaluation.

Illustrations

The following illustrations apply the concepts we have been discussing. We have assembled a data set of violent juvenile crimes in Dallas, Texas over a five-year period: 1998 through 2002. The unit of analysis is census tracts, of which Dallas has 234. We have available the following variables: tract number; total juvenile population in census tract; frequency of violent juvenile crimes; frequency of juvenile robberies; and frequency of juvenile assaults. In addition, we calculated offense rates for violence, robbery, and assault. The rates were calculated as follows:

Rate = Number of acts/juvenile population * 1,000

We used the unit of 1,000 as the constant because our juvenile population is in units of thousands rather than tens of thousands. We calculated offense rates because the frequency measure can be misleading. The volume of crime is partly a function of the population at risk (at risk to be an offender or a victim). Thus, a census tract could have a moderate volume of violent juvenile offenses and yet have a high rate because the particular tract has only a minimal number of juveniles. Of course the reverse can also be true, a tract can have a very high frequency but yet have a low rate because of the high number of juveniles at risk.

Table 14-1 reports for the violence, robbery, and assault rates for the following population statistics: minimum, maximum, mean, standard error, and standard deviation. Usually, we would not know the population values and the sample would be used to estimate the population parameters. But we

Table 14-1. Population Descriptive Statistics

	N	Min.	Max.	Mean	Stand. Error	Std. Dev.
Violence Rate	234	1.0	200.0	17.94	1.558	23.8334
Robbery Rate	234	0.0	41.7	3.39	0.371	5.6741
Assault Rate	234	0.0	153.8	11.78	1.019	15.5817

Table 14-2. Sample Descriptive Statistics

	N	Min.	Max.	Mean	Stand. Error	Std. Dev.
Violence Rate	47	1.0	55.6	16.54	1.988	13.6323
Robbery Rate	47	0.0	19.7	3.40	0.675	4.6259
Assault Rate	47	0.0	55.6	10.67	1.484	10.1768

have the population scores and we can use them to test the precision of the sample.

Estimation from a Sample

A random sample will generally reflect the properties of the population from which it was drawn, especially the population's central tendency. In theory, if one draws a random sample, then the mean of the sample serves as an estimate of the mean of the population. The principle underlying such a process is that the mean of any particular sample can be taken as an unbiased estimate of the mean of the population from which the sample is drawn. In general, a biased estimate is one that will systematically underestimate the true value, or systematically overestimate it, while an unbiased estimate is one that avoids this tendency. The unbiased estimate might prove to be either under or over the true value in particular cases, but it will not move in either of these directions systematically. It is roughly analogous to shooting arrows at a target. The archer who tends to hit below the bull's eye is systematically biased in one direction, while the archer who tends to hit above it is systematically biased in the other. An archer without such a systematic bias will hit below and above the bull's eye in equal measure, and occasionally he or she might even hit it dead center.

We will now draw a random sample and see how well our sample reflects the population of census tracts in Dallas. We will draw a 20 percent random sample using the simple random sampling procedure because all elements in the population (census tracts) are

easily enumerated and listed from 1 to 234. We use a table of random numbers and select 47 cases for the sample. The sample statistics are reported in Table 14-2.

Table 14-2 indicates that our 20 percent sample of 47 cases is different from the population of census tracts. How different are the point estimates obtained in the sample from their corresponding population values? All three of the maximum scores are lower in the sample and the mean of the total violence rate and the assault rate are lower in the sample while the robbery rate is slightly higher. Are these differences significant? To answer this question we must analyze the sample data.

The first thing a crime analyst should do is calculate confidence intervals around the sample means. The confidence interval is calculated in a very straightforward manner using the sample statistics and a t-value corresponding to the level of confidence and the degrees of freedom (i.e., $n=1$).

C.I. Pop. Mean (Φ) =Sample Mean (0) +/- t-value * stand error of sample mean

Table 14-3 indicates with 95 percent confidence that the interval within which the population mean is likely to lie actually includes the true score for the population mean for all three offense rates. Thus, our sample is a valid representation of the population from which it was drawn and any sample estimates that we use for analysis will be statistically valid.

Ordinarily, however, one would not know the population mean and the analyst would have to rely on the sample mean and the confidence interval as a reasonable approximation of where the true score lies. But, because we know the true score in the population, we can directly test whether the sample means differ from the true score. To accomplish this we will use a t-test but we could also have used a z-test. The t-test is used for small samples (<30 cases) or when the population standard deviation is unknown. Our sample consists of enough cases (47) to qualify for a z-test, but we are going to operate under the assumption that we do not know the population standard deviation. In any case, the results would be similar regardless of whether the t-test or the z-test was used.

$$t = \frac{0 \text{ (sample mean)} - \Phi \text{ (pop. mean)}}{\text{standard error of sample mean}}$$

Table 14-4 indicates that for all three offense rates, the sample mean is not significantly different from the expected population mean. The t-test scores are all lower than the required score for significance (t = 2.01; 46 degrees of freedom; .05 significance level). We may reject the alternate hypothesis that the sample means are significantly different.

Taken together, the results reported in Tables 14-3 and 14-4 provide statistical evidence that the sample estimates shown in Table 14-2 are a valid representation of the population scores for the total violence, robbery, and assault rates among juveniles in Dallas census tracts. We can thus confidently rely on the 20 percent sample to draw inferences about the population of all census tracts.

Sample Survey

Although we are principally interested in using the sample to estimate the three crime rates in the population, we might also be interested in conducting a citizen survey to gage public opinion about police performance. In this event, we would certainly want to know whether the respondents being surveyed lived in census tracts that were being sampled and had either low or high crime rates for the three crime measures. This neighborhood crime context could certainly affect the perception of the respondents who live in census tracts with high crime rates. Therefore, we also created a classification variable for each of the offense rate measures. This categorical variable has a score of 0 (low) if the particular offense rate in the tract is at or below the population mean and it has a score of 1 (high) if the rate

Table 14-3. Confidence Intervals

95% C.I.	Lower	Mean	Upper	Pop. Mean
Violence Rate	12.54	16.54	20.54	17.94
Robbery Rate	2.04	3.40	4.62	3.39
Assault Rate	7.69	10.67	13.65	11.78

Table 14-4. T-test Results

	d.f.	0.	Φ	s. error	t-score	prob. value
Violence Rate	46	16.54	17.94	1.988	0.7042	.4848
Robbery Rate	46	3.40	3.39	0.675	0.0148	.9882
Assault Rate	46	10.67	11.78	1.484	0.7480	.4583

was above the population mean. Table 14-5 indicates the number and percentage of census tracts that fall into the low or high rate categories for the three offense rates. These data show how census tracts might be categorized using a discrete measure and this measure could be incorporated into a sampling plan.

Table 14-6 provides the corresponding offense rate data for the for the 20 percent sample. These data indicate that the number and percentage of census tracts that fall into the low rate or high rate categories for the three offense types are different in the sample.

As we asked with the quantitative measures obtained in the sample, we now need to ask whether there is correspondence between the distributions of offense rate groups in the sample as compared to the population. To accomplish this, we use the chi-square test. Chi-square is a statistical test that compares the observed sample frequencies (Table 14-6) to the expected population values (Table 14-5) of a categorical variable to determine if the sample distribution differs significantly from the population. The chi-square statistic is calculated as follows:

$$\chi 2 \text{ (Chi square)} = \Sigma \frac{(\text{observed frequency} - \text{expected frequency})^2}{\text{expected frequency}}$$

The data in Tables 14-5 and 14-6 indicate that the sample scores depart somewhat from the expected population values. In particular, the sample slightly underestimates the low offense rate group for all three crime rates.

Table 14-5. Population Number and Percent of Rate Groups

	Violence		Robbery		Assault	
Offense rate	N	%	N	%	N	%
Low	152	65.0	167	71.4	157	67.1
High	82	35.0	67	28.6	77	32.9
Total	234	100.0	234	100.0	234	100.0

Table 14-6. Sample Number and Percent of Rate Groups

	Violence		Robbery		Assault	
Offense rate	N	%	N	%	N	%
Low	26	55.3	31	66.0	29	61.7
High	21	44.7	16	34.0	18	38.3
Total	47	100.0	47	100.0	47	100.0

Table 14-7. Chi-square Test of Rate Groups

Violence		Robbery		Assault	
$\chi 2$	prob.	$\chi 2$	prob.	$\chi 2$	prob.
1.936	0.1641	0.682	0.4090	0.620	.4309

However, the chi-square value shown in Table 14-7 indicates that the departures were not significantly different. The crime analyst may thus rely on the sample as a valid estimator of the distribution of low and high offense rate census tracts.

As it turned out, we are fortunate that there was no statistically significant difference found between the distributions of low vs. high crime rate census tracts in the population as compared to the sample. But, the reverse could have been true. To the extent that our sample differed from the population we would have introduced bias into our research. We would not have gauged properly the extent to which the underlying crime rates in an area affected public opinion about a variety of law enforcement functions, and indeed, may have affected citizen satisfaction with the quality of police services they were receiving.

Thus, a preferred approach would be to explicitly take into consideration the offense rate categories when drawing our sample. The approach would involve the use of a multi-stage sampling design and the procedure would be as follows. First, the census tracts would be stratified into low rate and high rate areas for either all three crime rate measures or one in particular. The proportionate representation of census tracts would be noted (e.g., 60 percent low rate and 40 percent high rate). Second, a random sample of tracts would be selected from within the strata so as to maintain the population proportion. Third, blocks within these homogenous tracts would be chosen at random. Fourth, households would be randomly chosen. Finally, a respondent would be chosen from among the household members.

This process would ensure that the sample perfectly reflects the population of census tracts and its precision would be enhanced as we would have explicitly taken into account the crime rate aspect of the census tract. Because we sampled from relatively homogenous units, the within group variance would be minimized then reducing the standard error of any sample statistics we chose to calculate. In turn, this precision reduces the size of the confidence interval around our estimates thus enhancing the confidence hat we can place in the likely population values.

Conclusion

This chapter has shown that a sample is a smaller representation of a larger group or population. Within this context, sampling involves selection of a portion of the population having a given characteristic. The relationship between the sample and the larger population from which it is drawn is very important in terms of statistical analysis and generalization. The sample selected should accurately reflect (that is, be representative of) the larger population from which it was selected if the results from the analysis of the sample data are to be applicable (i.e., generalizable) to that larger group. Random selection procedures are available for approximating the distribution of characteristics of the larger population, thus fulfilling the requirement of representativeness.

For some crime analysis studies the researcher may want to collect information on the entire target population, whether it be individual citizens, police districts, local citizen groups, particular geographical areas, or other units of analysis. In other situations it may be advantageous because of cost, time or theoretical considerations to gather data by taking a sample from the entire group. As a researcher you should address the issue of sampling on a study-by-study basis.

Sampling Rules

There are a few key decision rules that a researcher should consider when making a decision about whether to sample, as well as the type of sample to use. These are:

1. Estimated cost of collecting information on all members of the target group;

2. Time available to gather data;

3. Hypothesized relationships, based on theoretical assumptions, between specific characteristics of the target group and expected outcomes; and

4. Technical considerations dealing with sampling errors, such as estimated standard error and statistical significance.

In short, the specific circumstances surrounding a particular research project will determine the need to sample and the sampling method or combination of techniques to use. If a researcher decides to choose a sample, its size should be based on the level of confidence you wish to place in the findings. Generally, the larger the sample, the more confidence you can place in the findings. In this vein, the smaller the expected magnitude of the findings, the larger the sample needed to detect any differences that may be attributable to project activities. Similarly, the more detailed the analysis (for example, one that involves an examination of specific characteristics or subgroups of the sample), the larger the required size of the sample. There are several equations that may be used to precisely determine the size of the sample needed for various situations. These equations reflect: (1) the confidence level to be used to determine the significance of findings; (2) the degree of

accuracy within which you wish to estimate the population; and (3) some reasonable estimate of the values of any relevant parameters such as expected standard deviation in the sample. A researcher should consult with a statistician when addressing these technical considerations especially if he or she is going to determine sample size based on the expected results and degree of statistical significance desired.

Hypothesis Testing Rules

1. The lower the alpha value, the lower the risk of making a Type I error (i.e., rejecting the null when it's true);

2. The lower the alpha value the more "rigorous" the test; and

3. Increasing alpha value from .01 to .05 increases the chances of making a Type I error (i.e., saying there is a difference when there is not), decreases the chances of making a Type II error (i.e., saying there is no difference when there is) and decreases the rigor of the test.

These are only general rules and the researcher must ultimately determine on a case-by-case basis the tradeoffs between the conventional .05 significance value and the more rigorous .01 level.

15
Crime Mapping

Steven R. Hick
Sean Bair
Noah J. Fritz
Dan Helms

This chapter is designed to meet the needs of crime analysts new to the world of crime mapping, using a special class of tool called a geographic information system or GIS. (Much has been written about GIS, and we encourage readers to turn to a variety of introductory text books that address the broad field of GIS.) Within crime analysis, the use of spatial analysis to study crime is called crime mapping.

Crime mapping is a relatively new (it has only been widely used in police agencies since the mid-1990s) and highly influential technology. Like the Internet, searchable databases, e-mail, and other emergent technologies, the use of GIS has transformed the practice of police work, and crime analysis in particular. Like these other technologies, professional standards of GIS use lag in the law enforcement world. Unlike private industry, which often quickly embraces change and develops ways to use new technologies, law enforcement tends to be very tradition-sensitive, and adopts something new only after other professions have developed and proved it. In the case of crime mapping, this means we have some catching up to do.

This chapter provides the crime analyst with an introduction to and basic understanding of the foundation of maps and mapping. The crime analyst will be introduced to several basic techniques that enable the visualization and understanding of police-related data.

Maps and GIS

Cartography

The International Cartographic Association defines *cartography* as follows:

> "The art, science, and technology of making maps, together with their study as scientific documents and works of art. In this context may be regarded as including all types of maps, plans, charts, and sections, three-dimensional models and globes representing the Earth or any celestial body at any scale."[1]

What is a map? A map by definition is a graphic or visual representation of a portion of the Earth's surface. (For crime mapping we will ignore celestial mapping.) As map makers, we are constrained by map scale because we are limited to the amount of detail we can show as a function of the space in which we have to illustrate.

What is a Geographic Information System or GIS?

GIS is a collection of hardware, software, and people to collect, store, retrieve, manipulate, analyze, and display spatial data. When you break down the acronym "GIS" it is easy to understand what GIS is all about. The "G" stands for "geographic," so clearly it is necessary to have geography or spatial data. "I" stands for "information." The information is about the geography and is stored in the form of tabular databases. Finally, the "S" stands for "system," which represents the software and hardware required to link the tabular information to the geographic information. With this relationship between tabular data and

---

[1] Emil Meynen, ed., *Multilingual Dictionary of Technical Terms in Cartography* (Stuttgart: International Cartographic Association, 1973), 1.

geography, we have the ability to explore and analyze the world around us in an automated fashion and to make discoveries about our world that may not have been obvious before.

The GIS Enterprise

The typical GIS enterprise has several functional responsibilities. A small GIS department may find one person serving in many roles. A large GIS department may find a significant staff of people with unique responsibilities working together to ensure a successful GIS operation.

Most GIS departments have a manager or coordinator overseeing human resources, computer systems, software licensing, financial functions, and data administration. Larger organizations will have personnel dedicated to system operations with a system administrator, network engineer, system analysts, programmers, and the like taking care of computers and computer users. A database administrator maintains the core database and several database administrators may be employed to oversee different datasets. One person may be responsible for spatial or geographic data while another person oversees tabular data such as a police records management system (RMS).

Computer Hardware

There is really no specific GIS or crime mapping hardware. Most GIS software works in a Microsoft Windows environment on standard PCs or in a UNIX operating system on UNIX workstations. GIS software users are advised to take note of the minimum computer specifications required for their software. Random access memory (RAM) and central processing unit (CPU) speed are critical components to running GIS software without getting frustrated with computing

speed. Sufficient hard drive space is also important as GIS software uses a lot of space. In addition, the data created and used takes up a lot of fixed disk space as well. Do not forget some mechanism for backing up data, whether burning data to compact disks, backing up to magnetic tape, or maintaining redundant data on a second server.

GIS Software

There are many GIS software packages on the market today representing a broad spectrum of functionality and price options. An Internet search for "GIS software" leads to countless links for further exploration. Readers new to GIS must understand that we often refer to GIS as a toolbox. Much like a carpenter reaches into his toolbox to pull the tools needed for a specific job; the GIS professional reaches into the software to extract the tools needed to perform certain types of analysis. While perhaps oversimplifying the GIS software purchase, the more money you spend on software, the more tools you get. If you are new to the GIS or crime mapping profession, you must seriously consider the type of functionality you require and then purchase the software that closely matches your requirements.

Crime Mapping Applications

In addition to "off the shelf" software from major GIS vendors, several software applications have emerged in recent years focusing on the law enforcement and crime mapping community. Readers are directed to resources posted at the National Institute of Justice Mapping and Analysis for Public Safety Web site (formerly known as the Crime Mapping Research Center).[1]

---

[1] http://www.ojp.usdoj.gov/maps

Geographic or Spatial Data

Take a look out your window and consider all the features that occur in the real world. Make a list in your head. What do you see? Do you see roads, building, sidewalks, trees, and manhole covers? Do you see crime? I hope not, but where do crimes occur? Can we map these features? How? You've worked with road maps before to get from your home to your vacation destination with little difficulty. What information appeared on that map that you used? Was there information that did not appear on the map that you could have used? We collect or convert real world data into a computer-readable format so we can store and retrieve that data in an automated fashion. Then we can manipulate the data and analyze it to reveal relationships in the distribution, orientation, or proximity of data. When we analyze spatial data we are performing spatial analysis.

We have to begin with the dimensions of spatial phenomena. When we convert real world phenomena to map data, we create one of two types of spatial data models: vector data or raster data. Spatial data models are abstractions of the real world incorporating spatial features and their attributes appropriate for the mapping application.

Vector data is characterized by points, lines, and areas or polygons. Points, such as the location of a traffic accident are characterized by a single x and y coordinate. Lines, like streets, are characterized by a string of x and y coordinates that are linked together. Finally, a polygon, like a city boundary, is as a series of lines that start and end in the same place. Advanced vector data models incorporate topology. Topological relationships are built from simple elements into complex elements: points (simplest elements), arcs (sets of connected points), areas (sets of connected arcs), and routes (sets of sections, which are

arcs or portions of arcs). Redundant data (coordinates) is eliminated because an arc may represent a linear feature, part of the boundary of an area feature, or both.

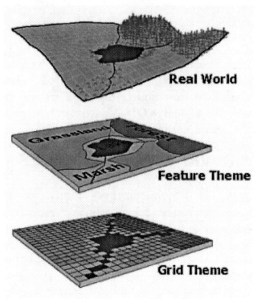

Figure 15-1: How the real world is represented on a map

The raster data model is characterized by an array of grid cells or pixels that are superimposed over the surface of the earth. Each grid cell in this array is assigned a numeric value for the feature on earth represented. The raster database model is particularly suitable for mapping data over a continuous surface such as elevation. In crime mapping, the creation of a crime density surface is a good application of the raster data model.

Spatial Data Formats

Each GIS software vendor has their own proprietary data format for storing spatial data inn the computer. In this day and age, moving data from one platform to another is fairly simple. Data standards have been adopted for the exchange of spatial data.

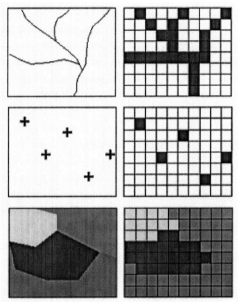

Figure 15-2: Vector data models (left) compared to raster data models (right)

In law enforcement, the two most popular software vendors are ESRI and MapInfo. ESRI software (which includes ArcView, ArcEdit, and ArcInfo; current versions are known collectively as ArcGIS) has the capability to work with topological data known as coverages, nontopological vector data known as shapefiles, and object-oriented databases known as geodatabases. The native MapInfo data formats are nontopological tables. Each of these vendors provides utilities to exchange data from one to the other. MapInfo can import coverages and shapefiles to tables. ESRI software can import MapInfo tables into shapefiles.

Another spatial data format of note is the Drawing Interchange File or DXF format created by Autodesk, Incorporated for use in their AutoCAD Computer Aided Drafting software. A DXF file is a specially formatted text file that can be viewed and modified with any text editor. Virtually every GIS software vendor has the ability to import DXF files.

Map Scale

All maps, whether published to paper or left on a computer screen, are reductions of the real world to a format more conducive to use on the desktop or in the police cruiser. Scale is the reduction of dimensions in the real world to dimensions in the map space as defined by paper or computer monitor size. Map scale will vary over a map as determined by the choice of a map projection, which is described in the next section. Map scale and map projection are interdependent. Map scale selection is an important consideration early in the mapping process as it dictates the level of detail that will be visible to the map reader thereby affecting the communication potential of the map. References to map scale are relative to the mapping environment or agency responsible for production of map series. Customarily, reference is made to large, intermediate, and small scale mapping. Given the same size sheet of paper, a large-scale map will show more detail in a smaller geographic area while a small-scale map will show less detail over a larger geographic area. On a small scale map of the world it would be difficult to illustrate the sidewalk outside your home. Likewise, on a large scale map of your town it would be difficult to also illustrate the location of other cities in the state.

The Shape of the World: an Oblate World and Flat Maps

Projections

If the earth was a perfect sphere and if globes fit in our pockets, map projections would not be necessary. However, we continue to flatten the near-spherical earth onto flat paper maps and flat computer monitors. When we flatten the globe, something has to give. Some distortion occurs moving from spherical to flat. Four characteristics are important when flattening the globe: shape, area, distance, and direction. One or more of these characteristics will "give." It is up to the cartographer to decide which characteristics are most important to the mapping project and then choose an appropriate projection.

So one of our first mapping challenges is to understand and deal with the problems associated with flattening out a nearly spherical world onto a flat map or flat computer screen. Take a juicy orange and cut it in half with each half representing a hemisphere of the earth. Eat the sweet, juicy part so as not to let a perfectly good orange go to waste while conducting a mapping experiment. Hold the now empty orange peel in your hand and smash it on the tabletop. What happened to the orange peel? It split into sections didn't it? This is similar to what happens when we flatten the spherical earth to accommodate flat mapping. Something had to give. The geometry of the sphere is distorted. When mapping, this could lead to problems when examining the shape of geographic features, or measuring distance, area, or direction. Welcome to the world of map projections. For many readers, the notion of map projections may be moot. If your jurisdiction is relatively small, such as that of a typical American city or county, the distortion rendered in map projection is small enough to be trivial in crime mapping. Your city or county surveyors won't consider this trivial, but you will hardly notice. Readers concerned with a larger geographic region or large state will want to strongly consider a map projection that limits distortion for measuring distance or area. Consider the use of the Lambert Conformal Conic Projection or the Universal Transverse Mercator Projection. Your choice will probably be guided by the projection in use by your agency's GIS department. If you do not have a GIS or mapping department and must go it on your own, then use the following

guidelines: if your jurisdiction has a predominantly east-west orientation (e.g., Colorado), use a conic projection such as the Lambert Conformal Conic projection; if your jurisdiction has a predominantly north-south orientation (e.g., Indiana), use a Transverse Mercator projection.

Map Datum

Datum by definition is a point of beginning or a place to begin measuring from. For example, when we measure elevation we measure from mean sea level (MSL). Mean sea level is a vertical datum. Measuring horizontally is a bit more complicated. Rather than focus on datum origins, it is probably more useful for the crime analyst or mapper to be able to identify the datum they are working in. There are myriad datum in use around the world. In the United States the two most popular datum include the North American Datum of 1927 and the North American Datum of 1983. Simply stated, as surveying and measuring technology improve, the ability to measure the Earth's surface improves. As a result, new datum are published periodically. Some readers may recognize datum in their region that are improved since 1983. With the advent of the Global Positioning System (GPS),[1] we have been able to improve our ground control network creating a High Accuracy Reference Network, or HARN. GPS users recognize the use of the World Geodetic System 1984 datum (WGS84) as the preferred datum in GPS mapping use. WGS84 represents a refinement of the ellipsoid by the United States Military. Shifting between datums can be trivial or substantial depending on your location. Consult your local GIS experts or licensed surveyors for details about preferred horizontal datum in your area.

---

[1] A worldwide navigation system that uses information received from orbiting satellites.

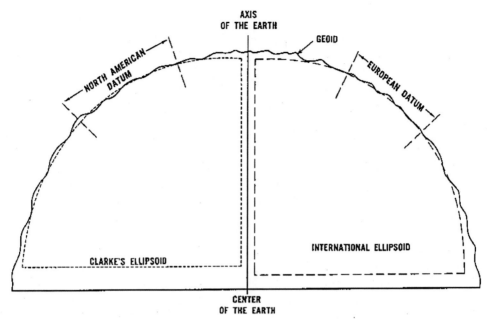

Figure 15-3: Positioning of different datums compared to the Earth's actual shape and axis

Coordinate Systems

When we collect and store geographic data in a computer we must have a spatial reference. A coordinate system is employed to locate a position in two- or three-dimensional space. The coordinate system is also defined by its origin, axes, and distance units. You should be familiar with latitude and longitude from your geography or earth science classes in school and you should be familiar with the Cartesian coordinate system described to you in high school geometry or algebra.

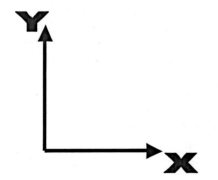

Geographic or Spherical Coordinates

A series of parallel lines running around the earth for measuring north and south from the equator are lines of *latitude*, or parallels. There is an equal space between each whole degree of latitude and the next. The equator has a value of zero degrees and the north and south poles have values of 90 degrees. Latitudes north of the equator are called "north latitudes" or are signified with a positive number; latitudes south of the equator are called "south latitudes" or are signified with a negative number.

Lines or meridians running from the North Pole to the South Pole are lines of *longitude*. Lines of longitude are not evenly spaced: they are furthest apart at the equator and converge at the poles. Measurement begins with a value of zero degrees at the Prime Meridian, passing through Greenwich (England), then measured in east and west directions from zero degrees to 180 degrees on the opposite side of the Earth.

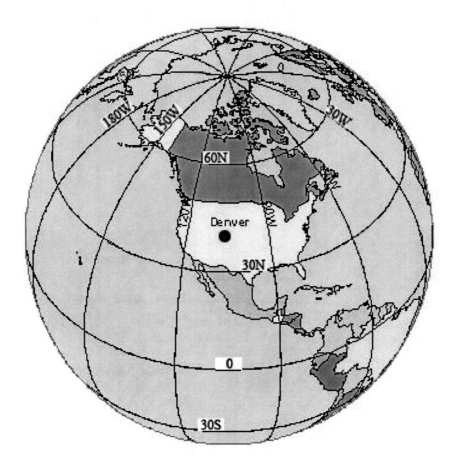

Figure 15-4: Latitudes and Longitudes

Cartesian or plane coordinates

Flattening out the globe allows us to use a Cartesian or planar coordinate system. This system helps us minimize distortion locally. Popular Cartesian coordinate systems include the Universal Transverse Mercator (UTM) system, customarily measured in meters, and the State Plane Coordinate System (SPSC), customarily measured in feet.

UTM Coordinates

The Universal Transverse Mercator (UTM) grid system has been widely adopted for mapping applications throughout the world. It is a metric system based on using the meter as a unit of measurement. UTM coordinates are derived from lines of latitude and longitude. The earth is divided into 60 zones in an east-west direction each measuring six degrees wide and given a numeric identifier from one to sixty beginning at the 180-degree line of longitude and then numbering in an east direction. There are 20 zones in the north-south direction with an alpha designation beginning at 80-degrees south latitude and increasing in a north direction terminating at 84-degrees north latitude. Identifying your location begins with a zone designation. Measuring in a north direction (*northings*) begins at the South Pole for southern hemisphere regions and at the Equator for northern hemisphere regions. To measure the northing or y-coordinate, begin at the South Pole and measure toward the Equator. To measure in the northern hemisphere, begin at the Equator with a value of zero and measure north toward the North Pole. In the southern hemisphere begin at the equator, now with a value of 10,000,000 meters and measure south approaching zero at the South Pole.

Measuring the *easting*, or x-coordinate, is a little more complicated. Each east-west zone has a Central Meridian corresponding to the line of longitude running through the center of the zone. For example, Zone 13 has east-west extents from 102 degrees west longitude to 108 degrees west longitude. The central meridian is 105 degrees west longitude and is assigned a "false easting" value of 500,000 meters. We then measure east or west of the central meridian adding to, or subtracting from 500,000 meters.

For a more comprehensive discussion of UTM coordinates, please refer to a text on map use and analysis or a military training manual.

State Plane Coordinates

As the name implies, state plane coordinates are designed for use at the state level in the United States. Because there are 50 states, there are 50 state plane coordinate systems. In addition to having 50 coordinate systems, most states are large enough to require that the state be divided into smaller zones running north-south or east-west to minimize distortion over increasing distances. Readers of this text in the United States are encouraged to contact their local GIS office or a local licensed land surveyor for specific

details about their state plane zone and coordinate system.

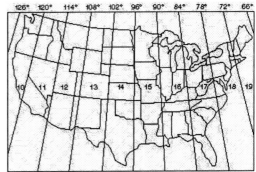

Figure 15-5: UTM zones in the contiguous United States

Like UTM coordinates, state plane coordinates are based on a Cartesian coordinate system measuring *eastings* in the x direction and *northings* in the y direction. Traditionally, measurements are made in feet, although metric equivalents have been published. The origin for the coordinate system varies by state and zone and is based on central meridians and standard parallels.

Which Coordinate System Should I Use?

At the municipal level in the United States, state plane coordinates are usual and customary. Cartesian coordinate systems like state plane and UTM are useful at the local level because they are generally used to map a smaller geographic extent thereby minimizing distortion resulting from flattening, or projecting, the earth's surface.

Much data available for download via the Internet is available in latitude and longitude, or in other geographic coordinates, and GIS software fortunately has the tools necessary for transforming from one coordinate system to another. It is important for the GIS user to recognize and understand what coordinates you are converting from and to.

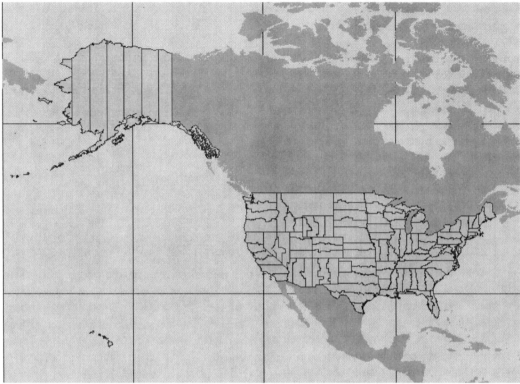

Figure 15-6: United States State Plane Coordinate Zones, North American Datum of 1983

Crime Mapping

We now turn to applying the principles and tools of GIS to crime and police data.

Crime Mapping Data
The Base Map

The first question the map maker must answer is "what is the purpose of the map?" One must always keep purpose in mind as this will dictate the level of map detail and the thematic data to be communicated. The cartographer usually begins the map making process with a set of digital map files often referred to as the base map. The layers of geography that actually constitute a base map are subject to interpretation, but usually base map layers include natural features like rivers, lakes, and coastlines as well as cultural features such and streets and roads, railroads, buildings, and city and county boundaries.

In law enforcement, streets are usually the most important geographic data layer to start with. Streets are stored in geographic databases as line segments commonly running from intersection to intersection. Therefore, each street segment is a unique feature in the database and has its own tabular data, including an address range.

There are other layers of information useful to the crime analyst. Consider the following list of layers of information that would be beneficial in crime mapping:

- Buildings with addresses
- Parcels with identification numbers
- Rivers and streams
- Lakes and ponds

- Utility infrastructure including electric, gas, telephone, cable, water, and sewer
- Schools
- Parks
- Businesses including pawn shops and liquor stores
- Shopping malls
- Automated Teller Machine (ATM) locations
- Military reservations
- Parks
- Bus routes and stops
- Boundaries, including municipal, school district, police districts, beats, and reporting districts

Vector map files are readily available from federal sources in the public domain like the United States Geological Survey (USGS) Digital Line Graph (DLD) data and the United States Census Bureau TIGER files.[1] Most local government agencies have a mapping or GIS department whose principal responsibilities include collection and maintenance of the agency's base map.

If vector base map files are not available, existing paper maps can be scanned and converted into a raster data format for use as a visual backdrop or frame of reference. Scanned maps should be georeferenced; that is, they must be referenced to a geographic coordinate system. Raster maps will not work for plotting crime data via address matching as we discuss in a later section of this chapter.

Police Data

The following paragraphs give brief descriptions of police data sources. For more information, see Chapter 10.

[1] TIGER is an acronym for Topologically Integrated Geo-Encoding and Referencing.

Calls for Service (CFS): In addition to map data, crime mapping requires crime data. Every time a 911 call is recorded, another entry is made in a database. After separating out the police-related calls from fire and emergency medical service (EMS) calls, the crime analyst has a database to start with. From this database the crime analyst can query those calls of interest. Perhaps false alarm calls are a nuisance, but because they may not be the responsibility of the crime analyst, they are therefore discarded or saved for another project on another day. To begin, a crime analyst may elect to query calls where call type is equal to residential burglary. Date and time are also critical attributes, and the crime analyst may begin selecting all crime types for the previous 24 hours of activity.

Records Management System (RMS): When police reports are typed in by a records clerk, entered by a voice recording system, or entered directly by a police officer, the data is stored in an RMS. There are myriad RMS vendors with many solutions and scalable products. The RMS becomes a primary source of data for the crime analyst.

There are other data sources in the police department that may be of interest and suitable for mapping. The gang unit may have a database of known gang members indicating their home and territory. Field Interview (FI) cards may be collected or entered into a database providing valuable information. Business license information may be beneficial for keeping track of commercial enterprises such as bars or liquor stores and the activity around them.

Working with Attribute or Tabular Data

Attribute data comes in many forms, and many of them may already be familiar to you. Following is a list of popular data formats easily integrated into a GIS:

Text files come in a variety of formats including comma delimited, tab delimited, and virtually any other field delimitation you care to use. Often you will see the file extension *.asc, *.csv and *.txt at the end of a text file.

dBASE files have become a de facto standard for data exchange. You will recognize the file extension *.dbf at the end of a dBASE file.

Microsoft Access has become an increasingly popular desktop office tool for database management. Access databases have the extension *.mdb. Microsoft Access is a relational database management system, meaning that you can have several database tables in the Access database that are related or linked together by a key field.

All GIS software products have the ability to create, link to, or import data from a database management system (DBMS). The afore-mentioned formats are prevalent in the law enforcement community. In larger enterprise GIS programs you will find the "big" relational database management systems by companies such as Oracle, IBM, Informix, and Microsoft.

Linking or Joining Tables

Often you will acquire a table of information that is not georeferenced. The table may however contain a field with some form of georeference. When that is the case, you have the ability to link or join your table to a table that is georeferenced, thereby giving you the ability to map new information. If two tables have a field in common, such as something simple like "State Name" or FIPS Code (Federal Information Processing Standard), with the name or number of each state appearing in the column, you could join or link the tables. You then have the ability to map new data because you have joined tabular or statistical information to a table that is georeferenced or mapped.

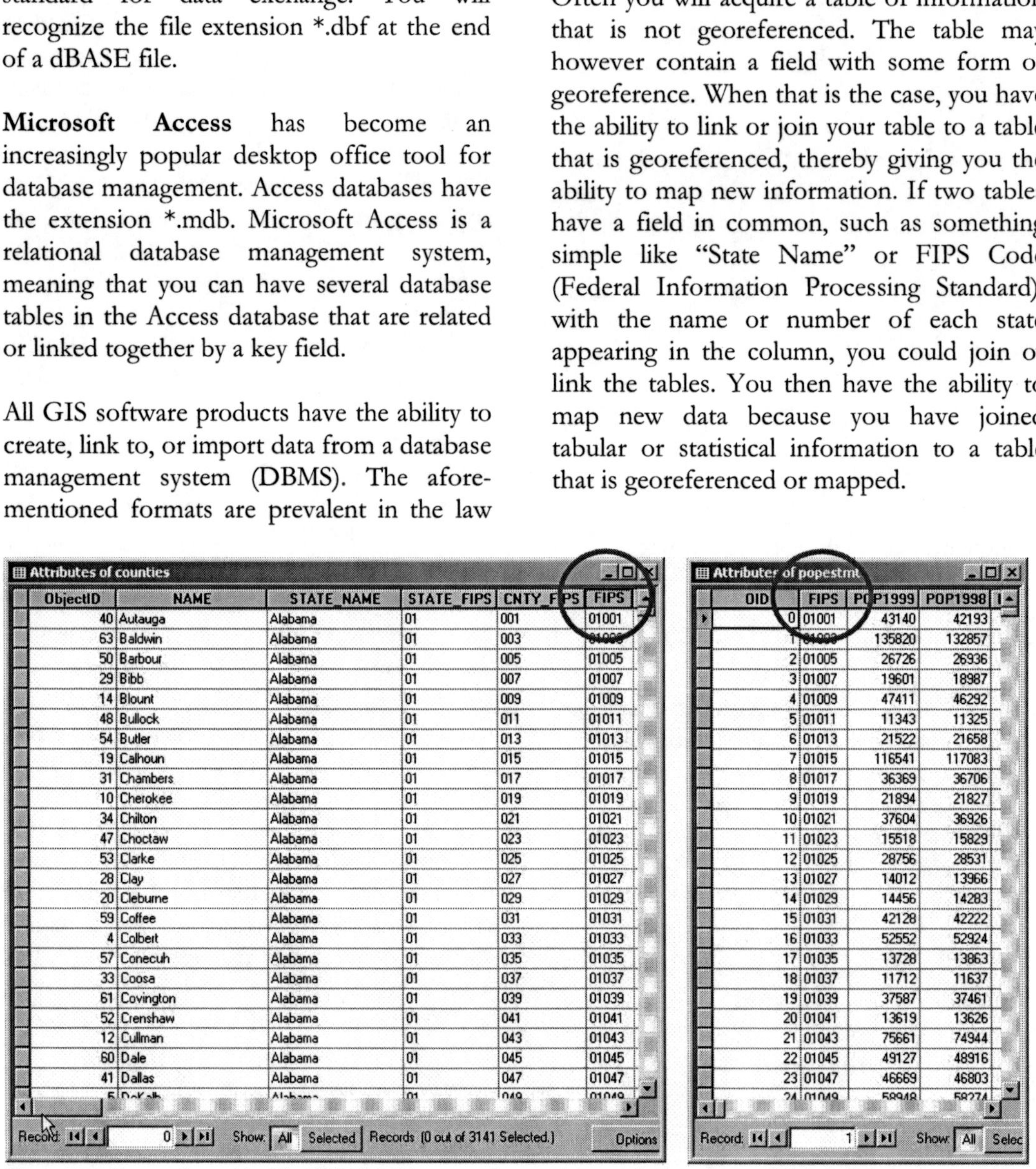

Figure 15-7: Two attribute tables. The "FIPS" field is common between the two and allows the two tables to be linked.

Crime Mapping Methods

Police departments are never at a loss for data. To use crime mapping is to take data from myriad sources and make the data appear on the computer screen or a published map. The following section explains one of the most popular techniques in crime mapping for converting tabular data files into mapped data: address matching.

Assigning Spatial Locations to Events (Address Matching or Geocoding)

We use a GIS to visualize data, specifically spatial data. GIS software has tools to turn tabular information with some form of spatial reference into data on a map. Once that data is on the map, we can commence data retrieval, manipulation, and analysis.

Geocoding by definition is the process of converting analog data into a computer-readable format. In law enforcement, most references to geocoding refer to one type of geocoding: address matching. There are other methods for converting analog or real world data into a format to be read by computer software. For example, most GPS receivers have the ability to record and store locations in a file that can be downloaded to the computer and converted into mapped data. Did you ever wonder how all the map data you see on the Internet or available for sale on CD-ROM came into existence? GIS technicians have spent countless hours digitizing paper maps using a precision mouse and a digitizing table. A digitizing table is like an electronic drafting table where the surface is underlain with an electronic grid that enables the person doing the digitizing to trace map features on a map taped down to the table top with a precision cursor. Locations are identified, converted into numbers including coordinates, and then transferred to the computer.

Address matching is "the ability to match an address component to its geographic location on the ground."[1] At a minimum two things are required: a street database and a database containing addresses such as crime records in the records management system. In a perfect world we would have a feature on a map corresponding to every possible address. The reality is that most of us record address ranges associated with street segments. The high and low address range is linked to each street segment. GIS software then locates specific addresses in our crime data "approximately" along a street segment. If your incident address was 150 Main Street and the street segment represented the 100 block with addresses ranging from 100 to 199, the GIS software would locate the address of the crime approximately 50 percent of the way down the block. Please note that this is not a precise location.

The illustration below comes from TIGER file technical documentation provided by the United States Census Bureau.

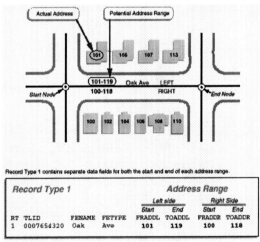

Figure 15-8: How address matching works. Source: U.S. Census Bureau, 1997.

[1] Glen Montgomery and Harold Schuch, *The GIS Data Conversion Handbook* (Fort Collins, CO: GIS World, 1993).

Address Matching Issues

The crime mapper must understand how address matching works and the inherent weaknesses associated with the technique.

1. **Street map data quality**: Imagine the difficulty associated with keeping street networks up to date in a GIS. New streets must be added to the street database while vacated streets must be deleted from the streets database. Street name changes are common as well. In older, more stable areas, the task may be minimal. In high-growth areas the task is large.

2. **Accurate address assignment**: In addition to keeping streets in the database, the address ranges must be correctly assigned. This task sounds simple, but is not. Cities and counties go to great expense to put crews in the field to verify correct address assignments along street segments.

3. **Street aliases**: Streets often have alternative names or local names. For example, interstate highways have an official numeric designation, but may also have a local name such as the "Blue Star Memorial Highway." Abbreviations may be common such as "MLK" rather that spelling out Martin Luther King Boulevard.

4. **Apartment buildings**: Apartment buildings generally have a single street address, but there are many units associated with that one address.

5. **Street type abbreviations**: Over time many abbreviations have been used to abbreviate street types. For example, the abbreviation for avenue may have been recorded as "AV" or "AVE".

6. **Police data**: How well are addresses recorded in your police data? Are there typographical errors? Are there spelling errors? Is there missing data? Are addresses listed approximately such as "in the 100 block of…?"

Data integrity is paramount in crime mapping. For that reason, an entire chapter in this text has been devoted to the topic of data integrity. Please see Chapter 7 for additional information about the importance of data integrity in law enforcement.

Visualizing Events on a Map

Visualization, for the purpose of this text, will be adapted from MacEachren and defined as the use of maps, whether on paper or computer, to make spatial contexts and problems visible to the map reader.[1]

In crime mapping, the first objective is to get events on the map. In previous sections we've discussed some of the considerations for the geographic base and the crime data. Once data has been address-matched, or geocoded, the crime analyst is confronted with points or dots on a map. The initial results may be overwhelming or they may be revealing. Certainly, having too many dots on the map leads to information overload and there is no reasonable expectation that an analyst can discern patterns from the information. Another issue that arises is when dots on the maps representing events in the database are co-located. In other words, two or more events have taken place at the same location. In GIS software, the dots lie on top of each other masking the fact that there are two or more features there.

---

[1] Alan M. MacEachren, *How Maps Work: Representation, Visualization, and Design* (New York: Guilford Press, 1995)

Spatial Queries

Early on in this chapter we defined a GIS as having the ability to retrieve information. Retrieving data via a map is known as a spatial query, and there are several different types of spatial queries.

GIS software includes a database management system, usually a relational database management system (RDBMS), to store attributes of the spatial data. GIS software also incorporates the capability of importing data from other database sources or accessing other data in database systems via links or connections such as Open Database Connectivity (ODBC). Database management systems support the concept of query to isolate a subset of data. *Find* is the simplest of attribute searches, usually with the intention of locating a single record. A *restrict query* enables the crime mapper to retrieve a subset of data by placing a restriction on the attribute of the data. For example, one could query a crime database by searching for all crime in a given month.

In a database, we have the ability to find or restrict our queries, not solely based on descriptive attributes (such as date, or type of crime), but rather on geographic features. Geographic or spatial features have special geographic attributes, such as coordinates and measures, length, area, and perimeter, that enable spatial queries.

Adjacency: Adjacency is the topological property of having an edge or boundary in common. Features sharing a boundary are in immediate proximity. You may ask: What jurisdiction is adjacent to mine? What other beats border Beat 12? On what side of the city boundary did the crime occur? Are our two rival gangs adjacent to each other?

Proximity: A buffer is a zone around a point, line, or polygon that is spatially related to the feature. Buffering is a popular technique in crime mapping. Creating buffers is just one technique for determining proximity. Points, lines, and polygons can all be buffered with GIS software. Creating a buffer merely entails determining what the radius, or proximity, should be around a specified feature. For example, if you wanted to determine a 1000-foot drug free zone around a school you select the school and use the buffer tool in your software. If your school is shown as a point feature in your map base, your result will be a circle with a radius of 1000 feet. If your school appears as a polygon more closely representing the school yard in your base map then your resulting buffer will be a polygon that resembles your school yard only much larger and with rounded corners. With buffering we can answer questions such as what is near by or what is the relationship between registered sex offenders and their proximity to schools?

GIS gives us the ability to manipulate data. Buffering is a manipulation of data. Creating a buffer creates new data that can then be used to do further analysis. After creating a 1000-foot buffer around your school you now have a new polygon in which you may want to query how many drug dealer suspects live or work within the buffer polygon.

Area: Area is the measure of a planar region. How big is, or what is the area of my police beat? How does the area of my beat compare with others?

Length or Distance and Connectivity: What is the length of a road segment? How long will it take me to travel from one end of town to the other on this road based on its length? Can I get there from here?

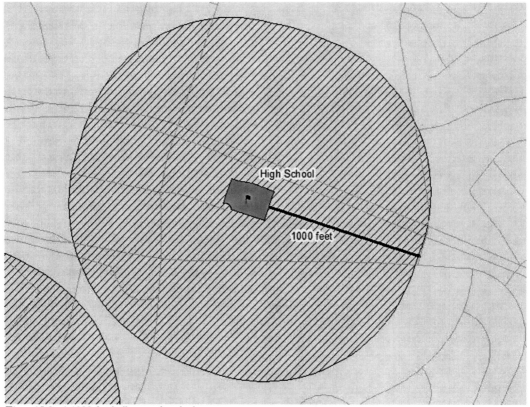

Figure 15-9: A 1000-foot buffer around a school

Levels of Measurement

Levels of measurement are the degree of subjectivity associated with measurement. The attributes associated with spatial data can be classified according to their level of measurement. There are four levels: nominal, ordinal, interval, and ratio.

1. **Nominal**: the root of the word nominal is "nom" which simply means "name." A nominal classification of data provides the location and the name of the feature.

2. **Ordinal:** the word ordinal comes from order and implies rank. For example, small city, medium-sized city, and big city would be an ordinal classification. You use small, medium, and large map symbols or dots to illustrate, but you cannot state how much bigger one city is than another based on symbology alone.

3. **Interval**: interval data provides numeric information for different classes of data. A "light crime area" may have 1 to 10 burglaries; a "high crime area" may have 11 to 20 burglaries. Interval data usually begins measurement from a datum or point of beginning; in this example, zero.

4. **Ratio**: ratio data is, as the name implies, a ratio of one value to another. For example we may classify data to look at the percent of crimes to total population for a reporting district.

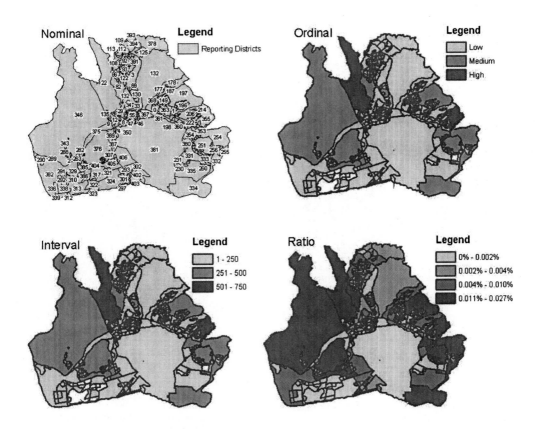

Figure 15-10: Crime maps using different levels of measurement

Data Classification

The purpose of data classification is to simplify complex geographic distributions into a presentation of the data that is meaningful to the reader. Data classification involves organizing data into groups or clusters based on a numeric or statistical distribution. There are two main components in a classification scheme: the number of classes into which the data is to be organized and the method by which classes are assigned. The number of classes is dependent on the objective of the analysis. Too often in crime mapping crime analysts rely on the default settings in their software for data classification. The natural breaks is the typical data classification default. Data classification

can be controlled by the crime analyst and therefore he or she should use a variety of data classification techniques. Different techniques will yield different views of the data. There are several common techniques available in most GIS software packages.

Natural Breaks: Most GIS software packages use the natural breaks technique as the default data classification option. This is a good technique for determining natural groups or clusters of values in the data. The technique looks for the "breaks" between groups of data values. Feature classes are set where there are relatively big jumps in the data. This technique is limited for time-series analysis such as comparing like time periods from one year to another because the range

329

of data may change significantly between years, making the distribution of data and therefore the natural breaks inconsistent between time periods.

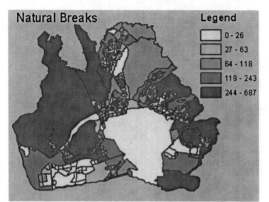

Figure 15-11: *A choropleth map using a natural breaks classification*

Equal Interval: The equal interval technique breaks the range of data from low to high into a number of equal subgroups or classes as dictated by the user. For example, the number of crimes per beat ranges from 0 to 250. To determine five classes, the GIS takes the range, 250, and divides it by five (50), and makes the categories each contain 50 (e.g., 0–50, 51–100, 101–150). This is an excellent technique for making "apples to apples" comparisons between data of different time periods, as long as the user sets up the same equal intervals in period one as in period two.

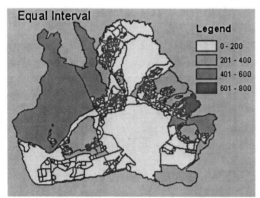

Figure 15-12: *A choropleth map using an equal interval classification*

Quantile: Quantiles throw an equal number of observations or data points into each class as determined by the user. If the user sets four classes of data (quartiles), 25 percent of the data or records will be in each class respectively. This technique can be very misleading depending on the distribution of the data. A quantile classification is well-suited to linearly distributed data.

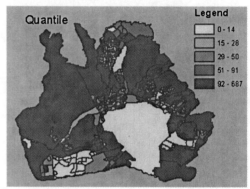

Figure 15-13: *A choropleth map using a quantile classification*

Standard Deviation: This technique should only be used when the data approximates a normal distribution. This technique calculates the mean of the data distribution and then maps one, two or three standards deviations above and below the mean.

Crime Maps

The following sections examine common crime mapping techniques to assist the new crime analyst in focusing on common and popular cartographic techniques that are useful in the law enforcement community for visualizing and interpreting, spatially, crime in their jurisdiction.

Most cartographers will identify three types of maps. General maps are "general" in nature, providing locations of data with place names attached. The street map in the glove compartment of your car is a general map. A second type of map is a chart. Those of you who fly or sail recognize that navigation charts show much more information than a road map, providing critical information for important things like determining runway or harbor approaches. The third type of map is a thematic map. Thematic mapping, as made obvious by the name, has a theme or tells a story. It illustrates the spatial distribution of a geographic phenomenon. A thematic map usually illustrates statistical data, but not exclusively. Crime mapping is one form of thematic mapping.

Popular crime maps usually take one of two forms: point symbol maps and area symbol maps. More and more crime mappers are also using a third type of map: a surface map.

Point Symbol Mapping

Point symbol mapping in crime mapping is the modern extension of the pin map. Do you remember when someone in the police department stuck different colored pins or thumbtacks into a map hanging on the wall in the police department to record where crimes were occurring? Now we have the ability to let the computer generate where those "pins" are placed electronically.

Dot distribution maps data back to the nineteenth century and the technique remains popular. In its simplest form, each symbol or dot on a map represents a discrete occurrence of the geographic phenomenon being mapped. Dot distribution maps are useful for illustrating spatial density. Difficulty arises when the data distribution is so dense that point symbols coalesce into a mass thereby destroying the original intent of the map: to show discrete event locations.

What about that address for an apartment complex where 100 units share the same site address? The odds are good that you respond to multiple calls at that single address.

To deal with the issue of co-located events, we use proportional or graduated symbol mapping. There is some difference between graduated symbols and proportional symbols. Graduated symbols are different sized symbols selected by the user to represent discrete data classifications. Proportional symbols are assigned by the software to represent each unique value in a range of point symbol data.

Use your GIS software to calculate the frequency, or count up the number of times an address is repeated in your database. Data integrity is essential. When calculating frequency your software looks for unique addresses. The address 123 Main Street and 123 Main St may be the same physical location, but because the street suffix is spelled out in one data entry and abbreviated in the second data entry, calculating frequency would only reveal one event at each address rather than two events at one address. There are many software tools on the market to help you clean your data to avoid problems such as these (see Chapter 7).

When you have calculated frequency, you can create a graduated symbol map. You will assign a different size dot to each count or a range of counts to show either an ordinal or interval classification of data.

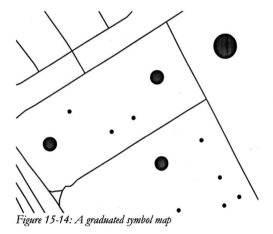

Figure 15-14: A graduated symbol map

How big should the dots be? How many dots should I show? There are several techniques for calculating and selecting graduated symbol sizes. Readers are directed to the text *Cartography: Thematic Map Design* by Borden Dent (see "Recommended Readings") for a more detailed discussion on graduated symbol mapping. There is a functional limit to the number of different symbol sizes that a map reader can interpret. Keep your audience in mind and keep your map simple. You will have a difficult time coming up with as many as seven graduated symbols and your map readers will also have a difficult time discerning the differences.

Choropleth Maps

Choropleth maps also go by the names *area symbol maps* or *statistical surface maps*. The difference between a pin or point symbol map and a choropleth map is that a point symbol map indicates a discrete location whereas a choropleth map indicates the aggregation of data over an area such as a police beat or a reporting district.

The first critical decision in choropleth mapping is selecting the enumeration area. The enumeration area is the geographic area or polygon you will use to analyze and illustrate your data. Are you mapping at the state level, county level, city level, census tract level, census block group level, census block level, police beat, or reporting district? You must decide the level of geography critical to your analysis and you must have data that can be mapped at that geographic level. Collecting data at the reporting district level is common in law enforcement. If your computer-aided dispatch (CAD) system or records management system (RMS) does not assign a reporting district number to each event, you will have to use the GIS to do a spatial join, or spatially assign the reporting district polygon to each event. With that

done, you can aggregate the number of events in each polygon and create a map with a ramp or range of colors that depict a range of data. Figures 15-11 to 15-13 are all choropleth maps.

Hot Spots

How does one identify a hot spot? First of all, how does one define a hot spot? A quick review of crime mapping literature reveals the following definitions of "hot spot":

- An area of high crime
- Events showing up in a cluster
- A single place with many crimes.

There are at least five ways to determine hot spots. The most popular seems to be simple visual interpretation. A 1999 National Institute of Justice study revealed that 77 percent of police departments surveyed used visual interpretation to determine hot spots in their jurisdictions. Most crime analysts "know a hot spot when I see it." This technique is not particularly statistically rigorous, but it is effective none the less.

Choropleth mapping is the second most popular technique for identifying hot spots, according to the aforementioned NIJ study. When using choropleth maps for hot spot mapping, you must consider the size of the polygon or enumeration area you are using. Large polygons may lead the map reader to overestimate the data presented. Areas that are too small may lead the map reader to underestimate the data presented. A bigger problem is mapping hot spots at the polygon level when the size of the polygons differs greatly. Small "hot" polygons may be overlooked by larger polygons that are not quite as hot. Choosing the correct data classification technique (equal interval, quantile, and natural breaks) will also have an effect on presentation of data and analysis.

For crime mappers that have the ability to generate a raster data set or grids, the option to perform grid cell or surface density analysis presents itself. Density surfaces are good for showing where point features such as crime are concentrated. For example, you might have a point value for each crime, but you want to learn more about the spread of crime over the city. By calculating density you can create a surface showing the distribution of the crime throughout the city.

The raster data model is defined as "cell data arranged in a regular grid pattern in which each [cell]…is assigned an identifying value based on its characteristics."[1] The boundaries of the grids are irrelevant. When draping a grid over the earth's surface, you cannot see the grid boundaries. The size of a grid cell is called its spatial resolution. The smaller the grid cell, the finer the resolution, enabling you to capture more detail. But additional detail is captured at the expense of increasing database size and complexity, hindering the performance capabilities of your computer. A larger grid cell choice will not consume as many computer resources, but it also won't let you make out much detail or yield meaningful results from your data. The raster data model is more efficient for certain overlay procedures.

Each grid cell in the array is also assigned a value based on its position. In density mapping, the cell value is calculated based on an underlying theme. To create a grid map of crime density, you must first map (geocode) crime or event locations; then determine your grid cell size. Then use the GIS software to calculate a crime density surface or grid.

Each cell's density is calculated by summing the crime points found in a specified search radius and dividing by the area of the circle in area units. By calculating density, you spread point values out over a surface. The magnitude at each sample location (line or point) is distributed throughout a landscape, and a density value is calculated for each cell in the output raster. Density maps are predominantly created from point data, and a circular search area is applied to each cell in the output raster being created. The search area determines the distance to search for points in order to calculate a density value for each cell in the output raster.

Density calculations can be made using simple or kernel calculations. In a simple density calculation, points that fall within the search area are summed and then divided by the search area size to get each cell's density value. The kernel density calculation works the same as the simple density calculation, except the points or lines lying near the center of a raster cell's search area are weighted more heavily than those lying near the edge. The result is a smoother distribution of values.

If we believe our data can be used to measure a value at every location but has not been, we can use interpolation methods:

Kriging: This interpolation method assumes that the distance or direction between sample points reflects a spatial correlation that can be used to explain variation in the surface. Kriging fits a mathematical function to a specified number of points, or all points within a specified radius, to determine the output value for each location. Kriging is a multi-step process; it includes exploratory statistical analysis of the data, variogram modeling, creating the surface, and (optionally) exploring a variance surface. This function is most appropriate when you know there is a spatially correlated distance or directional bias in the data.

[1] Montgomery and Schuch, *Conversion*, 1995

333

Inverse Distance Weighting (IDW): IDW interpolation explicitly implements the assumption that things that are close to one another are more alike than those that are farther apart. To predict a value for any unmeasured location, IDW will use the measured values surrounding the prediction location. Those measured values closest to the prediction location will have more influence on the predicted value than those farther away. Thus, IDW assumes that each measured point has a local influence that diminishes with distance. It weights the points closer to the prediction location greater than those farther away, hence the name inverse distance weighted.

If we interpolated a surface based on the count of residential burglaries, we would have discrete data at several addresses. Using interpolation techniques, the data would

suggest how many burglaries occurred at intermediate addresses between our actual burglarized addresses. This would be inappropriate as no burglaries occurred at those addresses. In this case, calculating a density surface makes more sense than interpolating a crime surface.

Many assumptions go into surface mapping. A notable one is that of a homogeneous surface, which does not exist in the real world. The crime density map that is based on grid cells fails to take into account natural or man-made barriers that may affect directionality of data density. The limits of the jurisdiction boundary will also affect results, as you seldom have data on the other side of the city boundary to include in your density or hot spot analysis. Analysts should consult with their software documentation for more information on surface mapping.

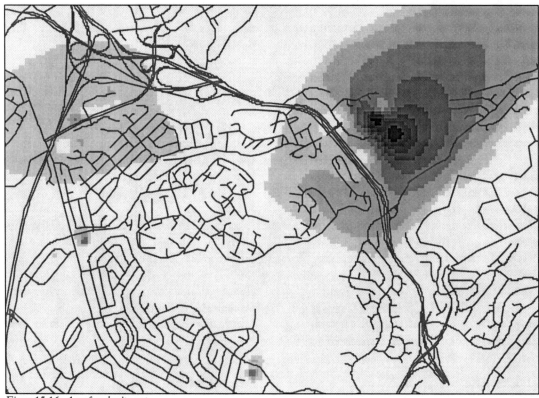

Figure 15-16: A surface density map

Spatial Analysis and Spatial Statistics

This is designed to be an introductory chapter to get a crime analyst headed in the right direction when crime mapping. In previous sections we have looked at the nature of spatial data, scale, and data classification. We also identified different types of thematic mapping techniques.

GIS software offers some statistical analysis capabilities, usually limited to summary statistics like mean, median, mode, standard deviation, and variance. There are software packages including some GIS that offer the advanced statistical analysis of spatial data. Spatial statistics include multiple regression analysis across geographic layers, trends in spatial data, and spatial autocorrelation. Spatial autocorrelation is the significant nonrandom arrangement of features in space.

It is beyond the scope of this book and chapter to cover all there is to know about spatial analysis. Crime analysts looking for more should consult their local colleges and universities and seek out specialized courses in advanced statistics, spatial statistics, spatial modeling, and spatial analysis.

Map Publishing

If you've read this far, you have learned about collecting or creating data, storing data on the computer, retrieving or querying data, manipulating data, and analyzing data. With that said and done, it is now time to display or publish your crime map. This final section will provide a quick mapping overview with simple cartographic guidelines.

Map Layout & Design

Map design is the sum of every element and decision that goes into map making. Map design "involves all major decision-making having to do with specification of scale, projection, symbology, typography, color, and so on."[1] Crime maps will include crime data usually focusing on one or two themes. In thematic map design, the cartographer, or map maker, has tremendous freedom in how they design their map. There is no rule book on what a map should look like. Larger map making agencies in the federal government such as the United States Geological Survey (USGS) and National Imagery and Mapping Agency (NIMA) and large private map making enterprises such as Rand McNally or National Geographic have templates and style sheets that they use to give their maps a customary look and feel, thereby relieving the individual cartographer of design freedom.

Symbology & Color

Choice of symbology is important. Some professions have standard map symbols that are recognized industry-wide. Firemen are familiar with hazardous material (HAZMAT) placards. No such standards exist in law enforcement and crime mapping, but software vendors such as MapInfo and ESRI have included symbol sets that are suitable for crime mapping.

Tradition and familiarity are powerful forces in cartography. The use of dots, squares, and triangles on a map is still a good idea, and research has shown that map users will respond correctly to simple and standard symbology.

Color choices are also guided by tradition and familiarity. There are conventional color choices. When you see a blue line or area on a map, chances are that you think of water. Likewise, red seems like an obvious color choice if you are illustrating hot spots on a

---

[1] Arthur Robinson and Barbara Petchenik, *The Nature of Maps* (Chicago: University of Chicago Press, 1976), 19.

map. We must also consider the connotative meanings associated with color. What color do we wear to funerals? Black is associated with sadness or melancholy.

Conventional color choices
- ☐ red—urban, built up
- ☐ brown—land surfaces
- ☐ blue—water
- ☐ yellow, tan—dry vegetation
- ☐ green—lush, thick vegetation
- ☐ black—man-made features

Connotative meaning of color
- ☐ purple—royalty, dignity, sadness
- ☐ blacks, browns, grays—melancholy, sadness, depression
- ☐ blues, greens—calm, security, peace
- ☐ yellow—cheer, fun, gaiety
- ☐ red, yellow, orange—excitement, stimulation, aggression

Map Components

Purpose

First and foremost you must ask yourself, why am I making this map? Did the chief request this? Am I making maps for weekly crime bulletins? Am I making this map for displaying in front of city council next week? Much like writing a term paper, you must decide the purpose and theme of your map. Keep it simple. Too many purposes and too much information on a map will confuse the map reader. Crime mapping is a flavor of thematic mapping. Try to stay focused on one or two themes when you make a map.

Audience

The second important question you must answer is "who is the audience for this map?" Am I making the map for the chief or for detectives? Is this map for display on the Internet making the audience everyone in the world with Internet access, or will it be displayed behind the agency's firewall?

When you decide on the audience, you will be in a position to determine how much detail to include and how complex the map must be. A map for analysts, detectives, and other police officers would provide much more detail at the street level about a series of crimes. A map prepared for presentation on your local access cable television channel will need to be simple because of the resolution limitation of analog television broadcasts. Which brings to the next topic: format.

Format

Early on in the mapping process you should select the format for your mapping exercise. There are three formats that come to mind right away: paper or hardcopy maps, digital-only maps, and Web maps for posting to the Internet. Paper maps will be discussed here because they are still the dominant mapping format in law enforcement. The rise of Internet mapping is encouraging, but much research must still be done on map visualization on the Internet.

When preparing to design and lay out a paper map, you must decide on the paper size that you will print on. Of course, your choices will be dictated by the printer or plotter that you have available. In the U.S., there are standard paper sizes available for off-the-shelf purchases. Those with a large-format plotter also have the option of purchasing paper on rolls measuring 36 or 42 inches wide.

Most folks have a standard LaserJet or Inkjet printer available, but are limited to letter size documents measuring 8.5" x 11" or legal size documents measuring 8.5" x 14". You may consider upgrading to a printer capable of printing B-size documents on 11" x 17" paper, greatly enhancing your mapping options with more paper space available. If you fold that map in half it still fits in a standard (A- or letter-size) document or report that you may be preparing.

Standard paper sizes:	
A	8.5" x 11"
B	11" x 17"
C	17" x 22"
D	22" x 34"
E	34" x 44"

Figure 15-17: Standard paper sizes for maps

Large format plotting on C-, D-, and E-size paper allows you to make large maps and posters suitable for displaying in large meeting rooms. Just remember to make symbols and text large enough to be viewed from greater distances on maps designed to be viewed from a distance. Make a draft copy of your map first and let your friends review it. Let your friends tell you if they can read the map from a given distance.

Orientation

You must decide whether to choose a landscape or portrait orientation. The default orientation will be set in your printer setup. Your map orientation is usually dictated by the orientation of your geography. This can be affected by your map design if you decide to insert photographic images or text boxes in the layout.

Scale

The scale of your map will be affected by the map format you choose. Remember that given the same size piece of paper, a large scale map will show more (large) detail, but a small area. A small scale map will show less (small) detail, but a larger geographic area. A larger map format will enable you to map at a larger scale and include more detail.

Your map must include a reference to scale for taking reasonably accurate measurements and so the map reader can interpret the relative distances between features. Most GIS software makes the insertion of scale simple. You can insert a bar scale, a representative fraction, or a text or verbal scale.

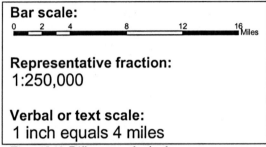

Figure 15-18: Different types of scale references

Title

Your map should include a descriptive title. This should not be difficult. Most map titles are placed at the top of the page, but this is not the rule. A map title should indicate the subject matter depicted on the map and may also include a reference to the time frame that the map data illustrates. For example, *"Residential Burglaries for January-March 2004."*

Legend

Your map is made up of symbology simplifying the real world into graphic images for ease of interpretation. You have taken events and selected the important features to map and interpret. Because you are using symbology you must include a map legend. The map legend explains what all those symbols and colors signify on your map.

Legend

CRIME

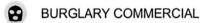 BURGLARY COMMERCIAL

 BURGLARY RESIDENTIAL

⚬⚬ CRIMINAL TRESPASS

Figure 15-19: Example of a legend

North Arrow

Your map should include a north arrow. Customarily north is "up" on a map, but that does not have to be the case.

Grid or Graticule

A graticule is a regular pattern of lines of latitude and longitude on your map used for spatial reference. If you are mapping a large area, these lines may be valuable for locating GPS coordinates.

A grid, or measured grid, is a pattern of regular spaced lines at a user-defined interval. You may want to illustrate a grid at 100- or 1000-foot intervals—whatever is appropriate and useful for your map scale—to assist the reader in estimating distances on the map.

Credits

You should give credit where credit is due. If your base map was provided by another department in the city, you may want to add a credit statement on the bottom of your map that says something like "*Base map provided courtesy of Gotham City GIS Department.*"

Disclaimer

It is becoming popular to add disclaimers to maps to avoid liability for misuse. Often you will see "*Map complies with National Map Accuracy Standards*" or "*Map for reference purposes only and not to be used as surveying instrument.*" An oft seen statement on police maps reads "*For Police Use Only*" or "*For Internal Use Only.*"

Summary

Exploring Crime Analysis was written to provide a crime analyst with the basic tools required to become proficient at his or her job. So too, this chapter on crime mapping provides the basic tools to become a good crime mapper. To be a good crime analyst, one needs training and experience. To be a good crime mapper, one needs training and experience.

In this chapter we looked at the definition of cartography and GIS. We now understand that there is a fuzzy boundary between the two disciplines. We have taken a look at the nature of spatial data and learned how to think of the real world elements in terms of the vector (points, lines, and areas) data model and the raster data model.

We delved briefly into the science of cartography with a discussion on projections, datums, and coordinate systems. If the earth was flat, this would be easy, but because the earth is not flat we are faced with problems when projecting the earth on a flat computer screen or piece of paper. And when all that data is stored in the computer we know we must store it in a coordinate system of some type—preferably a standard coordinate system such as latitude and longitude or state plane coordinates that facilitates integrating other data layers from our jurisdiction or neighboring jurisdictions.

We then took a look at the nature of spatial data. That plays an important role in how we map data. Is data discrete, occupying single locations, or is the data continuous, covering a wide area? In addition to the nature of data we looked at scale and the effects scale can have on our map presentations.

We examined data and getting data in the computer. Law enforcement agencies are rich with tabular data that can be address matched or geocoded yielding "dots" on a map.

Then we looked at how we classify data and the different map techniques available to us to make simple crime maps that tell a story or paint a picture of the data at hand. Point symbol maps are one class of thematic map, and graduated symbols are a useful tool for illustrating multiple occurrences of data at a single point. Choropleth, or area symbol mapping, is a popular technique when we aggregate data at the polygon level. When we map the data we must give consideration to how we classify statistical data. We defined and looked at examples of the most popular techniques: natural breaks, equal intervals, and quantiles.

Finally we wrapped up the chapter with a brief discussion of the essential map components and map production. Always keep in mind the purpose and audience of your maps. Then consider the best format for making your map and the scale that will work best. Include all the necessary map elements, such as title, legend, scale, credits, dates, disclaimers, and a north arrow, and you will be ready to make crime maps!

Recommended Readings

A Guide for Applying Information Technology in Law Enforcement. National Law Enforcement and Corrections Technology Center, 2001.

Antenucci, John, et. al. *Geographic Information Systems: A Guide to the Technology.* New York: Van Nostrand Reinhold, 1991.

Aronoff, Stan. *Geographic Information Systems: A Management Perspective.* Ottawa: WDL Publications, 1989.

Bair, Sean et. al., eds. *Advanced Crime Mapping Topics: Results of the First Invitational Crime Mapping Topics Symposium.* Denver: National Law Enforcement and Corrections Technology Center, 2001.

Berry, Joseph K. *Spatial Reasoning for Effective GIS.* Fort Collins, CO: GIS World Books, 1995.

Clarke, Keith. *Getting Started with Geographic Information Systems.* Upper Saddle River, NJ: Prentice Hall, 1999.

DeMers, Michael N. *Fundamentals of Geographic Information Systems.* New York: John Wiley and Sons, 2003.

Dent, Borden. *Cartography: Thematic Map Design,* 5th ed. Dubuque, IA: William C. Brown Publishers, 1999.

Goldsmith, Victor et. al. *Analyzing Crime Patterns: Frontiers of Practice.* Thousand Oaks, CA: Sage Publications, 2000.

Harries, Keith. *Mapping Crime: Principle and Practice.* Washington, DC: U.S. Department of Justice, 1999.

Longley, Paul A. et. al. *Geographic Information Systems and Science.* New York: John Wiley and Sons, 2001.

Montgomery, Glenn E. and Harold C. Schuch. *GIS Data Conversion Handbook.* Fort Collins, CO: GIS World Inc., 1993.

Obermeyer, Nancy J. and Jeffrey K. Pinto. *Managing Geographic Information Systems.* New York: The Guilford Press, 1994.

Robinson, Arthur H., et. al. *Elements of Cartography.* New York: John Wiley & Sons, 1995.

16
Effective Crime Analysis Writing

Barbara Brookover

Writing effectively is an art. There are basic elements, however, that when mastered allow anyone to write quality analytical expository narratives. Knowledge of the elements of effective writing, which include objectivity, accurate identification of audience, organization, determining relevant information, clear purpose, concrete and specific terms, an understanding of technique and style, and how to apply these elements, are key to successful crime analysis writing.

The question remains, why write effectively? Implementation of a new program, determination of staffing needs, and the re-design of beat boundaries (to name a few analysis projects) depend not only on the accuracy of information, but on the manner with which it is presented. The advantages of good writing are often overlooked and, as a result, information presented in written form is often misunderstood, incomplete, misleading, and ignored. This can cost individuals and organizations time, energy, and money. Whether you are writing a memo, proposal, or a report, the elements of good writing must be considered.

Expository writing, which exposes an idea or point of view by giving detailed explanations and definitions, is particularly subject to deficiency. Analytical writing, which takes the expository narrative one step further, is the primary writing style of the crime analyst. The need for clarity, conciseness, and efficacy in this type of writing is especially critical.

Sample Writing Assignments

On the following pages are two sample writing assignments based on the same data analysis. The samples are modified from the actual reports that were written; the type of complaint and the school names have been changed. As we examine the elements of good writing in the chapter, we will refer back to the samples.

Writing Styles
Definitions

Creative/descriptive writing tells a story that may or may not be based on fact. The intent of this type of writing is to provide a narration, not to inform, persuade, or justify. This is the type of writing found in novels. It is entertaining and often subjective.

Expository writing is distinguished from creative and descriptive writing because of the objective, direct, and specific nature of the content. An expository document explains who, what, when, where, why, and how. It is intended to inform, providing detailed information about a specific topic; therefore, ideas should be clearly identified and presented. Good expository writing has a narrowed topic that is easily identified by the reader and well supported by details, facts, and figures.

Analytical writing is a form of expository writing—concise and informative. Analytical writing, however, takes the details, facts, and figures included in the content and draws conclusions for the reader. When we analyze, we take something apart and find out what's inside, how it works, what its purpose and meaning are. Writing becomes analytical when the subject matter has been analyzed for the reader.

Noise Complaints at City of Anywhere Schools—SAMPLE A

Noise complaints have historically been excessive at school sites within the Anywhere School District. The complaints are the result of both sanctioned and non-sanctioned sports events, juveniles skateboarding and creating a noise disturbance on school grounds, dances, and concerts sponsored by the schools, and so on. During calendar year 2001, the Anywhere Police Department responded to 232 noise complaints at schools, dispatching 371 police units that spent a total of 127 hours. The number decreased to 181 noise complaints during 2002, requiring 304 police units that spent a total of 107 hours.

Noise complaints for the first quarter of 2003 total 145 at school sites. The 221 police units that have responded spent a total of 73 hours. At the current rate of occurrence, noise complaints will total 580 for the year, representing a 220% increase over the total noise complaints last year. The Police Department will dispatch 884 units and will spend 292 hours responding to noise complaints at schools within the Anywhere School District.

There are 35 schools within the Anywhere School District. The five schools with the highest number of noise complaints, January 2002 through March 2003, account for 30% of the total school noise complaints. The top ten schools account for 50%. The school with the highest number of noise complaints is Northridge School. Since January 2002, there have been 48 noise complaints at this school. Twenty-seven of these occurred January through March this year.

Attached are tables and reports that illustrate in detail the noise complaint problem at schools within the Anywhere School District during the past 12 month period, April 2002 through March 2003. According to the City of Anywhere Municipal Code Chapter 7.23, the Police Department has "…the right to discontinue response to any location that has ten or more noise complaint calls within a six-month period." Nine of the thirty five schools within the Anywhere School District currently qualify for discontinued response, each having had ten or more noise complaints during the past six month period.

Noise Complaints at City of Anywhere Schools—SAMPLE B

Thirty-five of the Anywhere School District (ASD) schools had a total of 276 noise complaints between April 1, 2002 and March 31, 2003. The following information is a brief summary for those schools.

By Month

	All Noise Complaints	Anywhere Schools (A.S.)	A.S. % of All Noise Complaints	A.S.% of Total ASD
Apr-02	531	17	3.2%	6.2%
May-02	593	5	9.8%	1.8%
Jan-03	487	27	5.5%	9.8%
Feb-03	552	52	9.4%	18.8%
Mar-03	639	66	12.2%	23.9%
Total	6775	276	4.1%	

The three months of 2003 account for 52.5% (145) of the ASD total (276) for the summary period.

March 2003 had the highest number of noise complaints with 66, approximately 23.9% of the ASD total for schools. March was followed by February 2003 with 52 noise complaints, approximately 18.8% of the ASD total.

ASD noise complaints for March 2003 (66) accounted for 12.2% of the total city noise complaints (539). The average percentage in the summary period for ASD noise complaints when compared to all noise complaint locations in the city is 4.1%.

By Hour and Day

	Sun	Mon	Tue	Wed	Thu	Fri	Sat	Total by Hour	Hour % of Total
0:00	2	2	1	1	0	1	2	9	3.3%

Much of the writing done in crime analysis is based on statistics, figures, and charts, developed as part of the analytical process. Presentation of the data without adequate written explanation can result in unanswered questions, incorrect conclusions, and misleading assumptions on the part of the reader. After analysis, a crime analyst is often expected to provide recommendations based on the results of the analysis. The purpose of the analysis may be to provide information so that others may make recommendations. Unless there is sufficient summarization of the data in the analytical written response, neither one of these outcomes is possible.

Examples

Creative/descriptive

Lock your doors and windows or you may be the next victim in the latest series of residential burglaries. From the time you leave in the morning until you return in the evening, your house is at risk. Hide your jewelry and record the serial numbers of stereo and video equipment, as these are the types of items most appealing to the thieves.

Expository

An increase in residential burglary has recently been identified in the City of Anywhere. During the past two months, 15 residential burglaries have occurred in beats 422 and 423. The crimes are being committed weekdays between 7:00 A.M. and 5:00 P.M.. Entry has been primarily through unlocked doors and open windows. No suspect information is available.

Analytical

During the 2-month period June through August, there were 15 residential burglaries in the gated community of Woodland Hills in the eastern section of the City of Anywhere, overlapping beats 422 and 423. This represents an increase of 75% when compared to the previous 2-month period. The burglaries are occurring between the hours of 7:00 A.M. and 5:00 A.M. Entry into the residences has been made via unlocked garage doors in 7 cases,

unlocked rear doors in 3 cases, open rear windows in 2 cases and through locked rear windows in 3 cases.

No suspect information is available. However, the type of property taken, which includes items easily concealed (jewelry and cash), as well as those requiring a vehicle for removal (stereo equipment and televisions), suggests the suspect may live within the gated community or associate with a resident.

The majority of entries were through unsecured doors and windows. It is therefore recommended that information be disseminated to residents in the target area regarding home security, specifically securing windows and doors.

Noise Complaints at City of Anywhere Schools

What writing style is used for Sample A?
What writing style is used for Sample B?

Sample A is written in an analytical writing style. The sample has the components of expository writing—a clearly defined topic (excessive noise complaints at schools in the Anywhere School District), and an explanation of who, what, when, where, and why. Additionally, the data has been analyzed and the sample includes an objective summary, including only the most important information to provide an overall picture of the extent of problem.

Sample B is written in an expository writing style. The sample has the required components—a clearly defined topic (excessive noise complaints at schools in the Anywhere School District), and an explanation of who, what, when, and where. Although the writing is factual and summarizes specific data elements, such as time of day and day of week, the summary does not provide an overall picture of the extent of the problem.

Objectivity and Point of View

Objectivity means free from opinions, personal feelings, and prejudices. When we are objective, we are detached, unbiased, and fair—fundamental characteristics of expository analytical writing.

Subjectivity involves the influence of our personal interests, prejudices, and emotions. Many crime analysis reports are based on data that has been identified, compiled, and analyzed using tables and charts sorted and evaluated in a variety of ways. This process is inherently subjective, resulting in myriad facts and figures. In the definition of analytical writing, summation was listed as a critical element. Summarizing the facts and figures and turning them into useful information also requires a degree of personal or individual interpretation about what should be included and what conclusions or recommendations follow from the data.

We have determined that crime analysis writing is an expository analytical writing style, which, by definition, is objective. We have also determined that there is a degree of subjectivity inherent to data analysis and the resulting writing process. How then, do we write effective crime analysis narratives that meet the requirement of objectivity?

Avoid the use of the first-person in analytical writing. Although the crime analyst selected the data for analysis, selected the analytical methods, conducted the analysis, and determined relevant information to include in the narrative, the narrative should not be written from a personal perspective.

Following are three statements presented from different points of view.

FIRST PERSON: *After careful analysis, I think a beat configuration consisting of eight beats would best meet the needs of the department because it provides for consistent citywide coverage.*

THIRD PERSON: *The committee recommends division of the city into eight beats, which provides equal field coverage throughout the day.*

ASSERTION: *Implementation of an eight beat configuration equally distributes calls for service activity, and with the current staffing plan, supports the deployment of two officers, per beat, per shift, providing equal field coverage throughout the city.*

All three statements are based on the same analytical process and the conclusion is the same for each—the city should be divided into eight beats. The first two statements, however, express the conclusion from a personal point of view, while the third, an assertion, simply states the conclusion as fact. Always support an assertion with evidence. If this is not possible because the evidence is inconclusive or only suggests a final outcome, this should be noted.

There may be occasional situations where personal perspectives are appropriate. An example would be when someone specifically requests that you, or a committee of which you are a participant, provide your opinion or recommendation. It would then be suitable to write an expository analytical narrative from a first person or third person point of view. Because credibility can be a factor, as well as the motive for the conclusion or recommendation, facts that support any conclusions must always be included.

Noise Complaints at Anywhere Schools

What is the point of view used for Sample A?
What is the point of view used for Sample B?

Both Sample A and Sample B are written objectively, asserting factual information. Opinions are not expressed in either sample.

Identification of Audience

Before beginning any writing project, it is necessary to identify your audience. Ask yourself two basic questions: Who is my audience? What do they need to know? Then answer the following questions.

- Why are you writing?

- What level of knowledge and experience does your audience have in the subject area you are writing about?

- What responses do you expect from your audience after they read your material?

- What will it take to get the responses you want?

- Are there responses you want to avoid?

- How will you know if your writing has accomplished the desired objective—are there feedback methods in place?

By considering these questions, you will meet the requirements of your audience. Potential audiences include your supervisor, fellow crime analysts, administrators, the general public, and patrol or investigative personnel, and may consist of individuals or groups of individuals. There may be occasions when information will be shared with more than one audience type, which may require separate written material for each.

The reader's level of knowledge about the subject matter determines the amount of background information to include. It also determines the level of detail and vocabulary. Too much background material serves as a review, causing the reader to lose interest. Too little background material and the reader may become lost. The same responses may result from too little or too much detail, which can leave the reader bogged down or

guessing. Terminology can overwhelm with its intensity or insult with its simplicity. Without the focus of a specific, well defined audience, your writing may be ignored, misunderstood, questioned, or discredited.

Analytical writing requires that details be communicated efficiently and clearly. Recognizing the knowledge and experience level of your audience allows you to provide the amount of detail they need, in an order that can be easily understood. Determining relevant information, or details, will be covered in a later section of the chapter.

Noise Complaints at Anywhere Schools

Who is the intended audience for Sample A?
Who is the intended audience for Sample B?

Police and school administrators were the intended target audience for both samples.

Sample A includes enough background information to describe the problem (the number of past noise complaints and the projected number if there is no intervention, activities that are generating the complaints, the effect on police resources for required responses, the schools with the greatest number of complaints), and enough detail to inform, yet not overwhelm.

Sample B provides background information that describes the problem statistically; that is, the number of complaints during the previous 12-month period. Many details are included that show the time of day and day of week of the complaints. This information is beneficial to individual school principals who must operationally eliminate the problem. It is of little value to administrators, who are interested in the big picture and are concerned about the entire school district. School principals are therefore the audience that would benefit most from Sample B.

Purpose

Two questions that assist with identifying your audience also help identify your purpose: Why are you writing? What outcome are you anticipating from your audience as a result of reading your written product? The purpose and the audience go hand in hand: write to get the results you want by giving your readers what they want.

By definition, the purpose of analytical writing is to present facts, explain a process, or define a concept. This would include writing to obtain funding for a proposal, to make a change in organizational policy, to provide instruction on how to complete job tasks, to impart information, to draw conclusions, or to gain credibility for a new crime analysis concept.

The purpose of your writing needs to be immediately clear to your audience. In a funding proposal, for example, the purpose is clear: to receive a financial award. The desired result may be hiring additional staff or implementing a new program. Proposal funding usually requires completion of specific objectives, which also need to be clearly identified. These objectives may require changes in organizational policy, for example. In this example, several written products, with different audiences and purposes, would be required.

To clearly define your purpose, it may be necessary to break down the overall topic into subtopics, identifying issues associated with each one. Ask questions about how your desired result can be obtained and carefully consider the answers. These answers will determine how successfully your document will be designed and the effects that it will have.

Once your document has been completed and disseminated to your readers, how will you know if your objective has been accomplished? Requests for a response or feedback can be verbal and expressed when the written document is delivered in person or as a follow-up to the written material. They can also be included at the end of the text, if appropriate: "If you have any questions or comments, please do not hesitate to contact me," or "I look forward to your response."

Noise Complaints at Anywhere Schools

What is the purpose of the writing in Sample A?
What is the purpose of the writing in Sample B?

Excessive police response to noise complaints at schools was an identified problem. The purpose of both samples was to impart information; to inform the target audience that the problem existed. The expected result was an awareness of the problem and a scheduled meeting with police and school administrative staff where accountability and corrective measures could be discussed, with the goal of reducing noise complaints and the resulting police responses.

The response or feedback mechanism was verbal contact with the initial recipient of the information: police department staff. They acknowledged the problem and passed the information along to school administrative staff, requesting a meeting after the information had been reviewed.

Because <u>Sample B</u> was directed toward school principals rather than police and school administrators, only <u>Sample A</u>, with accompanying data tables, was disseminated.

Details—Determining Relevant Information

Communicating details efficiently means giving your audience the relevant information they need, in an order that makes sense. Earlier in the chapter we discussed identification of audience. When evaluating details, consider the audience and what they need to know about your topic. If the information is not relevant, do not include it.

One method to determine the relevance of the details is to list them. Consider the topic you are writing about and then consider your potential audiences. List information relevant to the topic, considering what would be of interest to each audience.

Following is a list of details resulting from the analysis of noise complaints at the City of Anywhere Schools. Potential audiences include police department administrators, police department field personnel, school district administrators, school principals, and school staff (e.g., teachers, coaches).

INFORMATION	INTERESTED AUDIENCE
Cost of police responses to noise calls	Police administrators
City ordinance that allows for discontinued response to locations with repeat noise complaint calls	Police administrators School administrators
Number of police responses to noise complaints	Police administrators Police field personnel School administrators School principals School staff
Reasons for noise complaints	Police administrators Police field personnel School administrators School principals School staff
Times and days of occurrence of complaints	Police field personnel School principals School staff

INFORMATION	INTERESTED AUDIENCE
School sites with the highest number of complaints	Police administrators School administrators School principals School staff
Plans for continued monitoring of noise complaint volume	Police administrators School administrators
Recommendations for reducing noise complaints	Police administrators School administrators School principals School staff

Now that you have identified the information relevant for each audience, the next step is to rank the details in order of importance for each audience. The above example lists eight details and five potential audience groups. The number of details and potential audience groups will vary for each writing project. Thus, prioritizing or ranking ensures that only those that are most relevant and interesting are included. These should be presented in the ascending order of their importance and interest level to the audience. Exclude those that are of the least interest or have no real significance.

Noise Complaints at Anywhere Schools

Were the details relevant in Sample A? Were the details relevant in Sample B?

Based on the audience and purpose, relevant details were included in Sample A. Five of the above eight listed details were considered relevant to the target audience groups and were ranked in order of interest from most to least interesting.

Sample B includes three of the eight details in the table. These details are all of interest to school principals, who we determined were the target audience of this writing. Looking again at Sample B, let's evaluate the relevance of some of the details included.

81.2% (224) of the ASD total noise complaints happened between the hours of 5:00 A.M. and Midnight for all days of the week.

The writer is telling us that 81.2% of the complaints occurred during 79% of the day. Is this a relevant detail?

The weekend (Saturday and Sunday) accounted for 47.5% (131) of the total ASD noise complaints and had the highest per day average of noise complaints with approximately 65.5. In comparison, weekday (Monday through Friday) noise complaints averaged 29 noise complaints per day.

The writer repeatedly tells us throughout the narrative that Saturday and Sunday are the weekend and Monday through Friday are weekdays. Is this relevant? The statements that weekends had the highest per day average of approximately 65.5 and weekday noise complaints averaged 29 per day is misleading, based on the data listed in the tables included in the report.

82.8% of weekday (Monday through Friday) noise complaints happened between the hours of 4:00 A.M. and Midnight. The most prevalent hour for noise complaints was 6:00 A.M. with 15. Mondays accounted for 46.7% (7).

This statement tells the reader that 82.8% of weekday complaints occurred during 83% of the day. As with the previous statement regarding 81.2% of complaints occurring within 79% of the day, this information is not significant The time of day data has not been analyzed; it is simply stated.

Language

When the actual writing begins, language is an important consideration. Strong language skills promote a greater understanding of your material and a greater chance that your writing will have the desired result. If you

include concrete and specific terms, rather than abstract and general terms, your writing will be more interesting and will not require clarification.

Abstract and Concrete terms

Abstract terms refer to ideas or concepts—non-tangibles. Examples include good, bad, many, successful, responsibility, and rehabilitated. The terms are common and are used often, but can mean different things to different readers. The meanings of abstract terms can also change over time and with different circumstances.

Abstract terms should be used as little as possible in analytical writing. If they are used, the writer needs to understand that they are imprecise and may lead to misinterpretation. They may be necessary to describe ideas, but on their own, they are not informative and do not make points clear or interesting.

Concrete terms are the opposite of terms that are abstract; they describe tangible objects or events that are available to the senses. Examples include prison, guns, knives, buildings, pens, and pencils. These concepts are stable. Their meaning does not change over time or with different circumstances.

The title of a report *Successful Rehabilitation in Prison* includes one concrete and two abstract terms. The term prison is recognized and available to the senses; we can touch, see, smell, and hear a prison. We cannot, however, see, hear, touch, feel, or smell successful rehabilitation. Readers may misinterpret the content of the report before reading it due to their own interpretation of the terms. Recognizing this, the writer needs to be sure that abstract terms are clearly defined in the beginning and are supported by concrete terms and facts.

General and Specific Terms

While concrete and abstract terms are opposites, general and specific terms describe different ends of a range. General terms describe groups; specific terms describe individuals.

General terms can be confusing and vague when they describe broad categories of objects or events. Take the word "crime," for example. It describes unlawful acts, but is vague. Violent crime is more specific, describing unlawful acts against persons. It is still not specific enough, however, and may not be interesting to your audience. Terms such as homicide, rape, robbery, and assault describe specific violent crimes, which have clear meanings and which create greater interest. The general term crime, in the above example, may be the intended term, and specifying the various crimes would bog down the reader and take away from the overall topic of the writing. The details that make up the writing determine the language.

Analytical writing contains factual information that has been reviewed, evaluated, and summarized. Therefore, the words need to be specific and accurate, allowing the reader to understand exactly what the writer means.

Noise Complaints at City of Anywhere Schools

What language is used in Sample A?
What language is used in Sample B?

In Sample A, the introductory sentence contains the term excessive, which is an abstract term. It lets the reader know that, according to the police department, there are too many noise complaints to the schools and these complaints require a disproportionate number of police responses.

The number of complaints, which is listed within the same paragraph, provides an explanation for the term. All other language in the sample is concrete and specific.

Sample B contains concrete and specific terms.

Organize Your Writing—Executive Summaries and Analytical Outlines

Organization is another critical element in crime analysis writing. Because it is unlikely that your audience will have the time or patience to try to decipher a poorly organized report, memo, or paper, the point of the writing needs to be immediately clear.

Following is a portion of a memo that was written by a crime analyst, addressed to management level staff.

> SUBJECT: Past Due Billing/Non-Response Status
>
> To date there has only been one non-response location; the location's status was changed due to past due notices to pay on alarm fines and subsequent alarms at the location. The analyst needs information from finance, location name and address of past due notices sent, to facilitate in the identification and analysis of other locations that may cause or have caused consistent problems for the Police department...
>
> Please let me know if this information can be obtained.

The memo is poorly organized and although statements refer to the need for information, the purpose for needing the information and the specific information needed are not clear.

An **executive summary** is a method of organizing your analytical writing that allows readers to immediately find the information they are looking for. It takes the important results and conclusions of a report and summarizes them on one or more pages, depending on the length of the report. The actual report and associated data tables and charts are attached for further review, but their review is not required to fully comprehend the point of the report or paper.

An **analytical outline** is a method of organization similar to an executive summary. It allows the reader to find what they are looking for quickly and easily. Following is the format of an analytical outline. The background and introduction sections that are present in traditional writing are considered most effective if they are included in sections 1, 2 and 4. [1]

The analytical outline

1. The problem (What have you done and why?)

2. Your results and conclusions (What did you find out, and why is it important? What's your solution to the problem?)

3. Your recommendations (What should the reader do about your results?)

4. The two or three major details of your analysis, investigation or development (Here are the details of what I did and how I did it.)

5. Your conclusions (Restatement, in which you answer these questions: So what? And who cares?)

6. Appendices (The rest of the details.)

---

[1]T. M. Georges, "A Course in Analytical Writing for Science and Technology, Lesson 6," http://mywebpages.comcast.net/tgeorges/write/les6.htm (accessed July 28, 2004).

Noise Complaints at City of Anywhere Schools

Is Sample A an executive summary or does it follow the analytical outline?
Is Sample B an executive summary or does it follow the analytical outline?

Sample A is an example of an executive summary and it follows the basic format of the analytical outline. The results of an analysis of noise complaints were organized on one page, allowing the reader to immediately recognize the problem, results, and conclusions—the point of the writing. Numerous pages of associated data tables that illustrated the problem for individual schools and showed comparisons among schools were attached. There were no recommendations included in the summary because solutions were to be developed collaboratively between the Police Department and the Anywhere School District.

Sample B was also intended to be an executive summary. It consisted of multiple pages, however, and results and conclusions are not immediately clear. Data that was included in the attached charts and tables was also listed in the summary, along with additional statistics

Advantages of the analytical outline over a traditional one:

- Readers can find what they are looking for quickly and easily.

- When you begin with concrete results, you immediately get your reader's attention.

- You immediately expose your readers to your point of view, so that they will not judge your conclusions according to their own preconceptions.

- Your writing will be shorter and easier to write.

- By including the minor details in the appendices, you avoid cluttering your writing.

The executive summary or analytical outline method of organization should be a consideration in all crime analysis writing. This method can be used to provide a summary for monthly or quarterly crime statistical reports, for example, noting the increases or decreases in crimes, arrests, and calls for service in one page that allows the reader to know what is happening without having to page through numerous charts and tables. It also allows for immediate recognition of noteworthy activity.

Style and Technique

Earlier in the chapter we defined descriptive, expository, and analytical writing styles and reviewed the characteristics of each, emphasizing the expository and analytical styles. These can be approached in an infinite number of ways, limited only by a writer's individual style. The two writing samples evaluated throughout the chapter were based on the exact same data. They are, however, entirely different as a result of the distinctive technique and style of each author.

Skill in using components of style such as clarity, coherence, consistency, and conciseness, dictates the final outcome of the writing. Whether style and technique are inherent or learned, they must be adapted to the intended audience and purpose.

Clarity ensures that writing is uncomplicated, straightforward, and easy to understand. Clear writing also demonstrates error free

standard writing conventions (grammar, capitalization, spelling, punctuation, usage, and paragraphing).

Coherent writing is intelligible and articulate. Use of stylistic methods such as transitions, pronouns, repetition, and parallel structure ensure that ideas are linked to one another and have a logical order.

Consistency ensures that the same tone is maintained throughout the document. Whether formal or informal, personal or businesslike, the same tone or mood is consistently communicated to the audience.

Concise writing condenses your meaning into the fewest possible words, eliminating what your reader can easily surmise. This was discussed earlier as it related to the determination of relevant details. Use of the active voice is usually more direct and concise than the passive voice, and statements presented in a positive form are more concise than negative statements.

Summary

The analytical writing style is concise, informative, and factual. Objectivity removes any perceptions of bias and the consistent focus on the topic ensures that the memo, report, or paper will be read and understood. Effective crime analysis writing eliminates unanswered questions, incorrect conclusions, and misleading assumptions.

Crime analysis writing is effective when it incorporates the elements of good writing, including sufficient supporting details, clear purpose, logical organization, communicating a sense of completeness, and demonstrating an understanding of technique and style. Incorporating all the elements of good analytical expository writing into your written products ensures that, technically, your writing will be effective.

Every writer, however, has his or her own individual writing style. There are those that consider effective writing to be a science, and those that consider it an art. Both terms convey skill, ability, talent, proficiency, aptitude, and flair. Your own individual style determines the final product of your writing and allows flexibility in how the basic elements of effective writing will be incorporated into your piece. Experiment until you are satisfied that your writing is the best that it can be. This may require numerous drafts, but the final outcome will be worth the effort.

Recommended Readings

Georges, T. M. "A Course in Analytical Writing for Science and Technology." http:// mywebpages.comcast.net/tgeorges/write /les6.htm

Ross-Larson, Bruce. *Effective Writing*. New York: W. W. Norton & Company, 1999. This source book of proven tips and techniques provides all the tools needed to improve and refine your writing skills.

Rozakis, Laurie E. *The Complete Idiot's Guide to Grammar and Style*. New York: Alpha, 2003. The book takes you step by step through the basics of spelling, punctuation, and sentence formation to help you become an effective communicator of the written word.

Strunk, William Jr. and E. B. White. *The Elements of Style*. New York: Longman, 2000. The book approaches style by way of plainness, simplicity, orderliness, and sincerity. A well known, highly recommended book.

Williams, Joseph M. *Style Toward Clarity and Grace*. Chicago: The University of Chicago Press, 1995. A logical, expert, easy-to-use guide for achieving excellence in expression.

17
Crime Analysis Publications

Herb Williams

Who will use your crime bulletin? You spend hours going over information, reading reports, writing your analysis and producing maps, graphs, and charts. It's hard work. But do you really understand what the consumer wants and needs, and how to provide it?

Police are swamped with information: wanted posters, law changes, policies and procedures. Frankly, they get a lot of information that they don't even want. Does your crime bulletin look like every other memo from the front office? How will you make sure that your work—the information they really need—gets their attention?

This is not a chapter on how to create a document in Microsoft Word; it is a chapter on how to market an analysis product. This chapter will show you how to use your word processor to publish crime bulletins that officers will recognize as something they want, will remember, and will use. When you finish this chapter, you will have new knowledge and skills that will make you better at getting valuable information to the people who need it the most: the police officers and detectives on the street.

This chapter is divided into three main areas: "Understanding Your Audience," which discusses the need to give readers what they want; "Principles of Adult Learning," which will make your product easier to understand and remember; and "Points of Form and Style," which will address the hands-on skills of document publishing.

You may have noticed that two of the three sections don't mention the word processor. Ten years from now, we might not even use word processors anymore. Ten minutes from now, somebody will write a better program, and the editors will have to change the technical instructions in this chapter. So don't let the details keep you from seeing the big picture clearly. Your technical skills are important, but your brain is your most important tool by far.

Understanding Your Audience

Just because you think information is important does not mean that your audience will think it is important. The best analysts in the world know that their best work is wasted if it does not meet the needs of the intended audience. "[T]he analyst needs to ask directly for specific feedback from the customer. This is most effective if the analyst (and his or her management) has a collaborative relationship with the customer."[1] Why produce a detailed spreadsheet if all the customer wants is a pin map? So ask your customers what they want and how they want it, give them what they want, and then go back and ask if they used what you gave them.

Administrators need information for long-range, strategic decision-making. Workload per hour of the day is one example. Detectives need investigative support, such as analysis of burglary *modus operandi* (*m.o.*); shift commanders need to know where the hot spots are; patrol officers need to know who is running with whom. They don't necessarily care what the other units need.

---

[1] David Moore and Lisa Krizan, "Intelligence Analysis: Does NSA Have What It Takes?" *Cryptologic Quarterly* 20, no. 2 (2001), 8.

Give people what they want. Your mission is to analyze data and produce reports that tell people what they need to know. So if we're talking about, say, burglaries, the captain probably needs the spreadsheet, the detectives need the narrative comparing MOs, the lieutenants need the map, and the patrol officers need the mug shots. If you get feedback asking for a slightly different report, you should change your report accordingly.

If you have a reputation for giving officers the information that they want, the way that they want it, they will be more likely to read what you write. That helps everyone. When they use what you produce, they will be more likely to collaborate with you. That helps you to improve your work product.

Principles of Adult Learning

Now that you have everyone reading your crime bulletins, how do you get them to take action? This is where understanding how adults learn helps you. When you know how adults learn, you will write differently, and create your bulletins differently. You don't have to develop a lesson plan for every bulletin; but understanding basic principles will help you to present information in a way that makes it easier to understand and remember. That ease of grasp and recall is what will enable officers to take the leap from understanding the information to acting on it.

Let's face it: cops are a hard group to sell. The fact that most analysts are non-sworn only makes the job harder. Do not waste your credibility by telling people things they can't understand, or don't want or need. If you keep principles of adult learning in mind as you prepare your bulletins, you will be more likely to get the results you want. [1]

---

[1] Drawn from "Principles of Adult Learning" in *Methods of Instruction for Police Academy Instructors* (New Jersey Department of Law & Public Safety, 2003).

Adults Learn When They Are Ready

Since we are talking about members of a police department reading crime bulletins, we can assume that we have already met the threshold of job-relatedness. Adults are generally more ready to learn when the information is job-related. That's why we try to tailor the product to the intended audience, as discussed above. Additional motivators can be positive or negative.

Positive motivators include the intrinsic value in improving traffic safety in a given area (e.g., "Bulletin 03-21: Increase in Rear-End Collisions at Merge of Rt. 9 South and Green St."), or capturing a dangerous criminal (e.g., "Bulletin 03-22: Suspect in Sexual Assault."), or solving a long-term problem (e.g., "Bulletin 03-23: Thefts of Wallets from Gym Lockers").

Negative motivators include personal safety (e.g., "Bulletin 03-24: Armed Suspect Alert.").

Note that you do not have to tell the readers why they should be motivated to read the bulletin. However, you must be able to clearly identify a motivation for the target audience. If you cannot do so, then you need to redirect the bulletin to the appropriate audience. Every officer will be motivated to read about the armed suspect, but most detectives will wonder why you sent them a bulletin about traffic crashes. If they aren't motivated to read your bulletin, they will just throw it away, and they may not even bother to look at the next one you write.

What if the motivation just isn't that clear? How do you help the reader to get ready to learn? You can spell it out for them. Here is an example:

> **Bulletin 03-25: High-Volume Offenders**
>
> The Crime Analysis Unit has identified several previously unknown Township residents as high-volume criminal offenders, listed below.
>
> Extensive analysis has shown that the following Twp. residents, while never arrested in this jurisdiction, have extensive, current criminal histories. Any contacts with them should be documented, and where probable cause is found, thorough investigations should be conducted...

Patrol officers and detectives would love to have that information, wouldn't they? But if you don't show them why they should care, they might not read far enough to learn that there are a bunch of criminals hiding in their town. The first sentence spells it out. It speaks to the motivation, the readiness of the reader, to learn.

Adults Learn When They Understand the Reasons Why

Assume that there is a positive reception for your bulletins; readers expect to get what they want, and they are ready to get it. It's still not enough to simply say, as in the example above, that there is an undetected bunch of criminals in town. Your audience will be more likely to accept a statement like that if they understand why you say it.

You may be tempted to provide long explanations, or show how the statistics took you from point to point to conclusion. This is a temptation that should be avoided. If your readers need that much detail, they can find you at your desk. But you should provide enough explanation to reassure them that your statement is well-grounded.

In the example of the high-volume offenders, the bulletin said that extensive analysis has shown certain residents to be active criminals. Of course, you will keep all the supporting documentation in your files, but bulletins must be brief. So you might say:

> Traffic warrants for unpaid parking tickets indicate that several of these persons frequent known drug locations in another jurisdiction; their criminal histories show multiple convictions for drug possession, shoplifting, possession of stolen property, and other crimes, with several arrests in the immediate past twelve months. In addition, in the past two years, First Aid Squads have been summoned to nine of the twelve residences listed, for overdoses.

When the readers understand how you came to your conclusion, it makes it easier for them to accept it.

Adults Learn One New Thing at a Time

This principle goes hand in hand with the preceding principle: that adults learn when they understand the reason why. A large part of your job is helping your consumers understand how you came to your conclusions. When they are comfortable that your statements are reasonably drawn from the facts, they will accept your analysis, they will use your reports, and they will take you on faith even when they don't completely understand how you came to a conclusion.

Getting a group to that point of acceptance is no small task. You can only get there one step at a time. Since officers will rotate in and out of the department, you will have to repeat the education process over and over. That's okay; most of your customers will need to hear it repeated anyway.

If you are not meeting regularly with the people who use your reports, please start immediately. You need to meet with them to take in new information and to tailor the reports to their needs. But while you are there, you should take the opportunity to educate your audience on how you do analysis. You will do this a little at a time, making sure that there is good understanding of a topic before moving on to the next.

Remember how hard your statistics course was? How much harder would it have been if you hadn't learned one new thing at a time?

When new officers come into the group, you have an opportunity to go back and reinforce ideas you have covered before. Remember, people might not admit that they do not understand. They might just stop asking, and stop reading. If that happens, you have failed in your mission to deliver actionable information. The burden is on you to help your audience, one step at a time, to understand the material you give them.

This is also a good time to remind them about what you need from them to produce good reports. Common complaints among analysts are that reports are submitted with key information missing, names misspelled, associates not identified, and handwriting illegible.

Adults Learn New Things in Relation to Things They Already Know

Let's assume you are helping your audience to understand the reasons why you drew a certain conclusion, and you are introducing one new idea at a time. Where do you start?

Start from a point that everyone can understand. If you relate new material to things people already know, it will make it easier for them to follow. Here's an example:

Bulletin 03-25: Possible Gang Violence

There is a strong possibility of escalating gang violence in Patrol Area 5E.

Patrol Area 5E is known to be the primary residential area of the 18th St. Gang. Fourteen individually identified members of the 18th St. Gang live there, and have been arrested over sixty times for drug sales and possession, assaults, and weapons charges.

This area has had a recent surge of immigrants from the country of Boravia. Many of these immigrants are in the country illegally. Boravian language graffiti, including the tag "B-92," has been documented in numerous locations in Area 5E. 18th St. Gang graffiti has been found crossed out at the same locations.

The State Police Gang Intelligence Unit reports that an organizer for the Boravian prison gang known as "B-92" is frequently seen in Area 5E, and may be attempting to expand the gang's influence and drug trade.

There are enough indicators to believe that a gang conflict may be approaching. If the reports about the gang organizer are accurate, there is a strong possibility that gang violence will result soon.

Pictures of known 18th St. Gang members are attached. Pictures of suspected Boravian gang graffiti are also attached. Officers having any contact with suspected gang members should gather as much identifying information (names, addresses, associates, vehicles, tattoos,) as possible.

This bulletin doesn't just say that there is a possibility of violence between the 18th St. Gang and B-92, and then leave it at that. It walks the readers through the facts and the analytical process, one step at a time, starting with something they all know: the 18th St. Gang, in Area 5E, has many known members who have been arrested many times, and who are involved in drug sales and violence.

To help the readers understand why there is a strong likelihood of additional violence, the report gives them new information one step at a time: Area 5E has seen an increase in Boravian immigrants; many are here illegally; there is an increase in Boravian graffiti, possibly gang tags, around the 18th Street Gang's turf; a Boravian prison gang organizer has been reported in the area.

The last three principles work best all together: help your audience understand the reasons why by starting from something they already know, and proceeding one new step at a time. If your customers can understand your report more easily, they will accept what you say, remember it better, and take action.

Use As Many Formats As Possible (Just Not Too Much)

Earlier, we said that the captain probably wanted the spreadsheet, the lieutenant wanted the map, and so on. That's still true. Different audiences will want different formats for their information. When someone expresses a preference, you should try your best to give him or her information in that format.

However, it will make your task easier if you use multiple formats whenever possible. Some people learn better by reading, others by hearing, and others by putting their hands on the lesson. As crime analysts, we will normally be restricted to written information,

and that is where the primary focus of this chapter lies. The main thing for you to remember is that you are not restricted to text alone. You should supplement what you write with additional forms of stimuli: crime maps, tables, charts, pictures, and mug shots are just some examples of things you can include in your crime bulletins.

By all means, you should use other methods of communicating if you can. Talking to the various groups that depend on your reports is critical. It allows you to walk officers through the analytical process you use, to show them how you draw facts out of reports and how you draw conclusions; it allows you to pass around props, like a filed-down Honda key that car thieves use, or an authentic-looking fake license. You are not doing this to be an evidence technician; you are doing it because different people learn in different ways. Using as many senses as possible helps you reach more people, and helps you drive the point deeper than you could by using one format alone.

How much is too much? It depends. For a crime map that will go up on a bulletin board, go ahead and hang the spreadsheets next to it. Those who want to read the detailed breakdown of what times of day or what *m.o.* was used can do so. Most officers will simply look at the map. But for a bulletin, try to keep the main message to one page. You may include copies of warrants, call history for a location, or other supporting information on additional pages, but the text and one or two graphics (map, chart, or picture) should all fit on one 8½" x 11" page.

Wrap-Up

Talking to your consumers is not a word processing skill, but it will lay the foundations that support what you write later. It will help you to understand what they need and how they need it, and it will let you help them to understand how you got from point A to conclusion C. We agreed from the start that it is hard work; you not only have to gather and analyze the information, you have to get other people to understand it. These are the principles that help you to make it understandable.

A well-designed crime bulletin can take all these principles into account and still fit on a single page. And when you can do it—when you can get good intelligence out to the people who need it, and get them to understand it—you will be prompting effective action. When you do this well, everyone around you will see that you are an indispensable part of the public safety team.

Form & Style

In this section, we will cover some of the technical details of publishing a crime bulletin.

White Space and Bold Face: Because Nobody Reads Fine Print

Remember that overburdened officer we discussed earlier? The one who has to read fifteen memos from the bosses before he even gets his coffee? How much attention span does he have left by the time he gets to your crime bulletin?

Please give him a break. We all know that your report is the one he really needs to read. So make it easy on his eyes. Make it easy for anyone reading your bulletin to spot the really important parts. Here are some suggestions on format, gathered from the best, most experienced crime analysts all around the world.

Distinctive Header: Make your bulletin distinctive enough that anyone in the police

department can look at a stack of memos and pull out the crime bulletin. A word on color choices: if your bulletins are really popular, they will be copied by the simplest means possible: a black and white copier in the muster room. So make sure the header looks good in black.

No Fancy Fonts: After the header, keep everything else to one font type, one font size. You can set the sub-headings off with capital letters, (e.g., LOCATION, KNOWN ASSOCIATES or VEHICLE USED,) or in another font, as long as the information is easy to find and easy on the eyes. If a **suspect is known to be carrying a gun**, that should be in bold face.

Use White Space: Have you ever noticed that the details at the bottom of a contract are written in line after line of small print? That's because they don't want you to read it. We will do the opposite, because we want people to read what we write: keep paragraphs short, around three or four lines for a bulletin, and put spaces between each paragraph. The eye is attracted to readable print surrounded by white space.

Formatting—Eye-Catching, Not Eye-Sore: A good crime bulletin stands out from other documents. But distinctive should not be confused with flashy. Your crime bulletin may wind up in court one day, or in the newspaper. It has to look professional. Use lines, shading, boxes, pictures, and charts to highlight important information, but don't let your bulletin be mistaken for a used car advertisement.

Including Graphics

Let's not re-invent the wheel. You should be focused on the final product, not the steps that go into it. We already agreed that your word processing program will undoubtedly

358

be updated regularly, rendering some of these steps obsolete. Find a way that works for you. One of the nice things about Microsoft Word is that it gives you several different ways to accomplish the same results. If you have trouble, resist the urge to call the Helpdesk. You'll learn better if you research the answer for yourself. Microsoft has a Web site with a link to help you use their products better; so does every other major company that writes word processing programs. If you do not have Internet access at work, please show this page to your boss: it is imperative that crime analysts have Internet access (see Chapter 20).

There are many good programs available to help you manipulate pictures, adjust color and clarity, and even manage photo lineups to the highest legal standards. Adobe Photoshop is a very sophisticated program that allows for complex projects. The downside is that it requires some formal training to learn to use its full capability. ACD Systems' ACDSee, on the other hand, is easy to learn, and adequate for most basic tasks an analyst will need to perform. Use the right tool for the job.

Pictures make your bulletin much more readable and informative. They can include mug shots, photos of vehicles or disguised weapons, or anything else an officer may need to see.

First, you need to save your picture in a format you can manipulate. Depending on the software you're using, you might save it as a .bmp (bitmap), a .jpg (jpeg), or a .png (portable network graphics) file. There are many different formats available, and tinkering with them will help you to determine which one works best in different circumstances. If you are publishing your material on a Web-based system, .jpg images have enough detail to do the job, and nearly all browsers can read them. For printed documents, .png or .bmp files compress more data; you can expand them more easily, without losing resolution. Adobe Photoshop is one tool that can help you to improve resolution and adjust size, as well as enabling a wide variety of other tasks, such as cropping out mug shot cards for photo lineups, and adjust the brightness and contrast to make pictures better.

Most word processing programs have some basic tools for manipulating pictures, too. Resizing a picture is a simple matter of selecting it and then dragging the "handles" that appear along its borders. Dragging the corner handles ensures that the image's proportions remain intact. Some word processing programs (like Microsoft Word) can also crop, lighten, darken, and adjust the contrast of images.

Positioning images in relation to text can be difficult and frustrating, and it takes some practice to do it properly. By default, most word processing programs insert photos "in line with text," which means the photo is treated as a text character. Even if the photo is sized to take up only half the page, you cannot type next to it.

There are three ways to position text and images relative to each other:

1. Tables
2. Wrapping
3. Text Boxes
4. Columns

Examples of each are given on the next page.

Keyhole provides outstanding satellite images. See http://www.keyhole.com.

This is an example of a table used to arrange text and images. The first row of this table has a single column, and the second has two columns. We've shown the table gridlines (the dotted gray line), but normally you would not show them in a bulletin. Note that you can specify a "fill" for each cell, as in the first row.

This solution works best when the amount of text you want to present takes up about as much space as the image that will accompany it. We've had to add this extra sentence in to make the sizes match.

James J. "Whitey" Bulger

This layout was accomplished with text boxes (again, we've shown the borders). As you can see, text boxes can appear on top of images as well as next to them. The photos are of fugitives on the FBI's "Ten Most Wanted" list, obtained from http://www.fbi.gov.

As in tables, you can determine the border and "fill" of the text box. The text boxes over the photos are transparent, while this box has a patterned background.

Richard Steve Goldberg

In this example, the text is "wrapped" around the image. In Microsoft Word, this is accomplished by choosing the image and choosing Format | Picture | Layout | Square. Word also allows you to edit the "wrap points" of the image, so you can determine precisely how close to the picture each line of text gets. That works well for non-square images like this "yield" sign symbol. Note how the text follows the contours of the image.

Finally, text and pictures can be arranged in multiple columns. In Word, this is done through Format | Columns. You can apply a two-or-more-column format to an entire document, a single page, or a section of text, like here. This book—which, incidentally, was written and laid out in a regular word processing program—is mostly in two-column format, but it frequently switches to a single column (as on this page) to accommodate a table or image. (This section, however, occupies three columns with a line between.) See page 19, for instance, where the two-column layout is broken at the bottom to accommodate a table that must span the entire page width. Chapter 13 provides several pages in which both images and text are integrated in a two-column format.

Maps

The best thing about maps is that they convey so much information in a small amount of space. The next best thing about them is that they are easy to manipulate; you will treat them just like pictures, as described above. Here are some tips that will help you make the best use of maps.

- A map that looks great in a large setting may be too detail-rich to work on a small scale. Be sure to preview it before you go to print.

- A simple street map may be adequate for plotting crime clusters, but it won't show tool sheds and trees, and other hiding places and pathways that a good aerial photograph will show.

- The map that you use to analyze a situation may not be the best map to use when communicating information to officers. Analysis is one part of your job, and helping others to understand the situation is a different part of your job (see Chapter 1). Use the right tool for the job.

See Chapter 15 for more information about mapping and map design.

Tables

Tables are useful, but not as visually enticing as maps and charts. Try to team them up with a good caption to explain what they display, and remember the KISS rule: Keep It Simple, Stupid. Do not use tables that display too many different factors in a standard crime bulletin.

The nice thing about tables is that you can create or import them from another source, as you might do with a picture, or you can create one right in the document.

It's a fairly simple matter to take a table from a spreadsheet program (like Microsoft Excel) and import it to your word processing document. Many analysts use spreadsheets to track information and to perform data analysis. (See Chapter 18 for more information about spreadsheets.)

Table 17-1 was created in Microsoft Excel. But if you try to import an Excel table directly to Word, you will discover why it is called a spreadsheet program. It assumes that it will be printed onto a sheet of paper wider than your 8½" x 11" crime bulletin. Before you import that table, you need to make sure it will fit between the margins.

Alarms Entered into CAD 1997 through 2002*

Type	1997	1998	1999	2000	2001	2002	Percent Change 2001 vs. 2000	Percent Change 2002 vs. 2001	Total
Hold Up	555	477	442	487	392	357	-20%	-9%	2,710
Burglary	6,804	7,386	7,698	7,385	6,491	6,401	-12%	-1%	42,165
Fire	1,060	1,006	1,027	1,089	1,006	1,045	-8%	4%	6,233
Total	8,419	8,869	9,167	8,961	7,889	7,803	-12%	-1%	51,108

* General alarms with descriptions of Panic, Ambush or Duress were changed to Hold Up. Car alarms were deleted (approx. 50 per year). Medical alarms were also deleted (approx. 150 per year).

Table 17-1: a table pasted from Microsoft Excel

Copy the table from the spreadsheet program, and paste it onto your bulletin. If it is too wide to fit, you have some options:

- Re-size the width of the columns in the spreadsheet program, and then copy and paste again.

- Re-set the margins in your bulletin to allow a wider table. Don't push them out smaller than 0.1 inches. Remember to re-set them after the table.

- Print the table on a separate page using the "landscape" orientation rather than the standard "Portrait" layout.

You can create a table, like Table 17-2, in most common word processing programs. The spreadsheet option is the more common method, and the fastest, but there may be times when you want to simplify the data you present.

Area	Roof	Office Door	Win-dow	Truck Bay	Total
Down-town	2	6	3	0	**11**
North	3	8	4	13	**28**
East	2	5	2	8	**17**
Totals	**7**	**19**	**9**	**21**	**56**

Table 17-2: A table created in Microsoft Word

The main idea is to be comfortable with a variety of formats to help your consumers digest information more easily

Charts

Charts do a lot to make information easier to grasp. If you have saved a chart like any other picture, treat it like a picture. But you're more likely to create a chart in your spreadsheet program and import it from there.

Colorful charts are useful because they are eye-catching, but the black and white rule still applies: good bulletins will be reproduced by the most convenient means available, which is normally a black and white copier. Preview your charts in black and white to make sure they still make sense that way.

Too many colors will fail, even in a well-designed and adequately colored chart. Don't go beyond four contrasting colors, three or less is even less likely to confuse people.

Publishing Bulletins Electronically

Web publishing goes beyond the scope of this chapter, but here are a few suggestions that may help you to avoid the pitfalls identified by many analysts who have gone before you. Dreamweaver and FrontPage are very popular, user-friendly programs that many Web designers use. Putting your bulletins on a police intranet (see Chapter 20) in this format is a great way to get the information out to the people who need it.

It is imperative that you protect your crime bulletins from being changed after they leave your hands. You can easily imagine the mischief that would result from an improperly altered official document. Publishing in HTML is one way to prevent this. Another is to publish them as Adobe portable document format (PDF) documents. This way, you can distribute them as e-mail attachments, and they can be read or printed but not changed. However, your readers must have Adobe Acrobat Reader installed on their computers.

When using e-mail to send your bulletins, the same conditions apply as with paper: make sure the intended readers can immediately identify the message as a crime bulletin. Another consideration is how much information to put into the subject line. You need to include enough information for readers to be able to sort through their saved bulletins and find the ones of interest to them. For example:

TO: All Patrol Personnel
FROM: Crime Analysis Unit
SUBJECT: Bulletin 03-26: Prostitution in Downtown Area.

What if you wanted them to know that there had been a shift in *m.o.*, and that prostitutes were now frequenting the park where patrol cars couldn't see them? You can't fit that much information into the subject line. Getting to the point by the most direct route is an underrated skill.

Conclusion

Use the right tools for the job, but remember that your word processor is just a tool. You don't have to be an expert with it to do a good job, but you do have to know its capabilities. If you find a way to use it that works better than what is presented here, then you should use that way. These techniques are by no means definitive. Improvement and adjustment is not just a fact of life with computer programs; it is something to be desired.

Your most important tool is your mind. That's where you do your work, and it is where you need to have an influence on your customers. A good working knowledge of how adults learn will enable you to cut through all the static and give critical information straight to the officers who need it. Do your job with these principles in mind and you will never have to wonder if you have made a difference in peoples' lives.

18
Spreadsheets

Sean Bair
Noah J. Fritz
Dan Helms
Steven R. Hick

The primary analysis tool for most crime analysts is arguably the spreadsheet application. Crime analysts turn to their spreadsheet application in their time of need more than any other software available to them. Analysts use spreadsheet applications to calculate crime rates from year to year, calculate time series analysis, produce graphs and charts, and execute "what if" scenarios against available data. Many analysts also use the spreadsheet as their data repositories or means to pass data from one database type to another. In this chapter, we will explore the history of the spreadsheet application, its intended purpose, its contribution and place in crime analysis, and various methods an analyst could readily use with a spreadsheet application to address typical crime analysis problems.

History

In the realm of accounting jargon, a "spread sheet" or spreadsheet was and is a large sheet of paper with columns and rows that lays everything out about transactions for a business person to examine. It "spreads" or shows all the costs, income, taxes, and other categories on a single sheet of paper for a person to look at when making a decision.

In crime analysis, a spreadsheet is a software application used to store, manipulate, retrieve, and analyze data and produce statistical results. Before introducing the various uses of a spreadsheet application in crime analysis, it is important to understand the history of the spreadsheet to assist us in identifying its intended purpose.

The term "spread sheet" as it was originally used has its origin traceable well before the introduction of the microcomputer. References to the term "spread sheet" can be found as early as 1952 (e.g., first edition of Eric L. Kohler's *Dictionary for Accountants*[1]) Therein it is described as a worksheet providing a bidirectional analysis of accounting data (e.g., an accounting matrix in which the columns and rows constitute either debit and credit sides respectively or reverse).

It wasn't until the early 1960s that the first spreadsheet began to have its computer-based roots. Richard Mattessich pioneered the use of computerized spread sheets for business accounting. In his book, *Simulation of the Firm Through a Budget Computer Program*,[2] Mattessich provided the first examples of a spreadsheet application through print-out illustrations and proposed a spreadsheet computer program written in Fortran.

In 1978, more than a decade later, Dan Bricklin and Bob Frankston brought the spreadsheet computer program to the average computer user. Their program was called VisiCalc, short for "Visible Calculator" and it was marketed by Personal Software. In 1979, VisiCalc was first available for the Apple II computer.

One of the most significant challenges that Bricklin and Frankston had was from the Lotus 1-2-3 spreadsheet. Soon Lotus 1-2-3 was taking away VisiCalc's market share. Several factors eventually led Lotus 1-2-3 to take over from VisiCalc. While the 1-2-3

---

[1] Prentice-Hall, 1952.
[2] Homewood, IL: R.D. Irwin, 1964.

program looked very similar to VisiCalc, they made it more powerful and easier to use. VisiCorp (formerly Personal Software) had not upgraded or enhanced VisiCalc enough to keep ahead of the competition so in the end, Bricklin was forced to sell VisiCalc to the Lotus Corporation in 1985.

In 1987, Microsoft joined the spreadsheet marketplace with Excel. Just as VisiCalc lost ground to Lotus 1-2-3, Lotus lost a significant part of its market share to Microsoft's Excel primarily due to the ease of use, the graphical user interface that Excel provided, and its capability to operate under the Microsoft Windows operating system. Microsoft Excel clearly dominates the spreadsheet market today. Not too long ago, Lotus 1-2-3 was considered the "standard" spreadsheet. Excel now holds that distinction with an overwhelming market share.

The Spreadsheet Application

Every spreadsheet, no matter whose brand or what machine it runs on, has the same row and column layout, with each cell defined by its row and column position. The methods of using them vary only slightly. How numbers, names, and equations are entered in the cells is about the same. There are minor variations in how equations and formulas are written. The methods for producing graphs have minor variations from spreadsheet to spreadsheet. It is only when automating tasks by way of macros that the differences can become glaring. So, if you are proficient in one spreadsheet you can fairly easily use any other. Likewise, the examples provided in this chapter should apply to most spreadsheet applications, whether Lotus, Excel, Quattro Pro, or others. Before introducing crime analysis techniques using a spreadsheet, it is important to set a baseline for its nomenclature.

Spreadsheet Jargon

Row—A line of cells across the spreadsheet. Each row has a reference number or letter.

Column—A line down the spreadsheet. Column references are usually letters of the alphabet. However, some spreadsheets use numbers for both rows and columns.

Slot or **Cell**—A single "box" on the spreadsheet grid. Each cell can be identified by giving its row and column reference. The reference A5 would mean that the cell is in column A and row 5; it is the cell where row 5 crosses column A.

Labels—The text entries on the spreadsheet are called labels. Text is used to give names (headings) to the columns and rows so that, when the spreadsheet is studied, it is easier to make sense of the numeric data.

Status Area or Command Area—This area on the screen display gives information about the particular spreadsheet you are working on. The information will vary from program to program. The status line may include the contents of the cell being used: for example, text, numbers, and formulas.

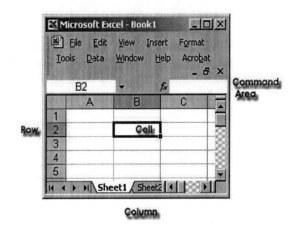

Figure 18-1: The components of a spreadsheet

"To Use or Not to Use": When to Apply Spreadsheets in Crime Analysis

Because of their ease of use and formidable power, most analysts turn to a spreadsheet application to perform just about everything. From calculating statistics, cleaning data, to uses as a data repository, even as a mapping tool, spreadsheets are a crime analyst's "go to" application. It's important to remember, however, the old saying: "Use the right tool for the right job." In addition to being arguably the most widely used application in crime analysis, the spreadsheet is also the most widely *mis*used application in crime analysis. In this chapter various uses for a spreadsheet application will be presented, while other uses will be discouraged. The following are some general abuses of a spreadsheet application and the reasons to avoid them:

- Spreadsheet models encourage the use of chaotic logic, where cells point to cells that point to cells, and can grow into random networks of calculation logic. This fact makes them attractive for applications such as neural networking, but can result in a "house of cards" of epic proportions when used as a crime analysis tool.

- They permit lots of easy off-by-one errors; although these tiny "mistakes," which result from the built-in imprecision of most spreadsheet functions, might seem trivial by themselves, they quickly add up.

- They generally are difficult to verify or audit. What formula was it behind what cell again? It's hard to know and keep track.

- They do not provide good tools for managing data either in terms of data entry or searching for details.

- Perhaps most importantly, despite their convenience, spreadsheets are not as robust a repository for information as many believe. This is by far the most routine misuse of the spreadsheet in crime analysis. Spreadsheets should not be used for data storage or as a data repository, given their limitations. These limitations will be discussed in the following paragraphs.

Besides the obvious product name keywords, Microsoft, publisher of two of the most popular spreadsheet and database programs in the world, chose these words to describe the applications when searching the Internet:

- **Microsoft Excel:** *spreadsheets, data analysis.*
- **Microsoft Access:** *database, database management, tables, queries.*

One primary reason why one would not want to use a spreadsheet application as a data repository is data limitation. Most analysts are only now becoming aware of the severe limitations in data size of a worksheet. The maximum number of rows that Excel can accommodate in a worksheet is 65,536. The number of columns (or variables) is limited to 255. One can see that with the record limit alone, most police agencies would be hard-pressed to open a year's worth of call for service records in Excel to perform a simple frequency on type of call or address. Even worse, depending on how data is entered into a spreadsheet, the user is typically never informed when record limits have been exceeded—any data beyond the limit is simply lost forever.

Another critical weakness is that spreadsheets are flat, rather than relational. Relational databases keep categorized data in unique tables and then relate records from each table to provide the most efficient possible way to show complete information about events. Flat files, on the other hand, must keep all fields—columns, in spreadsheet parlance—in one "table," the spreadsheet itself. This is a less efficient way to store information and results in rampant duplication of data. It also gives rise to a number of other potential errors. Although there are ways to join spreadsheets and make them behave like relational databases, this "Band-Aid" solution just contributes to the "house of cards" problems implicit in an over-reliance on spreadsheets.

For larger data sets, a more appropriate tool might be a statistical program. Spreadsheets are best used in crime analysis for tasks like:

- Calculate the crime rate from year to year assuming that each cell represents the total number of cases observed.
- Calculate time series analysis for crime series and patterns.
- Produce graphs and charts.
- Perform "what if" scenarios against available data.
- Calculate simple or summary statistics.
- Automate routine reporting or calculating tasks.
- Developing simple models for uses such as forecasting.

Detailed methodologies for many of these crime analysis functions will be described later in this chapter.

Data Issues in Spreadsheets: How to Structure Your Data to Maximize Your Result

Most spreadsheet applications can import and use a wide variety of data types, including server-based databases such as Oracle, SQL Server, or DB2. Accessing the more robust and complex database types typically involves

connecting to them through Open Database Connectivity (ODBC). Depending on the type of data you are connecting to, the spreadsheet program may have to modify or remove certain variable types. For instance, most advanced database types provide the means to store an Object Linking and Embedding (OLE) object such as a picture. Spreadsheet applications cannot read those variable types and will remove them during the import process. However, a spreadsheet application can handle the majority of the variable types available.

How Microsoft Excel Stores Dates and Times

Excel stores dates and times as a number representing the number of days since January 1, 1900, plus a fractional portion of a 24 hour day: ddddd.tttttt . This is called a serial date, or serial date-time. Excel can also define the date portion of a serial date as the number of days since Jan, 1, 1904. This mode is called the 1904-mode or 1904-system. The 1904 mode is used for compatibility with the Macintosh operating system and older Lotus 123 spreadsheets.

Dates: The integer portion of the number, ddddd, represents the number of days since Jan, 1, 1900. For example, the date Jan, 29, 2000 is stored as 36,544, since 36,544 days have passed since Jan, 1, 1900. The number 1 represents Jan, 1, 1900.

Times: The integer portion of the number, tttttt, represents the fractional portion of a 24 hour day. For example, 6:00 A.M. is stored as 0.25, or 25 percent of a 24 hour day. Similarly, 6:00 A.M. is stored at 0.75, or 75 percent of a 24 hour day.

Specific procedures for adding and subtracting dates and times will be provided later in this chapter.

Crime Analysis Formulas

The spreadsheet provides one of the most robust and efficient means to perform many of the common crime analysis related calculations. This section introduces many of those topics and provides examples on how to calculate them.

Common Crime Analysis Formulas

Percent Change. Percent change is perhaps one of the most widely used statistics in crime analysis. It could not be easier to calculate using a spreadsheet application. Percent change will provide us a result indicating the percentage of change from one value to another. This is useful in crime analysis to provide indications of whether crime is going up (positive percentage) or on the decline (negative percentage.) The formula is =(B1-A1)/A1 where B1 contains the most recent frequency and A1 contains the "historical" data. So, using this formula to calculate the percent change from year 2000 to 2001 where 2000 experienced 100 crimes and 2001 experienced 50 crimes would result in a value in cell A3 of -50% (assuming you formatted cell A3 as a percent.) An example of this calculation is provided in Figure 18-2.

So, to calculate percent change, simply subtract the old value from the new value, and then divide by the old value. Use the percent button to format the result as a percentage.

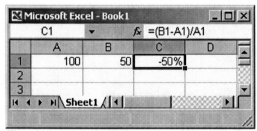

Figure 18-2: Calculating percentage change

Mean, Median, and Mode. The mean is the "average" of a group of numbers. Analysts are often required to provide average response times for emergency calls, average number of crimes per month, average length of time on a call, and so on. The mean is easily calculated in any spreadsheet application using canned functions. However, to manually calculate the mean, divide the sum of all numbers by the number of data points. The following chart illustrates the use of mean against a group of emergency response times. Notice how the mean is skewed because one of the emergency response times appears problematic—a response time of more than 100 minutes. For this example, perhaps the median response time might describe our data better.

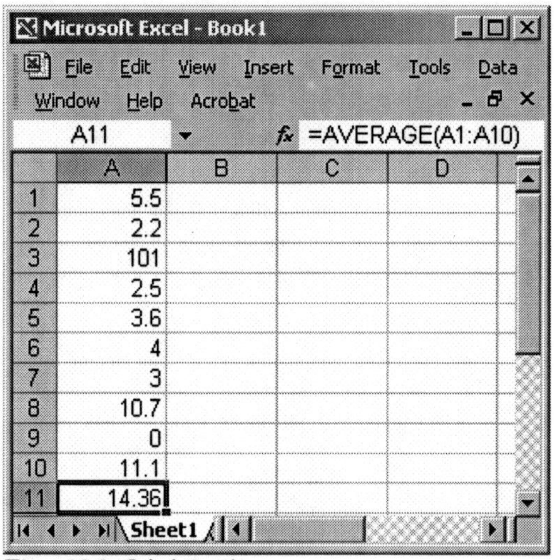

Figure 18-3: Calculating the mean

The median is the "middle" number of a group of sorted cases. For instance, 5 is the median number for the following group of cases:

1, 1, 1, 4, 5, 7, 7, 10, 202

The number 5 more accurately describes the middle for our group of cases and is not as subject to the pitfalls of outliers such as value

368

"202." When a group of cases contains an even number of data points, the median is the average of the two data points centered on the middle.

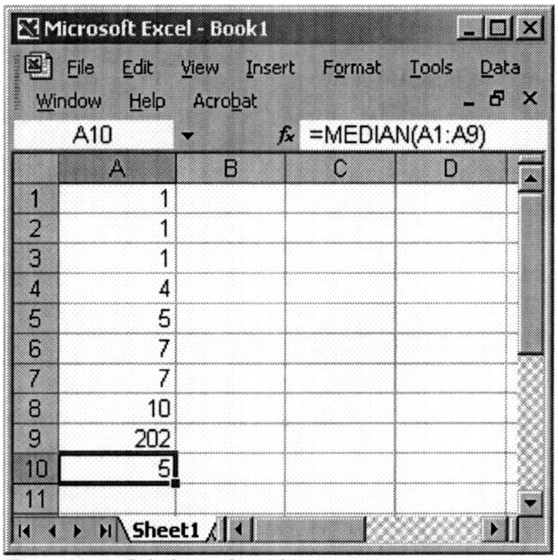

Figure 18-4: Calculating the median

The mode is the value that occurs most often in a series of numbers. The mode for our previous group of data points would be "1" because it occurs more often than any other number—3 times in all.

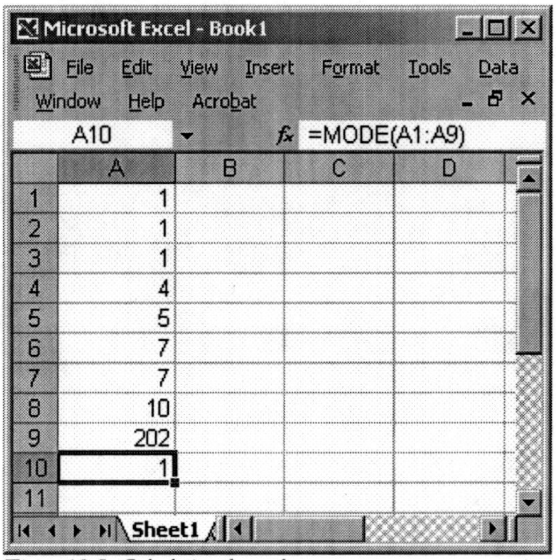

Figure 18-5: Calculating the mode

If no value is repeated, there is no mode. If more than one value occurs with the same greatest frequency, each value is a mode. Data points containing two modes are called bimodal. Data sets containing more than two modes are called multimodal. (See Chapters 10 and 13 for more on central tendency.)

Text Manipulation Formulas

Two of the most often used crime analysis text manipulation functions in Excel are concatenation and parsing. Concatenation is the process of merging multiple values in multiple cells into one cell. Parsing is the process of separating out a singular value in a cell to new values in multiple cells. An example of concatenation would be joining several cells containing components of an address (street number, direction, street name, street suffix) into one cell containing the entire address. An example of parsing data might be separating a string of words delimited by commas into several individual cells containing the data.

Parsing. Parsing is the process of taking text stored in one variable separated by some delimiter and separating the text into individual fields based on the delimiter. Parsing is most often used in crime analysis to separate a single address field into separate fields. The following illustration shows a single variable address and variables containing its parsed text.

There are various ways to perform parsing in spreadsheet applications. One of the quickest ways to easily perform parsing is using Excel's "Text to Columns" function. Here is a brief methodology of how to use the "Text to Columns" function to perform parsing. Before using this feature, make sure the column immediately to the right of the column you wish to parse is empty.

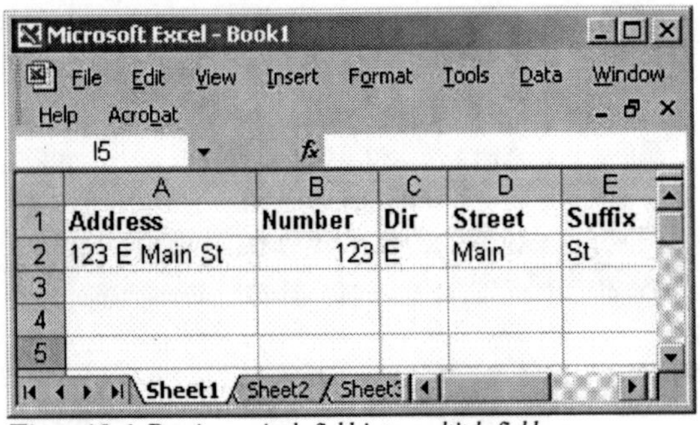

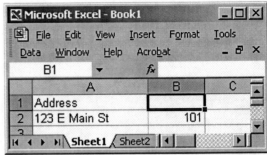

Figure 18-6: Parsing a single field into multiple fields

1. Select the data you want to separate (or select the column).
2. Go to menu Data | Text to Columns
3. Check the "Delimited" option button. Click "Next."
4. Select "Space"
5. Click "Finish"

Of course, data can be parsed using any of the other delimiters. You may wish to delimit your address field by the "#" sign. Often, the # sign is used to indicate the beginning of an apartment or suite number. By using this delimiter, you will separate your address from the apartment number resulting in a separate address field and apartment/suite field. Figures 18-7 and 18-8 illustrate this example.

Concatenation. Conversely, concatenation takes several values stored in separate variables and combines their values to create a single value. Again, most often in crime analysis the need to concatenate values is necessitated by the address variable.

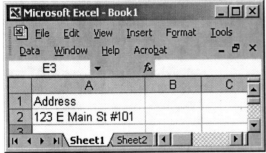

Figure 18-7: An address field before parsing out the apartment

Figure 18-8: An address field after parsing out the apartment

The concatenation process is similar to other functions performed in Excel or other spreadsheet applications in that we build a function to perform this process.

Notice how the concatenation formula displayed in the formula window contains double quotes (" "). It is necessary to include a space between our variable values otherwise the resulting value would look like this "123EMainSt". Unfortunately, often our data may contain spaces on the end of a variable value and sometimes it may not. The resulting concatenation might then have multiple spaces between values. In this case, another function may be necessary to "clean" our final address value. With the use of the "TRIM" function, we can remove extra spaces between words, leaving one space as a separator.

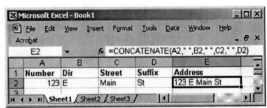

Figure 18-9: An address field concatenated from four separate fields

Table 18-1 provides additional Microsoft Excel text manipulation formulas commonly used by crime analysts.

Cell Value	Formula	Description	Result
A1=Sean Bair	=LEFT(A1,FIND(" ",A1))	Get the leftmost characters found before the first space.	Sean
A1=Sean Bair	=MID(A1,FIND(" ",A1,1)+1,LEN(A1))	Get all the text after the first space found.	Bair
A1=Sean Bair	=LEFT(A1)&MID(A1,FIND(" ",A1)+1,1)	Get the first character in the string and the first character of the first word found after the first space.	SB
A1=Sean Bair	=LEFT(A1) & MID(A1,FIND(" ",A1),LEN(A1))	Get the first character in the string and the remaining text found after the first space.	S Bair
A1=Sean Bair	=LEFT(A1,FIND(" ",A1))&MID(A1,FIND("",A1)+1,1)	Get the first word in the string and the first character found after the first space.	SeanB
A1=Sean Bair	=MID(A1,FIND(" ",A1,1)+1,LEN(A1)) & ", " & LEFT(A1,FIND(" ",A1))	Use the first space found to juxtapose the text before and after it.	Bair, Sean
A1=Banana	=LEN(A1)-LEN(SUBSTITUTE(A1,"a",""))	Find the number of occurrences of "a"	3
A1=22122001	=DATEVALUE(LEFT(A1,2)&"/"&MID(A1,3,2)&"/"&RIGHT(A1,4))	Returns a formatted date value.	22/12/2001
A1=September	=CHOOSE(MATCH(A1,{"January";"February";"March";"April";"May";"June";"July";"August";"September";"October";"November";"December"},0),1,2,3,4,5,6,7,8,9,10,11,12)	Find the numeric value for the month of September	9
A1=22/05/01 A2=5/12/99	=DATEDIF(A2A1"M")	Find how many months between A1 & A2	16
A1=15/12/01	=EOMONTH(A1,3)	Return the last day of the month 3 months from A14	31/03/2002
A1=18/02/01	=EDATE(A1,-1)	Return the date one month before A1	18/01/2001
A1= 22-	=VALUE(RIGHT(A1,1)&LEFT(A1,FIND("-",A1)-1))		-22
A1= -22	=ABS(A1)	Find the absolute value of A1	22
A1= 1995	=ROMAN(A1)	Return the Roman numeral equivalent for a number.	MCMXCV
A1= 25.499	=ROUND(A1,0)	Round the given number.	25
A1= 15.999	=TRUNC(A1)	Remove the decimal numbers from a given number.	15

Table 18-1: Common text manipulation functions. Both the EOMONTH and the EDATE functions are Excel Add-ins located in the "Analysis Toolpak"; if you use them without installing this Add-in, you will get an error message (#NAME?). To load the Analysis Toolpak in Excel, go to Tools | Add-ins and check the box next to "Analysis Toolpak."

Working with Times

Subtracting Times

Subtracting one time from another is difficult, since Excel does not handle negative numbers as times. When you enter a time without a date, Excel assumes the date is January 1, 1900, since it puts a 0 in for the date component of the serial number. For example, you cannot subtract 18 hours from 4:00 P.M., since this would result in a negative number (0.67 - 0.75 = -0.83).

You can get around this by entering a full date, subtracting a time from this, and then formatting the result as time-only. For example, to subtract 18 hours from 4:00 P.M., enter the 4:00 P.M. as "1/1/98 4:00 P.M." and subtract 18:00 from this. Formatting the result as hh:mm will result in "10:00 P.M."

Time Intervals

You can determine the number of hours and minutes between two times by subtracting the two times. However, since Excel cannot handle negative times, you must use an =IF statement to adjust the time accordingly. If your times were entered without a date (e.g., 22:30), the following statement will compute the interval between two times in A1 and B1:

=IF(A1>B1,B1+1-A1,B1-A1)

The "+1" in the formula causes Excel to treat B1 as if it were in the next day, so 02:30-22:00 will result in 4:30, four hours and thirty minutes. To covert this to a decimal number, for example, 4.5 (hours), multiply the result by 24 and format the cell as General or Decimal, as in the following example:

=24*(IF(A1>B1,B1+1-A1,B1-A1))

Rounding Times

For many crime analysis functions, it is useful to round times to the nearest hour, half-hour, or quarter-hour. The MROUND function, which is part of the Excel "Analysis ToolPack" add-in module, is very useful for this. Suppose you have a time in cell A1. In B1, enter the number of minutes to which you want to round the time; for example, enter 30 to round to the nearest half-hour.

The formula:

=TIME(HOUR(A1),MROUND(MINUTE(A1),B 1),0)

will return a time rounded to the nearest half-hour, either up or down, depending what is closest. For example, 12:14 is rounded to 12:00, and 12:15 is rounded to 12:30.

To round either up or down to the nearest interval, enter the interval in B1, and use either of the following formulas:

=TIME(HOUR(A1),FLOOR(MINUTE(A1),B1) ,0)

to round to the previous interval (always going earlier, or staying the same)

=TIME(HOUR(A1),CEILING(MINUTE(A1),B 1),0)

to round to the next interval (always going later, or staying the same)

Charting

One of the most useful features of a spreadsheet application is its capability to create beautiful and informative charts and graphs. The types and options available in most spreadsheet applications for creating graphs are virtually endless. Those that are most routinely used in crime analysis are presented here.

Bar Chart with Trend Line

A great use of a spreadsheet's graphing function is the bar chart with an accompanying least squares trend line. The bar chart by itself is a useful graph; however, by adding a least squares trend line to linear based data, you can visualize the linear or logarithmic progression of the data over time (e.g., increasing, decreasing or stable tempos, frequencies).

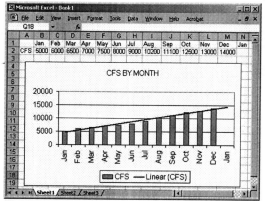

Figure 18-10: A bar chart with a trendline

Time of Day & Day of Week

One statistic widely misused in crime analysis is calculating frequencies by time of day and day of week. Often, there is a tendency to summarize the volume of incidents per day, summarize the volume of incidents per hour, and then combine the two results to state that the probability of something happening is greatest on the worst day at the worst time. This is an obvious misuse of the statistical results (see Chapter 11). However, one easy way to accurately depict the worst hour in a 168 hour week is to perform a tabulation by

hour of day and day of week and display those results using a 3D surface chart. If you structure the color scheme similar to that of a density analysis, the resulting graph will appear to provide "hot spots" on those days and hours that have the greatest frequencies. This is an excellent way to visualize the "density" of incidents over the 168 hour week. Likewise, an accompanying chart provides the necessary tabular data as reference. Figure 18-11 is an example of a time of day and day of week 3D surface chart. The chart has been converted to 2D to allow the reader to visualize density or elevation using graduated colors instead of height.

Excel Spreadsheet Automation

The following section provides automation description and examples using Excel.

There are two ways to automate tasks in Microsoft Excel—using macros or Visual Basic for Applications (VBA). Both have their advantages and disadvantages.

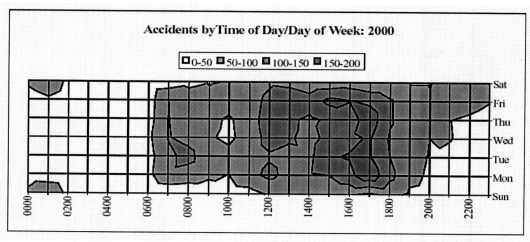

Figure 18-11: A surface chart showing the relationship between time of day and day of week

What Is a Macro?

A macro is simply a recording of keystrokes and mouse operations that can be played back later—as if a ghost was typing and clicking your mouse. A macro can be used to record a series of operations against cell data to obtain the same result each and every time while removing the need for user interaction. Because this process is done by the computer, the amount of time it takes for a macro to perform the same tasks as a human is exponentially less. For instance, you could use a macro to concatenate several fields into an "address" field instead of manually having to step through this complex process for various data sets. The trick to using macros is to know where the data is going to be when the macro needs to use it. If the macro you create will perform against data that is always structured and organized the same way, then creating and using the macro is easy. However, if the macro must make decisions about where data or variables are located, then the process becomes a bit more complex.

What Is VBA?

VBA, or Visual Basic for Applications, is a Microsoft programming language that allows users to enhance their products' core functionality. Most of the current Microsoft products, as well as other companies' software, provide a VBA interface and tools necessary to begin programming and enhancing and tailoring the product to meet their needs. For geographic information system (GIS) users, VBA is analogous to ESRI's scripting in ArcView. ArcView 3 provided scripting capability not by VBA, but through ESRI's proprietary Avenue language. (Similarly, MapInfo users will find analogous scripting using MapBasic.) ESRI has abandoned Avenue for VBA in their most recent releases of ArcGIS. This was

most likely due to VBA's popularity and ease of use. VBA is a simplified version of Microsoft's programming language—Visual Basic. There are numerous significant differences between VBA and Visual Basic, but the basic nomenclature is the same. Visual Basic is the most widely used programming language in the world today.

Differences

The question of which automation function to use when embarking on creating an automation is more about flexibility and user interaction than anything else. If your automation will not require user interaction, then a macro may be the automation choice for you. If, however, your automation must provide feedback to the user or make decisions based on user input, then you might want to consider VBA. Mostly, the decision is based on your ability to understand and program in the VBA environment. Short of learning the programming language of VBA, one quick way to get started learning how VBA works is to create macros. Macros use the same underlying VBA language. Therefore, when you create a macro, often an application will allow you to view the macro's "code," thus providing you an opportunity to see how functions and processes are written.

How to Create a Macro

Creating a macro in Excel is as simple as programming a VCR. (If the clock on your VCR is still flashing 12:00, please skip this section. If not, read on.) The process is more about planning than execution. Because the macro records every keystroke and mouse movement made, it is important to limit unnecessary commands as much as possible. Therefore, it is wise to first plan out what you wish to record and the mouse and keyboard movements you will make before recording; you might even write a "script" for yourself to follow: a set of instructions on what to click and type as you record your macro to make things run smoothly. Once you have a plan for which menus you will use, rows and columns you will manipulate, and the order you will perform them, creating a macro involves nothing more than pushing the Record button. From there, everything you do will be recorded. After you have completed all the steps in your plan, you can click the stop button to complete the recording.

The confusing part about macros is where they are stored and how to apply them to other spreadsheets. The default location to store a newly created macro is in the current workbook. Therefore, you would need to specify the location of the workbook containing the macro or have that macro's workbook open in order to use it in another workbook. To avoid this, change the default macro storage location to that of your "Personal Workbook." Storing the macro in your Personal Workbook will allow you to run the macro against any Excel file.

The other trick to macros and VBA has to do with absolute and relative cell reference. Absolute means that the reference in a formula will always look for the value in the specified cell, even if you copy the cell to a different location. The format for an absolute reference is A1 (referring to the cell located at column A and row 1). The dollar signs preceding either the column or row (or both) indicate which item should be absolutely referenced.

Relative references, which are the default, are in the column-row format (A1, E5, BD4405) and, if copied to a different cell, the cell reference changes relative to the new location. For example, if the formula specifies A1 and is copied to a new location

two rows down the new formula would specify A3. An example of a relative cell reference might be a cell containing the summary of a column of data. If the cell was at the bottom of the data (the last cell in the data), then making that formula relative would allow you to increase or decrease the rows of data while still maintaining the capability to summarize all rows.

By default, recorded macros use absolute cell referencing, which means that exact cell locations are recorded into the macro. The macro works only with the exact cells locations you use when you record the macro. When you record a macro with relative cell referencing, the actions recorded in the macro are relative to the starting cell location.

Conclusion

The goal of this chapter was to provide a fundamental understanding of the need and uses of a spreadsheet software application. The authors have only begun to scratch the surface of the available power of a spreadsheet application. Spreadsheet applications provide powerful tools to perform crime analysis but are often misused as data repositories or to perform complex statistics. Spreadsheets provide the means for crime analysts to carry out most of their day-to-day operations including data cleaning, basic statistical analysis, and the creation of beautiful charts and graphs. The spreadsheet can reduce the amount of work required of an analyst through automation using macros and VBA and free up an analyst to focus on more important matters. The spreadsheet application is a must-have tool for every crime analyst.

19
Analytical Charting

Christopher Mowbray

As humans are generally visually stimulated, the visual products produced by crime analysts are some of the most important contributions to the analysis process. At times, it is imperative that an analyst be able to take a complex set of data and present it in a visual way for it to make sense to the audience: investigators, patrol officers, superior officers, lawyers, judges, the media, and the public. Imagine taking all the information from an individual investigation and trying to explain it orally, without the use of visual aids, perhaps in a courtroom. Jury members and judges could easily be confused as the analyst attempts to explain links between people and entities by mouth. This process is simplified by the use of charts, maps, and other visual aids.

The preparation of analytical information takes knowledge of the specific types of charts, graphs, and other visual aids that may be required, as well as the software designed to aid in their creation and dissemination. One common misconception is that this all must be performed with expensive software packages specifically designed for analytical work. As important as this software is, it is not absolutely necessary in the creation of professional visual aids for an analysis product. For those agencies that are smaller or have more limited budgets, many commonly used office software packages can be used. There may be times when the analyst is unable to access certain high-powered, specific analytical software, and the office suite that came with his computer may be the only option. Thus, this chapter will begin with a discussion of many of the most

commonly created analytical visualization products and will progress into a more in-depth discussion about the types of off-the-shelf office software that can be used to create such charts. This will then lead further into a discussion of the benefits and drawbacks of both off-the-shelf software and analytically-specific software.

Though each organization or agency will have its own procedures and policies for creating analysis charts, there are certain conventions and principals that remain consistent throughout the profession. This chapter will illustrate and build on those common standards. A brief discussion of the commonly accepted practices will accompany each section, bearing in mind that the products each analyst will create could be substantially different from those pictured.

Types of Graphical Representations:

Many types of visual representations are available to the crime analyst. These are limited only by the analyst's imagination, as virtually anything can be represented graphically. The following section discusses many of the more popular graphical products that crime analysts use. Each subsection begins with a brief explanation of the analytical technique, followed by its uses. This will then lead into a discussion of the different computer software options that are available for its creation, and the benefits and drawbacks of using each option. We hope that analysts will use this information to make an informed decision as to which option is the best for use with their agencies, given their policies and procedures, as well as the software options at their disposal.

Link Charts

Link charts are sometimes called "circles and squares" charts. This format represents relationships by drawing lines between entities. In some instances, a circle would indicate a person and a square would be another entity, such as a business. These can prove to be especially beneficial where a large number of people, perhaps a gang, are associated to each other and a number of locations and businesses. Movements of entities, such as money and drugs, can also be represented in link chart format.

This is one of the most common forms of visual aids produced by analysts and as such is often one of the first products taught in many analytical courses. The capability to graphically represent relationships between people, places, and objects can greatly affect investigations and judicial proceedings. This is also one of the most widely used practices for organizing large quantities of information.

During an investigation, information is gathered from a number of sources, validated through proper investigative techniques, and placed into the link chart. This charting technique will therefore incorporate information from various sources into one analytical product, thus becoming an important piece of the analytical puzzle. It can be used in ways that individual pieces of information cannot: it also allows analysts to see indirect links between information that would otherwise seem unrelated or disjointed. Links between entities (people, places, things) can be very easily seen, analysis is made easier, and the presentation and explanation of the data is clearer.

Creating a link chart is simple: place a symbol or picture, used to represent individual entities, on the sheet of paper, either by hand or in a digital format, and draw straight lines between them. Conventions dictate that the lines used should be straight and avoid

crossing whenever possible. Should a line need to be bent, then it should be bent using an angular elbow. For example, Figure 19-1 is a representation of drugs being linked to a house (using a bent elbow).

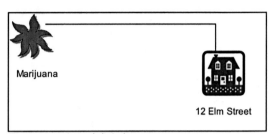

Marijuana

12 Elm Street

Figure 19-1: A simple link chart

Link charts afford the opportunity for analysts to indicate the reliability of the information. Common practice represents confirmed links with a solid line. Broken or dotted lines are used to indicate unconfirmed, weak, or possible linkages.

The use of colors and symbols are at the analyst's discretion or are dictated by the agency. i2's Analyst's Notebook, for example, has some pre-defined options as to colors and icons, although the opportunity for customization of link lines and entity icons is still present.

If several individuals or entities on a chart are linked to one common entity (for example, a business) they could be placed inside a box labeled with the name or address of the business with which each entity is associated (see Figure 19-2). Using this convention alleviates the problem of having to draw association lines between each entity and the common factor. This in turn simplifies the chart and makes it easier to ensure that lines do not cross. It also alleviates clutter, ultimately making the chart clearer.

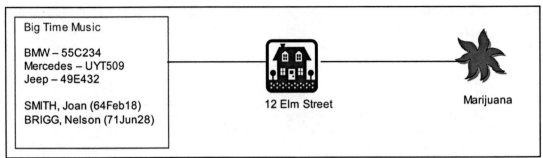

Figure 19-2: A link chart with a business. Multiple people and vehicles associated with the business are condensed in the business's box.

Figure 19-3 was created using i2's Analyst's Notebook. It is a very simple chart, but the information within it shows that a number of people can be associated to each other through vehicles, homes, bank accounts, and other associations. Using this chart, we can say that people are linked both directly and indirectly. With the chart, it is simple to

explain the connections between the people. Using Analyst's Notebook will also allow the analyst to change the icons to pictures of the actual entity being represented; therefore, pictures of the people could be substituted as well as a photo of the vehicle or house or any other entity present in the chart.

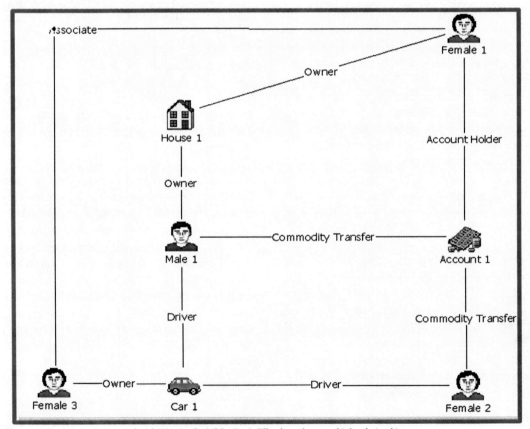

Figure 19-3: A link chart created with i2's Analyst's Notebook. The chart shows multiple relationships.

Organizational Charts

Almost everyone who has worked for an organization of more than several people has been privy to organizational charts. This is a method that shows, usually on a large piece of paper, how each person fits into the organization. It usually begins at the top with the owner or CEO, and then shows how he or she is linked to each of the vice presidents, and so on until supervision of the lowest ranks is shown. Most crime analysts are aware of this type of chart, as it also indicates the chain-of-command, a term common to police and law enforcement agencies. In the intelligence analysis world, these can be used to great benefit by showing the organization of an outlaw motorcycle group, a drug or street gang, or a fraudulently run company, to name only a few. For those familiar with genealogy, this is sort of a "family tree" representing the group.

There are some conventions to follow in the creation of organizational charts, though much of the formatting and aesthetics are left to the discretion of the chart's creator. Convention dictates that the "head" or most important and powerful people are at the top, and subsequently lower levels branch off to the bottom of the page. One may choose to include the names of the people who hold each position, depending on the space allotted for the chart, the mobility of the people in the positions, and the amount of detail the creator wants to show. As these charts are often used to represent a fluid organization, they must change periodically. The type of computer program used by the analyst determines the ease of such changes.

Organization charts are particularly useful when an analyst or investigation is focused on a group of individuals. These types of charts will provide a hierarchical structure to the group, providing easier analysis of organized crime groups or gangs, as well as groups of individuals where there could be an instigator or natural "ring leader." This facilitates infiltration and suggests possible lower-level investigation targets that, when taken down, may collapse the organization.

Figure 19-4 is an example of a typical organizational chart. Most analysts would place the names associated to each of the levels within the box as well. The example happens to be fabricated around a legitimate organization, but organized crime groups will often have an order that can be placed easily into a chart much like this one, as in Figure 19-5. These particular examples were created in Microsoft Word. Other products can be used to create identical charts.

Timelines

A timeline, a temporal analysis technique (see Chapter 11), is a very important component to any analysis package. Not only is it important to have a picture of the timing of a series of events, but so too is it important to be able to locate a suspect in time. Timelines can be both simple and complex, depending on the data one is analyzing as well as the amount of information available about the series or the suspect's past.

Imagine taking the stand in court and being asked to portray a whole series of events, both in the offender's life and in the crime series that included the crime(s) for which you are testifying. The story would become extremely difficult for a judge or jury to understand if there was no way of keeping the events straight in their minds. Therefore, the use of a visual document can be of great benefit. This document can then be used as a reference while you, as an analyst or investigator, recount the events that had an effect on the commission of a certain event.

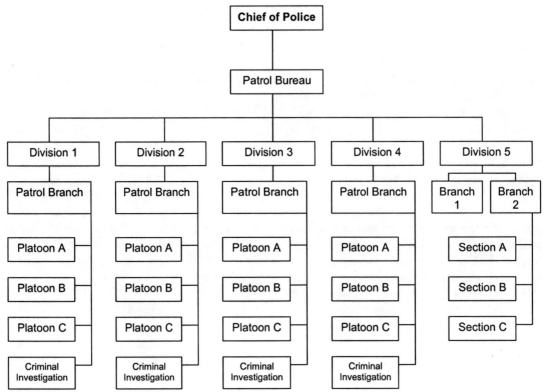

Figure 19-4: An organizational chart for a legitimate organization

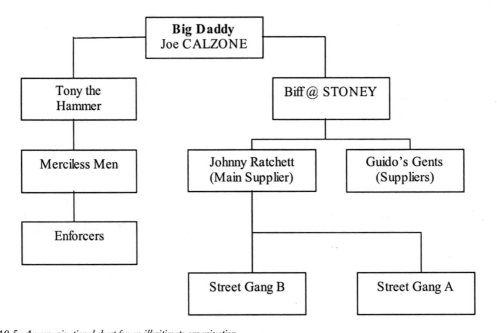

Figure 19-5: An organizational chart for an illegitimate organization

Although the influence of a timeline can be significant, its creation is relatively simple. As an analyst, you will have collected much information regarding the target event, including similar events that may have occurred previously. There will also be documentation of possible suspects from either previous cases or the target case. Therefore, each event could be placed on a timeline, indicating dates, times, days of the week, or years when each event occurred. This can aid in the determination of possible patterns in the behavior of the offender. One can then determine if any possible suspects follow that particular behavior pattern. Also important to document on a timeline could be incarceration dates and other law enforcement dealings. This can show offenders' behavior patterns and criminal activity escalation. This can become important in future charging, plea-bargaining, and sentencing.

Timelines can be based on periods of hours, days, months, or years. They can also be used on a single subject or multiple subjects—for instance, a timeline may plot the movements of the victim, witnesses, and offender on one chart. There must be an intersection in time and space between offender and victim for the crime to occur, and timelines can prove important for the determination of this intersection.

Information is the key to the creation of a timeline. One can plot almost anything on a temporal scale; therefore, investigators need to provide sufficient information as to the time frame of concern, as well as what types of activities they want plotted. Many investigators ask analysts to complete timelines for their files right at the outset. This can be a historical timeline of events leading up to the event, or a timeline of the event itself.

Adding events to a timeline, using certain computer programs, is relatively simple. Some of the most important information that can be contained within a timeline may not be criminal, but may show the buying and selling of commodities, such as homes (often with illegally obtained money), credit card transactions that indicate that the person is living well above his or her means, marriages, divorces, and other life-altering events. In addition to this information, one may indicate the time when the individual was incarcerated and thereby verify or impeach the alibis of possible suspects.

Not only will timelines provide necessary background into the event; they may also indicate an offense pattern for the offender that increases in severity or violence from petty crime to more developed (mature) criminal behavior, and even into organized crime. Timelines also have the capability to show organizational history for those involved in organized crime as they climb through the hierarchy of the group.

Figure 19-6 is a simple timeline created using Microsoft Visio. (For further examples of timelines using other programs, see the software section of this chapter.) This timeline indicates the charges leveled against the offender at certain times. Note the use of colors to differentiate between offense types.

Before creating a timeline, decide on the final output: what type of timeline do you want to create? Do you need a continuous line of events, or a series of linked boxes (much like a link chart)? How long a time must this span, and how long a time period is this going to encompass? The answers to these questions are going to dictate the type of chart that will ultimately be created and thus will also dictate which type of program you will use to create the chart.

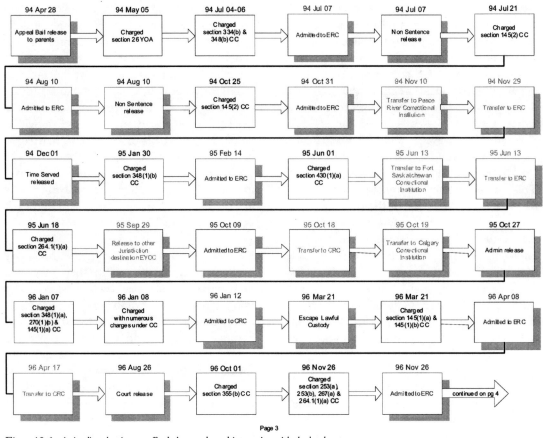

Figure 19-6: *A timeline showing an offender's custody and interaction with the legal system*

Photo Groupings

Groups of photographs can be placed on charts in either the link chart format or the organization chart format, or quite simply by being grouped together on one page. No matter the format, it is important that photos accompany the final analytical package, if only to show the faces of the target group. People are very visual and, as such, require this type of stimulus to learn more readily. By providing patrol members and investigators with a picture of a suspect, or known offender, they are more likely to remember the face or use it for future reference. An ideal way to accomplish this is to create stickers on ordinary label sheets for patrol officers to paste in their notebooks. This will

aid greatly in an investigation or if the patrol member happens along a separate file where the pictured person may play some role. In either event, further intelligence can be gathered and provided to the analyst.

Photo groupings are especially useful in gang analysis, by displaying all the known gang members, "hang arounds" and "recruits," either in a hierarchical chart—much like an organization chart—or simply as a group in alphabetical order. The analyst can then give copies of this chart to patrol members who are likely to find or have dealings with the individuals or to other specialized units where the individuals pictured may be important. One important place to offer these pictures is in the officer's meeting room. In this way, all officers are subjected to seeing the pictures every time they are on shift. Even if they are not paying attention to the photographs, the repetitive nature of seeing them continually will ingrain the image in their minds, and the next time an officer deals with one of the pictured subjects, the officer may recognize the suspect from the poster. The same holds true for the production of small booklets of pictures showing known gang members or groups of photos of other criminal or important groups. One may think of these as "class photos" of known street gangs or organized crime groups.

Mapping

Mapping is by far one of the most useful and currently one of the most widely used of all graphical or visualization techniques. Maps can be dynamic or static (meaning they can be ever changing or be created to show a single thing). Maps can be used to plot evidence, show the movement of people or objects, and show demographics surrounding certain scenes. We can also detect so called "hot spots" or hot beds of criminal activity by routinely plotting crimes on maps. Of course, maps are used in many contexts of crime analysis, and each are equally as important in their own right. We can use maps in the analysis of traffic patterns, movements of large crowds during rush hour, or even for closures of roads due to parades and protests. Maps are also useful for identification purposes and crime scene investigation, as well as in preliminary stages of raids and other police related endeavors.

There are many types of maps available to analysts, from simple pin maps or route maps to complex thematic maps, such as graduated symbol maps, choropleth maps, and surface maps. The definitions and uses of these maps are covered in Chapter 15.

Off-the-Shelf Software Options

There are several software options available to an analyst to create spectacular visual presentations for court briefings, analytical charts, and other products. One of the least costly options is to use readily available software that is present in most office settings. Not only is this easier on the budget, but it is easier to train personnel. All office settings that are computer dependent, like the analytical units of police departments, have some form of office software. Most of these include word processing software, spreadsheet applications, and presentation software. There are also products that can be added to the office packages that are specifically designed to create graphics. Therefore, analysts generally have all the tools they require available to them on their existing computer systems without buying analytically-specific software. The following section will discuss the most common software that is available in many offices and some additional uses for each one. This will be followed by a discussion on the benefits and drawbacks of each, and a comparison between off-the-shelf options and specific analytical software.

Microsoft Word

Microsoft Word or a similar word processing program is one of the most useful pieces of software in an analyst's arsenal. Almost every graphical product mentioned in the previous section can be created using the word processor. Word processors began as simple text programs; grew into valuable publication programs with many options for font and text sizes and color; and expanded into robust desktop publishing applications that now allow the user to add shapes, lines, graphs, tables, charts, borders, and images (see Chapter 17 for more).

Since the final analytical product will usually be printed, it often makes sense to create it in a word processor, thus saving the time that it would normally take to import or convert a chart created in a different program. Finally, most (and probably all) computerized police departments already have word processing software (most will have Microsoft Word); therefore, the cost associated with creating an analytical product is negligible.

Figure 19-2, a link chart, was created with a word processor. Most word processing programs offer the capability to draw lines and arrows, use shapes, inset text boxes with borders, and import pictures or other files. You can connect these objects together with straight or angled lines. Therefore, the link chart will follow the principals of link chart creation, much as if it had been created with analytical software. Similar principals can be applied in creating an organizational chart.

Photograph groupings may also be created with the word processor. Most programs will allow for the integration of graphics and pictures. A benefit of this process is that one can add photographs to any of the previously discussed analytical products. Word allows you to add captions to photos; text boxes can be used for greater flexibility in merging text with pictures.

Ease and cost are two of the benefits associated with creating analytical products using word processors. There are also some obvious drawbacks: analytical specific products are specially designed for the analytical function and, as such, have the appropriate templates as well as built in devices to facilitate analysis and the creation of graphical products. Editing can be difficult, as it is harder to move objects around the page without disturbing the formatting of the text. Finally, since the data in a word processing program is static,

changes in your analytical database will not automatically populate to your word processing document, as they would in a software program designed specifically for analytical charting.

Figure 19-7 shows how a simple word processing program can be used to visually display the same information used in Figure 19-3. This chart was created using Microsoft Word. Note the similarities between this chart and Figure 19-3 in the link chart section of this chapter. Although the Analyst's Notebook chart uses different icons and was easier to create, there are very few noticeable differences between the two charts.

Microsoft Visio

One of the most often used graphics programs, Visio is a very versatile product, capable of creating almost every product we have previously discussed. This graphics program has pre-defined entities such as circles and squares, geometric shapes, and other items such as office furniture. This enables the analyst to graphically represent a host of information types. Templates aid in the creation of organizational charts, timelines, and other visuals.

As in using a word processor, creating a product with Visio is a manual process, without dynamic links: whenever there is a change in the data that involves the movement of data or an insertion of new objects, changes must be made by hand.

Visio may be used to create link charts and organizational charts. It offers more options for arrows and shapes than word processors, as well as a standard set of boxes; however, the manual aspect is still present when a change must be made within the linkage chart. Several available templates make organizational charts very simple.

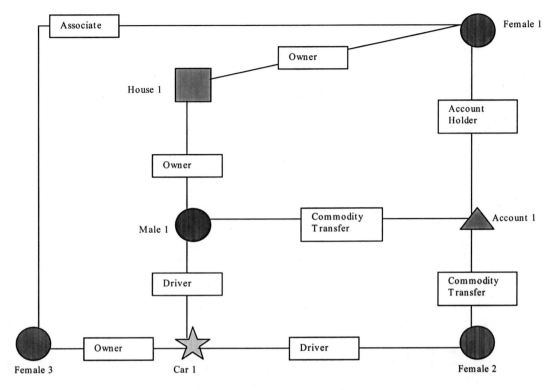

Figure 19-7: A link chart, identical in data to Figure 19-3, created in Microsoft Word.

Visio is commonly used to create timelines; in fact, next to Analyst's Notebook, it is probably the most often used product. Figure 19-6 provides an illustration of a timeline created using Visio.

Visio will be discussed in more detail in the analytical specific software section, as Paisley Systems has created its VisiSystem software on the Visio platform.

Microsoft PowerPoint

Microsoft PowerPoint is not only useful for creating powerful slide show presentations: it can also be used to create analytical products, which are then in an ideal format for digital presentations.

In an analyst's attempts to recreate the environment in which a crime has taken place, he or she must attempt to describe the area in great detail. This can be a difficult task if the person that is attempting to visualize the area has no previous knowledge of it. Pictures can help in that they will show exactly what the analyst is describing. Pictures and video clips can be embedded directly into a PowerPoint slide and these embedded objects can be "run" during the presentation, allowing you to expand the size of photos to show more detail, play video clips, and let the audience hear the sound files—turning your timeline or link chart into an interactive presentation. This can greatly aid in an investigative briefing or in a courtroom setting. The audience will be able to visualize the area and why it may have been targeted for the particular crime. This provides an analyst with the opportunity to create one presentation and show visual aids from different mediums within it; no changing of equipment is required. This is not only easier for the analyst involved but it also adds an air of professionalism to the presentation and bolsters the validity of the information as well as the reputation of the analyst assigned. See Chapter 9 for more information on effective presentations.

PowerPoint has similar options for adding shapes, text, pictures, charts, and other objects as word processing programs and Visio. It can also embed objects— organizational charts, timelines, and other visuals—created in other applications, or it can hyperlink to external files. As the program allows the user to create a custom slide size, very large documents can be created. This provides the opportunity for the analyst to create a large timeline and print it on a plotter. In the absence of analytical

specific programs, PowerPoint is probably a better option than a word processor, as the opportunity to see the entire slide is always present, and it is slightly easier to maneuver around. Many analysts have had much success using Microsoft PowerPoint slides as timelines (Figure 19-8). This enables the user to display the product on one screen digitally without the problem of conversion and creation of a new slide.

When using PowerPoint, however, be aware that embedded sounds, videos, and pictures will not print to a hard copy and are therefore beneficial only in a live presentation. Finally, when using PowerPoint, editing products is manual, and is as much a chore as when using a common word processor.

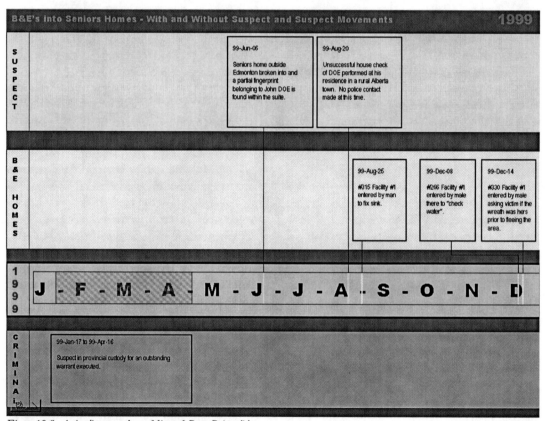

Figure 19-8: A timeline created as a Microsoft PowerPoint slide

Microsoft Access

An extremely useful product, Microsoft Access is a database program that enables the user to create a database and store huge amounts of information that is ultimately used for searching and analysis. Analysts have had much success using an Access database as a way of accessing information contained in a different database product. One example used by the Edmonton Police Service is an Access database search screen that actually pulls a series of tables out of a separate case management database. Through the use of a relatively simple Access database, the analyst was able to create a one-screen search tool allowing multitudes of information to be accessed with ease, thus enabling the analyst to perform his function more efficiently.

The use of Microsoft Access or another database program to build a simple database can solve the problems of changes in word processing or charting products. This technique was used by one analyst within the Edmonton Police Service for a single file he was analyzing. It was then used by several other analysts, and continues to be a well used product as it is simple to use and can be changed quickly to be investigation specific. This database allows an analyst to input date/time and comments involved in the event, as well as color code the event in several specific categories. The report that is generated from the database is then in color with a legend depicting the separate categories, as well as automatically placing the events in order. To add a new event, one simply types the information into the appropriate fields on the input form and the database automatically places it into chronological order without the analyst having to make changes. This is an excellent example of using the technology that is already available to combat a problem. Another of the benefits associated with using this type of system is that the analyst can keep updating the information as it becomes available and at the touch of the print button can update superiors or investigators as to the events associated with the investigation.

Figure 19-9 indicates an example of a timeline created from a database.

Photo groupings may also be generated from a database warehousing all the photographs. One may be able to produce a group of photos, each of which was given a specific code upon entry. At this point a query can be developed that will produce a report of the information requested, including the photographs, and can be custom designed to print in whatever format is required. This may be the most beneficial method as the database will house all the photos, or in cases where disk drive space is minimal will point to the photo path automatically.

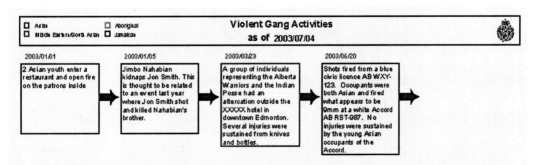

Figure 19-9: A timeline created from a Microsoft Access database

The creation of Access or other databases is not a simple process. There is a learning curve; however, once one is created, the process of modifying it for further uses can be relatively simple. As with all computer work, database design becomes intuitive with practice.

Microsoft Publisher

When creating large documents that are being distributed in a booklet or printed format, Microsoft Publisher is an excellent option. Some analysts may not give as much thought to the printing of their analytical package, but there are programs, such as Publisher, that are available to aid in the dissemination of a top-quality product. This enables the analyst to create a report in a booklet, or even a brochure style. This program is especially useful when the final product is to be bound for presentation to superiors or as court documents. Publisher is meant as a professional quality publishing program that is fairly easy to learn and use. This makes the final production and publication process much more efficient, especially when several copies of one document are required. The capability to add photographs and other files is made easier in publisher than in other document programs such as Word or WordPerfect, and it also allows these pictures and graphics to be moved around and placed in very specific locations, all the while leaving the written text and the margins set as per your request. In addition to these features, Microsoft Publisher allows one to choose several different paper sizes and folds and automatically adjusts the margins for proper printing to allow a binding application once the document has been completed.

Thus, common office software packages are extremely important and functional for analysts. Hopefully analysts will look on this software with some consideration the next time they are required to create some visual products. Although it may not be their first or ultimate choice, in certain situations where analytically specific software is unavailable, office software may be the only choice.

Analytical Software Options

There are a number of interesting and versatile products specifically designed to aid in an analytical capacity. Most of this software is more expensive than the off-the-shelf software discussed in the previous section and may not be as readily available. However, as this section will show you, there are obvious benefits to working with such software options. Once this software is purchased, the possibilities for its use are virtually limitless.

Options such as Analyst's Notebook by i2; VISI System by Paisley Systems; ATAC (Automated Tactical Analysis of Crime)—Bair Software; and Watson by Xanalys as well as others are available as analytical specific software options for criminal analysts. Several of these products will be discussed briefly in this chapter. It must be kept in mind that although certain products may be discussed in greater detail than others, it is not the opinion of the author, or the International Association of Crime Analysts that this product or software option is in any way better than the other options not discussed. One must also remember that in the absence of analytically specific software word processors and other common office software packages can be used to create similar analytical products.

i2 (the Analyst's Notebook)

This is probably the most widely used analytical software. A British product, i2 is designed specifically as a visualization program. There are several pieces to i2 that allow it to be very dynamic. Analyst's Notebook allows one to create link charts and diagrams with relative ease, and there is also a capability that creates timelines. Import functions allow telephone toll analysis to be completed in a matter of seconds, and still more import functionality through iBridge that allows information from virtually any database to be entered automatically and visualized. Once a chart has been created, iBridge then has the capability of further enhancing the product by expanding links and information from any entity already associated to the chart. This is particularly useful in criminal analysis as it allows for virtually limitless links between people and entities and can even identify links that were not obvious at the beginning. As the possibilities and uses for Analyst's Notebook are so diverse, this chapter is going to touch very briefly on a few very small items.[1]

Although this is an extremely useful product, there are also drawbacks to this system. One of the most prevalent is cost. A software solution from i2 in the form of Analyst's Notebook will cost about $5000 USD and a yearly maintenance fee and additional training fees are also charged. For larger agencies this is not much of a problem and the benefits far outweigh the cost burden. However, for much smaller agencies, whose budgets cannot handle such a costly endeavor, the benefits of using an i2 software option become diminished compared to the cost factor and therefore it would be advisable that they look at further options to create their visual products.

This program has automated many of the common functions in analysis. By opening a blank workbook, an analyst can create a link chart in relatively little time, with pre-defined links, entities, and other features. There are standard icons depicting almost everything a criminal analyst would require to build into a link chart, including vehicles, people, criminal organizations, nations, and businesses. Should the analyst require further entities, or wish to customize those already available with the package, then the option to import or create is available, as well as the option to import other files and photographs.

Analyst's Notebook is a graphical program used to make the work of the crime analyst more efficient. In a relatively short time, a host of different products can be created using this program. Information can be input to create linkage charts and posters, make sense of thousands of telephone records, and create timelines. The program then has the capability to put everything into an orderly graphical format that can be used both for investigative purposes and as a court exhibit.

The data required is dependent on the type of investigation being conducted as well as the type of output desired. For link charts, every entity, be they persons, places, or things, would need to be provided. Organizing phone records can be done using incoming or outgoing calls, time of day, length of call, or any other variable. Images can be entered into the link charts or blank notebooks to create linkage posters. For the production of a timeline, all events must be provided. If the events are presented in a digital format, such as an Excel file, it makes it easier and faster to create a timeline.

Analyst's Notebook can produce a product relatively quickly when provided with the proper information. There are a large number of products available and each takes different lengths of time to complete based on the information provided to the analyst.

---

[1] i2's Web site is http://www.i2inc.com.

There are certain terms that are used by Analyst's Notebook to describe the many functions and features of their product, some of the most common of which are the link notebook and iBase. The link notebook is the technical name for the worksheet used by the analyst when completing link charts and timelines in Analyst's Notebook. iBase is a database specifically used by Analyst's Notebook. It holds much of the information about entities on the link chart in what is called a card system. These are housed in the database and provide the analyst with the opportunity to either digitally import data or manually populate the card with the pertinent information.

Analyst's Notebook provides robust timeline creation capabilities. Analysts can input the data and an automated system provides the chronology. By using the timeline function of Analyst's Notebook, analysts can create multiple themes relating to several people or commodities and then ensure that they are linked by blending the lines together. There are flexible printing options that make use of the large-format capabilities of a plotter.

Figure 19-10 is a simple timeline made with Analyst's Notebook. This example shows both offenses (with the red exclamation point) as well as transfers of property made at local pawnshops. This shows a direct link between the burglaries and the pawned property. From an analytical perspective, this

is a very important piece of information, as we can plainly see that the individual involved is ridding himself of the property at his earliest convenience. Of course, this is only a small snapshot of the entire, and quite lengthy, timeline, although it still offers much insight into some of the criminal activity in which the individual is involved.

Analyst's Notebook was mentioned as an option for photo groups, in either poster or booklet form. This method is simpler than creating a database and is more user-friendly than a word processor, but the production of a chart using this method is not as intuitive as with a database. To create a photo group in Analyst's Notebook, one must enter each picture as an Object Linking and Embedding (OLE) object. This is automated and one can then add virtually limitless information to the bottom of the picture as a title. A drawback is that once placed on the page, each object must be moved manually to the new location as opposed to an automated system. And unlike database queries or reports, Analyst's Notebook cannot place photos in alphabetical order. However, Analyst's Notebook offers more flexible page and paper-size options than many database programs.

iBridge is another package offered by i2. As the name suggests iBridge is intended as a live "bridge" between a database and Analyst's Notebook. This enables link charts

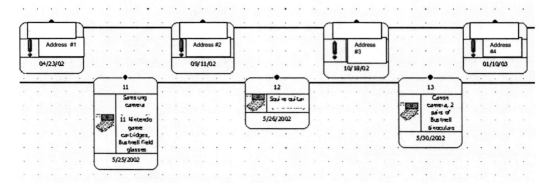

Figure 19-10: a simple timeline created with i2's Analyst's Notebook.

to be made with continuously updated, current information. By having a live link backward as well from all entities within the chart, the analyst is able to retrieve all current information from the database on any entity and the analytical process is made easier.

Query functions of the database can be made through iBridge. This allows for complex or simple queries to be made through the database and the results automatically charted. You can also then expand on any entity in the chart, again using the iBridge functionality. Expanding allows the analyst to focus in on one or a few individual entities in the chart and then expand the relationships relating solely to that entity. An explore function allows one to expand from one entity to the next. One of the most useful functions is the capability of iBridge to search the database and find a path between two identities. It does so by finding the shortest path between the two using all entities in the database. Of course, as this is a live connection, it will take only the most current and up-to-date information; thus, the chart may be ever changing, and the shortest path may become shorter as more information becomes available.

Multiple databases can be open at one time, allowing comparisons and contrasts between the two. This makes for ease in charting where different data sets may need to be combined. The results of separate investigations may be included on a single chart, and the paths between the two may be determined. When charting, you can only use one database at a time, but it is possible to combine entities on the chart.

"Common neighbors linking" is an expansion function. This means that you choose to include all entities that are linked to more than one chart entity. This can also be done on a chart that is already created without having to expand.

Like a good mapping program (see Chapter 15), i2's software offers analytical functionality that goes beyond strictly creating a visual product. Its tools allow the analyst to both analyze and communicate information, thus fulfilling the two "halves" of our profession, as discussed in Chapter 1.

Paisley Systems (VISI System)

VISI System is a product developed in Canada on the backbone of Microsoft Visio. [1] VISI System provides an almost identical product to i2's Analyst's Notebook; however, it is less expensive and works on a platform that is already available in most office environments. The following represents a quick overview of the products available through Paisley Systems and their VISI System software. Much like Analyst's Notebook, VISI System has several separate components that can either operate in conjunction to house all the data, or separately to perform individual tasks.

VISI*cais* is a database program for storing all data, complete with individual links and associations. VISI*link* allows analysts to produce link charts and networks from a number of different sources, such as databases, spreadsheets, and of course VISI*cais*. Query functions are completed using VISI*query*, which can function with VISI*cais* or be linked to external SQL or XML data sources. Customized reports may then be produced using VISI*report*.

---

[1] Paisley Systems' Web site is http://www.paisleysys. com.

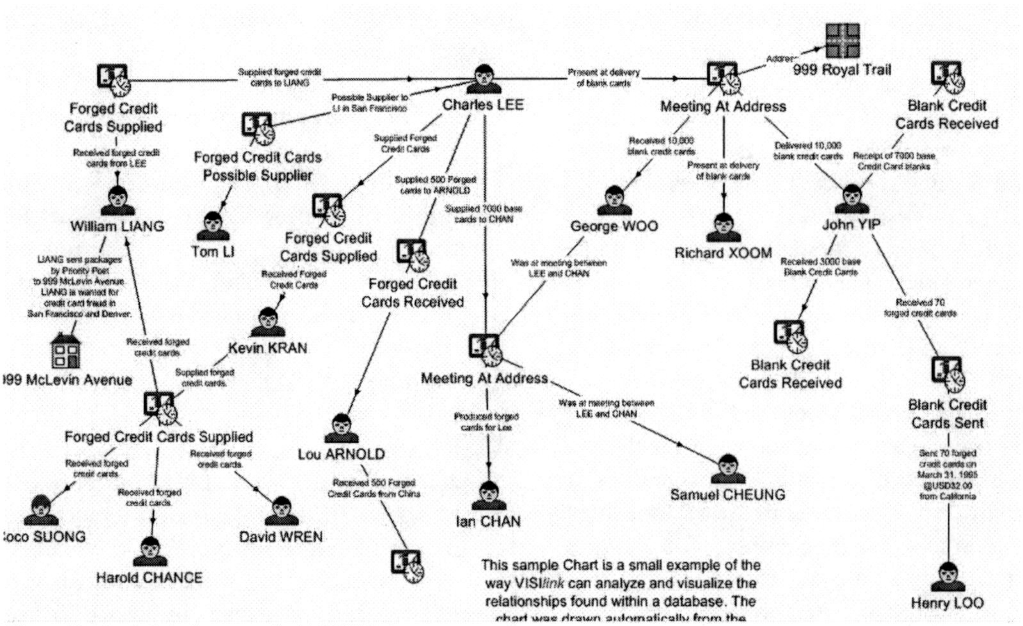
Forged Credit Cards Supplied
Supplied forged credit cards to LIANG
Possible Supplier to LI in San Francisco
Charles LEE
Present at delivery of blank cards
Meeting At Address
999 Royal Trail
Blank Credit Cards Received
Received forged credit cards from LEE
Forged Credit Cards Possible Supplier
Supplied Forged Credit Cards
Supplied 500 Forged cards to ARNOLD
Supplied 7000 base cards to CHAN
Received 10,000 blank credit cards
Present at delivery of blank cards
Delivered 10,000 blank credit cards
Receipt of 7000 base Credit Card blanks
William LIANG
Tom LI
Forged Credit Cards Supplied
George WOO
Richard XOOM
John YIP
LIANG sent packages by Priority Post to 999 McLevin Avenue. LIANG is wanted for credit card fraud in San Francisco and Denver.
Received Forged Credit Cards
Forged Credit Cards Received
Was at meeting between LEE and CHAN
Received 3000 base Blank Credit Cards
Received 70 forged credit cards
Received forged credit cards.
Kevin KRAN
Blank Credit Cards Received
999 McLevin Avenue
Supplied forged credit cards.
Meeting At Address
Was at meeting between LEE and CHAN
Blank Credit Cards Sent
Forged Credit Cards Supplied
Received forged credit cards.
Received forged credit cards.
Lou ARNOLD
Produced forged cards for Lee
Sent 70 forged credit cards on March 31, 1995 @USD32.00 from California
Received forged credit cards.
Received 500 Forged Credit Cards from China
Samuel CHEUNG
Ian CHAN
David WREN
Harold CHANCE
This sample Chart is a small example of the way VISI*link* can analyze and visualize the relationships found within a database. The
Henry LOO

Figure 19-11: A link chart created with VISIlink

As mapping is a key part of any analytical package, VISI Systems' fifth component is VISI*map*, which plots associations and links over geography to allow for easy identification of hot spots or other criminal activity nodes.

It is apparent upon viewing Figure 19-11 that the end result of VISI*link* and Analyst's Notebook are very similar.

Figure 19-12 shows an organizational chart created by VISI System. Note the similarities between this example and the charts created in Word and Visio in the previous sections of this chapter. As VISI System runs on top of Visio, the products will be virtually identical; however, VISI System allows for the automated import of data, thus saving valuable time in creating Visio charts.

Xanalys (Watson)

Another product that offers much the same functionality as Analyst's Notebook and VISI System, Watson by Xanalys (previously Harlequin) is specifically designed as a visual information analysis tool. [1] Watson provides the user with the capability to create and analyze link charts from a number of sources and merge these charts with each other. The example in Figure 19-13 shows associations between people and was created using Watson. Note, once again, how line and icon conventions make this chart similar to those created with other programs.

Xanalys also offers other products designed to aid in an investigational and analytical capacity. Quenza, for example, is a program used to extract text data and present it in a useable format. Powercase is a software option used for major case management, where information from the beginning to the end of an investigation can be housed and used in an analytical capacity.

[1] XANALYS's Web site is http://www.xanalys.com.

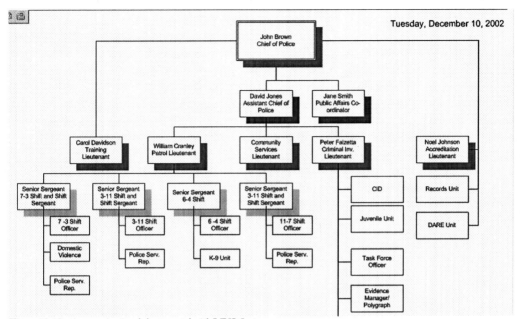

Figure 19-12: An organizational chart created with VISI Systems

Figure 19-13: A link chart created with Watson

Bair Software

Bair Software has created ATAC (Automated Tactical Analysis of Crime), which is a product that works with existing records management system (RMS) to aid in the statistical analysis of crime and thus in the deployment of resources.[1] ATAC works with any existing ODBC-compliant database. The program assists in both the identification and analysis of patterns and trends, as well as the dissemination of information based on them. It has tools that allow the automatic creation of charts, graphs, bulletins, and reports.

The examples presented above are by no means a comprehensive list of analytical specific software options available to criminal analysts; however, they do represent the most used and popular options available today. Refer to the list of recommended readings to obtain further options for analytical charting software.

Conclusions

As is manifest from this chapter, there are numerous methods that one can use to create analytical charts and other images. These range from relatively simple to very complex methods, and the software or computer programs used in their creation can run the same gamut. Having knowledge of the limitations of certain software allows analysts to make an informed decision as to the proper choice for them when tasked with producing an analytical product. The chapter is also meant as a tool to make analysts aware that they need not spend significant amounts of money on analytical specific software, as many commonly used office applications will do much the same job as the more expensive software although there are a number of drawbacks associated with the use of such common products. Of course, in the absence of any sort of computer software, one may always resort to the use of paper and colored pencils. Types of analytical charts, and the methods used to create them, are limited only by the analyst's imagination.

Recommended Readings

Ekblom, Paul. *Getting the Best Out of Crime Analysis.* London: Home Office, 1988.

Morris, Jack. *The Crime Analysis Charting.* Orangevale, CA: Palmer Enterprises, 1994.

Osborne, Deborah A. and Susan C. Wernicke. *Introduction to Crime Analysis: Basic Resources for Criminal Justice Practice.* New York: Haworth Press, 2003.

Stallo, Mark. *Using Microsoft Office to Improve Law Enforcement Operations: Crime Analysis, Community Policing, and Investigations.* Dallas: ACT Now, 2003.

Vellani, Karim H. and Joel D. Nahoun. *Applied Crime Analysis.* Boston: Butterworth-Heinemann, 2001.

---

[1] Bair Software's Web site is http://www.bairsoftware.com.

20
Working the Web:
Using the Internet and Intranet Technology

Julie Wartell

T he true means of success for any analyst is access to necessary and correct information. Much of this information, or the means to find the information, is available through the Internet. Hence, every crime analyst should have the skills to use Internet/intranet technology regularly. He or she needs to be comfortable with the technology and aware of the vast amount of data and resources available on the Web. As the technology advances and is made easier and more widely used, the use of the Web is a required tool in an analyst's tool box.

This chapter provides an orientation for newer users as well as some more advanced applications and resources for more experienced Web surfers. You will learn the immense significance of the Internet and the assistance that can be provided by it, how to "get around" on the Web, and how Internet research can facilitate the goals of analysts and make the analyst's job more efficient and effective. In addition, you will learn about the value of law enforcement agency Web sites—of creating crime analysis-related pages and using other agencies' sites.

The Internet

The Internet is a worldwide collection of computer networks connecting academic, government, commercial, and organizational sites. It provides access to communication services and information resources to millions of users around the globe. Internet services include direct communication (e-mail, chat), online conferencing (Usenet News, e-mail discussion lists), distributed information resources (World Wide Web, Gopher), remote login and file transfer (telnet, ftp), and many other valuable tools and resources.

According to the Computer Industry Almanac, the number of Internet users went from 544 million in 2001 to over 665 million in 2002. They expect this number to surpass 1 billion in 2005. The United States leads the total number with just under 161 million, but per capita ranks seventh.[1] If you think the number of Internet *users* has a lot of zeros, one study examined how much *information* exists on the Web. As of March 2000, the study estimated that there were 19 terabytes (that's 1 trillion bytes or 12 zeros) of information and 1 billion documents just on the "surface" Web.

Another way of describing the surface versus deep Web is "visible" versus "invisible." According to one of the Teaching Library Internet Workshops at the University of California at Berkeley,[2] "the "visible Web" is what you see in the results pages from general Web search engines. It's also what you see in almost all subject directories. The "*in*visible Web" is what you cannot retrieve ("see") in the search results and other links contained in these types of tools." So when one considers how much information is available visibly or on the surface through standard search strategies, it is difficult to fathom how much more lies beneath.

---

[1] Computer Industry Almanac, "USA Tops 160M Internet Users," http://www.c-i-a.com/pr1202.htm (accessed April 26, 2004).
[2] University of California at Berkeley Library, "Finding Information on the Internet: A Tutorial," http://www.lib.berkeley.edu/TeachingLib/Guides/Internet/About.html (accessed April 26, 2004).

A study conducted by faculty and students at the University of California at Berkeley attempted to measure how much information is produced in the world each year.[1] One major finding was that "the world's total yearly production of print, film, optical, and magnetic content would require roughly 1.5 billion gigabytes of storage. This is the equivalent of 250 megabytes per person for each man, woman, and child on earth." At the time, they also found that ninety-three percent of the information produced each year is stored in digital form.

When discussing the Internet, analysts should also understand (although not necessarily on a super-technical level) some related terms such as intranet, extranet, and Virtual Private Networks (VPNs). An intranet is:

1. A computer network connecting an affiliated set of clients using standard internet protocols, esp. TCP/IP and HTTP;

2. An IP-based network of nodes behind a firewall, or behind several firewalls connected by secure, possibly virtual, networks.[2]

While an intranet is similar to a Local Area Network (LAN), an extranet is more like a Wide Area Network (WAN). An extranet provides secure, authenticated access from remote locations to an intranet.

A VPN is a secure, private network connection built on top of a publicly-accessible infrastructure, such as the Internet. VPNs generally use encryption and strong access control for security.

Law enforcement agencies regularly use intranets, extranets, and VPNs due to the high level of secure information and access required. One example of an early use of this technology is Canada's Police Records Information Management Environment (PRIME) regional investigative intranet. Started in 1999, this system was used initially by investigators across British Columbia to share information, photos, and investigative leads regarding common cases. It provides an effective and highly efficient means to distribute data securely across an expansive geographic region. A February 2003 news release stated that PRIME, "will connect every municipal police department and RCMP detachment in the province, so information about criminals and crimes can be shared within minutes."[3] Another crime analysis-related use is to post the crime bulletins, statistics, and maps that have traditionally been published as hard copy and distributed via mail and face-to-face meetings. As Internet use becomes increasingly common, more and more cities, counties, and states are creating these secure, Web-based networks to share data and use common applications.

Surfing the Web

Anyone who has spent any time on the Internet knows that "surfing" the Web can be overwhelming. This does not always have to be true; there are efficient ways to surf. Three means for efficient surfing are selecting the appropriate search engine, targeting the most effective sites, and knowing some tools and tricks.

---

[1] Peter Lyman and Hal. R. Varian, "How Much Information (2000)," http://www.sims.berkeley.edu/how-much-info (accessed April 26, 2004).

[2] Intranet Journal, "Intranet Basics FAQ," http://www.intranetjournal.com/faqs/whatis/index.html (accessed April 26, 2004).

[3] British Columbia Ministry of Public Safety and Solicitor General, "New Crime-Fighting Technology Improves Public Safety," http://www2.news.gov.bc.ca/nrm_news_releases/2003PSSG0014-000205.htm (accessed April 26, 2004).

There are several dozen search engines available on the Web (see Appendix for list). Without getting too technical on how they work (most work relatively similarly), there are several recommended by Bill Ballwebber from the National Criminal Justice Reference Service in his "Web Searching Workshop."[1] These include Google, AllTheWeb, AltaVista, and iLOR. In addition, an excellent reference resource is http://searchenginewatch.com. This site keeps abreast of search engine technology, maintains lists of search engines, and provides searching tips and command language for the most common engines.

The Web Searching Workshop differentiates between search engines and offers multiple search strategies. Ballwebber notes that search engines are not created equal; superior search engines do the following:

- Cover a larger portion of the Web than other search engines.

- Excel at determining which results are most relevant.

- Frequently scan the Web for new Web pages and changes to Web pages.

- Support a wide range of search commands.

- Have clean interfaces, uncluttered by ads.

The most commonly used search strategies, according to Ballwebber, are:

- Putting phrases in quotes (to search as a phrase not individual words)

- Boolean operators (AND, OR, and NOT to link terms)

---

[1] Training material referenced with permission from author. Complete document available at National Criminal Justice Reference Service, "NCJRS Web Searching Workshop," http://www.ojp.usdoj.gov/ORIC/DenverICMC.htm (accessed April 26, 2004).

- Using an asterisk as a wild card (to search parts of words)

- Universal Resource Locator (URL) search (to search within a Web address)

- Domain searching (to search within a domain; for instance, ".gov")

- Link searching (searches all Web pages that link to the specified Web site)

There are several tools and tricks that you can use when surfing for information. If you know the name of the place but not the address, you can sometimes figure it out. Also, even good search engines sometimes find not-so-good Web sites. Finally, be sure to consider when searching that there are numerous interchangeable words and phrases in the crime analysis field.

Guessing the Address

Initially, you may want to try to guess the URL of the site you are looking for. Hints:

- For the domain name, most government agencies end in .gov; private companies in .com or .net, non-profit organizations in .org, and education institutions in .edu;

- Many governmental bodies use ci.cityname.statename.us (such as www.ci.redlands.ca.us);

- Try spelling out the name or using the acronym or abbreviation if they use one (such as www.cia.gov).

Backtracking

Sometimes Internet addresses change. Often, the address will only change its page title (the word or phrase after the last slash mark). If you find an invalid site address, try going backward one directory (or slash mark). Example: If you enter in http://www.access.gpo.gov/su_docs/gils/w hatgils.html and it does not work, try http://www.access.gpo.gov/su_docs/gils/ or even http://www.access.gpo.gov/

Synonym/Acronym Searching

Keep in mind that there are a lot of synonyms and acronyms for the concepts and organizations for which you are searching. Be sure to try them all. If you are looking for crime maps for a city, you probably want to search that city's name with "crime map," "crime statistics," and "crime analysis."

Now that you've done your search, how do you pick the most effective sites (out of the 894 or more that you got back)? The ones that come back at the top of your list (some search engines provide a percent match) are the most likely candidates to have what you've been looking for.

Not everything on the Internet is valid and should be used blindly. Most of you know that anyone can put just about anything on a Web site. When you are searching, be aware of the source of your results. If the reference site is governmental (.gov) or educational (.edu), it is likely to be legitimate. If a governmental or educational site links to a .com or .net, it is also more likely to be verified. The best method is to use common sense—if your statistics or leads that you have derived off the Web may have been put out there by John Doe, perhaps you should try to find additional back-up sources.

Doing Research on the Internet

Because the Internet provides access to such a vast amount of information, logic says that it is an ideal place to conduct research. This plethora of information that we've already established exists on the Web comes in a variety of formats. Some of the information is on agency Web sites, sometimes there are publications (either the abstract for the publication or, when you're really lucky, the entire thing), and there is also raw data to be analyzed or integrated into your analysis.

When conducting research on a problem, whether it's a crime or disorder problem or a process or program that your agency is considering or evaluating, there are a number of places to turn. Often, other police agencies have already researched or worked on a similar problem. There might be information available on their Web site or at least some contact information for further exploration about a strategy or program. In addition to other law enforcement agencies, there are a number of clearinghouses and organizations that either maintain publications or are knowledgeable and can reference academic and practical work. Many sites are listed in the appendix, but several are noteworthy and explained in more detail below.

National Criminal Justice Reference Service
(www.ncjrs.org)
Funded by various aspects of the federal government, NCJRS offers criminal justice information that supports research, policy, and program development worldwide. Federally-funded publications are available for downloading or ordering, and there is an extensive clearinghouse for searching.

Home Office Research Unit
(www.homeoffice.gov.uk/rds)
As the United Kingdom's criminal justice research division, RDS provides information that helps politicians and policy makers make evidence-based decisions and provide support to the police, probation service, the courts and immigration officials. RDS maintains statistics and publications that have been completed by staff and contractors.

Home Office Crime Reduction
(www.crimereduction.gov.uk)
This Web site provides community safety and crime prevention practitioners with information to reduce crime and anti-social behavior. Site includes Knowledgebase (interactive information service), a learning zone, toolkits on specific problems, and crime prevention advice.

Center for Problem-Oriented Policing
(www.popcenter.org)
A virtual Center to advance the problem-oriented policing field. Site includes POP guidebooks, relevant research, an interactive analysis activity, and links.

In addition to the resources listed above, other excellent starting points for research are non-profit organizations such as the Jill Dando Institute of Crime Science (www.jdi.ucl.ac.uk), the Police Executive Research Forum (www.policeforum.org), and the Urban Institute's Justice Policy Center (www.urban.org/content/PolicyCenters/Justice/Overview.htm.

Not only are there numerous organizations that have information available on the Web to read, print, and use, but there are also several sites that have the raw data available for analysts to download. The Bureau of Justice Statistics (www.ojp.usdoj.gov/bjs) posts crime and justice data such as UCR reports and National Crime Victimization (NCVS) surveys. The National Archive of Criminal Justice Data (www.icpsr.umich.edu/NACJD), a branch of the Inter-university Consortium for Political and Social Research at the University of Michigan, acquires, archives, processes, and provides access to computer-readable criminal justice data collections for research and instruction. The U.S. Census (www.census.gov) has demographic and geographic data that can be downloaded through various user-friendly

query tools. In addition, you may find that there are organizations in your jurisdiction that have downloadable data that will be useful for your mapping and analytical efforts. One example of this is the San Diego Association of Governments (www.sandag.gov), which provides the public with a wealth of free base map files for San Diego County.

Once you have decided to use a Web-based publication or online page, be sure to cite it appropriately. Citing online references is slightly different than traditional paper-published references. The American Psychological Association (APA) has been a primary resource for editorial style for many years. In the Fifth Edition of the *Publication Manual*, there is a complete section on guidelines for electronic resources.[1] It is noted that "electronic sources include aggregated databases, online journals, Web sites or Web pages, newsgroups, Web- or e-mail-based discussion groups, and Web- or e-mail-based newsletters." The following are example of proper APA citation formats.[2]

Online periodical:
Author, A. A., Author, B. B., & Author, C. C. (2000).
Title of article. *Title of Periodical*, xx, xxxxxx. Retrieved month day, year, from source.

Online document:
Author, A. A. (2000). *Title of work.* Retrieved month day, year, from source.

Communication via the Web

The Internet has increasingly become a means for communication, not only between

---

[1] American Psychological Association, "General Form for Electronic References," http://www.apastyle.org/elecgeneral.html (reviewed April 26, 2004).
[2] Editor's Note: *Exploring Crime Analysis* follows the Chicago style for documenting online references.

two individuals, but as a mass communication technique. Most well known, and used by almost everyone on the Internet, is e-mail. Also becoming increasingly popular is "instant messaging" or quick, written conversations. Additionally, there are e-mail lists, known colloquially as "listservs" (after LSoft's LISTSERV software) in which a large number of people are e-mailed the same message automatically through a Web-based server. A listserv may be moderated (where someone is reading the message before posting it to the group) or unmoderated (where all messages get posted). With the latter, the responsibility for proper behavior lays with the e-mail list participants. One example of the latter is the IACA Discussion List, but other ones related to crime analysis are LEAnalyst and Crimemap.[1] Another means of mass communication is a "forum" in which people can write in questions or comments and others can respond. Some forums are open to the public, while others are restricted to law enforcement personnel or registered users. Officer.com maintains a list of law enforcement-related forums at http://forums.officer.com/forums/.

One communication strategy that is also growing is for a law enforcement agency to receive communication and information from the community via the Internet. Departments may offer communication through an e-mail address, a form on the department's Web site, or an online survey. All are excellent means to get input and feedback from the community on neighborhood issues, crime problems, and police programs. In addition, some departments have begun using online reporting for certain types of crime cases that

are not emergencies and the suspect is no longer present. This not only saves the agency time and resources by not sending an officer, but allows the victims to file the report at their own convenience, and the information is automatically entered into a database or records management system.[2]

In addition to receiving information, law enforcement's use of the Internet to get mass information out to the community is also on the rise. Departments use Bulletin Boards, E-zines (online magazines), or mass e-mail notification. Bulletin Boards are Web sites where people can post and see messages about a topic. They are not moderated but can be useful for having "near-live" discussions. E-zines are Web-based e-mails of information with a magazine look and feel.

Mass e-mail notification works like a listserv except it is one-way communication. People sign up to be notified by the police department and receive an e-mail with information about a crime problem, crime prevention tip, or new police program. Some departments, such as San Diego Police (http://www.sandiego.gov/police/ewatch/faq.shtml), have implemented custom, mass e-mail notification programs, while others use a service, such as Silent Partner Alert (www.silentpartneralert.com).

Disseminating Information on an Intranet

As the Internet becomes more widespread, faster, and easier to use, an increasing number of departments are using secure sites (through an intranet, extranet, or VPN) to

---

[1] For more information and how to sign up for these e-lists, go to http://www.iaca.net/listserver/index.html (IACA), http://www.inteltec.com/leanalyst/ (LEAnalyst), and http://www.ojp.usdoj.gov/nij/maps/FAQs.html#ls (Crimemap) respectively.

[2] More information regarding online reporting can be found in Tom McEwen et. al., *Call Management and Community Policing: A Guide for Law Enforcement* (Washington, DC: U.S. Department of Justice, 2003), available at http://www.cops.usdoj.gov/mime/open.pdf?Item=913 (accessed April 26, 2004).

link to databases, post information, and provide a communication vehicle among law enforcement personnel. Agencies may use this type of Web-based portal to provide access to a secure, law enforcement-only database, such as the capability of allowing local agencies to access a state agency's system (e.g., parolees) or police personnel querying their own computer-aided dispatch or records management system. Crime analysts can securely distribute bulletins, post crime statistics and maps, and inform department personnel of products and issues in crime analysis. Not only does this save trees, but also a great deal of time and resources in making copies and mailing the information, as is currently done in most organizations. Although analysts should not eliminate attending meetings and spending face time with the officers and investigators, a large amount of information can be mass disseminated efficiently and consistently.[1]

Law Enforcement Web Sites

Law enforcement agency Web sites can add great value for departments' themselves, as well as for the community. Crime analysts should play an active role in creating and maintaining crime analysis pages on the site. Although there needs to be a balance between providing relevant and useful information to the public with privacy and confidentiality, the issues are far from insurmountable.

In developing a Crime Analysis Web page, the most important initial step is determining your agency's purpose.[2] Generally, the page

should accomplish the following: expand the audience; support community policing; increase the quantity, quality, and timeliness of information; provide the public efficient and timely updates; provide a means for efficient dissemination; allow for fewer requests; and reduce costs for providing information to the public. Once the objectives are prioritized, the following steps should be taken:

- Identify target audience.
- Determine citywide or organizational standards and format.
- Establish departmental committee to construct content and format.
- Develop the site (through a contracted Web developer or in-house development).
- Review process for new and updated information (accuracy and editing).
- Develop evaluation measures.

Crime analysis Web pages may include statistics, maps, figures, and other analysis-related products. The information needs to be accurate, current, and relevant for the community. It needs to be easily accessed and developed in a user-friendly format. Be sure to remember who your audience is. Once developed, Web pages are relatively easy to maintain, as much of the information can be automated. There are a wide array of crime mapping and analysis Web sites currently available (for a good list of sites with crime maps, see http://www.ojp.usdoj.gov/nij/maps/weblinks.html), and by doing some Web surfing, many more can be found. Be sure to check out what has already been done to get ideas, and talk to departments

[1] Several examples of secure sites are California's Parole LEADS, San Diego County's ARJISNet, and Lincoln (NE) Police. Because these Web sites are not public, the URLs have not been provided, but the agencies can be contacted directly for more information.
[2] Special thanks to Rachel Boba and Mary Velasco who provided a copy of their 2002 presentation done at

NIJ's annual crime mapping conference for this section of this training.

that have been through the development experience.

Using other agencies' Web sites is not only valuable for ideas for your own pages, but they also contain a wealth of information regarding their programs and efforts. Whether you are looking for comparative crime statistics or evidence of a crime prevention program that worked, be sure to "surf" efficiently. There are several online lists of law enforcement agencies (e.g., www.officer.com)—which can be helpful if you know the jurisdiction name and want to find their Web address. Yet, if you are generally surfing to find out which agencies worked on a particular problem or created a successful program (e.g., drug court), using the search engines and tools is much quicker.

Web-Based Training

As the popularity of the Internet has grown tremendously in the last five years, so has the opportunity for Web-based training. Online training, also known as distance learning, comes in a variety of formats. In general, distance learning allows the crime analyst to sit at his or her own computer and take a class that is being conducted anywhere else in the world. Specifically, distance learning can be synchronous (where the students and instructor are online and advance together) or asynchronous (where the students take the class and advance at their own pace).

Online classes can be a part of a university degree, such as at North Carolina State (http://www2.chass.ncsu.edu/aomp/ps498_crime.html) or be an entire degree, such as at Boston University (http://www.cjdegree.info/mcj/). They also may be topic specific, such as relating to insurance fraud (http://www.nicbtraining.org/) or specific to certain software, such as using GIS (http://campus.esri.com/). Classes vary

greatly in length, cost, interactivity (with the instructor as well as with the other students), and curriculum format. Some classes may have additional features such as CDs of information or online chat or discussion forums.

Summary: The Internet as a Resource

As discussed throughout this chapter, the Internet is vast and multiplying exponentially every day. In other words, the number of potential resources and links to valuable Web sites is massive. Although every attempt was made to include as many resources as possible that would assist a crime analyst in his or her job, the attached resource list is not exhaustive. These are the 250 (or so) resources that were known to the author and verified as valid addresses in July 2003; additional resources were added in November 2003. This list was compiled by extensive Web surfing combined with resource lists, training documentation, and Internet sites that contain numerous links that other analysts and law enforcement personnel have created before me.

The resources are categorized for easier intake into the following sections:

- Associations
- Clearinghouses
- Consumer Protection Sites
- Criminal Justice Information and Resources
- Directories/Search Engines
- GIS/Mapping Sources
- Grants and Grant Research
- Intelligence/CounterIntelligence
- International Policing Organizations and Resources
- Investigative Resources
- Law/Legal/Federal Agencies

- News Services
- Publications (Information/Technology Related)
- Statistics
- Technical Assistance Providers (Technology Related), and
- Training (Analyst-specific).

Some of these will be helpful for general job knowledge, some will aid in investigative analysis, and others for research and those miscellaneous requests that you get from your boss.

Not all aspects of this chapter will be used every day, but different sections can be referred to depending on your current project or need. As with anything, unless you are using the Internet regularly—for research, to disseminate or collect information, or as a training vehicle—it is very difficult to remember everything. Not only is the Internet constantly growing and changing, our jobs as analysts also continue to evolve. Hopefully, this information can aid in an efficient learning process and help us all become more effective in our jobs.

Online Resources for Crime Analysts

Associations

American Board of Criminalistics	www.criminalistics.com/abc
American Correctional Association	www.corrections.com/aca
American Society of Criminology	www.asc41.com
American Society of Industrial Security	www.asisonline.org
Canadian Association of Violent Crime Analysts	www.cavca.net
Federal Bar Association	www.fedbar.org
Forensics Science Society	www.forensic-science-society.org.uk
High Tech Crime Investigation Association	www.htcia.org
International Association of Chiefs of Police	www.theiacp.org
International Association of Crime Analysts	www.iaca.net
International Association of Law Enforcement Intelligence Analysts	www.ialeia.org
International Association of Law Enforcement Planners	www.ialep.org
International City/County Management Association	www.icma.org
International CPTED Association	www.cpted.net
International Society of Crime Prevention Practitioners	www.iscpp.net
Justice Research & Statistics Association	www.jrsainfo.org
National Association of Attorneys General	www.naag.org
National District Attorneys Association	www.ndaa.org
National Futures Association	www.nfa.futures.org
National Sheriffs Association	www.sheriffs.org
Urban and Regional Information Systems Assoc	www.urisa.org

Clearinghouses

Automated Index of CJ Info Systems	www.aindex.search.org
Central Banking Resource Center	patriot.net/~bernkopf
Federal Reserve National Information Center	www.ffiec.gov/nic
FedWorld Information Network	www.fedworld.gov
Financial Crimes Enforcement Network	www.fincen.gov
FirstGov: U.S. Government Information Source	firstgov.gov
Governing: The Resource of States and Localities	www.governing.com/govlinks/glinks.htm
IACP Law Enforcement Info Management	www.iacptechnology.org
Integrated Justice Information Systems	www.ijis.org
National Archive of Criminal Justice Data	www.icpsr.umich.edu/NACJD
National Center for Missing & Exploited Children	www.missingkids.com
National Check Fraud Center	www.ckfraud.org
National Clearinghouse on Child Abuse & Neglect	www.calib.com/nccanch
National Crime Prevention Council	www.ncpc.org
National Technical Information Service	www.ntis.gov
NCJRS Justice Information Center	www.ncjrs.org
Partnerships Against Violence Network	www.pavnet.org
Privacy Rights Clearinghouse	www.ucan.org/prc/prc4ucan.htm
Securities Class Action Clearinghouse	securities.stanford.edu
Transactional Access Records Clearinghouse	trac.syr.edu/aboutTRACgeneral.html
United Nations Crime and Justice Info Network	www.uncjin.org
U.S. DOJ OJP Information Technology Initiatives	it.ojp.gov
U.S. Government Printing Office GPO Access	www.gpoaccess.gov/index.html

Consumer Protection Sites

Better Business Bureau	www.bbb.org
Coalition Against Insurance Fraud	www.insurancefraud.org
Consumer World	www.consumerworld.org
Federal Government Consumer Information	www.consumer.gov
Federal Trade Comm. Consumer Protection	www.ftc.gov/ftc/consumer.htm
Lectric Law Library Consumer Rights & Protections	www.lectlaw.com/tcos.html
National Fraud Information Center	www.fraud.org
National Institute for Consumer Education	www.emich.edu/public/coe/nice/index2.html
Net Scam/Alert	www.netscams.com
Office for Victims of Crime	www.ojp.usdoj.gov/ovc
Taxpayers Against Fraud	www.taf.org
U.S. Postal Service Consumer Tips	www.usps.com/websites/depart/inspect/consmenu.htm

Criminal Justice Information & Resources

Center for Advanced Public Safety Research	www.newhaven.edu/psps
Center for Problem-Oriented Policing	www.popcenter.org
Community Policing Consortium	www.communitypolicing.org
CopNet	www.copnet.com
Crime and Intelligence Analyst Resources	www.geocities.com/crimeanalyst_2000
Crime Reduction Resources	www.crimereduction.gov.uk
Criminal Justice Links	www.criminology.fsu.edu/cjlinks
FBI Law Enforcement Bulletin	www.fbi.gov/publications/leb/leb.htm
Government Information Sharing Project	govinfo.kerr.orst.edu
Law Enforcement Links	www.leolinks.com
National Institute of Justice	www.ojp.usdoj.gov/nij
Officer.com	www.officer.com
Police Executive Research Forum	www.policeforum.org
Traffic Accident Reconstruction Origin (journal)	www.tarorigin.com/index.html
Urban Institute (Justice Policy Center)	www.urban.org
Web of Justice: CJ Internet Exploration Guide	www.co.pinellas.fl.us/bcc/juscoord/explore.htm

Directories/Search Engines

Acronym Finder	www.acronymfinder.com
Address Search Engine	www.addresses.com
AlltheWeb	www.alltheweb.com
AltaVista	www.altavista.com
Big Yellow pages	www.bigyellow.com
C/Net	www.search.com
Dogpile	www.dogpile.com
eMailman Finger (locating e-mail ownership)	www.emailman.com/finger
FoneFinder	www.primeris.com/fonefind
Global Yellow Pages	www.globalyp.com/world.htm
Google	www.google.com
Government Information Locator Service	www.access.gpo.gov/su_docs/gils
iLOR	www.ilor.com/searchblank.htm
InfoSpace	www.infospace.com
Internet Address Finder	www.iaf.net
Lycos	www.lycos.com
Metacrawler	www.metacrawler.com
NANPA Telephone Numbering	www.nanpa.com/number_resource_info
Payphone Project	www.payphone-project.com/search.html
Search Engine Resources	www.searchenginez.com
Starting Point	www.stpt.com

Directories/Search Engines (cont.)

Surf Point LinkExchange	www.surfpoint.com
Switchboard	www.switchboard.com
Telephone Information Source	www.555-1212.com
United States Post Office (Zip Code finder)	www.usps.com
WebCrawler	www.webcrawler.com
World E-mail Directory	www.worldemail.com
Yahoo	www.yahoo.com

GIS/Mapping Sources

Alexandria Digital Library Project	http://alexandria.sdc.ucsb.edu
Association of Geographic Information—Crime & Disorder	www.agi.org.uk/cdsig
Crime Mapping News	www.policefoundation.org/docs/library.html
Crime Prevention Analysis Lab	www.crimepatterns.com
Directions Magazine	www.directionsmag.com
Geodata: Federal, State, and Local Geographic Data	www.geodata.gov
Geography Network	www.geographynetwork.com
GeoSpatial Solutions Magazine	www.geospatial-online.com
GISLinx	www.gislinx.com
GISPlace	www.gisworld.com
GIS Portal	www.gisportal.com
GIS WWW Resource List	www.geo.ed.ac.uk/home/giswww.html
InfoTech Crime Mapping	www.infotech-europe.com/gis/crime-mapping.htm
NIJ Mapping for Public Safety	www.ojp.usdoj.gov/nij/maps
NLECTC Crime Mapping & Analysis Program	www.nlectc.org/cmap
Spatial News Crime Mapping Resources	spatialnews.geocomm.com/features/crimemaps/crimeresources.html

Grants and Grant Research

Catalog of Federal Domestic Assistance	www.cfda.gov
Chronicle of Philanthropy	www.philanthropy.com
Council on Foundations	www.cof.org
Environmental Grantmakers Association	www.ega.org
Foundation Center	www.fdncenter.org
Grantsmanship Center	www.tgci.com
National Network of Grantmakers	www.nng.org
Packard Foundation	www.packfound.org
Stern Family Fund	www.sternfund.org
U.S. Department of Justice Grants	www.usdoj.gov/10grants/index.html

Intelligence/CounterIntelligence

Center for the Study of Intelligence	www.odci.gov/csi
Central Intelligence Agency	www.cia.gov
Factbook on Intelligence	www.odci.gov/cia/publications/facttell
Kim-Spy Intelligence & Counter Intelligence	www.kimsoft.com/kim-spy.htm
Intelligence Professional	www.thepalmerpress.com
Intelligence Technologies International	www.inteltec.com
Interagency International Fugitive Lookout	www.usdoj.gov/criminal/oiafug/fugitives.htm
Terrorism Research Center	www.terrorism.com
United States Intelligence Community	www.columbia.edu/cu/lweb/indiv/dsc/intell.html
United States National Security Agency	www.nsa.gov

International Policing Organizations/Resources

Australian Institute of Criminology	www.aic.gov.au
Canadian Criminal Justice Resource Page	members.tripod.com/~BlueThingy/index.html
Criminal Intelligence Services of Canada	www.cisc.gc.ca
Home Office Research Development Statistics	www.homeoffice.gov.uk/rds/index.htm
INTERPOL	www.interpol.com/Default.asp
Jill Dando Institute of Crime Science	www.jdi.ucl.ac.uk
Justice Institute of British Columbia	www.jibc.bc.ca
Police Services of the UK	www.police.uk
Royal Canadian Mounted Police	www.rcmp-grc.gc.ca

Investigative Resources

Birth and Death Records by State	www.health.state.pa.us/HPA/obd.htm
ChoicePoint	www.choicepoint.net
Computer Incident Advisory Capability	ciac.llnl.gov/ciac
Dialog	www.dialog.com
Dun & Bradstreet	www.dnb.com
Economic Research Service (USDA)	www.ers.usda.gov
Equifax	www.equifax.com
Experian	www.experian.com
Genealogy Site (public data resources)	www.genealogy.com/00000229.html
Informus	www.informus.com
InterNet Bankruptcy Library	bankrupt.com
Internet Scam Busters	www.scambusters.org
Investigator's Guide to Sources of Information	www.gao.gov/special.pubs/soi.htm
Investigator's Little Black Book Online	www.crimetime.com/online.htm
Investigator's Toolbox	pimall.com/nais/in.menu.html

Investigative Resources (cont.)

KnowX Public Records Searches	www.knowx.com
LEXISNEXIS	www.LexisNexis.com
National Insurance Crime Bureau	www.nicb.com
Rapsheets	www.rapsheets.com
Research It	www.itools.com/research-it/research-it.html
Sex Offender.Com	www.sexoffender.com
Social Security Number Allocations	www.ssa.gov/foia/stateweb.html
Social Security Death Index	www.ancestry.com/ssdi/advanced.htm
Trans Union	www.transunion.com
Virtual Librarian	www.virtuallibrarian.com/index2.html
World's Most Wanted	www.mostwanted.org

Law/Legal/Federal Agencies

Code of Federal Regulations	www.gpoaccess.gov/cfr/index.html
Customs Service	www.customs.ustreas.gov
Department of Commerce	www.commerce.gov/
Department of Homeland Security	www.dhs.gov
Department of the Treasury	www.ustreas.gov/
Drug Enforcement Administration	www.usdoj.gov/dea/
Environmental Protection Agency	www.epa.gov/
Federal Bureau of Investigation	www.fbi.gov
Federal Bureau of Prisons	www.bop.gov
Federal Communications Commission	www.fcc.gov/
Federal Legislation (to search for Bills, etc.)	thomas.loc.gov/
Federal Register	www.gpoaccess.gov/fr/index.html
Immigration and Naturalization Service	www.bcis.gov/graphics/index.htm
International Constitutional Law	www.uni-wuerzburg.de/law/index.html
Law.com	www.law.com
Law Databases	www.internets.com/slegal.htm
Library of Congress	www.loc.gov
Secret Service	www.treas.gov/usss
U.S. Citizenship and Immigration Services	uscis.gov
U.S. Court of Appeals Federal Circuit	www.law.emory.edu/fedcircuit
U.S. General Accounting Office	www.gao.gov
U.S. General Services Administration	www.gsa.gov
U.S. Marshals Service	www.usdoj.gov/marshals
U.S. Postal Service	www.usps.gov
U.S. Supreme Court Cases	www.findlaw.com/casecode/supreme.html
White House	www.whitehouse.gov/

News Services

APB Online	www.apbonline.com
Associated Press	www.ap.org
CNN Interactive	www.cnn.com
Media Data Research Service	www.mediafinder.com
NewsLibrary	www.newslibrary.com/nlsite

Publications (Information/Technology Related)

Evolution and Development of Police Technology	www.nlectc.org/txtfiles/policetech.html
Federal Computer Week	www.fcw.com
Government Technology	www.govtech.net
High-Tech Dictionary	www.computeruser.com/resources/dictionary
Indispensable Info: Data Collection and Information Management	www.urban.org/nnip/pdf/indispen.pdf
Law Enforcement Product News	www.law-enforcement.com
Law Enforcement Technology	www.letonline.com
Law Technology News	www.lawtechnews.com/r4/home.cgi
NLECTC Technology News Summary	www.nlectc.org
StatSoft Electronic Statistics Textbook	www.statsoft.com/textbook/stathome.html
ZDNet	www.zdnet.com

Statistics

Economic Statistics Briefing Room	www.whitehouse.gov/fsbr/esbr.html
Federal Justice Statistics Resource Center	fjsrc.urban.org/index.cfm
Galileo Demographics and Census Data	www.usg.edu/galileo/internet/census/demograp.html
Government Information Sharing Project	govinfo.kerr.orst.edu
Grass Roots	www.crime.org
JRSA's Incident-based Reporting Resource Center	www.jrsa.org/ibrrc
NCJRS Statistics Publications	virlib.ncjrs.org/Statistics.asp
Population Reference Bureau	www.prb.org
Sourcebook of CJ Statistics	www.albany.edu/sourcebook
Stat-USA	www.stat-usa.gov
U.S. Bureau of Justice Statistics	www.ojp.usdoj.gov/bjs
U.S. Bureau of Labor Statistics	stats.bls.gov
U.S. Bureau of Transportation Statistics	www.bts.gov
U.S. Census Bureau	www.census.gov
U.S. Office of Highway Safety	safety.fhwa.dot.gov

Technical Assistance Providers (Technology Related)

Center for Criminal Justice Technology	www.mitretek.org/home.nsf/CriminalJustice/CCJTSite
Center for Technology in Government	www.ctg.albany.edu
Institute for Law and Justice	www.ilj.org
National Law Enforcement and Corrections Technology Center	www.nlectc.org
Office of Law Enforcement Technology	www.oletc.org
Institute for Intergovernmental Research	www.iir.com
SEARCH	www.search.org
U.S. DOJ Technical Assistance Guide	www.ojp.gov/training.htm

Training (Analyst-specific)

Alpha Group Center for Crime & Intelligence Analysis	www.alphagroupcenter.com
Anacapa Sciences	www.anacapasciences.com
Analysis, Consulting, Training Now (ACT Now)	www.actnowinc.org
California State Crime & Intelligence Analysis Certification Program	www.csus.edu
Canadian Police College	www.cpc.gc.ca
Crime Analysis Associates	www.crimeanalysis.net
International Association of Crime Analysts	www.iaca.net/Certification/training.html
NLECTC Crime Mapping and Analysis Program	www.nlectc.org/cmap
Police Training Calendar	www.policetraining.net

Glossary

administrative crime analysis. A broad category of analysis covering administrative and statistical reports, research, and other projects not focused on the immediate or long-term reduction or elimination of a pattern or trend. Examples include demographic change reports, crime statistics to support grant applications, creation of charts and graphs to support presentations, and creation of maps for special events.

analysis. 1) The element of reasoning that involves breaking down a problem into parts and studying the parts; 2) A process that transforms raw data into useful information.

call for service. An ambiguous term that, depending on the agency, can mean: 1) a request for police response from a member of the community; 2) any incident to which a police officer responds, including those that are initiated by the police officer himself; or 3) a computerized record of such responses.

clearance rate. The percent of reported crimes resulting in an arrest or an exceptional clearance according to the FBI's UCR program.

community policing. A philosophy and approach to policing that requires police to internalize their roles as community servants, to work pro-actively with the community to solve crime and disorder problems, to communicate frequently and effectively with community members, and to "personalize" police service based on community characteristics.

computer-aided dispatch (CAD). A computer application, or series of applications, that facilitates the reception, dispatching, and recording of calls for service. Data stored in CAD systems include call type, date and time received, address, reporting person's name and number, and the times that each responding unit was dispatched, arrived on scene, and cleared the scene. In some agencies, CAD records form the base for more extensive incident records in the **records management system** (RMS).

concatenation. In databases, the combination of multiple values stored in separate fields into one value stored in a single field. Analysts often must concatenate address components ("street number," "street," "apartment") into a single field ("address"). Compare with **parsing**.

content analysis. A technique for locating, identifying, retrieving, and analyzing documents for their relevance, significance, and meaning.

correlation. A statistical procedure designed to determine if there is a relationship between two variables.

crime analysis. The study of police incidents; the identification of patterns, trends, and problems; and the dissemination of information that helps a police agency develop tactics and strategies to solve patterns, trends, and problems. See pages 1–412.

crime mapping. The application of a **geographic information system** (GIS) to crime or police data.

crime report. A record (usually stored in a **records management system**) of a crime that has been reported to the police.

crime series analysis. The process in which an individual reads the content of police reports with the goal of identifying and analyzing a pattern of crimes that the reader believes is committed by the same person or persons.

criminal event perspective. A way of studying crime, rooted in **environmental criminology**, that considers multiple theories of offender, victim, place, and opportunity.

criminal intelligence analysis. The collection, analysis, and dissemination of information about criminals, particularly criminal organizations. Intelligence analysts hunt for leads on the structure and hierarchy of criminal organizations, the flow of money and goods, relationships and contacts, current activities and plans, and personal information about the participants, usually with the goal of arrest, prosecution, and conviction of the offenders involved.

criminal investigative analysis. An investigative process that identifies the psychological, physical, and behavioral traits of an offender based on the crimes that he or she has committed.

criminology. The scientific study of crime, criminals, criminal behavior and law enforcement.

data cleaning. A set of operations that replaces inaccurate or "dirty" data with correct or "clean" data.

deductive analysis. A type of analysis that applies broad theories or premises to individual situations. If theory tells us that most offenders commit crimes within x miles of their homes, for instance, we might deduce that an offender in a particular crime lives within x miles of the crime's location. Deductive analysis proceeds from the general to the specific. Compare with **inductive analysis**.

descriptive statistics. A set of measures that describe research data in terms of the frequency with which the variable occurs, percentage distributions, measures of central tendency and measures of dispersion around the mean. Descriptive statistics are used to describe the basic features of the data in a study; they summarize large amounts of information in an efficient and easily understood manner.

environmental criminology. The study of crimes as they related to places, including how crimes and criminals are influenced by environmental factors.

forecasting. Techniques that attempt to predict future crime based on past crime. Series forecasting tries to identify where and when an offender might strike next, while trend forecasting attempts to predict future volumes of crime.

geocoding. The process of converting analog data into machine- or computer-readable format—of translating addresses or numeric coordinates into points on a map. In law enforcement, most references to geocoding refer to one type of geocoding known as "address matching."

geographic information system (GIS). A collection of hardware, software, and people that collect, store, retrieve, manipulate, analyze, and display spatial data. The GIS thus encompasses the computer mapping program itself, the tools available to it, the computers on which it resides, the data that it accesses, and the analyst who uses it.

hot spot. 1) An area of high crime; 2) events that form a cluster; or 3) a single place with many crimes. Hot spots might be formed by short-term **patterns** or long-term **trends**.

hypothesis. An unproved theory tentatively accepted to explain certain facts.

inductive analysis. A type of analysis that draws broad conclusions about a phenomenon based on the study of its individual pieces—for instance, a profile of a pattern based on the analysis of its individual incidents. Inductive analysis proceeds from the specific to the general Compare with **deductive analysis**.

inferential statistics. Used to make decisions about a population. Inferential statistics are concerned with the statistical significance of sample results. Inferential statistics suggest statements about a population based on a sample drawn from that population.

law enforcement analysis. Processes, techniques, and products that provide information support for the mission of a law enforcement agency. **Crime analysis, criminal intelligence analysis**, and **criminal investigative analysis** are types of law enforcement analysis.

macro. A recording of user keystrokes and mouse operations that can be played back later. In spreadsheets, a macro can be used to record a series of operations against cell data to obtain the same result each and every time while removing the need for user interaction.

measures central tendency. Statistics that measure the "typical" value of a variable. See **mean, median, and mode**.

mean. The average of a series of numbers, calculated by summing the values and dividing by the number of values.

median. The score or potential score above which and below which one-half the scores lie.

mode. The value that occurs most frequently in a distribution of a variable.

modus operandi. Literally, "method of operation." It is a description of how an offender commits a crime. *Modus operandi* variables might include point and means of entry, tools used, violence or force exerted, techniques or skills applied, and means of flight or exit. Studying *modus operandi* allows analysts to link crimes in a series, identify potential offenders, and suggest possible strategies.

National Crime Victimization Survey (NCVS). A method of measuring crime rates that draws data from victims rather than from police agencies, thus attempting to produce a more accurate picture of total crime, rather than crime that is reported to police. The NCVS surveys 100,000 individuals aged 12 or over and collects data on types of crimes they have experienced, locations, times, physical settings, and characteristics of victims. but one that focuses on the experiences of victims.

National Incident-Based Reporting System (NIBRS). A national data reporting standard instituted by the FBI that builds on the older **Uniform Crime Reporting** (UCR) Program. NIBRS requires agencies who volunteer to participate to submit individual records, with several dozen variables, on certain crimes that they receive. It allows more in-depth analysis than UCR data but is more time-consuming for agencies to collect and transmit the data.

parsing. In databases, the separation of a value stored in a single field into more discrete values stored in separate fields. For instance, an analyst might parse a single field called "address" into its components: "street number," "street," and "apartment."

pattern. Two or more incidents related by a common causal factor, usually to do with offender, location, or target. Patterns are usually, but not always, short-term phenomena. See also **series, trend,** and **hot spot.**

population. In research, the theoretical "universe" or aggregation of individuals or items that are to be studied. The researcher draws a **sample** and tries to ensure that the characteristics of the sample will reflect the characteristics of the overall population.

police operations analysis. The study of a police agency's operations and policies, including its allocation of personnel, money, equipment, and other resources, geographically, organizationally, and temporally, and whether these operations and policies have the most effective influence on crime and disorder in the agency's jurisdiction.

problem. 1) An aggregation of crimes, such as a **pattern, series, trend,** or **hot spot;** 2) Repeating or chronic environmental or societal factors that cause crime and disorder.

problem-oriented policing (POP). An approach to policing articulated by Herman Goldstein. It teaches that police could prevent more crime, and better serve their communities, by crafting solutions to underlying problems rather than focusing on individual crime incidents. Problem-oriented policing relies on the careful analysis of crimes and their causes.

qualitative analysis. The analysis of non-discrete data—including observations, interviews, and textual content—in the attempt to find themes, patterns, and symbolic meanings, and to understand the nature of human interactions.

quantitative analysis. The statistical analysis and interpretation of numeric and discrete data, including central tendency, correlation, volume, and density.

range. The span or extent of a data distribution for a particular variable. It is calculated by subtracting the minimum value from the maximum value.

reasoning. The ability to draw accurate conclusions based on observations and knowledge of causes and effects.

records management system (RMS). A computerized application and database in which data about crimes and other incidents, arrests, persons, property, evidence, vehicles, and other data of value to police are stored.

sample. A manageable portion of a **population** that a researcher studies to draw inferences about the population as a whole.

SARA. A problem-solving model for systematically examining crime and disorder problems and developing an effective response. The acronym SARA stands for Scanning, Analysis, Response, and Assessment.

series. Two or more related crimes (a **pattern**) committed by the same individual or group of individuals.

signature. A personalized way of committing a crime that goes beyond *modus operandi,* usually not necessary to the commission of the crime but rather fulfilling a psychological need. An offender's signature links crimes in a **series.**

413

spreadsheet. A software application used to store, manipulate, retrieve, and analyze data and produce statistical results.

standard deviation. A measure of a data set's dispersion around the mean. Standard deviation helps determine how well the mean reflects the overall tendency of the data.

strategic crime analysis. A type of crime analysis that focuses on trends, problems, and their causes. Strategic crime analysis reduces crime through the implementation of long-term strategies and policies.

tactical crime analysis. A type of crime analysis that focuses on immediate patterns and series, with the goal of devising quick tactics to deter or apprehend an offender.

temporal analysis. The study of time and how it relates to events.

trends. Long-term increases, decreases, or changes in crime (or its characteristics).

Uniform Crime Reporting (UCR) Program. A U.S. standard of classifying and reporting crime that applies uniform categorizations to events and ensures that statistics reported by one jurisdiction are comparable to those reported by another. See also **National Incident-Based Reporting System**.

Visual Basic for Applications (VBA). A programming language designed by Microsoft that allows users to enhance their products' core functionality. Most of the current Microsoft products, as well as other software companies' products, provide a VBA interface.

Vollmer, August (1876-1955). "Father of American policing." Chief of Police in Berkley, California, 1905-1932; invented and instituted techniques, technologies, and processes that improved the effectiveness of police. Designed his beats in accordance with call volume; mapped crime; otherwise pioneered some of the first crime analysis processes in the United States.

Wilson, Orlando W. (1900-1972). Protégé of August Vollmer (q.v.). Police executive in many agencies, including Superintendent of Chicago Police Department, 1960-1971. Wrote *Police Administration* (1963), the earliest known text to mention "crime analysis."